I0188835

The Memorial (Yizkor) Book
of
Podhajce, Ukraine

Translation of

Sefer Podhajce

Originally Published in Yiddish
Edited by Me'ir Shimon Geshouri
Tel Aviv, 1972

Translation Project Coordinators and Editors:
Jean Rosenbaum
Mervin Rosenbaum

Published by JewishGen

An Affiliate of the Museum of Jewish Heritage - A Living Memorial to the Holocaust
New York

The Memorial Book of Podhajce, Ukraine
Translation of Sefer Podhajce

First Printing: May 2013, Sivan 5773
Second Printing: August 2019, Av 5779

Translation Project Coordinators and Editors: Jean and Mervin Rosenbaum
Translation funded by Jean and Mervin Rosenbaum
Translated by Jerrold Landau, unless otherwise noted
Layout and Editor: Joel Alpert
Image Editor:
Cover Design: Jan R. Fine
Publicity: Sandra Hirschhorn
Indexing: Tammy Weingarten

Published by JewishGen, Inc.
An Affiliate of the Museum of Jewish Heritage
A Living Memorial to the Holocaust
36 Battery Place, New York, NY 10280

"JewishGen, Inc. is not responsible for inaccuracies or omissions in the original work and makes no representations regarding the accuracy of this translation. Digital images of the original book's contents can be seen online at the New York Public Library Web site."

The mission of the JewishGen organization is to produce a translation of the original work and we cannot verify the accuracy of statements or alter facts cited.

Printed in the United States of America by Lightning Source, Inc.

Library of Congress Control Number (LCCN): 2013938331
ISBN: 978-1-939561-05-3 (hard cover: 554 pages, alk. paper)

Front Cover: Artwork from the original Yiddish Yizkor Book

JewishGen and the Yizkor Books in Print Project

This book has been published by the **Yizkor Books in Print Project,** as part of the **Yizkor Book Project** of **JewishGen, Inc**.

JewishGen, Inc. is a non-profit organization founded in 1987 as a resource for Jewish genealogy. Its website [www.jewishgen.org] serves as an international clearinghouse and resource center to assist individuals who are researching the history of their Jewish families and the places where they lived. JewishGen provides databases, facilitates discussion groups, and coordinates projects relating to Jewish genealogy and the history of the Jewish people. In 2003, JewishGen became an affiliate of the **Museum of Jewish Heritage - A Living Memorial to the Holocaust** in New York.

The **JewishGen Yizkor Book Project** was organized to make more widely known the existence of Yizkor (Memorial) Books written by survivors and former residents of various Jewish communities throughout the world. Later, volunteers connected to the different destroyed communities began cooperating to have these books translated from the original language—usually Hebrew or Yiddish—into English, thus enabling a wider audience to have access to the valuable information contained within them. As each chapter of these books was translated, it was posted on the JewishGen website and made available to the general public.

The **Yizkor Books in Print Project** began in 2011 as an initiative to print and publish Yizkor Books that had been fully translated, so that hard copies would be available for purchase by the descendants of these communities and also by scholars, universities, synagogues, libraries, and museums.

These Yizkor books have been produced almost entirely through the volunteer effort of researchers from around the world, assisted by donations from private individuals. The books are printed and sold at near cost, so as to make them as affordable as possible. Our goal is to make this important genre of Jewish literature and history available in English in book form, so that people can have the personal histories of their ancestral towns on their bookshelves for themselves and for their children and grandchildren.

A list of all published translated Yizkor Books can be found at:
http://www.jewishgen.org/Yizkor/ybip.html

Lance Ackerfeld, Yizkor Book Project Manager

Joel Alpert, Yizkor Book in Print Project Coordinator

This book is presented by the
Yizkor Books in Print Project
Project Coordinator: Joel Alpert

Part of the
Yizkor Books Project of JewishGen, Inc.
Project Manager: Lance Ackerfeld

These books have been produced solely through volunteer effort of individuals from around the world. The books are printed and sold at near cost, so as to make them as affordable as possible.

Our goal is to make this history and important genre of Jewish literature available in English in book form so that people can have the near-personal histories of their ancestral towns on their bookshelves for themselves and for their children and grandchildren.

Any donations to the Yizkor Books Project are appreciated.

Please send donations to:
Yizkor Book Project
JewishGen
36 Battery Place
New York, NY 10280

JewishGen, Inc. is an affiliate of the
Museum of Jewish Heritage
A Living Memorial to the Holocaust

Title Page of the Original Yiddish Yizkor Book

ספר פאדהייצע

רעדאַקטאָר : **מ. ש. גשורי**

פאַרלאַג פון דער פאָדהייצער לאַנדסמאַנשאַפט אין ישראל

תשל״ב ● 1972

Translation of the Title Page of the Original Yiddish Yizkor Book

SEFER PODHAJCE

THE PODHAJCE MEMORIAL VOLUME

Red. M. SH. GESHOURI
Published by
The Book Committee of „Sefer Podhajce"
in Israel

Foreword for the Translation and Publication of the Book

My maternal grandparents, Isaac Zinn and Sarah Lehrer Zinn immigrated from Podhajce to Texas in the 1890's. As a child, I remember hearing frequent stories about life in Podhajce. It was my pleasure to coordinate the translation project and underwrite the translation into English of the Podhajce Yizkor (Memorial) Book. Now the publication of this book will allow others not only to read about the tragedy of the Shoah that occurred there, but also learn of the rich history that existed there before the community was obliterated. With this new book we hope to keep alive the memory of the Podhajce Jewish community for descendants of people from the town and all others who might want to find out about this vanished community.

Jean Rosenbaum, March 15, 2013

Acknowledgements

Special thanks to the National Yiddish Book Center in Amherst, Massachusetts and the New York Public Library for supplying the high resolution images used in this book.

Special acknowledgement to Jean and Mervin Rosenbaum who both funded and coordinated the translation of the Podhajce Yizkor Book into English.

History of Podhajce and Historical Documents

The history of the town of Podhajce includes shifting national boundaries. In 1795, Poland temporarily ceased to exist as a country, and Podhajce became part of the Austria-Hungarian Empire. After World War I, it was once again a part of Poland until occupied by the U.S.S.R. in the early days of World War II. After World War II, it became part of the U.S.S.R. It is now in Ukraine and is called Podgaytsy. Its location is about 101 kilometers (60 miles) ESE of Lvov.

The first Jews settled in Podhajce as far back as the beginning of the 16th century. In the years 1580 to 1620, a great Rabbi there, Benjamin Aharon Solnik, became famous in the Jewish world because of his essay "Benjamin's Mess", which is a collection of questions and answers in matters concerned with "Halacha". (The synagogue in New York of those originating from Podhajce is called Benjamin's Mess). Towards the end of the 17th century, many Jews of Podhajce were massacred by invading Turks and Tatars.

According to the census of 1764, there were 1079 Jews in the community. During the 19th century, the Jewish population increased, and by 1910 numbered about 6000. However, Podhajce's importance declined, and by 1939, 3200 Jews remained out of a total population of 6000. The Jews were the dynamic elements in the town's economic and cultural life.

When war broke out between Germany and the U.S.S.R. in 1941; Podhajce was occupied by the Germans, and the Jews immediately became victims of attacks by the Ukrainian population. They were forced to pay fines, their movements were restricted, and they were subjected to forced labor.

In 1942, on Yom Kippur, the Gestapo and the Ukrainian police sent about 1,000 Jewish men and women from Podhajce to the Belzec Death Camp. The remaining Jews were ordered into a small Ghetto, where many died of typhus. A month later, 1,500 more Jews were sent to Belzec. (At Belzec, more than 95% of the arrivals were killed either immediately or very soon after their arrival.) On June 6, 1943, the annihilation was completed when, with few exceptions, remaining members of the community were shot and dumped into mass graves on the outskirts of the town. (This was three days before Shavuot, on the third day of the month of Sivan.) Since there is no way of knowing when specific people perished, Yahrzeit for all of the Jews of Podhajce is observed on that day.

(Information for this article came from this Podhajce Memorial (Yizkor) Book and the Encyclopaedia Judaica.)

Alternate names: Pidhaytsi [Ukrainian], Podhajce [Polish], Podhaitza [Yiddish], Podgaytsy [Russian], Podhaits, Pidayets, Pidhayets, Pidhajci, Podgaitsy, Podgajcy, Podgaytse, Podhaytse, Pidhajzi

Notes to the Reader:

Within the text the reader will note "{page 34}" standing ahead of a paragraph. This indicates that the material translated below was on page 34 of the original book. However, when a paragraph was split between two pages in the original book, the marker is placed in this book after the end of the paragraph for ease of reading.

Also please note that all references within the text of the book to page numbers refer to the page numbers of the original Yizkor Book, not the page numbers in this book.

Family Notes

Table of Contents

Notes from Translator:
[Y] denotes a Yiddish section.
[Y – number] denotes Yiddish, which corresponds to an equivalent section in Hebrew.
[Y – number S] denotes that the Yiddish article is a summary of the equivalent section in Hebrew.

The City in its Destruction

The Annihilation [Y]

Translator's Footnotes

1. This entry is not in the table of contents of the book.
2. Note, this section is a summary of the corresponding Hebrew article on page 49 (of the original book), rather than a full translation.
3. There is no note in the text about this section being a summary of the corresponding Hebrew section on page 47 (of the original book) – but it appears to be. It misses numerous dates, and does not appear to be a translation.
4. In this case, the Hebrew is a brief summary of the much longer Yiddish article.
5. The Yiddish appears to be missing the first two paragraphs that are in the Hebrew.
6. Two anecdotes are missing in the Yiddish.
7. Appears to be largely a translation of the Hebrew on page 229 (of the original book), but there are some differences.

[English page 3]

Preface

The town Podhajce is in the northern corner of Eastern Galicia in the neighbourhood of the towns Brody, Tarnopol, and Czortkow.

In the year 1939, before the outbreak of World War II, it had a population of 6000, 3200 of whom were Jews. The Jews were the dynamic element in the town's economic and cultural life, and like most of the towns in Galicia and Ukraina, it was a Jewish town in the full meaning of the word.

The first Jews settled in Podhajce as far back as the beginning of the 16th Century, and towards the middle of the 16th Century a regular Jewish community was already in existence. In the years 1580 to 1620, a great Rabbi, named Benjamin Aharon Solnik, who took up residence in Podhajce became famous in the Jewish world because of his essay "Benjamins's Mess" which is a collection of questions and answers in matters concerned with "Halacha" (the synagogue of those originating from Podhajce in New York is called Benjamin's Mess, after the name of the book by this Rabbi).

Podhajder Synagogue "Mas'sat Benjamin" (Benjamin's Mess) in New York

Podhajcer Synagogue in New York - the Holy Ark

Also after Rabbi Benjamin A. Solnik, great Rabbis who made the town's name famous in all the Diaspora, took up residence in Podhajce.

Towards the end of the 17th Century, 1667-1699, the Jews of Podhajce suffered from the invasion of the Turks and the Tatars, and together with their Polish neighbours they defended the town against the enemy. Jan Sobieski, the famous Polish King, repulsed the Turks from Podhajce in 1667, and in memory . of this event, an impressive monument was erected in the town (see photo on page 43).

The great suffering that was caused to Podhajce and the neighbouring towns during the period of the Turkish invasion, perhaps caused many to believe that redemption is round the corner and to join those believers in the false Messias Shabtai Zvi, 1626-1676. Also in the Frankish movement in the year 1750-1760, many of the Podhajce Jews participated, and some of them even went over to Christianity in 1759 together with Jacob Frank.

Upon the division of Poland in 1772, all Galicia passed to the Austro-Hungarian Monarchy. With the outbreak of World War I, in 1914, the Austrian rule in Eastern Galicia came to an end. During the years of the first World War the whole region was controlled by the Russian Army, and at the end of the war upon the establishment of the Polish State, In1918, all Galicia passed to the Poles.

[English page 4]

In 1939, the World War II broke out with the invasion of the German Hitlerite Army into Poland. During the first years of the war, up to June 1941, the Russians, who occupied Poland's border areas according to the Molotov-Ribbentrop agreement, ruled the town.

However immediately upon the outbreak of the war between Germany and Russia, the Russians were compelled to withdraw and the German army occupied the whole of Galicia and continued to advance eastwards within the Russian Ukraine.

In the first year of their rule, the Nazis confined themselves to the oppression of the Jews and depriving them of their fundamental rights of free movement, the purchase of requirements etc. Also various contributions which were collected by cruel means were imposed and many of the men were recruited to compulsory work in labour camps which were set up in the area. The labour camps were, in effect, death camps, where the Jews did hard labour and there was a shortage of food, and for the slightest offence, the "offenders" were shot dead.

The first "operation" in Podhajce was in 1942 on Yom Kippur. The Gestapo, helped by the Ukrainian Police, surrounded the city, took about 1000 men and women out of their houses and took them to the railway station. There the people were placed in great congestion into railway trucks and were sent to the Belsetz Destruction Camp. Only a few people succeeded jumping out of the truck whilst the train was in motion, and then returned to Podhajce.

After the first operation, a Ghetto was set up in a small part of the town and all the Jews were ordered to go into the Ghetto within 24 hours. Congestion in the Ghetto was very great, and consequently, typhus broke out. The Germans made surprise raids in the Ghetto from time to time and whoever was ill was shot dead. They could leave the Ghetto for one hour a day only to buy food from the neighbouring farmers and whoever was found coming back after time was mercilessly beaten up by the Ukrainian Militia who were guarding the entrance to the Ghetto.

The second operation was made a short time after the first. This time too, the victims were sent to the destruction camp, in the same way as in the first action.

During the whole winter period, there were no further operations. With the coming of the spring at Pesach time, rumours circulated that the town would be proclaimed as "Judenrein" (Jew free) and no Jew was permitted to remain in it. And indeed the Germans, some weeks later, announced that all Jews who remained in town must present themselves in the market square. Whoever could find hiding, hid and did not come to the market square. However only a few could find a safe hideout and the great majority of the Jews were concentrated in the market square from whence they were brought to

“Holendra”.There they were ordered to dig the big grave -a mass grave - and all of them were shot dead near the hole into which they fell. Many of them fell into the grave while they were still alive, after they were either seriously injured or not injured at all. More then 1300 Jews were killed and buried that day.

The third operation - the operation of annihilation of Podhajce Jews took place three days before Shavout, on the third day of the month of Sivan. On this date the organisation of Podhajce immigrants in Israel arrange for a yearly memorial Service in memory of the holy victims.

After this action about 800 Jews still remained. Three days later they were ordered to gather at the market place, whence they would be sent to the Ghetto of Tarnopol. But as they came to Zahajce they were ordered to dig a mass grave and all of them were shot dead and buried there.

[English page 5]

At the end of World War II, only some dozens out of the Jewish population of Podhajce and the surroundings - at one time numbering 4000 people - remained. The majority of the rescued came to Israel, part of them arrived in the United States and only a few isolated ones remained in Poland.

The association of Podhajce immigrants in Israel participated in some drives which were made to eternalise the Holy of the city, such as the planting of trees in the “Forest of Holy Victims” on the way to Jerusalem, and the setting up of a memorial tablet in the Holocaust Cellar on Mount Zion in Jerusalem.

At the same time it was the ambition of the association throughout the years of its existence to issue a Book of Memoires to eternalise the memory of the town and its Jewish inhabitants, and it is only now that we succeeded in materialising our subject.

In this Memorial Book many of those who originate from our town, participated writing on the following subjects:
Rabbi Wolf Firestone-Brecher of New York- The Rabbis of Podhajce in all generations; Dr. Baruch Milch - Characters from the Near Past;

Yehudit Hadar - The Hebrew School in Podhajce, the First Kindergarten in Our Town, easts in Our Town.

Yehuda Grüssgott - Synagogues, Cheders and Teachers; the “Kadima” Student'n Union; Memories of Meier Mass, the Hero of the Town;

Etty Gross - The Hebrew School; Characters from Podhajce; Memories on the Residents of “Stare Miasto”.

Dr. Michael Weichert - Impressions and Memories from Podhajce; Baruch Schatten- “Ha-Noar-Hazioni” movement (the Zionist youth); M. Brandwein - “Hashomer-Hazair” movement.

Chaja Reich and Devorah Shapira - Life of Jews in Zlotnik; Dr. Heller - Various memories; Dr. Pomeranz - Various memories.

Apart from the above mentioned memories, historical articles were written by the Editor, M.S. Geshuri, and Mr. Nachman Blumenthal and two historical monographies from Dr. Herman Adler and Chaim Virshovski were copied.

Memories from the War Period and Destruction were written by Nachum Pushteig; Henia Shourz, Genia Shourz, Dr. Baruch Milch, Shoshana Feigenbaum, Shlomo Teicher, Ada Weiss, Sima Weissman, Joseph Kressel, Sara Rotstein-Drori and Leah Feldberg.

Podhajcer Attending Yizkor Ceremony in Yaar Hakdoshim (Forest of "Holy Memories")

[English page 6]

Podhajcer Association in Israel

The first immigrants from Podhajce arrived in Israel at the beginning of the twentieth century, during the years 1919-1925. There were individuals and families whose motives for coming to the country were religion and tradition, like Jossel Frisch and the Rabbi of Zavalov, and others who came for economic or social reasons, as they were trying to build their homes in the new country, which was promised to the people of Israel. At that time, the first of the pioneer immigration left Podhajce. Those were organised in the "Achwa" and "Shomer Hazair" Associations and passed their pioneer training prior to their immigration.

The majority of these immigrants joined the Kibbutzim and part of them have up to this day remained within the Kibbutz movement. In the course of time, immigrants from other movements too, such as "Hanoar Hazioni" and "Hechalutz" came to the country, occasionally being followed by other members of their families. In the course of the years preceding World War II, the numbers of immigrants of all kinds from Podhajce increased, and in the course of time reached 15 to 20 complete families.

It is worthwhile mentioning that not all the immigrants who arrived in the country integrated here and stayed on. Those who did not integrate left the country. Some of them who returned to Podhajce unfortunately perished there together with the other family members during the Holocaust.

As was customary during those days, there was no organisational link among those in the country, who originated from our town, and it was everyone's endeavour to integrate in the entirety of the renewed nation in its homeland.

Only towards the end of World War II when the few remained, surviving the holocaust, who were saved in a miraculous manner, by hiding in bunkers or in forests or as refugees in Russia, or posing as "Aryans", arrived here, the necessity was felt for a special framework for countrymen who considered it their duty to help as best they could for the rescue, as well as the need for a reunion from time to time to the memory of the martyrs of their town and to eternalise their memory.

The association of those originating from Podhajce in Israel was founded in 1951 and towards the end of this year on December 2nd, 1951, the first meeting of the members of the association was held, and a provisional committee, whose members were Mordechai Merker, Jehuda Weissman, Malka Globus, Feivish Mosberg and the late Yehuda Roll, were elected.

It must be pointed out that our association was established belatedly, after there were many associations from various towns of Galicia and Poland.

During this period, there was, in effect, no connection among our countrymen and it was even difficult to trace their residences in this country; The first to act for the establishment of the association were Mrs. Nechama Merker(nee Stem) and her husband Mr. Mordechai Merker who invested a great deal of effort in assembling the Podhajcers through advertising in the press and on the radio.

It must be placed to the credit of the Podhajcers that they responded to the call of the Provisional Committee and in the first Memorial Service for the martyrs of our town, which took place at the Beit Hachalutzot on January 23, 1952, about 200 of the people of our town, the majority of whom arrived after the holocaust, participated.

[English page 7]

The first memorial service was followed by a long period of absence of activity, and only in the memorial meeting held in 1954, an active committee consisting of the late Meier Zerubavel-Zloczower (the engineer of the Tel-Aviv Municipality) and Mordechai Merker, Yehuda Weissman, Dr. Baruch Milch, Menachem Ettinger, Joseph Schachter, Zvi Goralnik, and the late Yehoshua Stamler, was elected.

The Committee was headed by Meier Zerubavel - chairman, Mordechai Merker-treasurer, Yehuda Weissmann - secretary. This time, too, it was due to Mordechai Merker's and his wife Nechama's efforts that the association's activities was revived and a new committee was elected, who started actual activities.

Since the committee of the association was elected in 1954, an annual memorial service for the.martyrs of our town is held on the 3rd day of Sivan, the day of the liquidation operation in Podhajce. The organisation committee has been active consistently since that time, performing some operations, highlighted by the publication of this book.

The first activity on the agenda was the planting of trees in the Forest of the Martyrs. This operation required the amount of IL1000-.which we had to pay to the Directorate of the Jewish National Fund. Without waiting for the organisation of the appeal of our members to take action, the members of the Committee convened and of their own money collected the sum required for making the agreement with the Jewish National Fund and only subsequently upon receipt of the consideration for the trees from the members of the association, the amount paid by them in advance was gradually refunded to them.

The second activity for eternalising the memory of the martyrs was the placing of a memorial tablet in the Holocaust Cellar. This operation was perfomed in 1964. At present the memorial tablet for the Podhajce Community is among the memorial tablets of its sister towns, which were destroyed in Galicia and Poland, and now, year by year before to the memorial service, our members proceed to the memorial tablets as to the tomb of their loved ones to pour out their bitter hearts and to moisten with their tears the cold stone symbolising the memory of our relations and dear friends who were murdered “al kiddush hashem”, for being faithful sons of the one and specific Jewish nation in the world. In financing the setting up of the memorial tablet, thanks to the initiative of our member Mr. Isser Roller the landsmanshaft of our town in the United States participated substantially.

[English page 8]

In the year 1964, the late Meeir Zerubavel who was the chairman of the association since 1954, up to the day of his death, passed away. Close to this date, Mr. Menachem Ettinger was elected chairman of the Association Committee, which office he holds up to the present day. During this period an energetic operation was launched for the publication of the Memorial Book of the Community.

The idea concerning the publication of the “Yiscor” Book to eternalise the memory of our Community was suggested as far back as 1961 by a number of members headed by Dr. Milch and Mr. Menachem Ettinger and his wife Bluma; however only in the year 1965 a special committee consisting of the members Dr. Baruch Milch, Menachem Ettinger, Yehuda Weissman, Shlomo Walden, Zwi Goralnik, Yehuda Grüssgott, Shraga Hessel, Mrs. Clara (Chaja) Stoop nee Milch, Baruch Shatten, Uri Milstock, Munio Brandwein and others, was elected. The Committee of the Book was entrusted with the task of raising the necessary funds for the publication of the book and concentrating the material for its printing - articles, testimonies, photos etc.

With the commencement of the operation and the appeal for the publication of the memorial book, we felt the necessity of giving the association a legal form and in the year 1965 we registered the organisation as an association in accordance with the Ottoman Law. Advocate Arie Ben Charutz worked out, voluntarily and free of charge, the statutes and had them approved by the authorities and we hereby express to him our gratitude and our esteem.

At the same time an energetic action was launched which made many and frequent session of the members of the committee necessary and which necessitated a great deal of work in sending of invitations, letters, circulars and questionaires to our countrymen in Israel and abroad.

One of the main difficulties with which the committee was faced was inherent in raising the many funds required for publishing the book.

The number of members of our association is not considerable and the majority of them are of moderate means. We applied several times to the Landsmanschaft of our town in the United States, but it was not easy to induce them to come to our help in our efforts to carry out the sacred task which we undertook.

In 1968, during the Passover holidays Dr. Milch, on the occasion of his visit to New York succeeded in organising a Committee consisting of the members Isser Roller, Jehoshua (Shia) Freedman, Mr. Gruber, Mitzio Frish, and Shlomo Reiss who undertook to assist us in the publication of the Book.

Party of Podhajcer in New York

Meeting of Podhajcer in New York

[English page 9]

During Dr. Milch's stay in New York, a meeting of our countrymen in the Synagogue of Podhajce emigrants was convened (named after the late Rabbi Benjamin Solnik the author of the book "Mas'at Benjamin") where Dr. Milch explained at length the subject of the publication of the book, urging the participants to assist in this task. This operation resulted in raising more than $1000.- which Mr. Roller collected from the Podhajce and surrounding emigrants, which amount was handed to Dr. Milch as the Landsmanshaft's contribution to the publication of the book.

Apart from this, only a few and isolated persons out of our countrymen responded by contributions ranging from $100 to $200 (according to a specification of contributors in the country and abroad attached to this booklet.)

The assistance of two Podhajcers in the United States namely that of Rabbi Wolf Firestone and Mr. Isser Roller must be particularly stressed. Rabbi Firestone himself wrote an article for us on Podhajce Rabbis in their generations and availed himself of every opportunity to urge the members of the Landsmanshaft to come to our help. Mr. Isser Roller and his wife Hanah (nee Grossman) continued in their activity for our interest. and remitted to us some hundreds of dollars which they collected among the members of our Landsmanshaft in the United States.

It is interesting to note that among our countrymen in the United States, who had an indifferent attitude towards the publication of the book and even showed opposition, there were also some "new immigrants" who arrived there after World War II, and who felt all the terrible events of the Holocaust. Even among the members who were elected to the Book Committee in New York, there were some who opposed this idea. There were also some among our countrymen in Israel who disassociated themselves from this activity, among them were such who were financially sound and those gifted with eloquence, who refrained from any material and spiritual participation in the publication of this book.

It was not easy to concentrate material for the memorial book. We addressed ourselves at every occasion to the Podhajce in Israel and abroad, requesting them to furnish us with descriptions and memories on the life of our town in the near and distant past so that the book may truly illustrate the status and significance of the Podhajce Community which was destroyed. In the course of time our call had a certain response and material was accumulated, which made it possible for us to contract an editor for putting it into print, by editing and translation.

The editor Mr. Sh. Geshouri also agreed to make an historical survey on the strength of the material found in various historic sources and thanks to this, at the beginning of the book, there is an interesting and comprehensive survey of the history, giving an idea on the history of the town and the Jewish Community in it from the beginning of its foundation up to the close of its tragic annihilation.

[English page 10]

There is also a contribution (in Yiddish) written by Mr. Nachman Blumenthal, who comes from our area (from the town of Borszczow) and a monography written by him on a forgotten author named Oizarkis, who lived in our town towards the end of the 19th century and the first years of the 20th century. We were also instructed by Dr. Kermish, the director of the archives of Yad-Va-Shem; and by the late Professor Abraham Weiss, who comes from our town and who, during the last years, lived in Jerusalem.

From the Yad- Va-Shem archives we received some important testimonies on the events during the period of the holocaust, which are included in the last part of the book, describing the destruction of the Jewish community in our town. This part also. includes a detailed report on the struggle to rescue a number of families, which was written by Mrs. Henya Shourtz of our town.

One of the most important and most difficult problems was the concentration of the names of the Holocaust victims of our town and the surroundings with a view to etemalising them in the book so that their memory should not pass into oblivion in the course of the generations.

A countless number of times we applied to the people of our town, stressing the great importance we attach to submission of full and properly arranged lists of the names of everyones relatives, friends and acquaintances; and indeed we received many lists of names of people who perished during the Holocaust, but there is no certainty that the list is indeed complete and that there are no defects and various distortions and we solicit our members indulgence and understanding for each phenomenon of this kind, only considering the objective difficulties with which we were faced.

Finally we would like to express our appreciation to all those who did not spare their efforts and time in helping us to publish this book, and in particular to the committee members Dr. Baruch Milch, Mr. Menachem Ettinger and his wife, Mrs. Clara Stoop and Messrs. Weissman, Walden und Merker, who carried on their shoulders the main responsibility for this extensive and prolonged activity. Our particular appreciation goes to those not of our town, who engaged in the publication of this book, to the Editor Mr. M. Sh. Gehsori, the proof reader Mr. Lindenberg and to "Ot" printing press, Tel-Aviv, who took care of the printing of the book, which is so precious to all of us.

Podhajcer Attending Yizkor Ceremony in Yaar Hakdoshim (Forest of "Holy Memories")

[English page 11]

Podhajce – After the Destruction

By Dr. Baruch Milch

My first meeting with the ruins of Podhajce was a short time after its final liberation. It was after a wearisome journey that I arrived at the place, on account of lack of regular transportation and the danger of raids.

It was in the summer, three months after the first liberation by irregular Soviet troops, who after a ten days stay in our town were compelled to withdraw eastwards and again leave the town and the surroundings under a cruel regime of the Nazis. For this reason I did not find the whole small group of Jews who remained here and were rescued, as part of them fled eastwards with the retreating Russian troops.

In fact, I was not present in Podhajce together with all my dear relatives and friends during the time of the main destruction and therefore did not have the "privilege" of seeing the destruction of my native town with my own eyes in its last hours, the town where I was raised, where I studied and where most of my dear and numerous family of more than twelve persons perished (my parents, two of my sisters with their husbands and children, my brother Joseph with his wife and two daughters). I did not then know that I remained the only one and the last of the entire family. Only some time later I found out that my younger brother, Nathan, who was recruited into the Soviet Army in 1940, fell near Stalingrad. I left my family as far back as 1939, and was expelled by the Soviets who found my family as being burgeoise, the same way they found this defect with other middle class Jewish families and they provided their identity cards with the "sign of Cain" - paragraph 1l. This tragic paragraph prevented aU those unfortunate holders of this certificate from full movement, and full access only to certain places. The possibilities of study for children were limited and and now they sometimes were in for criminal trials, jail and the like.

And now my tum came. As the son of a family with the ill-famed "paragraph II" in my identity card, I was transferred as a physician to another town - to the town of Tluste, Galicia, with a charming Jewish community, and fate wanted it, that I should remain there during almost the whole period of the Holocaust. My activity there is to some extent described in the Memorial Book that appeared on behalf of those who originate from this town, in Israel. In this town I lost my nearest family, who were murdered cruelly and tragically. My only son, aged 3, was buried alive in a mass grave while he was still embraced in the arms of my sister-in-law Clara Weinles, a beautiful 17 year-old girl, who during one of the "operations" got a bullet in her head and fell together with the child alive into the ditch together with hundreds of others killed. The same day they took with them, out of the bunker where I hid them, my mother-in-law the late Mrs. Rachel Weinles,whom they murdered. I found this out one day after I returned to town. In this town I also lost my first wife Peppi Milch nee Weinles who was taken out with her sister-in-law Eve and her 3 1/2 years old son from an underground hiding place in a field and both were murdered by the SS and their Ukrainian assistants. On arriving at Podhajce and at the first sight of my destroyed town, I imagined in my mind and in my heart all that it and its people underwent during the three years of the destruction when I was away. Even before I met with and talked to the Jewish people of Podhajce, before my eyes passed all the events and scenes of the "seven stages of purgatory" as I saw at Tluste and which was the fate met by all the Jewish settlements and communities in Poland, and suddenly before my

eyes there were again scenes of the Ghetto, operations, expulsions from homes, rooms full of hungry children and sick people with all kinds of infectious diseases. All the things that I already saw in another place and which was exactly similar to the goings-on here, since as a physician I had on more than one occasion access to places which were prohibited to others. I had the terrible "privilege" to come face to face with the horror. And again .I saw with my own eyes Jews with their bundles, property and belongings who were expelled from place to place, from village to town, from street to street, from house to house and from room to room, and I saw - my eyes were spared no sights - hundreds of human corpses of innocent people systematically murdered in a most satanic way and with every murderer's device. Some of them were caught and sent to camps from which they never came back, and they never saw the faces of their families, as happened with my abovementioned brother-in-law the late Auzias Walfish. Some of them were shot on the spot or died of starvation, of disease or of inhuman beatings. There were others who died a slow death of congestion, frost and bad clothing, of typhus and desyntheria, and by this proved and cruel method the Nazi murderers also destroyed our town Podhajce.

[English page 12]

However, my suffering was still greater when I brought up in my memory the town of Podhajce which once was a town full of Jewish life where there was a class of Jewish intelligencia, of Rabbis, of leading businessmen, of excellent craftsmen, scientists and men of repute and ordinary happy Jewish families, from amongst the people. And what is left of all this? Everything turned to dust and ashes, everything destroyed and not existing any longer. Jewish Podhajce strangled in the Ghetto, in cellars, in bunkers, in deep ditches, in forests, in camps and in mass graves. And then I fell into thoughts until my decision ripened not to refrain from any efforts until I will have succeeded to express in some way and to some extent and to eternalise in some form at least part of this big tragedy within the framework of the Memorial Book of our town, where the blood of my family, my relatives my friends and my acquaintances, were shed; a town which in my inner-most exists with all its might and the memory of which will never leave my thought.

It was Sunday when I arrived at Podhajce. In one of the main streets of the town, (Brezezianska) where they used to go from the Greek Catholic (Ukrainian) Church to the Centre of the town (Market Square), I met the majority of the Ukrainian population of the town and its outskirts on leaving the church, after they had finished their prayers. They were mostly youngsters and women with many children, all of them uninhibited and gay. When I looked at them I felt as if recently they underwent nothing, nor did they suffer from anything. They were all dressed in their Sunday best with holiday faces. They talked amongst themselves in a loud voice and even laughed, not paying any attention to the many stones on the repaired pavements, on which they walked, and which were taken from the tombstones of the Jewish Municipal Cemetery, on which the inscriptions, the names of the deceased and dates, were apparent.

It was at that time already that I was sure, that among the mass leaving the church there were many who collaborated with the Nazi gangsters and in those there were many who got rich from plundering from Jews. They were possibly not happy with the political situation and the regime upon the entry of the Soviets to our area. Howewer I saw and felt the satisfaction and gratification by the gentiles, which even included their good elements who saw murdering of the Jews as the finger of God, as a punishment for murdering Jesus... Some of them who hardly recognised me, said hello to me, wondering at the sight of their eyes as they did not believe that I remained alive, and certainly regretted it.

[English page 13]

It is very difficult to put on paper my feeling upon my coming to Podhajce and my meeting with the first of the survivors. I found that the survivors huddled together and lived in congestion, the only reason for this being that they wished to find some warmth and encouragement. I did not even find a grain of joy in this sad meeting. We were all pervaded by a heavy load of memories, nightmares, and tears strangled our voices.

We were still in a maze and had no mental capacity to get used to the idea that only we, the few who were here, survived with all our dear ones taken away from us. It was then that I remembered the saying of our sages: "anyone maintaining one soul of Israel is considered as if having maintained the whole world"; and indeed after this destruction and annihilation of our people in Poland and other countries, each surviving Jewish soul was considered a world of its own. I enquired into the tribulations of the life of every one of the survivors and as to how he succeeded in remaining alive. They finally gave in to my entreaties and opened their hearts to me. We heard of the horrid operations; of the operations of the Judenrat, on the "Ordnungsdiensten", on the plundering of the property and the various murderous methods up to the liquidation of the Ghetto, on expropriation and penalties. The atmosphere in the town was tense, about 70% of the Jewish residential homes, shops and synagogues were razed to the ground, and on the other hand, the majority of the other buildings, amongst which was the building of the great Synagogue, their appearance was like after a pogrom or a great fire. Not even roofs were to be seen, only broken windows and doors, bare walls and rooms without furniture. Only in a few houses of Jews there were Christians living past neighbours or farmers from the outskirts, some of whom were once employed with the Jews as workers, wood choppers, domestic servants and the like. With many, the plundered Jewish property remained. On the other hand, in the houses that were in a better condition, the government offices installed themselves and part of them were occupied by Soviet officials. Unfortunately, all my families houses, mine, that of my parents, my sisters and my brothers, remained intact and they were occupied by Christians of the folk or from Russia.

I entered my parents home, next to the Government house, on which the sign "POWIAT" was apparent. There I found two Christian families, one of our former domestic servant and the family of the worker who once was employed by my parents. On seeing me entering, I saw how surprised they were, and nevertheless they appeared as if they were happy that I survived whereas in point of fact, they were concerned for themselves and sad. They did not talk to me at all about the past, and only enquired what I was going to do. They suggested that I stay overnight with them and naturally I did not think of accepting their advice as otherwise I could not today have brought up these memories.

The few survivors who gathered from their hiding places, from the surroundings, from the forests and bunkers, all of them lived together on one house, that of Mordechai Lehrer in the centre of the town, fearing the nationalist Ukrainians who might want to destroy them, thus leaving no trace of the local Jews, who could one day testify against them or claim the return of the robbed property. We all went to the mass grave, to pray in public and to say Kaddish in memory of the martyrs, and only with the greatest difficulty could a "Minyan" be gathered as only two families remained alive completely, namely the Gross and the Shurtz family. The others were lonely men or lonely women. One of the survivors showed me a photo of a mass grave which was open, as some days before a government committee of "Shernik" came whose members went from place to place to investigate Nazi crimes.

[English page 14]

It was a heartbreaking experience to look at the photo where we saw the various parts of bodies of hundreds of people - men, women and children who were murdered. on the spot. According to the information I received, my parents, too, were murdered. there. This happened in the course of one of the last operations at "Holendra" in the direction of the Brzezan road out of town.

Mr. I. Schourtz standing next to the tombstone of the holy victims in Holendra

The ditch was now covered with fresh soil,entirely even and there was calm and tranquillity all round, not even the rustling of leaves or the twittering of birds, as is sometimes heard in a cemetery, as there was no tree on the spot. We took a big sheet of paper on which we wrote a brief history of this mass grave with dates. We introduced this sheet into a secure bottle which we closed and buried it very deep next to the grave. So far as for the history of this mass grave.

The following day I went out to the second mass grave of the martyrs of Podhajce and the surroundings which is at a greater distance from the town in the direction of the village Zahajce.

This visit was prone with the danger of death, as the road there was next to a Ukrainian village from which there was a danger on the part of the Bandero gangs. I was therefore warned not to expose myself to this danger by leaving the borders of the town by myself, as the intelligenzia was a special target they sought to liquidate .

I was moreover told that a week ago the only surviving Jewish pharmacist was murdered. This was Chaimke Weitraub, who went from Podhajce in a carriage to the neighbouring town Brzezany to bring some remedies and to reopen the local pharmacy, whom the Banderowce murdered in cold blood in the forest next to the village Muzilow.

I also understood that when the Germans declared Podhajce as Jew-free (Judenrein) they took the survivors of all the operations, who were strong people and in good health, under the pretext that they were being moved to the labour camp in Tarnopol (amongst them there was also the entire family of my brother Joseph) but when they arrived out of town they were all shot and murdered. Here on the spot of the mass grave an entirely different picture presented itself. Here on the place of the grave the soil sank for about one meter below the ground level of the surrounding area, which was all covered with thorns and wild flowers. In some spots there were holes and inclines, and it was really dangerous to pass on the spot. A special odour was felt, which helped to find the ditch. I stood there for about half an hour hanging around by myself on the spot, and again before my eyes passed the terrible scene of which I was an eye-witness at the time two days after one of the big operations at Tluste, where hundreds of Jews with their children were murdered and buried alive in a mass grave, and among them my only three year-old son.

[English page 15]

Then, indeed, two days after the murder, there was an entirely different picture from the present one. Then the ground of the mass-grave was raised above the level, and each time it was raised higher whereas in another place it sank. Between the furrow there were streams of blood and other liquids, and a terrible odour of death pervaded the air. In consequence of the gas emanating from the bodies which were buried alive, one could see individual limbs or some hand raised into the air, as if demanding revenge for the bloodshed. Also now when I stood in front of this terrible ditch, I found in the surroundings some remains, tom clothes, children's shoes, broken objects and fragments of silverware, which the victims got rid of in the last moments. In this terrible place also empty bullet shells and empty bottles, originating from the murderer's drinks, were lying around This sight made my blood run cold and the wrong cried up to heaven. In these moments, I was oblivious of the whole world, and I was enwrapped in this poor blood that was shed. When all this happened the heads of Governments in the various countries, who now talk highly about truth and justice, remained silent in their impotence to do something against the barbaric actions of the blood-thirsty Germans.

With a broken heart and eyes red from crying I left the fraternal grave. Gradually I came back to myself and I returned to town. I made a round of the town, and though it was an ordinary week-day, the sight of the town was as if on the eve of Yom Kippur- a quiet day without traffic and life, without open shops as in “olden days” before the Holocaust.

Cars were “non-existent”; apart from isolated carriages, no vehicles were seen and apart from some soldiers of the Red Army or Soviet Officials there was no living soul in the street. I also did a round. of the Jewish cemetery and found it fenceless, forsaken and neglected. The house with the room for prayers next to the door, and also the gate itself, were destroyed and only some high trees and remains of tombstones remained there on the whole area. It was indeed the rustling of the trees and grass that made one think that at any rate there was still the Holy Spirit in the air, guarding the dead buried beneath the soil, and it was as if the spirit was saying that not everything yet was lost and there was still a watchful eye.

Then I made for the great Synagogue which I entered, and which was deserted and open, doorless and windowless. Inside I did not find a trace of the Holy Ark, and only here and there bits of the Holy Books or bits of paper, written in Hebrew, were seen. Also here deadly silence of the vicinity, the sound of the draught through the windows and the twittering of the night bird made a terrifying impression, and I could not hold back my urge to cry. I saw God's House destroyed by the impure and was filled with feelings of anger and revenge for what was perpetrated by people claiming education and culture... It was not easy for me to leave the destroyed sanctity, where I once spent pleasant hours in the company of relatives and friends on Saturdays, holidays and week days alike and this brought up in my memory the poetry "the Holy City and its surroundings became the scene of shame and looting."

I left the synagogue, and looked round. Here was the centre of the town with the side Streets that once reverberated with gay Jewish life, now almost deserted, almost empty - a barren desert. The block of houses in the centre of the town, which existed for hundreds of years and the stores, ninety percent of which belonged to the Jews, were definitely destroyed and each time I passed through one of the streets, or entered a deserted house, it was as if I expected to hear the voices of living people, and it was some strange feeling that compelled me to run away quickly from the place.

[English page 16]

The Ghetto area offered a particularly shocking sight. I went into Moshe Lieblich's house, which during the Diaspora period served as a store for the property of the Jews who were murdered during the operations, and even then there were remains of clothes and broken tools of Jews who died. In my view it would be worth while to preserve those items as a Holy memory - but who is going to do this work?

I was at Podhajce three to four days and I scoured the town through its length and width and with my own eyes I saw the destruction of the Jewish community. I investigated and asked acquaintances and others about relatives and distant friends, when I found that none of my near or distant family had remained alive.

After I had arrived at the bitter and terrible "Full-stop", I could see I no longer had business in this town and I decided to leave it forthwith. However, even this was not of the easiest things, on account of lack of regular transport and danger on the roads. The majority of the local offices were only partly organised, and the same Ukrainians who previously collaborated with the Germans now were working there, and when I entered any office to get information or any assistance, these officials enquired into how I had succeeded to remain alive, when others perished, or: why did not the Jews defend themselves? And each time I had to give them again a new lecture on our precarious position during the Nazi period, though there was no need to add a great deal to what was common knowledge.

They were however unwilling to admit that each defence was doomed to failure, in view of the hostile Ukrainian neighbourhood, who helped the enormous military power of the

Germans. The fate of the Polish population bore witness to this, since after they had finished with the Jews they started liquidating the Poles in our surroundings, who did not succeed either to defend themselves. At that time I did not know about the uprising of the Jews of the Warsaw Ghetto; however, I told them about the passive resistance and defence with heroic deeds which occurred in many places and in Podhajce, for which I had evidence from the survivors.

I heard of the heroic death of the woman pharmacist Ornstein and Bertha Dauber and Leibush Lilienfeld, who poisoned themselves in the middle of the operation. They told me about the active resistance of a young man named Kovash Mates in our town- a former officer in the Polish Army -- who, while the operation was going on, drew a gun from his pocket and shot a German. Unfortunately this was not of much avail. Policemen got hold of the young man whom they did not shoot, but they beat him to death. The same day half of the Jewish Ordnungsdienst was wiped out. I pointed out to the officials, to whom I talked, the heroic deeds of the Jews and of the partisans, who inflicted all kinds of sabotage on the Germans, when for some time they lived under a clandestine Christian name or were wandering in the forest with anti-Nazi groups, as myself did when I was connected with the underground and the Polish resistance movement.

This was the only way of survival. There were cases, when after most of the family were murdered, some took up arms and others resisted without arms, and at a moment of lack of any other choice those defenceless mustered unusual courage and through heroic deeds succeeded in saving themselves in the last moment from annihilation. My narrations to the officials on the heroic deeds, while the sword of the destruction was on their very throats, sounded in their ears like cock and bull stories or fairy tales.

In my heart of hearts there is no doubt what they thought: pity that these few are still alive...

They showed no intention of assisting me in anything in my endeavour to leave the town and to return to my medical work as the Director of the Municipal Hospital at Zaleszczyki, where I was due to be back at a certain time.

[English page 17]

Fortunately, on Thursday a soldiers convoy appeared, which was en route to the Tarnopol district. I availed myself of this opportunity and joined it, and thus I succeeded to leave this God forsaken place, which at one time was so close to my heart. I took leave of a small group of survivors, as they did not concentrate in one place, fearing that they would be caught and sent to forced labour to the "Dombas" as was then customary, and the others were engaged in various preparations to leave the town where they suffered so much and where they were now left with their sad memories.

Particularly ardent was their desire to take advantage of the "repatriation law'" (the return of refugees to Western Poland) and thus to remove themselves more and more from this town, coming as close as possible to a safer place.

Everyone hoped to find some family or a good friend among the Jews of the United States or of Palestine, with the help of whom they would be able to reestablish themselves. On leaving the town, it was difficult for me to take my eyes off it and not look behind, and in my heart I thought: What a pity that there is one stone left in this town, and prayed to God that it would all go up in flames and that no memory of it or its inhabitants should be left, like Sodom and Gomorrah.

The whole town was worthy of the punishment of destruction after the annihilation of the Jews, since but for their help the Germans would have been incapable of perpetrating their crime of this total destruction. The Ukrainians were not embarrassed to admit that that is indeed what they wanted and no desire of theirs was more ardent than this, namely that there should not be a single living Jew left in the town, so that there would be no one left to strive for vengeance for the blood of his brethren whose only crime was their Jewishness and their Hebrew race.

I returned from Podhajce to Zaleszczyki, the place of my work, all broken from this sight in my native town and mentally depressed from the terrible crisis that befell my people. I did not believe that I could still muster strength to start a new and orderly life and to cut my losses, or that the tragedy that I underwent on the loss of my dear and beloved ones should pass into oblivion.

The fact that I did muster the strength and obtained new forces from nature and succeeded in reaching safe ground does not mean that we are free to forget our martyrs without erecting some memory for those who perished during the Holocaust of the Nazi period.

The crying voices of our martyrs ask for revenge. and we cannot turn a blind eye to what we were told in the Torah: " Thou shalt remember what Amalek did to you"

własnoreczny podpis

Jprawnia do przejazdów państwowy
irodkami komunikacyjnymi według u
aryfowych dla urzędników państwowy

Legitymacja nr. 47

Ob. Dr. Zielinski
Jan

ur. 20.6.1907 r. Podhajce

zam. Opola, Pl. Czerwonej Armii 5

zatrudniony (a) jest w Panstwowym Urzędzie Repatriacyjnym, Powiatowy Oddział w Opolu

w charakterze Lekarz
Kierownik Refer. Zdrowia

Ważna do dnia 31 grudnia 1945 r.

Opole, dnia 17 listopada 1945

Kierownik Oddziału

Dr. B. Milch Identity Card

[Page 6]

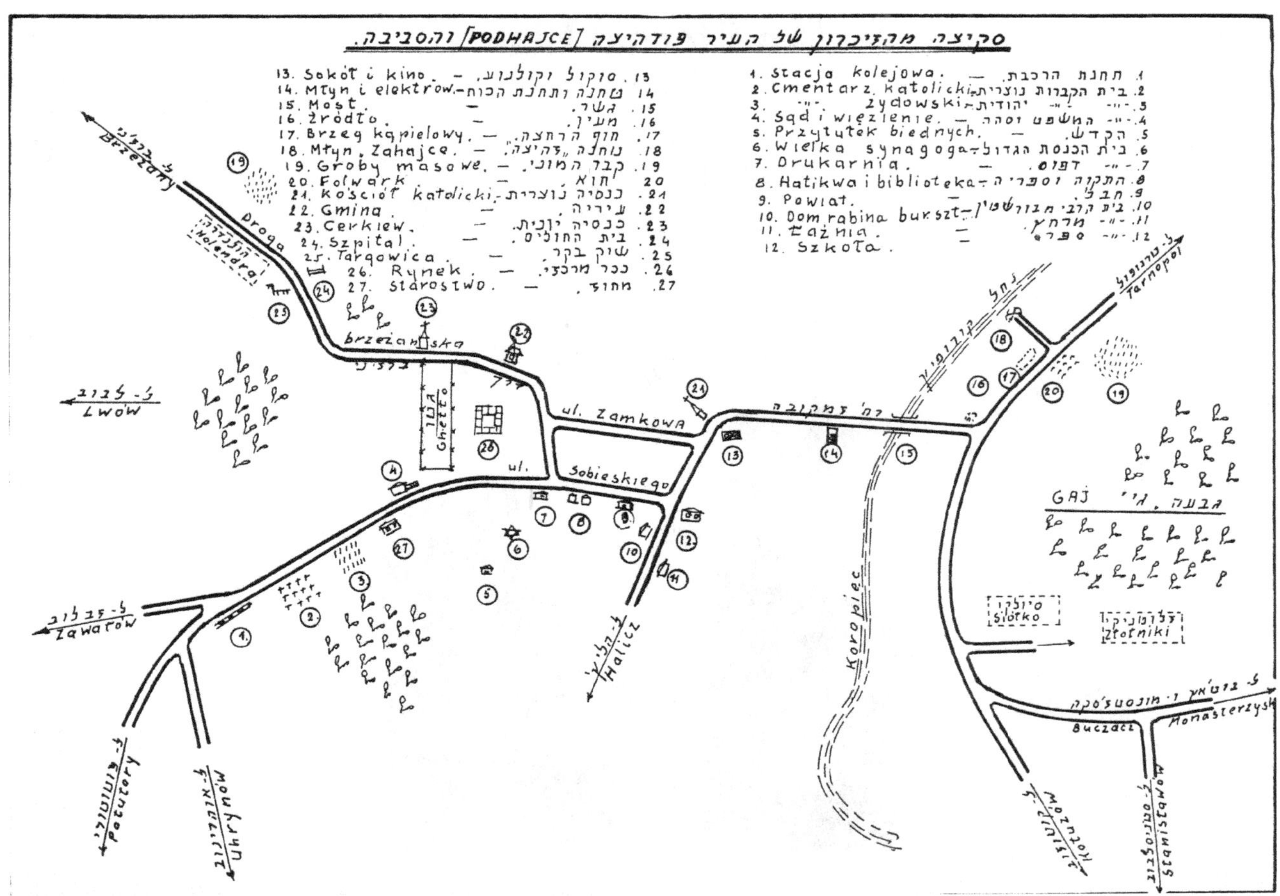
סקיצה מהזיכרון של העיר פודהיצה [PODHAJCE] והסביבה.
1. Stacja kolejowa. — תחנת הרכבת .1
2. Cmentarz katolicki — בית הקברות נוצרית .2
3. " Żydowski — " יהודית .3
4. Sąd i więzienie. — המשפט וסהר .4
5. Przytułek biednych. — הקדש .5
6. Wielka synagoga — בית הכנסת הגדול .6
7. Drukarnia. — דפוס .7
8. Hatikwa i biblioteka — התקוה וספריה .8
9. Powiat. — חבל .9
10. Dom rabina burszt — בית הרבי מבורשטין .10
11. Łaźnia. — מרחץ .11
12. Szkoła. — ספר .12
13. Sokół i kino. — סוקול וקולנוע .13
14. Młyn i elektrow. — טחנה ותחנת הכוח 14
15. Most. — גשר .15
16. Źródło. — מעין .16
17. Brzeg kąpielowy. — חוף הרחצה .17
18. Młyn, Zahajce. — טחנה „זהיצה" .18
19. Groby masowe. — קבר המוני .19
20. Folwark. — חוא 20
21. Kościół katolicki — כנסיה נוצרית .21
22. Gmina. — עיריה .22
23. Cerkiew. — כנסיה יונית .23
24. Szpital. — בית החולים .24
25. Targowica. — שוק בקר .25
26. Rynek. — ככר מרכזי .26
27. Starostwo. — מחוז .27
Brzeżany
Droga
brzeżańska
Lwów
Ghetto
ul. Zamkowa
ul. Sobieskiego
Zawarów
Potutory
Uhrynów
Halicz
Koropiec
Tarnopol
GAJ
Słotko
Złotniki
Buczacz
Monasterzysk
Stanisławów

Map from memory of the city of Podhajce and its surrounding area

[Page 7]

Introduction to the Book

An Eternal Light

Editor's introduction

The Editor Mr. M. Sh. Geshuri

With the appearance of this Yizkor book, another monument has been erected, another eternal candle has been added to those that have already been lit and erected in memory of the destruction and devastation, and another tragic link has been added to the terrible writ of accusation against Nazi Germany and its enterprise of murder against our people. Included among the pages of this book is another attempt to rescue the image of the community of Podhajce as it appeared to us from the pit of oblivion – a community that existed for hundreds of years, and now is no more and will never be again.

Podhajce, one of the countless towns in Poland and Galicia, excelled in well-rooted, vivacious Judaism with a tradition of hundreds of years, and an alert and lively Jewish community that was concerned for the existence of the nation and its future. In addition to this, the city excelled in its scribes, scholars, wise men and illustrious rabbis who were known also outside the bounds of the city and the country. The names of Podhajce natives were displayed gloriously in books and documents as people of worth and spirit. Whoever will leaf through the pages of this book will be thoroughly convinced that the community of Podhajce was focused upon the life of Torah and culture, and that its people were active in many and various fields of endeavor and effort. Exciting and sublime spiritual acquisitions found a resting-place in this locale, and with the passage of years, etched their seal upon any open heart, bent ear and sensitive soul. As they became absorbed, some of their bearers of the tradition became captivated by the charm to the point that they saw themselves as duty bound to join various movements and streams that arose and were established in their wake: some in order to enthusiastically and diligently shelter and protect the existence the fruits of consolidation of the tradition, its followers and leaders, and to transmit it to future generations – and others in order to undermine and weaken the edifice of the generations, and to establish the life of the nation and its national creativity upon new foundations that their parents would not have imagined. Throughout the generations, Jewish Podhajce lay between the freezing of tradition and boldly forging toward a change of order – a constant, energetic struggle between the old and the new. The community of Podhajce with its lights and shadows, its longings and agony, was a forging furnace for new concepts and ideas that took up wings in the spiritual life of our nation as it dug to renew its consciousness as in days of yore.

The reader who is a native of the city, who flies through the pages of the book, will certainly feel anew the overflowing wave of warmth flowing over his entire essence – an hour where the images are so recognizable and dear to him that they flash before his eyes, stand as if they are alive before him in their full splendor and glory. It will be an hour when the landscapes and places that were so familiar and precious to him once again appear before him and awaken associations from bygone days. It will be an hour when the events and experiences that were an inseparable part of his essence in the past and are etched on the tablet of his heart come forth, are restored before him and cause his soul and spiritual world to soar. The form and image of our native community, as it is seen in the book, will him to those days, laden with tribulation and grief but also crowned with beauty and hope, days when the body was mired in muddy abyss of the degenerate reality of the exile, but the spirit was floating toward the future in the heavens and seeing new worlds. Our book, that erects a monument to the destroyed community of Podhajce, is a document full of memories and tears of a well-rooted Jewish community, with its flourishing, thriving life full of energy, power and dynamism; and, on the other hand, the tragic days of the eve of the liquidation and the destruction.

Nobody would argue that were it not for the tragedy of the setting of Jewish Podhajce, the remnants of natives who live in Israel and in the Diaspora would not turn from their preoccupations and worries in order to perpetuate their city and all that happened to it. It seems to me that they would see no need for such, due to the absence of any trace of pretentiousness on the part of the survivors to enwrap themselves in the writer's cloak. That task of digging through sources and ancient scrolls would be left to the researchers of history, whose job that is. However the fact regarding Jewish Podhajce – along with other communities of Israel – the destruction in such a malicious and hair-raising fashion imposes the obligation to erect a monument of testimony for that community, to sanctify the memory of those dear personalities of the common folk and scholars, Hassidim and people of deeds who were active in that community. On the other hand, we do not boast that the material before us presents a comprehensive and exhaustive picture of Jewish Podhajce in all of its facets. It is not lost upon us that several eras, and many important institutions and events are missing from their place in the book, whether on account of a lack of historical sources, or time pressures that prevented some of the natives of the town from diverting themselves from their day to day concerns in order to clear their gaze toward a matter that has a spark of eternal life. Nevertheless, we believe that, despite these serious strictures, the material that is contained in the pages of this book is sufficient to present a survey, more or less, of Jewish Podhajce. We have invested so much effort and toil in order to give this community a monument among the other communities of Israel that were destroyed.

[Page 8]

A common principal in Yizkor Books is that they are written by people whose profession is not the pen. It is only the feeling of obligation and responsibility to perpetuate their city, so that it will not disappear and be silenced with the passing of the last of this generation that imposed upon them the challenge to take the writer's quill into their non-professional hands. As the editor of the book, I expended a great deal of effort in composing the chapters on the history of the community, on its rabbis and scholars, in order to reconstruct as well as possible the human landscape of the community. I can testify about myself that I did not perform my task in composing the historical material as a paid worker, but rather as a mitzvah[1] that is obligatory upon anyone who is able to help the activists who toil toward the end of publishing the book. In the merit of this miztvah, I succeeded in finding the sources that made it possible for me to edit the timeline, to discover the names of rabbis and scholars who lived in Podhajce. Had I not revived them and placed them into the book, they would have been consigned to oblivion. Therefore, I admit and confess that, not only am I not a native of Podhajce, but also I have never visited it. Nevertheless, I feel as if I have lived its life for more than several generations and breathed its air. With the book that lies before us, we will succeed to add another drop to the flask of tears of the nation, by describing the frightful deeds of the Nazi wild beasts and their assistants in Podhajce – may this be a fulfillment of our elementary duty regarding the martyrs of this city, and a discrete contribution to the broad literature of the Holocaust, regarding which it is fitting to quote the words of the composer of Akdamut[2]: “Even if the heavens were parchment and the forests quills...”

A feeling of duty toward the dear martyrs, and a discrete command to remember and memorialize awakened the vital need to establish this monument and conduct other acts of perpetuation. To all who worked on this matter, it is clear that the gathering of the material for the memorial book and other activities connected with its publication demanded special dedication. The decisive turn came with the activities that were started by Menachem Ettinger and Dr. Baruch Milch, who were the first who were aroused, and aroused others, each within his realm of possibility. Beyond this, they took upon themselves to toil tirelessly to realize this holy objective. Mr. Ettinger deserves special mention for his constant watchfulness and fundamental interest in everything relating to the book, especially for composing the list of the names of the departed and martyrs of the city. There is no doubt that without the great deal of help that he gave me, the idea of the book would not have moved from concept to actualization. Along with the two conductors of the task, thanks and blessings are to be extended to all those who gave forth their hand and enabled us to reach this point.

The book lies before you, natives of the city of Podhajce. It is ready to serve as a book of testimony and memorial, as a spiritual and living bond to bind us to the world of our past in Podhajce and its region, and to its Jewish life that once was and is no more.

Tel Aviv, Tevet 5632 (1972)

The presidium dais at the memory gathering in 1956
The speaker is Meir Zerubavel (Zloczower) of blessed memory

Translator's Footnotes

1. A commandment, or colloquially, a 'good deed'.
2. A complex, very beautiful liturgical poem, written in Aramaic that is chanted prior to the reading of the Torah on the first day of the festival of Shavuot. Akdamut was composed by Rabbi Meir ben Yitzchak, in Worms, Germany in the 11th century. The complete quote referenced here, as translated in the Artscroll Shavuos Machzor, is: "His (i.e. G-d's) eternal strength that could not be described even if the heavens were parchment, and the forests quills, if all the oceans were ink…"
3. *[Page 9]*
4. With the Publication of the Memorial Book of the Community of Podhajce
5. A Survey of the activities of the Association of Podhajce Natives in Israel

[This Hebrew text on pages 9-12 is equivalent with the "Podhajcer Association in Israel" article in the English section.]

The committee of the organization in the year 1958

**Standing from right to left: Pushteig, Shechter, Mayberger, Ettinger, Dr. Milch.
Sitting from right to left: Merker, Zerubavel (Zloczower)
of blessed memory, Weissman, and Stamler**

[Page 10]

The committee of the Yizkor Book in Israel

Sitting from right to left: Mrs. Clara Stoop, Dr. Kermish, Professor Weiss of blessed memory, Dr. Milch, Yehuda Weissman. Standing from right to left: Shlomo Walden, Nathan Brecher, Menachem Ettinger, Mordechai Merker, Yehoshua Stamler of blessed memory

[Page 11]

The presidium dais at the memorial
The Speaker is Mr. Yehuda Weissman

[Page 12]

The proofreader Mr. G. Lindenberg

Podhajce natives at the memorial to the martyrs of the city in 1969

[Page 13]

With the Publication of the Memorial Book of the Community of Podhajce

A Survey of the activities of the Association of Podhajce Natives in Israel

[This Yiddish text on pages 13-18 is equivalent with the "Podhajcer Association in Israel" article in the English section.]

The presidium dais at the memorial marking the 25th anniversary of the liquidation, with the participation of a representative of Yad Vashem

[Page 14]

A Hachsharah[1] group of Zionist youth from Podhajce and the region (1934)

Translator's Footnote

1. Hachsharah is a program for preparation for making aliya to the Land of Israel. Participants would study and practice skills, often agricultural skills, in preparation for their new life in Israel.

[Page 15]

Podhajce natives in Israel at the memorial to the martyrs of the city (1966)

[Page 16]

A meeting of the committee of Podhajce Natives in Israel

Sitting from right to left: Mordechai Merker, Dr. Milch, Menachem Ettinger, Clara Stoop, Yehuda Weissman, Shlomo Walden, Nathan Brecher

[Page 17]

Natives of Podhajce in Israel at a memorial gathering

[Page 18]

The presidium dais at the memorial in 1967
The speaker is Dr. Baruch Milch

[Page 20]

A drawing of the Great Synagogue of Podhajce with decorations on the topic of the Holocaust – produced by our fellow native the artist Chaim Buchwald

[Page 21]

Chapters of the Past

History of the Jews of Podhajce and the Region

by M. Sh. Geshuri
(An historical survey)

Introduction

A great merit fell upon the natives of Podhajce and its regions in Israel to perpetuate the memory of their city in a book. This was a city that was a center of its region, and in the merit of its people, rabbis and activists, its good name went out afar. This city, as any important Jewish city in Galicia and Poland, is deserving of a monument in our lives. Congratulations are due to those people who are able to donate to this precious task of granting eternal life to an important Jewish community, which was destroyed unto the earth by the hands of the enemy.

The city of Podhajce is not numbered among the fortunate communities that merited special descriptions by its residents in early generations or by eminent historians, as merited the principal cities of Galicia such as Krakow and Lvov, and even the cities of Zolochiv (the "exalted city" of Shlomo Buber) or Bolechow (the fruit of the pen of the activists Reb Dover Birkental). With the passage of generations, the rabbis of Podhajce indeed succeeded in publishing several books, but these books only deal with matters of Jewish law without providing the opportunity to peer into – not even in a general fashion – the lifestyle of one of the central communities of southern Poland of the 17th and 18th centuries. Nevertheless, several sources have been found that allow us to reconstruct and describe the life of the city during its various periods of existence – during the time of Turkish rule, during the time of the Council of the Four Lands, during the time of Shabtai Tzvi and Jacob Frank, during the time of Hassidism, and during recent times.

A. Podhajce in Upper Podolia

The population exchange in Podolia until the Slavic settlement. – From where did Jews come to Podolia? The Jewish settlement in Podol at the end of the 12th century. – Known cities in Podol with famous rabbis and known personalities. – The Sabbatean movement, Jacob Frank and his community, the Hassidic movement. – "The Berlin Haskalah" in Podol.

"Podhajce in Upper Podolia" – what does this mean? This title comes to teach us that there was not only one Podhajce in the Kingdom of Poland. If one looks into various encyclopedias, one will find more than ten settlements with this name in various regions, near Ludmir, Luck, Kremenice, and other places. However, here, we are dealing with the Podhajce that rose to the level of a regional city in eastern Galicia, and was situated on the banks of the Koropiec (Koropets) River. Aside from this, our Podhajce has its "letter of genealogy" as a daughter of the state of Greater Podolia that took on honorable place in the history of the Kingdom of Poland prior to the three partitions, and served as a place of residence for small and large Jewish communities throughout hundreds of years.[1]

The first settlement in Podolia took place in a very early period. According to the "Father of History", Herodotus the Greek, various tribes lived in Podolia as early as 500 years before the Common (i.e. Christian) Era. After the Roman Caesar Hadrian conquered the lands of Germany and Romania (in the second century of the Common Era), this area of land also fell under his rule. From the era of "The Wandering Tribes" and onward, various strata of tribes settled in Podolia. They differed from each other in religion: Praboslavs (Greek Orthodox), Catholics, Lutherans and Jews. The latter formed the majority of the civic population.

From the 14th Century until the second partition of Poland between Russia and Prussia in the year 1793, a succession of countries ruled Podolia, including the states of Lithuania, Poland, Russia, and Turkey. The name "Podol" appears from the beginning of the 14th century, and means "Lowlands" in Slavic languages. Podolia is located over a large area in the northwestern area of European Russia, bordered by Galicia and separated from it by the Zvoroce River. In 1793, the majority of this region, along with several other regions of the State of Poland, transferred to full Russian control. However, Upper Podolia remained affiliated with Eastern Galicia.

There are controversies regarding the origins of the Jews that settled in Podolia. Some historians believe that Jews arrived in Podolia from Russia and Poland, to where they migrated from Western Europe. However, there is another opinion that claims that the Jews came to Podolia from the land of the Khazars and the Crimean Peninsula; or from the Principality of Kiev from which they were expelled during the time of Vladimir Monomach in the year 1120. According to this opinion, a Jewish community existed in Podolia at the end of the 12th century, that was occupied in business, crafts, brokerage and leasing, and did very well. During the time of the Thirty Year War (1618-1648), they were joined by many German Jews from families that were well-known in Torah and wisdom. As long as Podolia was under the rule of the princes of Poland and Lithuania, the Jewish residents benefited from established rights, and their civic and economic situation was significantly better than that of their brethren in other areas. The study of Torah was also widespread among the people, and famous rabbis and scholars arose from there midst. However, this situation changed for the worse with the outbreak of the revolt of Ukrainian Cossacks in 1648. The revolt was directed against the Polish landowners, who oppressed the Ukrainian people. However, along with them, the Jewish residents of cities were greatly harmed. This era of oppression, tribulations, and fear of death by the sword of the enemy made the ground fertile for mystical delusions, and faith in miracles and supernatural salvation. These were the days of Shabtai Tzvi. Faith in his Messiahship spread throughout almost the entire Diaspora, including Podolia. This strong Messianic movement stirred up waves (primarily between the years of 1676-1700) and spread a spirit of hope in the hearts of the downtrodden masses. However, the bitter disappointment that came in the wake of this movement did not by-pass Podolia. It significantly shook up the lives of its Jewish residents. The situation became particularly bad when Jacob Frank, the heir to his Messianic movement, arrived with his followers. As a result of their being slandered by the Bishop of Kamenets Podolsk, a debate took place in that city between them and the rabbis who put them in exile. This debate ended with the imposition of a heavy penalty upon the Jews, the confiscation of volumes of Talmud from the entire region, and their public burning in the market square of Kamenets Podolsk (in the year 5518 – 1757).

[Page 22]

Indeed, the Hassidic movement arose in the middle of the 18th century as a healing balm for the nation that was broken and desperate from the burden of its tribulations. It was founded and established by Rabbi Yisrael Baal Shem Tov (the Besht), a native of the Podolian town of Okop. This Torah, which was reared and nurtured on the soil of Podolia, especially by the simple folk, broadened and deepened within a short period of time until it became a complete philosophy of life that enveloped all strata of the Jewish nation, despite the chasms between the various Hassidic groups. In spite of the opposition of rabbis and Torah scholars, it paved a path to the scattered Jewish people as a national movement full of content and meaning, and with a wide branched literature.

On the other hand, the Haskala movement also struck roots in Podolia. It was founded by the Jews of Western Europe ("The Berlin Haskalah"), and spread during the 18th century. It destroyed the "Wall of China" that surrounded the Jewish street, which was closed and sealed off from outside influences, and brought the spirit of the new times into it. Near Podhajce, Yosef Perel and Reb Nachman Kruchmal were active along with all of the renowned Haskala scholars who conducted a strong struggle to instill the light of the Haskalah into the dwelling places of Israel.

Podolia Jewry was then as always a living and vibrant part of Polish and Russian Jewry, and often gave of its liveliness to the soul of the entire nation. This situation did not change after the partition of Poland to two parts, with the larger part going to Russia and the smaller part included in Austrian Galicia. Galician Podolia encompassed the entire area from the left bank of the Dneister River until the border of Russia, and included the regions of Brody, Buczacz, Borsczow, Berezhany, Husiatyn, Zaleszczyki, Zvaraz, Tarnopol, Trembowla, Czortkow, Skala and Podhajce – all of them regions that were settled by small and large Jewish communities, that played an important part in all realms of life of this area of land. When destruction came upon our people in the Diaspora, they were also destroyed, and completely wiped out from the earth.

B. The Beginning of the Foundation of Podhajce

Legends and theories about Jewish settlement. – Podhajce as a small scale ingathering of exiles of Jews from various lands. – Podhajce as a border town. – The Tatar invasion of the city and its area. – The first Praboslavic population of Podhajce.

When was the city called "Podhajce" founded? Who were its builders? How did it develop and establish roots in the ancient and recent recesses of the past? How and when did Jews take hold of it, and who were their first neighbors in the city and region?

These questions and many questions remain without an answer and explanation. This is due to a simple reason: only few of the natives of the city known anything about the distant past of the city in which they were born and raised, or about the history of its Jewish population. Under these conditions, the only thing we can do is to gather the few pieces of information that can be gathered from various sources and join them together into as complete a description as possible of life in the city during the various areas.

"Red Russia", later to become Eastern Galicia, passed to the Poles in the year 1387, after it had been a source of contention for 200 years between local princes, and between Poland and Hungary. The Poles found a very sparse settlement there. In the east there were villages and towns that had been destroyed several times during the century, their residents having been killed by the Tatars and the Turks. For hundreds of years, a diversified population settled in this land, consisting of Poles who belong to the Roman Catholic church, Ukrainians who belonged to the Greek Catholic church, and Jews who established the civic foundation in all settlements of the region. Throughout all cities of the region, there was also a small Armenian minority who conducted business with the Armenians in Turkey, Kovkoz and Persia, as far as the large Armenian center in Isfahan. Biblical names were widespread among the Armenians of Galicia.

[Page 23]

C. The city in the Era of the Kingdom of Poland

The first document about Podhajce from the year 1519. – Jakob Buczacki, the owner of the city, receives a permit to establish a fair in the city in the year 1536. – Stanislaw Potocki, the hero of Poland, is buried in the Catholic church in the city in the year 1667. – Jan Sowieski with his army laid siege to Podhajce in the year 1667. – Ibrahim Pasha lays siege to the city in the year 1675. – The siege of the city by the Tatars in 1698, and their repulsion by the commander Felix Potocki.

The Jewish history of Podhajce and its environs in interconnected with the history of the gentile population. Therefore, it is necessary to survey everything that the Poles did for the benefit of the city from a national and state perspective, and the lot of the Jews in these attainments.

The first document in which the name Podhajce appears is from 1519. This document specifies that Jakob Buczacki, the Bishop from Chelm, was the owner of the city. However, it is silent about the date of the founding of the city, and does not tell how it fell into the hands of the bishop. Podhajce is also mentioned in a document from 1516, in which Bilski relates that the Polish commanders Kaminecki, Lanckoronski and Tyborowski were defeated in Poland by 500 Tatars. The fought bravely and were finally defeated.

It would seem that Jakob Buczacki was the one who began to work for the development of the settlement of Podhajce, in that he influenced the king to establish a fair day in this city in the name of its holy population. A short time thereafter, the ownership of this city passed to the hands of the Walaski family. Nikolai Walaski, the prince of the Sandomierz palace (kasztalan), founded a fair in 1536 under the name of Holy Marcyn, with the authority of a permit from Zygmunt I. He was the king who established the German law (Magdeberg) in 1539 rather than the Polish Russian law out of feelings of gratitude to Walaski. Fairs served as a means of development for the cities at the time. In the year 1590, Zygmunt III issued a permit to Marcyn Walaski to transfer the fair to a more appropriate day, to the day of "withdrawal", at a time when the market day was convened on Saturday. In 1630, the city passed on as an inheritance to the Potocki family, and at that time, the members of this family began to be called and to sign their names with the name Podhajce.[2]

The first concern of the Potocki family was the establishment of a Roman Catholic church as a counterweight to the Greek Catholic church that had been founded by the Ukrainian population. Stanislaw Rewer Potocki, the bearer of many high titles from the kingdom, was buried in this church in 1667. He was born in 1579, and throughout his long life served as royal Hetman, ruler of the Krakow region, and one of the well-known army captains of the state. At first, he fought near Gozow in 1607, and from that time, he participated in all of the wars conducted by Poland throughout sixty years, without concern for his health, property, or many estates. He stood at the head of the army in 46 battles against the Vandals, Russians, Wallachians, Turks, Tatars, and Cossacks, during the rule of three kings.

Jan Sowieki had his beginnings as a commander in the year 1667 on the plains of the city of Podhajce, when he stood at the head of 12,000 fighters of the best of his army against the Tatar and Cossack troops who inundated Podolia and laid siege to Podhajce. For two weeks, the army of Poland held out bravely against the enemy army, which consisted of approximately 80,000 Tatars and 24,000 Cossacks. They even organized a surprise attack that caused great losses in the enemy camp. In the meantime, the Sultan found out that the Cossacks who had a treaty with the Poles started a rebellion. He established a peace treaty with Poland and promised to be their ally. This show of strength made the name of Jan Sowieki famous throughout Europe as a proud commander "whose head rises a hundred-fold over the shoulders". The writers of Poland wrote a great deal about the siege of Podhajce. In the letters of Captain Sowieki to his wife from the besieged city, he boasts about the fortifications of this city. In 1687, when he was already king of Poland, Sowieki came to Podhajce for a second time in order to view the battlefield upon which he forged his first glory.

Already then, Podhajce was one of the largest and most splendid cities in the "Russian district". According to the description of Dalirak, a Frenchman from the court of Jan Sowieki, the city had paved roads, five churches, and an old palace with mighty towers, high porches and surrounded by moats. In his words about the population of the city, the Jews are numbered in the first rank, followed by the Wallachians, Armenians, Poles and Ukrainians.

The incessant attacks of the Tatars, which did not by-pass Podhajce, strongly hurt the city and its inhabitants. The walls were broken, part of the palace was turned into a ruin, and many houses were destroyed. In 1675, Ibrahim Pasha laid siege to Podhajce. After the city surrendered, he destroyed its houses and brought its inhabitants to captivity under the guard of his general, Mowiecki. A decision of the Polish Sejm in 1677 declared that: "Out of a desire to reconstruct our kingdom from the ruin and damage that was inflicted upon it by our enemies, and taking note of the rights of Count Potocki who is full of mercy, we grant to Podhajce – the estate of Potocki – freedom from all taxes for 12 years."

In 1698, when Felix Potocki, the ruler of the Krakow region and Hetman of the Polish crown, was persecuted by 40,000 Tatars, he selected the walls of the palace of Podhajce as a support. In the battle, conducted with great fury and lasting for four hours, the Tatars lost many men and were forced to retreat from the palace that was located in the outskirts of the city. They set it on fire along with the loot that they could not take with them.

The very active Polish statesman Ignace Potocki was born in Podhajce. In the middle of the 18th century, all of the estates of Podhajce transferred to the ownership of the Bilski family, and from them transferred to the hands of Caspar Roglinski, the ruler of the Infeland region, around 1782. Podhajce, along with all of the developing area – Rudnik, Lisa, Urinos, Kosozov, Yasheniovchik, along with the farms of Zagaytsy, Holandra and

Syulka[2] – became part of the estate of the Principality of Czartoriska, who set up his summer palace in the city in the latter period.[3]

[Page 24]

The city was located on the banks of the Koropiec River, a river of 75 kilometers in length, with two banks in Podhajce. It passed through Podhajce to Monastiryska and Zaleshchiki, and empties into the Dneister on its left. The area of the region of Podhajce is crossed from north to south by three rivers – Strypa, Zlota Lipa, and Koropiec – which are tributaries to the Dneister. Early on, these rivers created many ponds and pools, so that each one of them became a sort of chain of ponds. The fish in these ponds served as a source of livelihood for the poor population, in particular during those periods when the harvest of the fields was destroyed by enemy soldiers and garrisons. The ponds and pools also served as a natural protection for the fortresses and palaces that were built from the outset in such protected areas.

D. The Beginnings of the Jewish Settlement of Podhajce

Near the city – the Jewish cemetery with ancient monuments. – When did the Jews of Podhajce organize into a community? – Rabbi Aharon Solnik, the author of the "Masat Binyamin" responsa book (1602). – Podhajce under Turkish rule from 1672-1699. – Persecution and tribulations against the Jews by the Turks. – The special "Slicha"[3] for the events in Podhajce by the author Reb Zeev Wolf the son of Rabbi Yehuda Leib Mrazni.

The government lists of Russia and Poland from the year 1550 make mention of the origin of the Jews in Podolia. The gravestones that were found there prove that there were Jews there several hundred years before that period. The elders of the city of Podhajce tell of an old cemetery with ancient gravestones that existed next to the city. The question is for how many years did the Jews live in the city without an organized community, whether because of their small number or because the local Jews were not interested in organizing themselves for various reasons. It is known that Podhajce served as a point of passage for merchants who moved from east to west and west to east, and the Jews played a central role in the world in business, for they maintained contact with the Jews of the west (Germany, Austria and other lands), and the east (the lands of Wallachia and Moldavia, Turkey and others). It would make sense that Podhajce, which served for a period of time as a transit point for Jewish merchants, became the location of a small or large Jewish community with the passage of time, and only after they had succeeded in establishing themselves there did they establish an organized community with rabbis and other clergymen[4].

In 1602, the name of a rabbi in Podhajce is already mentioned, a fact that points to the existence of a Jewish community in the city. This rabbi was the well-known author of the "Masat Binyamin" responsa book, which was written by Rabbi Binyamin Aharon the son of Avraham Solnik. Matters related to the roots of folklore are also mentioned in that book. Facts about the appearance of clothing in his days are mentioned in the book (section 80): the article of clothing that was called "mantle", whose top covers a person's neck, and which continued to wrap around and descend to below the knees, having no sleeves or any such things. It was the custom of the elders of Krakow to wear it in the synagogue during the types of prayers, etc. That "mantle" is not worn at home nor in the marketplace -- The "Rok" is only found in the Kingdom of Poland. It was customary to wear it even when sitting at home, and sometimes a "pleitza" would be sown on it, made out of the skin of foxes or other animal or cattle skins. This is called a "shoib", and it warms the body and protects it from cold.[5]

The "Masat Binyamin" responsa book (section 67) deals with the custom of the bride and groom seeing each other prior to the wedding. The question: A young man became engaged to a girl from the city of Ostia. The young man came to see the bride, as is the custom of all the land, and the gift was passed by his face[4]. (The groom was from the city of Podhajce, and the time was at the beginning of the 17th century.) Excerpts of this book are brought down in various books.[6]

The changes of government that overtook Podhajce also left their mark on the life of the Jews. The city was under Turkish rule for a period of 27 years (1672-1699). According to reliable sources, the border of the Turkish dominion reached the bog of the Dneister, and the city of Kamenets Podolsk was the capital city where the Turkish Pasha resided. In general, the relationship between the Jews and the Turks was particularly peaceful, and during the time of the expulsion from Spain (1492), the gates of the empire were opened wide to the many refugees who fled from Spain and other lands of Europe where they were persecuted. With the passage of time, the Jews gained great influence in the business and economic life of Turkey, and several of them obtained high positions, and even became statesmen. With the conquest of Podolia, the business relations between Turkey and the Jewish merchants of Podolia reached to Koshta and Smyrna (Izmir). However, the fierce battles between the Poles and the Jews instilled great fear upon the Jews in Podolia, and impoverished them economically. Despite this, it is hard to understand why the Turks afflicted the Jews of Podhajce in the year 1676. No information or sources remain about this event, except for the "Slicha" that was composed by Reb Zeev (Wolf) the son of Yehuda Leib and was published in his book "Geffen Yechidit" (Berlin 1699). This is a Slicha that had not caught the interest of researchers until now. We have to thank the Jewish researcher Ch. Y. Garland who included some memories of this event in his book "The History of the Decrees

against Israel", that testify to its historical importance. I will bring it down in its original language.

[Page 25]

In the year 5537, there was a decree in Podolia. The author of the book "Geffen Yechidit" (A short book of great quality, that deals with matters of moral chastisement and fear of Heaven in clear language, dealing with Heavenly issues and issues of reproof, may its author be thought of meritoriously. He was one of the intellectuals, and in this small composition, he displays his expertise and sharpness. He is our rabbi and teacher, Rabbi Zeev Wolf the son of Rabbi Yehuda Leib Mrazni, etc. Amsterdam) wrote an elegy about the martyrs in the prayer that he wrote. These are his words there (folio 24, side 2). The acronym at the beginning of the stanzas is "I am the small one Zeev Wolf"[7]:

I wrote a "Kel Maleh Rachamim[5] for the martyrs and prisoners in the region of Podolia, 5437 (it should have said, 5436). I signed the beginnings of the stanzas, "I am the small one Zeev Wolf".

G-d full of compassion, who avenges blood, how great were the tribulations that came upon me, they happen (it should have said it is only evil[6]) all the days.

[7]The souls of the poor and innocent, they are like the animals that fall among the captives, and school children who fall like sheep and goats, many have become hidden among the gentiles.

The portion of meat and fatlings should be divided among two brothers, the father goes childless, and cries, "where is my child".

The smoke sent its hand to his father in Deitz, and the abnormal enemy came and shot, this killing took place in the summer in the community of Podhajce.

Trembling overtakes me when I hear about it, Torah scholars, men of wisdom, the young of the flock were dragged out, and murder came to the land; there is much killing by Kedar[8] of those bloated with hunger.

How did a voice from heaven come down and issue a decree regarding those as lowly as a hyssop and high as a cedar, to be cut down like cumin and rice.

With lamentation and tears the places of Israel respond, who are left desolate without inhabitants, and you oh G-d exist for ever, why is their no voice and no sound.

Woe to those who have been lost and will not be forgotten, scholars who take hold of swords, shields and spears[9], many are laid down in the places of the sacrifices.

Regarding these I weep, about the great agony and oppression, of the sublime people, who went up from the second exile.

You oh G-d why are you silent, as the wicked swallow up the righteous and plot evil against him, everything in the city has been destroyed, and they have been completely expelled.

To whom shall I utter my woe, and who will stir up strife, regarding those who you call your children, of whom very many have been taken captive, and have been murdered with abnormal deaths.

Open the gates of heaven, to hear the cry of the poor, to take vengeance on the blood that was spilled like water, and to bind their souls in the bonds of life.

Take revenge on behalf of the Jewish people, from Kedar and Ishmael, and repay their deeds, and may the redeemer come to Zion, Amen.

As well, the scholar Yomtov Lipman Zunz (1794-1886)[10], one of those who laid the foundations of scientific research into Judaism, and one of the greatest researchers of the Jewish people of that time, makes mention of this elegy in his book "Literaturgeshichte". However, even he does not tell us anything about this decree, which is not mentioned in any books.

The content of this Slicha reveals a small amount and hides a great deal. In this Slicha, we read about a tragedy that occurred to the Jews of Podhajce, on account of a libel or pretext that took place against the Jews of the city, without exposing the factors that caused it. As a result, the Jews of Deitz (Podhajce) paid by being murdered and taken captive. Nevertheless, it is good that this important document on the events that took place in Podhajce was saved from oblivion, and that we are able to include it in its original in the history of this community.[8]

E. The Jewish Community of Podhajce

The Jewish community – "A kingdom within a kingdom". – The rabbis and activists of Podhajce in the ledgers of the Council of the Four Lands. – The collection of taxes by the community. – The book "Birkat Yaakov" by Rabbi Yaakov the son of Baruch of Podhajce.

The Jews, whose relative population in Poland and Russia was larger than in any other country in the world at that time, were a world unto themselves, not only in religion and lifestyle, but also in society and economics. It is no exaggeration to state that they were like "a kingdom within a kingdom".

The Jews had one great advantage – their general umbrella group, the Council of the Four Lands, which represented them before the government, negotiated in their name, and issued decrees for the benefit of the community. The restrictions, denigrations, and special heavy taxes that the Christian law imposed upon the Jews from the time that the Roman Caesars accepted Christianity as their religion, were liable to wipe them out, were they imposed with their full force and strength. Yisrael Halperin did something good for us when he labored to collect an anthology of decrees that were written and recorded in the Legers of the Council of the Four Lands (Jerusalem, 5705), to give them to us. This book serves as a mirror into all of the cities and towns in the Kingdom of Poland. One can learn a great deal from it. Podhajce is not passed over in this book, and the names of its activists and rabbis who were in contact with this council are mentioned.

The Jews of Poland were subject to three authorities: to the town council and landowner (poretz) in each city (if the city was privately owned), to the central government of the state, and to their own government, which they held in the highest of esteem since it was a bone of their own body. Rabbi Dovber of Bolechow, when he mentions the name of one of the Jews who filled the role in the independent leadership of the community, never neglects to call them by their rightful title: "The mediator of the Council of the Four Lands", "The head of the country", "The chiefs who are the heads of the countries", "The chief captains and leaders" – when he describes those people. These are repeated often in his book.

The community under local Jewish government conducted all matters of the Jewish community, both physical and spiritual. It presented itself as the representative of the entire local community before external forces – the king, the priests, the poretzes (landowners), etc. In order to fund its activities, the community had to impose internal taxes. Some taxes were collected directly from every resident, some were included in the prices of daily necessities such as the yeast tax, and some were paid for the services of the community on behalf of its residents, such as shechita (ritual slaughter), or the communal weights and measures. The prime

task of the community was to administer the collection of the Head Tax. This tax was imposed in the middle of the 17th century as a tax on every Jewish community in the entire country, and was evaluated to the value of tens of thousands of gold coins: with time, the tax increased, and at the beginning of the 18th century, its value reached 220,000 gold coins. The Council of the Four Lands would apportion this tax and set the value of the tax upon each and every community. There were serious negotiations between the communities and the council with regard to the apportioning of this tax, for frequently, a certain community was unable to pay the amount imposed on it. The community then turned to the heads of the council with a detailed memorandum, "with letters written by the communal council with clear language, and in Hebrew.", as it requested relief from the Head Tax.

[Page 26]

After a time, the Polish authorities realized that this means of imposing a general levy upon the Jewish community as an organized body was not beneficial for them, so they turned over its collection to a central representative of the Jews. With the general recession that afflicted the Jewish community during the 18th century, its foundations of security were shaken, and there was a need to invest large sums to conduct life and maintain ones property, the Council became bogged down with many debts, and was not able to pay its obligation to the state coffers. The Poles asked themselves if it would not be better to impose a personal tax upon every Jew without the intermediation of the Council. If that were the case, the Council would no longer be needed. There were various other internal factors that weakened the strength and authority of the Council: disputes and controversy, the interjection of private interests onto the public benefit, the rule of a small number of wealthy people over the masses, the decay of the impoverished people, etc. All of this led to the abolition by the Poles of the central Jewish government in 1764, and the imposition of a direct tax of 2 guilders a year upon every Jew above the age of 1. This tax would also be collected through the communities. The administration of this new tax required a census of the Jewish population. To this end, the government set up a special committee in each city consisting of communal leaders and headed by the Polish landowner. These committees were given the responsibility of enumerating the Jews. From the material that remains in the archives about this activity, we can learn many details about the number of Jews, their family composition, and to a reasonable extent about their occupations. In the introduction to the summary of the enumerator in one of the cities of Poland, it is stated in Hebrew: "Today is the day that the sound of the census taker will be heard in the city, and each person will stand for enumeration". Indeed, the Jews of Podhajce also "stood up for enumeration". In 1765, 1290 Jews were enumerated in Podhajce itself, and 1548 in the entire community. The harsh decree regarding collecting a tax in equal amounts from each person caused the poor to absent themselves from the census.

In one of the sections (section 149) of the ledger of the Council of the Four Lands (that also relates to Podhajce), the "matter of the absentees" is discussed: that is to say, those who refrain from paying taxes. There, note is made of a special privilege of King Wladyslaw IV of Poland from March 25, 1635 (6 Nisan 5395) that establishes the enactments of the council regarding the absentees, as well as enactments regarding other matters. Six copies of this remain; one of them included in "Birchat Yaakov" by Rabbi Yaakov the son of Baruch of Podhajce (Lvov 5506, ad the end of the book, sections 111-133). The aforementioned section is from the year 5384 (1624), a date that confirms the ancientness of the Jewish settlement in Podhajce[9].

F. During the Decrees of 5408 and 5409{11}

The anti-Polish Chmielnitzki movement in Reisin{12}. – The Decrees of 548 and 5409 regarding the fairs of the country. – "The evil Chiel the enemy of Israel. – the "Third destruction" of Polish Jewry. – The destruction of the community of Podhajce. – The war of defense of the Jews along with the Poles. – Descriptions of the destruction in the book

"Yaven Metzula" by Reb Natan Hanover. – The freeing of the Jews of Podhajce from taxes by the "Russian Sejmik".

The Decrees of 5408 and 5409 did not come suddenly. During the 17th century, the region of Halitz, including Podhajce, endured great suffering from the invasions and attacks of the Tatars, Turks, and later the Cossacks and Russians. The Cossack attacks began in the 17th century. In 1615, a difficulty battle against Cossack troops took place in Rohatyn near Podhajce. Hetman Zolkiwski succeeded in killing them and cutting off their commander, who was taken to be executed in Lvov.[10]

The Ruthenians from Podhajce and its environs joined the anti-Polish movement that was nown by the name "Chmielniszczyzna" that spread from Ukraine to Reisin. They joined forces with the Ruthenians from neighboring towns in conducting military actions and attacks against the estates of the Polish noblemen around the city, and threatened that not one "Liach" (Pole) would remain alive. The Ruthenians of Reisin were filled with hatred against the Catholic faith, its convents, and its churches.

In 1648, the large revolt of Bogdan Chmielnitzki broke out in the eastern borders of the state. The year 5408 (1648) was a year of tribulation for the Jews of Poland. The Jews of Podhajce were also severely afflicted. In April 1648, Chmielnitzki led his army from the Zaporoza region in the west, and defeated the Polish army, under the command of Potocki and Kalinowski from May 6-15. This brilliant victory was the portent for the outbreak of the general revolt of the residents of Ukraine. They attacked the Poles and Jews in the villages, cities and towns. In every place, they destroyed, pillaged, and murdered without mercy. The fate of the Jews was terrible. The full measure of hate of the farmers and the Cossacks was unleashed against them. They fell by the hundreds and thousands along the roads. Jewish property went up in smoke. Women and children were murdered or taken captive.

As with all the communities of Podolia and Reisin, Podhajce also suffered from this tribulation. Its effects were felt until the middle of the 18th century.

[Page 27]

The number of victims from Podhajce is unknown, but it was certainly no less than the number in other towns. At the time, the Jews fought hand in hand with the townsmen. The Jewish population defended the city along with the Christians. They were armed with guns and gunpowder, and even served in the artillery corps.

The disaster[13] that befell the Jews in this era is described in many documents, whose authors witnessed the bloody sword with their own flesh. The best of the descriptions is by Reb Natan Hanover of Zaslow. He was in that city until July 25, 1648. Hanover's composition, "Yaven Metzula" ("Deep Mud") is a first class source about the destruction of those days. It is used by many historians. From his words, we can see the path of Chmielnitzki's army from its beginning until the Zhivachov agreement (August 1649). Jewish chronicles speak of 100,000 victims in 500 destroyed communities. The issue of refugees was particularly severe: "Many of them are our co-relgionists. They went out from their lands, and were expelled from their places and habitations, and have now found rest and repose, since the land is not sufficiently quiet and peaceful to enable those distant to to their homesteads".[11]

The situation of the Jews worsened after the tribulations of 5408. The destruction was so great that the "Ruski Sejmik" that entered Halitz on December 23, 1675 formulated a legal recommendation asking the Sejm to reduce the head tax upon the Jews of Reisin, since entire communities were destroyed and were not able to pay taxes (in translation from Polish: "For they all fell in Buczacz, Tarnopol, Podhajce, and all of the wojewodas (regions), and therefore they are not able to pay taxes"[12]. Indeed King Jan Sowieki III was correct when he established in a memorandum of July 27, 1694 that the Jews of Reisin "suffered more than other Jews from the passage of the armies and enemy attacks".

G. Well-known Rabbis and Yeshiva Heads in Podhajce

The many tasks and responsibilities of the rabbis. Rabbi Moshe and Rabbi Yehuda Leib his son, among the first rabbis of the community of Podhajce. – Rabbi Binyamin Aharon Solnik, the author of the book "Masaat Binyamin". – His son Rabbi Yaakov fills his place as the rabbi of the city. – Rabbi Moshe the son of the Shach during the time of the Turkish conquest. – Rabbi Moshe Katzenelenbogen (a descendent of the prince Shaul Wohl). – Rabbi Zecharia Mendel, the author of books. – Rabbi Meshulam Zalman the son of Rabbi Yaakov Emden. – Rabbi Aryeh Leib, the author of "Lev Aryeh".

As we come to survey the history of the rabbis and their situation hundreds of years ago in the Jewish communities of Poland, the fact stands out before us that well-known rabbis who were great in Torah served specifically in the small and medium sized towns, rather than in the large cities and metropolitan areas. There was a simple reason for this: the great rabbis searched for quiet places where they would be able to study Torah and Divine service without interruption. Thanks to this, Podhajce as well had famous rabbis, whose names flutter out from books filled with Torah and wisdom. From among those that earned a name in rabbinical literature, we will mention here only the names of famous rabbis that served in Podhajce, or were born there and moved to serve in other communities, from the period of Polish independence prior to the partition. The community of Podhajce and its rabbis became known in the Jewish world, and the rabbis of Podhajce maintained a correspondence with well-known rabbis of the capitals of Europe, who would also visit the city from time to time and attempt to assist in the organization of local matters to the best of their abilities.

Who was the first rabbi of the community of Podhajce, and who issued the recommendation to appoint him? Certainly one should have been able to find details about this in the first ledgers of the community; however since the community of Podhajce was destroyed by the Nazis along with all of its documents – we must salvage from the literary sources at least the names of some of the rabbis of the city, whose compositions in various topics, primarily in responsa and Jewish law, preserved their memory for future generations. Similarly, it is possible to be assisted by the inscriptions on the monuments of the rabbis of the city, and of rabbis from Podhajce who died outside of their communities and merited to have fancy monuments with suitable inscriptions.

From among the first rabbis of the community of Podhajce, we must mention two, a father and son, who are mentioned in the books "Anshe Shem" and "Matzevet Kodesh". These are the rabbi and Gaon Rabbi Moshe and his son the rabbi and Gaon Rabbi Yehuda Leib. The following is the text of the monument on the grave of Rabbi Yehuda Leib in Lvov.

"Yehuda was faithful to G-d and the holy nation, he was a leader and Gaon, the holy candelabrum, expert in the recesses of Torah in its revealed and hidden{14} forms, he toiled in Torah day and night, and was the head of Yeshiva here, and the head of the rabbinical court of the community of Podhajce, our rabbi Rabbi Yehuda Leib the son of the great rabbi Rabbi Moshe who was also the head of the rabbinical court of Podhajce, who spread Torah in Israel, toiled in Torah, and made his nights like days, and enlightened the eyes of Israel, taught the nation of G-d how to walk in the ways of Torah, and taught many students who were great in Torah and who drank of his waters. In the merit of this may his soul be bound in the bonds of eternal life. He died on the 11th of Cheshvan 5473"[13].

Rabbi Binyamin Aharon (the son of Rabbi Avraham) Solnik, was of the greats of the wise men of Poland in the 5300s, an outstanding student of the Rema and Maharshal, and the friend of Rabbi Yehoshua Falk (the Sema), Rabbi Mordechai Yaffa (the Levush) and the Maharam of Lublin. He served in the rabbinate in Podhajce and other places. He was thought to be one of the outstanding scholars of the generation, and all of his decisions and teachings were accepted by the people of his generation with great respect. He was the author of the book "Masaat Binyamin" (Krakow, 5393) that includes 112 questions and answers that he responded to those who asked him about Halachic matters. He also authored a book on the Chalitza ceremony{15}, and a book on the setting of the yearly calendar, neither of which still exists. He occupied the rabbinical seat of Podhajce for approximately forty years, from the year 5340 to 5380 (1580-1620), and was a member of the Council of the Four Lands. He died after he had reached 90 years of age, in the year 5380 (1620).

[Page 28]

One can read about the author of the "Masaat Binyamin" and the place of his service in the words of the Gaon, the author of "Pnei Yehoshua", in one of his responsa regarding the law of priestly impurity (that was printed in the responsa Maamar Mordechai by the Rabbi Maharam of Duesseldorf, section 56). In his words, he mentioned three great Gaonim who were Cohanim and who lived in the area of Lvov and its region, including the Gaon the author of Masaat Binyamin. The following are his words there: "It is clear that in the community of Lvov there are very great people, writers such as in our community... including the author of Masaat Binyamin." The author of Klilat Yofi (Krakow 5648) continues by touching on only main points about the aforementioned Gaon, as follows: "Indeed, it is already known that the Gaon Rabbi Aharon the son of Rabbi Avraham Solnik, the author of the Masaat Binyamin responsa book, was one of the great rabbinical decisors of that time, from whose waters we drink. Later Gaonim rely on his precious and honorable book with regard to practical Halacha. The Gaon was a student of three pillars of the world: The Rama, the Maharshal, and the Maharash the son of Rabbi Yehuda who was called by the name Maharash the Second. He had two grown sons and one daughter. His first son was the Gaon Rabbi Yaakov, the author of the book Nachalat Yaakov on Rashi's commentary of the Torah. He is also mentioned many times in the responsa of his father the Gaon, and he also had a correspondence of questions and answers with the Gaon, the author of Meginei Shlomo (the Responsa book Pnei Yehoshua part 2, section 67). His second son was the Gaon Rabbi Avraham who was an omen for his generation, and whose splendor and Torah light shone first on Tarnopol. Later, he was the head of the rabbinical court and a Yeshiva head in Brisk of Lithuania{16}. His daughter Leah was married to the Gaon rabbi Menachem Mann, the student of the Gaon Moshe Ish Chai, the head of the rabbinical court of Presmisla, the author of the book Mateh Moshe. As well, the children and grandchildren of the author of Masaat Binyamin were all great and mighty men of Torah, including the Gaon Rabbi Leib, the Yeshiva head and author of the Shaagat Aryeh responsa book, and the Gaon Rabbi Liber Charif, a Yeshiva head in the community of Krakow. Even during his younger days, the author of Masaat Binyamin was one of the great rabbis of Krakow, still during the life of the Rema and also after his death. Later, he set up his Yeshiva and study hall in the state of Silesia, and from there he expressed his questions and doubts to the Gaon the author of Sheerit Yosef of Krakow. He then to the State of Poland and set up his residence in the community of Podhajce, where he served as the head of the rabbinical court and the head of the Yeshiva, as is described in his book in several places. There he reposes in honor.[14]

After the death of the author of Masaat Binyamin, his eldest son, the Gaon Rabbi Yaakov, the author of Nachalat Yaakov (a commentary on Rashi's commentary on the Torah), ascended to the rabbinical seat of Podhajce. According to his words in the introduction to his book, he did not leave a son after him to take his place in the rabbinate of Podhajce, so we do not know the period of his rabbinical service in Podhajce.[15]

According to a eulogy that is found in one of the books that is attributed to the Rabbi Y. of Belzec, it is stated that a rabbi by the name of Rabbi David served in the 5300s in Podhajce. He died in the year 5393. No other details remain of his rabbinical or private life.

One source in our book mentions the name of a great rabbi who served in Podhajce. His words are as follows: "At the Jazelowicz fair the following agreed upon this warning: the great luminaries, the great Rabbi Mordechai, the head of the rabbinical court and Yeshiva, head of the community of Podhajce and the community of Rzeszow, and one other rabbi, and this matter took place in the year 5440." In another place, it is stated that to replace the well-known Rabbi Aharon Shmuel Kaidanower, the rabbi of Krakow who died in Chmielnik during his travels on the 12th of Tammuz 5436, they appointed in Rzeszow, Rabbi Mordechai from his place of residence in the community of Podhajce, and he became one of the great rabbis of his generation.[16]

The eldest son of the rabbi and Gaon Rabbi Shabtai Katz (the Shach){17}, Rabbi Moshe, served as a rabbi in Podhajce. The city was conquered by the Turkish army during the time of his tenure, and Rabbi Moshe succeeded in evading the Turkish captivity, as he related in the introduction to the two books of his father that were passed to him as an inheritance, that is Nekudat Hakesef and Takfu Kohen that he published in Frankfurt am Main in the year 5437 (1677). In his introduction, he also tells a little bit about the city of his tenure, Podhajce, as follows: "Time has passed, and I have not been able to fulfil my obligation as I had thought, for the yoke of my Yeshiva has been weighing upon me, and my place of residence is the community of Podhajce, a joyous city, a city with everything in it, the Torah of G-d is in its midst, a faithful and praiseworthy community, from which go forth people of knowledge and wisdom; during the war with the Turks, they went into captivity without mercy or grace, and they have become a proverb and a byword, and the G-d of most high saved me, and I went to Mount Morim the inheritance of my fathers, and when I wished to dwell in peace I found no peace and quiet, and the tribulation of he who gains more knowledge gains more anguish caught up with me, for fire was sent from above and the entire community was burnt with the blink of an eye."

The rabbi and Gaon Rabbi Moshe Katzenelenbogen, who occupied the rabbinical seat in Podhajce for some time, was also of great lineage. He was the son of Rabbi Shaul Katzav (a shortened form of the longer name Katzenelenbogen), a descendent of the prince Shaul Wohl and the Gaon the author of Masaat Binyamin. After various libels and tribulations, he went to serve in the rabbinate in Anshbach, Bavaria, where he reposes in honor. Rabbi Moshe's brother-in—law, Rabbi Zecharia Mendel, was a native of Podhajce. I will write about him specially.

Rabbi Zecharia Mendel (the son of Aryeh Leib) was a native of Podhajce. He was a scion of the Maharshal and Rema. He studied Torah from Rabbi Yaakov Yehoshua, the author of Pnei Yehoshua. The Jews of Podhajce followed after him, for they took honor in his honor. He served as the rabbi of Frankfurt auf Oder for the final decades of his life, where he published his books "Menorat Zecharia" (5536) – novellae on tractate Shabbat and sermons on the Sabbath and festivals, "Zecharia Meshalem" (5539) – novellae on tractates of Talmud, 'Zecharia Hamevin" (5551) – on foundations of philosophy and Kabbalah. He died in Frankfurt auf Oder on the 24th of Kislev 5552 (1791). The following is engraved upon his monument: "The enlightened rabbi, great Gaon, G-dly Kabbalist, etc., who never left the tent of Torah, and taught many students in his youth and old age."[17]

Two rabbis by the name of Reb Moshe served one after the other in Podhajce.

[Page 29]

After the aforementioned Rabbi Moshe Katzenelenbogen, Rabbi Moshe the son of Menachem Nachum was chosen as rabbi of the city. He signed an approbation of the book "Birchat Yaakov" on the Choshen Mishpat section of the Code of Jewish Law[18] on Elul 2, 5478 as follows: "Signed by Moshe, the son of our rabbi and teacher Rabbi Menachem Nachum of Premisla, who graces the holy community of Podhajce". This is almost the only detail that remains about him for us.

Rabbi Yisachar Dovrish, the head of the rabbinical court of the community of Podhajce, was one of the geniuses of the generation already during the life of his father Rabbi Yaakov Yehoshua of Krakow and Lvov, the author of the Pnei Yehoshua book of novellae. In 5501, he issued an approbation on an edition of the Choshen Mishpat section of the Code of Jewish Law with three commentators, the Sema, the Shach and the Taz. One of his responsa became known for its sharpness and expertise in the responsa book of Rabbi Chaim Cohen Rappaport. At the end of the answer, he signs as follows, "On Sunday, 24th Tishrei 5504, signed by the holy Yisachar Dov the son of the Gaon Rabbi Yaakov Yoshia, May G-d preserve him." However, he did not live long. As he was passing through the city of Berlin, he became ill and died on the 22nd of Cheshvan 5505[18]. He left behind a son who was a great scholar, the Gaon Rabbi Tzvi Hirsch Rozanish, the author of the book Tesha Shitot (Lvov, 5560).

No less than the aforementioned rabbis of Podhajce was the lineage of the rabbi and Gaon Rabbi Meshulam Zalman the son of Rabbi Yaakov Emden, one of the important scholars of the Ashkenazic world in the 18th century, the son of Rabbi Tzvi Ashkenazi the Chacham Tzvi, who was known especially for the controversy that he stirred up against Rabbi Yonatan Eibeshitz. This controversy spread like burning fire throughout the Jewish people in all of their places of habitation, and involved not only scholars, but also the masses of Jews. It divided the nation into two camps, and there was no end to the desecration of the name of Heaven and the name of Israel caused by this controversy. It was the causes of the decline of the honor of Torah in the Ashkenazic world.

Apparently, Rabbi Meshulam Zalman served as the head of the rabbinical court of Podhajce thanks to the connections of his zealous father with the city administrators. From there, he wrote a letter (in the year 5517 –1756) to his father that was published in the book "Edut Leyaakov", that starts with the heading: "A letter of his son the peaceful{19} rabbi and Gaon Meshulam Zalman the head of the rabbinical court of the community of Podhajce." From there he was accepted to be the head of the rabbinical court of the Hamburger Synagogue in the large city of London, from where he gave an approbation to various books, including the book "Kiseh Melech" in the year 5529 (1769). Likewise, we find a letter of friendship from him to his father the Gaon Yaabetz{20} about the miracle of Mikliva[19].

Rabbi Aryeh Leib, the author of "Lev Aryeh" was a rabbi and preacher in Brody. Earlier, he was a rabbi in Podhajce. He excelled in his "Pleasant sermons and sharp words that are sweeter than honey and honeycombs". These were published by his grandson Rabbi Yaakov Levi in the name of "Sefer Nachalei Dvash". He died on the eve of Rosh Chodesh Adar 5578 (1818)[20].

One can also ascribe importance to the rabbis of later generations in Podhajce for various reasons, regarding their genealogy, for they were related to families of rabbis and Gaonim known throughout Poland and its neighboring countries, and also on their own account, due to their great knowledge and valuing of Torah. The equivalent factor among them is that all of them knew how to hold Podhajce, the city of their tenure, in esteem as an honorable city for Polish Jewry, and they caused the city to be known to the many.

Note in this section, Translator's Footnotes are designated by { } brackets. The footnotes designated by [ ] brackets are the text footnotes.

Translator's Footnotes

2. From among these places, the only ones that I found in JewishGen Shtetlseeker near Podhajce are Zagaytsy and Syulka.
3. A "Slicha" (literally "apology" is a poetical liturgical prayer recited on fast days and days of penitence.
4. I am not sure of the intent of this expression, but I believe that it meant that he was chastised.
5. "G-d full of compassion" – the introductory phrase of the most common of memorial prayers.
6. The difference in Hebrew is only whether or not the one word is split into two. In this and the previous emendment, I believe that it is either Garland or Geshuri who is emending the text.
7. From this point, some of the poetry is paraphrased by the translator, due to its obscurity.
8. A Biblical tribe equated with the Arabs.
9. A euphemism for the tools of prayer. See Rashi on Genesis 48:22.
10. Generally known by his secular name of Leopold Zunz.
11. Gezerot Tach VeTat (the Decrees or Visitations of 5408-5409 / 1648-1649) refers to the tribulations endured by the Jewish people during the Cossack uprising of Bogdan Chmielnitzki.
12. Reisin is a term that means "White Russia", but it is not necessarily geographically equivalent with the modern sense of the term (i.e. the modern republic of Belarus).
13. It is interesting to note that the Hebrew word used for this 'tribulation' or 'destruction' is 'shoah', here and in several other places in the text – the term used in Hebrew to denote the Holocaust. This should give some indication of the cataclysmic severity of the Chmielnitzki devastation upon Eastern European Jewry.
14. I.e. Mystical or Kabbalistic.
15. Chalitza is the ceremony of releasing a woman from the need for Levirate marriage.
16. Brest-Litovsk.
17. The Shach is the acronym for one of the most prominent commentators of the Code of Jewish Law (Shulchan Aruch).
18. The section of the Code of Jewish Law (Shulchan Aruch) dealing with jurisprudence.
19. A play on the word 'Meshulam'.
20. The acronym of Yaakov the son of Tzvi.

H. Podhajce as a Center for Sabbateanism in Galicia

Podhajce in the region of Sabbatean influence. – It became a nest of the Sabbatean sect after the Turkish conquest. – The visit of the preacher Chaim Malach to Podhajce. – The battle of Yaakov Emden with the Sabbateans of Podhajce. – The preacher Rabbi Yisachar of Podhajce is suspected of Sabbateanism. – The influence in Podhajce of Elisha Schorr, the Sabbatean from Rohatyn.

During the days of the Movement of Shabtai Tzvi, Sabbateanism spread in a significant fashion throughout the southeastern region of Reisin, and found supporters also among the circles of rabbis and scholars. The faith in Shabtai Tzvi penetrated here primarily from the Turkish Jews who settled in Podolia and Reisin during the time of the Ottoman conquest. They succeeded in spreading this faith among the Jews of those regions. This movement, along with the Frankist movement that followed, did not by-pass Podhajce. According to Rabbi Yaakov Emden (Yaavetz), who conducted a strong battle orally and in writing against Sabbateanism during the middle of the 18th century, Podhajce was known as a nest of believers in Shabtai Tzvi. One should not be surprised about this, for from a geographical perspective, Podhajce was located in the region of Sabbatean influence along with the cities of Horodenka, Glinyani, Nadworna, Tysmienica, Rohatyn, Buczacz, Komarno, Zbaraz, Zolochev, and Kamiunka – all of which were known as bastions of Sabbateanism.[21]

The bitter disappointment that came with the conversion of Shabtai Tzvi did not put an end to the Sabbatean movement. After the death of Shabtai Tzvi (1676) the belief that the soul of the Messiah is imprisoned in the husks[21] and will reappear as the redeemer of Israel spread among his supporters. The Sabbateans broke up into various factions. The successor of Shabtai Tzvi, Yaakov Krido and his son Brechia, accepted the Islamic faith openly, and simultaneously maintained their Sabbateanism. They created a unique sect called "Donma" that blended Islam with the faith of the Messiaship of Shabtai Tzvi, and continued to exist through time. The ideologue of Sabbateanism was Michael Avraham Cardozo (died in 1680), a Marrano who became an enthusiastic Sabbatean. He wandered through various lands and preached that Israel should wait for the deeds of Shabtai Tzvi, about whom Isaiah prophesied "and he is counted among the sinners" (Isaiah 53). Therefore, the Sabbateans must become converts like their Messiah. The Sabbateans permitted themselves to engage in acts of lewdness, and saw such as deeds of holiness that hasten the coming of the Messiah.

The contact with the Jews of Turkey, most of whom were Sabbateans, assisted the spread of Sabbateanism throughout Ashkenazic Jewry of Podolia, and when

the contact between Podolia and Lvov was restored in the wake of the peaceful seer of Karlovitz (1699), this movement set up roots also in Lvov and its environs.

In Podhajce as well, there was a significant group of Sabbateans, who at first worked underground so as not to arouse anybody's suspicion. They remained in contact with the emissaries of Shabtai Tzvi, at first with Chaim Malach, a native of Poland who went to Turkey at the end of the 17th century to join Shabtai Tzvi. He arrived through Vienna to Poland in the year 5460 with the aim of strengthening the faith in Shabtai Tzvi. During this visit, he traveled around Reisin in particular, since he knew that Sabbateanism had already taken hold there, and had won over a recognizable number of followers. He toured

Zolkova, Horodenka, Podhajce and Buczacz, and won over followers to Sabbateanism through his sermons[22].

[Page 30]

After the failure of the Hassidim who made aliya headed by Rabbi Yehuda Hassid of Siedlice, Chaim Malach came to Poland for the second time in the year 5475. However, this time, the Chacham Tzvi warned his brother Rabbi Shaul, who was the head of the rabbinical court of the community of Krakow, about this sect, and especially about the "evil angel" Chaim Malach[23]. After Malach left Reisin, the Sabbateans of Podhajce maintained contact with Moshe Meir of Kamiunka – one of the most important propagandists of Sabbateanism in Poland, with his brother-in-law Fishel (Feivel) of Zolechov, and with the preacher Rabbi Yisachar of Podhajce. We can surmise that they were also in contact with the well-known Sabbatean of Zolkova, Yitzchak Keidaner.

Rabbi Yaakov Emden relates that the Sabbatean emissaries sometimes presented themselves as peddlers who circulate between towns, but they mainly presented themselves as preachers and remonstrators. The people of that generation tell about their means of propaganda, that they knew how to attract the hearts of simple people by giving lectures in homiletics, such as from Ein Yaakov. Through questions and explanations of the confusing legends, they slowly turned the naïve hearts toward their secrets with "smooth language", they began to show them hints of Shabtai Tzvi in Midrashim and the Zohar, until they had instilled the "belief" in their hearts. In 1713, Rabbi Naftali Cohen writes regarding the Sabbateans that they have special ceremonies on the Sabbath, they sing songs based on Shabtai Tzvi, and they take a picture of Shabtai out of their bosoms during dances, and hung and kiss it – things that are similar to what is told about the customs of Chaim Malach and his sect in Jerusalem. Rabbi Naftali accuses them of speaking pleasantly to people and drawing them into their apostasy.

Rabbi Yaakov Emden specifies the names of those who follow the new path. He says, "These are the names of the head of the accursed sect in Poland, in places where they are scattered: Zolkova, Podhajce, Rohatyn, and Grodok." Perhaps Podhajce was better known to him than the other places, for his son served as the rabbi there before he moved to London, and he told his father everything that he knew about Podhajce. The writings of Rabbi Yaakov Emden are full of accusations against those places. However, the names repeat themselves in the lists of the Frankists. Some of these cities preserved the tradition of their Sabbatean groups until the Nazi Holocaust[24].

The Podhajce natives who Yaakov Emden castigated "the entire autumn" included the preacher Rabbi Yisachar "who is considered by them to be a great and pious man". Regarding him, he states that after difficulties that arose in Podhajce, this preacher went to the Domna in Salonika, and after a while he was one of the rabbis of Jacob Frank, who showed him many antinomist hints in "old books". For what reason did the anger of the zealous Emden lash out against the "preacher" of Podhajce? He was one of the children of Rabbi Yaakov Yehoshua, the author of "Pnei Yehoshua", (1681-1756) who was chosen in 1718, after the death of the Chacham Tzvi, as the rabbi of Lvov and its region. He was one of his companions who fought with him against Rabbi Yonatan Eibeshitz. However, Rabbi Yaakov Yehoshua was not lacking for "troubles" despite his brilliance in Torah, for a short time after he was chosen as the rabbi of Lvov, one of the mighty parnassim of Lvov attempted to place his son-in-law on the rabbinical seat after Rabbi Yaakov Yehoshua's contract expired. After he left Lvov, he moved to Buczacz, the place of residence of his in-law Rabbi Aryeh Leib, who was at the time the head of the community of Buczacz. He was wealthy, and also a Torah scholar, and was nicknamed by the people "Reb Leibish the head of the state". Shifra, the daughter of Rabbi Aryeh Leibish was married to the son of Rabbi Yaakov Yehoshua, that is Rabbi Yisachar, the head of the rabbinical court of Podhajce. It seems that politics and zealously went hand in hand here, and the brilliance of the people who were hurt by their hand was not taken into account[25].

I. The Two "Baalei Shem" of Podhajce.{22}

Aside from great rabbis and Torah geniuses who conducted their work in the community of Podhajce, there were also two Baalei Shem, who busied themselves with the writing of amulets based on Holy names. Baalei Shem went through many incarnations through the generations. In the 17th and 18th centuries, there were also many Baalei Shem who were not scholars at all Their true or apparent power was in the healing of the sick, and that is what attracted the attention of the community on frequent occasions. This was an intermixture of a practical Kabbalist who works through prayers, amulets and oaths; and a popular physician who was familiar with potions made from animals, plants and inanimate objects. The two Baalei Shem who are discussed here were natives of Podhajce, who were raised and educated in the spirit of Torah and tradition. Due to the tribulations of the times and various other factors, they were forced to wander afar to find a place for their activities outside the country. Both of them lived during the same era, and both were involved to some degree in the Sabbatean movement that had set itself up in Podhajce as well. Both of them are mentioned in the books of the zealous Rabbi Yaakov Emden, who apparently was familiar with all of the Jewish communities in various countries and cities. In general, the name Podhajce appears in almost all of the books of that era, which is proof that this city played an important role in

Jewish life. The dispute between Rabbi Yonatan Eibeshitz and Rabbi Yaakov Emden did not by-pass it.

[Page 31]

These two Baalei Shem were born in Podhajce and lived there for a certain period. We have no information regarding their way of life there. Despite this, we are not exempt from presenting here the few details about them, gleaned from various books. From this, it is possible to learn as well about Jewish Podhajce of that era.

a) Rabbi Shmuel Yaakov Falk – ""Doctor Falk", the Baal Shem from London

There were three main stops in Falk's long life. His native city of Podhajce, Furth Germany, and London, England. He lived from 5468-5542 (1708-1782). We do not know for how many years he lived in Podhajce, and why he left it to move to Furth. We only know that he arrived in London in 1742, when he was 34 years old, and lived there for 40 years until his death. He resided permanently in London, with the exception of visits to Paris that were related to his work.

According to the inscription on his tombstone in London, he was "the son of Rafael the Sephardi". This does not mean that his origins were from the Jews of Spain or Portugal , but rather that he belonged to the new Hassidic movement that worshiped in "Sephardic style" (Nusach Sephard). His family name was Falk. This was a family of illustrious rabbis who gave honor to the name. The renowned Gaon Rabbi Yehoshua the author of "Pnai

Yehoshua" bore this name, as well as the famous decisor of Jewish law, Rabbi Yehoshua the son of Alexander HaKohen, who was known by the acronym of Sema on account of his book "Sefer Meirat Einayim". It would seem that our Baal Shem is related to this family. His appellation of "Baal Shem" (given to him by himself or by others) brought with it a halo of awe and honor. He was a Kabbalist and mystic, and was revered by many of his generation. The reason for this reverence was his activities as a wonder worker, at which he was apparently quite successful.

There are almost no details about his activities in Podhajce, just as there are few details about the events of his life. Such information is available from articles in various books that appeared in our generation (such as "Maagal Tzvi" by the Chida – Rabbi Chaim Yosef David Azulai); books of disputation by the zealous Rabbi Yaakov Emden, especially the books: Hitavkut, Gat Derucha, and Shevirat Luchot Haaven; the diary that the Baal Shem left after him, that is now found in the library of the Beis Midrash of the United Synagogues of London.

The years that Falk lived in Podhajce began at a time when various movements and cults of misleaders and the mislead, Kabbalists and Baalei Shem, false prophets, Sabbateans and Frankists, Hassidim and Frankists, Hassidim and Misnagdim. All of these laid fertile ground for the activities of Baalei Shem and miracle workers. One of the factions that arose during that era was that of Yehuda Hassid, who wished to hasten the coming of the Messiah by fasts and suffering. He and his friends left Poland in 1700 to go to Jerusalem. During their travels, they passed through Furth, Germany, via the Tyrol and Venice. Nobody knows who inspired Falk to establish his residence in Furth. Perhaps he wished to wait for his teacher Yehuda Hassid, and to go to the Land of Israel, and only by chance remained in Furth. We only know that Falk's mother also came to Furth, where she died and was buried. After some years, a monument was erected on her grave by order of her son. It is also known that Falk sent various sums of money to the community of Furth, and he left it a significant sum of money in his will. All of this was apparently in recognition of the assistance that the community granted to his mother.

Details about the activities of "Doctor Falk" in Germany are brought down in the letters of Archenholtz[26]. He tells that a noblewoman by the name of Daharnatzov relates in her memoirs about "unbelievable wonders" that were performed by Falk in the presence of several men of wonders. In Archenholtz' opinion, it is possible that these wonders succeeded because of Falk's special knowledge of chemistry. During one of his travels, the mysterious doctor came to Westphalia, and the government of that land became angry because he refused to reveal hidden treasuries. They sentenced him to death by burning, as a wizard. He fled to London (in 1742) in order to save himself, and lived there for forty years, until his death. The story of his flight to London is also mentioned in the writings of Rabbi Yaakov Emden, who states along everything else that Falk married a woman with a lame limb while he was living in Germany. We do not have full faith in this information, since Rabbi Yaakov Emden was always prepared to believe any bad report about those who were suspect in his eyes. Falk had no children, and apparently he adopted a child by the name of Gavriel.

The era of London was the longest era in Falk's life. He was received nicely when he arrived there, just as other refugees were received nicely when they arrived in that city, without being excessively interrogated about their past and their deeds. It would seem that Falk continued to work in the "hidden matters" there as in Westphalia, albeit in a more cautious manner. He gained a following of those who had faith in him on account of his works of wonder, of people who saw these works as supernatural. Among the wonders that were told of him was his ability to light a small lantern that would burn for several weeks without fuel. When there was a need for coal, he would only have to whisper a Kabbalistic incantation, and clumps of coal would slide obediently into the cellar of his house. Table utensils that had been pawned would find their way back to the closet, against all the laws of nature. When a fire threatened to destroy the Great Synagogue of London – they tell of him – he stopped the progress of the fire by writing four Hebrew letters on the doorway of the synagogue.

Word of such events spread quickly among people. Here, we find the same close relation with high people. Archenholtz mentions the name of a royal prince, who, during the course of his search for the philosopher's stone, turned to Dr. Falk, who refused to receive him. The Chida (Rabbi Chaim Yosef David Azulai) mentions in his book "Maagal Tov" (page 136) in which he described his travels . When he visited Paris in the year 1778, he met with the nobleman De Suma and the noblewoman De Krona, who saved several Jews from the claws of the Spanish Inquisition. She hinted to Rabbi Azulai that the Baal Shem of London taught her practical Kabbalah. This exposure angered the honorable scholar, who surmised that Falk maintained close relations with the strange nobleman Baron Theodore De Neuhauf, when he headed the Corsican revolutionaries against the Ginoazes who crowned the king. After he was expelled, he settled in London in 1749. The displaced king strengthened himself with the hope of restoring his fortune by finding treasures that were buried in the depths of the ocean. For assistance in this endeavor, he turned to an elderly Jew who visited him during the time he was in jail. (The rabbi identifies him as the Baal Shem we are now discussing.) Falk also mentions the mysterious meeting with Prince Chortoriski (apparently Adam Chortoriski, 1734-1823), the ruler of Podolia; as well as with a person by the name of Immanuel whom he describes as a "servant of the king of France" (Louis XVI. Similarly, it seems that the Baal Shem gave an amulet ring to the Duke of Orleans, with the aim of assuring him the royal crown. It is told that this ring was sent by Phillip Egalita prior to executing a Jewess named Juliet Gosho, who sent it to her son, Baron De Charter, who was later on crowned as King Louis Phillip. Prior to his death, the king bequeathed the ring to the nobleman De Paris, and it is surmised that today, it can be found in the Satuv house in Svikenheim. Similarly, our Baal Shem was not hidden from the eyes of the well-known Jewish philosopher Shlomo Maimon, whose autobiography (published by Lageblum, Tel Aviv) tells that in the midst of a Kabbalistic discussion, he was told that there was a G-dly man who has lived in London for a few years and works wonders with the power of the Kabbalah. Maimon doubts this, but those with whom he discussed promise him that they saw with their own eyes that this Baal Shem lives in Graphenhagen. He an answer to them in philosophical style, stating that he does not doubt at all the truth of their stories, but it is possible that they had not checked into the matter carefully enough, and they relate to what their eyes see as with any practical matter.

[Page 32]

In a letter of one of his friends, Zusman Sachnovitz, it is stated regarding Falk: "His house is lit by silver candlesticks on the wall, along with a central candelabrum with eight sticks, made of pure silver. Even though it could only hold enough fuel for one day and one night – it continued burning for three weeks. On one occasion, he remained in his home isolated for six weeks, without food or water. At the end of six weeks, when ten men gathered together and came to him, the found him sitting at his work chair, wearing a gold turban and a gold chain around his neck with holy names etched onto it. In truth, this man was unique in his generation with his knowledge of holy mysteries. I cannot relate about all the wonders that he performed. I offer gratitude that I am numbered among those who dwell in his shadow." It is possible that all of the festive and coquettish behavior of Falk was performed to make an impression upon his visitors and to instill in them faith in his works, from which he earned a great deal of money[27].

Zusman's letter reached Rabbi Yaakov Emden, who felt it proper to express his opinion about Falk in the following language: "Regarding Falk – everyone knows his machinations and foolishness. I have never seen him: however many people have told me that he comes from Poland, and he attempts to know all the secrets of practical Kabbalah, through which he is able to expose hidden treasuries. This matter led him to confusion when he was in the state of Westphalia, and the local authorities wanted to burn him alive as a wizard and sorcerer, however he fled to England. He even married a woman in Westphalia, a woman whose behavior aroused many complaints. Then he went to London. There he found many supporters, especially among the middle class. Several wealthy Christians also placed their faith in him, asking them to expose treasures in the sea and on land. He succeeded in tricking the owners of wealthy ships, upon whom he wasted much money. Now he is poor and impoverished. Thanks to these machinations, he rose to a life of wealth and comfort. However, he spent a great deal of money on foolishness in order to ensure that he had a good name, until he was sometimes forced to borrow money from businessmen. Despite all this, it seems that he is a boor and an ignoramus. He presented himself as a Kabbalist. However, all that he wrote and spoke about was nothing but foolishness, which is not understandable to anyone. Nevertheless, as long as Falk did not attempt to mislead the people, I did not pay attention to him and his bad behavior. When his household administrator Zusman began to conduct propaganda on his behalf, I found it necessary to expose his face." These are the words of accusation that Rabbi Yaakov Emden issued against Falk, and require no interpretation. However, there is no accusation of Sabbateanism, and even Zusman's letter has no hint of such[28].

The important bankers Aharon Goldschmid and his son Gershon were among Dr. Falk's friends. They gave him appropriate advice regarding his business. He became wealthy during his last two decades of life. He lived in a tavern in the Wolkloz Quarter, where he set up a synagogue that was served by two cantors. We find him using vehicles for transportation. He loved books, and in the diary that he left behind, we find lists of books for the study of grammar, philosophy, and polemics. He maintained contact with the chief rabbi Rabbi David Tavli (the son of Shlomo Zalman HaKohen Schiff), and the rabbi of the New Synagogue, Rabbi Moshe Meyers. He was

well accepted by the masses, and paid great attention to the doing of good deeds. He died on April 17th, 1782 and was buried the next day in the cemetery on Glubb St. The inscription on his gravestone notes that during his forty year sojourn in London, he observed Torah and commandments, and distributed all of his wealth to charity. The image of the Baal Shem that remained after him, is portrayed by someone from his generation as follows: "When he walked outside, he was covered with a flowery cloak, blending in a surprising manner with his long, white beard, and the appearance of his noble face."[29]

[Page 33]

In summary, it should be stated that this Podhajce native spread the fame of his city throughout the capitals of Europe. The Baal Shem of London was a known person in London and outside of it, and the name of Podhajce was precious to him throughout his life.

b) The Baal Shem and Kabbalist Rabbi Moshe David of Podhajce

The renowned Kabbalist Rabbi Moshe David of Podhajce was of the same generation of Dr. Falk the Baal Shem of London. He was born in Podhajce and lived there for a number of years as an honorable Kabbalist and Baal Shem. It would seem that he had many followers in the city, for Zusman Sachnovitz, who found him in London, describes him as follows: "He was famous in the state of Wolhyn, he was the Kabbalist, renowned man of G-d, our rabbi and teacher Rabbi Moshe David, may G-d preserve him, who is called Rabbi Moshe David the Baal Shem from the holy community of Podhajce"[30]. It is further written there: "The renowned Rabbi Moshe David, may G-d preserve him, is an elderly, great Kabbalist, who formerly used to live in the community of Podhajce, and became known there as a Baal Shem"[31]. This honorary appellation is not given to just any person. This testifies that the bearer was renowned in his deeds and his Kabalistic knowledge. He first became known as a Baal Shem in eastern Poland.

We know almost nothing about the history of Rabbi Moshe David the son of Tzvi in his birthplace of Podhajce. His name, Rabbi Moshe David of Podhajce, indicates that this city was his place of residence for a certain period of time. We learn from one of his sermons that he was born in 5466 (1706). We do not know what were his deeds in this city, on account of which he was persecuted, excommunicated and expelled. He would certainly have had friends and relatives there without us hearing anything about him. The information about his actions would have come to us from his opponents and enemies, particularly from the time that he lived in the Land of Germany. The information is sufficiently detailed but quite one sided. Only echoes come to us from the time that he lived in Altona, after he came into the field of interest of Rabbi Yaakov Emden and other zealots on account of his close contact with Rabbi Yonatan Eibeshitz and his son Wolf. There is no doubt that were it not for the stubborn persistence of Emden in his war against the Sabbateans, we would not even have known the name of this Kabbalist, as he is called in his description: "The Baal Shem and Sabbatean Rabbi Moshe David of Podhajce"[32].

It would seem that Rabbi Moshe David of Podhajce is not numbered among the leading Sabbateans, for he was lacking their vivid imagination and strength of expression. He did not represent the generation of the creators of the Sabbatean tradition, but rather the generation of the weakening. He did not appear as a personality who imprinted the seal of Sabbateanism, and perhaps this is why his life is characteristic of the life of other persecuted Sabbateans. The complexity of his doctrine is characteristic of the complexity of the third generation of Sabbateans[33].

Rabbi Moshe David understood very well why he was being persecuted. He knew that his persecutors approached him with the idea of "all of Israel is responsible for each other". Since he did not contemplate separating from the community of Israel, he stood up against the principle of general responsibility, and claimed the rights to his personal belief. "What does it concern them whether or not I believe in Shabtai Tzvi" – Moshe David called out to his persecutors – "You are not responsible for me, and you will not be called upon to pass judgement. It is enough that you look after yourselves. If it is within your power, do not permit me to enter the Garden of Eden. However here on earth, leave me alone, for you and I are alike". These words reveal to us what was in the heart of this believer who was persecuted on account of his belief. He was not the only one who thought like this – that a Jew is allowed to believe in Shabtai Tzvi provided that he observes all of the commandments. Thus did he distance matters of faith from the hearts of those who trust in flesh and blood.

Why did he leave Podhajce? We have no details about this. Apparently, the hand of his oppressors and opponents brought him to this. He did not bid farewell to Poland after he left Podhajce, but rather moved to other places. It would seem that he wandered from place to place, wrote amulets, and did wonders, apparently earning his livelihood in this manner. Emden relates that in Rogoza, in the Posen region, the court of law exposed the content of his amulets, and he was expelled from town on a wagon filled with dung. He was also expelled from Lissa (also in the Posen region), apparently at the same period of time. Rabbi Yaakov Emden apparently exaggerates when he states that "he was exiled and expelled from the entire Land of Poland". However, there is no doubt that he was indeed expelled from various places. It is stated in a different place that in Rogoza, he distributed amulets "that contained pleas for help". He was forced to leave the city on account of the cholera epidemic that broke out. From there he moved to Lissa and to other places.

We have sufficiently detailed information on the history of Rabbi Moshe David only from the time that he lived in Germany. He came to Fiurda in the year 5518 (1768). Various sources tell of his deeds there, such as the letter of Rabbi David Strauss, the head of the rabbinical court of Fiurda,to Rabbi Asher Enzel, the head of the rabbinical court of Grabfeld; and the letter of one of the administrators of the community of Fiurda, Rabbi Yaakov Falk, to the administrators of the community of Altona. An important addendum to these two aforementioned sources is found in the letter of Rabbi Asher Enzel, the head of the rabbinical court of Grabfeld, to Dr. Strauss, in which he writes that "the man that is referred to as the Baal Shem, named

our rabbi and teacher Rabbi David the son of Rabbi Tzvi who lived in your important encampment (that is Fiurda) for three months and left there with a good and great name". Independent sources tell of the events of Rabbi Moshe David after he left Fiurda. They related that Rabbi Moshe David traveled from village to village and from place to place after leaving Fiurda. From the letter of the aforementioned head of the rabbinical court of Grabfeld, it is possible to see that Rabbi Moshe David revealed secrets from "mystical wisdom" also in Grabfeld, and with his harsh words with which he disparaged the scholars of the revealed Torah, he aroused suspicion in the heart of the head of the rabbinical court, who ordered that his books and writings be examined[34].

[Page 34]

The majority of information that remains about Rabbi Moshe David comes from the period of time that he spent in Altona. He first arrived in Altona in the year 5519. He also visited London that year. Rabbi Yaakov Emden surmises that he went to London because he "found no rest" in Altona, and in order to "befriend his likeness", that is Shmuel Falk the Baal Shem of London. Several details regarding the visit of Rabbi Moshe David in London are found in the letter of Eliezer Zusman Sachnovitz[35]. He tells that Rabbi Moshe David resided in the home of Shmuel Falk and participated in his magic. Rabbi Shmuel Falk wrote an interpretation of his secrets for him. Rabbi Moshe David wrote a detailed letter to Rabbi Yonatan Eibeshitz on the matter of Shmuel Falk "and told of the great wonders and wonders of the man, that is the holy man who is a man and not a man, and with the purity of his tongue he said such and such, that leader of leaders, that great man, about whom is hinted in rectifications 69, 106, 71, and 74, and about whom Rabbi Shimon Bar Yochai said pure words about the secrets that were revealed, as is said: and he will give strength to his king and raise up the horn of his Messiah". Rabbi Yaakov Emden relates that Rabbi Moshe David was expelled from London in disgrace, but he brings no proof to his words, which are not corroborated in any other source.

Rabbi Moshe David was received honorably in Altona by Rabbi Yonatan Eibeshitz, who brought him close and tended to all his needs. From various documents brought down in various books, it is proven without doubt that Rabbi Moshe David was active in Altona as a teacher among the Sabbateans, and as a preacher among the non-believers. "His net was spread" among a very wide circle. It is natural that his closeness to Rabbi Yaakov Eibeshitz and his son Wolf – who appeared in Altona at that time with his full splendor of wealth – made him into an attractive personality. His discussions and sermons were especially liable to arouse suspicion and doubts in the hearts of opponents of Sabbateanism. When Wolf Eibeshitz to Altona and set up a Beis Midrash in his home, he appointed Rabbi Moshe David as the head teacher and prayer leader. Some people say that Rabbi Moshe David was a friend and partner in Kabbalah study of Wolf Eibeshitz himself.

One can surmise the relationship between Rabbi Yonatan and Rabbi Moshe David from a response that he wrote to Rabbi Yitzchak Halevi Ish Horwitz (one of the rabbis of the Kloiz in Brody at that time) of Glogow, from which it is possible to understand the grievances, complaints and demands regarding Rabbi Moshe David (the letter is brought down in the book "Hitavkut"). One can especially see the fact that a man such as Rabbi Moshe David, known as a Sabbatean, was a friend of his son Wolf Eibeshitz and taught Kabbalah in his house, while he demanded the expulsion of Rabbi Moshe David from Altona. The response of Rabbi Eibeshitz is a very important document. At first, he claims that until the arrival of Wolf, Rabbi Moshe David was "discrete", something that was indeed possible, and we have no direct proof to the contrary. Secondly, he claims that Rabbi Moshe David is only one of the teachers in the house of Wolf, who pays him an inflated salary. After answering several questions to other complaints, Rabbi Eibeshitz claims that not only is there no proof that Rabbi Moshe David sinned at all, but rather the opposite: he is a holy and pure man. He opposed the demand of Rabbi Yitzchak to expel Rabbi Moshe David from Altona. However, the "guardians of the city" of Altona were not silent, and attempted to accomplish this themselves. In the middle of the winter of the year 5521, Rabbi Moshe David was forced to leave Altona. He went to Norden that is in the state of Friesland. Rabbi Yonatan gave Rabbi Moshe David a letter of recommendation, addressed to Rabbi Elya of Norden, in which he wrote: "Since a pious and G-dly Kabbalist such as Rabbi Moshe David had to go there because of the situation, I ask that you take him into your home and sustain him in his old age... and I am coming only to inform you that I guarantee him, and the payment for his food can be demanded from me. It is a great Mitzvah to sustain him appropriately." This letter is an interesting document, which shows that Rabbi Yonatan remained faithful to Rabbi Moshe David despite everything, and did not hesitate to issue a letter of recommendation to a man that was forced out of Podhajce on account of Sabbateanism. Rabbi Moshe David went to Norden and remained there for a period of time. His persecutors caught up to him there as well. Rabbi Yaakov Emden relates that Rabbi Moshe David went from Norden to "disgrace in the Land of Hungary and died among the uncircumcised". However, we cannot know what of this is historical truth and what is literary spice[36].

The personality of Rabbi Moshe David, a native of Podhajce, is very concealed. Perhaps the religious researchers can deal with this, for he is considered to be a veteran Sabbatean. Indeed, there is one such researcher in Israel who wrote a special monograph about him, which was before my eyes as I wrote this chapter.

[Page 34]

J. Jacob Frank and the Frankist Sect in Podhajce

The incarnation of the Sabbateans as Frankists. – The change of guard also in Podhajce. – The rabbinical ban on Frank and his sect. – The Prince Marcyn Radziwil turns toward Judaism and maintains contact with the Frankists in Podhajce. – Jacob Frank visits Podhajce. – The Tzadik Rabbi Shlomo of Podhajce fasts. – The slander of Judaism by the Frankists to the bishops. – Jews of Podhajce join the mass conversion to Christianity of the Frankists. – The despair of the Jews in Podhajce "after the deed".

During the period of the Shabtai Tzvi movement of 1665-1676, there were many Jews in Podhajce who were caught up in the belief that Shabtai Tzvi was the true Messiah. After he and many of his relatives converted to Islam and the

Sabbatean movement weakened, Podhajce was significantly taken by the enthusiasm toward messiahs[37].

[Page 35]

After a few years, when Frank appeared with his doctrine and unique way of life, many Jews of Poland and Galicia followed after him. There were also Jews in Podhajce who followed after him, and the city became a flash point for that movement as well[38].

Jacob Frank did not come to Poland from the east, for he himself was a native of the town of Korolowka in Eastern Galicia. He became involved in Sabbateanism, and from 1752-1755, he lived in Izmir and Salonika, the centers of the secret "Domna" sect of Sabbateanism, where he came into contact with its leaders and was influenced by them. Later, he declared himself to be a messiah and founded a sect that was a form of continuation of Sabbateanism. However, instead of the asceticism that was preached by the early Kabbalists, Frank stood for complete freedom, and giving into the bodily desires "for the sake of the commandment". When he to Poland in 1755, many believers followed him. The center of the sect was at first in Lvov, where Frank organized a mystical festivity accompanied by sexual licentiousness, whose goal was to hasten the redemption through the gates of impurity, similar to Sabbateanism. After his bizarre deeds became exposed in Lvov, Frank moved to the town of Lanckoron in 1756. However, he and his followers were caught there during a service that was accompanied by an orgy, and in an examination in front of the rabbinical court of Satanov, it became clear that the members of this sect participate in licentiousness and swap wives. The rabbinical council of the Four Lands, which convened in Brody in 1756, declared a ban on Frank and his sect. All members of this sect became a target for severe persecution from the Jewish community[39].

Indeed, after the weakening of the movement of Rabbi Yehuda HaChasid that made aliya to the land of Israel, his followers still roamed around the Carpathian region. They attracted a significant number of followers. When Jacob Frank appeared on the scene of Sabbateanism, these Sabbatean centers in Reisin and Podolia became fortresses of the Frankists. Podhajce was a significant center of Sabbateanism in Poland, and maintained contact with important Sabbatean activists in Poland, including the preacher Rabbi Yisachar of Podhajce. With the change of guard of the Sabbateans to the Frankists, various nests of Sabbateans continued to exist and conduct activities. The Frankist movement was also quite active in Podhajce, and the paths of the leaders of the sect passed through it[40].

Prince Marcyn Radziwil, who became interested in religious issues, maintained contact with the Frankists in Podhajce. He even visited Jacob Frank in 1759. Radziwil was a strange personality. He was born in 1703, and was sent abroad at age 15 to study in academies. In 1728, he married Alexandra Balchaca the granddaughter of the well-known Polish writer Waclaw Potocki. He was interested in the sciences, particularly medicine, chemistry, physics and music. His wife died in 1736, and in 1737 he married Marta Trambacka. Then, he began to busy himself with metaphysical problems and religious research. He decided to seek out and choose for himself the best religion, and he chose Judaism. He studied Hebrew and Yiddish. He distanced his Christian servants from his courtyard and employed only Jews in his estates. According to the Polish writer Niamcowicz, Jews would gather in his home on Sabbath eves to partake of the Sabbath meal, consisting of fish, noodles and pudding. He ate only Kosher food, and wore Jewish garb on the Sabbath. The noblemen of his family declared him to be mentally ill, especially when it became known that he maintained a harem in his palace, and that only Jews are found around him. Through their efforts, King August III ordered a trustee to be appointed over him. Marcyn Radziwil died in 1781.

At the beginning of his appearance, Frank tells that when he was in Poland for the first time in 1656 "I conducted more special activities in Berezhany, Rohatyn, Sworow, and I did other such things, so that everybody was mixed up. I even made other such mix-ups of this nature among the Polish noblemen, and later you can see what this did to them." Immediately after he arrived in Rohatyn, the lewd celebrations began, similar to those of Lvov. Frank continues to relate: "I spent approximately one week in Rohatyn, and from there I traveled to Podhajce. There, some of the people accepted my doctrine. There, Elijah the Prophet appeared to me in a dream, in the same form that I had seen him previously, and told me that they would take me and my entire group to jail in Lanckoron, and that they would also take our horses. I immediately told this to the members of our group." These are the strange words that Frank relates about his wanderings from city to city, and the followers that he acquired.

The shame of the Frankists in Podhajce was revealed by a woman, whose husband demanded that she perform a forbidden act. The husband promised her that several great scholars have agreed that this is a rectification and commandment at this time, for their preacher Rabbi Yisachar of Podhajce, who was held by them as a great and pious man, commanded thus. Finally the matter became known, and those who rebelled against the authorities were fined a large sum (Ledgers of the Council of the Four Lands, page 70). According to testimony that was given to the rabbinical court of law in Satanov, even prior to the coming of Frank, they conducted their prayer services as was done during the time of Shabtai Tzvi, and added the name Yaakov [i.e. Jacob] to the name Shabtai – Yaakov Shabtai, with the special description, "he is the true god and the king of the universe, our true messiah, aside from whom there is no other god, neither above or below or in the four directions of the world, therefore we bow, prostrate ourselves, praise, revere, sanctify, make our king and extol the name of the great and mighty king Shabtai Tzvi."

Frank further tells of his adventures: "When I traveled from Ivani to Lvov through Podhajce, many gathered to go with me. I told them that I am going to change my religion, and I attracted many to follow me. When you hear that I have become the master of these people who go after me, and that the entire world gives me honor, you will know that the Satan – and not the true god – leads us..."

[Page 36]

Even though he was elderly, Elisha Schorr, who was a preacher in Rohatyn, joined the early followers of Frank, since he saw him as the faithful continuation of Sabbateanism. His sons Shlomo, Natan (Lipman) and Leib also joined. The sons of the Schorr family played important roles in the events of Lanckoron. After their deeds were revealed, they placed themselves along with Frank under the protection of Cardinal Dembowski, and though their efforts, a debate was arranged with the rabbis of Lanckoron. Elisha Schorr and his son Shlomo participated from the Frankist side. They and three of their friends signed "the copy of the claims and answers" on behalf of their sect[41].

It is interesting to note that the names of rabbis of several cities are mentioned among the rabbis who persecuted the "sect" in Podolia and Reisin: Kamenetz, Sharigrod, Mezhibozh, Tomaspol, and others, without mention being made of the rabbis of the Galicia region. There is no doubt that in Podhajce, there were also many who did not join the Frankists. According to the historian Meir Balaban, during that time, there lived in the city a Tzadik Reb Shlomo, who repented completely throughout his life, fasted, and immersed in the mikva [ritual bath] daily. He was a Tzadik who certainly protected the honor of traditional Judaism and Torah. However, it would seem that the voices of the opponents of the sect were not heard, and there were no people who were brave enough to go against them. Only in Rohatyn itself, did the local rabbi speak out against the Schorr family and their deeds. The local rabbi, Rabbi David Moshe Avraham, was called the name Ada"m by the people of his generation – the initials of his name. He was the author of several books. According to his family tradition, he was "the man who fought with a strong arm against the group of evildoers, and he girded his sword, the sword of G-d, and beat them until defeat, are these not the impure evildoers who took hold of the path of Shabtai Tzvi, may his name be blotted out, headed by the impure evildoer Elisha (Schorr) who lived in Rohatyn at the time, and was called Elisha of Rohatyn."

The followers of Sabbateanism in the form of Frankists, who were persecuted by those who were faithful to the Torah of the rabbis, finally separated from Judaism, and spread false libels about it, including a blood libel during the debate in Lvov in 1759. Along with Frank, who took on the name "Josef" after his apostasy, many members of his sect converted, including some natives of Podhajce. The following were included among the apostates: Shimon the son of Shlomo and Chaya, David Leizerowicz, Bartholomiew Zwirzchowski. Among them we find the name of an apostate from Podhajce, Dominik Wolfowicz[42].

Frank bragged about his deeds and the influence he had on his believers in Podhajce. This is what he writes about one of his journeys: "When I traveled from Ivani to Lvov and I passed through Podhajce, many Jews came to me there and told me that they are prepared and ready to convert. I only accepted those upon whose heads I saw a 'light'. I rejected approximately thirty people upon whose heads I did not see a light. In Lvov, a Jew by the name of Chaim from Podhajce approached me. He had come to Lvov, and begged me to accept him. I looked upon his head and did not see the sign, so I did not want to accept him. However, other believers approached, and urged and begged me to accept him. I told them that he would not remain a believer forever, but I would give in to their will. I accepted him against my will. Now when I came to Warsaw, I heard that he to Podhajce to Lvov, and once again became a Jew."

Frank bragged and told wonders and great deeds about himself: that Elijah had come to him (and from there I traveled to Podhajce and saw in a dream Elijah the prophet, whom I had already seen before); that an angel from heaven went after him to Poland; and that he is able to do wonders in heaven and earth. Through acts of deception, he showed his fellow believers how a green flame surrounds his head with a halo, and a wheel of fire in the shape of a moon would explode. Among everything, he described his relationship with the redeemer that would be born: "I never believed that the redeemer would be born a second time... But my intention was about the 'secret of the bread' in the Catholic faith, and this too I never learned from anybody. However, when I went to the Catholic church in Podhajce for the first time when the service called 'mass' was being conducted, the idea came to my heart that the body of the redeemer is hidden in the bread, and I bowed to this bread as did all of the worshipers." Through his cunning, Frank knew how to mislead the masses with his guile, and a large group of several hundred people from several countries followed after him. In Podhajce as well, many people followed him. However, after their deeds and actions became known, his opponents turned to the overseer of the estate of the owner of the city of Lanckoron, who put Frank and his followers in jail after he was convinced that these reports were true. The rabbis severely excommunicated Frank in the city of Brody, with the blowing of a shofar and the extinguishing of candles{23}, and forbade anyone from marrying into the group, for their children are bastards{24}, their wives are adulteresses, their bread is the bread of gentiles and their sacrifices are the sacrifices of the dead. It was also forbidden to include them in any holy act. It was decreed that every person was required to search after them, to turn them in, and to expose their evil deeds. This ban of excommunication was proclaimed in many cities in Poland, printed with the name "Cherev Pipiot" [Double Edged Sword], and sent to all Jewish communities. Rabbis from Lvov and its region, Brody, Skole, Gloga, Zbaraz, Zmigrod and other places signed the ban against the sect of Shabtai Tzvi and the Frankists. There were no signers from Podhajce, Rohatyn and many other nearby cities.

The members of the Frankist cult made haste to take revenge on their Jewish brethren. In accordance with his command, his supporters gathered in Rohatyn and took council as to how to take revenge on the Jews, and how to insult the Jewish masses. They slandered the Jews to the government officials with vain and false libels – that the Talmud, which is the basis of the Jewish religion, is completely filled with nonsense and trickery, and teaches and commands them to murder Christians and drink their blood. They requested that Bishop Dembowski convene a meeting of the greatest rabbis to debate religion with them, and then it would be proven with actual facts that the Talmud is filled with slander, jealousy and hatred against Christians, and only the book of the

Zohar, which is holy and also honored very much in the eyes of the rabbis, teaches the true faith. This is not the place to discuss at length that debate and the decree to burn the books of the Talmud. There were members of the sect from Podhajce who were involved in this desecration, and there were also some of them who regretted, repented and continued to be faithful Jews.

[Page 37]

In 1759, approximately one thousand followers of Frank left Judaism. A detailed list about a large portion of Frankist cult (508 souls, including 155 men and 120 women) who changed their religion in Lvov was preserved, and was published with notes in the Polish language in the well-known book by Kraushauer on Frank. This list is interesting from many perspectives. In many cases, it notes the place of origin or residence of the people. Thereby, it is possible to establish the place of origin of more than two thirds of those listed. The largest centers were in Busk, Rohatyn and Podhajce in the Lvov region, and in smaller communities near Satanov. We will now mention the names of the members of the sect in Podhajce: in September 1759 – David Leizerowicz (the son of Leizer); Yosef who took on the Catholic name of Bonwentura Podhajci upon his conversion, and his daughter Malka who converted and took on the name Mariana Bonwentura; the son of Moshe of Podhajce who took the name Franciscus Sirapicus; Pesach – Josefus Pioscki, his son Moshe – Ludowicius, his daughter Dvora who changed her name to Roza Bakaninzis; Chava the maid of Moshke became a Christian and took on the name Manania Szaunska; the second daughter Dvora (?) received the name Salucia Anna Piosicka; a different Jew called Moshka the son of Eliezer received the name Tomasz, and his wife changed her name to Marianna. Shimon the son of Shlomo and Chaya the son of Sheva[25] also were among those who became Christians. In October 1759, the following people became Christians: a girl named BatSheva who received the name Franciska Bonwentura Podhajcka; Marianna the daughter of Chaim and Chana. In April 1760, the following people became Christian: Franciskow and his wife Katrina Gruszecki of Podhajce. In July 1760: Yankel the son of Aharon who received the name Grigorius Jakubowski da Podhajce, as well as Izak the son of Pesach who changed his name to Franciscus Benedictus Aronoski[43].

Here it speaks only of "the known ones" according to what is found in the archives and the lists. It would seem that there were also those whose names did not appear for various reasons. There were also natives of Podhajce who converted to Christianity in other places. The following people converted in Kamenetz Podolsk in November 1760: Anna the daughter of Shimon and Sofia Jablonski, whose parents had previously converted. Aside from these, apostates are mentioned on other occasions – Jews from Podhajce such as Sofia Podhajcka and others.

Those who converted to Christianity rose to the rank of nobility in accordance with Polish law, as is shown by their new names. Among the "fathers" of the apostates, there are included some high ranking noblemen who are known in Polish history.

Among those close to Frank was a certain Piotr, whose Jewish name had previously been Nachman[44]. He was the son of Natan Nota of Podhajce, the brother-in-law of Reb Hirsch Witlisz, a communal leader from the city of Opatow, the father of Reb Yehuda from there, the father of the Gaon Rabbi Yechezkel Landau of Prague, the author of the "Noda Biyehuda" responsa book, the son-in-law of the leader Rabbi Yechezkel Pesach, who was the son in law of the Gaon Rabbi Yitzchak Shpitzkof, who settled in the community of Chanczyn in his youth{26}. His father, Natan Nota of Podhajce, was also considered to be one of the followers of the sect of Shabtai Tzvi, and it is mentioned in the Book of Zealousness that his brother-in-law Rabbi Hirsch Witlisz persecuted him, and his son joined the community of Frank. This Piotr was one of the second group in the race that Frank, his wife and several people close to him conducted on the ramparts that surrounded the city and fortified it to the right of the Church of Holy Barbara. At the end of this race, it is told that the "Master" (Frank) sat and said about Piotr, "Why are you standing? And now what?" Piotr answered, "This thing I cannot do..."[45].

Two faithful Hassidic traditions are told about the reply of Rabbi Yisrael Baal Shem Tov of Medzibozh to the event of the large scale apostasy of the Frankists, that affected various cities and towns. He said: "Upon all of you that became apostates, the Divine Presence weeps and says: as long as the limb is connected to the body there is hope that there will be a healing, but once a limb is severed, it has no possible rectification, for every Jew is a limb of the Divine Presence" (The Praises of the Baal Shem Tov). His grandson relates that the Baal Shem Tov said, "two holes were bored through his heart through this deed"[46].

During the period when it seemed that the Frankists had the upper hand, when it seemed to them that the rulers and bishops of the church were standing at their right hand, they caused great trouble to the Jews. In a letter of the Lvov mediator Reb Chaim Kormasz to the activist Reb Dover of Bolechow, interesting details are included regarding Frank's stay in Podhajce. Kormasz' father suffered greatly from the persecutions of the Frankists in that town, and the situation reached the point where, through their recommendation, he was imprisoned and chained in iron chains by order of the city owner Potocki. He was freed from his imprisonment only thanks to the intercession of the communal leaders[47]. The name of Rabbi Herschel Galni (Reb Tzvi Hirsch the rabbi of the tailors in Brody) is similarly mentioned. The evil people who joined him "were all from Podhajce, and caused troubles to the opponents in Podhajce until the time of the first debate. In a note there it is mentioned that Podhajce already had a large number of Sabbateans at the beginning of the 18th Century, and that Chaim Malach carried out a great deal of activity there. It is no wonder that the Frankists also struck deep roots there.

The first followers of Jacob Frank in the region of Podhajce came from the secret Sabbateans in Galicia. However, they had already disappeared from the borders of Galicia at the time of the Austrian conquest, for they went with their messianic leader to Brunn (Brno) in Moravia. From there they moved to Germany and settled in the town of Offenbach near Frankfurt am Main. After the death of Frank, the connection between members of the sect was severed, and it ceased to exist.

Note in this section, Translator's Footnotes are designated by { } brackets. The footnotes designated by [ ] brackets are the text footnotes.

Translator's Footnotes

21. A Kabbalistic term for the opposite of holiness.

22. A Baal Shem is someone who performs miraculous deeds or delves into Kabbalistic secrets by pronouncing a name of G-d.
23. These are symbols used during a formal act of excommunication.
24. The word is 'mamzerim' – i.e. bastards in the Jewish religious sense.
25. The use of the 'son of' is strange, as Chaya is generally a female name.
26. Rabbi Yechezkel Landau is a very famous rabbi (1730-1793) of Prague. Aside from him, I do not know why the author has brought down such a complex chain of relations in this case – other than to show that the converts to Christianity were related to some prominent Jewish leaders.

[Page 38]

K. Podhajce at the Beginning of Hassidism

Hassidic leaders near Podhajce. – The debate about the identity of Reb Adam. – Reb Adam as an influence upon the Baal Shem Tov. – Visits of the Baal Shem Tov to Podhajce? – Reb Nachman of Horodenka, Reb Gershon of Kutow, Reb Mendel of Premishlan, Reb Baruch of Kosow. – The chasm between the Hassidim and Misnagdim[27] in Podhajce. – A grandson of the Zydachow dynasty as Admor in Podhajce. – Reb Yitzchak Izak Menachem the Admor in Podhajce.

Around the time of the battle with the Frankist movement, the Hassidic movement arose like a blossom. Its founder was Rabbi Yisrael Baal Shem Tov (known as the Besht). The cradle of this movement was almost at the gate of Podhajce. It is not known why Jewish Podhajce did not succeed in serving as a center of Hassidism as well, as it served as a center for Sabbateanism and the Frankist movement. Indeed, Podhajce was known for its extremism in Hassidism as well. Its Hassidim were especially enthusiastic and its Misnagdim were especially zealous. However, the greatest leaders of Hassidism were not located in Podhajce itself, but rather in neighboring cities, some close and some farther away[48].

However, before we spend some time on the personality of the founder of Hassidism, the Besht, we will first devote a few lines to the legendary character of Reb Adam Baal Shem. As is known, it is mentioned in “Shivchei Haabesht” that the Besht received secret and mysterious letters about the Torah from “Reb Adam”. This person has not been identified to this day. There are researchers into the development of Hassidism who relate to the entire story mentioned there as a legend without historical basis, especially when it became known that the name Adam was not customarily used by the Jews of Poland at that time. However, from the publication of the book in the year 5578 (1818) we learn that the people mentioned there were known in their locales and lands, and this Reb Adam is known until this day in the circles of Hassidim from the area of the cradle of the Hassidism of the Besht in Eastern Galicia, and many legends were told about him in the city of Rohatyn near Podhajce, where he served as the rabbi and head of the rabbinical court. His name was Rabbi David Moshe Avraham, and the people of his time called him by the acronym of Reb Ada”m. He wrote the book “Tiferet Adam” and several other books that exist in manuscript form. One of them was published in Lvov in the year 5655 (1895) under the name “Merkevet Hamishneh”. Its content is a broad commentary on the Mechilta of Shmot[28]. The memory of the great Ada”m lives to this day. A few words about his activities are published at the beginning of that book. That book had approbations from its time by Rabbi Chaim Kohen Rappoport, the head of the rabbinical court of Lvov, and Rabbi Yitzchak Landau, a rabbi of the region of Lvov. Prior to the publication of the book, Rabbi Yosef Shaul Nathanson added an approbation. Rabbi Uri Zeev Salat describes the author as “the great Gaon and holy man of G-d”. He further writes: “The man who fought with a strong arm against the evil group and raised his sword, the sword of G-d and beat them to destruction, are these not the impure evildoers who followed the evil path of Shabtai Tzvi may his name be blotted out, headed by the impure one Elisha Shar"i who was nicknamed through the city of Rohatyn and was called Elisha of Rohatyn... From my master and teacher Rabbi Y. Sh. Nathanson, I heard about mighty things about this holy author, that were told to us by our holy ancestors."

The grandchildren of the author relate in their introduction to his book that after his battle with the Frankist, the Besht came to him: "and our grandfather told us that our master the Besht came to him in his full glory and informed him that it was ordered from heaven to give him good and beneficence on account of his zeal, the aforementioned zeal of the G-d of Hosts, similar to the zeal described in the Torah of Pinchas the son of Elazar the son of Aharon the Priest, who was given the covenant of peace[29]". The publisher of the book (of the Nagelberg family) similarly describes in his introduction: "I have heard from our elders, who heard from their fathers, that before the Ark of G-d[30] was taken to the Heavens, the Besht came to visit him, and to serve him as a scholar. The Besht said to the rabbi and author: "Rabbi, bless me", and he put his two hands upon him and blessed him. The Besht said after he left: I believe that the rabbi has died, for I saw the Heavenly Hosts going forth to greet him, and I heard that the great people of his generation called him Reb Adam". We do not know the year of his birth or death. He died in Rohatyn and left a large family that continued to live in Rohatyn. If the meeting with the Besht were not a legend, the rabbi would have died between the years 1749-1760. As is known, the Besht died in 1760 (5520).

The Hassidic movement first spread through Podolia. Its founder Rabbi Yisrael Baal Shem Tov was born around 1700 in the town of Ocop. This small town in Podolia, on the border with Wallachia, had a small Jewish population. We do not have any historical data from which we can determine the time of the revelation and activity of the Besht. We know approximately his birth date and death date. From the legends of his life, we know that he lived in the mountains around Kosow and Kuty. It is possible that he also came to Brody on occasion, and possibly also Podhajce, but he never appeared in public.

According to the author of "Seder Hadorot Hachadash", 37 close followers and students of the Besht merited to receive Torah from his mouth. His brother-in-law Rabbi Avraham Gershon of Kutow, a great scholar and Kabbalist, the friend of the well-known Rabbi Yechezkel Landau of Prague (the author of the Noda Biyehuda) left the exile in the year 5507 and settled in the land of Israel. Rabbi Nachman of Horodenka was numbered among the students of the Besht in Galicia. He was one of his most faithful students. The motto that was always on his lips at every occasion was "this is also for the good". The Besht laughed and said, "It is good that you were not living in the time of Haman, for you would also have said that the decrees of Haman are for the good". Reb Nachman was present in Medzibozh at the time of the death of the Besht, and would come on occasion to supplicate at his grave. When he decided to make aliya to the Land of Israel, he went to prostrate himself at the grave of the Besht and ask his permission. When he from his grave, he proclaimed joyously, "The Besht commanded me to travel to the Holy Land". He made aliya in the year 5524 (1764)

to the Land of Israel along with Rabbi Menachem Mendel of Premishlan. Simcha, the son of Rabbi Nachman, married Feiga, the granddaughter of the Besht, the daughter of Hodel (Eidel). Rabbi Nachman of Bratslav was born from that marriage in 5532 (1772).

[Page 39]

Prior to the journey of Rabbi Mendel of Premishlan to the Land of Israel, the Kabbalist Rabbi Baruch of Kosow visited him and stayed with him for several days. Rabbi Simcha of Zolovitch, the son-in-law of Rabbi Shlomo of Rovno and the author of the book "Ahavat Tzion" ["Love of Zion"] was also on that journey. The doctrine of Besht Hassidism began to spread in the land of Israel and nearby lands due to that journey. The students of the Besht saw in this a sign that Hassidism would eventually spread through all lands. Rabbi Yechiel Michel, the preacher of Zolochev, was considered to be the right hand man of the Besht, and he was one of the chief disseminators of the doctrine of Hassidism in Galicia.

If we follow the path of the Besht in the period before his revelation and afterward, we will find that for the most part, he moved about in the area close to Podhajce. Around the year 5490 (1730) Rabbi Yisrael set up his residence in the city of Tlust in Galicia. From time to time, he would make the rounds in nearby communities and villages, teaching Torah to the children of the tax collectors. It may be that the community of Podhajce was not pleasing to him, since it had served as a center of Sabbateanism and the Frankist cult. This suspicion may have kept him from preaching his words in that city. Indeed, despite the failure of the Sabbatean messianic movements even before the sects had ceased in Poland, there were still secret remnants of the Sabbatean cult in Galicia. Their members included scholars, Kabbalists, rabbis and preachers who had become spoiled and now stood at the head of these groups. The well-known zealot Yaakov Emden directed his anger at them. It is known that even after the excommunication of the Sabbateans by the rabbinical council in Lvov, there still remained many who were rooted in their sins and who remained partly in one camp and partly in the other.

The Hassidic movement arose after the despair that pervaded among the masses after the failure of the messianic movements of Shabtai Tzvi and Jacob Frank. The failure of these movements created a vacuum in Jewish society, which was thirsting for social support and spiritual sustenance. In such circumstances, the Besht knew how to attract the masses to him, by preaching that everybody is equal before G-d, whether a scholar or simple person. It is not the study of Torah that is the main thing, but rather uprightness of heart and pure intention. He opposed the excessive fasts and self imposed suffering, by saying that "self imposed suffering causes sadness", and the service of G-d must be done through joy. On account of this, remnants of the messianic movements, who had abandoned their customs, joined Hassidism.

The community of Podhajce was among those who apparently was not completely given over to Hassidism, nor completely to Misnagdut [opposition to Hassidism]. Therefore, there was a chasm in it between the Hassidim and Misnagdim. The opposition to Hassidism apparently came from the rabbis of the city, most of who were scholars and geniuses who had not become involved in Hassidism. It is not known whether the Gaon Rabbi Nota, the head of the rabbinical court of Podhajce, whose name is known as a renowned Kabbalist and great scholar, was a Hassid, or apathetic to Hassidism. It seems that in order to preserve the peace, no Admor of the various dynasties in Galicia wished to set up residence in Podhajce, even though various Tzadikim did come to visit their Hassidim in the city, to conduct table celebrations{31}, and bestow good upon their Hassidim. They even brought with them the spirit of joy and sweetness of the Hassidic melody.

Thus, Podhajce remained as a city without an Admor, until one of the grandchildren of the well-known Tzadikim decided to establish his residence in Podhajce in 5669 (1909). This was Reb Yitzchak Izak Menachem, the paternal grandson of Rabbi Yitzchak Izak the Tzadik of Zydaczow, and the son-in-law of the Tzadik Rabbi Nachum the son of Eliezer of Uzipol, who was the son of Rabbi Yehuda Tzvi the Tzadik of Strettin, the author of many books: "Imrei Tuv" on the Torah, "Imrei Ratzon" on the tradition of Genesis, "Imrei Bracha" on the legends of the sages, "Imrei Chaim" on the 613 commandments. Rabbi Yitzchak Izak Menachem served as an Admor of Podhajce from 5669 until 5703 (1943). He was considered to be a pious and holy Tzadik, and hundreds of Hassidim followed him. He died in the city of Podhajce on the 13th of Adar I, 5703, during the Nazi Holocaust[49]. The son of Rabbi Zeidele was saved from the Holocaust and continued serving as the Bursztyn Tzadik in New York, U.S.A. Podhajce and Bursztyn natives in New York rest under his shadow and work for his benefit.

The neighboring cities were unlike Podhajce – which lived its internal societal life without the direct influence of Hassidism. Starting from the beginning of the 19th century, Hassidism under the influence of Rabbi Yehuda Tzvi Hirsch Brandwein of Strettin took root in Rohatyn. The Rebbe was the student of Rabbi Aryeh Strelisker who was called "Hasaraf"[32], who was the student of the Tzadik Rabbi Shlomo of Karlin. Rabbi Yehuda Tzvi was one of the well-known Admors in the first half of the 19th century. He had great influence among the Jewish masses in Eastern Galicia. He was particularly noted for giving "segulot" [spiritual remedies] for illnesses and to women who were having difficulty in childbirth. The Maskilim of Tarnopol fought against him and informed the authorities about his seguolot and kemiot [amulets], for they saw this as extortion of money from the Hassidim.

His eldest son Reb Avraham inherited the position of Admor from his father. After him, Reb Nachum became the Admor in Strettin when he was only 18 years old. After a few years, Reb Nachum moved to Bursztyn, and was an Admor there until 1914. Most of his Hassidim lived in nearby cities, in which they set up kloizes[33] of Bursztyn Hassidism.

Aside from Strettin Hassidim, there were also Hassidim of Belz, Czortkow, Husiatyn, and others in Podhajce.

[Page 40]

L. Under Austrian Rule

Podhajce under Austrian rule. – The census of 1772. – Decrees and ordinances against the Jews. – The head tax, meat taxes, and Sabbath candle tax. – Tax collection by Jewish lessees. – With a strong hand and cruelty. – The struggle against Jewish garb. – The transfer of Jews to agriculture. – Public schools for Jews. – The rabbis of "Mitaam". – The drafting of Jews and the exemption from the draft by paying a tax.

With the annexation to Austria I the year 1772, recognizable changes began in Jewish life in Galicia, including in Podhajce. The situation of the Jews in Podhajce was particularly difficult during the first years of Austrian rule. They especially had difficulty in becoming accustomed to the new conditions, which were different from those in Poland.

During the first four years, the communal structure remained the same as it had been during the Polish era. Until 1785, all of the Jews of Galicia were organized in accordance with the "Jewish regulations" of Empress Maria Teresa of the year 1776. They were organized into a unique body that was headed by "the chief directorship of Galician Jewry". The organization was liquidated in the year 1785, and no other institution arose in its place. With the publication of the Jewish regulations of Josef II on May 27th, 1789, and the regulations of tolerance on May 7th, 1789, a standard order was established regarding Jewish matters throughout Galicia, that brought in its wake decisive changes in communal life.

The community of Podhajce was also organized according to those regulations. As in the rest of the small and medium sized communities, a communal council with very limited authority stood at the head of the community of Podhajce. It was required to listen and adhere to any request of the central government. The community was responsible for all government taxes imposed upon the Jews. According to the Jewish regulations of 1776, the communal council was made up of six members, and according to the regulations of Josef II, the number was reduced from six to three members, who were chosen for three years. Aside from the communal heads, heads of the Chevra Kadisha (burial society), synagogue administrators, and others were chosen. The cadre of communal officials consisted of the communal secretary (scribe), communal administrator, cantors, synagogue beadles, ritual slaughterers, and undertakers. The conducting of religious affairs was in the hands of the rabbi, who was also chosen by communal electors for a term of three years[50]. However, according to the regulations of 1785, the office of communal rabbi was cancelled. Only religious teachers and cantors were chosen instead. According to the regulations of May 7th, 1789, the communal heads received a salary from the communal coffers. This regulation was the cause of great competition at the time of elections for the position of head of the community.

Already in the days of Jewish autonomy in Poland, many competed for the office of communal Parnas (administrator), a position that brought honor to its holder. In Podhajce as well, the communal elections never took place without divisions, without complaints and slander about those elected, and accusations of imposition of illegal taxes – that is that they imposed all of the taxes among the non-wealthy classes, while they protected themselves and their families. (according to the archives of the internal ministry in Vienna.) Disputes and controversies often broke out upon this stage, that invited libel, slander to the government, and all types of lies and accusations.

Immediately after the Austrian conquest, the Austrian government took drastic measures with the aim of changing the status of the Jews at once, and getting them accustomed to new conditions. The Jews were inundated with a wave of instructions, regulations and directives that only caused chaos. Only after some years did the bureaucratic Austrian authorities in Vienna, Lvov and the regions of Galicia begin to recognize and understand that one cannot suddenly effect all of the changes in the lives of the Jews with drastic measures.

Our nation has always looked upon a census as a serious danger to human life, and the Torah commanded that one can only conduct a census by means of "a monetary contribution for each head" (Exodus 30, 12). If the Jews of Galicia were suspicious of the census conducted by the Austrian government, this was not a vain fear, for after the census, laws appeared with the purpose of limiting the freedom of the Jews, reducing their numbers, or at least inhibiting their culture and removing their sources of livelihood. On December 6th, 1772, the first "Patent" of Baron Fragen, who took care of Jewish matters, placed the responsibility upon the communal heads and rabbis to provide a detailed accounting on the status of the community, its property, income, expenditures and debts, the number of communal administrators and rabbis, and the numbers of people in its region of jurisdiction. They had to list the names of heads of families and their family members, with their ages and sources of livelihood. Such a detailed census had never been carried out before in any part of the world. Not for love did the government wish to know this information, but rather to impose special heavy taxes on them, and to prevent the Jews from sneaking across the border. Any Jew who was not registered in the year 1772 was later registered as an alien.

1,370 Jews were registered in the region of Podhajce in the census of 1765, including 1,079 in the city itself. The number of Jews in the entire "occupied region" was approximately 225,000, from among a general population of 2,308,100 – that is to say, they were 9.6% of the population. This percentage was considered to be very high in the eyes of those who regarded the Jews as a damaging element toward the Christians and the state. The large number of Jews frightened the Austrian officials in Galicia, and they devised cruel decrees that were not equaled even in the middle ages, in order to free themselves from this "national plague". These were like the decrees of Pharaoh in his time, in the spirit of "let us act cunningly toward them lest they multiply" (Exodus 1, 10). A short time after the census, the Jews were forbidden to marry off their children without asking permission from the commission, and this permission was only given after great effort and after paying a high tax. The commission issued another edict: to expel all "Jewish indigents". And how great was the number of Jews who could be classified as "indigents",especially since everything was given over to the whims of the presiding official, and if the official was a lover of bribes, anyone who could not pay the bribe was liable to be expelled as an "indigent".

[Page 41]

The government sent the Jewish indigents to the Polish border, as if Poland was their native land, and it had the responsibility to support them. Poland refused to accept these indigents, and commanded the border guards to refuse them entry. These expulsions continued from 1781 until 1789, the year when the Jews were granted rights equal with all of the citizens of the country, and it was forbidden to expel a resident on account of poverty. That year, the harsh restrictions on marriage in Galicia were also repealed.

The decree regarding marriage permits caused a situation where most of the marriages were not "valid" according to Austrian law, and the children born of these marriages were considered "non-legal" and were called after the name of the mother. Even after the repeal of this decree, there were many cases of "non-legal" marriages, since the law included restrictions on the age of marriage, and the age was apparently set too high for Orthodox Jews. Often, "legal" marriages took place many years after the wedding, in order to ensure that the children would have the status of legal children and that they would be permitted to be called by the name of the father. This situation continued until the beginning of the 20th century, with the outbreak of the First World War in 1914.

In the year 1774, the government raised the head tax, which had been set in Poland at the rate of 300 Kreutzer, to 1 Guilder. Aside from this tax, an income tax of 4 Guilder a year was imposed upon the Jews. In 1784, Josef II repealed the income and property tax.

In its place, the following were instituted: a) A household tax of 1 Guilder for each family; b) a marriage tax; c) a Kosher meat tax in accordance with the type of meat. In 1797 the domestic tax was repealed and replaced with a Sabbath candle tax and a sales tax. In the event that the income from the meat tax and the candle tax were not sufficient, the sum was made up through an additional tax. The meat tax was called "payment for tolerance and protection".

With the imposition of the meat tax, that brought with it great profits for those who were occupied in its collecting, disputes broke out between various communities. The tax was given as a monopoly to a tax lessee, who was given the responsibility to collect the Kosher tax as he saw fit, and to forbid shechita (ritual slaughter) for many butchers. This situation made it possible for those butchers who worked hand in hand with the lessee to raise the price of meat at their whim – a matter that angered the population, especially the poor. The banned butchers also complained that the ban on slaughter jeopardized their livelihoods. Occurrences such as this took place in every community, caused hatred and jealousy, and disrupted relations between people. The Sabbath candle tax, which every Jew was responsible for, was also difficult. Several strata of citizens were exempt from this tax: a) people engaged solely in agriculture; b) military men and their wives; c) widows of army men; d) unmarried men and women living with their parents, relatives, or friends; e) business assistants, apprentices and household employees who were unmarried or widowed.

The masses of people in Galicia were downtrodden because of the oppression of the lessees of the meat and candle tax. This era, which was known as "licht fachter" and "fleisch fachter"{34}, is etched in the memories of the people through various anecdotes and stories about cruel and inhuman methods employed by the lessees in collecting the taxes. These means bordered on robbery and theft. The tax lessees were often the communal Parnassim, and the authorities would turn the anger of the Jewish residents against them.

Aside from the burden of impositions and taxes, the communities of Galicia were without exception also burdened with the responsibility of paying off the debts from the days of Jewish autonomy in Poland; the debts of the central bodies – the Council of the Four Lands, the regional councils, and the individual communities. In a law of August 28th, 1787, the Jews of Galicia had to obtain German surnames. Thus began the process of Germanization of the Jews. From that time, the rabbis were bound to conduct their official duties only in the German language.

In 1821, the matter of Jewish garb entered to the order of the day. Already in the regulations of Josef, section 47, the Jews of Galicia were required to cease wearing by 1794 the traditional garb that set them apart from the rest of the segments of the populations. Only rabbis were permitted to wear such garb. However, the actualization of this regulation was cancelled on May 28th, 1790 on account of the opposition of the Jews. When the central government in Vienna concerned itself with the preparation of new Jewish regulations during the years 1816-1820, the question arose once again about whether it was reasonable to forbid the Jews from wearing traditional garb by force of law. The head of the Galician Gubernia, Baron Hauer, recommended the inclusion of a specific ban on Jewish garb in the new legislation. He also had the support of wide circles of Jewish assimilationists. When the wider Jewish community found out about the intentions of the Gubernia to carry out the recommendations of Baron Hauer, a protest movement arose amongst the Jewish masses. The Jews of Podhajce also expressed their opposition. Its communal heads turned to the government and requested the continued permission to wear Jewish garb. Among other reasons, economic reasons were also given, for the change of garb would cause new expenditures for the Jews that they could not afford. The other communities of Galicia submitted similar petitions. Apparently, this was an organized effort from a single source. Finally, the plans were shelved, and the storm abated.

In the framework of the regulations regarding Jewish life in Galicia, Kaiser Josef II demanded that a portion of the Jews be transferred to agriculture. Jews who were prepared to turn to agriculture, were promised a

50% reduction in the toleration tax, and later a complete exemption. That year (1785) Josef II commanded the founding of Jewish settlements in Galicia. Through a special decree, the communities were required to immediately began settling 1,400 families from Galicia on the agricultural settlements. Podhajce contributed 9 families to this requirement. In 1822, 40 families of the region of Berezhany transferred to agriculture. Of these, 24 were settled on the accounts of the communities and 16 on their own accounts.

[Page 42]

The Jewish regulations of Josef II (from March 20th, 1785) also commanded the Jews to establish public schools. The authorities were interested in attracting Jewish children to public schools that opened up starting from 1782. Since they did not succeed at this, the communities were asked to found public schools in 1785. Once again, the Jews did not fulfil this demand. Then, strong orders were given that made the communities responsible for ensuring that children would be required to attend public schools until the age of 13.

The school in Podhajce existed until the liquidation of the educational network in 1806 – a liquidation that came on account of the negative relation of the Jews to this. Despite all enticements, punishments and fines, they refused to send their children to these schools out of fears that their attendance would lead to apostasy.

In 1788, a great disaster happened, in the form of an ordinance that obligated Jewish youth to serve in the army. This was a great innovation in the life of the Jewish people, who had not been used to this for hundreds of years. It is no surprise that a great tumult arose among the Jews with the publication of this law. Many youths left the land and scattered throughout the world, or hid from the government emissaries. About a year later, Kaiser Josef II wished to lighten the situation somewhat. He ordered that the Jews only be put into certain areas of service, that they be provided with Kosher food, and that they not be assigned difficult labor on the Sabbath. In 1804, the actual draft into the army was replaced with a draft tax. It is known that in 1853, members of the communal council of Podhajce gathered together and decided to collect the sum of money required to free the community from the draft of its youth into the army. To that end, they imposed a special tax on the flour for the baking of matzos. The salt merchants also collected a special payment to this end, and in 1855 a ban was threatened upon any merchants who did not wish to fulfil this decision. Only in 1878 was the obligation of army service once again imposed upon Jewish youth from the age of 21 and above, as it was imposed upon the rest of the segments of the population.

Note in this section, Translator's Footnotes are designated by { } brackets. The footnotes designated by [ ] brackets are the text footnotes.

Translator's Footnotes

27. Misnagdim are opponents of Hassidism.
28. The Mechilta is a Biblical commentary on Shmot (Exodus) from Mishnaic times. The analogous commentary to Vayikra (Leviticus) is known as the Sifra, and on Bamidbar and Dvarim (Numbers and Deuteronomy) is known as the Sifrei.
29. Numbers, 25.
30. Seemingly a nickname for Reb Adam.
31. A "table celebration", or "tisch" is a gathering of Hassidim with their Hassidic leader (Admor) over a meal.
32. A Saraf is a fiery angel.
33. A kloiz is a Hassidic prayer hall or informal synagogue.
34. Licht is 'light' and Fleisch is 'meat'.

M. The Situation of the Jews After the Revolution of 1848

The revolution of 1848, which brought changes to the internal statesmanship of the Hapsburg Monarchy, awakened many hopes within the Jews of Galicia as well. They believed that a good and firm future awaited them from all perspectives.

Their interest was at first toward the repeal of the two taxes that were difficult and despised by them – the kosher meat tax and candle tax. Indeed, after a period of unclearness and various rumors regarding the repeal of these taxes, the parliament decided on October 5th, 1848 to repeal all of the taxes upon the Jews. Similarly, the Jews were declared to be equal citizens with regard to all rights and duties that were upon the rest of the residents of the land.

In the first census that took place in Podhajce in the year 1765, 1,548 people were enumerated in the entire community, and 1,290 in Podhajce itself. Starting from 1870, a census took place every ten years. We have access to a detailed table of the number of Jews in the city, and their percentage with respect to the general population.

Year	General population	Number of Jews	%
1870	4,570	2,742	60.0
1880	5,943	4,012	67.5
1890	5,646	3,879	68.7
1900	5,790	3,757	64.9
1910	5,576	3,497	62.7
1921	4,814	2,872	59.7
1931	5,743	3,124	54.4
1939	6,000	3,155	53.0

We do not have detailed information about the sources of livelihood of the Jews of Podhajce. There exists an accounting of the business and work departments in Brody from 1876-1881 which details the number of those working in the various branches of business and labor, without a breakdown by nationality[51]. According to this accounting, there were 1,281 craftsmen and workers in the city and region, and 350 who worked in business. It would appear that, similar to other cities, almost all of the merchants and a large portion of the craftsmen in Podhajce were members of the Jewish community.

Starting from the beginning of the 20th century, decisive changes took place in the professional makeup of the Jewish population. Many young people completed their courses of study in high schools and became lawyers, doctors and engineers. However, due to the special relationship of the Polish authorities with the Jews, many remained without employment.

The Jews of Podhajce were among the first to whom the nationalist idea came. In one of the Hebrew newspapers from 1876, a writer describes Podhajce as being dissimilar from neighboring towns “that live in darkness and are hidden from the light of the world”, so that a new light will not penetrate its rays to them. However, it follows in the footsteps of the large cities, and warms itself toward ideas that offer a solution to life in the Diaspora. In Tishrei 5636 (1877), a group was founded in Podhajce that had the purpose of “reading timely letters in the holy language and in the language of the land”.

[Page 43]

Members of the "Achva Tzeira in 1935

A monument in memory of the war against the Turks under the leadership of Jan Sowiecki in the year 1667

A group of youths who were members of "Hanoar Hatzioni" (1930)

[Page 44]

The members gathered daily in a premises that they rented, and discussed the mysteries of the times. The organization selected for itself the name "Meeting Place of Jewish Citizens" (Izraeliteshes Birgerliches Kasino)[52].

At the time of the beginning of the emigration of Russian Jews to outside lands, voices were heard in Galicia demanding that the stream of refugees be directed to the Land of Israel rather than America. It is interesting that the Viennese "Alians" branch in Podhajce, which was headed by the Maskilim Yehuda Leibush Alerhand and Shaul Schorr, collected money for the benefit of the refugees of Russia, and sent it to Vienna with the condition "That the money that is sent by the help organization (Alians) only go to those who are going to Palestine, and not to the exiles in America.[53].

On the other hand, the anti-Semitic movements, which sprouted in Galicia in those days and were modeled after such movements in Germany and Vienna, also influenced the situation of the Jews. The matter of Jewish lessees of land in Podhajce was of particular influence. In the year 1891, two assimilated Jews leased lands in Podhajce from a certain insurance company in Krakow. This matter angered the Polish noblemen, who demanded that the travesty be rectified, and that the contract issued to the Jews be nullified, since they were strangers in Poland. The leasing of lands to Jews was regarded as a unpatriotic and anti-nationalist deed. The Polish noblemen in the regions of Podhajce and Kolomya gathered even together in a convention and strongly protested the deeds of the group. This matter caused a strong anti-Semitic outbreak in the Polish newspapers, and angered the spirit of the Jewish intelligentsia. Influenced by this situation, most of the members of the committee of the "Agudat Achim" decided to abandon the assimilationist idea and to concentrate their educational activities only among the Jews[54].

The "Ahavat Tzion" organization, that was founded in Vienna by Peretz Smolneskin and Dr. Reuven Birer in the year 1884, was accepted with great admiration among the Jewish community. It decided to establish a settlement in the Land of Israel for Jewish farmers from Galicia. Immediately after the founding of Ahavat Tzion, Dr. A. Zaltz began to concern himself with purchasing a tract of land for the Galician settlement. He was invited by Baron Edmond Rothschild to come to Paris, and on September 7th, 1897, a contract was signed between him and the representatives of the Baron stating that Ahavat Tzion purchased an 8,600 dunam tract of land in the Galilee for 50 families. Dr. Zaltz decided to call the moshava Machanaim. This was the Arab village of Kibaa that was found between the Rosh Pina moshava and Mishmei Hayarden. The news of the purchase was received with great joy in Galicia. Elyakim Getzel Perel of Podhajce, age 30, was among the group of 11 settlers who were sent to Machanaim in November, 1898[55].

With the spreading of the Chibat Tzion movement and the development of Zionism, the revival of the Hebrew language also took place. Various organizations were founded for the speaking and nurturing of the Hebrew language among those who had set their eyes upon Zion. The Hebrew newspaper Hamagid that appeared in the Prussian city of Lyck made its way to various areas among the cities of Galicia. Its absolutist recommendations aroused anger in the Zionist circles, and there were those that advised banning Hamagid and supporting the Zionist newspapers of Galicia. There were a few writers in Podhajce who published essays on Jewish life in the city and the events therein. Thus, readers in other cities were able to obtain some idea about the Jews of Podhajce. They started in

Hamagid and continued on with articles in other newspapers. Hamitzpeh, which was published in Krakow under the editorship of Shimon Menachem Lazar, published articles from time to time by people who concealed their identities with pseudonyms. Similar articles were published in Polish, German and Yiddish publications. Even the Machzikei Hadas newspaper of Agudas Yisroel did not neglect to mention Podhajce[56].

The First World War, the invasion of the Russian armies into Eastern Galicia in August 1914, and the events of the war that did not skip over any settlement in Galicia, left their mark upon the community and the Jewish population, who for the most part escaped westward. The activities of the community and its institutions ceased. Civic life, including Jewish life, only resumed their normal course at the end of the First World War in 1918. The community began to operate in a normal manner, and acted to the best of its abilities until June 1919. At that point, the Polish army conquered the city, and the Polish authorities opened their offices. The era of Polish rule in the life of the community of Podhajce began.

Notes and Sources

1. The settlement of Jews in Podhajce was always free and unrestricted. This may have been due to the fact that it was a city in Podol, and its ownership changed from time to time. The prime sources of information of Jewish Podol are: a) Galicia and its Jews (research into the history of Galicia in the 18th century) by A. Y. Breuer, Mossad Bialik, Jerusalem; b) the Book of Kamenetz-Podolsk and its Environs, published by the Organization of Natives of Kamenetz-Podolsk and its Environs in Israel, Tel Aviv, 5725 (1965); c) The Book of Chronicles of Podolia and the Ancient History of the Jews There, by Menachem Nachum Litinski, Odessa, 5655 (1895).

2. For the first information about Podhajce, see the entry of Dr. Meir Balaban in The Hebrew Encyclopedia (in Russian), edited by Y. L. Katznelson, published in St. Petersburg.

3. Podhajce played an important role in Polish history. In the chronicles of the kingdom, it is listed as a place where well-known commanders of armies and Polish kings encamped. However with regard to the Jews, it was one of the communities where they did not lick from honey. Some of their tribulations are mentioned in books.

4. Even the spelling of the name "Podhajce" went through many incarnations in the Polish language and other languages. The spelling of the cities kept writers busy in Yiddish as well, and even more so in Hebrew. The Jews of Poland did not preserve the principles of original names of cities and towns, and therefore, differences in spelling of the name arose in Hebrew as well. I mention this detail here only in passing, for it does not interest us here to deliberate about the issues of the name.

[Page 45]

5. See: A. A. Harkavi in "New as well as Old"[35] in the addendum to the seventh volume of "History of the Jews" of Tzvi Graetz, chapter 7, page 32.

6. Despite the fact that the book "Masaat Binyamin is a responsa book, it includes folklore material. Therefore, it attracted the attention of wise men more than other books.

7. Zeev Wolf the son of Yehuda Leib was the author of the Slicha that was published in his book "Gefen Yechidit" (Berlin, 1699).

8. According to the Book of Buchach, the Jewish population of Upper Podol became impoverished after the war with Turkey to such a degree that the Polish nobility of the region issued a specific directive to its representatives of the Sejm in Warsaw, asking the king to free the Jews of Tarnopol, Podhajce and other cities of the region from the head tax, for "Divine law commands every person to stand at the right of his fellow".

9. Podhajce is one of the places for which we did not succeed in identify the names of representatives and activists, despite the fact that the material of the Council of the Four Lands is collected into a special ledger – even though there is no doubt that there were representatives in that council from Podhajce.

10. The Rohatyn Yizkor Book.

11. The Pinkas of the State of Lithuania

12. "Akta Grodzakia", volume 24, Page 398, number 205.

13. The only source on them is from the books "Matzevet Kodesh" and "Anshei Shem".

14. Rabbi Binyamin and his book "Masaat Binyamin" are mentioned several times in the book "Luchot Zikaron" of Chaim David Friedberg, second edition, Frankfurt am Main, 5664 (1904).

15. Some of the details can be found in the introduction of his book, published in Constandina.

16. See some details about him in the aforementioned book "Luchot Zikaron", page 97.

17. hese details are found in the book "History and Activities of People of Renown", Part 1, by Reb Eliezer Landshaut, Berlin, 5644 (1884).

18. We find details about him as well in the aforementioned book "People of Renown".

- Rabbi Tzvi Hirsch took his place in Podhajce. Words of Torah about him are published in various books.

19. See the book "Important Cities of Israel"[36], volume 6, Brody, by Dr. N. M. Elber, Mossad Harav Kook, 5716 (1956), Jerusalem

20. The Pinkas of the Community of Rohatyn and its Environs (published in Jerusalem by the Organization of Rohatyn Natives), includes information about Podhajce as well, where the emissaries of Shabtai Tzvi succeeding in winning over followers.

21. See the article "The Sabbatean Movement in Poland" by Gershom Sholem, in the book "The Jewish People in Poland", Jerusalem, 5714 (1954).

22. Much is written about Chaim Malach in the book "History of The Frankist Movement" by Meir Balaban. He is mentioned to some degree in all of the literature about the Sabbateans and Frankists.

23. The name of the city of Podhajce is mentioned in almost all of the many books of Rabbi Yaakov Emden, who fought strongly against the followers of those movements, as he saw in them a serious danger to the existence of Judaism. On account of his hatred of Sabbateanism, he had exaggerated suspicions and boundless zeal. Podhajce had a prime place among the Jewish settlements of Podolia that were attacked by his sharp pen, perhaps because one of his sons served in the rabbinate there for several years. His son supplied him with ample information.

24. See the book "Torah Hakedosha", page 70, by Yaakov Emden, and see what his written about him in the testimony of Dover Birkenthal of Bolekhow in his book "Divrei Bina".

25. The book of Archenholtz "England and Italy" (in German, volume 1, page 249).

26. Dr. Falk, the Baal Shem of London, a native of Podhajce, was known also among Christian scholars in the central cities. His name is mentioned along with his photograph in various encyclopedias, in the Jewish Chronicles of London, in the book "Hitkavkut" by Yaakov Emden (Altona, 5532). His name in London was known as a doer of charity and good deeds. He left behind a charitable fund.

27. It should be pointed out that the words of Emden about Dr. Falk come across as hesitant, with the feeling that despite all of his zeal, he was not able to inflict great damage upon him, since Falk has earned for himself an honorable position in London, that grew still greater after his death. Furthermore, in the diary that he left behind, there is not a trace of Sabbateanism.

28. The photograph of the Baal Shem of London is brought down by several historians (including the writer Gershom Bader, a native of Galicia, who spent many years in New York), just as is the photograph of Rabbi Yisrael Baal Shem Tov of Mezhibozh. This was noted by Dr. Avraham Shwadron of the Hebrew University of Jerusalem. See also the books "Lachasidim Mizmor" (Jerusalem, 5696 / 1936, page 136).

29. The Kabbalist and Baal Shem Rabbi Moshe David of Podhajce found great support from Rabbi Yehonatan Eibeshitz of Prague, after Rabbi Yaakov Emden lashed out against him in fury and mentioned him negatively in almost all of his books. It would seem that he was forced to leave his native city of Podhajce on account of his Sabbateanism, and to wander from city to city in different countries. Rabbi Moshe David is mentioned in the books of Emden: "Hitavkut", "Gat Derucha", and others.

30. Gershom Sholem also searched after the path of Rabbi Moshe David of Podhajce, and mentions him several times in his works, such as his article "Information about Sabbateanism from the Books of the Missionaries of the 18th Century" in "Zion" volume 9, 5704 (1944), page 30.

31. Some details about the time period in which he lived in Poland can be found in the special monograph that the researcher Chaim Warshawski dedicated to Rabbi Moshe David in the Zion Quarterly, year seven, Jerusalem, pages 73-93. We can also find details about him after he left Poland and his native city of Podhajce.

32. See the book "Edut Beyaakov", page 70.

33. In his aforementioned work, Warshawski mentions the exchange of letters between Rabbi David Strauss the head of the rabbinical court of Fiurda and Rabbi Asher Enzel the head of the rabbinical court of Grabfeld, as well as to Rabbi Yaakov Falk, one of the Parnassim of Altona.

34. The letter of Zusman Sachnovitz sheds light on the visit of Rabbi Moshe David to London. In general, we get the impression from all that was written about Rabbi Moshe David that he suffered great tribulations on account of his being persecuted by his enemies, headed by the zealot Emden.

35. The book of David Kahana, "The History of the Sabbatean Kabbalists and Hassidim" in the series "Even Hatoim" also serves as an important source about he history of Sabbateanism in Podhajce. In it, Podhajce is mentioned in the same breath as the cities that had many Sabbatean followers, including Lvov, Zolokiv, Klatzkov, Rohatyn, Podhajce, and Horodenka. Rabbi Yisachar the Magid of Podhajce, "who was considered to be a great man" is mentioned among the many who were persecuted (page 176).

36. In the section "Even Miluim" in the aforementioned book, Podhajce is mentioned among the other cities that were led astray by Chaim Malach and believed his words with complete faith (according to the book "Edut Yaakov").

37. In the section "Even Afel" in the aforementioned book, it is written that Frank came to Poland in the year 5516 (1756). He was empty of Talmudic study, and was only expert in the books of the Zohar and writings of the Kabbalists.

38. See the book "Frank and his Followers" by A. Krozhar, that was translated from Polish into Hebrew by Nachum Sokolow with some omissions. In the original Polish book, there are documents and facts that are not in the Hebrew book, that was published in Warsaw in the year 5653 (1893).

39. By surveying the book "Frank and his Followers", it is possible to get the impression that Frank visited Podhajce often as an official and unofficial guest. He is portrayed as succeeding in his activities there. See page 148 of chapter 4, where he boasts about the followers that he gained there.

40. In the Pinkas of Rohatyn and its Environs, in which Podhajce is mentioned several times, a great deal of space is devoted to Elisha Schorr, whose family was among the first to join the Sabbatean movement. Rohatyn was near Podhajce.

41. In the Hebrew book "Frank and his Followers", there are scattered facts about the isolated acts of apostasy from among the followers of Frank in Podhajce, without

[Page 46]

there being a more complete list of the large-scale apostasy of approximately 1,000 followers of Frank. Jewish Podhajce played a recognizable role in that apostasy.

43. See the article of Dr. N. M. Gelber: Three Documents about the History of the Frankist Movement in Poland in "Zion", year 2, Jerusalem, 5697 (1937), page 326.

44. A significant place is given in the book to Piotr, formerly Nachman the son of Natan Nota of Podhajce. It seems that he as well was not among those who were overly convinced. See chapter 16, page 218.

45. The writer A. Sh. Stein, in his book "And the Fire Left Ashes" – a historical novel about Frank and his community (Alef, Tel Aviv, 5717 (1957) mentions Podhajce countless times. The following is written about Piotr of Podhajce: "Piotr, he is Yerucham the son of Natan Nota of Podhajce, is supported on the branch of a pine tree. He was one of the first believers, one of the leaders and educators of the sect, with a white face, adorned with a black beard, with curly hair, rebellious, with eyes glowing like coals. He cleaved to the master with love and devotion. The spirit of Frank was good to him in that area, in the forest, near his believers. "Take one of the sisters for you Piotr", Frank said to him, "I see that you are depressed. Depression is a sin, and a mistress is good for depression and black moods. It awakens the influence – why do you stand?... Do I not do such deeds in open before your eyes, in order to actualize all that I prophesy to you?" Yerucham whispers however, "This thing I cannot do..." (Page 277).

46. Rabbi Nachman of Bratslav, in "Likutei Haran".

47. See the article "Three Documents Regarding the History of the Frankist Movement in Poland" by Dr. N. M. Gelber in "Zion", year 2, Jerusalem, 5697 (1937).

48. There were rabbis that suspected that Hassidism had a connection to Sabbateanism, so a dispute broke out between Hassidim and its opponents. It would make sense that this fact kept the Jews of Podhajce from joining Hassidim. On the other hand, one should take note of the fact that Podhajce was not far from Tarnopol, from where the light of enlightenment emanated to the entire region from the days of Yosef Perel, and many Jews became captivated by this light.

49. For details about him, see the book "History of People of Renown", section 1, New York, 5710 (1950), page 2.

50. Throughout the region of Bursztyn, Bobrka, Chodorow, Strelisk, Premishlan, Podhajce and Rohatyn there were no rabbis[37], but rather decisors of Jewish law. They all received an annual salary ranging from 25 to 120 Florins.

51. See the Polish "Geographic Dictionary" regarding Podhajce.

52. See the article of A. David Polisiuk in "Hamagid", November 1, 1876.

53. On this principle, the branch in Podhajce appealed through "Hamagid" to all of the branches with the request that each city should sent its leaders to Vienna and "request that only those who go to the Land of our fathers should be helped and supported by the donated money, so that they could purchase fields, plant vineyards, and till the soil there. Then the idea of a settlement in the Land of Israel will move from potentiality to reality" (Hamagid 1882, issue 29, July 26, page 237).

54. See the book "The History of the Zionist Movement in Galicia" by Dr. N. M. Gelber, volume 1, pages 149, 154.

55. See the chapter "Founding of the Machanaim Camp" in the aforementioned book, page 362.

56. "Machzikei Hadas" issue 18, February 22nd, 1907; "Washcod" Polish weekly of the Zionist organization in Galicia; "Neuer Morgen", Lvov July 11, 1933; "Chawilia" May 15, 1937; various issues of "Hamagid"; various issues of "Hamitzpeh".

City Center

Note in this section, Translator's Footnotes are designated by { } brackets. The footnotes designated by [ ] brackets are the text footnotes.

Translator's Footnotes

35. In this list of notes, I translate the titles of the books when the translation is meaningful in English. If the title of the book is not meaningful (i.e it is a play on words of the author's name with reference to a biblical verse – as is often the case in books of responsa), I left it in transliteration.
36. Israel here refers to the Jewish People.
37. I.e. official rabbis.

[Page 47]

Table of Historical Dates of Podhajce

A. General

1463	The Podolian wojywoda [leader] Jakub Buczacki founds two parishes and the Roman Catholic Church in the city.
1519	Under the influence of the owner of the city Jakub Buczacki, the king grants the right to hold a fair day in Podhajce.
1539	King Zygmunt bestows upon the city Germanic law rather than Polish and Russian law.
1579	Stanislaw Rewer Potocki, a mighty and famous army general, is born.
1590	Marcyn Walaski receives permission from the king to change the day of the fair to a more fitting day.
1630	Members of the Potocki family of noblemen set up residence in the city.
1630	The market day is changed to Saturday.
1663	King Jan Kazimierz and his camp remain in the city for several days
1667	Jan Sowiecki is besieged in the city for two weeks, and a peace treaty is signed with the enemy on October 16.
1667	The city is described by the Frenchman Daliran, one of the court men of Jan Sowiecki.
1670	A second description of the city by the German traveler Vardom.
1675	Podhajce is besieged by Ibrahim Pasha. It is destroyed and its residence were sent to captivity along with the guarding troop.
1677	Podhajce was freed from all types of taxes for 12 years in accordance with a decision of the Sejm.
1687	Sowiecki visits the city as King of Poland, and looks on the battlefield where he reaped his first praise.
1698	Feliks Potocki, the Hetman of the Crown of Poland is pursued by various battalions. He finds security in the walls of the fortress. He took a stand there until the enemy retreated.
1772	Podhajce transfers to Austrian rule.
1870	There are 4,570 residents of the city.

B. Jews

1420	There are old gravestones from this date in the old Jewish cemetery of Podhajce. In the 16th century, Jews lived in Podhajce – according to Meir Balaban
1602	The Rabbi and Rosh Yeshiva of Podhajce for 40 years was Rabbi Binyamin Aharon the son of Avraham Solnik, the author of the "Masaat Binyamin" responsa book. He died in 1620 (5380).
1633	The book "Masaat Binyamin" was published in Krakow on 43 pages (5393).
1648	During the years 5408-5409, the revolt of the enemy of the Jews, Bogdan Chmielnitzky, may his name be blotted out, took place. Many Jews were murdered, and the community of Podhajce was destroyed.
1650	A synagogue for the Jews was erected similar to the church.
1665-1676	Many Sabbatean Jews could be found in the city of Podhajce.
1667	Jews fought a war of self defense shoulder to shoulder with the citizens during the time of the siege of Podhajce.
1672	Podhajce, defended by Jews as well, was conquered by the Turks, and remained under their control until 1699.
1676	The Turks perpetrated a pogrom in the city. Many Jews were murdered, and many were taken captive. Reb Zeev Wolf the son of Rabbi Yehuda Leib authored a Slicha, which was published in the book "Gefen Yechidit" (Berlin 1699).
1676	The Polish Sejm freed the Jews from paying taxes for 12 years on account of their defense of the city.
1680-1690	(5460) Chaim Malach, the Sabbatean emissary, visited Podhajce.
1696	(5456) Reb Moshe David the Sabbatean Kabbalist from Podhajce was born (he died in 1766 – 5526).
1708-1782	The well-known Baal Shem of Podhajce, Reb Chaim Shmuel Yaakov Falk, a native of Podhajce who lived in London.
1746	The book "Birkat Yaakov" was published in Lvov by Rabbi Yaakov the son of Reb Baruch, a rabbi in Podhajce.
1750-1760	Visits by Rabbi Yisrael Baal Shem Tov to Podhajce, Tlusti and the region.
1756	Yaakov Frank appeared in Poland, and visited Podhajce many times.
1759	Jewish families from Podhajce were among the Frankists who participated in the mass conversion to Christianity on November 17.
1764	The Council of the Four Lands, which had representatives from Podhajce as well, was

disbanded by the Polish Sejm.

1765 The first census of the Jews of Poland. 1,290 Jews were enumerated in Podhajce, including the rabbi of the city, Hirsch the son of Dovber.

1745 5505, Rabbi Yisachar Berish, the rabbi of Podhajce, died. He was the son of the "Pnei Yehoshua", the head of the rabbinical court of Frankfurt am Main (22 Cheshvan).

1788 The first draft of Jews into the Austrian army. It was later transmuted to the transfer of an exemption tax.

1790 Nine Jewish families of Podhajce moved to earn their livelihood through agriculture with the help of the government.

1791 5552, Rabbi Zecharia Mendel the son of Rabbi Aryeh Leib of Podhajce died. He was a rabbi, author, and representative to the Council of Four Lands.

[Page 48]

1855 The head of the community of Podhajce was dismissed by the government.

1876 The obligatory draft for Jews.

1876 5636. The founding of the organization for the reading of works in Hebrew and other languages in Podhajce, called "Beit Aseifat Ezrachei Yehudim" (The Meeting Place of Jewish Citizens).

1879 5639. Rabbi Yitzchak Izak Menachem Eichenstein was born. He was the Admor in Podhajce from 5689.

1880 5,943 people lived in Podhajce, including 4,012 Jews.

1881 Yehuda Leib Elerhand and Shaul Schorr founded a branch of the Israelite "Alians" of Vienna in Podhajce.

1890 5650. Dr. Michael Weichert, jurist playwright, and well-known reviewer was born in Podhajce. He died on March 12, 1967 in Tel Aviv.

1895 5655. Rabbi Dr. Nachum Werman, great scholar and author, was born in Podhajce. He died in Israel.

1898 Elyakim Getzel Perel of Podhajce was among those who made aliya to the Land of Israel. He settled in the Machanaim settlement in the Galilee. At the end of the 19th century, there was a large fire in the city, and 2/3 of the Jewish houses went up in smoke.

1896 5656. Rabbi Avraham Weiss, a Professor of Talmud who lives in Jerusalem, was born in Podhajce.

1876 There was an article in Hamagid from November 1 about Podhajce by David Polisiuk.

1900 "Congregation Rodef Shalom Anshe Podhajce" was founded in America.

1901 The "Podhajcer Young Men's Benevolent Association" was founded in America.

1895 Congregation "Masaat Binyamin Anshe Podhajce" was founded in the United States.

1903 The "First United Podhajcer Congregation" was founded in America.

1905 A general Talmud Torah was founded in Podhajce by Rabbi Shalom Lilienfeld.

1905 Rudolf Szwager was the first Jewish lawyer in Podhajce.

1905 Binyamin Kutner of Podhajce was chosen as a member of the region committee of the Zionist organization of Lvov.

1906 A branch of Poale Zion was founded in Podhajce

1906 The Admor Rabbi Yitzchak Meir of Kapuscince visited the city and donated significant sums to the Talmud Torah and various communal institutions.

1909 Rabbi Shalom HaKohen Lilienfeld died on September 31 at the age of 53.

1914 The Austrians retreated from Podhajce, and it was conquered by the Russian armies who attacked the Jews.

1918 A branch of Hashomer Hatzair was founded in Podhajce.

1919 Pogroms were perpetrated against the Jews at the end of October.

1920 During the war of Poland against the Bolsheviks, Petliura's troops came to the city, followed by the Bolsheviks, and caused trouble for the Jews.

1929 A charitable fund was established by the communal council.

1930 A Jewish cooperative bank was founded in the city as a branch of the Jewish cooperatives of Poland.

1931 The Kadima students corporation was founded in Podhajce.

1931 300 Shkalim[{38}] were sold in Podhajce during the elections to the Zionist Congress.

1933 The Zionists won in the elections to the Podhajce community. Five members were elected.

1939 There were 3,155 Jews in Podhajce out of a population of 6,000.

1939 The U. S. S. R. invaded Podhajce in October.

1941 The Nazis entered Podhajce on July 6 at the time of the outbreak of the war of the Nazis against Russia.

1942 The first aktion in the city took place on Yom Kippur, and the ghetto was established the following day.

1945 Russian Partisans appeared in Podhajce in March.

3rd of Sivan – The Memorial Day to the Martyrs of Podhajce and Environs.

The "Nes Tziona" group of Hashomer Hatzair (1931)

Translator's Footnotes

38. A shekel (plural shkalim) is a token of membership of the Zionist organization.

[Page 49]

The Rabbis of Podhajce in their Generations

by Rabbi Wolf Feuerstein

The small town of Podhajce, my birthplace that is between the cities of Berezany and Buchach in eastern Galicia, was a city filled with scholars and scribes 400 years ago. Its rabbis were Torah scholars whose renown spread through all the lands of the Diaspora. The greats of Israel from near and far debated Jewish law with them, and students from all corners of the land streamed to them to drink their words with thirst. A unique one of them was a Yeshiva head and head of the Diaspora[1], a cedar of Lebanon, great in Torah, the Gaon and great decisor Rabbi Binyamin Aharon the son of Reb Avraham Solnik, the author of the Masaat Binyamin book of responsa. He occupied the rabbinical seat in Podhajce for forty years, from the year 5340 – 5380 (1580-1620). Most of his responsa were accepted as Halacha throughout the entire Jewish Diaspora. Our great rabbi was beloved not only in his own community on account of the proper ways in which he led it to ensure its internal and external security, but his good renown also spread afar on account of the large Yeshiva that he maintained in our town, from which he spread Torah and wisdom. There, our rabbi delved into the Torah of G-d, not leaving its tent day and night, until the point that his Torah proclaimed him to the outside, and he merited in being counted among the members of the "Council of the Three Lands". He continued to ascend in influence until he became the head of the council. In order to complete the topic, and also to the honor and glory of my native city which was prior to the Holocaust the burial place of my scholarly, honorable and modest mother Chana the daughter of Reb Chaim Mordechai Fueurstein of blessed memory, and which was the burial place of her fathers and grandparents of blessed memory, I will enumerate the names of all of the great rabbis who occupied the rabbinical seat in our town throughout a period of 365 years, from the year 5300 (1540) to the year 5665 (1905).

The two rabbis of Podhajce who preceded the author of Masaat Binyamin were:

a) The rabbi and Gaon Rabbi Moshe.

b) The rabbi and Gaon[2] Rabbi Yehuda Leib his son (Matzevet Kodesh and Anshei Shem)[*1]. The following is the text on the gravestone of Rabbi Yehuda Leib in Lvov.

"And Yehuda went down to the faithful nation of holy people, he is the great Gaon, the pure menorah, expert in the compartments of the hidden and revealed Torah, toiling in Torah day and night, the head of the Yeshiva in this place, and the head of the rabbinical court[3] of the holy community of Podhajce, our teacher and rabbi Rabbi Yehuda Leib the son of the great rabbi our teacher and rabbi Rabbi Moshe who was also the head of the rabbinical court of Podhajce, who spread Torah throughout Israel, toiled in Torah, and made his nights as days, enlightened the eyes of Israel, taught the people the path of Torah that they should follow, and established many students who were leaders of the generation, who drunk from his waters. In this merit, may his soul be bound in the bonds of eternal life. Died on the 11th of Cheshvan 5373 (1633)."

c) Masaat Binyamin. The rabbi and Gaon, head of the Yeshiva and head of the Diaspora, the pillar of teaching, the scion of holy ones his name is his glory[4], our rabbi Rabbi Binyamin Aharon the son of Reb Avraham Solnik may his merit protect us and all Israel, amen[5]. Who was known by the name

Masaat Binyamin

A student of the Ramah[6], the Maharshal[7], the rabbi and Gaon Rabbi Shapira the author of "Mavo Shearim", and Maharash II[8]. He maintained discussions with the Ramah, the Levush, the Maharam Lublin[9], and the rest of the leaders of the generation, many of whom were relatives by marriage. Later he taught Torah for several years in Krakow at the end of the days of the Ramah and following his death. During his younger days, he was also the rabbi of the entire State of Silesia for a brief period. Then he was appointed as the head of the rabbinical court and the head of the yeshiva of the holy community of Podhajce, where he occupied the rabbinical seat for approximately 40 years. He died there at the age of approximately 90 years old in the year 5380 (1620), and there he reposes in honor.

His sons were Rabbi Avraham, the head of the rabbinical court of the holy community of Tarnopol, and later the head of the rabbinical court and head of the Yeshiva in the holy community of Brisk of Lithuania. He maintained discussions with the Bach[10] and the rest of the greats of his generation. The second was Rabbi Yaakov, the author of the book Nachalat Yaakov on Rashi's commentary on the Torah, who took his place as the rabbi of the holy community of Podhajce. His son-in-law was the Gaon Rabbi Menachem Mann, the head of the rabbinical court and head of the Yeshiva in the holy community of Vienna. His descendents included the Gaon, the author of the Shaagat Aryeh, the head of the rabbinical court of the holy community of Metz, the Gaon the author of Knesset Yechezkel, the head of the holy community of A"hv[11]. Many of the leaders of the generations to this day are related to him.

The books he wrote are: The Book of Chalitza[*2], the Book on Issues of Laws Pertaining to Women, Novellae on the Four Turim, and first and foremost, the book of Responsa of Masaat Binyamin. Those who followed the Masaat Binyamin are:

d) His eldest son the Gaon Rabbi Yaakov of holy blessed memory, the author of Nachalat Yaakov, a commentary on the commentary of Rashi on the Torah[12]. He took the place of his father and

did not leave behind a son to take his place (see the introduction to his book printed in Constantina).

[Page 50]

e) Rabbi David who died in the year 5393 (1633). He wrote the book Tiferet Yisrael. A eulogy is found about him in the writings of the R"I of Belzec (Neubauer's list, paragraph 989.

f) The Gaon Rabbi Mordechai of holy blessed memory, the head of the rabbinical court and head of the Yeshiva of our community and also the holy community of Rzeszow. The researcher Ch. D. Friedberg writes the following about him in his book Memorial Tablets:

"Presently I have found in a large collection the manuscript of the Gaon Rabbi Yitzchak, the head of the rabbinical court of Tysmienica, in section 100 at the end of the discussion on the Aguna[*3]: In the fair of Jazlowiec, the great luminary, the great rabbi Rabbi Mordechai the head of the rabbinical court and head of the Yeshiva of the holy community of Podhajce and the holy community of Rzeszow has agreed to this leniency." In the introduction to the book Brachot Shmuel by Rabbi Shmuel Keidaner, he tells of himself that he left the holy community of Rzeszow and was accepted as the head of the rabbinical court of Frankfurt am Main[13], and later in the holy community of Krakow. Rabbi Mordechai, originally from Podhajce, filled his place in Rzeszow. He was one of the great rabbis of his generation. (In his approbation to the book Daat Yekutiel).

g) After him, the Gaon rabbi Moshe Kac, the eldest son of the Rabbi of the entire Diaspora[14] Shabtai Kac, the author of the Shach, of holy blessed memory, occupied the rabbinical seat in our town. He brought to print two books of his father that came to him as an inheritance in 5437 (1677) in the city of Frankfurt an der Oder[15]. These are the books Nekudot Hakesef and the book Takfu Kohen. These are his words in the introduction to the books: “For a long time I did not fulfil my duty as I had intended, since the yoke of my Yeshiva was upon me. I formerly lived in the holy community of Podhajce, a pleasant city, a city that has everything, with the Torah of G-d in its midst, a praiseworthy and faithful city, with people of wisdom and understanding. During the war with the Turks they were taken prisoner without mercy, and made into a proverb and a byword, and the G-d of High saved me, and I went to the mount of teaching to the inheritance of my fathers”, etc.

h) After him, the Gaon Rabbi Moshe Katzenelenboigen, the son of Rabbi Shaul Katz”av occupied the rabbinical seat in our town. He was a descendent of the prince Shaul Wahl and the Gaon the author of Masaat Binyamin. After he was imprisoned on a false charge, the people of Ansbach, Bavaria redeemed him and appointed him as head of the rabbinical court of their city. There he reposes in honor. (From the introduction to the responsa of Shaar Naftali, and the book Yesh Manchilin, Oxford manuscript, by his son the Gaon Rabbi Pinchas Katzav, and in the book Gedulat Shaul, and the book The History of the Schorr Family.) His brother-in-law was the rabbi and Gaon Rabbi Zecharia Mendel of Podhajce, who was known as Zecharia the Prophet, who was the head of the rabbinical court of Buchach, and who died in Frankfurt an der Oder. The following is written on his gravestone: “Here is buried the son of holy ones, a descendent of Rashi, the Tosafot, the Maharshal and the Ramah the author of the Mapa, the great rabbi and kabbalist our Rabbi Zecharia Mendel of Podhajce, the son of Rabbi Leib the head of the Yeshiva of the holy community of Lvov and region, who gave classes at the Chevra Kadisha and Talmud Torah, and did not move from the tent of Torah, and set up many students in his youth and old age. He is the author of the work “Menorat Zecharia”, “Zecharia Meshulam”, and “Zecharia Hamevin”. He further left behind many letters that spread from his wellsprings outside. He died and was buried with a good name on Tuesday the eve of Chanukah 5452.”

i) After Rabbi Moshe Katz”av, Rabbi Moshe the son of Rabbi Menachem Nachum was appointed. He wrote an approbation to the book Birchat Yaakov on the Choshen Mishpat section of the Code of Jewish Law. This is what is written there: The approbation of the great and famous Gaon and rabbi Rabbi Moshe of blessed memory who was the head of the rabbinical court of the holy city of Podhajce. It is signed on the 2nd of the month of Elul 5478. (There is also an approbation from the author of Pnei Yehoshua in this book.”)

Signed by Moshe the son of Menachem Nachum of Premislaw who lives in the holy community of Podhajce.

j) His place was filled by the great Gaon Rabbi Yissachar Dov Berish the son of the sharp Gaon Rabbi Yehoshua the author of Pnei Yehoshua. His responsa that he answered in Metz during the life of his father to the judge Rabbi Gershon of Koblenz is found in the book of responsa Kiryat Chana, sections 41, 42, 43, and 44, signed by Yissachar Dov the son of my father the great rabbi[16] the Gaon Yaakov Yehoshua may G-d save and redeem him[17], who lives in the holy city of Podhajce. The Gaon the author of the Pri Megadim in his book Tevat Gomeh brings down words of Torah that he heard in his name. In the book of responsa of the Gaon Rabbi Chaim Cohen Rappaport the head of the rabbinical court of Lvov, there is a responsa from him signed on Sunday, 24th Tishrei 5504. He gave an approbation in the year 5502 to the book Mari Tzvi. His son was Rabbi Tzvi Rosenes, the head of the rabbinical court of Lvov. He had intended to set up his residence in Metz and to be a Yeshiva head there, but he died on the way. His honorable resting place was Berlin. He died on Tuesday, 22 Cheshvan 5505. (Anshei Shem).

k) After him, the rabbi and Gaon Rabbi Meshulam Zalman the son of the Gaon Rabbi Yaakov Emden occupied the rabbinical seat in our town. From there he wrote a letter to his father in the year 5517 (1757) (Edut Leyaakov page 57) as follows: A star went forth from Jacob and a scepter and lawgiver arose, the gates of wisdom, the pure words of G-d, forged silver refined sevenfold, his soul and memory are the desire of my heart, that is the honor of my master and father the chariot of Israel, may G-d stand for him and his holy ones, the renown rabbi and Gaon, the great luminary, the holy lamp, pious, may his light shine in the honor of the holiness of his glorious name[18], our rabbi Rabbi Yaakov may his light shine. And he signs there: To this point I have spoken with the fire of my zealousness, the house of Jacob is a fire and flame that burns the evil ones who wished to swallow the pleasantness of Jacob,

the implements of his ancestors are in his hands, a zealous person the son of a zealous person, the zealousness of scribes is written in the book of righteousness that is his book, as the soul of the father so is the soul of the son who waits to see him and to bless in his name and serve him. The small one of Israel Meshulam Zalman the son of the renowned Gaon the holy lamp our rabbi and teacher Rabbi Yaakov. The responsa begins: A letter of his son the great luminary[19] Rabbi Meshulam Zalman may G-d protect and save him, the head of the rabbinical court of the holy community of Podhajce.

[Page 51]

From our city, he was accepted as the head of the rabbinical court of the holy community of London. From there he gave his approbation to the book Kiseh Hamelech in the year 5529 (1769).

l) After him the rabbi and Gaon Rabbi Tzvi Hirsch occupied the rabbinical seat in our town. (See the book of responsa Meir Netivim by the rabbi and Gaon Rabbi Meir Margolis the head of the rabbinical court of Lvov, page 22, where he writes as follows: a responsa to my in-law the Gaon Rabbi Tzvi Hirsch the head of the rabbinical court of Podhajce.) A question from him is published in the responsa book of Rabbi Chaim Kohen Rappaport, section 54. Works of Torah in his name were published in the book Divrei Chachamiv Zolekow, 5514 (1757).

m) After him, our rabbi and teacher Rabbi Simcha Rappaport, a great Gaon in his generation, ascended the rabbinical seat in our town. He is the son of the Gaon Rabbi Chaim Kohen Rappaport the head of the rabbinical court of Lvov. He died in the year 5585 (1825) (see Daat Kedoshim page 164, (Anshei Shem).

n) The rabbi and Gaon Rabbi Shmuel followed him as the head of the rabbinical court. The rabbi and Gaon Rabbi Eliezer HaKohen was a member of his rabbinical court. In the responsa book Neta Shaashuim by the rabbi and Gaon Rabbi Tzvi Hirsch, you can find several questions that were posed to them (sections 61, 66, and others). The following is written there:

"Two crowned heads of great intelligence to understand and teach, that pair of rabbis, their glory is like a pleasant olive, the rabbi, the great luminary[20] Rabbi Shmuel the head of the rabbinical court of Podhajce, and the renowned sharp rabbi Rabbi Eliezer HaKohen may his light shine on that community. A question to them on the issue of an Aguna." The responsa is signed on Wednesday, 16th of Av, 5542 (1782). Rabbi Shmuel is mentioned in the Pri Tevua responsa, section 54.

Rabbi Yosef Aryeh Brecher of blessed memory
the father of Rabbi Chaim Mordechai Brecher
of blessed memory and Rabbi Wolf Fueurstein
may his light shine

o) Our teacher and rabbi Rabbi Aryeh Yehuda Leib, a great and renowned Gaon the author of Lev Aryeh, was appointed in our town following them. Later he was appointed as the head of the rabbinical court in the city of Brod during the days of the Gaon Rabbi Efraim Zalman Margolis. He has a responsa in the responsa book Beit Efraim on the section of Yoreh Deah, and a work Lev Aryeh on tractate Chullin. In the responsa book Neta Shaashuim, you can find several responsa to this rabbi. This is the text of one responsa in section 12: Much peace to a great man, my honorable friend, the rabbi and sharp great luminary, expert in wisdom and books, may his light shine, honor to his glorious name, our rabbi and teacher Rabbi Aryeh[21] Yehuda Leib the head of the rabbinical court of teacher of righteousness[22] in the holy community of Podhajce." His approbation was given to the books Nachal Eshkol (5564 – 1804) and Mekor Hachachmah (5574 –1814).

p) The great rabbi and Gaon Rabbi Nota was the head of the rabbinical court after the rabbi "Lev Aryeh". This is what Rabbi Shmerler wrote in his book The History of the Rabbi and Gaon Rabbi Avraham David, the head of the rabbinical court of Buchach, the author of Dat Kedoshim, who died on the eve of Rosh Chodesh Cheshvan 5601 (1841): "In this days, our rabbi and Gaon obtained another faithful friend, the illustrious rabbi and expert Gaon Rabbi Nota of blessed memory, the head of the rabbinical court of Podhajce. There was a deep love between them. The Rabbi and Gaon Nota poured water on the hands of the Rabbi and Gaon Rabbi Meshulam Pressburger the head of the rabbinical court of Tyemienica, and on the hands of the Gaon the author of Neta Shaashuim (the father in-law of the author of Daat Kedoshim). His friends were the Gaon Rabbi Yaakov of Lissa the author of Chavat Daat and the rabbi Rabbi Aryeh Leib HaKohen the author of Ketzot Hachoshen. Like them, he was pious in all of his ways and righteous in all of his deeds. Students who had the ability to stand in the tents of Torah with the help of a man who guarded its doors streamed to him from all corners of the land to hear learning from his mouth". Etc.

q) After him, the rabbi and Gaon Rabbi Shimon Meller was appointed in our town. In the responsa book Beit Yitzchak by the rabbi and Gaon Rabbi Yitzchak Shmelkes, section 7 on the Orach Chaim, laws of Tefillin, one can find a responsa to that rabbi. The following are his words there: "Peace and blessings and all good Selah[23] to my friend the sharp rabbi and expert in all rooms of Torah our rabbi and teacher Rabbi Shimon Meller may his light shine, the head of the rabbinical court of Podhajce."

[Page 52]

Rabbi Chaim Mordechai Brecher and his wife

r) After him, his place was filled by his son the rabbi and Gaon Rabbi Yonah. A responsa from the Gaon Rabbi Yitzchak Shmelkes can be found in section 104. These are his words: "On the 5th of Cheshvan 5525 in Berezany: Blessings and peace to the fine, excellent youth Rabbi Nota Yonah Meller the son of the rabbi and Gaon the head of the rabbinical court of Podhajce."" Rabbi Yonah Meller traveled to Stanislawow, and there he reposes in honor.

s) After him, a native of Podhajce, the Gaon, great in Torah and good deeds, Rabbi Shalom the son of Rabbi Chaim Mordechai Lilienfeld of blessed memory was accepted as the head of the rabbinical court. In the responsa of the Maharsha[24] by the Rabbi and Gaon of the generation Rabbi Shalom Mordechai the head of the rabbinical court of Berezany, you can find a responsa to that rabbi: "To the honor of the great rabbi, etc. our Rabbi Shalom Lilienfeld, the head of the rabbinical court of the holy community of Podhajce." After the death of the aforementioned rabbi, there was no other rabbi leading Podhajce, but rather three judges: the righteous teacher Rabbi Avraham Eisen, the righteous teacher Rabbi Feibish Szwarc, and the righteous teacher Rabbi Wolf Haber.

In New York, the natives of our town accepted my brother Rabbi Chaim Mordechai Brecher of blessed memory to be their rabbi and teacher in the synagogue Masaat Binyamin of the natives of Podhajce. My brother, great in Torah and good deeds, was a grammarian. He proofread the Yehoash Bible, the Torah Shleima, the Mandelkorn concordance, and others. He died on the 14th of Cheshvan 5726 (1966), at the age of 86. May his soul be bound in the bonds of eternal life.

A Hymn to the State of Israel

by Rabbi Chaim M. Brecher

I wrote this on the day that the establishment of the state of Israel was authorized by the United Nation on the 15th of Kislev 5708 (November 1947), that is the year 1878 of our exile, when I am 68 years old less two days.

Our hope has not yet been fulfilled
This is our ancient hope
To inherit the land of our fathers
As a faithful covenant from on high.
However its beginnings have become revealed
To the wandering daughter of Zion
The high right hand has turned
To turn mournful ones to its borders.
After the tribulations of our Diaspora
In flames of hell and slaughter
The matter of our righteousness came forth
The dawning of our salvation as a sprouting blossom.
The dawn of our salvation in the corner of the land
That the council of nations graced us upon
We will take a step and increase our strength
And what was taken from us will to us.
The land will to its owners
As all of our seers have prophesied
The Nation of Israel will live upon it
Despite the eyes of all of our enemies
Our state shall sprout and flourish
It will raise its glory like a rose
The Right hand of our Creator is before us
A dancing serpent and sea monster.
Our hope will yet be fulfilled
This is the ancient hope
To inherit the land of our fathers
A faithful covenant from on high.

[Page 53]

Words about the Personality of Rabbi David Lilienfeld

by Meir Pickholz

Rabbi David HaKohen Lilienfeld was one of the last of the important rabbis of Poland. He occupied the rabbinical seat in Podhajce, filling the place of his father Rabbi Shalom HaKohen Lilienfeld, who was renowned as a Gaon, and authored various halachic words. To our dismay, his works were not published. They were at the printers at the time of the outbreak of the Second World War, and they did not succeed in publishing them.

Rabbi Lilienfeld was the scion of a dynasty of rabbis that existed for approximately 170 years. The first of this dynasty was Rabbi Nathan Nota Galiczer, who was also a rabbi in Podhajce. The rabbis who occupied the rabbinical seat in our town in the latter generations are buried in a special row near the entry gate to the cemetery in Podhajce. The first in this row is Rabbi Nathan-Nota, from whom the family spread out.

Rabbi David Lilienfeld possessed a very broad level of knowledge. He obtained his knowledge from private lessons, for since he was the son of the rabbi, he was not able to attend the government school in those days. He had fully mastered the Polish and German languages. His speeches in Polish were filled with meaning and content. He delivered a lecture on every Polish national holiday, and his lectures were always acceptable to the powers of the civic government. He also impressed the hearts of all who saw him on account of handsomeness and splendor of his countenance. He concerned himself with all matters, small and large, in the community of Podhajce: including matters of representation, legal matters, civic matters, etc. Similarly, he answered every resident of the town who required his opinion. He was a Zionist with his heart and soul. In 1925, he was a candidate of the Mizrachi Party in the elections to the Polish Sejm. He fulfilled his rabbinical duties without any expectation of reward, for he had large businesses, including flourmills and rental houses.

His younger brother Yosef Leibish Lilienfeld was ordained as a rabbi when he was still young, however he did not occupy himself in the rabbinate. He was a dedicated Zionist and an educated man. He was fluent in Polish and German, and also spoke English. He had several daughters, and his economic status was very good.

The brother-in-law of the two brothers, Rabbi Zusha Pickholz, was a young man graced with all fine traits. He studied with his father-in-law Rabbi Shalom Lilienfeld during his youth, and received his rabbinical ordination from him. He was also an educated man with progressive ideas. He was a Hassid of Belz and was a close confidant of the Belzer Rebbe. He had a similar relationship with the Rebbe of Czortkow, Rabbi Israelinov. He was the head of the Machzikei Hadas organization of Podhajce, and conducted a daily Talmud class in the Beis Midrash of the city. He was the grandson of the rabbi from Lukacz, whose lineage traces back to the kingdom of the House of David.

The building of the Polish public school, across from the house of David Lilienfeld

[Page 54]

Rabbis of Podhajce – Notable Men

Brought from encyclopedias and manuscripts

Rabbi Zecharia Mendel (the son of Aryeh Leib) of Podhajce

A rabbi and author in the first half of the sixth century of the sixth millennium (the 18th century according to the secular count). He was born in Podhajce to his father Rabbi Leib of Buchach, who was a scion of the lineage of the Maharshal and the Rama. He studied Torah from Rabbi Yaakov Yehoshua the author of the Pnei Yehoshua. He served as a rabbi and preacher in Frankfurt an der Oder during the latter decades of his life. There, he published his books: Menorat Zecharia (5536), novellae on Tractate Shabbat and sermons on the Sabbath and festivals; Zecharia Meshulam (5539), novellae on tractates of the Talmud; Zecharia Hameivin (5551) on principals of philosophy and Kaballah. He died in Frankfurt an der Oder on the 24th of Kislev 5552 (1791). The following is engraved on his gravestone: “The rabbi, the illuminary, the great Gaon and G-dly kabbalist, etc. who never left the tent of Torah, and established many students in his youth and age.”

*

Of his many students (of Rabbi Yaakov Yosha) who served before him when he lived in Lvov, Berlin, Metz, and Frankfurt am Main, we will only mention one here, that is Rabbi Zecharia of Podhajce who attracted many people with his sermons and his admonitions in the city of his residence, Frankfurt an der Oder near Berlin. He died there, and the following lines are engraved on his gravestone:

The son of holy ones, of the lineage of Rashi, the Tosafot, the Maharshal and the Rama the author of the Mapa, the rabbi, great illuminary, G-dly Kabbalist, our rabbi and teacher Rabbi Zecharia Mendel of Podhajce, the son of the our rabbi and teacher Rabbi Leib the head of the holy community of Lvov and the region, who gave classes here at the Chevra Kadisha Talmud Torah, and did not depart from the tent of Torah. He established many students during his youth and old age. He is the author of Menorat Zecharia, Zecharia Meshulam, and Zecharia Hameivin. He also left after him many letters so that his wellsprings can spread outward. He died and was buried with a good name on Tuesday the eve of Chanukah 5552. For more on this rabbi, see Hagdolim Hachadash 1, 19, 2, section 7, and side 43 b of section 62, and further.

(From "The History of Men of Renown and their Activities" by Eliezer Leizer the son of our rabbi Meir Landshuta of holy blessed memory, section 1, Berlin, 5644 –1884).

*

The Rabbi and Gaon Rabbi Yissachar Dov

Rabbi Yissachar Dov, who was known as Berush, was the student of his uncle the Gaon Rabbi Hirsch who was the head of the rabbinical court of Halberstadt from the year 5478. Rabbi Berush was a rabbi in Podhajce. The response that he answered to Metz during the life of his father to the judge Rabbi Gershon Koblenz Mazia are published in the responsa book Kiryat Chana section 41, 42, 43, 44. His signature there is Yissachar (with the double shin)[*4] Dov the son of the Gaon our Rabbi Yaakov Yosha may G-d protect and save him, who lives in the holy community of Podhajce. The rabbi, the author of the Pri Megadim, in the book Tevat Gomeh page 70 folio 2, brings down some words of Torah that he heard from him. In the responsa book of Rabbi Chaim Kohen Rappaport the son of Simcha (Lemberg 1861) at the end of the responsa that pertains to Lah"a[*5], a response from him can be found, signed on Sunday, 24 Tishrei 5504[*6] by the small Yisachar (with one Shin) Dov the son of rabbi Yaakov Yosha may G-d protect and save him. In Tesha Shitot of his son the Gan Rabbi Hirsch Rosenes, we find some novellae of Berush his father. He intended to settle in Metz and to be a Rosh Yeshiva there. As he traveled from Podhajce to Metz via Berlin, he took ill and died there. The following is engraved on his gravestone:

"Here is buried the jug of manna, the mighty warrior in the army of Torah, the sharp rabbi, our rabbi and teacher Rabbi Yisachar Berush the son of our famous rabbi and teacher Rabbi Yehoshua may G-d protect and save him, the head of the rabbinical court of Frankfurt am Main. He died and was gathered unto his people on Tuesday 22 Cheshvan 5505. Dedicated by his grandson whose name is among us Yisachar Dov Berush the son of our rabbi and teacher Mordechai Tzvi HaKohen Yolles of blessed memory in the year of Yisachar Dov Hacohen (5617)[*7].

(From "The History of Men of Renown and their Activities" by Eliezer Leizer the son of our rabbi Meir Landshuta of holy blessed memory, section 1, Berlin 5644 – 1884).

Rabbi Yitzchak Izak Menachem Eichenstein of holy blessed memory
The Admor of Podhajce

He was born in the city of Zydaczow (Polish Galicia) in the year 5639 to his father the Admor, the holy rabbi Rabbi Shlomo Yaakov of holy blessed memory, the son of the Admor the holy Gaon[*8] Rabbi Yitzchak Izak of Zydaczow of holy blessed memory. He was educated by his maternal grandfather the holy Gaon Rabbi Avraham Horowitz of holy blessed memory, the head of the rabbinical court of Szendiszow. He got married in the year 5656 to the righteous Rebbetzin Miriam of blessed memory (died on the 13th of Shvat 5684) the daughter of the Admor Rabbi Nachum of Burstyn of holy blessed memory (of the famous Admors of his generation). He is the author of the holy book Imrei Tov on the Torah, Imrei Chaim on the 512 commandments, Imrei Bracha on tractates Brachot and Shabbat, Imre Ratzon on the cantillation of the Torah. He served as an Admor in the city of Burstyn from 5625 to 5675. He then moved to Stanislawow. He died on the 15th of Elul 5665. He is the son of the righteous Admor Rabbi Eliezer of Stretin, the son of the holy renowned Admor Rabbi Yehuda of Stretin of holy blessed memory. The wife of the holy Rabbi Nachum Burstyn of holy blessed memory, the righteous and renowned Rebbetzin lima of blessed memory, was the daughter of the Admor, the holy Rabbi Tzvi Hager the head of the rabbinical court of Pytszinzyn, the son of the righteous Admor Rabbi David of Zablotow (the son-in-law of the holy Gaon Rabbi Moshe Leib of Staszow), the son of the renowned holy Gaon Rabbi Menachem Mendel of Kosow of holy blessed memory.

The Admor of Podhajce of holy blessed memory served as an Admor from the year 5669 until 5703 in the city of Podhajce. He was righteous, pious, and holy, famous through the entire state of Galicia. Several hundred Hassidim followed his light. He died on the 13th of Adar I 5703 in the city of Podhajce.

(From "The History of Men of Renown" section 1, page 2. The chief editor is Rabbi A Rand. New York, 5710 – 1950).

[Page 55]

*

Rabbi Dr. Nachum Werman (Wahrmann)

He was born in Podhajce, eastern Galicia, in the year 5655 (May 7, 1895) to his father Rabbi Yisrael (of the family of Rabbi Avraham David of Buchach, the author of Daat Kedoshim on Yoreh Deah) and to his mother Etia the daughter of Nachum Silber. He studied in cheders and in the Beis Midrash. When he was 12, he moved with his parents to Czortkow, where his father obtained a position in the court of the Admor Rabbi Yisrael Friedman (a descendent of Rabbi Yisrael of Rizhin), as a teacher and educator of his grandson Shlomo (who is today an Admor in Tel Aviv). His father taught him along with the grandson of the rabbi.

When he was 16, he traveled to his father's brother in Frankfurt am Main. He concluded the Civic Real School in 1917 and traveled home to serve in the Austrian army. After the end of the war at the end of 1918, he to Czortkow, and participated in Zionist communal and educational activity as a member of the Tzeirei Tzion committee, a group head of the Hashomer youth movement, a teacher of evening Hebrew classes, and other such activities.

He to Frankfurt in 1919. He studied in university for three years. During that time, he served as the principal of the Hebrew school, and he directed the cultural work of Hechalutz. He transferred to the university of Guesin, where he was examined in Semitic languages, Biblical science and ancient history. He received his Ph.D. His dissertation topic was: The Sota (the law of the unfaithful wife) in Tannaic literature. He taught for three years in the Rabbinical school of Breslau, and received his rabbinic ordination.

He married Paula the daughter of Eliezer Shipman in 1929. That year, he was chosen as the regional rabbi of Lower Silesia in the city of Ilza. For the final five years of his ten years of service there, he also lectured about Talmud and history in the Breslau Rabbinical School.

During the time he lived in Germany, he also participated in Zionist and literary activities. He was a delegate to the national council of German Zionists, and he published scientific articles in the Monthly of History and Judaic Science (in German), and research articles in special books (in German). He published "Giving the Sota to Drink during the Time of the Temple (Breslau 1933), and Conditions and Support in Hebrew Law (Breslau 1937).

He made aliya in the spring of 5699, and then became a teacher of Hebrew, Bible, Jewish law, Jewish lore (Aggada) and history in elementary and high school in the school of Kiryat Motzkin, the local delegate to the committee of Hebrew Language, a member of the council of the Israeli Institute of Folklore and Ethnology, a member of the Union of Religious Scribes, a participant in the cultural work of the town, and of the community of Haifa as a teacher of evening classes, a lecture in Ohel Shem and Mussafim Leshabat, and various other institutions. He continued his research into the Festivals of Israel and their customs, and published articles on these topics in the Hagalgal weekly, the Nerot Shabbat bi-weekly, the Edut quarterly, and in the Moadim book on sections of Jewish law, published by the Real School of Haifa, 5707.

He was the chairman of the teachers organization in the school in Kiryat Motzkin, a member of the national committee of the Yada-Am group, a participant in the Hatzofeh daily and the Had Hamizrach weekly (published in Jerusalem) and in the Yada-Am stage of Jewish folklore.

In the month of Nissan, the final work of Wahrmann in Jerusalem was published by the Bamberger Printing Press. It was a pamphlet "Sources for the History of the Decrees of Tach and Tat[*9]; prayers and penitential services for the 20th of Sivan."

(From the Encyclopedia of pioneers and builders of the Jewish settlement by David Tidhar, volume 3, second edition. Given to publication by his daughter Esther.)

Losses

Rabbi Chaim Mordechai Brecher of blessed memory

In New York, the famous Hebrew grammarian and researcher into traditional order of prayers and the meaning of the cantillation notes of the Bible, Rabbi Chaim Mordechai Brecher of blessed memory died at an old age (he was 87). For decades, he served as the chief adviser for several publishers in America (Shilo, Ktav, the Slazinger Brothers, and others), in setting the traditional orders of prayers and the cantillation notes in the books of the Bible that were published by them, with glosses about the order of prayers and their vowel signs. Rabbi Brecher was particularly known for his proofreading of the bilingual Bible that appeared in its Hebrew edition with the Yiddish Yehoash translation on the side. He added to this book important notes on matters of tradition. He was also a great Talmudist, and compiled comprehensive dictionaries clarifying Talmudic concepts, which were included at the end of editions of the Gemara published in New York.

He left behind his widow, two daughters, a son, and grandchildren. May his soul be bound in the bonds of eternal life.

Text Footnotes

1. Reish Metivta and Reish Galuta – Yeshiva head and Diaspora head. (Translator's note: a Reish Galuta is a term used for the leader of the exile during the Babylonian era. Here, it would be used colloquially for a leader of great prominence.)
2. Hrh"g – Harav Hagaon (Translator's note: the rest of the text footnotes of this chapters are expansions of acronyms of names and titles used in the text. I expanded them in full in the text, with the exception of commonly used acronyms of names, but I include the footnotes here for completeness.)
3. Ab"d D"kk – the head of the rabbinical court of the holy community.
4. Z"k Sh"t – the scion of holy ones, his name is his glory.
5. Zy"a vechy"a – his merit should protect us and all Israel, amen.
6. H"Rma – the rabbi Rabbi Moshe Isserles.
7. Maharshal – Our rabbi Rabbi Shlomo Luria, the rabbi of Lublin.
8. M"harash II – Our rabbi Rabbi Shlomo of Lublin.
9. Mahara"m Lublin – Our rabbi Rabbi Meir of Lublin.
10. The Bach – the rabbi Rabbi Yoel Sirkis, a rabbi in Krakow, called by the name of his book "Bayit Chadash".
11. Ah"v – Altona, Hamburg and Undsbach, three communities that united at the end of the 17th century.
12. Ah"t – On the Torah.
13. Ff"dm – Frankfurt am Main.
14. Rcbh"g -- the Rabbi of the entire Diaspora.
15. FF"da – Frankfurt an der Oder.
16. A"a Moh"g – My master and father, our great teacher.
17. Nr"u – May G-d protect and save him.
18. Kksh"t – the honor of the holy name of his glory.
19. Hmh"g – Hamaor Hagadol
20. Hmaoh"g – Hamaor Hagadol.
21. Ksh"t Mohr"a – the honor of his glorious name, our teacher and rabbi Rabbi Reb Aryeh.
22. Abd" umo"tz – head of the rabbinical court and teacher of righteousness.
23. Vcht"s – and all good, Selah.
24. Maharsha – Our teacher Rabbi Shmuel Eidelis, a rabbi in Ostraha.

Translator's Footnotes

(noted in the text as [*x])

1. These are the names of his works, by which he was known.

2. Chalitza is the law relating to the ceremony of releasing a woman from the obligation of levirate marriage. Deuteronomy 25:5-10.

3. An Aguna is a deserted wife, whose husband has left without granting her a divorce, or has disappeared without evidence of his death. Such a woman is considered still bound to the husband, and is not permitted to remarry, unless an opening for leniency is found.

4. The Hebrew name Yissachar contains a double Shin, with the second one being silent. Although the full name has the double Shin, in the Yiddish phonetic form, the second Shin would commonly be dropped.

5. I am not sure of the meaning of this acronym.

6. According to the Jewish calendar, the 24th of Tishrei (the day following Simchat Torah) can never fall on a Sunday. There must be some minor transcription error here.

7. In rabbinic poetry, such as on gravestones, years are often tied to acronyms of names.

8. There is a long acronymic title here that I skipped.

9. The Chmielnitzky uprising.

[Page 56]

The Sabbatean Kabbalist Rabbi Moshe David of Podhajce

by Chaim Wirszowsky

(A section from a survey on his personality, wanderings, and life path)

If it had not been for the stubborn persistence of Rabbi Yaakov Emden in his war against the Sabbateans, it would be doubtful if we would even have known the name of the kabbalist, the Baal Shem and Sabbatean[*1] Rabbi Moshe David of Podhajce. Our knowledge of him stems, at least for the moment, only from the letters of debate of Yaavetz[*2], in which he is mentioned dozens of times, not only in the words of the zealous rabbi himself, but also in testimonies and letters relating to Rabbi Moshe David. From these documents, a few fragments remain for us from the words of Rabbi Moshe David, and a few praises that one of his followers said about him. However, the knowledge that we have about the events of his life, primarily from the words of his enemies and persecutors, are very sparse and coincidental. Nevertheless, by examining and dissecting them, we are able to not only expose a portion of the story of the life of Rabbi Moshe David and to obtain somewhat of an idea of his personality, but also to paint a fascinating portrait of the Sabbatean underground as it existed and operated. Similarly, we can learn no small amount about his ties with other Sabbateans of his era, and about the principles of his doctrine. Here, I feel duty-bound to point out that the remnants of the doctrine of Rabbi Moshe David would be to me like a sealed book, had not new vistas of understanding the Sabbatean doctrine been opened up by incisive research of Professor Gershon Sholem regarding Berechya, the head of the Sabbateans of Salonika[1]. I am indebted more to the research of Professor Sholem and the words that I heard from his mouth more than I can point out in the body of this article, and I am happy to emphasize this with my words of thanks as a preface to my article.

A.

Very little is known about the events of Rabbi Moshe David the son of Tzvi[2] of Podhajce (or Podhajcer) before he appeared in the land of Germany. His name testifies that the city of Podhajce, which was an important Sabbatean center[3], was his native city, or at least the place where he lived for a long period of time. From one of his sermons (that will be dealt with later) we learn that he was born in the year 5456 (1696)[4]. Our sources do not tell when and how he became an adherent of Sabbateanism, and about his deeds in Poland on account of which he was persecuted, expelled and excommunicated. We primarily hear echoes from the time that he lived in Altona, due to his close contact with Rabbi Yonatan Eibeshitz and his son Wolf, when he entered the field of interest of Rabbi Yaakov Emden and other zealots.

Rabbi Moshe David was a kabbalist[5] and Baal Shem who first became known in eastern Poland. Zusman Sachnowitz, who met him in London in the year 5519, writes about him: "He was known in the area of Wolyn, he was a kabbalist, a renowned man of G-d, our rabbi and teacher Moshe David may G-d protect him, who is known as Rabbi Moshe David the Baal Shem of the holy community of Podhajce[6]." It is further stated there[7], "the renowned rabbi and teacher Moshe David may G-d protect him is very elderly, a great kabbalist. He previously lived in Podhajce, and was known as a Baal Shem." (Yaavetz in this manner obscured the two sources and turned them into words of derision.) Other information about his deeds in Poland comes to us from the mouths of his enemy, who of course only saw him from one side. In the letter of Pesach the son of Yeshoshua of Lissa[8] we read among everything else: "Here we have in the house of the rabbi a guilty elder may his name be blotted out, Moshe David. Indeed, it is known to all that he is one of those who was persecuted and expelled from Poland, of the accursed sect." We can learn more about the past of Rabbi Moshe David from Yaavetz himself. In his book "Beit Yonatan Hasofer" he writes (page 17 folio b): "The guilty accursed one (from the words used in a ban of excommunication. Yaavetz purposely chose this language that implies apostasy.) Moshe David, who misled many in the holy community of Rogozany and also through the amulets that he issued written with nonsense. Since a plague, G-d protect us, fell upon that community after this disgusting person filled the place with filthy amulets, a court deliberated, found him to be a Satan[9], and expelled him from the city. He was also expelled from the holy community of Lissa and other places on account of his disgusting deeds. Furthermore, it was testified regarding him that he abandoned the permissible and ate forbidden food (according to Avoda Zara 39 folio b). Also in Prstice, they saw him strangling chickens and eating them[*3]. Those acquaintances who knew him said that for many years, he did not eat ritually slaughtered meat, and he was also suspected on having relations with married women." From these few words of the Yaavetz, we can learn several details. They must be analyzed in detail. We have already seen that Rabbi Moshe David was a Baal Shem. From what is related here and in other sources[10], it seems that he wandered from place to place, wrote amulets and performed wonders – like the Baal Shem Tov and other Baalei Shem – and he apparently earned his livelihood in this manner. In Rogozno (Posen region) a court of law exposed apostasy in his amulets, and he was expelled from the city on a wagon filled with dung[11]. He was also expelled from Lissa (also in the region of Posen), apparently in the same timeframe. Yaavetz exaggerates, apparently, when he states that Rabbi Moshe David was "excommunicated and expelled from all of Poland"[12]. However there is no doubt that he was accurate when he mentions his expulsion from various places[13]. We have supporting testimony to this from one of the letters of Avraham HaKohen of Zamosc, who writes on Rosh Chodesh Cheshvan 5520 (Shamush Book, chapter 2, page 2): "And it was when G-d expanded things for us and justified our case in the city of Warsaw, we then took the appropriate opportunity to judge the evil men, sinners and rebels – including of course the iniquitous evil person Moshe David of Podhajce, who was excommunicated and banned in our state for several years already." Later, when we will deal with the events of Rabbi Moshe David in the land of Germany, we will see that he appears there not only as a Baal Shem and worker of wonders, but also as a Sabbatean teacher and preacher. Therefore, it is perhaps fair to surmise that during his wanderings through the communities of Poland, he occupied himself not only in the writing of amulets that secretly borer the symbols of his faith, but he also attempted to win over souls. It is especially important to note his visit to Prstice in Moravia. In such an important Sabbatean center, it was possible for Rabbi Moshe David to learn a great deal, and also perhaps to teach. It is interesting that especially in that place, according to the testimony of the Yaavetz, he was seen strangling chickens and eating them. If this testimony is true, the matter was no coincidence. We must remember that the Sabbateans in Prstice belonged to a radical branch of the movement. Therefore, it is no wonder that a Sabbatean would permit himself to behave with more freedom and less caution in Prstice, for there he was amongst his own. Yaavetz states that it was told to him that Rabbi

Moshe David accustomed himself to eating non-kosher food, and he was also suspect in marital infidelity. If these statements are true, the way of life of Rabbi Moshe David proves that he was numbered among the radical Sabbateans. However, we must not ignore the fact that there is no corroboration of this testimony from any other source. Indeed, such transgressions were commonplace among the radical Sabbateans, and in the eyes of the Yaavetz, all of the radical Sabbateans and sins of this nature were relevant to his cause. More important is the fact that there is a sound principle to believe the words of the information of the Yaavetz regarding a less common matter. I mean the amulets of Rabbi Moshe David. Yaavetz relates that in the amulets that were opened in Rogozno, "words of nonsense were found". The three letters of "shua"[*4] are none other than the acronym for woof and warp "shti vaerev", that is to say, the sign of the cross was drawn in these amulets. This is a surprising and astonishing fact, which demonstrates the way some elements of Christian faith were intermingled in the Sabbateanism of Rabbi Moshe David, an intermingling that found its expression in the inscription of the classic symbol of Christianity in an amulet of a Jewish Baal Shem. This fact demands interpretation. However, until I attempt to find the historical meaning, we are able to debate its veracity.

Text Footnotes

1. Published in Tzion, sixth year, books 3 and 4.
2. There his father is mentioned in only one document. See Hitavkut (Disputation) first printing, 72 folio a, (Lvov, 56).
3. See the Doctrine of Zealotry first printing, 33 folio b, 59 folio b. During his time, Chaim Malach, the student of Berechya, was also active there. See the Testimony of Yaakov 51 folio a; G. Sholem Berechya, etc. "Tzion" sixth year, page 123, and further on; D. Kahana, the History of the Sabbatean Kabbalists and Hassidim , section 2 page 176. Issachar the Sabbatean preacher from Podhajce is also known, see the Doctrine of Zealotry, 34 folio a.
4. See the continuation of the article in Tzion, seventh year, pages 86-87.
5. Thus is he called in the letter of Fiyortza. See Disputations, 103 folio a (Lvov, 56, folio b).
6. Disputations 127 folio b (Lvov page 71).
7. 126 folio b (Lvov 69 folio b).
8. Written in Kislev 5520 to Rabbi Yechezkel Landau, published in the book Disputations, 51 folio a and further on. The citation brought later on is found on page 51 folio b (Lvov, 25 folio b, a zealous youth from the Yeshiva of Rabbi Yonatan Eibeshitz who went public to pillory the Sabbateans in Altona.)
9. Yaavetz nicknames him in several places with the name of Satan, for the letters of Moshe David are numerically equivalent to Satan. See Disputations, 48 folio a, 50 folio a (Lvov 27, folio a, 28 folio b).
10. See the continuation of the article in Tzion, year seven, pages 79-80.
11. Disputations 103 folio b (Lvov 57 folio a).
12. Ibid. 48 folio a, 103 folio b (Lvov 27 folio a, 57 folio a).
13. Aside from the previously mentioned source, see also Disputations 38 folio b (Lvov 20 folio b): "Only go and inquire in the holy community of Rogozno and the holy community of Lissa, aside from other places in Podolia."

Translator's Footnotes

1. A 'Baal Shem' (literally: master of the name) is a Kabbalist who works wonders by using the name of G-d.
2. Yaavetz is an acronym of Rabbi Yaakov Emden.
3. It is forbidden to eat the meat of birds and animals unless they have gone through the process of shechita (ritual slaughter).
4. Shin vav ayin – "shua". I translated this as nonsense, but a literal translation is not entirely clear. It is clear from the text that the sign of the cross is implied.

[Page 57]

Dr. Falk – the Baal Shem from London

by Rabbi Dr. Herman Adler

Chaim Shmuel Yaakov Falk, who was known by the name "Da Falk", Dar. Falk or Dr. Falkon (approximately 1710-1782) is a cryptic and not well understood personality. He lived in London for approximately 40 years, and was known as the Baal Shem of London. The level of awe and respect that was intertwined with this name for more than 100 years is exposed to a large degree by recent research. Indeed, the veil of mystery that was borne by this personality has turned with time to shrouds; despite the many investigations and new revelations as to why he hid behind the veil. This personality is of interest because he is connected with a movement which has left tracks in Judaism to this day. He also came into contact with many of his generation who are worthy of attention, and he had close relations with personalities of influence in the Jewish community of London. The sources about his life story are very few. They include: a) mention in various books that appeared in his generation; b) information from books of disputations by Rabbi Yaakov Emden, the Book of Disputations and Gat Drucha (published in Lvov, 1877), as well as "Shvirat Luchot HaAven" (The breaking of the tablets of iniquity); c) his diary which passed to the possession of the late Rabbi Shlomo Hershel of holy blessed memory, the chief rabbi of London, today in the library of the Beis Midrash of the United Synagogues. The diary, that is described by Dr. Neubauer in the catalog of that library (number 127) includes 59 octavo pages and is written in Rabbinic Spanish and German cursive. It consists of a strange intermixture of diary material, explanations of dreams, details of charitable donations, lists of books, biblical texts, names of angels from kabbalistic books, receipts ofinim[1] and alcoholic liquids, accountings for exchange of money, lists of pledges, etc.

His place of birth is not known definitively. That which is implied in the transcription of Mr. Pichutto of Aleksandrow, that his place of origin was Furth, is not correct at all, for engraved on his gravestone is

"that he came from the country", and Emden, who lived in his generation and apparently knew his entire past very well, specifies that he came from Poland. It is almost certain that he was born in Podhajce, a city in Podolia, from which also came his friend Moshe David. Nothing is known about his father, aside from the statement that his name was Rafael the Sephardi. This does not imply that his origins were from the Jews of Spain and Portugal, bur rather that he belonged to the new group of Hassidim who called themselves Sephardim, since they adopted the Sephardic prayer rite.

[Page 58]

Despite the fact that the false Messiah Shabtai Tzvi died in the year 1676, specific groups that believed in his Messiahship continued to exist in Judaism. This gave rise to sects, some of which who intermingled Torah and Kabbalah. One of these sects was founded by Yehuda Chasid, who taught that the coming of the Messiah would be hastened by living a life of suffering. He and his friends made aliya from Poland to Jerusalem in the year 1700, passing through Furth, Tirol and Venice. Did Falk arrive in Furth with the intention of waiting for the actions of his teacher, and making aliya to the Holy Land? We know that his mother died in Furth and was buried there, and at a later date, a monument was erected over her grave in accordance with his instructions. The community of Furth claims that she helped him when he was in difficulty – a claim that is substantiated by the fact that he sent sums of money to the community of Furth at various occasions, and in his will, he left her an appropriate inheritance from the fortune that he left behind.

Was Falk a member of the Sabbatean movement? Thanks to the work of Professor Schechter, we have the ability to uncover the connection between Falk and Sabbateanism, for he cites several sources and turns his attention to various places in the books of Yaakov Emden, where he castigates Falk with a poisonous tone as a member of the sect, nicknaming him “the master of the demon”.

Such accusations cannot be accepted definitively. Emden saw the purpose of his life to emulate his father Rabbi Tzvi Ashkenazi and to put an end to the apostasy that endangered the moral life of Judaism. He authored several books on the sources of the false Messiah and his faithful supporters. The prime reason that Emden attacked Falk was the matter of his friendship with Moshe David of Podhajce, upon whom he spread his protection after he was expelled from various communities of the continent. Nevertheless, it is reasonably accurate that Falk felt himself close to him, to his fellow native, since he was also a student of the school of Rabbi Yehuda Chasid. The second reason for the castigation of Emden was the amulet that bore the names Shmuel and Tzvi. Indeed, there were many other Shmuels in Jewry aside from Shmuel Falk. We can also state in Falk's merit, in his book that is known, that nobody ever looked askance at him, and that nothing can be found that can support the strong castigation of Yaakov Emden. Nevertheless, one other thing is certain – that he was a kabbalist and that he boasted of magical powers. He lived in an era when many misleaders and misled people were floating around Europe. Among them were misled people who claimed that they were able to reveal mighty treasures through the staff of magic, incantations and amulets. These were people of the type of Schriffer and Caliostro. This was an era where people dreamed of the philosopher's stone and the potion of the essence of life, at a time when even the great giants of science deceived themselves and their fellows that they were able to turn silver into gold through the means of the dark science of white magic. Other examples of the deeds of Falk in that era are related in the book of Arkenholtz, who states that a noblewoman of the name of Da Ranchov, who died in France in the group of marshal Da Kamp, tells in her published memoirs about works of kabbalah and magic that were performed by Falk in front of her eyes on the land of Brunsweig and the estates of her father, in the presence of many wonderful personalities whose names were mentioned in that book. In the opinion of Arkenholtz it is possible that the “unbelievable magic was performed by him” came as a result of the fact that he had specific professional knowledge of chemistry. During one of his trips, this mysterious doctor reached Westphalia, a place where the authorities – who were in uproar on account of his delving into hidden treasures – condemned him to burning, as was the custom with witches. Falk saved himself from this punishment by fleeing, and he arrived in London. Emden cites a letter that at that time, Falk married a woman with a questionable past. This fact cannot be true and correct, since Emden was always prepared to believe in desecration of the Name by those who were suspect in his eyes of being apostates or supporting Sabbateanism. Falk had no children. However in his will, he mentions the name of his stepson Gedalia.

He was received pleasantly in London, in the manner in which that country related to refugees who arrived there, without excessive inquiry into their past. It would seem that he continued there with the ideas that brought him into conflict with the authorities of Westphalia. However, apparently he acted in a more cautions manner. He acquired a reputation with his wondrous deeds that were seen as beyond bounds of natural. Among the wonders that were told of him, his ability to light a small lantern without oil that would remain lit for several weeks stands out. When he requested coal, he would only have to whisper a kabbalistic incantation, and the pieces would slip obediently into his cellar. Metal table utensils that he dragged to a lender on ropes would find their way back to his table, contrary to the laws of nature. When a fire threatened the Great Synagogue in London, it was said that he stopped the progression of the fire by inscribing four Hebrew letters on the door lintel.

When he first arrived in England, he apparently earned his livelihood as a worker of wonders, playing on the nonsensical beliefs of the masses. The books of his generation as well as his diary that he left behind give evidence to information of mysterious trips to the Forest of Accusations, and from there, explanations about meetings that took place, and chests of gold that were buried there. Did he keep his treasures in the aforementioned forest in order to test, to exalt, or to melt?

[Page 59]

The Baal Shem continued to attract a crowd of followers by cloaking himself in the cloak of holiness. In one letter that was preserved by Yaakov Emden, written by Falk's friend Zusman Shachnowitz, he is described as some sort of sublime person. His room is illuminated with silver lamps on the walls and with a central eight-branched chandelier made of a solid piece of pure silver. Even though it only held enough oil to last for one day and night, it remained lit for three weeks. On one occasion, he closed himself off in his house in isolation for a period of six weeks, without food or drink. At the end of that period, ten men gathered to enter to him. They found him sitting on a royal throne, with a golden miter on his head, and around his neck a gold chain with a gold star upon which holy names were inscribed. "Indeed, this man is unique in his generation on account of his knowledge of holy mysteries. I cannot describe to you in detail all of the wonders that he performed. I consider it a great honor and mercy that this man found me worthy to be numbered among those who sit in his shadow and wisdom."

News of events similar to these spread very quickly to the outside world. We find him maintaining close relations with people of high rank. Arkenholtz mentions one royal prince who turned to Dr. Falk in his search for the philosopher's stone, but left disappointed as he was rebuffed by him. The Chida (Azoulay) mentions in his little book that describes his travels that when he visited Paris in 1778, he met the nobleman Da Suma and the noblewoman Da Krona, who saved several Jews from the talons of the Spanish Inquisition. The noblewoman implied to Rabbi Azoulay via an innuendo that the Baal Shem of London had taught her practical kabbala. This revelation raised the ire of the honorable scholar. It seems that Falk maintained close relations with the eccentric adventurer Baron Theodore Da Neuhauf, who was coronated as the king of Corsica because he stood at the helm of Corsican revolutionaries against the Genoans. He was later exiled and settled in London in 1749. The exiled king fortified himself with the hope of his good fortune that had soured by revealing treasures hidden in the depths of the ocean. To actualize his desire, he turned to an elderly Jewish rabbi for help. (The rabbi is identified as our Baal Shem). Falk mentions a mysterious meeting with Prince Czartoryski, apparently Adam Czartoryski (1734-1823), the ruler of Podolia, and with a personality by the name of Emanuel, who was described by him as "a servant of the king of France (Louis XVI)". Similarly, the Baal Shem gave a ring as an amulet to a duke from Orleans in order to assure him the royal crown. This ring, it is related, was sent by Philippe Egalite to a Jewess by the name of Juliet Gusho, who transferred it to her son, Baron Da Charter, who later became King Louis Philippe. Before his death, the king bestowed the ring to the nobleman Da Paris, and it is assumed that today it is found in the House of Stob in Twickenham.

The bankers Aaron Goldschmid and his son George were among the most important friends of Dr. Falk. They are frequently mentioned in his diary as having given him wonderful advice in business affairs. He became a wealthy man during his final two decades of life thanks to his investments in lending and speculation, and successful business investments. He lived in a spacious house in Welclose Square, where he established a synagogue served by two cantors. This synagogue also had a sukka. We see him using riding utensils on his travels, which he swapped constantly. He loved books, since he was a man who studied a great deal. In his diary, we find a list of books that he possessed, including books of grammar, philosophy and disputation. He maintained contact with the chief rabbi Rabbi David Tavli (our Rabbi and Teacher David Tavli the son of Shlomo Zalman HaKohen Shiff), the author of a book of responsa and sermons that was published with the title "Lashon Zahav" (Golden Tongue) by Rabbi Gabriel Adler and the new rabbi that was appointed in the New Synagogue, Moshe Meyers.

Just as we do not have information about the means that he attained his wealth, we also do not know how he disbursed it. He was of good status, he was liked by people, and concerned himself greatly with the performance of good deeds. In his diary, we find several hints to the disbursement of sums of money to charitable needs. In his will dated April 14, 1782, preserved in the archives of the United Synagogue, he appoints Aaron Goldschmid, his son George Goldschmid and his son-in-law Leon Da Simons as executors. His main bequest was two small Torah scrolls in a silver ark, and annual payments of 100 Sterling to the Great Synagogue; annual payments of ten guineas to the Beis Midrash of the Ashkenazim and Sephardim; twenty guineas to the community of Furth for various charities; ten guineas to the chief rabbi of the era, and other sums for distribution to the poor. These annual payments were distributed in an organized manner by the supervisors of the United Synagogue. However, on account of low , the sums became smaller. He died a few days after he arranged his will, on April 17, 1782, and was buried the next day on the Glebe St. Cemetery, Mile End. The inscription on his grave notes that he observed the Torah and Mitzvot during his forty years of living in London, and he disbursed all of his money to charity at the time of his death. His portrait, now in the possession of V. H. Goldschmid, was drawn by Kopley, and testifies to the talents of the artist. The following is the inscription on his grave.

Here is buried Sh. Y. Ch. (Shmuel Yaakov Chaim)

[Page 60]

An elderly man of fine stature, the important man who came from the state, the complete scholar, the kabbalist, our rabbi and teacher Rabbi Shmuel the son of our rabbi and teacher Rafael of holy blessed memory, who was known throughout the land and far off isles. For the forty years that he was here, he erected the banner of Torah and service, fulfilled the Torah, commandments and statutes, and at the time of his death, he disbursed all of his great wealth to several distinct charities. In this merit, may the Creator of the Heavens and the Founder of the Earth bind his soul in His Garden of Eden with the other righteous people, and may he merit to arise at the time of the resurrection with all the dead of Israel who will eventually arise. He died with a good name on Thursday, 4 day of the month of Ziv that is the month of Iyar, and was buried with honor and eulogies the next day, Friday, the 20th day of the Omer, 5542.

May his soul be bound in the bonds of eternal life.

This illustration corroborates the image of the Baal Shem that was described by those of his generation. He "was walking outside wearing a floral suit that was suited to his long white beard and noble facial expression." Relating to him, we can make use of the famous words of Pope with a small change: "if some human failings fell to his lot, look at his face, and this will all be as if it was not."

From English by M. Sh. Geshoury

M. M. Oyzerkes

In memory of a forgotten Yiddish writer

Mordechai Mendel Oyzerkes was born in Podhajce in the year 1848. He worked in the distilling industry, producing liquor from potatoes, and wandered a great deal through Galicia, Russia and Romania. Later, he to his hometown and became a private teacher.

We know very few details about his life and chronicles. Apparently, his father was also a private teacher. In any case, he was so taken by the special ambience of people of this profession, that he dedicated his first book to describing this reality. "The Private Teacher" was also the name of the book, which served as a sort of autobiography of the author. In his introduction to his book, he admits and confesses that his knowledge comes from private study, and not from a teacher or a guide, and from contact with people during his many days of travel. He goes on to describe the challenges of a private teacher, who must bear all of the nonsense of the children of the wealthy in order to earn his livelihood, and the disparaging relationship with their parents, who provide his livelihood.

Oyzerkes' motif and style of writing draws from the influence of the Haskalah literature, with a clear style in order to educate and guide the reader. His entire story contains lessons, and frequently these lessons are expressed explicitly. However his primary positive trait is that he chooses topics from the life going on around him. The expressions, the mottoes, the blessings and curses that are found in plentiful fashion in his books are a comprehensive treasury of the style of speech that was commonplace among the residents of Galicia in those days.

Of his wide-ranging creations, only a few books were published, as follows:

1. "The Private Teacher". Appeared in three volumes, published in Podhajce in 1897, 1898, and 1900.

2. "The New Generation" – scenes from life of the present, published in Lvov in 1905.

3. "Father Married Mother", a novel based on real life, Lvov, 1905.

4. Portraits from the life of the Jews of various classes. Podhajce, 1908.

Nothing is known of his literary bequest, the place of living, and his fate.

It is clear that Oyzerkes did not gain much satisfaction from his livelihood as a teacher or an author. He loved his land of Galicia, and its people. Along with this, he mercilessly castigated their deficiencies. He finally left Galicia at the end of his days in order to find rest in the land of the future, America. However, he disappeared completely from our eyes in this vast expanse of land. All that is known is that he died in 1913, in the 65th year of his life.

From the Yiddish monograph by Nachman Blumenthal.

Translator's Footnotes

1. I am not sure what this term means.

[Page 61]

Life in Podhajce Through the Mirror of Journalism

Extracts from Hebrew newspapers

Podhajce, Tishrei 5637 (1878)

Our town is one of the small ones; but not like the small towns of the region that still dwell in darkness and gloom, without a scintilla of the light of wisdom. Rather, it is like its sisters, the large cities who make forward strides at all times in accordance with the spirit of the times, and constantly ascend in sophistication. Similarly, our city also learns to better itself and seek knowledge. Recently, the choice people of our town founded a movement to read periodicals in the holy tongue and vernacular languages of the country. They rented two large rooms in a fine and proper house, where the members gather every day. This place is called "The Gathering Place of Jewish Citizens" (Israelitesh Birgelichers Casino). They established a charter and sent a message to the state representative (Staatshalterei) to approve and confirm it. The place will open to the members on October 1. I wish to express my thanks to the honorable people who made efforts to found this organization. These are: the honorary chairman Reb Shmerel Rosmarin and his vice chair and honorable treasurer Reb Alexander Gelber. The third honorable person is Reb Yehoshua Kahana who was the first to have this idea.

To the dwellers of the small towns in our land, I call out: Look upon the city of Podhajce, look and do like it. For how long will you sit lazily without doing anything? Arise from your foolish slumber! Is not the light of wisdom penetrating to your houses, and are you closing your eyes from seeing the shining light of wisdom? Wake up! Become people who know how to discern between the light of wisdom and the darkness of the fool, and then you will be called a wise and learned nation.

A. David Polisiuk

"Hamagid" year 20, issue 42, 14th Cheshvan 5637.

*

Podhajce, Tammuz 5642

To the editor of Hamagid, Shalom! You have been, for some time already, a seer, whom G-d has put in place to stand on the lookout as a periodical to inform the House of Jacob what is going on with its brethren who are spread and scattered in all corners of the world among various nations. From the time I met you and started to engage you in the Hamagid periodical, from the time you started to publish and edit it even during the days of Rabbi Silberman of blessed memory, your purpose has been solely to unite far off hearts. You have preached to and reached out to the nation that is drawn out and worn, at times to abandon the forlorn path and the not good circle, in which our enemies find in this movement a pretext to accuse of iniquity; at times with words of admonition and sharp words of reproof, to speak and teach them the proper path upon which to walk, to do only good and right, and to find grace in the eyes of the nations amongst which they dwell.

If you see oppression of the poor and miscarriage of justice in the state, you would be the first to take a shofar to your lips, to call people to arms, to collect funds, and to provide them to the mistreated oppressed ones. Even now, you take no rest when you see your brothers in deep trouble and disgrace. You awaken and arouse, you do not favor the great and you do not play favorites with the princes of the people, who turn their eyes to the free lands and find our Jewish brethren there, you admonish them, and your motto is "The Land of Beauty"[1]. You were the first who raised in your periodical the notion of "settlement of the Land of Israel", and Jerusalem entered into your heart twenty years ago already with your wonderful article "They will be saved with and calmness" (Hamagid year 6). Your precious articles have always struck roots in the hearts of the readers.

Our brethren in this city as well, we founded a branch of Alliance Israelite Universelle of Vienna with the assistance and efforts of my wife and intelligent friends, Reb Yehuda Leibush Alerhand and his vice Reb Shaul Schorr may they live. This group numbers 4 members from our city and surrounding area. Through the efforts of my aforementioned friends, the local group collected donations of money of the sum of approximately 140 coins to assist the downtrodden of Israel. We sent the collected money to the Alliance Israelite Universelle group in Vienna with the note that it is the will of the chapter that this money be sent to assist only those going to Palestine, and not those going to America. The organization responded to our local chapter with a letter that our desire will be carried out, and the money will only be disbursed those going to The Land of Beauty. Therefore, how wonderful would it be if a branch of the Alliance Israelite Universelle organization would be established in each and every city, and when they send their money to Vienna, they would request that only those who are going to the Land of our Fathers will be assisted and supported through their donations, so that they could purchase fields, plant vineyards and plough its land, so that they will draw and satiate themselves from the splendor of its glory, for there is a blessing there. The honorable organization will fulfill their desire, and then the idea of settlement of the Land of Israel will speedily move from potential to actualization.

A. David Polisiuk

Hamagid, year 26, issue 28, 10 Av 5642, page 237.

*

Podhajce, 3 Adar, 5647

To the author of Hamagid, Shalom and blessings!

In Hamagid issue 7, in "News in Israel", you brought down an announcement from the Drohowicer Zeitung that the Jewish community in the city of Brzostok gave their thanks to Mr. Izidor Rosmarin, the postmaster of Brzostok, who informed the regional minister (Bezirkshauftman) and also the postal administration in Lvov about the "circular" from Basle, Switzerland, to place seals on copies of the books of the Code of Jewish Law, and to precede this announcement with the header 'Chasid Oha"e'[2]. The community of readers will consider

Mr. Rosmarin to be a Christian because of this. Therefore, I see it as my personal duty to proclaim in Hamagid that Mr. Rosmarin is a Jew, the son of one of the honorable people of our town Mr. Shmerl Rosmarin may he live, who was given a golden souvenir with the crown of the state as a prize. Even though he is a Jew, he is still worthy of being praised and thanked for his action to ensure that many Jews in our land are appointed as postmasters. In our city as well, there is a Jewish expeditor employed at the post office, and numerous others were inspired to do as he did. Mr. Rosmarin is not embarrassed to be known as a Jew, and his face does not blush in the midst of the community of Christians when he states that he loves his people!

[Page 62]

Mr. Izidor Rosmarin has come a few days ago to visit his parents' home, and when I visited in his parents home, he informed me that the group in Basle Switzerland has sent its notice to the post offices promising to give the sum of 10 marks for the effort of the post office of placing the seal into the books of the Code of Jewish Law that are copied through that organization. Mr. Rosmarin showed me the letters of thanks that were sent to him. He also said that letters of thanks were also sent to the postmaster from Shipner.

A. David Polisiuk

Hamagid year 31, issue 10, 13 Adar 5647, page 74.

*

The Murder of a Jewish Family Near Podhajce

A.

In the nearby village of Ribnik the innkeeper took ill a few weeks ago, and traveled to the city of Podhajce to consult with doctors. His wife, who remained alone at home, asked her brother-in-law, her sister's husband and another family member, as well as her 17 year old younger sister, to stay with her until her husband would from the city in good health. On the night of the 14th of June, thieves broke into the house, murdered the wife of the innkeeper, her sister, her brother-in-law, and cut off their heads with an axe, leaving behind a young child knowing that he would not have the power to avenge them. In the morning, people came to the house and found the housewife and her sister lying dead in their bed, with bloodstains on the walls. The two men were found in the field outside the house, and they were not able to determine how they got there – whether they were dragged outside by the murderers after they got there, or whether they fled outside out of fear of the murderers. The murderers were not found.

The blood of the innocent cries out from the earth "a stone from the wall calls out and a beam from the wood answers". It was a horrific site to see the elderly father rending his garments, clapping his hands on his thighs, and tearing the hair from his scalp over the murder of his two daughters and son-in-law. The shrieks of the bereaved mother ascended to the heavens over the slaughter of an entire family as pure burnt offerings: "the fruit of my womb, would it be that I died instead of you. I will go down to my daughters and son-in-law in mourning to my grave." Who did not weep when he saw the young child bereft of his mother. His father is lying on the sick bed, and his illness is worsening. His mother has been murdered. Where will he go now? Woe to the eyes that see thus.

The victims were brought to the city in coffins. The doctors performed an autopsy and found a fetus in the woman, for she was pregnant. This soul is also considered among the victims. It can justly be said that "they were four who were five".

The murderers saw no reward for their crime. They spilled innocent blood and did not take any money, for in their haste to perpetrate the murder they tired of searching for the hiding place of money – and they fled. They only found the accounting ledgers, in which the debts owed by the farmers to the innkeeper were recorded, which they tore to pieces.

Hamevaser, Hebrew weekly, Lvov, June 16, 1865, issue 23.

B.

These are the results of the investigation by the judges of our city. In that village, a certain Christian served as the forest ranger, who was known as a troublemaker and a lover of strife. He was with the farmers of the village when they came to conduct an investigation in the hotel in the evening of the day in which the murder was perpetrated. When the judges revealed that he too was in the house in which the murder was perpetrated that night, they began to suspect that his hands spilled the blood. They issued a command to conduct a search in his house. During the search, the found a Jewish skullcap, a bloodstained sickle, and a cloak that had been washed in several places. The judges determined from these items that the forest ranger shed the blood of the innocents. The guards shackled his hands and feet, and sent him to jail. When the court case took place, he denied that he participated in the murder. However, the judges brought his daughter, a young girl to court, and asked her, "Was your father in his home that night?" She answered, "when my father home and entered his room, he took off his coat and put on a new coat. He then washed the coat that he took off". When the owner of the hotel home, he identified the skullcap as his own. Then the murderer confessed the act of murder that he perpetrated.

From the Hamevaser weekly, Lvov, August 4, 1895.

*

Life of the Jews of Podhajce in the weekly Hamitzpeh

A.

From the Progression of the Communities

Instead of the column "From the Mud of the Communities" that frightens the heart of every faithful Jew, I will try to make a good beginning to the new chapter "From the Progression of the Communities". Let this path be a sign to all cities of our land, to compete with us, to add to it more and more, to cause joy to all who love our nation.

At a time when all of the rabbis of our land are slumbering, and along with them, the communal leaders are sleeping a slumber of laziness, and in the midst of this, the best of the powers of our nation are going to ruin, and our children are growing up without Torah or worldly ways, or are becoming assimilated with the gentiles with their energies being spread to a different nation – our rabbi, the head of the rabbinical court Rabbi Shalom Lilienfeld may he live long arose in our city, the Gaon of our people, glorious in Torah and wisdom, and founded the General Talmud Torah in a pleasant manner that is equitable to every person. Hassidim, average people and enlightened people are all happy with our rabbi, the Gaon may he live long, who always knows to walk with his wisdom in the spirit of all householders. He has displayed his wisdom to us this time as well, by forging a compromise and doing the will of each and every person. To the Hassidim he gave their Hassidism and to the enlightened people he gave their enlightenment. The teachers will not be lacking in livelihood even one iota. The program is simple in its arrangement. The teachers that were up to this point each the masters of their own affairs have now gathered together under one banner, the "banner of Torah and Awe of Heaven", under the supervision of a supervisor and chief teacher, an expert, who is in awe of the word of G-d. Until now, the students of one teacher were from several classes, but now each class is under one teacher, and the teachers are divided between different classes. The youngest children are together, and study under the natural "Hebrew in Hebrew" system; those who study Chumash, Rashi and Bible are together, and those who study Talmud and Halachic decisions are together. To those who are most pious and desire only the old educational stile, "Cholem alef is oy"[3], a few teachers remain outside the general organizational structure. The teachers are given an appropriate salary, each in accordance with his work and needs of livelihood, but by no means less that what he was earning until this time. In this manner, everyone comes to his place in peace, and with the help of G-d, a knowledgeable generation will be educated in the spirit of Torah, ways of the world, and fear of Heaven.

[Page 63]

B.

The Students Taking their Exam in the Beis Midrash

Our rabbi and Gaon, accompanied by the elite of our city and its wise people, dedicated the days of Chol Hamoed to examine the teachers and students in the Beis Midrash, in order to ascertain the order of grades and classes. When I saw the spectacular site, when all of the lads gathered to the place of the examination, I said in my heart: perhaps now the time has come for the fulfillment of the words of the Gaon Rabbi Sheptl the son of the Shela in his book "Vavei Amudim" – and these are his words, "By the life of my head, my innards are cut in my memory as I recall how when I visited the holy community of Amsterdam, I saw the children learning Torah from Bereshit until Leenei Kol Yisrael[4], then all of the 24 books of the Bible, and following that, all of Mishna. When they got older, they began to study Gemara, commentators and Halachic decisions. I wept about this. Why is this not done in our land? Would it be that this custom would spread throughout the entire Jewish Diaspora. What harm would come if a child would fill himself up with Scripture and Mishna until his is 13 years old, for he would reach his objective within one year, which does not happen in our learning style. By the life of my head, if the chief Gaonin of the land would band together, establish an order, and set up a style of study in this manner, there is no doubt that it would be the will of G-d that this endeavor should succeed." See the source for his full statement on this matter.

The old city of Podhajce, the place where the Gaon the author of the Masaat Binaymin lived and now reposes in honor, as well as other greats of Torah (see what the Gaon the son of the Shach wrote in his introduction to the book Nekudat Hakesef, as follows: My chief place of residence used to be the holy community of Podhajce, a city which has everything, the Torah of G-d in its midst, a praiseworthy and faithful city, from which came forth people of wisdom and understanding, etc.), this city will be the first to Torah to its rightful place, and our rabbi and Gaon will be the one who begins this. He preaches properly and fulfils properly, for he took upon himself to teach an in-depth class a few hours each day in the general Talmud Torah. The wealthy people of our town are duty-bound to support this great endeavor, so that it should not falter. Those who toil in this should not stumble from the obstacles in their path, and shall not suffer setbacks, for the institution is worthy of toil, and overcoming all obstacles. If those that make the effort succeed in this, they will serve as examples for other cities to strengthen Torah. They should only be strong and vigorous.

Afikoman[5]

Hamitzpeh Krakow, issue 43, 28th Tishrei 5666 (October 17, 1905).

C.

The Fight of the Rabbi of the City Against Anti-Semitism

Many newspapers, including American ones, have reported on the grave danger that was hovering over the heads of thousands of Jewish residents of Podhajce and region at the time that the Ruthenians were gathering, and their salvation through the efforts of our rabbi and Gaon Rabbi Shalom Lilienfeld the Kohen, the head of the rabbinical court of our city. Each newspaper reported in its own style. It is also my fault, for I did not inform Hamitzpeh at the appropriate time, due to a reason that was beyond my control. Now, dear editor, in order to do your will, I wish to ascribe truth to its proper place, and describe the matter as it was, so that our brethren should know that Israel is not bereft of people who are able to protect their nation and honor, even in this orphaned generation.

Several days before the Ruthenians gathered in our city, the life of our brethren here was hanging on the line. A death pall, in the full sense of the term, hung over us, for inciters made the rounds from town to town and from city to city in order to incite the wild masses to perpetrate pogroms against the Jews, as did their brothers in Russia, for the whip was let loose by the government. Fear grew day by day, for the masses were convinced and ready to believe everything. It seemed as if it were true that the blood of the Jews was permissible to them, and they would not be afraid to publicly threaten the Jews, saying: you only have so and so number of days left to live. Despite the fact that our rabbi and head of the rabbinical court, whose honor was great in the eyes of the minister of the region, went to the minister together with our honorary communal leader Mr. Rotenberg to ask him to protect us, and he promised to protect us well, this was not sufficient to assuage the fear of in the hearts of the Jews, for who did not know that 20 or 30 gendarmes are as naught when faced with thousands of ruffians coming with the power of permission. Many of our brethren were prepared to leave the city, with all of their property and wealth. Our rabbi made no small effort, in his sermon on the Sabbath prior to the gathering, to calm the masses of our brethren who were prepared and armed for the day of the battle, for the residents of our city knew that our rabbi is trusted in the eyes of the state, as in the gates of Torah and science, and they believe every utterance that emanates from his mouth as the words of a luminary. However, what man is able to cut the heart of this fellow, to tell him
not to fear at the time when a sharpened sword is placed upon his neck? And furthermore, what is the situation if that man is part of that fear. However, our rabbi is a man of success with no equal. He is assisted from Heaven, and G-d grants success to everything that he does. The day of the Ruthenian gathering was set for Thursday.

[Page 64]

Throughout the days of the week, those who intended to gather came to find their place, but could not do so, because the Poles who were their mortal enemies did not grant them place to gather. This increased the confusion tenfold. However our rabbi knew how to take advantage of the situation. He saw what was happening and seized the opportunity. Despite the attitude of the Poles who always have ambitions against his honor, he made a dangerous step of self-sacrifice, and turned the parlor of his large fortress-like home over to them[6]. On Thursday morning, when ten thousand Ruthenian men and woman began to gather, and the rabbi's parlor was too small to hold all of those assembled, our rabbi permitted the chief spokesman Dr. Bochinski to ascend through the large parlor to the balcony, and to speak from there for a few hours.

The masses, laden with their bags and sacks to be able to collect the booty, were not able to wait. They waited to hear from the speaker, “strike and pillage the Jews”. However, with the assistance of the Rock and Redeemer of Israel, to our joy, they heard otherwise. Bochinski, who had for the moment turned into a friend of ours, spent half his wrath pouring fire and brimstone onto the Poles who are attempting to destroy the Ruthenians (according to their words). He then suddenly turned to the Jews to say: do not think my brothers, that only us Ruthenians are oppressed and downtrodden by the hand of the Poles. Our Jewish brethren are with us in this tribulation. They are also crushed under the burden of this nation. They are tormented and downtrodden by these high people, etc. etc., and we must love them with brotherly love, walk with them arm in arm, fight for their rights as for our rights, etc. The speaker continued – go and see, of all the houses and meeting places of Polish Podhajce, we were not given a place to gather. Even the regional office (Rada Powiatowa) that exists only because of our money is closed before us. Only the rabbi, the rabbi of the Jews who is good and does good, turned his house over to us in mercy and justice. It is a shame on the Poles. Give honor to the Jews. Give honor to the Podhajce rabbi. All of those gathered shouted out loudly: Honor to the rabbi. Honor to the Jews. Shame on the Poles. The speaker told them: repeat! They repeated. A third time! They repeated a third time and countless more times. His concluding words were: to your tents in peace, with proper decorum. Do not cause trouble along the way. Love the Jews. Always seek their peace and good. The masses listened to him and conducted only a small demonstration in the streets of the city, singing national songs. At every stop they called out and repeated: Shame on the Poles! Honor to the Podhajce rabbi! Honor to the Jews! At the end, the entire gathering stood in front of the regional office and shouted out loudly: Shame on the marszalek! Honor to the rabbi. Then they to their homes in peace. The Jews had joy, gladness and honor[7].

It is appropriate this day to inscribe this in the annals of Jewish history, and about our exalted rabbi, whose name is “Shalom”[8], and who should stand for blessing and praise for generations upon generations.

The new courthouse

A similar event to this took place to us now with respect to the new school, the "General Talmud Torah", that was founded by our rabbi this year, and through which our city gains splendor and serves as an example to all of the cities of our land, as is already known to the readers of Hamitzpeh. Other cities such as Seret, Bolszowce, Zablotow, and others, are already jealous of us and wish to follow suit. In recent days, the elderly Gaon of our generation, the Light of the Exile, from whose water "of knowledge of Torah" we drink, our rabbi Shalom Mordechai HaKohen the head of the rabbinical court of

[Page 65]

Berezany, sent special messengers to our rabbi and Gaon in order to study the organization of the institution so that a similar general Talmud Torah can be founded in his community.

The slander of the Biks and their organ "Slowo Polskie" upon us and our Torah had no small amount of influence upon the officials of our town. One day, all of the Talmud Torahs were closed by the regional minister without given any positive or negative reason. At that time, the Admor and Tzadik of Kopyczynce may he live long lived honorably in our city. This Tzadik mourned over the closing of the school as he would over the destruction of the House of G-d, for he loved Torah greatly, and he had great satisfaction after he examined the students of each grade, and found that even the students of grades 5, 6 and 7 knew their lessons in Mishna and Talmud by heart. As a token of thanks and satisfaction, he granted proper support to the Talmud Torah fund. Our rabbi went to the regional minister accompanied by the head of the community. It was for naught. The regional minister was ill in his home, and in the interim, the cheders were closed and the youths were going around idle. We almost gave up. However, our rabbi thought otherwise. He girded his loins, and went to see the regional minister in his sickroom. Our rabbi talked harshly to him and asked him for the reason why the school was closed. The regional minister answered him lovingly and positively, and told him that he was very distressed since he never heard anything bad about this school, but it would be a form of rebellion against the Poles and the government, etc. However, our rabbi from whose lips grace flowed knew what to answer him. He convinced him that this would only be religious progressiveness, without any political taint. On the contrary, on the contrary, etc. The minister believed all his words, and issued an order that very day from his bed to open all the cheders.

After all of these events, I cannot conceal the truth that our honorable communal leaders were assisted greatly by him in every good and positive endeavor, and they were indeed supporters of Torah. This was also a benefit and a good omen regarding him, as a man whose words were listened to, knowing that he had the fear of Heaven. Apparently, there are other urgent matters in our city that require rectification, and I hereby request in the names of those who seek the peace and welfare of the city that they assist our exalted rabbi and Gaon, may he live long, in paying attention to these matters with the help of the honorable communal leaders.

Afikoman

Hamitzpeh, Krakow, Adar 19 5666 (1906), issue 11, third year.

D.
The Death of Rabbi Shalom HaKohen Lilienfeld of holy blessed memory

The festival of Sukkot, our time of rejoicing turned from a festival to a day of mourning and weeping for the Jews of Podhajce. On the first day of the festival of Sukkot at 8:00 a.m. our rabbi the exalted Gaon Rabbi Meshulam Lilienfeld HaKohen the head of the rabbinical court of Podhajce passed away in the 53rd year of his life. He was buried that day with great honor near the grave of the Gaon the author of the Masaat Binyamin. It was not only our own city that has become orphaned from this mighty Gaon, but also the entire House of Israel, for in this orphaned generation we do not have many rabbis who possess the great talents that he did. His Torah and wisdom gave him renown among the greats. Many communities wished to offer him the rabbinical seat. However, his prolonged illness thwarted the development of this pleasant rose, and somewhat darkened the sun that was able to shine from one end of the world to the other.

The writer of these lines, who already wrote many letters to Hamitzpeh abut the greatness of the late Gaon of holy blessed memory, is forced this time in great sorrow to suffice himself with these brief words. The Comforter of Zion will comfort the entire house of Israel with imminent redemption and with good and faithful shepherds.

Pesach Brandsdorfer

Hamitzpeh, Krakow, issue 42, 30 Tishrei 5670, (October 15, 1909)

E.
The Choosing of a New Head of the Rabbinical Court in Podhajce

Our bereaved community has arisen from its mourning when its Parnassim, the president Mr. Rotenberg and his vice Mr. Kinter, Mr. Gutman and Rabbi Mendel Grynberg from Stanislawow with the news that the rabbi and Gaon Rabbi Yonah Meller agreed to accept the rabbinical post in our city after having left it 22 years ago and living honorably in Stanislawow, with Torah and divine service. At first the Gaon refused to to his source, having merited two benefits in Stanislawow. However, he was not able to withstand the urging of our communal notables. He had mercy upon the orphaned community and agreed to be the head of the rabbinical court. The city of Podhajce rejoiced and was glad. The eyes of all members of community, almost without exception, turned toward this honorable rabbi, in whom resides both Torah and wisdom, and see him as a salvation and comfort for our ancient community. Here, we impatiently await his arrival this coming Chanukah. The entire community expresses its gratitude to our Parnassim who immediately felt the absence of a rabbi, and hastened to appoint him, to Torah to its proper place. For the rabbi and Gaon Rabbi Y. Meller is a native of our town. He was educated in it, and originally occupied its rabbinical seat. He was known by everyone as the "Rabbi from Podhajce" during all the years that he lived in Stanislawow. I hereby wish the people of our community and the rabbi Mazel Tov.

Pesach Brandsdorfer

Hamitzpeh, Krakow, issue 49, 20 Kislev 5670 (December 3, 1909)

"The Wide Street" opposite the courthouse building

A first aid course in 1941. Dr. Kornowicz is in the center

Members of the Kibbutz Podhajce

Translator's Footnotes

1. "Eretz Tzvi" is a poetic term for the Land of Israel.
2. The meaning of this sentence is not entirely clear. It seems like that he informed the post offices that a certain seal must be placed in the copies of the Code of Jewish Law that pass through the post.
3. A reference to the rote teaching of the Hebrew letters and their sounds.
4. The first and last words of the Pentateuch.
5. Obviously a pseudonym.
6. 'Them' here refers to the Ruthenians.
7. An almost verbatim rendition of Esther 7:16.
8. Shalom in Hebrew means 'peace', and by stating his name in quotes here, there is a double entendre.

[Page 67]

From the Past

History of the Jews of Podhajce

by Nachman Blumenthal

1. Name and History of the City

The name of the city appears in the sources in various forms. Here we will deal with the Hebrew and Yiddish sources. In the Hebrew sources, we find various spellings of the word[1]: Podhaitz in the ledgers of the Council of Four Lands; Pohitz in the Birchat Yaakov book by Rabbi Yaakov the son of Rabbi Baruch of Pohitz, Lvov (1745); Podhaitze – "Hamagid"; Podhaitz – in a booklet published in Przemysl in 1906; Podheitzi – G. Kressel in the Lexicon of Hebrew Literature, 5722 (1962). There were authors who used differing version in the same work. In a single edition of the Hebrew "Hamagid", it is written once as Podhaitze and once as Podhitze.

We also find various versions in Yiddish literature: Podheitze – "The Private Teacher", Drohobycz 1897; Podheitz – R. Mahler, Warsaw, 1958; Podietz – Weichert, Memories, Tel Aviv, 1960; and even Podgaitze – Pages on Yiddish Demography, Statistics and Economics, 1923, number 3. In ordinary Yiddish, the word is pronounced as Pidhaitz or without the 'yod' as Podaitz. In that respect, the Yiddish version is closer to Ukrainian than to Polish.

The name of the city stems from the large forests (gaia, haia) between which the settlement is situated[*1]. The settlement itself is situated in a valley surrounded by densely overgrown hills. The sources emphasize the fine position of the city that was founded later, which attracted tourists and guests. The great Polish composer Friedrich Chopin used to enjoy staying over there on account of the beauty of the area[*2]. With the growth of the settlement, the forests were cut down to a large degree. Fields and gardens near the houses took their place.

The settlement was already known at the beginning of the 15th century. In the year 1463, the Roman Catholic (Polish) church was erected. In the 16th century, the Greek Catholic (Ukrainian) church was erected, which was built like a fortress. Aside from this, there was a castle, and walls surrounding the city. In the middle of the 17th century, a Frenchman who was among Jan Sowiecki's court men, Daleran, describes the city in 1667. Among the residents of the city at that time, Jews, Wallachians, Armenians, Poles and Ukrainians are mentioned[*3]. Everything was wiped out by the frequent battles that took place there. Only ruins remained from the castle, and a beer brewery was erected in its place.

Podhajce was a city from the beginning of the 16th century. It obtained the privilege of conducting a major annual fair, aside from the weekly fairs for the nearby towns. Podhajce obtained the Magdeburg rights in 1539, which helped the development of the city. From the year 1630, Podhajce became the place of residence of the Potocki Polish magnate family.

Podhajce was situated upon the road through which the Tatars, and later the Cossacks and the Turks would invade Poland. The Polish army commanders (hetmans), as well as the Polish kings, Jan Kazimiersz in 1663, Jan Sobieski in 1667 and 1687, and August II in 1698, spent time in Podhajce. In 1675, Podhajce was plundered and destroyed by the Turks (Ibrahim Pasha). In 1698, the Polish military, headed by King August II, drove out the Tatars[*4]

Podhajce transferred over to Austria in 1772

[Page 68]

חידושי דינים

תם ונשלם שבח לאל בורא עולם

היום יום ו' פרשת וישמע יתרו י"ז שבט שצג לפ"ק

שער הספר והדף האחרון של הספר „משאת בנימין" מאת הרה"ג בנימין אהרן סלניק ז"ל (נדפס בשנת שצ"ג — 1633)
שער־בלאט און לעצטער דף פונם ספר „משאת בנימין" פון הרה"ג ר' בנימין סלניק ז"ל (געדרוקט אין יאר שצ"ג — 1633)

The cover page and last page of the book Masaat Binyamin, by the rabbi and Gaon Rabbi Binyamin Aharon Solnik of blessed memory. Published in 5383 – 1633

[Page 69]

Jews in Podhajce

It is difficult to assert when Jews first settled in Podhajce. According to Meir Balaban[*5], Jews arrived there during the 16th century. According to other sources, Jews came there much earlier. Two known Polish scholars state that the Jewish cemetery in Podhajce is much older than the Christian one, and that the oldest monuments date from the year 1420[*6]. Regarding the old times of the city, that same researcher mentions the "Interesting synagogue which is completely similar in structure to the local Greek Catholic church, which was built in the year 1650." According to the authors, the similarity is because the synagogue was first designated as a house of worship for the Aryans, and later given over to the Jews[*7]. In 1602, there was a rabbi there, which means that there was already an organized, independent Jewish community with a significant number of Jews. The rabbi was Rabbi Binyamin Aharon the son of Avraham Solnik, a known author of responsa under the name "Sefer Masaat Binyamin"[*8].

The Jews fought alongside the Christian population at the time of the battles around Podhajce, defending the walls of the city during the time of the siege in 1667. The same thing happened when the Turks invaded the city in 1672. Jews took part in defending a portion of the walls, and the remainder was defended by the Polish population of the city. The Turks invaded the city twice: on July 22, 1673 and in 1676. They razed the city to the ground, and some of the Jews who did not succeed in escaping or hiding were killed or taken prisoner[*9].

The Sejmik[2] in Halicz decided after that, on account of the service of the Jews in the war, to present a request to the chief Sejm in Warsaw to free the Miastszanes[3] and Jews of Podhajce for twelve years from paying royal taxes. The Sejm approved this on December 3, 1676[*10]. The Sejm in Warsaw dealt with this matter once again on April 18, 1701, and decided to continue to free the city from the aforementioned taxes for a longer time, for the city had suffered greatly from the battles in its area [*11].

During those years, the Jewish community played a great role in the spiritual life of Jewry. A full tier of rabbis and scholars lived and were active there. Since there was no printing press in Podhajce, they printed their books in outside cities that had printing presses, and they mentioned the name of their community on the title page. The book "Masaat Binyamin" by the aforementioned Rabbi Solnik was published in Krakow in Cheshvan of 5363 (1633)[4] by his grandson Rabbi Chaim Menachem Mann.

In 1672, the Turks crossed the Polish border and took over Podolia (below Podhajce). They remained there until the year 1699. They perpetrated a pogrom in the city in 1676. Many Jews were murdered, and others were taken prisoner. A selicha (penitential prayer) by Wolf the son of Rabbi Yehuda Leib remains and was published in the book "Gefen Yechudut" which was published in Berlin in the year 1699. When he later to Podhajce, the city was in disarray after the Pogrom that the Turks had perpetrated. The selicha begins with "Kel Maleh Rachamim"[5]. The Podhajce rabbi Moshe the son of Shabtai Cohen, who succeeded in escaping from prison, tells about it in the introduction to the book "Nekudot Hakesef" which was published in Frankfurt an der Oder in 1677[*12].

We know of the following from among other rabbis and sages who lived in Podhajce:

Yaakov the son of Baruch of Podhajce, the author of the book "Birchat Yaakov", which was published in Lvov in 5506 (1746).

Meshulam Zalman the head of the rabbinical court of the community of Podhajce, the son of Rabbi Leib the son of Shaul (approximately 5511 – 1751).

Yissachar HaMagid of Podhajce (from the same time). Yaakov Emdem considers him as an adherent of Sabbateanism, although "he is considered by them to be a great and pious man"[*13].

*

At the beginning of the 18th century, the Sabbatean Chaim Malach settled in Podhajce, and attracted a great number of adherents. Thanks to him, "Podhajce was an important center of Sabbateanism"[*14]. Another Sabbateanist was known – over and above the aforementioned Yissachar HaMagid of Podhajce – from a later generation, Rabbi Moshe David of Podhajce, who was born in Podhajce in the year 5456 (1696). A ban of excommunication was imposed upon him and he was forced to leave the city. He later settled in Altuna, Germany, where he died in the year 5526 (1766).

[Page 70]

There were Jews from Podhajce among those who became apostates at the time of the Frankist movement. In 1759, 508 Jews became apostates in 1759, including the following from Podhajce: David Leizerovitch, Jas (Josef) who took the new name Podajcki upon receiving his baptism. His daughter Malka also became an apostate and took on the name Mananna; the son of Moshko (Moshe) of Podhajce took on the name Franciscus Seraficus, Pesach from Podhajce – Josefus Piesecki, his son Moshko (Moshe) Lodowicius, his daughter Dvora changed her name to Roza Bananenzis. Chava the maid of Moshko also became an apostate and took on the name Manannia Szajnska, her second daughter took on the name Saloma Anna Piasecka. Another Jew, Moshko, took on the name Tomasz Elazanius Podhajciecki, his wife – Mananna There was also a seven year old girl among those who became apostates. She took on the name Franciska Bonawentura Podhajciecka.

In 1760, Yankel the son of Aharon became an apostate and took on the name Gregorius Jakubowski da Podhajce, and Pesia Ickowicz took on the name Franciska Benedictus Aranska. On November 9, 1760, Anna the daughter of Shimon and Zofia Jablonski became an apostate in Kamenetz-Podolsk. Her parents had become apostates earlier. Aside from these, others Podhajce Jews became apostates on other occasions, such as Zofia Podhajiecka, and others. According to Polish statutes, the apostates became members of the nobility, which means they joined the ranks of the szlachta[6]. This is also indicated by their names. We find important Polish aristocrats among those who were baptized[*15]. The text of the oath was in Polish.

*

The final rabbi of Podhajce in independent Poland was Rabbi Hirsch (Tzvi) the son of Berl Dov. His name is included among the list of Jews in Podhajce that was produced through the census of 1765.

After Galicia was taken over by the Austrians, the center – not only administrative – transferred to the regional city of Berezhany, where the seat of the headquarters of the regional rabbinate was located. Only an "ordinary" rabbi, a religious leader, remained in Podhajce. However, his salary was more than the other rabbis in the other communities, aside from Berezhany. It is no surprise that the city grew with it scholars, and with its high cultural and moral achievements. The emphasis often stemmed from the great bygone generations, the writers and correspondents of the city, who had written in the various Jewish and Hebrew journals for decades. A. David Polisiuk writes in Hamagid in 1876 that Podhajce is not like the other surrounding towns which sit in darkness and are shielded from the world so that no new light would Heaven forbid penetrate into them. On the contrary, Podhajce acts like the large cities, moving toward progress and the ways of the Haskala.

In Tishrei 5666 (1876), an organization was founded in Podhajce with the purpose of "reading the periodicals in the holy tongue and the vernacular." It rented two rooms in an appropriate house, in which the members gathered together every day. The name of the organization was "Meeting Place of Jewish Citizens" (In German: Izraelitishes Bergerliches Kasino").

After enumerating the activities regarding obtaining certification from the civic administrator in Lemberg, and enumerating those who stand at the head, the correspondence ends with a call to the small towns: "Look at the city of Podhajce, take note and do as it does. Arise from the slumber of folly. Wake up and become like people who know how to differentiate between the light of intelligence and the darkness of the fool, and then you will be called a wise and understanding nation."

The same correspondent did not neglect to send other correspondences to the same periodical, about their other important problems. He always invokes the great past of Jewish Podhajce.

After Austria took over Galicia, the situation of the Jews deteriorated. The country was cut off from its earlier sources and had not yet set up contact with the rest of Austria. The Jews also had to become accustomed to the higher taxes that were imposed upon them by the Austrian regime, and also to the national projects to Europeanize them.

[Page 71]

A new tribulation crept up; they began to draft the Jews to the army (1788), and one was able to evade the draft for a fee. The money had to go to a middleman. We know that in the year 1853, the community members gathered in Podhajce and decided that in order to collect the tax to free the community from the army, they would impose a special surcharge on flour for matzos, which would go to the communal coffers. All merchants who dealt with salt similarly decided to impose a special fee for that purpose. In 1855, anyone who would not abide by that decision was threatened with a ban[*15]. Later, the Jews had to give over either money or a quote of people. In 1852, the region of Berezhany had to provide 58 soldiers (1,281 in all of Galicia). In 1878, general military duty was imposed upon the Jews in a similar fashion to the gentile community (from age 21). This applied to all healthy males, without exception.

The Jews had the duty to pay the various taxes: for candle lighting on Friday nights, for having a wedding, for kosher meat, etc. Cliques were formed which ruled over the community and used the Jews for their own self-benefit. Clashes arose between the head of the community and the Jews. In 1855, the head of the community was even removed from his office by the regime[*16].

As well, the communal elections were not democratic. The voters were divided into categories; who belonged to the intelligentsia, who paid the most taxes – these are just a few – belonged to a higher curio which elected a greater number of members to the communal council than the lower curios to which belonged the masses and the remainder of the residents who paid the lowest taxes (known as etat). The communal elections themselves – Galician elections were a byword – were rife with forgery, just like the general elections. Those whom the authorities approved of were elected. Thus was the situation in the Austrian era, and thus was the situation later under the Poles.

With this situation, there was friction between Jews until the outbreak of the First World War; the Jewish community became the seat of backward elements, and was run for the most part by designated officials. This came to an end after the rise of Poland, when democratic elections were conducted, and every individual had only one vote.

However, new tribulations began at that time. The authorities would interfere with the elections, and not approve all candidates. On occasion, especially in the later years, they would dissolve the communal council if they found something inappropriate in their eyes. Instead of elected members, they would nominate a government commissar who would rule with the power of the regime behind him.

In general, the community concerned itself solely with religious matters, with everything else being run by the Polish decree. The community took the name "Gmeina Wyzaniowa", and had to concern itself solely with the religious needs of the community: a cheder, a rabbi, a cemetery, a bathhouse, and the like, and to some degree with social assistance.

If at times the community allocated in its budget a specific sum for a worldly cause, such as a secular school, the national funds, and the like, the Starosta would impose penalties, and in such a case, appeals to the Wojewoda[7], to the higher authorities or the interior minister would not help

If the authorities approved of a communal head, he would remain in his position without elections for a long time, not infrequently until death. This would especially be the case in smaller cities. There were also cases, often connected with livelihood, where the honor was transmitted hereditarily.

The head of the community of Podhajce at the beginning of the 20th century was Leib Rottenberg. He remained in office until the beginning of the world war.

In independent Poland, the Zionists would enter the communal elections with their own list. Eventually, they did so in cooperation with like minded organizations. However, during the elections, they were not able to obtain the approval of the Starosta, without whose approval the elections would not take place. A regime commissar would be appointed from among the assimilationists, who was, of course, from the "Party of the Regime".

Such a commissar existed in Podhajce in the year 1927. His name was Ratner. He was a wealthy Jew, and he threatened that whoever would not vote for his list during the elections (which the regime finally confirmed after intervention from the Jewish nationalist elements) would be persecuted. The Polish administration had the appropriate means to do this, and they would gladly apply it against Jews whom they could easily accuse of anti-government activities, etc.[*17]. They could also take other frightening actions, such as removing concessions, raising the government taxes, etc.

[Page 72]

The "Cywila" writes regarding Ratner's machinations (May 13, 1927) that he agreed that only 260 Jews would take part in the list of those entitled to participate in the elections., and after reclamations, it was agreed to register another 180 names. In total, this was 440 who were registered for the election, at a time when their numbers in the city were more than one thousand. These were the known tactics that were used in Galicia earlier during the elections to the Austrian parliament, to the Landrat of Galicia, and so on.

With the intention to help "his" party, the Starosta forbade the use of Yiddish in the election rallies. This made the publicity work more difficult, for the Jewish masses did not understand any Polish. When Dr. Adolf Rothfeld from Lvov, a member of the Zionist executive in Poland, came to an election rally and spoke in Yiddish, The delegate of the Starosta interrupted him and did not let him speak until Dr. Rothfeld would switch to Polish. At the beginning of his speech, he stated that he would raise an interpellation about this in the Polish Sejm

The Zionist organization achieved victory in the communal elections of 1933. They won five mandates (Engineer David Lileh, Dr. Zalman Dik, Michael Kohn, Chaim Lehrer, and Moshe Weintraub). On the other hand, the list of the Husyatiner Hassidim won only one mandate, as did the Yad Charutzim (workers) and the Aguda, who elected the assimilationist Tovia Ratner[*18].

However, the victory did not last for long, for the authorities dissolved the communal council and nominated the court officer Pastel as a government commissar. He immediately removed all allocations from the community budget that were designated for Jewish national interests[*19].

In an article from Podhajce that was published in the Cywila of Lemberg in those times, the communal activities were described. It seems that they conducted all of their activities in an orderly fashion. They chose a special committee chaired by Ch. Funken in order to renovate and improve the old cemetery. They helped the Gemilut Chasadim fund, the committee for social assistance, etc.

[Page 72]

2. The Number of Jews in Podhajce

From what we can see, it appears that Jews were the majority already at the beginning of the 17th century. We are missing further details, but we can deduce that there was never any shortage of them. Neither the Polish government nor communal institutions knew this at that time. It is possible that the Jewish community itself did not even know this. We have a sign of this, for in order to know precisely the head-tax of the Jews, the Polish government had to conduct a Jewish census in Poland. In the second half of the 18th century, shortly after the first partition of Poland in 1765, we have the first official (however less precise) number of "Jewish heads" in Podhajce, despite the fact that we had the right to take sufficient precautions during the election for various reasons.

According to the census of 1765, there were 1,290 Jews in Podhajce itself, and 1,548 in the entire region. In 1870, the Austrian regime conducted a census every ten years. We bring down here a table of the general population of the city, and the number of the Jewish population, as well as the percent of Jews in the general population from the years 1870-1939.

Questions of religion, nationality and mother town were a very important part of the population censuses in Galicia.

Until 1910, Austria did not recognize the Yiddish language in the censuses, and the Jews had to indicate one of the official languages, mainly Polish or German. Thus, in the census of 1900 it came out that 76.56% of the Jews of Galicia speak Polish, 10% German, and the rest "European" languages.

[Page 73]

Year	General Population	Jewish Population	%
1870	4,570	2,742	60.0
1880	5,943	4.012	67.5
1890	5,646	3,879	68.7
1900	5,790	3,757	64.9
1910	5,576	3,497	62.7
1921	4,814	2,872	59.7
1931	5,743	3,124	54.4
1939	6,000	3,155	53.0

Even later, during the time of the Polish regime, when Yiddish was recognized as a language, the official Polish authorities made efforts to reduce the number of Yiddish speakers. In the census of 1921, 2,872 residents of Podhajce registered themselves as Jewish by religion, but only 2,543 Jews chose Yiddish or Hebrew as their mother tongue. It is hard to believe that in such a Jewish town as Podhajce, there were indeed 329 Jews who considered themselves to be Poles and spoke Polish in their homes.

Dr. Avraham Stop continues along this theme in the Book of Tluste, and writes the following anecdote: A Hassidic Jew entered the conscription office along with an escort who must instruct him what to say. The Polish officer asks him what type of education he has, what language does he speak to his children, what type of books he reads. The Hassid must ask his guide after every question, "What is the master saying?" Finally the officer asked the Hassid what nationality he should register him as. The escort responded, "You see that he is a Pole, write down Polish..."

3. With what do the Jews of Podhajce Occupy Themselves

We do not have precise information about this. The question is almost unsolvable to this day. From the fragments we can surmise that during the years 1876-81, in the entire area, there were: 5 glazers, 3 lathers, 1 clockmaker, 17 blacksmiths, 7 pot makers (clay pots), 1 brick maker, 4 bakers, 2 butchers, 2 greizler[8], 6 millers, 17 liquor distillers, 12 tailors, 16 shoemakers, 5 furriers, 2 bednares[8], 13 carpenters, 7 pharmacists, 1 bathhouse attendant, 5 coachmen, 10 barbers and surgeons (the two occupations went together), 2 mechanics and opticians, 18 plough makers and wheelwrights, 1 bag and net maker, 1 weaver, 3 wheel makers, 9 restaurateurs.

As we know from other cities as well, most of the tradesmen were Jews. The statistics do not support this[*20]. Altogether there were 1,281 tradesmen in Podhajce.

The following merchants were in the region: 4 iron merchants, 12 salt merchants (a government monopoly), 21 mill professionals (apparently they worked independently and thereby were considered as millers), 1 liquor merchant, 78 propinators (innkeeper or tavern keeper), 1 linen merchant, and 1 agent.

The following were in the free professions: 1 notary, 7 brokers, 1 leaser of forests for cutting, 1 owner brewery owner, 13 owners of mines, 27 leasers of goods and speculators[*21], 3 wood handlers, 3 owners of brick kilns, 59 small scale businessmen, 13 fur and leather traders, 9 meal and cereal businessmen, 26 mill owners, 2 merchants of women's dresses, 1 chimneysweep, 42 wheat tradesmen, 5 silk and cloth tradesmen, 5 tradesman of spices and similar items, 3 tradesmen of axle grease, 3 tradesmen of clay pots, 2 dealers in second hand clothing, 3 cattle merchants, 3 tradesman of tar.

The following industrial enterprises were located the area: 1 beer brewery in Podhajce, 16 mines (one in Podhajce), 8 pot makers in Podhajce, 24 watermills, one factory of agricultural machines in Siulki.

The general problem of employing Jews in practical jobs began to be discussed during the final years of Poland's independence at the time of the Four Year Sejm (1768-1772). Of course,

nothing came of it. After that, when Austria took over a portion of Poland, primarily Galicia, the ruler (at first Maria Theresa, then her son Kaiser Josef II) attempted to change the occupations and means of livelihood of the Jews. At the same time, they tried to attract them to agriculture. However, almost nothing came of this. According to the plan, in the year 1786, in the entire region of Berezhany, 64 families had to settle in the countryside. In fact, there were only 40 Jewish farmers in the year 1822. 16 did so with their own means, and 24 with the help of the community[*22]. Later, the number further declined.

Regarding shopkeepers and stall owners – In the entire region of Berezhany, in the year 1826, there were 1,827, of whom 1,820 were Jews; in 1827 there were 2,015, of whom 1,824 were Jews[*23]. At that time, in the entire region there were 18 merchants with their own firms, of whom 17 were Jews[*24].

[Page 74]

This situation did not change much until the final years. New tradesman and new merchants arrived. Their numbers grew. However, a new domain arrived – the free professions. Podhajce had a relatively large intelligentsia, with many lawyers, doctors, ordinary students, and those who had already concluded their studies but who could not find any work due to the attitude of the Polish regime towards the Jews.

The first lawyer who settled in Podhajce was – it seems – Rudolf Schwager, who had an office there until the outbreak of the First World War. We find his name in the Jewish folk's calendar of Gershom Bader (for the years 1905-1909). In the same timeframe, that same source mentions two doctors: Arnold Landau and Michael Salpeter (we can note that the first names of the members of the Jewish intelligentsia were assimilated). Prior to the First World War, Dr. Wilhelm Neuman was in Fuchuk.

Prior to the Second World War, more than ten people were engaged in those two professions.

4. The Final Rabbis of the City

In the Hebrew periodical Halevanon (Mainz)[*24] from the year 1878, we find n the section "From the Writings of Writers" a correspondence written from Podhajce by David Polisiuk, who was already known to us. In the beginning, he writes about the city of Podhajce as it once was: "What we had from days of yore, and what we lost and are lacking at this time, our fathers told us and we know them, and our elders told us, this time it is told to you: In days of yore, our community was at the pinnacle of its splendor, like all the large and faithful communities. They were not lacking in righteousness, uprightness, Torah and wisdom. We still hear a lofty voice speaking words from the commentaries of the son of the Gaon the author of Siftei Kohen, and how golden are his words: My place of rest in strength used to be in the holy community of Podhajce, a pleasant community, a city with everything in it, the Divine Torah is in it, it is a faithful and praiseworthy city, from it stemmed people of wisdom and understanding (from his preface to the Code of Jewish Law, Yoreh Deah section, printed in Lvov, 5625, 1865). The head of our community was the Gaon the author of Masaat Binyamin – a mighty lion crouched there by the name of Lev Aryeh who was a light sown for the righteous." After him the Rabbi and Gaon Rabbi Natan Neta Galitzer of blessed memory held the rabbinic seat. He was fearless, and openly stamped out any bad thing. He died approximately 40 years ago, and left behind a grandson, Rabbi Shimon Meller, a young man. The elders of the city were against making him their rabbi: "How can they set their eyes upon such a young rabbi who is still a lad". However, the "brazen men of the generation raised their foreheads", and they "helped him with their strong hands to ascend the rabbinic seat despite the will of the righteous and pure ones". Now he is already old. He has left the city and moved to Stanislawow, where he inherited a large fortune and a large house from his father. The city heaved a sigh of relief, believing that now they would choose a new, capable rabbi. "However we erred apparently", for the rabbi left behind a son, Rabbi Yonah, who was still quite young. The entire population of the city opposed giving him the crown of the rabbinate." His father came to his assistance, "and dispersed money like dust among the wealthy people of our city." All of them suddenly agreed to the new rabbi, and inscribed their consent."

This picture is too dark to be true, and we wonder why the Levanon printed such a letter at all. From other places, we have other opinions against the Meller rabbis (see the article about the rabbis in our book). His son, Rabbi Yonah Meller, was a rabbi for a long time (until the end of the 19th century), and the shochtim (ritual slaughterers) were happy with him.

Following him, Rabbi Shalom HaKohen Lilienfeld[*25] became the rabbi in the city. There are many stories about him, which in some cases border on the miraculous. At the beginning of 1906, the Ruthenians wished to make a large assembly

in the city, and this threatened the Jews of the city as well as the provincial residents with a great danger. The rabbi and Gaon Rabbi Shalom Lilienfeld HaKohen, the head of the rabbinical court of our city, saved them. How so? First, he went with the head of the community to the Starosta to request help. He promised to help. But what could 20-30 policemen do against myriads? The rabbi, however, calmed down the community, urging them not to flee from the city, "For the rabbi is also expert in matters of state, just as he is in the gates of Torah and science." The events took place like this:

[Page 75]

The Ukrainians did not have a place to hold their rally, for the Poles did not want to give over their Sukol Hall. The Ukrainians were enraged. What did the rabbi do? He gave his own house. "Despite the will of the Poles who always were careful about his honor, he took a dangerous step, one of self-sacrifice. He turned over the hall of his large house to them." When the Ruthenians gathered together, approximately ten thousand men and women, and the hall seemed too small, "our rabbi permitted the chief spokesman Dr. Bachinski to ascend to his roof through the large hall, from where he spoke for several hours."

And he, who was supposed to talk against the Jews, spoke in favor of the Jews and against the Poles. He said the following about the Jews: "Our brethren the Jews are brothers to us in this tribulation. They are also suffering under the burden of this nation... And we must love them with brotherly love – it is a shame upon the Poles. Give honor to the Jews." The crowd, hearing such a speech, was calmed down. The author of the correspondence writes unassumingly, under the name "Afikoman".

In the year 1907, Rabbi Shalom HaKohen Lilienfeld issued a proclamation to the Jews that tens of thousands of them should sign a petition to Kaiser Franz Josef, asking him to repeal the new "procedure" whereby Jews can be summoned to court on the Sabbath to give testimony. "Is it not known that the government is not content with those who throw off the yoke of Torah and commandments, and this is the way to protect the religion and its adherents? The rabbis should arouse themselves to present a request to the high government to repeal these improper procedures[*26].

After the death of Rabbi Lilienfeld, no new rabbi was chosen. A group of three rabbinic judges took his place.

5. Eminent Householders

At the end of the book "Kach Yevarech Yisrael" (Thus Shall Israel be Blessed) that was published by the rabbi of Jezierna L. Y. Manzan, Przemysl 1905 we the following names from the residents of Podhajce among the "name of prominent ones" who contributed money toward the publication of the book to enable its publication.

The renowned rabbi and Gaon Rabbi Shalom Lilienfeld, the head of the rabbinical court:

Rabbi Yosef Bergman
Rabbi Pinchas Hecht
Rabbi Reuven Helfandbein

I believe that among the Holocaust survivors of Podhajce, there are still people who remember these Jews and who can tell us who they are.

In Hamagid (1906), we find other articles, aside from those written by the aforementioned Polisiuk, written by the maskil Chaim Moshe Silberschitz from Podhajce.

Other correspondents, of that time or from an earlier time, often conceal themselves with “witty” pseudonyms. However, usually, the people in the city knew very well who they were. The correspondent himself made sure of this.

6. Zionism

Anti-Semitism grew greatly in Galicia at the end of the 19th century. The main reason was the difficult economic situation of the population, especially the peasants who did not have their own land, or had very little of it. In Podhajce, there was another reason for this: the Jewish agricultural workers of the Polish landowners.

In 1891 in Podhajce, two assimilated Jews leased land from an insurance company in Krakow. The Polish aristocracy complained against this and demanded that the contract be annulled. They organized a unified and open protest against this. As well, the Polish newspapers spoke out sharply against the “foreigners”, and in connection to this, conducted anti-Semitic agitation directed toward the peasant masses. Because of this agitation, the Polish landowner classes had to fight against the Socialist streams that were beginning to spread at this time, as well as against those, non small number of whom were Jews, who were propagandists-theoreticians or ordinary requestors. The Polish anti-Semitic parties declared a boycott against Jewish businessmen, and in general against Jewish economic institutions, such as banks and the like.

On the other hand, the will of the Jews not to leave things be grew. Many Jewish assimilationists who had hoped that, with the help of the Polish sympathizers, they would obtain full equal rights and assimilate into the public, recanted, to Jewry and became disseminators of Haskala and progress amongst Jews. In 1881, Yehuda Leib Alerhand and Shaul Schorr founded in Podhajce an affiliate of the Israelite Alliance of Vienna, which had 40 members from Podhajce and the region. They collected money and sent it to the center in Vienna with the purpose of helping only those who would be making aliya to the Land of Israel, rather than general Jewish emigrants who are traveling to America[*27]. Aside from this, the affiliate turned through Hamagid (number 29, from July 26, 1892) to all other affiliates of the Israelite Alliance suggesting that they also designate their collected money solely for those who are making aliya to the Land of Israel[*28].

[Page 76]

Teachers and students of the general public school

Members of Hanoar Hatzioni in Podhajce

Members of the Hechalutz organization in the year 1931

[Page 77]

The words quickly led to action. In November 1898, 11 Jews were sent from Galicia to the Land of Israel to settle in the Moshava of Machanaim. Elyakim Getzl Perl of Podhajce, a 30 year old man, was among them. They arrived in the Land of Israel on December 1, 1898[*29].

We also find Podhajce in the list of the 75 chapters of the Zionist organization in Galicia of those years. Binyamin Kutner of the Zion organization of Podhajce was among those chosen to the regional committee of the Zionist Organization of Galicia, whose seat was in Lemberg[*30].

The yearly annual meeting of the Zionist organization took place in October of that year, in which the old committee (whose secretary was Y. Messer) was dismissed, and a new one was chosen consisting of: chairman Binyamin Kutner, vice chairman – B. Margolies, secretary – L. Salpeter, treasurer – L. Lilienfeld, librarian – M. Kohn, economic matters ("Gospodash") – Y. Falber, and members without special functions – K. Sternshuss, Y. Wolf, Y. Zeidler, H. Milch, and Y. Shapira[*31].

In December of that year, we read in Woschod number 49 from December 6, 1905 that a private Hebrew school, a Talmud Torah, was established. The correspondent from Podhajce announces that in that school they study like in the former cheders, and suggests that the Zionist organization should take responsibility for that school.

They conducted publicity work among the masses, collections for the Zionist funds, cultural work, readings, performances, etc. The organization remained in a constant battle against the Jewish socialist Party (Zydowska Partija, Socialistitszna), which worked hand in hand with the Polish Socialist Party and struggled against the idea of Zionism. There were organized evenings in Podhajce in which members of each party spoke. In one such evening, M. Schorr spoke sharply against the representative Dr. Buch. The crowed agreed with the speaker, and the opponent lost the opportunity[*32].

On another occasion, in December 1905, Zion helped conduct a mourning program regarding the pogroms in Russia. Rabbi Lilienfeld, and Messrs. Marienberg and Schorr delivered speeches. Money was also collected for the displaced people[*33].

A convention of Poale Zion took place in Podhajce in the year 1906[*34].

In 1907, at the time of the elections to the Austrian parliament, the Zionist candidate Dr. Gabel came to Podhajce to deliver his political speech. However the rabbi of the city did not allow him into the synagogue. The assimilationists who were in confederation with the Poles – in a factional publicity page in German, they were called "Jews who were enemies of the regime" – were supported by the Orthodox. They conducted their election campaign using such means.

However, the Zionists did not give in, and they finally convinced the rabbi to permit the election rally to take place in the synagogue. Dr. Henryk Gabel came once again to Podhajce. A large crowd came to hear him, including many Ruthenians (Ukrainians), with whom the Zionist organization was in confederation for the elections[*35].

In the elections of that year, Dr. Henryk Gabel was indeed election n the region of Buczacz, Monasterzyska and Podhajce. Aside from him, two other Zionist deputies were elected from Eastern Galicia: Dr. Adolf Stand and Dr. Arthur Miller.

[Page 78]

Members of the Hechalutz organization in the year 1931

Lineup in the summer camp of Young Achva near Berezhany

Young Achva in Podhajce

[Page 79]

On the other hand, not one Zionist candidate was elected n the later elections of 1911. The following assimilationists were elected: Stern (from the region of Buczacz), and Dr. Steinhaus (from Zolkiew – Rawa Ruska – Sokol). The system of Galician elections worked in such a good manner.

In December 1910, Zion organized a Chanukah evening in Freundlich's large hall. The hall was overflowing. Y. Schorr from Lvov and Sh. Margolies from Podhajce spoke. In the artistic segments, artists from Lemberg performed[*36].

The Zionist organization conducted its work in this manner within the political-cultural realm at that time, and was more advanced than larger cities in Eastern Galicia.

The Zionist organization grew strongly during the Polish era, after the First World War. The Z.P.S. disappeared, and the Jewish national workers parties came in its place: Poale Zion, left and right, the Bund and the “Reds”.

The city remained a nationalist Zionist city until the end, and therefore its Jews suffered not infrequently, first from the organ of the regime (Starosta), and from the assimilationists, whose numbers were negligible, but whose power and influence over the regime and communal organ was large.

The vast majority of the Jews from the city took part in all the Zionist funds, and also in the Zionist observances (20th of Tammuz, the Balfour Declaration, and general events the proceeds of which were designated to Zionist purposes.) The Zionist deputies of the Sejm were often invited to report on current events, etc. (Somerstein in August 1934, etc.)

For the most part, the general open ceremonies took place in the synagogue. At times, a major speaker was brought in from Lvov (on the 20th of Tammuz, 1927, the Sejm deputy Dr. Bernard Hausner, etc.) Aside from the general Zionist organizations, other Zionist organizations were active in Podhajce, but their influence was much smaller.

As well, the youth organizations such as Achva, Hashomer Hatzair, and Haover conducted their activities in the city.

Achva was the largest youth organization. It had its own chapter in Podhajce, and published its own publication called Gloss Achwai. According to number 4 (July 1935), three members from Podhajce were to travel to the Land of Israel that month: L. Fisch, L. Scherer, and G. Hessel. Aside from this, there was a "den of youths" in Podhajce, the number of members of which reached 65. In 1935, that chapter organized a Hachsharah in Nadworna, and in the year 1936 it organized two summer colonies: Ormien near Berezhany and Sielce near Sokol.

7. Schools

In the former independent Poland, the regime did not involve itself at all with the education of Jewish children. The Jews themselves concerned themselves with this. Later, when Austria took over the government, strong ordinances were issued the aim of which was to Europeanize the Jews in general, along with the children and school graduates. They began to persecute the cheders and melamdim, and encouraged the Jewish youth to seek out the government schools and to learn the vernacular as well as the government language. Of course, the Jews tried as much as possible to evade these edicts.

We bring the following anecdotes which describe how the Austrian regime dealt with those areas.

In 1806, there were 533 Jewish children in the government schools in the entire region of Berezhany[*38]. We first find Jewish children in the open schools approximately 80 years later when the statute regarding compulsory education was issued. In the meantime, Jews studied, as always, in cheders, Talmud Torahs, Yeshivas, or alone under the supervision of their fathers, grandfathers, or other good and pious Jews.

Even later, at the end of the 19th century, modern (private) Jews schools began to appears, which complemented the general government schools with Jewish studies, or they had permission from the government to completely replace it[9].

From the former Austrian official statistics[*39], it can be seen that in the Podhajce region, there were the following Hebrew schools:

[Page 80]

Year	1894 - 1895	1897 - 1898	1899 - 1900	1901 - 1902	1905 - 1906
Schools	2	3	3	5	6
Teachers	2	3	3	5	6
Students	44	70	72	145	149

There was no Baron Hirsch school in Podhajce. It seems like this pious town was against founding such a school. The Baron Hirsch foundation supported six students here, who studied trades with various tradesmen during the 1903-1905 school years. The Hirsch allocations supported them and paid for their studies.

A yearly accounting was published by the foundation in Vienna from 1896 to 1914. There was a synagogue in the city called the Baron Hirsch Shul. It is possible that it was established in a house that had been dedicated as a school, but this did not come to be.

In 1904, a General Talmud Torah was set up in Podhajce through Rabbi Lilienfeld. A notice about this was published in Hamagid (December 1, 1905, number 8): "For the children of the poor and rich together, set up with proper order and appropriate and effective supervision." There were six classes in the school. "Every student will study at the appropriate grade level. The subjects include: a through knowledge of our holy tongue, Bible, Mishna (Berachot, Pesachim, Yoma, Sukka, Beitza, and Megilla)[10]. Simple Gemara (tractate Berachot), Gemara with the Tosafot and Rosh (tractate Pesachim)." Every subject is taught in a designated hour according to the curriculum: "And in every grade there are two teachers, one who supervises the order to ensure that the students pay attention to their studies, and one to teach the appropriate lesson – and over them is a head teacher – a principal who is in charge of examining the students on their studies at every occasion." Both Hassidim and enlightened people study at the school. The rabbi and Gaon Rabbi Shalom HaKohen may he live long took interest in the Talmud Torah. He sent emissaries to find out how the Talmud Torah is conducted, and apparently, he also visited himself. (Hamitzpeh, February 16, 1906).

The renowned Admor, Rabbi Yitzchak Meir Heshel may he live long of Kopachintsy, came to Podhajce in the year 1906. He examined the students, and was very happy with the situation. He donated 26 crown to the school, and before he left the city, he gave a 20 crown gold coin to the chief advisor of the school, Mr. Kutner, as well as all the money he had collected through his visit[11], which was greater than 100 crown. He also gave 13 crown to "support the poor in the hospital with kosher food" (Hamagid, February 23, 1906). The article was sent to the newspaper by Netanel Shechter, the secretary of the General Hospital.

Interest in the Hebrew school, and for learning and understanding Hebrew, grew as well with the growth of the activity of the Zionist organizations.

(In 1931, the school had 250 children and 3 teachers – Cywila, May 22, 1931.)

8. Credit Institutions

In 1929, the communal council established a charitable fund. According to an accounting that was given to the general meeting of the membership in May 1931, throughout the duration of two years, interest free loans to the sum of 20,000 zloty were given out. Over 150 merchants and tradesmen benefited from this. The fund was supported by the constant support of the communal council[*40].

About a year later, a cooperative bank was established, which decided to affiliate itself with the Jewish cooperatives of Poland. The headquarters of the Zwi¹zek ¯ydowskich Spó³dzielni (Association of Jewish Cooperatives) was located in Warsaw, and the headquarters for eastern Galicia was located in Lvov. The bank called Zwi¹zek Kredytowy Spó³dzielczy (Cooperative Credit Union) was founded in the year 1930. According to the balance from the year 1932, the turnover was 70,445.12 zloty; the revenue was 2,204.01 (Przegland Spó³dzielczy year 7, number 1). In 1933, the sum shrank to only 30,190.02 zloty. This fact also points to the economic destruction of the Jews in the town.

9. Podhajce "Duckmakers"

In S³ownik Geograficzny (Geographical Lexicon), in the section which discussed Podhajce, the Jews were given such a "compliment": "The Jews of Podhajce were known for their cunning in business and their dishonesty." I do not know the basis upon which the author issued such a judgment. He offers no substantiation or corroboration, so I believe that he arrived at that conclusion from the words that he certainly heard: "Podhajce Duckmakers" (Certainly that expression also existed, in some form or another, in Ukrainian.)

That source of expression was imparted (in writing as well) in various forms[*41]. I wish to give over as well the variant that I heard from my mother (a niece, the daughter of the brother of the Gaon of Berezhany Rabbi Shalom Mordechai HaKohen), and also from the region from my childhood in Borszczow.

[Page 81]

A gentile from the town came to the fair in Podhajce to sell a calf. He stood for a very long time, and nobody approached him. Finally a butcher approached him and asked him: "What do you want for the duck?" The gentile became very angry and shouted at the Jew that it was a calf and not a duck. The Jew went away. The gentile continued further on until he came to another Jew, who asked the same question. The gentile left him also in anger, but already with a quieter voice. This continued for a third and fourth time, until the gentile came to the conclusion that it might indeed be a duck and not a calf, since so many people said this. When a Jew approached him at the very end of the fair, the gentile did not argue with him, but only demanded a good price for the duck. They conducted the usual business negotiations, until the Jew finally purchased the merchandise. Both businessmen went on their ways, and both were happy: the Jew because he purchased a calf cheaply, and the gentile because he received a good price for the... duck.

10. City Council

As they did with the elections to the community, the Jews campaigned for their representatives on the city council. First and foremost the opponents were the Poles and Ukrainians, and following that, the Jews against each other. Often, the Jewish side attempted to create a general Jewish block in order to increase the chances of the Jews.

At times, they also attempted to form a coalition with the Poles and Ukrainians in order to create a common list, but this did not always succeed.

Such a unified list was formed during the 1927 elections to the city council. The Jews had 29 mandates, the Poles 11 (7 Miestszanes, 4 Endekes), and the Ukrainians 4 (Anda).

The following are the names of those elected: 17 Zionists: David Lile, Dr. Shlomo Dik, Dr. Malvina Landauawa, Binyamn Zeidler, Mechel Kohn, Oszias Gottesman, Dr. Zygmunt Rottenberg, Dr. Nathan Reichman, David Cimet, Hirsch Moshe Weintraub, Moshe Liblich, Dr. Avraham Finkel, Moshe Orenstein, Magister Shmuel Eker, Chaim Funk, Julius Hassenkorn, Dr. Leon Salpeter; 10 Nationalist Jews: Dr. Henryk Notik, Shmuel Fisher, Avraham Moshe Ridkes, David Lilienfeld, Tovia Ratner, Oscar Haber, Chaim Lerer, Dr. Leon Gross, Suesia Kahn, Dr. Julius Fell; 2 non-aligned: Herzl Falber, Eliahu Rasmak.

The magistrate chose a Pole as mayor, and Engineer David Lile as deputy mayor.

In May 1931, the city council was dissolved and a government commissar was put in place with a nominated council (Cywila, May 22, 1931). On the first meeting of the council, after the opening of the meeting by the commissar, the Jewish representative Dr. Salpeter took the floor and protested that there is only one Jewish representative on the council whereas in the previous vote, there were 29 Jews out of 48 city councilors. (Cywila, May 15, 1931).

In the elections which finally took place in May 1934, the Poles received 8 mandates (Sanacia – 5, Endekes – 3), the Ukrainians received 2, and the Jews received 6 (4 Zionists, 1 Orthodox, and 1 assimilationist). (Neue Morgan, May 30, 1934).

11. The Final Years before the Destruction

In a correspondence from Podhajce that appeared in the Neue Morgan on June 22, 1932, the correspondent (whose pseudonym was R-D) complains that the economic crisis caused the destruction of Jewish existence. Many businesses closed or transformed their stores to... soda water.

[Page 82]

The credit institutions of the city included the Gemilut Chasadim fund and the cooperative bank, which were created from local funds with the aim of mitigating the need of the fallen merchants and tradesmen. They granted loans with good conditions, but this was too small. According to the article the community itself became impoverished. Nevertheless, they tried to help in whatever ways were possible: good subsidies for orphans; providing wood for winter; matzos for Passover as well as potatoes and financial support; proper free prescriptions for the ill. However, this was not sufficient.

This picture, completely depressing, which incidentally was not limited to the city of Podhajce, was from the year 1932. From that time, the situation for the Jews certainly did not improve, and anti-Semitism increased in Poland especially after Hitler came to power in Germany. There were calls for an economic boycott against the Jews. Political machinations of the government also increased, both from the political parties and the incited masses.

The situation came to physical actions against the Jews. The Jew did not feel secure with his life when he saw that the economic basis of his existence was going under. The national cooperatives of the Poles and the Ukrainians who wanted to establish their own economic life on firm grounds, for their own reasons, became more independent and wished to distance the gentiles from the Jewish stores, the Jewish workplaces, and the Jewish intelligentsia.

The Jew felt impoverished, abandoned and alone. His entire hope was for Jewish unity, for the eventual assistance that the Jews abroad would be able to give him, but this too was not sufficient. The need was too great. People began to look for the possibility to leave Poland. However, the world was locked to Jewish immigrants. Even the gates of Palestine were locked for Jews. Only a few fortunate people were able to go there.

Such was the situation of the Jews in our area at the time when the Second World War broke out to the misfortune of the world and to the Jews in particular. This decisively destroyed the Jewish community in Poland, simply wiping it off the map.

12. The Podhajce Landsmanschaften (Societies) in America

A brief overview of the Podhajce organization in America in the year 1939 – just before the outbreak of the Second World War[*42].

1. Congregation Masaat Binyamin Anshei Podhajce was founded in the year 1895 with 25 members. In 1938, it had 200 members. It had a mixed makeup, with 10% being American born. The language of its meetings was Yiddish. Its aim was to maintain its own synagogue, to have a plot in the cemetery, to engage in mutual help, and to support local philanthropic institutions. Its secretary was Gelle.
2. Congregation Rodef Shalom Anshei Podhajce was founded in 1900 with 30 members. In 1938, it had 200 members. 75% were workers, 20% were American born, and 5% were not natives of the city. The purpose of the organization was to support the old home and local institutions, and to maintain their own synagogue and cemetery. The secretary was Joe Weiser. It had only 170 members in 1939. That year, they sent 1,600 dollars to the old home for Maos Chittin (Passover assistance)[*43].
   They supported their native city with 1,500 dollars a year. Aside from this, they maintained a fund for their own members who were in need. The secretary of the organization was A. Freundlich.
3. The Podhajce Young Men's Benefit Association was founded in 1901 with 50 members. It had 125 members in 1938. The majority were workers. 2% of them were not Podhajcers (they were from the region, or they married Podhajcers). 30% of the members were born in America. They met twice a month. Yiddish was the language of their meetings.
4. First United Podhajce Congregation Anshei Sefarad was founded in 1903 with 10 members. In 1938 there were 100 members. It had a mixed makeup. 40% were American born, and 5% were not natives of the city. Yiddish was the language of its bi-monthly meetings. They maintained the Talmud Torah in the old home. Aside from this, they supported local institutions with 100 dollars a year, maintained a synagogue, had a fund for those in need, and concerned itself with a cemetery for the deceased, etc. It secretary was Julius Schorr.

[Page 83]

Text Footnotes

1. Slownik Geograficzny, volume 8, page 384.
2. Baedecker: Das Generalgouvernment, 1943. Page 232.
3. The manuscript comes from a Frenchman who was among Jan Sowiecki's closest confidants. Doleran. 1661.
4. According to Balinski-Lipinski: Balinski-Lipinski: Starozytna Polska.
5. Yevreiskaya Encyclopedia, volume 12, page 641, 1913. The article was written by Meir Balaban.
6. A. Czolowski Bohdan Janusz: Przezlosc I zabytki Wojewodztwa Tarnopolskiego. Page 180, 1926.
7. Ibid.
8. Yevreiskaya Encyclopedia – We can confirm "historical vignettes" about the rabbi; this does not mean that there was no rabbi (rabbis) previously. Only that we are lacking sources about this.
9. Mateusz Miezes: Udzial Zydow w wojnach Polski. Warszawa 1939, Str. 162.
10. The same in S³ownik Geograficzny, volume 8, page 386. However, there, Jews are not mentioned. Ibid. Pages 167-8.
11. Miezes, page 180.
12. Moshe Steinschneider (Moritz Steinschneider), Die Geschichtsliteratur der Juden. 1905. Pages 183, 186.
13. The ledgers of the Council of the Four Lands, Section 5678 (note).
14. Chaim Wirszowski: The Sabbatean Kabbalist Reb Moshe David of Podhajce, "Zion", 5702, note 3.
15. M. Balaban: Spys Zydow, page 4. It also brings the text of the oath.
16. Philip Friedman, page 144. Note 5.
17. Cywila, May 6, 1927.
18. Neuer Morgan, August 4, 1933.
19. Neuer Morgan, August 20, 1934.
20. Slownik Geograficzny, volume 8, page 388.
21. Characteristically, they provided for the needs of business and industry chambers in Brody, where the article was composed. It is completely clear that Jews were intended here.
22. Steiger, page 258.
23. Ibid., page 257.
24. This was a weekly supplement in Hebrew to the Izraelite, which was published in German in the city of Mainz (Magentza).
25. See the Jewish People's Calendar.
26. Machzikei Hadas, New York, 18, February 22, 1907.
27. Dr. N. M. Gelber: History of the Zionist Movement in Galicia, pages 237, 268-9.
28. A. David Polisiuk, the correspondent from Podhajce, gave over the sum of 140 florins to Vienna, noting that the chapter desires that the money should only be used to assist those who are going to Palestine, and not those who are immigrating to America. The headquarters agreed with this, and the correspondent concludes: How good it would be if in every city, a branch of the Israelite Alliance would be founded – then the idea of the settlement of the Land of Israel would move from potentiality to actuality.
29. Gelber, ibid., page 362.
30. Ibid. Pages 511-512.
31. October 11, 1905, Lemberg, 44 (Polish weekly of the Zionist Organization in Galicia (Woschod).
32. Woschod, from February 14, 1906 – a correspondence from Podhajce.
33. Ibid., December 6, 1905.
34. Ibid. October 31, 1906.
35. Ibid. October 18, 1907.
36. Ibid. January 6, 1911.
37. According to Neue Morgan, Lvov, from July 11, 1933. [Translator's note: footnote 37 is not marked in the text.]
38. Steiger, page 133.
39. Gronski, table 25, page 45.
40. Cywila, May 22, 1931.
41. In the YIVO information, from the years 1937-1938; Dr. M. Weichert: Memoirs, volume 1, Tel Aviv, pages 11-12.
42. The Jewish Landsmanschaft in New York, 1939. Published by Y. L. Peretz writers union.
43. Galicianer Yearbook, April 23, 1939.

Stara Targowicz Street

Translator's Footnotes

1. I transliterated these spellings into English, and did not spell out the Hebrew spellings in full.
2. A Sejmik is a local parliament (as opposed to the Sejm, which is the main parliament). See http://en.wikipedia.org/wiki/Sejmik
3. Citizens of the city.
4. Cheshvan of 5363 would correspond to the year 1632.
5. G-d full of mercy – an opening phrase of many memorial prayers.
6. Szlachta is the Polish nobility: http://en.wikipedia.org/wiki/Szlachta
7. The Starosta is a regional government leader, and the Wojewoda is the regional parliament.
8. I was not able to ascertain the meaning of these professions.
9. I assume that this means that they had the right to set up their own curriculum.
10. Mishnaic tractates dealing with the holidays.
11. Known as 'pidyon' (redemption) – money given to a Hassidic Rebbe by his followers during an audience

[Page 84]

The Golden Chain of Podhajce Rabbis

by Rabbi Wolf Firestone (Fierstein)[1]

Approximately 400 years ago, the town of Podhajce, my birthplace, was a city full of scholars and learned people. Its rabbis were great in Torah, and were famous throughout all Jewish communities. Rabbis from near and far used to write to them regarding various problems in Halacha, and students from all countries used to come to learn with them. The greatest and most important of them was the rabbi and Gaon Rabbi Binyamin the son of Reb Avraham Solnik, the author of the Masaat Binyamin book of responsa. He occupied the rabbinical seat of Podhajce for forty years (1580-1620), and his responsa were spread out to every place that Jews lived. He instilled order into the Podhajce community. First and foremost he founded a large yeshiva, where students came to study Torah and wisdom from his mouth and from his assistants. He also studied there, and fulfilled the verse, "and you shall toil in it day and night". He became even better known in the Jewish world, for he was selected to be a member of the "Council of the Three Lands". He later became the head of the council.

In order to perpetuate the memory of the rabbis of Podhajce, and to give honor to my native town, where my mother Chana of blessed memory, the daughter of Reb Chaim Mordechai Fierstein and all of her ancestors are buried, I wish to enumerate here all of the rabbis who occupied the rabbinical seat of our city from the year 5300 until 5665 (1540-1905).

The two rabbis who preceded the author of the Masaat Binyamin were the rabbi and Gaon Rabbi Moshe and his son Rabbi Yehuda Leib. Rabbi Yehuda Leib is buried in the Lemberg cemetery. Great praises about his personality are inscribed upon his gravestone. It is mentioned there that both he and his father were rabbis in Podhajce.

The third rabbi was, as mentioned, the rabbi and Gaon Rabbi Binyamin Solnik. His eldest son, Rabbi Avraham, was the rabbi in Tarnopol and later in Brest Litovak. His second son Reb Yaakov was the rabbi in Podhajce after his father's passing. He composed a book titled "Nachalat Yaakov" – a commentary on Rashi's commentary on the Torah. He was the fourth rabbi of our city. He had no son to take his place.

The fifth rabbi was Rabbi David, the author of a book called "Tiferet Yisrael". He died in the year 5393 (1633). He was followed by Rabbi Mordechai of holy blessed memory, who had previously been a rabbi in Rzeszow.

The seventh rabbi was the rabbi and Gaon Rabbi Moshe Kac, the eldest son of the famous rabbi Rabbi Shabtai Kac, who is known as the author of the Shach. He was followed by the rabbi and Gaon Rabbi Moshe Katzenelenboigen, the son of Rabbi Shaul Katzenelenboigen, who can trace his lineage to Rabbi Shaul Wahl (who was the king of Poland for one day), and to the Gaon the author of the Masaat Binyamin. His brother-n-law was the rabbi and kabbalist Rabbi Zecharia Mendel of Podhajce, who was the author of several books.

After Rabbi Moshe Katzenelenboigen, Rabbi Moshe the son of Rabbi Menachem Nachum was appointed as the new rabbi. He was followed by the great Gaon Rabbi Yissachar Dov Berish, the son of the Gaon Rabbi Yehoshua the author of the Pnei Yehoshua.

The eleventh rabbi was the rabbi and Gaon Rabbi Meshulam Zalman, the son of the Gaon Rabbi Yaakov Emden. Later, he was appointed as a rabbi in London (around 1769).

After Rabbi Meshulam Zalman, the rabbi and Gaon Rabbi Tzvi Hirsch occupied the rabbinical seat. Following him was Rabbi Simcha Rappaport, the son of the Lemberger rabbi Rabbi Chaim Kohen Rappaport. He died in the year 5585 (1825).

After them was the rabbi and Gaon Rabbi Shmuel. His name is mentioned in various responsa books. After him, Rabbi Aryeh Leib was appointed as rabbi. He was a great Gaon, who is known as the author of the book Leiv Aryeh.

After the author of Leiv Aryeh was Rabbi Nota. Rabbi Nota is mentioned as a great and important rabbi in various books.

After Rabbi Nota, Rabbi Shimon Meller was appointed as rabbi, and following him, his son Rabbi Yonah Meller.

After Rabbi Yonah Meller, the Gaon Rabbi Shalom the son of Rabbi Chaim Mordechai Lilienfeld was appointed rabbi. He was born in

Podhajce. After he died, nobody was appointed as a new rabbi. His place was filled by three rabbinical judges, the righteous teachers Rabbi Avraham Eisen, Rabbi Feivish Szwarc, and Rabbi Wolf Haber.

[Page 85]

In New York, the natives of our town appointed my brother Rabbi Chaim-Mordechai Brecher of blessed memory as the rabbi and righteous teacher in the Masaat Binyamin synagogue. He was great in Torah and good deeds, and a great grammarian. He annotated the Yehoash edition of the Bible, the Concordance of Shlomo Mandelkorn, and other books. He died on the 14th of Cheshvan 5626 (1966) at the age of 86.

May his soul be bound in the bonds of eternal life.

{An abridged summary of the article in the Hebrew section of the book.}

A Few Lines About Rabbi David Lilienfeld

by Meir Pikholtz

{This is equivalent with the Hebrew article on page 53.}

[Page 86]

(An abridged summary of the article in the Hebrew section of the book {Hebrew article is on page 56}[2])

Dr. Falk – the Baal Shem of London

by Dr. Herman Adler

(An abridged summary of the article in the Hebrew section of the book {Hebrew article is on page 57})

[Page 88]

Important Historical Dates for Podhajce[3]

1420	Beginning of the Jewish settlement. The oldest gravestones in the cemetery are from that year.
1580	Rabbi Binyamin Solnik, the author of the Masaat Binyamin responsa book, was the rabbi in Podhajce until his death.
1667	Jews fight together with all the citizens against the Turks and Tatars.
1676	The Turks overrun Podhajce and perpetrate a pogrom against the Jews.
1676	The Polish Sejm exempts the Jews of Podhajce from paying taxes for a period of 12 years, on account of their oppressed state and as thanks for their help in the battle against the Tatars.
1680-1690	Chaim Malach, a follower of Shabtai Tzvi, comes to Podhajce several times.
1696	Rabbi Moshe David of Podhajce, a well-known kabbalist and follower of Shabtai Tzvi, was born in Podhajce. (He died in 1766).
1708	Rabbi Shmuel Yaakov Falk, the "Baal Shem of London" was born, apparently in Podhajce. (He died in 1782 in London).
1745	Rabbi Yissachar Berish, the rabbi of Podhajce, the son of the Pnei Yehoshua, died on the 22nd of Cheshvan 5505[4].
1746	The book Birchat Yaakov by the rabbi of Podhajce, Rabbi Yaakov the son of Rabbi Baruch, was published in Lemberg.
1756	Jacob Frank appeared in Poland, and came to Podhajce several times.
1759	The last Frankists, including several families from Podhajce, commit apostasy in Lemberg on September 17, 1759.
1765	The first census in Poland. There are 1,290 Jews in Podhajce.
1772	The entire area of eastern Galicia, including Podhajce, comes under Austrian rule.
1790	Nine Jewish families of Podhajce settle on farms with the help of the Austrian regime.
1791	In the year 5552, Rabbi Zecharia Mendel the son of Aryeh Leib died. He was a well-known rabbi and author of books.
1876	A "club" for the reading of periodicals was founded.
1879	Rabbi Yitzchak Izak Menachem Eichenstein, who was the Podhajcer Rebbe until 1929, was born.
1895	The founding of the first Podhajce organization in America.

1896	Rabbi Avraham Weiss, the renowned Talmudic scholar, was born.
1909	Rabbi Shalom Lilienfeld died on September 31 at the age of 53.
1941	On July 6, the city fell to the Nazis.
1942	The first aktion in the city took place on Yom Kippur. The 3rd of Sivan is the yahrzeit of the martyrs of Podhajce and region.

Translator's Footnotes

1. Although this is a summary of the longer Hebrew article on page 49, I have translated it in its own right, as it simplifies much of the flowery language, and is therefore much easier to read. Interestingly enough, there are a few facts in the Yiddish that do not appear in the Hebrew – such as the cryptic comment about someone having been the king of Poland for one day (although this is documented – see http://www.maxpages.com/nodabyehuda/samuel_j_katzenellenbogen_1521
2. I generally did not translate the Yiddish abridged summaries of the Hebrew articles, unless there was an overriding reason. In these cases, the hyperlink points to the original article.
3. This Yiddish section is not a translation of the dates on page 47. Although this Yiddish date list is far briefer than the Hebrew date list, there are some dates in each section that do not appear in the others. No author is listed for the Yiddish date list.
4. There is a mistake in the English year here. The English year would be 1744. Hebrew Years and English years always have the same final digit – except that the Hebrew year starts in September or October, so the first few months of a new Hebrew year still correspond to the preceding English year. Cheshvan is the second month of the year, and would fall in October or November.

[Page 89]

M. M. Oizerkes

by Nachman Blumenthal

Podhajce was represented with its own writer in the new Jewish literature in the Yiddish literature – Mordechai Mendel Oizerkes. The word "Podhajce" is written under the author's name on the title page in one of his books, "The Private Teacher". The author apparently took pride in his home town even from so far away! Perhaps he thereby wished to hint that what he was writing about had a connection with Podhajce, even without mentioning the name of the place from where he came? It is entirely possible.

Oizerkes was born in Podhajce in 1848. During his young days, he worked in a liquor distillery. He traveled widely through Galicia, Russia (Odessa) and Romania, and reached as far as Constantinople. Then he and settled in his native town, where he earned his livelihood as a private teacher (in people's homes). In his lexicon, Zalman Reisen even notes that Oizerkes was a lawyer. He certainly meant that he was a legal assistant, for Oizerkes had never studied this subject.

Oizerkes wrote in many genres: novels, plays, songs with their own tunes, etc.

After becoming acquainted with his published novels – and many of his writings never saw the light of day and we can assume that they were lost – we cannot agree with the opinion of Zalman Reisen, who referred to them as "novels of literary trash". On the contrary, they always had a healthy moral, and many accurate details are woven in that portray the lives of Jews in the small and medium sized towns and villages from his time and his place (Podhajce, Lvov, etc.) in a very realistic fashion – as the author himself demonstrates in the names of his books. From this standpoint, they have a great value. It is also worthwhile to praise the Yiddish words and idiom that stem for the most part from the "Germanic"[1] languages (Galician Yiddish German), according to the mode of that time).

Oizerkes died in 1913 at the age of 65 in America.

We have very few details about his life. Apparently, he had a difficult childhood and youth. Apparently, his father was a private teacher, and his mother died when he was born. His book "The Private Teacher" seems to be a sort of literary autobiography (in which he discussed excessively – under disguised names – more about his fellow townsfolk than about his own self). In his introduction to his own book, he states the following about this: "Believe me – he means the "dear reader" – that I know of no professional teacher, even for one solitary lesson, who earned bread from one mode, and already worshipped many forms of idols". We can assume that he was describing the parents of his students, who in his time had already began to seek people with secular education (students, academics) rather than riff-raff, as well as his own students to whom they wished to impart worldly education aside from the traditional subjects. Regarding such "antics", the author states that he would not wish to learn with someone of that nature. For he only wishes to "learn to dance". "Dancing with the Angel of Death" – adds the mother of the student, who was angry for she is paying futile money to the teacher...

A private teacher – that is his teacher himself – also comes through in his story "The New Generation", and from his words and the words of the parents to the children, we can even find out what he taught, and how much he charged for a "lesson".

First of all, one learns "how to write properly" (of course, not in Yiddish), then they read a Yiddish card that came in the mail, a "newspaper page", they make a calculation; -- indeed, of course to speak and read a bit of Polish and German. In "Private Teacher", we even have almost a shorthand protocol for a German lesson. The author reads a

sentence and translates it into clear German. The students must repeat it in their own words, but they intermix Polish and Yiddish words. The author hears this and corrects them.

For his difficult labor – the older students frequently disparage him and do not want to put their heads into his doctrines at all – for coming to the students' homes for an entire month, the teacher is paid (if no fault is found with him) ten crowns for an entire month! And if, Heaven forbid, he became ill and did not come to the lessons, they deduct 12 kreitzer (24 heller) for every missed day. This is the manner that his "bread givers", of course wealthy people, conduct themselves.

[Page 90]

Just as he lived alone, he died alone. One can see that after his death, nobody called, nobody wrote any personal memories or literary evaluations.

He took up writing in his middle years, after he from touring the world. As he himself states, he had enough life experiences and adventures, and this spurred him on to demonstrate to his readers how to live and protect oneself from the errors that others have stumbled upon. He himself had no formal education. It seems that he only completed four classes in the gymnasium, and did not learn any trade. In describing his acquaintances and his environment, the author demonstrates directly and indirectly through general principals what is good and what is bad, which protagonist is an honorable person and which is a devil. Sometimes he gives over the moral in brief passages, such as for example: "How good is it when one learns a trade" (the name of a chapter), and of course in that chapter he describes that the Jew with a trade is a respectable Jew, has a livelihood, performs necessary work, at the time when others are "*shurkn*", playing cards, and conducting dark business, etc.

According to him, "to be an ignoramus is a great error". A second golden thought of his.

We can see from this that Oizerkes strove for excellence. He was an erudite Jew, not steeped in "sciences" – but he wanted to be a disseminator of the haskalah ideals and spirit from the progressives in his times.

However, aside from his writing, which had great influence upon his readership – which was not small and his work did fulfill their needs – he himself had to concern himself with livelihood. How? In the aforementioned preface he states that he wishes to "present the situation" in the right light, as it truly is. He must therefore involve himself with the wealthy Jews whose "situation" is so lofty, and it was they who hired him as a private teacher. In truth, the author does not give the name of the place, but it was in a small town like Podhajce, and it is not too difficult to figure out what the author was talking about. Indeed, he states in the preface that he is afraid of those who are well connected, but he describes it nevertheless!

The author explains "the difficulties of every strata of society, nobody is passed over–today this is an error and a crime". Thus were they persecuted until death.

In his first book that he published, he turns to words of sadness and weariness:

"Go forth, my poor child, into the world. And when someone laughs at you, you must not make anything of it. Then you should know that you have encountered a completely simple and uneducated person. And a poor child must already know that he should laugh at this..."

The relationship of the wealthy people to him, who had to endure his criticism and apostasy – was probably the reason for his immigration to America. However, as has been stated, even there he had no luck.

Actually, he did not "emigrate", for to America, one escapes. However, as the author writes in one place regarding his connection with one of his protagonists who escapes "to Columbus' land" (for he made a girl pregnant) – "only bums travel to America". (The New Generation, page 100). However, we do not know the actual reason that compelled the author to travel to "Columbus' land".

[Page 91]

From Oizerkes' rich creations, very few appear in book form – only the following:

1. "The Private Teacher, Portraits of Galician Jewish Life". By M. M. Oizerkes, Podhajce, Drohobycz. Printed by A. H. Zupnik, 1897. (120 pages).
2. "The Private Teacher..." Second Section. Drohobycz. "*Ferlag Des Farpasers*"[2], 1899, (131 pages).
3. "The Private Teacher..." Third Section, Drohobycz, "*Ferlag Des Farpasers*", 1900 (153 pages).
4. "The New Generation", portraits of the present time, published by Shmuel Horn, 5665 (1905), (173 pages).
5. "Father Took Mother", A novel of the Present. Published by Shmuel Horn, Lemberg, Alembekov 7. 5665 (1905). (172 pages).
6. Portraits of Various Jewish Strata. Podhajce, 1908.

Where Oizerkes literary legacy remains, and whether it still remains at all – is unknown to us.

The author was very concerned about anyone pilfering from him, Heaven forbid, or reprinting his books without his knowledge. Therefore, he always included the appropriate warnings on the title page, such as "all rights reserved" or "reprinting is forbidden".

Aside from this, he included the following remark: "Every book which does not have my insignia (stampiglia) is considered as stolen."

The "stampiglia" was a stamp with red ink: Lwow-Lemberg, Hebrew teacher – Samuel Horn.

However all the warnings – it seems to me – helped him little. I doubt if the income from the books covered the expenses.

It was not out of riches that he left the city and set out for America.

Incidentally, we have already seen what type of an undignified opinion Zalman Reisen had of Oizerkes. Nevertheless, when Gershon Bader published the first volume of his lexicon (letters aleph – yod), under the entry "The State and its wise people – biographies of erudite people and writers whose cradle was in Galicia" Oizerkes is not even mentioned. It was only Reisen of all people who took up Oizerkes' unjust treatment. It is possible that, "One sees it in the other". Reisen felt that G. Bader had committed a wrong with respect to Oizerkes, for "His novels were very popular with the public, a form of Galician Sh"M[3] " We are happy to hear that the Podhajce residents were included in the reading public at that time (most certainly these common folk whom the author intended were primarily girls and housewives). However, on the other hand, we must as well take up again the injustice perpetrated against Oizerkes, in that Reisen places him on the same plane as Sh"M, whereas Oizerkes deserves to be placed on no less of a plane than Izak Meir Dik of Vilna, if not higher... and Izak Meir Dik is considered by Reisen to be a veritable writer. In his article "Galicia in Yiddish Literature", Reisen gives us new details about Oizerkes life. Bader once wrote to him that he (Bader) knows Oizerkes well. "At the time when I was the editor of the Lemberger Tagblatt, I had in my file a full bundle of his stories of which I did not even publish one. As far as I know, he used to travel around to distribute his books, and large circles 'loved him', as they say in America."

In this manner, by writing about Oizerkes so nonchalantly, Bader not only wronged him, for a published article in the Lemberger Tagblatt would have helped him greatly, if not materially then at least morally – but he also committed an injustice against Yiddish literature; for where are those narratives today? Even Reisen comes to the following conclusion: "I believe that Oizerkes does not deserve to be entirely forgotten (? ! N. B.) when one writes about the history of Jewish folk literature in Galicia." In order to write about a writer, one must know his work! And where is Oizerkes' written work?

As much as I do not want to castigate Zalman Reisen's opinions and his own persona – I knew him personally and maintained a correspondence with him for some time – I must state that in Reisen's evaluation of the Oizerkes' creations, one can plainly feel the completely negative attitude to a Lithuanian and Galician Jew.

Oizerkes remained lonely in life and lonely as a writer, completely immersed in his own straight path, influenced by nobody. Nobody took note of him in literature. Nobody wrote about him, and therefore, Oizerkes remained in a situation where he did not develop as a writer. This is a shame, for he had kernels that could have sprouted, that could have developed and gone higher and higher, and could have advanced him. However, the outside stimulus was lacking.

[Page 92]

{Three title pages of Oizerkes books. The German translation appears next to each one. Each one is stamped with the seal of “Yosef Archives in Jerusalem”}

דער טאַטע האָט
דיע מאַמע גענומען

ראָמאַן אוים דער געגענוואַרט

פאָן

מ. מ. אויזערקים.

פערלאַג פאָן שמואל הארן, לעמבערג, אַלעמבעקאָוו 7.
נאַכדרוק פערבאָטען.

לעמבערג, תרס"ו.
דרוק פאָן א. סאלאט.

Der Tate hot die Mame genimen
Roman aus der Gegenwart, von **M. M. Ojserkis.**
Verlag von SAMUEL HORN, Lemberg, Alembeków 7.
Nachdruck verboten.
Druck von E. Salat, Lemberg, 1905.

Father Took Mother
A Novel about the Present
By
M. M. Oizerkes
Published by SHMUEL HORN, Lemberg, Alembekow 7.
Copying is prohibited
Lemberg 5666
Printed by A. Salat
SAMUEL Horn
Hebrew Teacher
Lwow – Lemberg
Der Tate hot die Mame Genimen
Roman aus der Gegenwart, von M. M. Ojserkis,
Verlag von SAMUEL HORN, Lemberg, Alembekow 7.
Nachdruck verboten
Druck von E. Salat, Lemberg, 1905

דער

פריוואטלעהרער

בילדער אויס דעם יודישען, גאליציישען לעבען

פאן

מ. מ. אויזערקים

פאדהייצע.

דראהאביטש.

דרוק פאן א. ה. זופניק.

Druck von A. H. Żupnik in Drohobycz.

1897.

The
Private Teacher
Portraits of Galician Jewish Life
By M. M. Oizerkes
Podhajce

Drohobycz
Printed by A. H. Zupnik
Druk von A. H. Zupnik n Drohobycz

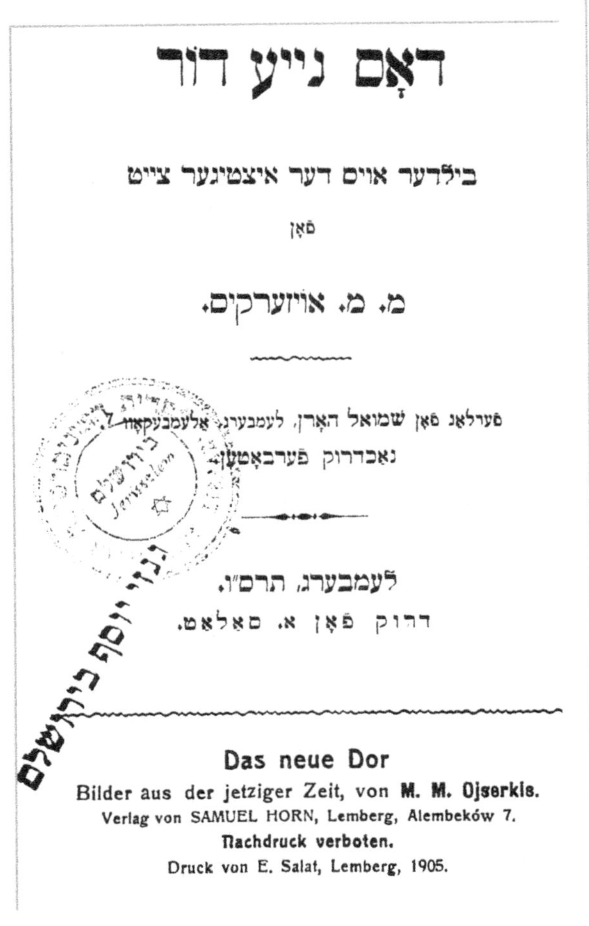

דאָס נייע דור

בילדער אויס דער איצטיגער צייט

פאָן

מ. מ. אויזערקיס.

פערלאג פאָן שמואל האָרן, לעמבערג, אלעמבעקאוו 7.

נאכדרוק פערבאָטען.

לעמבערג, תרס"ו.

דרוק פאָן א. סאלאט.

Das neue Dor

Bilder aus der jetziger Zeit, von **M. M. Ojserkis.**

Verlag von SAMUEL HORN, Lemberg, Alembeków 7.

Nachdruck verboten.

Druck von E. Salat, Lemberg, 1905.

Das Neue Dor (The New Geneation)
Portraits from the present time
By
M.M. Oizerkes
Published by Shmuel Horn, Lemberg, Alembekow 7.
Copying is prohibited
Lemberg 5666
Printed by A. Salat
Das neue Dor
Bilder aus der jetziger Zeit, von M. M. Ojserkis
Verlag von SAMUEL HORN, Lemberg, Alembekow 7.
Nachdruck verboten.
Druck von E. Salat, Lemberg,1905

[Page 93]

What were the merits of Oizerkes' books? His topics were taken from Galician Jewish life of that era, where he himself comes from, and we believe that he took his topics from events in Podhajce, which he knew in full detail.

He polishes up the events somewhat, makes them interesting, (extraordinary events), and exaggerates when describing both the good and bad characters. He states in his aforementioned preface, he himself was a witness to the "facts" that he describes. However, it is difficult to take at face value that so many fortuitous events took place in one place and unfolded as he described them.

He describes good, ideal people and bad people. The bad ones persecute the good ones, who must defend themselves from them. However, finally, things end up well. Everything is in accordance with an enlightened Jew who believes in progress. Oizerkes was no exception in this detail. To his credit, we should emphasize that there is no lewdness in his narratives. The idea was always a moral one. Good is rewarded, evil is punished, and finally, after a crisis in family life, the man turns to his wife, and everything is good and well. In one word, it is a story like all other stories...

So what of it then? Oizerkes had a good eye. He precisely observed the spirited people, the sources of their poetic personalities, and portrays their essence accurately and realistically. The external characteristics come out better – as if from a world of German-Yiddish gibberish – would a Maskil have better understood his different Galicia? However, we do find a large number of pure Yiddish words, curses, genuine Yiddish idioms, etc.

Now you read and see for yourself how the "Deitshmerish"[1] rings in the following excerpts.[4]

"He stands there overcast; I would certainly want to rip off the spodek!"

"Somewhat of a loafer" "I make a footbath for you."

And when a woman comes to a wedding and is unable to dance "She indeed (the word '*takeh*' with an 'n' sound at the end!) has the face of mockery, like a dressed up ram." "He went as if on foreign feet." "*A linen knish.*"

"One sweet man and a golden brother-in-law" "Once he was silenced with silliness". "Not with a spodek!"

"A head to absorb the learning, she had, such a year for my and your enemies, dear reader."

"You foolish bigot!" – "Every poor person is a charitable person!"

And if there is a commotion in the house, the protagonist does not shout out: "*shta tam* what are you doing?", And another Ukrainian word: "*Hovorei meni do sraki*" (Private Teacher, page 36). Did they not talk this way in Podhajce? Was this not ordinary Jewish folk, which touches the heart?

And now an old matchmaker comes to a maiden: She feels like meeting her, who had a relationship with a lad, "Who had made graduation", and suddenly such a disgrace: a matchmaker! She talks to her – the modern "educated" maiden: "who crawls to her like something else? Do not provide for me."

The matchmaker, who was no fool, and was familiar with an honorable man, knows about the relationship and wishes to proceed with her match, goes to the father of the maiden and calms him, even though he himself knows everything and "carries around a belly full of secrets, but everything remains with me." Thereby, she wins over the father...

The author does not merely wish to tell over to the reader a fine, interesting story and thereby entertain him. He does not merely wish to educate him about good things, about good deeds, and deter the evil. He does wish to teach him something concrete, first and foremost... German. For example, when he makes use of a German word which is not common among the people, he includes a Judeo-German version in parentheses. On another occasion, he translates such an international word, with the explicit objective of teacher the reader, civilizing

him, and turning him into a European! I am certain that when reading his books, people did not merely read the story with great interest, but also learned things: words, ideas. Aside from this, from the subject matter one could learn proper behavior, the art of ideal rhetoric, and how to conduct oneself in a cultured fashion in society, on the street, etc.

[Page 94]

He explains the relevance of his language in the introduction to "The Private Teacher". "The people in the book speak German. Not because the author wishes to demonstrate that he knows a bit of German. Heaven forbid! But rather because a teacher with students, students who are successful one with the other, and they all speak only German with officials. Such German that today's civilized Jews must be familiar with. I do not know deep German, and it should not be pronounced. Have no fear – my friendly reader."

Even the writing technique of our author is old fashioned and quaint. The author, aside from when he is telling a story, talks personally with the reader: "Dear Reader" (and not only at the very beginning of the narrative). He might also say: "You must know, dear reader, that Moshe had a melancholy, choleric temperament; but perhaps you do not know what this means, so I will explain it to you..." He indeed describes it, and explains over two entire pages that temperament is the same as the condition or the nature of the human blood – in coarse Yiddish "*dos geblit*" – and that researchers have found that there are four human temperaments, etc. etc.

On another occasion, the author has mercy on the reader, when he deviated from the path (of telling the story) and on the path of science, as he explains, "I do not wish to make you, reader, tired, so I will be brief..." He then continues on with the story until he forgets himself a second time...

And when he finally brings the mother together with the father – who had been separated and had already become old through the course of the long story – he gives over a moral to the young readers: "This couple, I mean our couple, felt like producing a young Jewish couple, who would get married on G-d's head (!! – N.B.), my readers would understand very well that they must think about this a bit. End."

Here too one can see the private teacher, the great pedagogue!

He concludes the lesson, but this cannot be enough, one must work independently with the teacher. The reader, after concluding the narrative, has enough material to ponder and review. The author does not want the reader to take him for his word. A student must not stick a finger in his mouth; on the contrary, the reader himself must attempt and come to his own realization that the author is correct! And I place before you the fact that they did indeed discuss, debate and even vote on the problems discussed in his books in far off corners of Eastern Galicia, from where the protagonists hailed... Only when one comes to the "end" does the author take the reader by the hand, over houses and homes, over small towns and large cities, over oceans and deserts. You understand that you are accompanied by such a good guide, so the "dear reader" need not have any fear; for he will be led to the happy ending.

*

"I guide the reader into one house, one that is called "a *balabatish* house"[5] in Galicia, which implies that the head of the household is doing quite well." This is certainly good, a fine house, but the head of the household does not like him (or the reader).

Later he guides him, may we be spared, in to a prison. Earlier, he warns the reader that he should have no fear, for he would be with the author, thank G-d, and they would be able to leave the prison. The protagonist of the story would remain there, and this would also not be for long, for he is an honorable man, but the evil ones spoke against him...

These are his own words, taken from the chapter: "In the Isolation Cell". First the author explains why he guides the unfortunate reader to this place: "I must now take my reader to a place that is very sorrowful; believe me, dear reader, I would sincerely like to spare you this, for I know... (it is) an iron cage – – – but it cannot be thus, I must visit our good Friedman there, and naturally, I must take along my devoted readers..." Incidentally, Friedman also wishes to say a sad word there...

[Page 95]

It was indeed gloomy in the isolation cell, but the author had a good heart, and did not keep the reader there for long. Only Friedman must remain there unfortunately, even though he is an "honest man" – and there was a mix-up. However, the author does not neglect him there, and the eighth chapter is already called "Friedman is Free". Truth must be victorious! This is a comfort for the reader, who has gone through so much, and perhaps indeed saw themselves as living through Friedman.

The author often feels that the reader cannot endure the great tension until the appropriate answers that he pines for finally come: he already wishes to know the ending. In the interim, the author appeases him: a miracle occurred: from the evil women came a righteous woman. And the puzzle is already set out – in the interim. This reminds me of another episode from another story of the author – where he writes about another type of problem in a similar fashion: the child is unfortunately very hungry, but dinner is still far off; what did the devoted mother do? She gave the child in the interim... a "*faltshikl*" (little portion)! This way he could hold out until dinner! But if one turn from an evil person into a righteous person overnight, please, if you will (and incidentally, the author knows well that the reader, whom he has surrounded from all sides, wishes this and even more!) know this – read the pair of calm chapters which will explain to you how this came about.

Here is another thing about Oizerkes' literary technique. Most of the material in his narratives is discussions between his characters, and if momentarily there was no second person in the scene, he allows the person to talk to himself or to brood out loud. Thus something happens in the plot. The reader learns very important things, often deep secrets that the author did not or was not able to make obvious to the reader earlier in a different manner.

From this we see how easy it was for his narratives to make scenes and dramas. On the other hand, if he places a character into a scene, he makes an introduction and presents him to the reader. He will already know something, and he will know more later "My dear reader, I must first introduce you to Mrs. Kessler's tenant, or before I let our story unfold."

The author plays the role as an eyewitness to what he writes about, as if he heard and saw everything, and what he did not see – he does not know! He does not take the reader with him everywhere; for example, in "*Tzezeit Un Tzespreit*" ("Wildly Scattered") (1, 7), he writes about the mistress of the house who sits in a corner and dreams. He states, "To write about her stature and her eyes, I must wait until she awakens." And indeed, when she wakes up, opens her eyes and stands up, he describes her stature and eyes. In other cases, he apologizes for not giving over such details, since, "Unfortunately, dear reader, I cannot tell you this, because I myself do not know." (ibid. page 61). On another occasion, he gives a different answer; for example: "About the separation (of the man and his wife), I do not wish to tell this to the reader so as not to sadden him (ibid, page 57). However, the reader already got the hint, and already felt very well the pain of the separation. (The author knew this very well, but he "makes himself as dead").

And in another place: the author tells about an honest Jew, a faithful person in the forest: "Whether the Jew was a wealthy man, this I cannot tell the reader, for I have not seen the bank books with the balance." This appeals to primitive and naïve readers – and such were Oizerkes' readers! -- They are convinced that everything that he says is absolutely true; he is therefore alone!

The author also consults with the reader and asks him how he likes things, whether he agrees with him – the author. The author places before the reader a question which must certainly be an original question to this type of reader: Why is the good bad and the bad good? And he explains as follows: "One must be a philosopher in order to understand the answer. However I am not even remotely a philosopher[6] so it would be brazen of me to attempt to answer. I beg the beloved reader my boldness for delaying. Let me chatter. I expect that you, Heaven forbid if not, have understood my meaning. Every one of you has intelligence. I wish to sharpen your minds, and that will hurt nobody" (Private Teacher, 3, page 7). Thus does the author ingeniously lead the reader into philosophical questions and... explains them.

[Page 96]

Oizerkes does not state from where the themes of his novels stem. Many facts that he relates in his stories stem without doubt from his hometown. People who still remember that time will certainly recognize which of the true residents of the town are hidden under the newly invented name of a protagonist in the novels. Furthermore, when he writes about certain events and institutions, they certainly have a basis in what he saw with his own eyes in his hometown: such as "Zion Organization", an "Official Casino", a people's kitchen, "*tombale*", "Our city". "The lawyer settled in Podhajce" – this is certainly referring to the first lawyer in Podhajce, with whom Oizerkes might have worked as an assistant, etc., etc.

However, the author was not only afraid of people with dark characters, with whom he might have worked for a living; unintentionally, he also deals with the observant (nevertheless a Maskil Jew!) In one place he states that unfortunately, piety along does not save a person from crime, for the only "pure human character is the right closet". And he soon comes to the following: "I do not claim, Heaven forbid, that the observant are criminals". However have the Orthodox forgiven him for this statement? I believe not (In the story, they take revenge on the teacher, and they throw him into a pit.)

In another place he states: "The reader must be afraid to read about the rabbi, for it is bad; believe me, my dear reader, that a rabbi, a priest (He, the heretic, does not even use the customary "*lehavdil*"[7], which would have fit in very well here.), even a good Jew would have also made (and not created!) the same penalty as a thief ("which I am not"), a murderer, or even a heretic who smokes on the Sabbath, Heaven forbid. You have nothing to fear, and are permitted to listen."

A few words about Oizerkes' orthography:

The written word that consists of a Hebrew root with Yiddish prefixes is interesting; he writes the root in Hebrew and the accessories in Yiddish, and separates the parts with an apostrophe. *Ge'ganve't* or *geganvet.* The author also has the question of his own style. He writes: "*gefateret*" (page 112), '*gemosert*" (3, page 136), "*gepoelt*" (3 page 150). He Hebraizes the second part of the word, the suffix and writes it along with the "*sav*", a letter which is used solely in Hebrew words. For in Yiddish, one uses the letter "*tes*".

He uses mnemonics and abbreviations in places where one usually does not do so. For example, he often uses the abbreviation F"m (*Feh, Mem*) for the name of the Friedman, the protagonist of the Private Teacher, which comes out very often. He also uses the short form *Beis, Ayin*"*Gimel* for "*Baal Agala*" (wagon driver); *Beis Ayin*"*Mem* for "*Baal Melacha*" (worker); *Kuf*"*Mem* for "*Kerker Meister*" (jail master)! When he uses a mnemonic, it is a sign that the word is used often, and it shows that the jail is a beloved accessory in his stories, one of his favorite themes. The ideal teacher sat in jail on one occasion (perhaps also the author?)

Despite his love for his homeland of Galicia, he does not idealize it in his stories:

"I hate Galicia" declares the author often in the name of a protagonist ("*Tzezeit*", page 81). "It is better to remain in Vienna, in New York." There (in Galicia), there are bad people, Orthodox serpents. Fanatics, superstitious people and pious thieves rule there." For these reasons, he also calls his homeland: Foolish (*narishe*) Galicians, or silly (*fardripete*) Galicians (Private Teacher, 2, page 35).

"I want to express appreciation for my brethren, the Jews of Galicia, for I love them sincerely, but this does not work out, for the blunders which they commit cannot be overlooked. They perform the commandments of external show. With the commandments they earn "credits and importance" (3 page 131).

*

A Maskil, a poor man, with an pure character and a heart full of humanity and decency, a loner, isolated from the world, he finally left his beloved Galicia and sought out a place of refuge in the new world, in America, which was so different than Galicia. However, in the great and endless expanse of America, our author disappeared completely from our eyes...

Translator's Footnotes

1. The word used here is "Deitshmerish". In the Weinreich Yiddish / English dictionary, this word is translated as "Too much like German (said of modern German words or phrases sporadically used in Yiddish but not accepted by cultivated stylists)."
2. "*Ferlag Des Farpasers*" literally means "Publishers and Editors". I suspect that here it is intended to be the name of a publishing company.
3. Evidently the acronym of an author.
4. In translation, the Germanic mode of Yiddish will not be evident. Anyone wishing to study this concept must read the original. These snippets were meant to illustrate the jargon used by the author, and, taken out of context, are difficult to translate. I left some words in transliteration, as they would loose their meaning in translation.
5. *Baal Habayit* (literally master of the house), is a term used for a patrician or well to do head of a household.
6. The word used here is "*untershalg*", which seems to me 'trace of' (i.e. I am not even a trace of a philosopher). The author of the article placed a (!) after this word to express his surprise as to its usage.
7. *Lehavdil*, literally "to differentiate", is an interjection often placed to separate between a holy and profane topic – here it would have fit in well between the mention of the rabbi and the mention of the priest.

[Page 97 and 98]

Chapters of Memories

Members of the Achva Kibbutz

The Zeev group of Hashomer Hatzair
From right to left: Aryeh Dik – perished;
Meir Marbech – living in the Land;
Shlomo Klein – perished;
Yaakov Horowitz (lawyer) – perished

Members of Beitar in Podhajce

[Page 99]

Chapters of Memories

From Podhajce to Jerusalem

by M. Sh. Geshouri

(In appreciation of the personality of Professor Avraham Weiss of blessed memory.)

There are names that have become an idea. A person sets a goal for himself, dedicates all of his strength and energy to it, and it becomes a symbol to him. There are individuals who have been able to dedicate their entire lives and thoughts to one activity, to develop it in their personality and to become fused with it, so that the enterprise becomes their memorial. Professor Avraham Weiss of blessed memory was one such unique person.

He had many stations in his life, beginning in his birthplace of Podhajce and ending in the midst of Jerusalem, where he lived for his last years. He was exalted with his Torah, character traits, and splendid with his renown. He was a man whose entire life was dedicated to cleaving with Torah. He was a man of Talmud and study, possessing many spiritual treasures, dedicating his entire being and essence to the spiritual development of scholars, nurturing them and awakening in them a love of Torah. All of his students stood out as people who appreciated Torah and its students.

Rabbi Avraham Weiss spent the days of his childhood and youth in his native city of Podhajce, in which he was born on the 26th of Nissan 5656 (1896). At the time, Podhajce was one of the cities of Eastern Galicia which was rooted in the tradition of Torah and Jewish values. It had many scholars who were known for their Torah and awe of Heaven. The sounds of Torah burst forth from the Beis Midrash of the city through most of the hours of the day, for students studied there in shifts. Rabbi Avraham Weiss took his first steps in this atmosphere, and he received his education in cheders and the Talmud Torah as all Jewish children in those days. He quickly became known as a genius in Talmud and Halacha, and was considered to be one of the best and most promising youths. He spent his best years in Podhajce. Even though he settled into other cities far from his city after he left, the atmosphere of his hometown never departed from him. In his letters to his family, he always took interest in what was happening in the city.

He continued his studies in Vienna, the Austrian capital. There, he concluded his studies in university (1921) and in the Rabbinical Seminary (1922). When he to Podhajce with the titles of rabbi and doctor, he got to know Torah greats from close up, as well as their methods of study and behavior. These were the first years of Polish independence, when the political barriers between Congress Poland, Austrian Galicia, and parts of the German regions of Silesia and Posen were broken down and united once again under Polish rule, and the relations between the leaders of the country and the Jews were unclear. However, Rabbi Avraham Weiss, with his exalted spirit, could not even go a short way without making use of his blessed talents. Already in 1922, he taught in the Hebrew school in Bialystok, without turning to the rabbinate and earning his livelihood from his studies. Later, he served as a Talmud teacher in the Teacher's Seminary in Warsaw, and in 1927 as a Talmud teacher in the Tachkemoni Rabbinical Seminary and the government seminary for teachers of religion in Warsaw. When the “Center for the Wisdom of Israel” was founded in that city in 1928, with the purpose of training secondary school teachers for religion and Jewish history, and modern rabbis for the communities of Poland, Rabbi Avraham Weiss was one of the first teachers, along with Professor Moshe Schorr, Professor Meir Balaban, the poet Yaakov Kohen, the historian Dr. Schipper, and Dr. Mordechai Broide – all of blessed memory.

His style of teaching in general was one of “not getting angry and not playing favorites”, especially with respect to the commentators. With his wisdom and boldness, he permitted himself at certain times to disagree even with the early commentators. Truth and the search for truth were to him the prime policy in his learning. He was expert in both the Babylonian and Jerusalem Talmud, and on rare occasion, he would teach according to the Jerusalem Talmud rather than the Babylonian Talmud[1]. He loved those students who came to the institution directly from the Yeshivas, and who continued to wear the garb that was traditional of Orthodox Yeshiva students in Poland during their first years there. Professor Weiss himself, in contrast to the other teachers of the institution, continued to wear his long traditional garb, in which he dressed himself meticulously and impeccably. He was happy when one of the former Yeshiva students had difficulty with a Rashi, Bartenura, or Tosafot[2]. On such occasions he would reveal himself before the students with a full measure of his sharpness and wisdom. From among the students of the institution, he met his wife, Penina Kramer, who excelled in her Talmudic knowledge.

He was promoted from time to time. In 1932, he was appointed as the rector of the Institute of Jewish Wisdom, since he was also a talented administrator. Even though his primary focus was in teaching, he did not abandon research. He published manuscripts of Talmudic research, research anthologies, and Jubilee books. In 1929, his article "About the Babylonian Reality" was published in the second volume of the writings of the Institute of Jewish Wisdom; in 1931, he published "Notes on the Babylonian and Jerusalem Talmuds" in the Jubilee book in honor of Dr. Broide; in 1935 he published "The Ancient Source of Expressions" in the Jubilee book in honor Professor Moshe Schorr. In 1937-1939, close to the outbreak of the war that led to the Holocaust, he was still able to publish in volume eleven of the Writings of the Institute his article "The Babylonian Talmud in its Literary Context" (a: Expressions b: Discussion topics). He was also one of the activists of the Mizrachi movement in Poland.

[Page 100]

At the outbreak of the Second World War, he was able to recognize the Nazi enemy in Warsaw. His various discussions with his acquaintances testify to the level of fear that Professor Weiss had during the era that preceded the war, and over what happened to him under German occupation, when he was appointed as a member of the first Judenrat of Warsaw. In March or April 1940, Professor Weiss and his family had the opportunity of going abroad and immigrating to the United States. There, he began a new era of his life, for when he arrived there, he was immediately appointed as a professor of Talmud at the Yitzchak Elchanan Rabbinical Seminary of Yeshiva University in New York. However the difficult tribulations that he endured in Poland had a strong effect upon him, and therefore he did not succeed in publishing his scientific research. His books were not distributed appropriately, and therefore are not known to the masses. He lived in The Bronx, one of the boroughs of New York City; however he never stopped thinking about aliya to the Land of Israel. In the meantime, he sent his eldest son to Israel. He joined one of the religious kibbutzim. His beloved and revered student was the poet Shlomo Dikman, who died in Jerusalem in 1965. Several other scholars who were saved from the Nazi and Soviet infernos were numbered among his students.

On the occasion of his 70th birthday, Yeshiva University in New York published a Jubilee book in his honor, with the participation of the greatest scholars of Talmud research in the world (New York, 5723, 1963). The following books were published by him: The Complete Reality of the Talmud (New York 5703); The Creativity of the Savoraim[3] (their role in the creation of the Talmud, Jerusalem, 5713); About Talmudic Research (New York, 5715); The Judicial Order (research into Talmudic jurisprudence, New York, 5718); About the Literary Creativity of the Amoraim[4] (New York, 5722).

His desire to make aliya to Jerusalem immediately after his retirement was actualized. When he retired from work, he made aliya with his entire family to Jerusalem, and was accepted as a professor of Talmud at Bar Ilan University. His wife Penina Weiss, with the assistance of her husband the professor, succeeded in writing her memoirs of the tragic events under the German government in Warsaw, and the experiences that they endured in the Warsaw Ghetto. These memoirs enrich our knowledge of the Holocaust era in Poland. These memoirs are kept in the Yad Vashem archives in Jerusalem. His wife died approximately one year before her husband. From that time, he was depressed. When his students from the institute of Warsaw who survived and had made aliya to the Land of Israel came to comfort him over the loss of his wife, he hinted to them that his world is not full without Penina. Indeed, one year after her death, he his own soul to his Creator. Woe for those who have passed away and are not forgotten.

At the conclusion of the sheloshim (thirty day mourning period) after the death of Professor A. Weiss, a memorial ceremony was arranged in the synagogue of Bar Ilan University. The Minister of Religion Dr Zerach Warhaftig discussed his personality. He was eulogized as well by the rector of the university Professor Ch. Z. Hirschberg of the division of Israeli History, who knew the late man well, and was able to describe his many interests and activities throughout his life; Professor Yitzchak Gilat the head of the Department of Talmud; and Dr. Chaim Levin, who served as a lecturer of Talmud in the department in which Professor Weiss also lectured.

With his death, an unusual personality passed on, a man with a sharp intellect and great knowledge in Jewish studies, a communal man of great action and great merits. May his soul be bound in the bonds of eternal life.

A meeting of the committee in the home of the chairman Mr. Ettinger with the participation of Professor A. Weiss (at the head of the table). To his right is Dr. Kormish of Yad Vashem.

[Page 101]

Podhajce

by Dr. Michael Weichert

Dr. Michael Weichert of blessed memory

Podhajce is a city in Galician Podolia. In Polish, its name is Podhajce and in Ukrainian Pidhajci. However, the Jews of Podolia did not pronounce the "ha" correctly and did not differentiate between "Halelu" and "Chalelu". To them "Hershel" was "Ershel". Therefore, the name of the town to them was Podeitz[5]

As in most of the cities of Galicia, Podhajce had a derogatory nickname. They would say Korkovanei (the gizzards of) Lemberg, Raavtani (the gluttons) of Stanislawow, and the "katchkemachers" (duck makers) of Podhajce. Why katchkemachers? Because of an event that took place.

On the second day of the fair, a farmer stood up – in Galician Yiddish, every farmer was simply called a "goy" – who had brought a calf for sale. A Jew approached him, felt the calf, and asked:

"What is the price? For how much are you selling this duck?"

"I don't have a duck. I am selling this calf that you see.", answered the gentile.

"Calf? Where?", said the Jew in surprise, "I refer to this duck".

The villager pulled his spectacles toward himself.

"What duck? You see that this is a calf. Perhaps your vision has dimmed? Did you go blind?"

"What is he talking about? He called a duck a calf."

The villager stood and spilled out all of his bad dreams, and the Jew stood his own.

"Do not be angry. Why should we argue? Let's ask other people."

They called other Jews from among the passers by, and the all agreed that this was indeed a duck. The Jew had a big bargain. He purchased a calf and paid for a duck. From that time, they called the Jews of Podhajce "katchkemachers".

When a Jew from a city of Galicia would have a dispute with a Jew of Podhajce, he would immediately spout out: Podhajce katchkemacher. Or he would remind him that he comes from a town that starts with a "Po" and ends with a "ts". It was difficult to be a Podhajcer in Galicia.

In Polish history, Podhajce is praised for its pedigree, which began to stand out already in the beginning of the 16th century. After some time, in 1663, King Jan Kazimierz of Poland spent some time there, as he was waiting for his battalions to go together with them to Ukraine. Four years later, a camp of 80,000 Tatars and 24,000 Cossacks camped out there for two weeks against King Jan Sobieski and his army of 12,000 Poles. Thanks to the brave stand of the latter, the Sultan was forced to make peace with Poland. In 1675, the Sultan destroyed the city and exiled its residents. In 1698, the royal Hetman (Commander) Feliks Potocki was repelled to there.. He was attacked by 40,000 Tatars who pursued him until Podhajce.

The Jews of Podhajce did not know any of this, and if they did know it at one time, it had by now been forgotten from their hearts. At the end of the 19th century, an Austrian "bezirkshauptmannschaft" was set up in Podhajce. That is to say: a regional government, or in Polish, a Starostowo.

Podhajce was a clean and polished city. In its center was a large square paved with stone, known by the Jews as the marketplace. From there, wide streets extended out in both directions, one leading to the splendid Roman Catholic monastery and the other to the large Greek Catholic Czorkwa. The Jews called both of them "kloister", one of the Poles and the second of the "goyim" (gentiles).

The marketplace had two story homes, some with balconies. Father away from the marketplace, two story homes became rarer. For the most part, the one story houses were surrounded by gardens. On one side there were flowers, and on the other, there were vegetables and fruit trees.

In one of these small houses, on the road that led from the Greek Catholic church to the bridge and directly to Bzan (in Polish Berezany), and to the left to "Kalombis" (pits of flowers), where Jewish lads would go walking on Sabbath afternoons with their girlfriends, lived my paternal grandfather, Reb Yossi. That section of the city was called "the old city", and in days of yore, it was the "gmeina" (community) itself, since children who were born in that area were registered in their birth certificates as having been born in "stary miasto" (old city).

[Page 102]

Behind Grandfather's house there was a very large field of apples, pears, cherries, gooseberries, corn, fox-grapes, kidney beans, beans, cucumbers, beets and other vegetables. Aside from this, there was a portion of the field that was ploughed, planted with wheat and harvested with his own hands. Near the house, which with the passage of time sank further and further into the ground, he built a large stone stable that he rented on an annual basis to the Austrian authorities for the royal colts, and to which they brought the city horses. There was a large field behind the stable, surrounded by a high fence, and thin barriers, where pairs of horses would be placed together.

Grandfather was a tall Jew with a straight back, a tanned face, and a reddish-blond beard. He was recognizably different from the other Jews of Podhajce. This was felt in particular in the Beis Midrash. During my youth, I spent my summer vacations in Podhajce, and Grandfather took me to worship with him on Sabbaths, and to recite the Kinot (dirges) on the night of Tisha BeAv. Grandfather's prayers were without shaking his body and moving his hands, without groans and sighs. He would stand straight and present his supplications before the Creator of the World with clear pronunciation. On the night of Tisha BeAv, he sat, like the rest of the worshipers, on an overturned prayer podium and with his shoes off. However, his Kinot were not accompanied by weeping and tears. He uttered his complaints against the Creator over the destruction of the Holy Temple and the exile of His sons among the gentiles.

Grandfather did not live in peace with the town. He hated all injustice, and it was difficult to appease him when he took up his complaint with his fellow. He never requested anything for himself, and therefore, he was not afraid of the Parnassim and the power brokers in the community. He had his own outlook on the world and on man, and he spoke publicly that which he felt in his heart. More than anything, he loved cleanliness and order: in clothing, in the house, in the garden, in the field, and in interpersonal relations and relations between generality and detail.

For all his days, Grandfather's aims were filled with purpose. He did not know of sickness and did not know doctors. He came to visit us during the summer when he was 75 years old. Mother rented a room for a few weeks in the home of our relative in the village of Mikuliczyn in the Beskid Mountains, a two hour train ride from Stanislawow, where we lived. The renowned internist from Lemberg, Professor Gluzinsky, would spend his entire summer in a nearby village. He was well accepted by Jews, who streamed to him from all corners of the country. Father and Mother asked Grandfather to go to the professor so that he could examine him. They had to plead a great deal until he agreed.

The professor examined Grandfather, felt and examined, and started asking questions:

"Do you drink?" – "Heaven forbid", answered Grandfather.

"Hmm...", smiled the professor, "perhaps you can describe to me your daily regimen?"

"I get up early and go to the field or the garden. When I from my work, I worship and eat breakfast."

"Do you taste anything before breakfast?"

"I have something to drink"

"How much?"

Grandfather indicates with his hand about ½ a cup.

"What do you drink? Liquor?"

"Not at all – Okoweit[6]."

"When do you have a second drink?"

" Before lunch."

"Again Okoweit?"

"No, usually rum."

"And before dinner?"

"Again shehakol"[7]

"For how long have you being doing this?"

"From the day that I came under my own control."

"But you said that you don't drink?"

"This is also included in drink?"

The professor laughed and Grandfather got angry:

"Perhaps I seem like a drunk in your eyes, Mr. Professor?"

"Heaven forbid, but to drink spirits twice a day, rum or regular vodka, is worse than getting drunk from time to time. You have to refrain from the cup."

After this, Grandfather complained to us that we tricked him and "dragged him into the bag", as the expression goes, and that the doctor searched and found an illness with him. A few months later, Grandfather died.

Grandmother was the opposite of grandfather. Her name was Rachel. She was short, but healthy, strong, and very diligent. She never rested, for she was always busy and occupied – in the home, in the kitchen, in the garden. She was a woman of valor without equal, and work literally burned beneath her hands. All corners sparkled with cleanliness. She was very intelligent and pleasant to her fellow. She loved sharp retorts, and knew how to answer appropriately whenever necessary. However, she did this with a smile on her lips and in good spirit. I never saw her angry or heard her raise her voice. Nevertheless, with her strong hands, she maintained the entire enterprise of running the house and ruled over her husband, her daughters, her daughters-in-law, her in-laws, and her grandchildren – and was loved by them all.

Grandfather had five married children, three boys and two girls. The eldest Reuven left when I was still a child to go to America with his family. He was sixty years old at the time, and in his first letter, he complained that at the time of his old age, he was forced to bundle himself out and set out for a far-off and strange land. The second son Ezra spent all of his time in Podhajce, lived in a nearby cottage surrounded by a garden, and earned his livelihood with difficulty, primarily with in the merit of his wife Riva. She was a healthy and strong woman, whose strength was greater than that of three men. She worked in the garden, bundling bundles of textiles to sell to customers.

[Page 103]

They had two sons and a daughter. The daughter took after the mother. She was blessed with a healthy body and fiery red hair. When it was time to get married, the aunts whispered for a long period of time, they found for her a husband who would eat strong food and drink strong drink. The eldest son, Hershel, was a scholar. He married the daughter of Yisrael of Ritin – as the Jews called another large town in Podolia – Rohatyn. He was a quiet, good-hearted man, with large, blue eyes and a splendid, blond beard. Whoever saw him was not able to find any fault in him. During the world war, he was drafted to the "Andsturm". He was dressed up in army fatigues without any delay, given a gun, and ordered to guard the bridge. Since he had never been a soldier, and was unfamiliar with army regulations, he fell asleep on guard duty. The battalion was made up of Ukrainians. One of them came to him, stole his weapons, and tattled on him. He was brought before a military court.

The soldier with the long, blond beard and the large blue eyes made a strange impression upon the judges.

"What is your profession?"

"A Talmudic commentator", he answered.

He was exonerated.

Hershel loved to learn and teach. However since he had many children, he was forced to run a textile store in Rohatyn. He had a business, but not necessarily a livelihood. He would travel to Lemberg every few weeks to purchase merchandise. He was not a successful businessman, similar to Grandfather and all of Grandfather's sons. When he once complained to my father that his store is not providing him with a livelihood, Father asked him how he calculates the price of the merchandise for the customers.

"I add profit atop of the price that I pay in Lemberg."

"And what about the expenditures for the trips to Lemberg, the rent of the store, and all the various taxes and fees?"

"About this I never thought."

This was the type of merchant that my cousin Hershel was.

Yankel, the second son of Uncle Ezra, was not a "mench"[8] during his youth. He got up and went to America. There, his situation did not improve very much, and when he a few years later, he became a person of the community, and began to go out in a streimel and silk kapote. Since in America, as the news reached here, Yankel was not observant of the commandments, not particular about Jewish matters, and also not a scholar, family members would murmur among themselves abut Yankel's streimel and kapote.

Grandfather married off his eldest daughter, Tauba, to someone from Podwolcziska on the Russian border. His son-in-law, a Jew of stature with a black beard, well-kept and combed as is proper, was the only one in the family who would travel to the Rebbe. He had large businesses, and his home was a wealthy home. He had ten children. When his luck took a turn for the worse and his businesses failed, he immigrated to America with all of his family. His first letter began with the words: "I, Simcha Nathan Wilner, in America". Apparently, his fortunes were not good in that country. In his second letter, he wrote: "In the home, one father succeeded in sustaining ten children, whereas here, ten children do not succeed in sustaining one father."

The youngest daughter, Sarache, lived with her husband Hirsch Wolf Grynspan and their three children – a son and two daughters – in Grandfather's home. She toiled hard all her days for a morsel of bread for her family.

Podhajce was not far from Tarnopol, from where the light of the Haskalah shone onto the entire area already from the days of Yosef Perel. Many youths were attracted to that light. Grandfather's third son, my father Beirush, was also attracted to it. He was expert in small letters. He read and studied, but at the same time he glanced into Hashachar of Smolenskin and turned his ear to the sweet voice of Bat Hashamayim.

He married the daughter of Lozer Galart of Stanislawow. This grandfather of mine from my mother's side was a great scholar, and had his rabbinical ordination. He struggled against boorishness and hypocrisy, and he concerned himself with teaching his daughters not only Bible, but also Polish and German. He suffered no small amount from the zealots of the city, and only his scholarship and importance in the Torah circles saved him from embarrassment and disparagement. My mother Sara, Grandfather's third daughter, was tall and pretty during her youth, and remained that way throughout her life. She was intelligent and lively. She was not a "Bshao" (a disparaging term used by the Jews of Galicia). My father was tall and thin, with the red beard of a Misnaged[9]. He was divorced from his first wife. He was a Podhajcer. He knew that he would not be able to make an impression upon a girl from Stanislawow, so he made a pretext to ask a Torah question of Reb Lozer Galart, and through that entered into a conversion with him – the way things worked out also with his daughter Sara. The knowledge, discretion, modesty and refinement of the young man could not but make an impression upon the wise girl. Later, when Grandfather told her that they are proposing a match with her from this young man of Podhajce, she began to see him in a different light. Reb Lozer, who chose matches for his older daughters, urged his third daughter to agree to this match. She did the will of her father, whom she loved with all her soul. Shortly thereafter, the marriage contract was written up, and the wedding was arranged.

The couple moved to Podhajce, and one year later, on May 5, 1890, the young woman gave birth to a male child who was named after his grandfather Michael. At the time of the Pidyon Haben (Ceremony of the redemption of the firstborn), when the large, strong baby was brought in on a silver tray decorated with watches and gold chains, the joy of both sides was incalculable. After many years, father merited having a kaddish[10], and my maternal grandfather had the first male child

in the family. At that time, the train did not yet reach Podhajce. During those days, the train wagons would carry the travelers as if in a fever, to the point of shaking up the inwards, as people used to complain at that time.

[Page 104]

My mother had no desire at all to live in provincial Podhajce. She also longed greatly for Grandfather, and she urged my father to move his home to Stanislawow. In Podhajce, my father earned his livelihood from the wheat business. In Stanislawow, it was difficult for my father to attain any status. During the early period, my father remained in Podhajce, and on Sabbaths – not every Sabbath – he came to Stanislawow. He never uttered a word of complaint. However, as time passed, mother explained how difficult it was for him to live with Grandfather in Podhajce; how burdensome was the tiring journey in the wagon; the necessity to be cut off from his wife and child, to whom he was very attached; and the difficulty of having to have his bed on the bench-bed in Grandfather's house. In those times, the homes of the Jews had long, narrow benches with legs, containing straw stuffing inside. During the day, it served as a bench, and night the cover would be removed, and bedding would be placed on the straw.

A corner in the center of the city
From right to left: the home of Dr. Pik,
the home of Weintraub the shochet, the home of Tsimet.

From my earliest youth, I enjoyed "measuring distances", as my mother called it. In Podhajce, I would go forth and wander through all the streets. I was just over three when we moved to Stanislawow. There too, I would set out toward the edge of the city, and reached the bridge over the Bistrica. In this manner, the era of Podhajce had not yet left me. I would visit Podhajce during my vacations. Even when I was already a student in the gymnasia, I would love to visit Podhajce and find out what was going on in the city, especially with the Jews. I visited Podhajce for the last time during my vacation one year before my matriculation exams. At that time, I also visited one of father's nephews in the nearby town of Berezany, whose family name was also Weichert. I visited Podhajce once again during the vacation between grade 7 and grade 8, with the intention of setting out for Vienna after my matriculation exams. I wished to bid farewell to Podhajce. Grandfather and Grandmother had already not been alive for several years, but I was attracted to the area of my grandparents' home, that was so near and dear to my heart. When I would come to spend my vacations in Podhajce during my youth, I would get up early, walk in front of the small house, and turn to the left on the wide main road. For many years, the memory of the appearance of that road remained with me, as well as the aroma of the morning air. Often, the two of them, the scene and the aroma, would appear to me in a dream with splendid clarity. This would even happen when I was awake. To this day, it is sufficient for me to breathe the morning air, and that same sharp aroma and impressive scene would come to my mind once more.

From “Paths and Journeys of Life” by M. Weichert , Tel Aviv, 5628 (1968).

Translator's Footnotes

1. The Babylonian Talmud was compiled later than the Jerusalem Talmud, and is therefore considered more authoritative in general (with the exception of certain tractates that only have a Jerusalem Talmud).
2. Rashi and Tosafot are the primary Talmudic commentators. Bartenura is a commentator on the Mishna.
3. The Savoraim is the term for the generation of scholars who immediately followed the redaction of the Talmud.
4. The Amoraim is the term of the scholars of the Talmudic era. (Tannaim is the term for scholars of the Mishnaic era.)
5. The author uses the spelling of Podeitz through the article, including in the title. However, I am using the spelling Podhajce, which is the convention for this translation.
6. I am not sure of the identity of this drink.
7. Shehakol is the blessing over most types of drink.
8. Literally a “human being”, meaning here a “decent person”.
9. Probably a more meticulously groomed beard than that of a Hassid.
10. Kaddish is the prayer recited by a child after the death of a parent. Meriting to have a 'kaddish' is an expression that means 'merited to have a son'.

[Page 105]

Pleasant Scenes that Ended with the Holocaust

by Dr. Immanuel Heller

A general view of the city with the bridge over the Koropiec River

Our city of Podhajce was situated in a beautiful area. A mountain covered with forests and groves towered over it with it being in the valley. Thus did it get its name "Podgiatz" – the city that is at the foot of the grove.

In the valley at the foot of the mountain there is a pond shaped like a narrow strip that extends for several kilometers until Bialokrynica that is on the way to the town of Zlotniki. The Koropiec River also flows through the valley.

The soil of the city and the area is reddish black and fertile. It yields a bountiful supply of grains – wheat, corn, barley, oats, etc. The fruit trees in the city and the environs provide tasty, sweet fruit for the populace – apples, pears, plums, cherries, etc. The children would pluck these fruits for their pleasure, and they would often home with stains on their mouths and hands from these fruits.

From the market square in the center of the city, one road leads to the train station. Its length is approximately two kilometers, and it is decorated on both sides by trees, some old and others planted in our days. It passed by the Christian cemetery and continued on through fields, until the train station. The train from Lvov, which passed through Potutory and Berezany to Premishlan, and then to Lvov, passed by twice a day.

Connection between the city and the train station was maintained by the wagon drivers of the city. In the summer, wagons hitched to two horses served this purpose, and in the winter, they used special sleds called "Zalobnies", which were furnished with furs to cover the legs of the traveler. More than once, during the harsh days of winter, a snowstorm hit, and piled up mounds of snow on the route to the train. The sleds passed over them with difficulty, swaying from side to side. The wagon drivers in their tall fur hats looked like Cossacks, who appeared to us as figures from the imagination during our childhood, without any attachment to reality. They held long whips in their hands to whip and urge on the horses. However, in general, they would whip the air, for the well fed horses did not require any urging, and performed their job faithfully, without waiting for the whip to strike their backs.

For many years, peaceful and calm relations, and even relations of friendship and brotherhood, pervaded among the three segments of the population, among the three nations that belonged to three different religions: Jews, Roman Catholics and Greek Catholics. To serve them, there were three types of houses of prayer in our city: an old synagogue that was erected, it is told , in the days of King Jan Sobieski, the Roman Catholic church for the Poles, and the Greek Catholic church for the Ukrainians, who were called by the Jews by the general term "goyim".

A small Polish house of prayer (Kaplica) stood over the valley. It was erected in memory of the battle against the Tatars in the year 1667, in which King Sobieski attained his first acclaim as an army captain. From there, a splendid panoramic view of the city of Podhajce, the suburb of Zahaica, the pond and the river flowing through the valley spread out before the viewer.

There was a flourmill in the area between the pond and the river. Close to it there was a sawmill – called "Tartak" in the vernacular. An electric generator, which provided electricity for the populace, was established there a few years before the outbreak of the Second World War. The Roman Catholic Church and the public school were also located in that area.

There were no industrial enterprises in our city. The only tall chimney in the city was that of the monastery. Twice a day, at 6:00 a.m. and 5:00 p.m., a prolonged siren was heard throughout the city, that proclaimed the beginning and end of the workday in the sawmill.

As in all the cities of Galicia, the majority of the Jewish residents were small scale merchants or craftsmen. In the latter years, the percentage of those professing academic professions, primarily doctors and lawyers, increased significantly. A certain portion of the residents earned their livelihood from growing fruit trees and selling their fruit. Indeed, many residents had fruit orchards and vegetable gardens next to their houses, not for earning a livelihood.

[Page 106]

One of the most widespread and beloved crops in our area was corn. The stalks would reach to the height of a person, or even more. Cooked or roasted kernels of corn were a treat for the children. I can still taste the taste of the corn that I enjoyed in abundance during my childhood. It tasted like almonds or edible chestnuts, which did not grow in our area.

Autumn would come a short time after the ripening of the corn. Piles and piles of golden ears of corn would be placed out to dry on the rooftops. Only the stocks with their broad leaves remained standing in the fields and the gardens, waving to and fro in the autumn wind and making a sound that could be heard from afar.

My grandfather Hirsch Leib Horowitz of blessed memory, also loved nature, and enjoyed tending to his garden. As if in a dream, I remember him from my childhood, as he was hoeing the furrows and planting various vegetables, or grafting apple trees. This labor was not for his livelihood, for he was well-to-do. He did this only for enjoyment, and he did it willingly and enthusiastically.

The monastery

A deep depression fell during the 1930s, which marked the end of the peaceful and serene life of the Jews of our city of Podhajce. Suddenly, unemployment increased, there was a shortage of cash, and there was a slowdown in all branches of business and trade. The youth saw no way to get themselves set up in life. The number of youths who wished to immigrate, to make aliya to the Land of Israel or to immigrate to other countries, increased daily. However, this too was fraught with difficulties, and only few were able to overcome them.

Hitler came to power in 1933. A dark wave of coarse, ominous anti-Semitism overtook Germany, and its influence was felt throughout Europe, and came to our town. At first, people refused to believe that this nonsensical talk would find an attentive ear in society, especially in such a cultured land as Germany. However, the reality was more ominous. Thus arrived the year 1939, the year of the outbreak of the Second World War, and later the years 1942-1944, the years of the Holocaust and destruction for the Jews of Europe.

Difficult battles took place on the banks of the Volga and the foothills of the Kavkaz Mountains. On the main routes, on trains and on the roads, army battalions, implements of war and armaments streamed eastward to the front, to the interior of vast Russia. The travelers had the following motto: "The wheels are turning to victory..."

On the trip westward, broken airplanes and broken people, thousands and tens of thousands of wounded made their way back. This was aside from those who fell in battle and whose burial place was in the soil of Russia.

However, the area of Podhajce was not on the main route, but rather on the side routes, and during the first months, calm prevailed more so than would be expected during such times. Hundreds of people were absent from the city. Some of them went to Russia with the retreat of the Russians, and others were enlisted to work by the Germans. There were also a few who joined the partisans.

Once again the golden days of autumn arrived, when nature scatters its beautiful treasures with a wide open hand and a generous spirit. Leaves turned yellow in the gardens under the partly cloudy autumn skies, and the dried out leaves of the cornstalks made their sounds. The days were still warm, but the nights were cool. People began to worry about winter, which seemed to be a harbinger to war, poverty, cold and hunger...

Thus did the Days of Awe – Rosh Hashanah and Yom Kippur – approach. The small amount of news that came from the far off front indicated that the conquests of the German Army stopped going "according to plan", and that they were not succeeding in conquering the fortified cities that stood in their way. Hitler promised for the thousandth time that he succeeded in pulverizing the bones of the Russian army, but the situation was such,

as if out of spite, that the bones of the Germans and their allies were being pulverized more and more. The retreat and defeat of the Germans was becoming more and more real.

In the meantime, the city was closed off. It was a besieged city surrounded by the enemy. Jews were forbidden to leave the city, and nobody knew what each day would bring. The Hitlerist newspapers were filled with provocations and threats, and the atmosphere of a pogrom was hanging over the world.

[Page 107]

Finally the "angels of destruction", the men of the S.S. and Gestapo in their black uniform with the symbol of death – the skull of death – sewn to their hats, arrived. They arrived on the Eve of Yom Kippur, knowing clearly that the day was holy to the Jews, and that they would be all in the synagogues, or would have gathered in their homes for prayer. Aside from this – there was no place for anyone to escape.

The city was surrounding by the S.S. men and the militiamen. They began to remove the Jews from their homes and sending them to the train station. In the process, they mercilessly beat the Jews with whips, sticks, and the butts of their guns. Only to hurry them on as much as possible! Only to confuse and degrade the people so that they would have no thought of flight or resistance.

My grandfather Hirsch Leib Horowitz took heed of the sounds of weeping and screaming that came from the Market Square of the city, and fled to the garden. However, where was there to hide? Aside from the few trees and patches of grass, there was one small area where the cornstalks still stood crowded together, where one could hide without being noticed.

However, the Nazi beasts of prey did not come alone. They brought their dogs to help. They broke into the house and removed Grandmother Ethel. When they saw that her husband was not in the house, they hurried into the garden. The dogs immediately noticed the man hidden among the cornstalks, and grandfather was removed from his hiding place and dragged to the train station under a rain of blows. There stood the death cars, which brought the Jews on their final journey to the Belzec death camp.

The clear autumn sun looked down from above and continued along its path of ages. The branches of the trees rustled in the abandoned gardens, and quietly dropped their leaves...

Synagogues, Cheders, and Teachers

by Yehuda Grussgott

In the imagination of a Podhajce native, the name "Shil Gasse" (The Street of the Synagogue) brings to mind three ideas: the social stream, the external-architectural stream, and the cultural stream.

From a social perspective, this was the neighborhood of the poorest Jews of the town, the neighborhood of the porters, water drawers and simple craftsmen. Their huts, made out of poor material, stood in rows, with a narrow alley separating one row from another. Often, only a mutual wall separated them.

Only one house stood out in the neighborhood, the house that had an attic and a porch – the house of Avramche Walden (Avramche the teacher). The neighborhood was called Shil Gasse because most of the synagogues of the city were located there, headed by the central synagogue – Di Groise Shil – a name that it received because it was one of the largest and most impressive buildings in the city, both in height and in area. On the Jewish street, the synagogue served as a unit of measure of size and height. People would say: "as high as the synagogue", "as large as the synagogue". We children would compete and say: "Shloimo shot the slingshot to the height of the synagogue", "Yankel shot a stone up to the roof of the synagogue". It was said that a monastery used to be located in that building, and one of the heirs of the noblemen of Podhajce gave it as a gift to the Jews in the 17th century (?)[1] in order to serve as a synagogue. In the years between the world wars, when the Zionists "conquered the government" of the communities, the Great Synagogue began to serve as a meeting place and gathering place for all the Jews of the city. There, we celebrated the national days of remembrance, the anniversary of the Balfour Declaration, the Yahrzeit of the leader of the Zionist movement and visionary of the Jewish State Binyamin Zeev Herzl, the yahrzeit of our national poet Ch. N. Bialik, etc. At the time that such celebrations or memorials took place, most of the Jews of the city would close their businesses, don their festive clothes, and stream to the synagogue in order to listen to the speakers and lecturers. There as well, prayers were conducted on days of national – i.e. Austrian or Polish – celebration, with the participation of delegates of the government and Jewish population. In the two wings of the house near the church there were two small synagogues, that of the bakers and that of the tailors. However, the community of worshippers was mixed, and included no small number of merchants.

Opposite the Great Synagogue was the old synagogue called "the City Beis Midrash". During all hours of the day, until late into the night, the building was filled with Jews studying Torah, and on the benches near the giant oven, the "loafers" or wandering Jews would doze. At the approach of the festivals, particularly Passover, when they whitewashed and conducted repairs in the house of the teacher, the cheder would transfer to the Beis Midrash for two weeks. The prayer halls of the Hassidim of Chortkov and Belz were located on either side of the lobby of that building.

The Great Synagogue

[Page 108]

To the east of Great Synagogue were two small synagogues opposed each other. In one of the them, the Hassidim of the Husyatiner Rebbe worshipped – and it was called the Husyatiner Kloiz. A bit lower down was the synagogue of Yad Charutzim. Two well-known cantors served in these two synagogues. Both differed in their style of prayer and in the melodies that they used for various segments of prayer. They placed their stamp on the prayers and each gave a different and unique meaning to their prayers.

On the High Holy Days, people came to the Husyatiner Kloiz from all parts of the city to hear the prayers and sweet voice of Getzel Perel, who would conduct prayers with the accompaniment of his son Eliezer, who today lives in Safed. In the Yad Charutzim Synagogue, known as the "Temple", the prayers of Aharon Shmuel Ettinger inspired the hearts of the worshipper. He is the father of Menachem Ettinger, the chairman of our organization in Israel.

The synagogue known as the Baron Hirsch Synagogue was located in the northern section of the city. The cheder of Baruch the teacher was in that neighborhood. There, the level of learning was similar to that of the cheder of Reb Davidl. As a result of this proximity, the students of Baruch the teacher "ruled over" the Baron Hirsch Synagogue.

In the quarter in which the fortress was located, on the street known as the Schlossgasse, stood an old synagogue constructed out of hewn stones. It was known as the Schlossgasse Shil – the Synagogue of the Street of the Fortress.

Near the Christian neighborhood, almost at the edge of the neighborhood, stood a synagogue colored in bright bronze-like brown, which was called the Synagogue of the

Furriers. It was of beautiful form. Its walls were decorated with Biblical themes. The internal furnishings of the synagogue were also unique.

During the time of Soviet occupation, from 1939-1941, several of the smaller synagogues were converted to workshops. This included the Yad Charutzim Synagogue, which was turned into a shoemaking shop in which Jewish and gentiles shoemakers worked.

We will to the neighborhood of the synagogue, the Shil Gasse. All of the cheders were located in that area, and the sounds of the studying of schoolchildren could be heard at all hours of the day. Four year old children would come there to commence their study of the Aleph Beit with Avramche the teacher, and they would reach the second level of Chumash.

[Page 109]

In this cheder, the Jewish child made his first acquaintance with the printed word and the world of scripture. Only few children in the city did not pass through this passageway on their route to more advanced studies. Here the children studied in comfort, under the supervision of good people: Avramche the teacher and his wife Frieda were good hearted people with warm souls. They had bright faces, and took care of guests.

At times, the Rebbe would wave the tail-stick (kanczuk blez) with the intention of quieting the chattering crowd. However, he would always hit the table top, as if by chance. This would cause joyful chatter and increasing laughter. Then, the face of the teacher would brighten up again.

The second level of study of Holy Scriptures took place in the cheder of Shmil-Leib (Shmuel Leib). There, we studied all of the weekly Torah portions in Chumash, and we became familiar with the cryptic script of Rashi. We were awed by the stories of might in the Former Prophets[2]. This was called the study of "verses". The crowning goal of our studies was the study of several tractates of Gemara: Bava Metzia and Bava Batra.

We commenced our high level Bible studies with Reb Dovidl. A completely different atmosphere prevailed there. There we reached majority, and reached the age of commandments. There, our eyes were opened to the world that revolved around us. There we began to debate issues of our world. There as well, at the end of our Talmudic studies, we separated our ways and became Maskilim or Yeshiva students. However the memory of the crowded room in which we ripened and matured, the memory of the visage of our rabbi (the nickname Rabbeinu had for us at this point a different meaning) was etched deeply in the hearts and spirit of his students. It was a full patriarchal image, full of life, but bent with age; eyelashes covered with red, and sickly eyes hidden beneath thick eyebrows; a high forehead and a large, bald head, covered with a skullcap that miraculously did not fall off the forehead; a wide, white beard which always showed signs of aromatic tobacco, which he would carry in a horn shaped vessel that he made with his own hands. He would also make the tobacco with his own hands. This work seemed like alchemy from the middle ages. He would grind the tobacco in a grinder, filter it through a special filter, and add some sort of liquid, apparently for color and aroma. He would conduct this process diligently and with concentration, as if he was preparing incense for a mysterious service in the Temple.

Reb Dovidl was graced with deep knowledge of Talmud. Above all, the power of religious ecstasy that exuded from his personality could be felt. Some sort of secret beamed out from him – a secret that was hidden not only in the pages of the Book of the Zohar[3], that he carefully hid and concealed from us. However, he would talk about this secret that was beyond grasp, of this world and the World To Come, in his prophetic language, with parables and visions, as we would accompany him to the old Beis Midrash behind the gentile neighborhood at the time of sunset. During the difficult and cruel years of the Second World War, in any place that we found ourselves by force of fate, in the wide expanses of the Soviet Union, during the days of blood and nights of terror of the Nazi occupation, in the lands of the west of Mandate Palestine – in all of these places, those visions of the time preceding the End of Days jumped and flickered about, at the time of tribulations created by the world and man.

In his prayers, Reb Dovidl requested that he would merit in passing from this world before the evil comes. Indeed, he died at an old age, approximately 90 years old, during the terrible cholera epidemic that broke out at the end of the First World War.

The people of Podhajce tie a secret to his death no less wondrous than that of his life and personality. "To greet death", he would say, "One must prepare as if greeting a great festival, with nobility and an exalted spirit". Thus did he do. As he lay convulsing on his sickbed, he ordered his household to prepare everything, without forgetting his small volume of the Zohar, which was suddenly found under his pillow. This was wondrous, for the members of the household claimed that nobody gave it to the old man, and he himself did not arise from his bed. In his final moments of suffering before his death, when consciousness to him and his thoughts became clear, he asked that they place a key in his grave. He asked to look at the key, and he studied it for some time...

His funeral was the largest one in the city in those days. They placed the key in his grave, as he commanded, in order to lock up the hungry mouth of the ground from the victims of the cholera epidemic. Indeed, after this, the mortality rate of those who were ill decreased. People then would say that when Reb Dovidl went down to the grave, he locked up the mouth of the ground from further victims of the terrible epidemic. The great friend of the youth died. Their distinguished teacher went on his way. A man whose entire life was without blemish passed away; a righteous man went down to his grave.

May these lines of memories of one of his many students serve as a monument to his memory, after the monument on his grave was removed from its place in the Jewish cemetery of Podhajce by the hands of the barbarians in order to serve as the foundation stone of the house of some gentile, or a stone on the sidewalk in a gentile neighborhood. We, his students, hereby erect for him a memorial in the book, in our independent country – the State of Israel.

Translator's Footnotes

1. The question mark in parentheses is in the text.
2. The Former Prophets consists of the books of Joshua, Judges, Samuel I and II, and Kings I and II.
3. The Zohar is the main book of the Kabbalah.

[Page 110]

Memories of the Hebrew School in our City

by Yehudit Hadar

The Hebrew School in 1923 with the teacher Kurtz
Thirteen of the students are in Israel, and one is in the United States.

As I have been informed, there used to be a Hebrew School in our city under the directorship of the distinguished teacher Brecher, a resident of Podhajce. The teacher Brecher was a Hebrew teacher in our city for many years, but one bright day, he packed his suitcases and set out for America along with his family. In the meantime, until another qualified Hebrew teacher arrived, all sorts of youth, mainly students who had already mastered the Hebrew language, gave classes in Hebrew.

Many of the residents of our city were not satisfied with this situation, and attempted to bring a good, experienced teacher to our city. Their efforts bore fruit, and they succeeded to bring a teacher by the name of Rozen to our city. He arrived in our city before fitting premises for the Hebrew School could be found. After a short time, they succeeded in renting appropriate premises for the Hebrew School at the home of the Pulver family. The premises had two large rooms that could hold 30-35 students. I still remember the first day when the students gathered in the Hebrew school, the welcome and the first conversation of the teacher Rozen with the students, who were very much taken by him at that time. The teacher Rozen was of average height, approximately forty years old or slightly older. He arrived in our city from the town of Zlotniki. He had the high forehead of a scholar, and his visage exuded intelligence and good heartedness. People would say about the teacher Rozen that he was an expert in Talmud and a good pedagogue. We began our studies in an elementary fashion, and we paid great attention. In the meantime, other students joined us, and other courses were opened for beginners and those more advanced. We studied Hebrew, grammar and Bible for one hour each day, and the studies were conducted in an orderly fashion. One bright day, the teacher Rozen did not appear at our class. We were worried. Then the rumor spread that the teacher Rozen left our city for unknown reasons, and we were left once again as sheep without a shepherd.

We suffered greatly from the lack of a teacher, for we had become accustomed to our studies. After a short time, a young man, tall and with an erect posture, arrived in our city. His appearance exuded nobility and honor. He was a refugee from Russia and his name was Goldstein. He accepted upon himself the leadership of our school, and quickly exerted his authority over the students. He introduced a new style of learning, and imbued a completely different character to our school. The classes were conducted in literary Hebrew, unlike the teacher Rozen, who taught us in a biblical style. In addition to Hebrew, grammar, and Bible, we also studied literature and song with the teacher Goldstein. Form time to time, we also performed small plays on a wooden stage, such as "The Binding of Isaac", "The Flood", "King Saul", etc. Goldstein intended to settle in our city, for he was still a young man of 28. However, the Polish government opposed his residency in the city and ordered him to leave. I believe that he was commanded to leave Poland since he was a refugee from Russia. The school reached a state of crisis after he left.

After Goldstein left, there were a few teachers in the city, but they did not succeed in striking roots, since they were not as successful at teaching as their predecessors, and their students were not able to get used to them. In the meantime, the students dispersed, and we lost the premises at the Pulver home,

for it was difficult for the remaining students to pay even the rent. Once again, the committee or the group of donors concerned themselves with bringing a Hebrew teacher to our city at any cost. They got up and went to Lvov, the big city, where there was a Tarbut teacher's seminary. After much searching, they brought a Hebrew teacher to our city. He was a bachelor, approximately 29 years old. His externals did not offer much promise. He was tall, and his face did not exude anything special. He seemed like an ordinary young man, and at first it was difficult to get accustomed to him. However, here the adage was fulfilled: do not look at the container, but rather what is in it. After we succeeded in finding two gigantic rooms in the home of Dr. Avner and the classes started – we were forced to admit that we erred in judging the teacher Kurtz by his appearances. He was a teacher who was graced with all fine talents, with a proper approach, a fitting mode of relating and great patience. In short, he was a genuinely wonderful teacher. The classes started with a small number of students; however, with the passage of time, all of the students who had previously dispersed to the school. All of them to the students' benches, and the school bustled with many students. Almost 90% of the youth studied in Hebrew courses. That teacher by the name of Kurtz, whose externals did not promise much, knew very well how to win over the hearts of the students with his wonderful style that caused the students to absorb very quickly, and with his great dedication. He not only succeeded in winning over the hearts of his students, but he also won over the heart of a young woman who married him. He then settled in our city. Since his wife was a native of our city, people stopped worrying about Hebrew teachers, and the members of the committee breathed a sigh of relief.

[Page 111]

In the meantime, Rozen, the former teacher, to our city. He along with Kurtz did their share in developing the Hebrew school in a fine fashion. The school remained in existence until the outbreak of the Second World War, in which the students perished along with their teachers and parents. The school ceased to exist with the loss of Jewish life in the city.

One thing is certain and agreed upon by all of those who survived, most of whom live in Israel – that the Hebrew school of Podhajce provided its deep power and influence in educating its students in Zionism and the Land of Israel.

Students of the Hebrew school of Podhajce with the teachers Kurtz and Rozen

Reb Yechiel Meller

He was born in the city of Podhajce on Dec 7,. 1822. In his youth, he went to live in Stanislawow with his father, where he was educated in the manner that was customary of the cheders of that era. He studied only Talmud and Halacha. At the age of 16, he married a woman from Lvov, and there he began to learn the German, French and English languages, and delved into their literatures. When Mr. Stern began to publish his Kochvei Yitzchak periodical in 1945, he asked him to become an assistant in preparing the articles. He agreed, and many of his articles were published in all of the 26 editions. He also wrote several satirical stories that were published in Hanesher and Haet, published in Lvov.

In 1883, the first section of his book Nitei Neemanim, an anthology of all of his various articles, was published.

[Page 112]

The Hebrew School in Podhajce

by Etty Gross

Is it possible to tell of the Zionist activities in Podhajce and not mention the Hebrew school? And if the Hebrew school was already mentioned, is it possible to fail to mention the names of the two teachers, Mr. Kurtz and Mr. Rozen.

First, I want to establish without any doubt, that the school stood at the head of all Zionist activities, even though it was a cultural rather than a political institution. I was numbered among the veteran students of the school. I began to study in the school at the age of 9, and I studied there for many years.

Did the school suffice itself with only teaching the Hebrew languages? Certainly not. The study of the Hebrew language was only a means of implanting in the students the love of the Land of Israel, the love of the Jewish nation, and faith in its eternity. Indeed, these topics were not included in the curriculum of the school, but the point was made at every day, at every hour, and at every opportunity. Every holiday was celebrated at school as well, and at every holiday, the religious and national aspects were stressed together. For each holiday, we prepared a play, a party, or an excursion. There was no holiday that was devoid of content for us, and each holiday had a different theme.

For Passover, we learned the four questions and sung Chad Gadya; on Lag Baomer and Tu Bishvat, we would go out on excursions; for Shavuot, we would decorate the school with a great deal of greenery. The school imparted to us the love of the Land, which was far away from us only from a geographical perspective. The Kinneret, the mountains of the Galilee, and the Jezreel Valley were not merely geographical locations for us, but names tied to the pioneering struggle to renew the life of the nation upon its land.

Various clubs were active in the school. We published a wall newspaper, and there was Hebrew speaking club whose members took it upon themselves to converse only in Hebrew.

However, the material state of the school did not improve, apparently, for it always moved to a different location. We studied in a variety of locations. The rooms were not always comfortable, and in the winter, there was not always heat. I recall that many times, we would sit in coats during the winter, and write with gloves on our hands.

However, what did the cold matter in comparison to the warmth and enthusiasm that was found in the school. The two teachers were loved by us, even though each one had a different temperament. Mr. Kurtz was enthusiastic, emotional, and calmer; whereas Mr. Rozen was more exacting and demanding. They complemented each other, and each had his own personal charm. Their work was very difficult. They were very dedicated, despite the fact that the material conditions were not easy.

The work of the school was great and blessed. The values implanted in our hearts, and the knowledge imparted to us, helped many of us in our absorption in the Land.

An evening class for the study of Hebrew with the teachers Kurtz and Rozen

[Page 113]

The first Kindergarten in our City

by Yehudit Hadar

In our city, there were several families who attempted to found a kindergarten, rather than to send their young children to the cheder and the Rebbe. The activists worked hard in order to actualize their thoughts and to find the first kindergarten teacher. A few of the residents of the city, Zionist activists, traveled to Lvov (that is Lemberg), from where they brought a Hebrew teacher, for there, there was a seminary for teachers and also kindergarten teachers. After some effort, they found a kindergarten teacher. The activists rented three rooms from the Walgrif family. The rooms had several good traits: they were large, spacious, and well ventilated. There was a lovely garden surrounding the house. After the rooms were rented, the efforts to furnish the kindergarten began: small tables, small chairs, a closet, etc. were needed. After furnishing the kindergarten, they once again traveled to Lvov to bring various games for the kindergarten. In the meantime, the mothers prepared the toddlers for the important event, that they would be soon attending a Hebrew kindergarten where they would learn to speak Hebrew, to sing in Hebrew, and even to play in Hebrew. The children, who spoke Yiddish or Polish in their parents' homes from the time they were born, waited impatiently with great childhood curiosity for the day when the studies in the kindergarten would commence. Indeed, the awaited day arrived.

In the morning of that day, at 8:00 a.m., the mothers dressed up their young children in a dandy fashion, and they came with their sons and daughters to the kindergarten building. A swarthy young woman, tall, and graceful, stood on the steps of the kindergarten, and she introduced herself to the parents and children with an enthusiastic smile. When all of the children who had registered in the kindergarten had arrived, the kindergarten teacher invited the children inside with a pleasant wave of her hand.

The children had barely entered the kindergarten, when they scattered in every direction, and touched all of the objects, toys and games with their hands. On the first day of kindergarten, the children already learned how to say "Shalom, Todah, and Bevakasha" (Hello, please, thank you). The kindergarten teacher, Rivka Folkenflik, was very patient. She explained to the children and taught them the names of each toy or game that the children took into their hands. After time, the children learned to play together, not to hit, and not to grab a toy from the hands of another child. They learned how to eat nicely, to wash their hands before eating and after eating. The children learned good behavior, and the parents were very satisfied.

It was no wonder that when one of the mothers removed her child from the cheder or the rebbe, who taught the young child with the dry letters of the alphabet, and transferred him from the cheder to the kindergarten, the child would feel himself freer. At first, he would conduct himself with some restraint or laziness, however with time, he would participate in the games and performances of the children, such as "The Children of Mattathias", "The Hashmonaim", and by Chanukah, the child already knew how to sing the song "A little jug, a little jug, it gave its oil for eight days". The child would play among the other children with pride and seriousness in the role of Judah the Maccabee. The young children would conduct a conversation among themselves with importance and clear intent: "I am great, I am the brave Judah. I am the Maccabee Poyadim to Palestine"[1]. He wanted to say: "I will grow up and be brave as Judah Maccabee, and I will travel to Israel."

The kindergarten teacher taught the children to give in, to assist each other, and to be independent. The studies bore fruit. In the winter, for example, the children helped each other tie the strings of their hats or button the buttons of their coats. The kindergarten teacher Folkenflik, graced with extreme patience and an appropriately objective attitude to each student, without concern for the parent's status, served as a fine example to many of the parents as well, who at first objected to their children playing with certain other children. The kindergarten teacher succeeded in imparting to each boy or girl the love of the Homeland through various means: through words, brief stories, or little songs of the Homeland. She even imparted to the children a feeling of honor to adults, and a willingness to help their fellow. Thus, this kindergarten teacher, the first in our city, succeeded in winning over the hearts of the children and their parents, and in implanting in them a love and dedication to their nation and Homeland. She was an example for the young children, who to this point went about aimlessly. She was the one who imparted the spiritual basis in the hearts of the children.

The kindergarten teacher Folkenflik should be praised and thanked for her dedicated work for the children of our city, who were a source of pride to their parents.

The Hebrew school

Translator's Footnotes

1. I am not sure of the translation of the term Poyadim. I expect it is a vernacular term.

[Page 114]

The General Zionist Youth Movement in our City

by Baruch Schatten

At the outset of my words I wish to admit that it was not with ease that I came to write the following lines about the General Zionist Youth Movement in Podhajce. However, after I realized that if I would not perform this brief task, the situation would result in a diminution of the image of the Zionist youth movement of our fine town that once was and is no longer. I wished to prevent that the section on the youth of Podhajce should be described from one side only; how is it possible to skip over this group of youth who were the splendor of the young generation, the generation of continuity of pioneering, whose activity was not restricted to the city itself, and whose influence was felt on a national level as well.

We are speaking here about the following organizations: Achva, Young Achva (the children's organization), and the Hebrew youth movement that later changes its name to the Zionist Youth.

During the years 1926-1927, the residents of the city raised the flag of general Zionism as expressed in the national movement of that time, with an aim of educating and preparing the young generation to fulfil the roles that the nation has imposed upon them, with the perspective that one should not look upon the building of the Land as a monopoly of one class only (the workers), but should rather be an enterprise that belongs to all classes of the nation. It is fitting to mention the fact that the Zionist youth movement arose in an era where there was a crisis among the youth, when their ideological foundations were crumbling and they were standing at the crossroads.

The new motto was: realizing the fundamental Zionist idea without excuses. Indeed, the realities proved that it is possible to exist and to live, to build and be built up without depending on the ideological code of the camp of the "world of tomorrow". The General Zionist youth movement struck roots in the World Zionist Organization and in the Jewish street. Throughout the Diaspora and the settlement in Israel, hundreds of branches arose, as well as units for pioneering hachshara. The lively center existed, as is known, primarily in Eastern Galicia, that is Lvov. It is no wonder that the General Zionist movement flourished in this region, and its activities stood out in the development of the Hebrew settlement of the Land of Israel until the outbreak of the Second World War.

Members of the Zionist Youth Organization (1930)

[Page 115]

Zionist youth in Podhajce

Zionist youth in the year 1935

Zionist youth

[Page 116]

Achva Kibbutz

Members of Hechalutz in the year 1931

Hachshara Kibbutz of members of Achva (1934)

[Page 117]

Members of the Zionist Youth

Standing from right to left: Friedberg, Shimon Kramer, Fisher Jopiter.
Sitting right to left: Dr. Iziu Liblich, Dr. Ber

Zionist youth

In Podhajce, several Zionist youth organizations existed as I mentioned above: Achva, Zionist Youth, and Young Achva. Similarly, there was an Achva hachshara kibbutz whose members worked in the local flourmill and the sawmill (tartak in the vernacular) that was next to the river outside the city. The kibbutz received support and encouragement from the local Zionist organizations. The Jewish community in our city excelled, to our good fortune, in the love of the nation, and extended full support and encouragement to the Hebrew youth.

As far as I remember, the following people stood at the head of the local committee of the Zionist organization: Dr. Rotenberg of blessed memory (a lawyer) and the engineer Dr. Lilla of blessed memory, whose houses were always open to anyone who turned to them. It was a real experience for us to work with them. I feel a special duty to mention Dr. Dik, who spread his support with a generous hand and an open heart to the general Zionist movement in particular. Dr. Dik was a noble personality, with a warm Jewish heart, who conducted himself modestly with his fellowman.

Achva was composed of people of the age 18 and over from the popular circles. Young Achva consisted of youths from the ages of 13-18. Young Achva arose with the purpose of renewing and injecting of young blood into the popular Achva movement, to prepare the generation of those who would continue on, and to instill scouting education, love of the homeland and a desire for personal realization into the youth. The chapter of Young Achva in our city was one of the largest chapters in the region. It was able to conduct a summer camp and conventions, and issue publications. Thanks to the activities of the heads of the movement, it succeeded in imprinting its stamp upon the entire movement.

[Page 118]

Members of the Young Zion
Standing, Lubchia Katz, Freda Heller, Fanchia Gross
Sitting Freda Stadmauer, Dr. Max Sar, Malchia Gross

Members of Young Achva (1936)

Moshe Erda of blessed memory served as the head of the Achva chapter of Podhajce. He also served as the secretary of the community in our city, and the chief intermediary between the Jewish national organizations and the government. Aryeh Kurtz of blessed memory also served as head of Achva. He was a teacher in the Hebrew school and conducted wide branched cultural and spiritual work. Similarly, it is fitting to mention the members Buchwald and Polisziuk. The members of the Zionist youth were primarily students of the high school. Shlomo Walden, Elka Gotstein and the writer of these lines were the heads of that organization.

Achva published booklets entitled Glus Achvaj (in Polish) and Young Achva, which were published by Weinless' publishing house. The following participated in these publications: Leon Shourz who was also one of the heads of Young Achva, Moshe Erda, Dr. Dik, Schatten and others. This publication was dedicated to issues of the day and to educational problems of the movement. It was compiled in the Polish language.

With recognition to the special merit of the local chapter of Young Achva, the writer of these lines was invited in 1936 to the Achva center in Lvov in order to lead the national youth organization.

In conclusion, I have not fulfilled my obligation if I do not point out the good relations and joint activity that pervaded among the various local youth organizations. With regard to the overriding national interests, preference was given to the general interests over the interests of each individual faction.

[Page 119]

The Youth and Hashomer Hatzair in Podhajce

by Avraham Brandwein

A group of Hashomer Hatzair members

From right to left: Meir Zoloczower of blessed memory, Elu Reich of blessed memory, Dov Bezen of blessed memory, Yehoshua Poliszuk of blessed memory, Avraham Marbuch, Mordechai Oren (Orenstein)

Hashomer Hatzair, 1920-1921

Podhajce, a typical Jewish town, is situation in a lovely area, with abundant greenery, forests and rivers. Koropiec, the small river, that was made fit for the breeding of fish by the creation of two large ponds, served as an attraction for the citizens of the city on festivals and Sabbaths. The rich river foliage, bulrushes and numerous lily pads formed lovely islets in the clear blue water that decorated the ponds. However, they disturbed the local youth from enjoying themselves in the water in swimming great distances.

The government dam created a waterfall, which increased the enjoyment of the youths throughout the summer and was a source of pleasure for the adults who came on Fridays, the eve of the Sabbath to refresh their bodies prior to the Sabbath rest.

On both sides of the river, there were meadows rich with sweet vegetation, in which cows and ducks grazed, satisfying their hunger under the supervision of shepherds. Our Jewish youth found in them a place to enjoy reading and study, with the mats of grass serving them as a soft mattress, and the rays of sunlight tanning their white, fine skin.

The pond did not stand forlorn in the winter. A heavy layer of ice covered its surface. Tens and hundreds of young people would enjoy themselves skating on cold, icy days, as they found an outlet for the youthful energy that was locked up in them.

The river, the pond, and its surroundings were centers for the multitudes of children and youth throughout all the days of the year. A sloping hill towered over the river, covered with fresh young trees in the summer and snow in the winter, adding beauty to the general landscape. This forested hill knew how recount the countless activities of the Hashomer Hatzair chapter, discussions and debates, planning of activities, scouting activities, and ordinary hikes for reading and relaxation.

The industrial area was on the other side of the river: the sawmill, the flourmill, and finally – the power mill. These were the largest employers in our city. The elementary school and Sokol house were nearby, and the Catholic church opposite them.

The Jewish homes began from that point and onward, and extended to the center. The center – in the shape of a large, round open area – had a concentration of stalls and was surrounded by stores, residential dwellings and places of employment, all together. Streets and alleys spread out from there in all directions. The population of the city of Podhajce was spread out among them. Thus was the general landscape; the Jewish landscape in the midst of this picture excelled in its liveliness, activities, and well developed mutual assistance.

Hundreds of Jewish families that were scattered throughout the 72 villages of the neighborhood regarded this city as the spiritual center and the place in which to find assistance at the time of difficulty. Jewish life was lively, and the events of the Jewish world found expression in the Jewish street. The 20th of Tammuz, the day of the Balfour declaration, the bloody events of the Land of Israel in 1921, the laying of the cornerstone of the Hebrew University of Jerusalem, and – on the other hand – anti-Semitic occurrences in various places – all of these aroused special feelings among the Jewish population.

[Page 120]

The leadership of the Hashomer Hatzair chapter in the year 1931

Veterans of Hashomer Hatzair, 1920/21

Jewish family life was very well developed in the broad sense of the term. Each family served as a warm corner that wove the character of the Jewish boy or girl. From the immediate family, the family atmosphere broadened to the extended family through visits on Sabbaths and festivals, and forged the living bond between the Jewish past and present, to the Jewish mission. Not infrequently, meetings and spending time together took place in the context of general events that were arranged at the synagogues in order to forge the character of the Jewish youth and deepen the commitment to the national mission. The cheder in its earliest days, the Tarbut Hebrew School with teachers and educators such as Shimshon Rozen of blessed memory and Aryeh Kurtz of blessed memory, great in Torah and wisdom, and filled with the love of Israel and the love of Zion – established a firm and strong base as a bond to the past, to the Hebrew language and to the national revival movement in all of its branches. The young person, who was filled to the brim with a Jewish atmosphere from his home, his family, and his teachers in Tarbut, received food and energy to heal his exile oriented soul and to raise his Jewish stature. If we study the composition of the Jewish population of Podhajce and its region, we will see that it included hundreds of extended families who maintained their family ties throughout many years. On holidays and festivals, the family ties centered around meals and visits, which strengthened the ties between relatives and magnified the joy of the festival. The First World War scattered them to various places. After the ceasefire, they gathered together again and forged anew their mutual way of life. Waves of disturbances afflicted the state, starting with the anti-Semitic outbreaks of the Poles and ending with Petliura's gangs, which led to a literal pogrom. Pillage of the houses and stores marked the climax of 18 hours of disturbances by the Petliurchiks. The adults and children hid in their cellars and attics. From the corner of my hiding place, I saw Mr. Binyamin Kitner of blessed memory, one of the leaders of the local Jewish community, tied to the water well waiting to be executed unless someone would bring a ransom for him. The shots of the Bolsheviks who pursued them from the direction of the mountain scattered the Petliura gangs, and my father of blessed memory freed Binyamin Kitner from his fetters.

These days of wantonness passed, and the Jewish community organized itself in the subsequent days. Schools opened, and food packages were distributed by representatives of the assistance organizations of America. The large buns and glasses of cocoa that were distributed to the children were particularly tasty. Means of livelihood were not readily available, and the vast majority of the Jews made use of this merchandise.

In this situation of a weak economic base, without political standing – the young generation of children and youth who felt the reality of the exile on a daily basis came of age. This feeling served as the impetus for national and social awakening among the youth, who were not satisfied with life solely in accordance to the traditions of the fathers, but rather searched for a remedy and wished to forge its own path, a path of liberation, of upright stature and national pride. Students from our town who studied in the large cities brought with them the winds of pleasantness and renewal. During the vacations from their studies, they brought together the finest of the studying youth and established the Hashomer Hatzair chapter in our city. This was in the years 1918-1920. The founders of the chapter included Dr. Marbuch of blessed memory, the engineer Zoloczower (Zerubavel), Mr. Jopiter and Mrs. Hala Messing (Lebel) may they live, and others.

The lectures, excursions, scouting activity – all of these in the bosom of nature among the green fields and forests awakened a revolution in the hearts of the youth, who generally spent their time studying in the walls of the cheder or the Beis Midrash. In those days, a lively group of youth got together with initiative and founded Hechalutz. Mr. Menachem Itinger, Mr. Buchwald and others were among its first members. These two groups, the group of studying youths and the Hechalutz group, worked together throughout the years in the midst of the local Jewish youth. They were not satisfied with preaching and explanations alone, but they transferred over to practicality, and made aliya to the Land in 1921. The entire town accompanied them, some with esteem, some with reverence, some with lack of faith, and some with opposition to their deeds. This aliya had a strong echo that extended and strengthened. Other Shomrim or other pioneers made aliya.

[Page 121]

Veteran girls of the Hashomer Hatzair chapter

Standing from right to left: Messing, Malka Weitzis, Freida Lerer, Sheindele Lerer. Sitting: Rozia Rozmarin, Haber, Mrs. Marbuch

A group of Hashomer Hatzair members

From that time, the Hashomer chapter continued it activities uninterruptedly, weathering the crises that broke out from time to time. For the most part, these crises were created by the lack of leadership and direction due to the aliya to the Land of the veterans of the chapter. The Zionist activity in the city increased yearly, along with the activities of the Hashomer Hatzair chapter. All strata of the youth organized themselves and joined up with the chapter, despite the opposition of the majority of the parents. The opposition to the movement arose from a variety of reasons. Some were opposed to our Zionism, some to our Socialism, and some to both. Some were opposed to the mingling of boys and girls, and some to the distancing of their children from the ways of tradition. In this atmosphere of lack of support and even opposition, Hashomer Hatzair forged its way into the ranks of the younger generation and became the central force of the youth of the city. With time, the Zionist circles provided moral, material and communal support to the Hashomer Hatzair chapter. They presented us as "patrons" to the authorities, and we always found a warm and open heart from them at times of difficulty. Thanks to their advice or assistance, we were not infrequently saved from difficult situations. The Hashomer chapter turned into a warm corner for the boys and girls of age 13 and above. Its activities digressed significantly from education work, and encompassed various communal areas.

In the chapter, the youth enjoyed an atmosphere of friendship, camaraderie, national pride and social justice. The youth who had witnessed the exile with their own person, the life of poverty, unemployment and lack of hope, found here the vision for a creative and free life in the Land of their dreams: with the sweat of their brow they will revive desolate areas, with their own hands they will establish settlements and protect with weapons life, honor and the future of the Jewish homeland. All of this came to expression in many discussions on many Sabbath eves – discussions that were accompanied by songs filled with longing for the Land and its landscape. There, they learned to value and honor the status of workers, and to desire to turn into a creative people. They recognized the lack of economic, political and national status of the Jewish people in the Diaspora, and laid plans for the actualization of the liberation from all this and the creation of a new life. Here, the recognition that the Jews must live by overcoming their fears, and not recoil from conflict with gentiles, penetrated into the hearts of the members of the chapter. This indeed happened that on one of the days of the festival of Shavuot, at a time when a group of 14-year-old boys and girls were engaged in a scouting activity on the hills outside the city, they were attacked by stones thrown by shepherds. The youths entered into a battle with stones, and did not flee from them, as had been the custom until that time.

[Page 122]

A Hashomer Hatzair chapter (1938)

The Aryeh group of Hashomer Hatzair

Some Podhajce natives in Hashomer Hatzair Kibbutzim at a festive convention in Merchavia, on the occasion of the jubilee of the movement in 1963

A group of friends in Hashomer Hatzair (1934)

[Page 123]

A Hachshara group of counselors of Hashomer Hatzair in the year 1924

There was no Zionist activity in the city in which the chapter did not stand in the forefront: parades on the anniversary of Dr. Herzl's death on the 20th of Tammuz, on the day of the laying of the cornerstone of the Hebrew University – all of these included appearances of the members of the chapter in their fine costumes. In activities regarding the Jewish National Fund, the Tarbut School, the public library, and the Hatikva hall, elections – in every place the Hashomer chapter served as the nerve center. The Tarbut School included hundreds of children and maintained itself solely by its tuition fees. Collection of money from the parents took place throughout the years by members of the chapter on a voluntary basis. They participated in hachsharah (Zionist preparation), counseling, organizing, in activities of the League for the Working Land of Israel, and in the leadership of Hechalutz. This was a constant support in Zionist activities, against the various streams that swept through the Jewish street.

Eras of upturns and downturns affected the Jewish street, and these negatively influenced our lives in the Hashomer chapter. The economic recessions of 1924 and 1929, felt through the country and the cities of Poland, caused disappointment among the youth and sowed seeds of despair and apathy among their ranks. An interruption in aliya, unemployment, growing anti-Semitism, and the rise of fascism – all of these caused defections from all of the youth movements in the city, leading to their disbanding. The Communists took advantage of the disarray among the youth and increased their strength. The Hashomer chapter maintained its stand even during this era, despite the losses that it suffered, and continued with its activities with conviction and faith that there was no other way. Through the struggle for the soul of the youth, the chapter overcame setbacks and established young reserves for the leadership of the chapter, so that it could continue its activities after its graduates leave for the Land or go on hachsharah. As usual, they found support and assistance through the "patronat" (The group for the supervision of the scouting youth and Hashomer Hatzair) who remained faithful to the Hashomer spirit and its values, and came to their assistance in front of official organizations who related inimically to the chapter. In the years 1934-1939, the members of the leadership committee of the chapter were Dr. Baruch Milch, Dr. Morgan (the young), Professor Grussgott, Dr. Rozia Kestenblatt, Dr. Yaakov Horowitz of blessed memory, and others. In the years 1938-1939, the eve of the outbreak of the war, a time of rising tensions, the connection between the committee and the chapter strengthened further. They all felt that disaster was impending, and they must strengthen themselves internally and find a way to continue on through any reality that might ensure.

The war broke out with all its fury. A flood of tribulations came upon Podhajce like a thief, drowning everything in fire and blood. The end came even to the Hashomer chapter.

[Page 124]

The Kadima Student Corporation

Crescat Vivat Floreat Kadima
by Yehuda Grussgott

A group of academics – sworn friends
From right to left: Dr. Ber – who remains in Poland, the teacher Kestenblatt who perished, the veterinarian Matis Kohn who perished

From among the many youth organizations that were officially or unofficially affiliated with political parties, the Kadima student corporation that arose in Podhajce in the year 1931 should be noted. This was not exactly a pure academic corporation, since gymnasium students also belonged to it. At the founding meeting of the organization, mutual material assistance among the students was set as the prime goal of the corporation, through forming social connections that will be expressed in joint activities.

Indeed, only a few people were given some sort of one time financial assistance (it is not known from which fund), however, they all enjoyed the "colors" (embroidered ribbons – see the picture), both the "poskim" and the "borshim". Each corporant had to find a girl who would be willing to embroider the "colors". Since the girls did not hasten to volunteer for such, several members such as Suzia (Sara) Orenstein of blessed memory (the sister of Mordechai Oren, a captive in Prague) Salka Haselkorn of blessed memory (the wife of Adek Gang of blessed memory) Lorka Weinglas (the wife of Leon Milch) took it upon themselves to sew the first colors for the first festive meeting "Boda". All of the work took place in the home of the Orensteins. The emblem of the corporation was a heart shaped shield, with the initials of the Latin words "Crescat, Vivat, Floreat Kadima" (Grow, Live, Flourish Kadima) embroidered upon it.

The corporation was only active during the summer vacation and the festival times, when the youth who studied in universities and high schools to their homes. They, the sprouts of the youth and splendor of Podhajce Jewry, were many, many...

Then the joyous "Bodot" and "Bidot" would take place, at first at the home of the legal magister Ira Margolis of blessed memory, who was the father and founder of the corporation and its first leader. In time, he became an experienced corporant in the Kadima of Lvov, and still later its president. I recall the "Bodot" in the home of the engineer Lila of blessed memory. His son Misio of blessed memory was later the president of the corporation. In the latter period, the gatherings took place in the Tikva home. The "Bodot" were filled with various games and entertainment. Anyone who entered in the middle of the evening would immediately find a pretext to mock the bubbly youthfulness of those gathered. In the "Bibot", we would turn to each other not with our first names, but rather with the nickname that was given to each corporant, a nickname that would bring a smile with its ring and meaning, such as: Egvenia, Amba, etc.

We would sing various songs and verses there. I remember a number of stanzas, which I bring with a freeform translation:

Arise to battle!
My nation the sword!
Cast forth your oppressive fear,
Grab a sword of fire in your hands!
The seat of Zion,
We will capture with might,
Affix a yoke to the sickle
At the time you go to the oppressive dust.

There was no shortage of songs of despair and disappointment, that were characteristic of the corporation. For example, the following:

I sit in a dark cellar,
With my cup filled with liquor.
Oh, how good is it for me – I will think –
Nobody will speak to me...
My red nose, my bulging belly –
I do not care, to hell;
I will take a cup in my hand,
And sip, and sip, and sip...

[Page 125]

We were young, and the pessimistic atmosphere of these songs passed quickly. It was happy and pleasant, and we did not feel any worries for several hours. Veteran corporants, old masters, "Alte Herren" served as "patrons" of the corporation. I remember the final "Bida" in which the engineer David Lila and the lawyers Notek and Rotenberg participated. There are also less pleasant and heartwarming memories: including the social excommunication that was imposed upon all members who refused to join the corporation and related to it with reservation due to differences in world outlook or other reasons. A member was liable to "rugchia" (revocation of membership) for not obeying the excommunication. This was considered to be a great shame and disgrace. However, not all of us agreed to such a hasty penalty.

With the passage of time, it became more and more clear that the corporation was becoming a tool of specific parties in the election campaigns for local Zionist organizations, for delegates to the Zionist congresses, and to the Polish Sejm. At that time, internal schisms became exposed, which caused the departure of many "brothers".

Finally, without knowing by whom and when, the corporation ceased to exist. However it is possible to sum up that during its three years of existence, the corporation filled a vital role in the social landscape: it forged a living connection and interconnections between the generations among the intelligentsia of the city – between those with academic professions (doctors, lawyers and teachers) from one side, and the studying youth (students of institutions and high school graduates) on the other side. To this day, it unites us with the strong ties that began then, during our bright youth.

Academic youth on an excursion (1933)

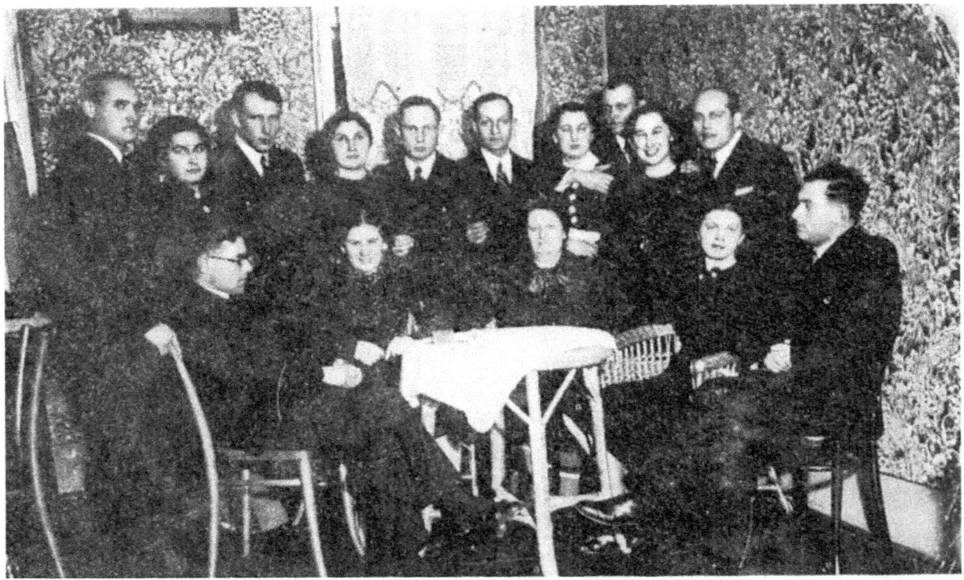

A group of academic youth in the house of the Weinless family (1938)

[Page 126]

Meir Mass the Hero of our Town

by Yehuda Grussgott

A cottage stood for many years, toppling over and sunken into the ground. The years brought its windows nearer to the ground, and one had to bend down significantly in order to peer inside. That cottage, bent with age, stood next opposite the synagogue of the Hassidm of Husiatyn (The Husiatner Kloiz).

In this cottage lived Chana Mass with her two children, Meir and Sheindele. A strange story was told about Chana's husband and the father of her children. Many years had passed since the man abandoned his family and immigrated to America. His tracks were lost. There were indeed those who claimed that the husband of Chana Mass would send money on occasion, albeit only to his children and not to his wife. My memory goes back to those years when the grandfather Itzi Mass was alive and lived in the cottage. In truth, I don't know why they called the old man Mass – if I am not wrong he was Chana's father. Chana was burdened with the yoke of running the household. From her one could obtain dairy products such as fresh milk, cheese and butter. Chana sold fowl. Homemakers would come to her to purchase "a quarter of a fowl", a duck, a wing or a foot, and in the winter – duck fat.

One day in the summer, wagons started to unload heaps of stone and bricks next to the dilapidated cottage. They grew and formed into cubes upon cubes. The town noticed this, and everyone asked the question: "How can poor Chana afford to build a house?" The questions remained without answers. Within a short time, a one-story house, built with red bricks, arose in place of the cottage. However, the secret remained a secret.

More than this, the character of Chana's son, attracted and enchanted the people of Podhajce. His full name was Meir Mass. This was a strange thing in a town where everyone had a nickname or an adjunct name to their first name. Meir was known for his strength, braveness and brazenness already when he was in cheder. The child, about ten years old, was the leader of all the children of the neighborhood, the "Shil Gasse" neighborhood. He was tall, with long legs, and nobody was his equal in running and jumping. He had muscular arms that were long in relation to his body. They were always in motion. His hair was fine, smooth and light blond, and his cheeks were always rosy. A strained expression was always upon his long face, upon which his long, aquiline nose stood out. His clear eyes, blue as the sky, peered out restlessly upon his surroundings. He was more like a "gural" (mountain man) than a student, both in his external appearance and his love of freedom that was ingrained in his soul. Meir was a master at throwing stones afar. A stone from his hand would reach the roof of the tallest building in the neighborhood, the Great Synagogue – a huge building whose style and awesome appearance reminded one of a fortress or castle. Meir also excelled at shooting stones from a catapult, and nobody was his equal with a slingshot.

It was impossible to measure up to him in the game of buttons, because of the precision of his shot, the force of his throwing against the wall, and more importantly, by his ability to measure the distance between two buttons by opening his fingers between the index finger and the thumb. His superiority was clear, his victory was expected from the outset, and it was dangerous to compete with him, for all of the buttons of his opponent would quickly end up in Meir's pocket. In the game that was usually accompanied by outbreaks of laughter, shrieks and whistles that spread through the neighborhood, Meir was the central personality in the Jewish neighborhood. Already when he was a child, people feared him, revered him, and loved him all at once, on account of the fact that his height and strength exceeded all others of his age. He was brave of heart, jolly and friendly. By nature he was goodhearted, and he pursued justice. His strength and braveness did not make him into a pest. On the contrary, he had social sensitivity. He felt an injustice against his fellow and supported him. We always saw him standing up for the weaker one. We, the children of the Jewish neighborhood, were proud of him. People of the Christian neighborhood who would attack Jewish children, beat them, and pick their pockets were frightened of Meir. In order to frighten an attacker and chase him from the Jewish neighborhood, it was sufficient to call out "Meir, Meir". Thus was Meir from his childhood, from his cheder years.

Meir Mass During the First World War and the 1920s

That Hercules of childhood, the Hercules of the Street of the Synagogue and the exclusive realm of Jewish life, grew up and became a central figure in the older youth of Podhajce, both Jewish and gentile. Meir became the mighty person of the youth of the right bank of the Koropiec River, the place where the regional city of Podhajce was located with its Jewish, Polish, and Ukrainian residents. He became the center of dispute between the local youth and the village youth of the village of Syulka on the high left bank of the river. The reason for the misunderstanding between several of the youths on each side, that led to the protracted "war" between the youth of the city and the youth of Syulka is not known to me now, but I remember the facts well.

Each afternoon, the youth of both sides gathered in the meadows that were on both sides of the Koropiec River. The offensive would begin with the shouts of Hurrah from hundreds of mouths of the youths of age 13-20. Weapons included slingshot stones, nails,

screws other remnants of items that were used by the Austrian troops in the erection of barbed wire barriers. (The front and the trenches in the First World War passed through the length of the Stripa River, a distance of 2 miles from Podhajce. It was the nearest flank and served as a battleground for brief skirmishes between the Russians and the Central Forces several times during the war.) The results of the competition were decided mainly by the appearance of Meir Mass on the battlefield, which always sowed fear and terror among the youths of Syulka, and injected additional strength into the city side. Meir pushed forward with a volley of stones and projectiles, and conquered the ruins of the liquor still on the hill, that was the fortress of the side of the farmers. Thus did Meirke the "Jew boy" become the hero of all the city yo++uth. He was our pride, he represented our ancient tradition, a tradition of bravery and strength, from the times of David and Judah the Maccabee. Thanks to him, the hatred and violence that were the lot of the Jewish children at the hands of the children of the non-Jewish neighborhood, were forgotten for a long time.

[Page 127]

In the wake of the First World War, several independent states arose from the ruins of the Austo-Hungarian Empire, including the State of Poland.

Several national conflicts grew and strengthened in Poland, whose new borders encompassed several national minorities. The national consciousness of the Ukrainians took on the form of extremism and anti-Semitism. In this realm, with regard to relations with the Jews, there were no differences between the Poles and the Ukrainians. The Jewish Population found itself between the hammer and the anvil, prone to inimical relations on either side. The anti-Semitic policies of the new Polish government expressed themselves in various economic restrictions imposed upon the Jews.

A partial view of the Market Square (Rynek)

The Polish youth of the Endek stream perpetrated disturbances in the universities. Boycotts against Jewish stores and attacks on stalls were daily occurrences during that era.

The Ukrainians in the eastern regions of Poland also searched for ways of actualizing their anti-Semitism in various forms. I wish to mention one of them here, for it serves as a background to the growth of the new character of Meir Mass. The army draft would take place every year in the regional city during the months of May and June. Youths of the age of the draft, 21-year-olds, would come to the draft committee from all villages of the region. Among them were several villages whose residents were known as instigators of strife and conflict. Holhocha was one such village. Its residents were tall, blue eyed, and light haired, appearing in their externals more like a Germanic tribe than Ukrainians. They would march to town for the draft in orderly groups, in formation, dressed festively with embroidered linen shirts fastened to their necks with a red ribbon. Their caps were tilted backward. They accompanied their march with popular and nationalistic songs, sung in fine voice.

One year, in 1936 or 1937, the youth of the suburbs of Halicz [1] decided to demonstrate that they were true sons of their village that was known for infamy. After their enlistment, they went to the taverns to get drunk as was their custom. After they had become inebriated, they went out to the marketplace, where the majority of the stalls belong to Jews. They began to pillage the meager property, and they injured several Jews. A tumult arose in the city. Quick as lightning, the news reached Meir Mass and another Jewish strongman, Binyamin Goldberg, who was nicknamed "Binyamin Kotlar". These two, certain

of their strength, appeared in the marketplace among the hundreds of wild, fiery draftees. The two of them removed the harness straps from the wagons that stood in the marketplace, and burst into the gang of hooligans waving them about. A tumult arose among the proud, haughty village youth. When they saw that several of their number had been whipped and were bleeding, they retreated from the battle field in a wild retreat, through all of the streets and alleys of the city to the direction of the suburbs of Halicz, with Jews such as Mass and Goldberg tailing after them. Thus did two brave Jews, of which Meir Mass excelled in his diligence, save the Jews of Podhajce from the attack of Ukrainian nationalists, and perhaps even from a pogrom, for such an incident was liable to easily escalate into a pogrom.

[Page 128]

This was a spontaneous act of Jewish self-defense. It was effected by two brave Jews, who attracted other Jews to them with the strength of their heart, primarily those merchants who had been injured in the disturbance. The name of Meir Mass was raised once again on the lips of all the residents of Podhajce. To Jewish consciousness, he was a hero, whereas with regard to the non-Jews, there were feelings of astonishment on the one hand, and hidden jealousy and hatred on the other. The years passed, and we children grew up. Each of us chose our path in life in accordance with our economic opportunities. For some reason, Meir did not choose a concrete path. "He sits on the neck of his mother", they would say about him. The truth is that with those conditions and opportunities that the Jewish youth had between the two wars, it was difficult to forge proper means of livelihood, taking into account all of the previous attitudes that were common among the Jews, especially among those of the middle class, with regard to handiwork and physical labor in general. Meir joined the Achva pioneering youth group, went through hachsharah, but did not succeed in obtaining the awaited certificate for the land of Israel. In this situation, similar to that of his friends, the Second World War overtook him in 1939.

Shortly after the outbreak of the Second World War, the Red Army entered the areas known as Western Ukraine and conquered them. However, the Russians did not remain for too long in Eastern Poland. When the war between Germany and Soviet Russia broke out in June 1941, the Russians were forced to retreat from all of the areas that they had conquered. Then, our city as well fell into the hands of the German murderers. The first ones to begin with the murder of the Jews and theft of their property were the local Ukrainians. Murder was imprinted upon their blood and souls, and they were prepared to murder a person for a pair of shoes. The Germans, who perpetrated their own murderous deeds in accordance with a higher command, would say that in this matter they have much to learn from the Ukrainians... They also began to set up local S.S. units, and with the protection of the Germans, they began their systematic murder of the Jewish population.

The second phase of the murderous actions was the enlistment of Jews to hard labor and their transfer to work camps. In this endeavor as well, the Ukrainians were the most active. The first to be enlisted to work and removed from the city were members of the Jewish intelligentsia, with the intention of preventing the Jews from organizing by the removal of the intellectual forces. Along with them, they searched out the strongest and bravest of the Jewish population, first and foremost Meir Mass. Several Ukrainian S.S. men overtook him, fell upon him, beat him until he lost his strength, and transferred him to the Kamieniolom Work Camp, the hardest camp in our region. There, they kept a special eye out for him. Already within the first days of his arrival there, they shot him to death for “disobedience” or “opposition”.

This was the bitter and tragic fate of Meir Mass, similar to the fate of hundreds of strongmen like him among European Jewry.

A group of pioneering youth in Podhajce

Translator's Footnotes

1. I am not sure why it mentioned Holhocha in the previous paragraph, and a suburb of Halicz in this paragraph. According to shtelseeker, Holhocha is about 20 miles from Halicz.

[Page 129]

Holidays and Festivals in our City

by Yehudit Hadar

Throughout all generations, holidays and festivals were honored guests in public and private life. They brightened up the mundaneness of all the days of the year. Throughout all of is history, the Jewish nation preserved these spiritual treasures, that united it into one unit. Our national poet Ch. N. Bialik painted a lovely and artistic portrait of the festivals: "The festivals are exalted above the landscape of the weekdays, just as mountains are exalted above the landscape of the earth. Every tall mountain, and each one that is taller than its fellow, testifies about changes and movements and shifts that took place under this mountain during several ancient eras, and compounded one upon the other, raising it recognizably above the landscape and lifting it upward. Similarly, each festival testifies about deep movements, at times volcanoes, that took place beneath the ground of the nation, not only once but many times, one after another. Indeed, when we come to dig and investigate beneath the national festival, we find beneath it layer upon layer and stratum beneath stratum. There is not just one reason for the festival, but rather many reasons." (Bialik, "Words by Heart").

Indeed, the Festivals of Israel were similar in all Jewish cities and communities. Nevertheless, it seems that each community celebrated its festivals in a style unique to its community. It seems to me that we celebrated out festivals in Podhajce with a unique style to our community, with a spice whose secret was known only to the Jews of our city. If someone from our city would celebrate the festivals in other cities, it would seem that the flavor of the festival of Podhajce was removed. Therefore, I feel that our Yizkor Book should give over some impressions of the festivals in our city.

The First Day of Rosh Hashanah, and the Observance of Tashlich

As usual, the people of the city were busy with their affairs. Nevertheless, the atmosphere of the approaching Days of Awe could already be felt a few weeks prior to Rosh Hashanah. This was especially felt the week before Rosh Hashanah, when all the Jews of the city would arise early for Selichot.

According to tradition, the first day of Rosh Hashanah took on the characteristics of a festival and a Day of Judgment simultaneously. The day of judgement was set to judge all living beings, and therefore it was appropriate to worship on that day with awe and fear, more than any other festival of the year. For us, even though the people gathered in the synagogue, which was filled to the brim, no joyous smile was seen on the face of the worshipers, who conducted themselves with more seriousness and somberness than usual. They knew and felt that on this day, they would be brought to judgement before the King of Kings. All of their activities were to ensure that they would be victorious in the judgement, and therefore they all prayed from the depths of their hearts with extra devotion.

A break took place after the Shacharit service. Some of the worshippers, men and women, left the synagogue, and would wish a good and blessed year to anyone whom they met. After the recital of "Lamenatzeach Livnei Korach Mizmor" the shofar blower blew the tekia-shevarim-terua, whose sounds reverberated upon the walls of the synagogue. The sounds of weeping could be heard from the women's section. A holy silence enveloped the worshippers, who stood bent over before the Judge of the entire earth. During the Musaf service, the shofar sounds were divided into three groups: Malchuyot, Zichronot, and Shofarot. The sounds of the shofar frightened, but also excited and aroused, the hearts.

The content of the prayers also influenced us greatly, especially the moving Unetane Tokef prayer. Then, I was not able to overcome my emotions, and my eyes filled with tears. The authorship of this prayer is ascribed to Rabbi Amnon of Mayence, who was tortured and died in sanctification of the Name on Rosh Hashanah. During this prayer, we feel the suffering of the author, and the prayer from our hearts and the request that G-d have mercy upon his nation and that the shofar sounds would speedily herald the redemption and the coming of the Messiah poured out as if by itself. At the conclusion of the service, the worshippers to their homes to partake of the afternoon meal, to rest and to regain strength, so that they could set out from their homes in groups to the rivers and ponds for the Tashlich service.

After a rest of a few hours, the movement began anew in the city. From all the streets and lanes, the Jews, men, women and children left their homes wearing streimels, hats, scarves and kerchiefs of various colors. They set out toward the rivers. The sound of the crowd, laughter and light conversation accompanied the walkers on their way to the Tashlich service. Some of the faces were bright and smiling, and others were serious and somber. Some were even sad to the point of tears.

The crowds of worshippers reached the river, and their lips uttered the Tashlich prayer, whose main theme is to "cast to the depths of the sea all of their sins". In order to symbolize the casting off of sins in a realistic manner, people would overturn the pockets of their clothes and shake them out over the water. The prayers of Tashlich expressed the state of mind of the believing Jew on Rosh Hashanah. How great is the meaning embedded in the verses of David the son of Jesse: "From the depths of despair I call out unto G-d, G-d answers me broadly". No less exalted is the meaning of the words of the prophet Micha the Morashtite: "Who is a G-d like you, bearing sins and overlooking the transgressions of the remnant of His inheritance, He does not hold anger forever, for He desires mercy."

The Tashlich prayers finished, and the personal oppression was lifted from the heart. However, the masses of worshippers remained standing at the banks of the river without moving. The last rays of sunlight lit up their faces. As I looked around, I saw the bent forms of those standing in prayer at the banks of the river straighten out. Their eyes shone. All of those people begin to show signs of life once again, as they turned their pockets inside out and scattered crumbs of bread upon the water. Their voices echoed afar as they read the concluding verse of Tashlich: "They shall not shoot and not destroy on my Holy Mountain, for the land is filled with knowledge of G-d like the water that covers."

[Page 130]

The Reb Meir Hirschorn Beis Midrash

Kol Nidre

It was the late afternoon of the eve of Yom Kippur. The Jewish stores were closed and locked. The concluding meal had ended – this ritual meal consisted of stuffed fish, soup, crepes (kreplach) of the kappores chicken, and a main course. During the meal, the piece of chala was dipped in honey, and the shehecheanu blessing was recited over grapes from the Land of Israel. At the end of the meal, the streets of the city were filled with Jews, old men and youths, and even old and young women – each of them setting out to their own synagogue: some to the Meir Hirschorn Beis Midrash, some to the Great Synagogue, and some to the synagogue on the Street of the Palace (Schloss-Gasse). During the latter era, my family and I worshipped there. We had seats that we had inherited (in Yiddish, "A shtot"). The seats were on a long bench, with a reading platform upon one which could place one's Machzor (festival prayer book) and other items. The synagogue was well lit. Aside from the regular lights, there were dozens of wax candles burning. These were the memorial candles for those who had departed from the land of the living.

A holy silence enveloped the synagogue. The cantor, wearing his white kittel and enwrapped in his tallis, stood before the teiva (reader's lectern) surrounded by a choir. He read out the proclamation prior to Kol Nidrei, that starts with "With the permission of G-d and the permission of the congregation", in holiness and purity. The words emanating from the mouth of the cantor moved the hearts of the listeners. I glanced at the worshippers, looking for the "sinners" [1] – however I saw before me only upright, honorable people of all classes, wearing white kittels and wrapped in tallises. My soul wandered about; it became clear to me, and I foresaw that that evening – the evening of penitence and forgiveness – the Judge of the Land will remove our harsh decrees, for the Jews of our city and also for the scattered Jews wherever they were.

When the time of Kol Nidre arrived, the congregation stood up in unison. Not even a low whisper was heard in the hole. Only from the women's section could be heard the sounds of stifled weeping. Then the sweet voice of the cantor was heard, starting the singing of Kol Nidre in the ancient melody. It is impossible to describe the holy awe that enveloped the congregation during the Kol Nidre prayer, which the cantor repeated three times, one after the other, raising his voice each time. Even though the contentof the prayer is merely the annulment of vows, the historical background of this prayer – for it served as the release from vows and oaths for the Spanish Marranos – imbued it with its importance and awakened the holy awe in our hearts. The melody of Kol Nidre contributed in no small manner to the creation of that special atmosphere that even influenced any gentiles and moved them to visit the synagogue on the night of Yom Kippur. This atmosphere fell upon the congregation immediately after the serious and splendorous declaration of "With the permission of G-d and the permission of the congregation", that served as a prelude to Kol Nidre. For who among Israel can say with a full heart that they are not among the sinners...

After Kol Nidre, the cantor intoned thrice "And the entire congregation of the Children of Israel will be forgiven, and the stranger that dwells in their midst, for the entire nation has stumbled", and the congregation repeated after him. The tension rose once again at the time of the recitation of the "Yaale" hymn. The sound of stifled weeping, strengthening more and more, burst forth from the women's section. The adage says "women's come to tears easily", and this was particularly felt during the services on the Days of Awe. During the night of Yom Kippur, there were many fitting opportunities for the shedding of tears, especially during the recitation of the penitential prayers, during the recitation of the confessional "for the sin that we sinned", etc. The common factor of all these prayers was the theme of repentance and the begging of forgiveness. Tears are appropriate for these themes. Thus it says explicitly, "May it be Thy will, You who hearken to the sound of weeping, that you put our tears in your flask for preservation..."

[Page 131]

One of the prominent characteristics of the atmosphere of the synagogue on the night of Kol Nidre was the heavy air and stifling heat that emanated from the dozens and hundreds of burning wax candles. At the end of the service, all of the worshippers went out to the fresh air of early autumn, with their faces aglow and their eyes sparkling, as they wished everyone "May you be sealed for the good" (Gmar Chatima Tova). Even after I left the synagogue to set out for home, the echoes of the melody of Kol Nidre accompanied me, that moved the hearts of millions of Jews throughout the earth in the midst of this day, and united them in prayers for the realization of the desires of our souls, along with wishes for a good sealing of fate for the entire Jewish people.

Yom Kippur in the Synagogue of our City

Early in the morning of the day of Yom Kippur, the women prepared food for the entire day for their children, for most of them remained in the synagogue all day on this fast day, and only a few went home during the time of the Torah reading for the break. The men would remain in the synagogue all day wrapped in their tallises and wearing their white kittels, without shoes or with slippers. The girls would sit in the women's section and converse among themselves, while the adult women and old women would sit and peer into the book of Techinot (women's petitions) or one of the other books designed for women. The prayer leader, with his white, festive garb, would stand before the lectern near the Holy Ark, ready to begin the morning service, feeling the great sense of responsibility imposed upon him as the representative of the congregation on the Day of Judgement.

After the Psukei Dezimra service, the cantor and worshippers would move over to the main part of the Shacharit service. He would sing "The King Sitting on the high and loft throne" in the traditional chant, as the congregation and choir answered after him. The Shacharit service of Yom Kippur is very long, but the traditional melodies blow a spirit of life into the recitation of the prayers, and they are pleasant to the ear. Those who were musically inclined among the congregation would assist the cantor by responding at set times. The Shmone Esrei of Shacharit is punctuated by hymns and poems that are unique to that day. In these prayers, the early generations bequeathed to us a long litany of traditional melodies and tunes, transmitted to us from generation to generation. Each year they sound as new, filled with the pleasantness and energy of youth.

After the Shacharit service, the Torah reading takes place from the portion of Acharei Mot, in which is mentioned the deaths of the two sons of Aaron the Priest, who were punished with the full measure of the law. The portion is read with the special melody for the Days of Awe. This melody is the cause of many debates among cantorial researchers who find in it remnants of centuries old Eastern motifs. Others disagree and say that this melody dates from the era of the First or Second Temple.

Of all the service of Yom Kippur, Musaf was dearest to us. We young people were interested with all the strands of our souls in the mysterious spirit that envelops this prayer, especially the wondrous segments of the Avoda section, which expresses the soulful embrace of the nation in its ancient glory at the time of the enactment of the holy service in the presence of large crowds and the glory of the King in the Holy Temple by the High Priest. The prostrations of Aleinu and the Avoda made a special impression upon us. The festive yet melancholy melodies penetrated the hearts, and the vision of the kneeling and prostration would move the thinnest strands of the heart, and instill fear and awe into it.

Prior to Musaf, after the Torah reading, the memorial service (Yizkor) was announced. It is the custom to pray for the souls of the dead and to pledge to charity in memory of their souls. In the Av Harachamim prayer, the souls of the holy martyrs who gave up their lives in Sanctification of the Divine Name, and the victims of the Holocaust are also mentioned. At the time that Yizkor is recited, those whose parents are alive leave the synagogue, so as not to create an opening for the Satan, and not to arouse the evil eye. During the Yizkor service, many women saw it as a propitious time to express their personal prayers. A middle-aged woman sat near me. Among her other petitions, she asked the Dweller On High to have mercy upon her daughter who had reached marriageable age, and send her match to her, so that she should not remain Heaven forbid as an old spinster. Another woman who sat near me asked the Dweller On High to grant her strength to sustain her orphaned children honorably, so that she would not Heaven Forbid require the assistance of flesh and blood. Heartrending cries were also heard from the old women, who pleaded with all the warmth of their souls, "Do not cast us away at the time of old age, as our strength fails do not abandon us". In general, during Yizkor, the crowding in the synagogue increased due to the presence of orphans and widows who came to recall the souls of their dear departed. People who were not seen in the synagogue all year would come to this service.

[Page 132]

A certain disarray pervaded in the women's section during Yizkor and thereafter. Not all of the women were familiar with the Machzor, and many required the assistance of their neighbors who were more expert than they. There was no small number of women who also prepared appropriate equipment for the services: Machzors, the Korban Mincha Siddur, Chumashes with Yiddish translation, and also Tzena Urena. With all the trees, the forest could not be seen.

The Unetane Tokef prayer aroused a stormy spirit with the women. Its tragic content would touch the hearts of all the worshippers, especially the hearts of the women. Fear and trepidation overtook the worshippers during the recitation of this hymn, which was recited by everyone with emotion, and at times with wailing. The weeping was great during the time of the recitation of the section, "On Rosh Hashanah it is written and on the fast day of Yom Kippur it is sealed, who shall live, and who shall die, for none merit before Your eyes in judgement". On the other hand, the shepherd's melody of "Kevakarat" (As a shepherd..) was enchanting and refreshing. On more than one occasion, women fainted in the midst of this hymn from the great emotion, and the doctor or their relatives had to be summoned. This accentuated the serious spirit of the moment, but on the other hand, it disturbed the service and impinged on the holiness.

The Avoda section came toward the end of the Musaf service. This describes in a dramatic fashion the service of the High Priest on Yom Kippur during the time of the Temple. The congregation of worshippers, already tired from the fast and the long service, became alert once again during the Avoda service. The cantor sang "And the Priests and the people gathered in the courtyard.." in the traditional melody, and as he arrived at "They would kneel and bow down", all of the worshippers would fall on their faces as during the days of yore in the Temple. The content of the Avoda service was filled with warmth, and it appeared as new in our eyes each year. With natural longing for the splendid life of days gone by, the worshippers sung the concluding stanza: "Indeed, how splendorous was the High Priest as he left the holy place in peace".

With this, the Yom Kippur prayers with all their experiences were not over. After the Mincha service came the Neila service as a conclusion to the prayers of Yom Kippur. The day turned into twilight. The wax candles cast a gloomy light, and all the worshippers felt as if a new spirit entered into their beings, and new powers were granted to them. Since this service was the last of the services of the day, one says "and seal us" instead of "and inscribe us". Here, we also take the Dweller On High to task, and complain to Him about the disgrace of his nation that has been pillaged and displaced, and the disgrace of His holy city of Jerusalem, "I recall G-d and am astonished, as I see every city built up on its base, and the city of G-d lies lowly to the pit". The Neila service concludes with the recitation of Shma Yisrael, the blowing of the shofar, and the declaration, "Next Year in Jerusalem!"

After the weekday evening service, the congregants disperse. The women and children hurry home, while the men remain next to the synagogue to recite the Sanctification of the Moon in groups.

Simchat Torah Festivities

The Sukka was very dear to us, even though as women we were exempt from this commandment. Our hearts were proud and wide with it. In the Sukka, warmth of heart and refinement of the soul pervaded. However, the height of our joy was obviously reserved for the day of Simchat Torah.

The scene of the synagogue on the night of Simchat Torah was heartwarming and full of charm. The youth of the People of Israel were sitting on the benches, on the reader's podium (bima) and even on the worshippers' lecterns, with paper flags in their little hands. There was no toddler who did not long to go among the adults and fill a most important task: to raise the flag of the Jews with a high hand and outstretched arm. Atop the flag was a red apple, upon which was a small candle. The children were joyous at the advent of Simchat Torah, for on that day, they felt themselves equal with the adults. Furthermore, they would receive various sweets. At nightfall, the children of the city marched to the synagogue beside their fathers for the hakafot (Simchat Torah processions), as they waved their small flags with pride. That night, the girls were also permitted to participate in Simchat Torah in the synagogue, albeit not in the hakafot themselves. The synagogue was fully lit, and light and joy radiated from all faces. The children were overexcited from the great joy and enthusiasm. At times it seemed as if all of the festivals that preceded Simchat Torah, such as the days of Selichot (penitential prayers), the Days of Awe, Sukkot and Hoshana Rabba were nothing other than a preparation for Simchat Torah, when we would all declare with mirthful joy and deep seriousness: "You were shown to know..." (Ata Hareita) [2].

How splendid was the hakafot procession around the bima in the synagogue. Everyone would encircle the bima, from the rabbi of the city to the water carrier. The children would follow after them with their flags in their hands, and even the girls would intermingle among the boys, and sing and dance. After the cantor concluded the reading of the verses of "Ata Hareita", the hakafot were distributed.

[Page 133]

With great noise and incessant tumult, a voice would call out from the bima, "So and so the son of so and so, give honor to the Torah!". After all of the Torah scrolls were removed from the Holy Ark, the procession would begin with the cantor chanting "Ana Hashem Hoshia Na" (Please G-d, save us). After the hakafa, those who made the circuit would start to sing and dance, accompanied by the young and the old. The first hakafa would conclude, and the shamash or gabbai would once again stand up and declare the customary text: "So and so the son of so and so, give honor to the Torah!". Thus went the second hakafa, and then the third and fourth. After each hakafa, joyous and mirthful songs and hymns were sung, and the dances were repeated. The hakafot were progressing in full force. The congregants were proud, their faces were aglow, and the joy of the festival was set upon them. Those who received the honor of the hakafot each did their part standing up, each in a different voice and different style. That is to say, the text was the same for everyone, but each person had his own voice and special melody, and each person was somewhat unsure and frightened about his own voice, so the verse came out confused and mixed up, in opposition to the will of the recitor. The strophe, "Helper of the poor, please save us" aroused special interest for the worshippers. Among those who kissed the Torah scrolls that were held in the hands of those honored with the hakafa were the women and girls, who bent their heads over the benches to kiss the Torah scrolls. This time, they were granted permission to kiss the holy Torah, and they made haste to place their soft lips upon the silk coverings of the Torah scrolls. The older boys, who already knew in their hearts the meaning of the kiss of a girl, would cunningly, during the crowding, place their hands between the Torah covers and the lips of the girls, so that they would receive the kiss. Laughter would break out among those who witnessed this, and the face of the girl would redden from shame. Those who were honored with the hakafot were given great honor. For the first hakafa, they generally honored the rabbi and important people of the city. The procession of the bright flags of the young children was one of the most precious ceremonies of Simchat Torah. The festival of Simchat Torah was considered as a national festival, in which men, women and children took part. The participation of children in this festival was very noticeable, and it is no wonder that the children would await impatiently all year.

A Purim celebration in the Shomer Hatzair headquarters, 1938

Purim in our City

The night of Purim was not that different from all other nights of the year. With the exception of the reading of the Megilla and the eating of hamantaschen, the evening was completely ordinary. As the adage goes, "The farmer is not a brother, the guilder is not money, fever is not an illness, and Purim is not a festival." What is this referring to? To the night of Purim. This was not referring to the day of Purim itself and the following evening – the day was a festival, a festival in every way, and it is possible that this was the most joyous of all festivals of the year.

After the fast day of Taanit Esther, we went to the home of my uncle and grandmother to hear the Megilla reading. The children were equipped with their graggers (noisemakers) in honor of Purim, and they would make noise with their graggers whenever the name of Haman was recited during the Megilla reading. The next morning, my uncle went to the synagogue, and our aunt spread a white, shiny tablecloth on the table, upon which she places a large chala, and all types of cookies and hamantaschen, bottles of wine and liquor, as well as an earthenware plate with a great deal of coins in the denomination of 10 or 15 agorot (groszy) in order to distribute to the poor. In the morning of Purim, the Megilla was once again read in the synagogue, and once again, the children spun their graggers and banged the lecterns to blot out Haman. However, the noise in the morning was measured. When we left the synagogue, we saw that the stores were open, and everyone was conducting their business like an ordinary weekday, we felt bad and the taste of the joy of the festival was dampened. However, salvation came in the second half of the day, when the stores were closed, and we had light and joy. People began to prepare themselves for the Purim feast, and begin to distribute Mishloach Manot (the giving of food portions to each other). The bearers of the gift packages spread through the city. The door of our house was not closed for several hours. One was still talking, and the next one came.

Toward evening, our uncle and all the invited guests gathered around the table. With a feeling of contentment, our uncle cut the Purim challa lengthwise, in memory of the situation with Agag the King of Amalek, upon whom King Saul had mercy and left alive despite the order of the prophet Samuel to not have mercy upon the seed of Amalek. The prophet was forced to rend him in half with his own hands in the city of Gilgal. The table was bedecked as on a festival, with a variety of food and drink. Our aunt had just served the fish, and the door opened, and a group of youths dressed in masks and costumes entered. These were the "Joseph Players" troupe, which would annually make the rounds to the houses of the city notables and perform the play of the sale of Joseph. This was a complete and splendid play, with expertise and tradition, both with respect to the content and with respect tot he play itself. The performance drew tears from our eyes, and at the conclusion, the actors received their reward, both in the form of money from my uncle, and with a "Lechaim" over drinks and various baked goods. As this troupe left, a second group of disguised people entered, who performed the play of Queen Esther, Mordechai the Jew, and King Achashverosh. They also received their reward for their performance. Aside from the troupes, many children dressed in masks came. They entered the room of those partaking in the feast with great noise and tumult, as they would sing various songs and hymns. We would sit and listen to their hymns and jokes, as our souls were filled with enjoyment. One of the hymns that sticks in my mind is as follows,

"Happy Purim angel, where I go I fall;
My beard is long, my wife is ill,
Today is Purim, tomorrow is not
Give me a coin and toss me out."

[Page 134]

There were various plays. Not all of them were performed well by the actors. However, every play was performed with alertness and feeling. The performance of the Sale of Joseph was particularly well received, for it was always a great experience for the audience. Everyone enjoyed it, and lovingly remembered it and its wonderful melodies. This play would either be elongated or shortened, depending on the time that the actors had and the importance of the hosts.

The Mishloach Manot played an important role in this holiday. The bearers of gifts spread out through the city with their napkin-wrapped platters in hand. The door of the house did not close for several hours. There were two types of Mishloach Manot: those to relatives, family, and general friends, and those to clergy. It was easier to arrange the Mishloach Manot for the clergy – for them the main thing was the hard, clanging coin that was placed atop of it. It was more difficult to prepare Mishloach Manot for members of the family. For these, it was usual to study carefully the gifts that were received, and to ensure that the gift was designed in such proportions so as not to cause embarrassment, Heaven forbid. The men did not pay attention to this entire matter. However, the women saw it as very important, and treated it seriously. Often, the issue of Mishloach Manot caused an argument in the family...

Women were among those who came to request Purim money. This included "pious women" who served as the focal point of the offering of assistance in the city, whether to the sick, the poor, or householders who had come upon hard times and required financial help in their time of need. The students of the Hebrew school and members of the youth movements, such as Hashomer Hatzair, Achva, Hechalutz, the Revisionists, etc. were also not absent. They came with the Keren Kayemet (Jewish National Fund) boxes in their hands, and asked the Jews of the city to donate generously. Indeed, the Jews of our city distributed their donations on the day of Purim generously and with an open hand. As the celebrants were of good spirit with wine, they raised their voices in song, primarily with the hymn of "Shoshanat Yaakov" (The Jews of Shushan were glad and joyous as they together saw Mordechai dressed in purple), with the Yiddish addendum, "Haman wished to murder the Jews, but he himself was hanged". My uncle added his own verse to this hymn: "Master of the universe, may the downfall of Haman be visited upon all enemies of Israel, and may the grace of Queen Esther be poured upon all the daughters of Israel."

Slowly, those feasting would turn to joking and lightheartedness. The drinking was as customary "without bounds". The joy aroused song, and the song became more enthusiastic. The hours of the night would be spent in song and dance, with joy and pride beaming from every face, with the hope and comfort that all the enemies of the Jews would thus be destroyed and would never arise again. Our aunt added that everyone who starts up with the Nation of Israel should meet the same end as the evil Haman, and all those at the table answered simultaneously, "Amen, Amen, may it be His will." The guests took leave of our aunt and uncle with kisses and good wishes, promising to visit again soon. They left the house with a joyous heart, a light gait and an exalted mood.

The Keren Kayemet LeYisrael (Jewish National Fund) Committee:

Muniu Buchwald, Moshe Erde of blessed memory, Engineer David Lilla of blessed memory, Tzvi Goralnik

---

Translator's Footnotes

1. The proclamation before Kol Nidre is a permission to worship with "sinners".
2. "You were shown to know that G-d is the L-rd, and that there is none other than He", a verse recited at the opening of the hakafot ceremony on Simchat Torah.

[Page 135]

Experiences and Figures from the Recent Past

by Dr. Baruch Milch

Many years have passed since I moved away from my forlorn town, and many experiences still remain with me in their full brightness, even with their negativity and faults. These are experiences that warmed my soul during the days of my youth. Their shadow always accompanies me, and their shadow lies deep in the depths of my spirit. It is appropriate to bring them to paper as a memorial candle for what was and is no more.

Regarding Nationalism and Anti-Semitism

The Ukrainians and the Poles were two small nations crowded together in eastern Galicia, and were subjugated by many other nations through the course of centuries. At the conclusion of the First World War, they found the time opportune to fight with each other and sow death and destruction among their two nations, and coincidentally among we Jews who lived among them.

In the wake of the national antagonism between the Ukrainians and the Poles in our region, anti-Semitism spread with greater force among the gentile population, both the city dwellers and country dwellers. As a result, they began to organize themselves, and they began a bitter struggle against the Jewish merchants, doctors, lawyers and other professionals. They set up cooperatives ("Kolko Rolnici"). From that time, there were Polish or Ukrainian stores who utilized anti-Semitic mottoes. This situation began to cause a downturn in the Jewish livelihood. The economic foundation of many families was weakened or destroyed. On the other hand, the anti-Semitism caused a national Jewish awakening among the youth and the adults, who began to understand that the foundations of our existence in the Diaspora were weakening and disappearing, and that the only way for them was to turn to Zionism, pioneering, and aliya to the Land of Israel. This Zionist awakening many assimilationists to the bosom of Judaism, and caused a decisive change in their lives.

The Zionists in the city conducted strong activity, particularly in light of the aspirations and expectations to get to a Jewish state that were aroused at the time of the Balfour Declaration and the San Remo proclamation. The influence of anti-Semitism was felt in various professions of the Jews. It was known that the Jewish practitioners of the free professions and the crafts were among the best, and they had earned the trust of their customers who depended upon them for everything. Nevertheless the worm of anti-Semitism destroyed the human feelings that existed earlier in relations between the peoples of the region. In Podhajce as well, the Zionist camp was enriched with good and fresh spirits. Ordinary residents who were not organized in the Zionist organizations also drew close to Zionism, including people who in general were distant from Zionist politics and factionalism. This gave a strong push to Zionist and

factional activity in the city.

Dr. Landau, the elder of the physicians of the city, who was accepted by all of the residents of the city and the region, would visit the synagogue only once a year, on Kol Nidre night. Nevertheless, he had a warm Jewish heart, and his wife was known in the city as a dedicated activist for the benefit of the orphans and poor, and to all acts of charity and benevolence. A second doctor from among the most popular in the city was Dr. Dik, a veteran Zionist, the chairman of the Keren Kayemet LeYisrael (Jewish National Fund) committee and other national organizations. After them came Dr. Heller, who weighed more than 100 kilo. The farmers of the region related to him with trust, as a paradigm of good health. However, his obesity also caused his sudden death as a result of a heart attack. The personality of Dr. Reichman also stood out. He was the scion of a well-connected family (his mother was the sister of Rabbi David Lilienfeld and the daughter of the renowned Rabbi Shalom Lilienfeld), and also a communal activist. Dr. (Mrs.) Chaia Kressel-Torten, Dr. Chaim Walger, Dr. Rafael Freud, the younger Dr. Heller, Dr. Baruch Milch and others were among the excellent doctors. From among the lawyers, it is appropriate to mention the Zionists Dr. Notik, Dr. Salpeter, Dr. Morgan, Dr. Rotenberg, and the three lawyer brothers Dr. Pomeranz, Dr. Marbech and Dr. Yaakov Horowitz. The later was a Zionist and communal activist who was particularly dedicated to the affairs of the youth. From among the engineers, the most active in he community and Zionism were Engineer David Lila, Engineer Hirshberg and others. From among the judges, teachers and government or municipal officials, there were some Jews at the time of the birth of the State of Poland, but they were gradually dismissed from their jobs. There were a few Jewish farmers in Podhajce. As well, there were a few Jewish farming families in each village of the region. However, almost all of them were also occupied in some sort of labor or business.

At this opportunity, I should note that most of the Jewish parents sent their children to high school and encouraged them to take the matriculation exam in order to gain the degree of "Matura", that added glory and prestige to its holders. However, the "hell" for the Jewish youth only began after receiving the matriculation certificate, when the gates of the higher Polish schools were locked before them because of the "numerus clausus" (quotas), particularly in the professions of medicine, engineering, and the like. Some of these youth began to spread through the lands of Europe, to live the life of wanderers in the large cities of Austria, Czechoslovakia, France, Switzerland, Germany or Italy, in order to study the professions that were forbidden to them in their native country. This was no easy matter

from an economic, technical or financial perspective, as well as with respect to the knowledge of foreign languages, etc. I was also among these youths, and I set out for Prague, Czechoslovakia in order to study medicine. I concluded my studies there. The measure of suffering was not complete even after all the wanderings, for after the conclusion of the studies, when some of them to Poland with their diplomas in medicine, pharmacy, engineering, etc. they were forbidden to work in their professions. The "nosterificia" protocols began again, and not everyone succeeded in obtaining one. There were those who did not at all to Poland, for they set themselves up in a variety of countries throughout the world, or they made aliya to the Land of Israel. Such people included Dr. Marbech of blessed memory, Dr. Yisrael Liblich, the engineer Shulwolf, and others. Furthermore, entire families made aliya to the Land before the war of destruction and the Holocaust, such as Ticher, Mosberg and others.

[Page 136]

The Jews of Podhajce in their Struggle between the Ukrainians and the Poles

In the struggle between the Ukrainian and Polish populations, the Jews of Podhajce found themselves between the hammer and the anvil. In the years 1933-1934, the antagonism between the ruling Poles and the majority Ukrainians in eastern Poland grew. The Ukrainian nationalists employed all sorts of terrorist activity against the Polish rule, such as the bombing of bridges, railways and public buildings, and setting the homes and farms of Poles and Jews on fire. The Polish authorities were forced to employ oppositional activities called "pacificacia" (pacification). The authorities imprisoned many of the Ukrainian youths and intelligentsia, closed their schools and even issued a directive to the Ukrainian population that they were responsible for ensuring the protection of the bridges, communal buildings, etc. during the evenings and nights. In the interim, an incident took place with a Jewish student of the Podhajce Jewish youth who sat at home all day occupying himself with his studies, and only went out to walk in the fields outside the city and enjoy fresh air in the evenings. The police caught him and suspected him of damaging government property. The Jewish student suffered murderous blows from the police, who brought him to the police station and accused him of attempting to ignite one of the houses because he was a Communist. In order to accuse him, it was sufficient for the political official of the police (Mr. Bierant) to know that this youth was once a member of Hashomer Hatzair in the city, which was always suspected of extreme left leaning ideology and was considered close to the Communists, Anarchists, etc. An extremely unpleasant situation was created here, until the elders of the city, headed by Rabbi David Lilienfeld himself, felt themselves duty bound to make great efforts to save the Hashomer Hatzair member from libel, and to convince the police (who knew the truth) that a "misunderstanding" had occurred, and that the evil decree should be revoked.

Shortly after this incident, the student left Poland and made aliya. He established a fine family, and to this day, he works in a responsible position and lives a life of happiness and peace. Thanks to this incident, he was saved from the Nazi talons, whereas most of his family who remained in Podhajce perished in the Holocaust.

A group of Admorim from the region of Podhajce at a spa

About the Trust of the People of Podhajce in Admorim

Faith was always a primary tenet of Judaism. Whoever was not numbered among the believers was considered a denier of basic principles who has no share in the Nation of Israel. Obviously, there were those whose religious faith and national connection was pure and refined, as well as those who became involved in all sorts of nonsensical and vain beliefs. The Jews of Podhajce were generally people of boundless faith. I will now tell about several incidents connected to the faith of the people of Podhajce.

I recall one of the stories of Father of blessed memory that took place in Podhajce during his childhood at the end of the 19th century, when a large fire broke out in the city, in which about one third of the houses of the city burnt down. The fire spread extremely rapidly and transferred from street to street in a large-scale fashion, wreaking havoc upon the homes. It is interesting to note that the vast majority of the burnt homes belonged to Jews. The fire began in the center of the city, in the home of a Jewish family named Milsztok. This house was rebuilt after the fire. It burned down once again during the First World War and was once gain rebuilt by someone named Leib Weiss (nicknamed Leibele Trask).

This story that I want to tell relates to this house and its burning. Some time before the fire, one Rebbe, a great Tzadik, came to the city accompanied by his Gabbai in order to remain for a while in the city amidst his Hassidim and those close with him, as was usual during those days. The Hassidim received him well and put him up in one of the homes of the wealthy people of the city next to the Milsztok home. One Sabbath morning the Rebbe got up and wished to worship in the synagogue that was near his house. To get there, he had to pass through the yard of the Milsztok house, which had a wide, long corridor. Suddenly, two girls of the Milsztok family came out of the house and stood on both sides of the path through which the Rebbe was to cross. The Rebbe did not want to pass between two women, and the Gabbai requested that they vacate the place to let the Rebbe pass. However, they refused to move. The Rebbe was forced to to the home in which he was staying, feeling hurt. "It is unfortunate that I cannot worship in the synagogue this Sabbath", he said. On account of the insolence of the mischievous girls, he let a curse slip through his lips, saying: "A place with girls such as these will eventually be burnt". Indeed, so it was. A few weeks later (the Rebbe had already left the city some time ago), a large fire broke out in Podhajce that started precisely in the home of the Milsztok family. Even though the fire broke out by chance, all the people of the city believed that the fire came as a punishment from Heaven because of their disparaging treatment of the Rebbe.

[Page 137]

A more or less similar incident affected the Rotner family in Podhajce (the father of the head of the community, Tobiasz Rotner), who were considered to be one of the most honorable families of the city. During a dispute, he greatly embarrassed one of the great Tzadikim of Galicia (The Rebbe of Kopyczynce or the Rebbe of Czortkow). After this, he became the father of several children who were lame or deaf from birth. All of the people of the city saw this as a punishment from Heaven.

I will tell here another story that is connected with the faith of the people of our city. In its time, it was our custom to conduct most of the weddings in the city in the wide open space next to the Great Synagogue (Shil Gasse). In connection to this, they would relate in the city that once, a wedding took place there of a young couple whose moral character was suspect. Suddenly, the earth opened up its mouth, and the groom, bride, and many of those present were swallowed alive. Immediately thereafter the earth closed its mouth, and it was impossible to save even one of those who had been swallowed... After this terrifying incident, a tall stone monument was erected n the place where this took place, next to the back wall of the Great Synagogue. The people of the city would come there during the month of Elul, conduct a memorial service, and throw garlic, as if in a cemetery. I witnessed this custom with my own eyes, and I was never able to find anyone present who was able to tell me additional details about this incident. The fear of the place rested upon the adults who visited there, and the children were afraid to go close to the place, especially during the evenings. Apparently the fear of the place hovered over those who knew something about what had taken place there, but they were reluctant to talk about it.

The author of the book Masaat Binyamin, who served as a rabbi in Podhajce, became known as a Gaon in Torah and good deeds. A wreath of legends was woven around his popular personality. These legends were transmitted from generation to generation, but most of them have been forgotten with the passage of time. I know one legend that is connected to this old-time rabbi and Tzadik, whose name is mentioned with awe and reverence by natives of our city to this day.

This was the story: This old-time rabbi preached to the congregation in the Beis Midrash on designated Sabbaths. His words included topics of morality, as he preached about good behavior between man and G-d as well as between man and man. The rabbi would deliver a sermon especially on Shabbat Hagadol (the Sabbath prior to Passover) and Shabbat Shuva (the Sabbath between Rosh Hashanah and Yom Kippur), and he would arouse the audience to Torah and repentance. Prior to his death he said that the people of the city are not worthy of reciting the verses of the Yigdal prayer in the Shacharit service [1] on account of the many Apikorsim (heretics) who are found in the city. As a sign that his words are correct, he said that after his death, a certain tree would grow overnight over his grave. Several people of the city told me that indeed, the words of the rabbi came true. When I visited the cemetery in the city, I saw with my own eyes the old, tall tree that was hovering atop the grave of the rabbi and Tzadik

The Admor of Bursztyn

Podhajce was a typical Galician city, with all of its positive and negative attributes. In its last generation, most of its Jewish residents were Maskilim with progressive and liberal outlooks. Some had academic education, such as the engineers, doctors, lawyers, teachers, etc. The Jewish youth of the town was composed of all types of youth groups from Hashomer Hatzair to Bnei Akiva. There were also student corporations. Indeed, there was also no lack of Hassidim, who gathered around their Kloizez. The Rebbe of the city, who was known as the Bursztyn Rebbe, had no small amount of influence. His house, or more accurately his court, was located in one of the lovely corners of the city. It was a courtyard surrounded by trees. There were also many gentiles who related to him with honor. On Sabbath days, many Hassidim would gather around the Rebbe's table. They particularly came to hear the Rebbe's Kiddush and wishes of Lechaim from his holy mouth. There were also Shalosh Seudot (the third Sabbath meal) and Melave Malkas (a meal following the Sabbath) at the conclusion of the Sabbath, that attracted many of his Hassidim and those who revered him, including many Jews of our city. Many of the youth of the city would also come to be present for his fine Kabbalat Shabbat (The service of welcoming the Sabbath), Melave Malka celebrations, Purim feasts and Passover Seders, that were conducted with all of their traditional and popular ceremonials until the light of the morning. It is interesting to note that particularly during these celebrations, the area around the Rebbe's courtyard served as a comfortable and attractive meeting place for the youth and young couples.

The Rebbe himself was a man of middle stature, stout of body, having a serious face, splendid in his attire and modest in his mannerisms. He did not have

a unique income for his livelihood and the sustaining of his court. He lived from gifts from people of the city, which his Gabbai collected weekly from steady donors. However, the Rebbe's court was always bustling with the poor and hungry, who were provided with bread and various food. On Sabbaths, Purim feasts and Passover Seders, the court was always filled with people who were not members of the Rebbe's family, despite the fact that his own family was large enough: two daughters, a son, and their families. The wedding celebrations of the Rebbe's children were important and impressive events in the city.

[Page 138]

Rabbi Yitzchak Izak Menachem Eichenstein of blessed memory, The Admor of Bursztyn

The degree of influence that the Rebbe had in Podhajce can be discerned from the following incidents. In the years 1915-1916, during the time of the First World War, the Austro-Hungarian armies retreated from the city to the west, and in their place came the armies of the Russian Czar, which included people of a mixture of various Asiatic origins such as Circassians, Uzbeks, Kyrgyzes, and others who brought with them the germs of the dangerous illness of cholera from their countries. This illness was accompanied by an atmosphere of hunger, filth and dirt that pervaded with the change of armies. A shortage of medicine and cleaning materials was felt in all places. All of this made itself quickly felt by the population. The situation was quite bad in our city as well, and people fell like flies in the Jewish community. This serious illness often attacked people suddenly with diarrhea and severe stomach pains that continued incessantly until their life was snuffed out. A relative of mine Dr. Wilhelm Neuman, in his position as regional physician, made a great effort to fight the dangerous illness and enable the population to cope. He arranged sanitary assistance on each street with groups composed of Jewish and non-Jewish citizens of the city, who ensured cleanliness, distributed some food to the hungry, buried the dead, etc. On account of the shortage of medicine, everyone was instructed to eat more garlic, and the children always walked with a necklace of garlic around their necks. At the time, my late father was the head of the sanitary division in our area, and it was easy for him to obtain the garlic. As a result, the entire house was filled with the aroma of garlic, and we were not able to look at garlic for many years after that on account of this. In truth, the danger of communicable disease was greater in our home, for father would often make the rounds in the houses of the sick and dead. The pleas of our dear mother not to endanger us were to no avail, and he continued fulfilling his role faithfully. To our good fortune, no tragedy happened to us. Half of the street we lived on was emptied of people who had passed away. At that time – during the time of danger that was hanging over every person in the city – the lot fell upon the Admor of Bursztyn to act in accordance with his righteousness.

First of all, he advised us to construct a life sized mannequin and to arrange a burial ceremony for it as is done for any Jew in an honorable place in the cemetery. The advice of the Rebbe was carried out. A large crowd of Podhajce natives participated in the funeral. However, the results were the opposite, for as a result of the massive crowding in one place, the epidemic strengthened. Then the Rebbe offered a second piece of advice – to arrange a "black wedding". He advised to arrange a communal wedding of a poor boy and girl on the accounts of the city, and that the entire population should participate in it. A "groom" was speedily found – his Gabbai, Reb Yitzchakl , and the "bride" was the maid of his household Sarale, who had worked as a maid for many years with a variety of people. Both of them were between the ages of 30-40. The wedding was arranged in the Great Synagogue, and a large group participated. Nevertheless, this means also did not serve as a protection against the plague. The new couple themselves were not a source of contentment for those who arranged their marriage, for they separated after a short time.

The epidemic continued to take its toll. During those days, the well known teacher in our city, Rabbi Davidl, died at over the age of 80. He was a modest scholar, by whose hand several generations of our townsfolk, I among them, were educated in the study of Torah, Bible and Talmud. He was a faithful and dedicated teacher, who spread Torah in our city at all times of the day and night. Then, the Rebbe of Bursztyn offered a new piece of advice; to prepare a large brass key and place it in the hands of the departed Reb Davidl. His students sat all day and night on the floor of his house around his body, and studied Mishna for the elevation of his soul. A large funeral took place the day after his death, and the pallbearers carried him along with the key to the gate of the cemetery. This deceased man had been chosen to permanently lock the gate of the earth in the face of the plague. The matter took place. Indeed, the epidemic ended after some time, either because of the locking of the ground before the plague by the key in the hands of the departed Reb Davidl, or because of the sudden departure of the Russian army who fled for their lives, and the appearance of the Austo-Hungarians with all types of medicine. However, the Jewish population believed with a full heart that the salvation came through the power of the Rebbe

[Page 139]

Holidays and Festivals of Joy...

It is difficult to forget the lovely festivals in our city, through which our nation displayed its spirit in the most open fashion. They served as a clear lens to the treasures of our people and its spiritual world. Every holiday had its customs and mores. On Rosh Hashanah at the time of Tashlich, most of the people of our city would gather around the Koropiec River. The youth would ignite bonfires on its banks, and dance to their light with song and joy. Hikes would be arranged on the lovely days of Passover. The hikers would be wearing new, splendid clothes and shoes. Most of the hikers would go outside the city with their children, to the tall hill called "Gei", where they would play with nuts and other types of games.

The fact that Yom Kippur is listed among the rest of the festivals of Israel is proper evidence that this day is not a day of agony and mourning, but rather a holiday and festival. How great was the influence of the Eve of Yom Kippur and Kol Nidre night. In the afternoon, all business and stores were closed quickly. Everyone finished their work and prepared for the festive meal that preceded the fast. Family and acquaintances met with their elders to wish them that may be sealed for a good life. Then they went to the synagogue for Kol Nidre after lighting the traditional large candles. The custom of wearing white clothing on the Days of Awe was particularly impressive – particularly for the prayer leader who wore a white cloak (Kittel) under his tallis, as a symbol for the forgiveness of sins. The atmosphere that pervaded prior to the recitation of Kol Nidre elicited unusual attention. Not infrequently, Christians would show up in the synagogue for Kol Nidre, as well as Jews who were distant from religion and had not visited a synagogue all year. The atmosphere seemed like that of angels and seraphim, and an unseen eye hovered atop the city and atop all of us. How great were the preparations in my father's house on the Eve of Yom Kippur. In the morning, everyone would arise early for the Kapparot ceremony. Breakfast was eaten very early. When father from the first Minyan at the synagogue, he would run his store to conduct a bit of business. From there he would hasten to the bathhouse, and home for a simpler than usual lunch. On his way, he would arrange a few more purchases. He would grab the hands of anyone he met along the way and give them heartfelt greetings for the upcoming year and for the approaching Day of Judgement. In the afternoon, he shut his store and hurried to the synagogue for Mincha. When he , the entire family was already waiting: my brother Yossi, his wife Mintzia of the Hecht family, and their daughters Libchia and Malchia; my sister Dvora, her husband Yehoshua Walfish and their four children; my youngest sister Bronchia, her husband Marcus Hauring and their two children; my youngest brother Nathan (all of them perished in the Holocaust during the war with the accursed Nazis). All of them came to wish our father Zelig and mother Rosa (nee Lippa) a good year and a Chatima Tova (being sealed in the book of life), to drink a cup of wine together with wishes for a good life, and to taste an apple dipped in honey. On occasion, some of them stayed with us for the meal preceding the fast. This meal was always ample and festive, but was concluded in haste, so that the cup of tea after the meal was emptied while standing already. Mother lit the candles, and then the entire family went to the synagogue for Kol Nidre. Father hastened to be one of the first in the synagogue, for as Gabbai, he was responsible for arranging various matters with the cantor, arranging the seats, making sure that the candles would be lit in a specific place by the gentile, collecting and counting the money from the plates that were set out for the Keren Kayemet and various charitable institutions, giving instructions to the Shamash, etc. Similar customs and arrangements were common among most other Jewish families in our city. The light of the many tall candles sparkled out through the windows. Everyone hurried to the synagogue with excitement for Kol Nidre.

The material relating to the Jewish holidays and festivals is great and rich. Every city and town had a unique atmosphere for the festivals. In general, the Jewish holidays were festivals of joy in every place. The gladness was great during the holidays. I have already mentioned briefly the holidays of Purim and Passover. There were also numerous customs for the festival of Shavuot. The houses, the synagogues, and the streets in the Jewish quarter were adorned with flowers and decorations. This imbued the entire city with a festive atmosphere. No small amount of attention was also given to the food for this festival, upon which it was customary to eat a special dairy meal in addition to the meat meals. The women would cook three cornered pastries stuffed with potatoes mixed with butter and cheese. Should we not mention the festival of Simchat Torah and its customs in the synagogue, about which it is said that anyone who did not witness the festivities on Simchat Torah has never witnessed joy in his life? Simchat Torah was primarily celebrated with the Torah processions (hakafot) that took place evening and morning in the synagogue. The hakafot were conducted with a sublime spirit accompanied by singing and dancing. Even the children would participate in the festivities, joining in the hakafot by following behind the adults with colored paper flags. All of the ceremonies in the synagogue on Simchat Torah included songs and hymns. The joy was especially great with the with the Chatan Torah and Chatan Breishit [2], who arranged kiddushes in their homes with drinks, wine and liquor poured out as water. I recall that many Jews would get drunk and shout out mockingly "Cursed be Mordechai and blessed be Haman". The day of Simchat Torah turned into a first class national holiday that encompassed the entire nation, from young to old, women and children, and instilled upon them all a spirit of joy and mirth, a spirit of hope, comfort and encouragement for good days to come...

[Page 140]

Purim Players in Podhajce

The Jews of Podhajce would also celebrate Purim in their joyous style, "With noise, food, drink and entertainment". Among the Jews, there were four Purim plays that did not depart from the Purim stage until the era of the Holocaust. These are "Achashveirosh Play", "The Sale of Joseph", "David and Goliath", and "Jacob and Esau". These plays fit in well with the Purim theme from the Megilla. Mordechai was the second to the king in his Diaspora county of Persia; Joseph did not become lost in a strange country, for he rose from slave to second to the king in the Land of Egypt; David, the young Jew, defeated the giant gentile Goliath; Jacob purchased the birthright from Esau and ruled over him.

In Podhajce, there was a traditional annual performance on Purim by the "Joseph Players". The performance was put on by the local Jewish water drawer of the town, the father of eighteen children, short in stature with a small beard and a smile that never departed from his lips. His nickname was "Yosele the water carrier". Some time before Purim, he would arrange rehearsals for the play, in which most of his children participated. If one or two would be missing from the ten sons of Jacob our father, he would invite children from the poor neighborhood to make up the number. His troupe would appear every Purim in the homes of all of the honorable Jews, with special costumes befitting the Bible. They would portray the sale of Joseph to Egypt by his brothers, how he lived as a prince in Egypt, how the elderly father (our forefather Jacob was played by himself) arrived in Egypt to ask Joseph to free his sons who were imprisoned as suspects of espionage [3], and how finally the identity of Joseph was revealed, etc. It is interesting to note that these plays always served as a source of decent income for several poor families in the city, so that they would be able to purchase matzos, fats and potatoes for the upcoming holiday of Passover. In the latter years, this Purim play turned into a source of income for the Keren Kayemet LeYisrael and the Keren Hayesod.

Youth Movements and National Life

The day of the Balfour Declaration, that was declared by the British Foreign Minister Lord Balfour on November 2, 1917, authorized as well by other governments, and included in the British Mandate of 1922, turned into a day of joy and gladness and a portent for the beginning of the redemption for all of the youth organizations and movements in the city. This declaration recognized the rights of the nation of Israel to the Land of Israel, its historic birthplace.

Similarly, the anniversary of the death of Dr. Herzl, the 20th of Tammuz, was marked by every Jewish community with a public gathering at which they reminisced about the memory and activities of Herzl, whose name had become one of the most revered, precious and famous among the Jewish people of the Diaspora. His name was a symbol of the longing for national pride, independence, and the renewal of the glory of the nation. From the day of the death of our national poet Chaim Nachman Bialik on the 21st of Tammuz 5694, the two memorial days were observed simultaneously – that of the political leader and the poet. On these memorial days, despite their festive character, it was permitted to do all work, and the stores were open. However, many Zionists closed their stores and places of work, and paused from work on those days. The Hebrew school was closed, and some Jewish children did not attend the public school. Each year, parades of the members of the various parties took place on the streets of the city. The members of the youth groups and the children of the Hebrew school would gather next to the Hebrew school, and from there they would march through the main streets, arranged neatly in rows, to the Great Synagogue, where a large crowd of people from our city, Zionists and others who were curious, were gathered. The chief spokesman was always Mr. Moshe Liblich of blessed memory, a veteran Zionist in our city. Following him, representatives of the various youth groups and teachers of the Hebrew school would address the gathering. At times, special representatives of the headquarters of the movements would come to speak that day about Dr. Herzl, the Zionist movement, and the Land of Israel. The majority of the Jewish houses were decorated on those days with pictures of Dr. Herzl and blue and white flags. Of course everything was done with permission, in accordance with the permits received from the Polish authorities. Obtaining the permits was not among the simplest of matters. They were only received after difficulties and struggles.

Despite the attitude of the Polish authorities to the Jews, even to those who were born in Poland, we should not skip over the national Polish holiday of May 3rd, which was celebrated in Poland in memory of the national charter, the constitution of May 3rd. On that holiday, all of the businesses, work places, offices, schools, etc. were closed. There were also Jews who saw it fitting to adorn their houses on that day with the red and white flags of the state, and the pictures of the president of the state and members of the government. On that day, large, splendid parades took place, in which groups from all strata of the population participated, as well as representatives of the villages of the area (of which there were more than 70), with their special multicolored costumes. The place of the Jewish community of the city was also not absent that day. Its delegates always had the rear place in the parade. This situation was also repeated with the groups of school children, and the Jewish children marched in the rear. Incidents sometimes took place where the Jews were accused of disrupting the order of the parade, or of not decorating their homes in the appropriate fashion. The Poles regarded this as a great desecration of their holiday. This matter was always associated with many difficulties. The parades often served as negative influences, where the Polish patriots became drunk. At times, these "patriots of the nation" became unruly and began to pillage the Jewish neighborhoods. Indeed, our Jewish brethren would foresee what was to take place, and were prepared for any circumstance. They would even organize themselves to protect their lives and property. The butchers, smiths, porters and others were especially involved in this.

Despite all this, the people of Podhajce were forced to participate in the festivities, to march in the parades, willingly or unwillingly, and to dance at the joy of those who were as distant from them as east is from west. The Jews of Podhajce were no different in this regard than those of the other cities and towns of Galicia.

Moshe Liblich of blessed memory
one of the first Zionists in our city

[Page 141]

A group of members of Gordonia
Sitting from right to left: Yisrael Glazer,
Nathan Brecher, Uri Milsztok, Izak Gotstein

Members of Hechalutz in Podhajce, 1930

Members of Beitar (Brit Trumpeldor) in Podhajce

Translator's Footnotes

1. Yigdal is a hymn that contains a summary of the 13 principles of faith.
2. On Simchat Torah, the yearly Torah reading cycle is concluded and begun anew. Chatan Torah is the person chosen to have the aliya at which the concluding section of the Torah is read. Chatan Breishit is the person chosen to have the first aliya of the Torah – following right after Chatan Torah.
3. This fact is not in accordance with the Biblical narrative. Jacob only went to Egypt after the identity of Joseph was revealed to the brothers.

[Page 142]

Members of the leadership of Beitar
In the center, the chairman of the chapter Friedler, to his left Natan Milch (fell near Stalingrad)

Regarding the Youth Groups, Cheder Education and the Hebrew School

Since we are discussing the youth groups of the city, it is worthwhile to mention that almost all of the parties and movements that existed in Poland existed in our city, including: Hechalutz, Gordonia, Hanoar Hatzioni, Achva, Bnei Akiva, and others. However, the Hashomer Hatzair movement was the strongest. We were also not lacking an academic student corporation and illegal Communist groups.

With regard to the study of the Hebrew language and literature, most of the youth of the city began their aleph beit studies in the cheder. In my time, this took place with Avromche Melamed (Walden) or Aharon Melamed (The Red), and their helpers (the belfers). Later, the children studied Chumash and Rashi, Bible, Gemara, etc. from the renowned Reb Davidl, his neighbor Rebbe Leibishl, Rebbi Meirl (on Schloss Gasse) and others. Aside from this, there were older youths in the city who would study Torah in the evenings from the three rabbinical judges of the city: the head of the Beis Din Eisenstein, the judge Haber and the judge Schurz (the son of the Rebbe of Zawalalow) from whom I studied along with the son of Rabbi David Lilienfeld. We studied for many hours with them at night, despite the fact that we were students of Gymnasium at the same time. From among the townsfolk there were also people whose souls longed for Torah. At night, and at times even during the day, they would sit and occupy themselves with Torah, whether in the synagogues, the Beis Midrashes or private homes.

The first teacher, whose name was Brecher, taught the Hebrew language (in the Sephardic pronunciation), both spoken and written. In my time, Koretz and Rozen were also Hebrew teachers. In their merit, we should point out the happy fact that most of the youth of all factions studied in the Hebrew school during the day or with evening classes. These two teachers worked hard to accustom the youth to Hebrew. They were the central point for the instilling of the love of Zionism and the Jewish homeland.

[Page 143]

Economic Life and Anti-Semitism

To this point, I have told about religious and traditional life, feelings and faith, accepted paths of life, etc. However, we cannot ignore the economic factors, the staff of bread of the Jews of Podhajce. Similar to other cities and towns in Galicia and Poland, the Jews of Podhajce and its region were not only divided into Hassidim and non-Hassidim, but also into merchants who had stores and warehouses for wood, grain, coal, iron, etc. For five days a week (except for the Sabbath and Sunday), the stores, offices and warehouses were open as usual. Thursday was the weekly market day, when thousands of farmers from the nearby villages would come in with their wagons laden with the produce of their land and their manufactured items. The wagons of the villagers filled the center of the town, the areas of the city marketplace as well as the side streets. Merchants of the area also arrived with their stalls that day, and participated in the business and barter. The farmers brought fruits, vegetables, eggs, fowl, butter, cheese, as well as cattle and grain. After they sold their merchandise, they would go to the stores to purchase their household needs. On the market day, the entire city was filled with movement and a deafening din. Whoever went out that day to the streets of the city would be startled by the sight of the sea of thousands of heads, walking through the market or standing next to the stalls of the various peddlers, filled with all sorts of items, pants, coats, shoes, boots, and other such merchandise. The Jewish merchants, men and particularly women who were a unique group among the Jewish population of the city, played the main role in the market square. The hands of the women merchants were industrious, and they began to make use of their own language of sorts, a sort of constant banter. With the aid of this language, their hand was always on top. This fair also served as the gathering place for professional thieves, drunks, hooligans and men of the underworld who found a wide open field in the crowds for their activities. On occasion, the market day provided an occasion for an organized attack by anti-Semitic groups upon a Jewish merchant or stall, causing conflict and bloodshed. At times like this, Jewish self-defense became active. On many occasions the conflict concluded with the local police arresting the defenders rather than the instigators of the conflict and the attackers who had caused bloodshed...

In our town, a certain farmer of the region named Pilko the Drunk became known. He was quite wealthy and loved to tipple. On account of his drunkenness, he sold some of his land every year. When he became drunk on Thursdays he would hasten to the city, run through the streets and shout aloud, “Jews to Palestine”. Unintentionally, he thereby filled a Zionist role, declaring that the Jews are duty bound to to the Land of Israel.

The main source of income of the Jewish merchants, peddlers and craftsmen in this city was on the Thursday market day. This day was a “day of blessing” for the Jewish population of the city. It was the source of livelihood for almost all the people, and provided them with their household needs for the entire week. Despite the sporadic incidents of strife and conflict, the days of the fair passed peacefully. Indeed, there was a difference between the fair days during the period of Austrian rule and those of the period of Polish rule. The Austrian gendarmes attempted to keep order with full force of the law, and succeeded in this. This situation took a turn for the worse during the Polish era.

Characters and Nicknames

In the space of every Jewish city and town in Galicia, there were stories, fables, legends, mottoes, and jokes that formed a rich and variegated folklore. Some of these were based upon historical facts that were adorned with stories of wonders. Some were fables of a moral theme, jokes, legends from the middle ages, as well as stories from people of our time. Stories of all of these types were told in Podhajce as well, and there is no doubt that some of this vast storehouse of material that floats around the space of our old community is worthy of being written down. It is possible to preserve some of the important folkloric material that relates to our town. However, without doubt, we will have to suffice ourselves with a little, literally "the tip of the fork". Even this will not be in a complete fashion.

One of the most notable items is that almost all the residents of the town had a nickname aside from their regular name. At times, a nickname would be given to the residents of an entire city. The residents of Lvov were called "Lemberg Pipekes", the residents of Berezany were called "Berezaner Kremalkes", and the residents of the town of Przemysl were called "Przemysler Horse Thieves", etc. Our city of Podhajce had the name "Podhajcer Duck Makers" (Podhajcer Katchke Machers). What is the source of this nickname? Regarding this, we have a long story that is brought in the memoirs of our fellow native Michael Weichert [1]

The nicknames that were added to the names of most of the residents of the city, in addition to the true family name, was another matter that was often humorous. For example, Yehuda the "lo" (The no), since always expressed a negative opinion and expressed his "lo" with stress of the vowel. The nickname "Pious man" was given to a certain Moshe the Pious who always brought home several poor people on the Sabbath for food, drink and lodging.

[Page 144]

The nickname "Abba Kalika" (Abba the cripple) was given to someone whose hand was somewhat paralyzed. "Leibish Mareni" was given to someone who, despite being a Hassid, loved to extend his hand to the young village girls who came to his store. A Jew by the name of Levi had the nickname "Levi Parch" (Levi the rat) because of his large bald spot. Each year on Shabbat Hagadol, when the city hoodlums would stand by the gates of the synagogue and accompany the worshipers who were on their way home with shouts and "cat howls" with various "musical instruments" (such as tin plates, pots, jars, etc.), this Levi would prepare cake, wine, and fruit as a fine snack for these hoodlums, instead of shouting at them as did the others. Nicknames were given to other citizens, such as "Muchia Puta" (Silly Muchia) to someone who was not overly intelligent, or "Yosha Kalb" (Yosha the Calf) for the same reason; "Yoel Natkes" – because he was too smart; Leib "Tziutzia Veyitzia" became he had many relatives; "Itzia Drong" because of his tall height, etc. The nickname of one Jew of our town by the name of Leon Weiss aroused great interest. He was a wealthy Jew, a merchant of hides and shoes, and he was known as "Leibele Trask" ("Leibele the Smack") because he was short and he would become angry or upset easily. His wife was taller than him, and when he would argue with his wife and wish to slap her on the face, he would jump up and shout out "I will give you a smack" or "you will get a smack". Thus did he gain the nickname "Trask". Regarding this nickname and its bearer, it is told that once a shoe wholesaler from Lvov came to town to visit several merchants, including Mr. Weiss, who were delinquent in their payments. When the wholesaler descended from the train car, he asked one of the passers-by, "Where does Mr. Leon Weiss live?" He was answered that there was nobody in the city by that name. As the merchant continued on asking his questions to several other passers-by, each one of them could not answer his question. The wholesaler thought that there was a matter here of a man who did not exist, and the name signed on the contracts was nothing other than a forgery. Only later when he was meeting with one of the shoe merchants, he was answered, "I am sure you are searching for Leibele Trask, who is known to us by his nickname". Thus did the wholesaler find the person for whom he was looking.

The water drawers of Podhajce were considered to be one-of-a-kind characters. Almost every part of the city or street had its own water drawer, who had the rights to provide water to the residents of this neighborhood. The largest street of the city ("Di Breite Gasse" – The Wide Street) and the surrounding area was considered the "territory" of Yosele the Water Drawer and his sons, who are known from the section on the Purim plays. "Mordechai the Water Carrier" and his wife Zelda the dull-headed has the rights to draw water on Schloss Gasse. On Holenada, this job was fulfilled by Rachele and her son Moshe, and we should not wax lengthy about this. Often, disputes broke out between the water carriers regarding competition between several houses of families, and also regarding prices. This was similar to the disputes and struggles that would break out between some of the shochtim (ritual slaughterers) who on occasion conducted their disputes in manners that were not acceptable to Jews, and also at times in unseemly fashions. Not infrequently, these matters would reach the authorities, an involvement that instilled shame and caused great unpleasantness.

Schloss Gasse – the Street of the Castle

The Crazies of our Town

The veteran of them, who was nicknamed "Pasulki-Drefki" was a short Jew with a long beard who lived by the mercy of the city. He would go from house to house every Friday with two large sacks to collect challas, fruit, and other food items. His main craziness was politics. He would gather fragments of newspapers on the streets. He would always approach the telephone poles and hit them with his cane, thereby "discussing" about all types of countries, kings and statesmen. Later, when he continued going from house to house to collect food, he would inform the residents of the city about all types of political news, in accordance with his opinion. He had a special affinity for Bulgaria, and most of his proclamations were "Praise Bulgaria", until he got to the topic of Sarajevo, the city that caused the First World War.

The second crazy in the city was loved by everyone, even the Christians. He was Moshe Chaim. Whenever anyone tripped along the way, he would approach him, pat him on his back and call him by his profession with the addition of the name "Abba" (father). He would call a baker "Father of Bread", a shoemaker "Father of Shoes", etc. He would call the Christian regional official "The Father of the City". He was always happy with his lot, pleasant, dressed well, and with his great naivety he was able to receive his needs from everyone easily. He worked as a water drawer from time to time, providing for certain houses. He would give all the money he collected to his elderly mother, "Mother Rivcha". He never requested donations. He loved to eat, and meticulous about eating good food. Therefore, he looked good and his health was strong. However, his tendency to gluttony hastened his end. As was related to me, one Seder night, he went from one Shulchan Aruch (Seder meal) to another, and a third, and he ate a great deal at each place. During the night he was attacked by strong pains and treated them with hot water bottles. When real medical help arrived, it was too late.

[Page 145]

It is interesting to note here one episode that was characteristic of Diaspora Jewry and connected to Moshe Chaim, despite the fact that he was crazy. During the year of 1914-1915 of the First World War, after the Austrian army retreated from its positions and the armies of the Russian Czar advanced westward and entered our city, they immediately declared a curfew at specific times. However, this Moshe Chaim did not understand the order, and he went outside. The soldiers captured him, imprisoned him, accused him of spying, and tried him as a spy before the military court. However, the collective responsibility of the Jewish people in a time of tribulation was awakened in our city as well during that time came to the salvation of Moshe Chaim. After he was imprisoned, the Jews of the city felt themselves in an intolerable situation, and they worked diligently to free him.

The Russian army commanders who were stationed in our city knew that among the Russians, Circassians, Cossacks and other peoples of Russia that comprised the Russian army, there were also Jewish soldiers. They were also not oblivious to the fact that there were also Jews in the Austrian camp, and that on both sides of the front, Jews spilled their blood for a matter that bore no relationship to them. For such was the lot of the Jew in every country, to spill his blood on the alter of the "homeland" in which he was living. From that time, the nickname "Margel" (spy) was added to Moshe Chaim's name, or as he called himself "Ein Spien".

This situation of the drafting of Jews to the armies of various countries resulted in tragic situations during battles between the enemy camps. Not infrequently, at a time when shooting took place between the two sides, one would hear the cry of "Shma Yisrael" from the "enemy", and it became clear that the two combatants were Jews who resided in two enemy countries. I know of a specific incident of two brothers of the Lippa family from the village of Telyache near Podhajce, who met together, one from the side of the Russian army and the other from the side of the Polish army. At night, at the moment they were about to shoot at each other, it became clear that they were two brothers, and thus they were miraculously saved from death.

The Family Life of "The Eternal Jew"

Aside from a few families in our city, most of the Jewish population in Podhajce was composed of several large, extended families, such as the Horowitz, Fiszer, Perl, Haber, Stein, Milch, Itinger, Lilienfeld, Polisziuk, Pomeranz families, and others. There were also certain other families whose connections were more or less loose, but who would join together on days of joy or anguish, and became one body in the family of the wandering Jew. The situation was similar in Podhajce, on account of the mutual responsibility and joint suffering. On the one hand, we cannot ignore that in our city there were people who never met, never came in contact with each other, and never talked with each other for various reasons. However after the Holocaust, when very few were left, one from a city and two from a family, this situation improved. Today, if two natives of our city meet in the Diaspora, and even more so in Israel, they have a common language and mutual family warmth. The Holocaust survivors regard themselves as one large family, without concern for their various classes. The hearts of them all ache over the destruction of their community, and they find comfort in their survival and their reestablishment in independent Israel, that has once again become the homeland for all scattered Jews.

An Incident that Took Place with Binyamin Kitner of Podhajce

I have touched on the story of various families in our city, and I feel that one should not pass over the incident that took place to Binyamin Kitner of our city, who was a wise and pleasant man, honored and liked by his fellow. This interesting and sad incident took place in the years 19190-1920, when the Poles fled westward and the Bolshevik armies penetrated quickly to Warsaw. (Then, the "Miracle on the Wisla River took place, and the Bolsheviks fell and retreated eastward to Russia.) During those days, remnants of the Ukrainian nationalist soldiers and the inimical armies of Petliura roamed about the No Man's Land between the Polish and Bolshevik fronts. This No Man's Land touched Jewish settlements in many places. For quite some time they did not know for which side and for the benefit of whom they were fighting. However,one thing they knew very well: to rob, to pillage, to murder, and they especially placed their eyes upon the Jews.

[Page 146]

Thus came the turn of Podhajce. When several dozen armed soldiers came to our town riding on horses, the people of the city did not realize that they were from Petliura's gangs, and the Jews went out to the street to greet "the new rulers". Their commander asked that the elders and notables of the city be sent to them. Binyamin Kitner and Mr. Eizenstein the head of the civic court were sent as representatives of the Jews. It was thought that they were about to establish a provisional government in the city, and these were the men fit for the task. However, at the moment when both of them appeared before the captain, he drew his revolver and informed them that they were arrested as ransom, adding that within six hours, the residents of Podhajce, especially the Jews, must bring specified quantities of hides for shoes, textiles, food, etc. as fines. Failing that, the two men would be killed, and there would be many difficulties in the city. Thus, the people of the city found out who these soldiers were, and with whom they must deal...

The two men were imprisoned in an isolated house, and the Jews quickly began to collect the "contribution". In the meantime, the ruffians spread out among the Jewish homes at the edge of the city and began to rob and beat the Jews, and rape the women. However, fortunately, after five hours of the rule by Petliura's gangs in the city, several soldiers of a Soviet battalion appeared suddenly, as evening fell, from the east atop the Gei Hill, and shot several gunshots over the city. Confusion and fear overtook the Petliurists. They began to prepare for defense, and the soldier that guarded the two prisoners was called up for defense. The prisoners seized the opportunity and escaped through the window to the next house, where they changed their clothes, donned the clothes of farmer women, and hid. Thus they were saved from certain death, for the soldiers later to search for them. These soldiers caused difficulties in the city all night, and only in the morning did they flee westward to the town of Zawalow. The situation was shakier there, and the local Jews paid with the blood of several victims who were murdered by the ruffians.

A day or two later, the Bolsheviks entered the city and began to impose their rule. The leadership of the city and the local militia was given over to one of the poor Jews of the city, a second class tailor who had a left leaning outlook. His name was Getzel Berg, and from that time, he had the nickname Getzel the Commandant. The Kitner family had a large house with many rooms in the city. This was formerly a hotel. Getzel the Commandant entered the home of Mr. Kitner and evicted him from most of the house, leaving him` 1 and his family with only one room as living quarters. He claimed that this was a command from the Soviet authorities, and as mayor, he required these rooms for offices. Kitner answered the order without any opposition, adding a few words to the Comrade Commandant: "Thank G-d that the leadership of the city has to the hands of a Jew".

Another Jew, of whom many of the city did not appreciate his virtues and qualities, entered into the history of the city during that brief period. He was a carpenter and also a local merchant by the name of Davidzili (David) Heiden, a short Jew with a long beard and peyos that he kept behind his ears, a naturally white face and other trappings of a Hassid. He worked in business as a side job. He was a good carpenter by profession, but since this profession did not sustain him appropriately, he also ran a small store for sewing materials, which was tended to by his wife. Despite the fact that he had a lot of business from his professions, he was not particularly wealthy. Just as he was short in stature, he lived most of his life in a small, short house, half of which was sunken into the ground. Only in the later years, when his family grew and his children (two sons and two daughters) grew up, did he began to add on to his small house with his own hands, and add three or four additional rooms, for dwelling and also for a workshop. He was a man of energy, strength, wisdom, and he had a good heart. He was expert in "the small letters" and knew how to study a page of Gemara. In the morning or evening, he would sit alone or in the company of Aharon the teacher and study Torah. He was a good prayer leader, and on holidays, they loved to listen to his sweet prayers and melodious voice. He would invite a poor guest to his table every Sabbath to eat at his table. On the Sabbaths and festivals, he would sing the hymns accompanied by his children, and his neighbors on the street (including me and my family) enjoyed listening to their singing. In addition, he was a communal activist, who distributed contributions with an open hand. He often succeeded in promoting peace between disputants. I recall the dedication celebration that took place when he moved to live in one of his new rooms. At that time, he donated a Holy Ark to one of the synagogues in which he worshipped, and his wife also gave a gift – a Parochet (ark cover) with fine embroidery, which she made herself. He put great energy into promoting peace among the shochtim in their dispute with the city. He did a great deal to ease the straits of the children of Mendel the Undertaker, who were hungry and did not have sufficient clothing. He did not pay attention to those of the city who said, "Such is an appropriate punishment for Mendel the Undertaker, for when he was the guardian of the cemetery (in which he resided), he did not act properly, and thereby caused disgrace to the cemetery." Heiden concerned himself as well with Itzele the Musician at a time when his livelihood was not sufficient for all his needs, even though he was beloved and desired in the city as a jester and chief musician at all of the weddings in the town and region. Thanks to his intercession, he got an additional job as the guardian of the local bathhouse. From that, he also obtained his rent money. Heiden gave over the key to the back door of the large Beis Midrash to youths who were hiding from the government police, at a time when they were busy losing weight as a protection from being drafted into the army. He only asked of them that they study a bit of Torah in addition to playing cards. Heiden spread his protection upon Hershele the Satan (nicknamed the Lying Rebbe) when his neighbor wished to complain to the government against him for disturbing them day and night with his shouts, for Hershele would worship in his house on Shul Gasse (the Street of the Synagogue) in a loud voice morning and evening, and he disturbed the sleep of his neighbors. In his travels to other cities, he presented himself as the Rebbe of Podhajce. He had a long beard with long peyos, small, deep eyes, and wore a black, long kapote and white socks. Only, he did not know how to study Torah...

Before he reached the age of 50, Heiden took ill with intestinal cancer, and underwent an operation in the Jewish hospital of Lvov. I was present as well at the time of the operation. It was successful itself, however due to the lateness of the operation, complications, unsanitary conditions, and failure to use antibiotics in those days, he died, to the grief of all who knew him. His entire family was murdered during the murderous war of the Nazi Germans. His eldest son Shaul served as a soldier in the Polish army and was captured by the Germans. His friend Taubenkiwel who survived said that Shaul tried to flee from his confinement, and the German guards shot and killed him.

[Page 147]

The leadership of the T. O. Z.

Standing from right to left: Pepa Milch (nee Weinless), Yaakov Shear, Hela Sperber, Magister Gang, Mania Kitner of blessed memory, the lawyer Notik, Dr Tartan-Kressel of blessed memory, Michael Kohn, the court official Mr. Shleicher. Sitting from right to left: Mrs. Shear, Mrs. Dr. Gross, Mrs. Morgan, Mrs. Dr. Rott

Allof blessed memory

Conclusion

The article is too brief to describe everything. I know and feel that with all my writings, I have not fulfilled my duty to the extent that it assuages the conscience. It was a bold and difficult experience to write on paper about a reality that is no more. I feel difficult pangs of conscience regarding the personalities and characters, each one of whom had a recognizable influence upon the city and the community. More than twenty years have gone by since the bloodbath in the cities of Poland, but the voices of my brothers and friends, relatives and family members burst forth from the group and demand that we establish a memorial to the pure souls. However, how can we respond to this serious demand? Who can plumb into the magnitude of the Holocaust?

Our city, with what is old and new in it, was destroyed in a cruel manner at the hands of the Germans and their troops. Fate did us a good turn in that a small remnant of the large family that was Jewish Podhajce remained. This town is worthy of a memorial in our lifetime, for in it we saw the first light of the world, in it was revealed to us the light of the rebirth that brought us to the designated Land, to live in it and revive it, to built it and be built up by it. It is fitting that the few survivors of it who remain among the Holocaust survivors, scattered in various Diasporas and also in Israel, will do everything possible to maintain the soulful connection that beats in our hearts for that town that was and is no longer. It is not the nostalgic longings for the Podhajce of the Diaspora, with all of its positives and negatives, that attracts us to it to remember it and inscribe it upon the tablet of our hearts, but rather the love of our parents' homes and our families who are lost for us forever. Their memory will never depart from our hearts. In order to fulfil the verse "and you shall relate it to your children that day" in its broadest meaning, it is the duty of all of us to tell not only of the suffering and difficulties prior to the Exodus from Egypt, but also about the cruel times of the decrees of annihilation in the Nazi war of destruction.

The bright images of our dear martyrs and the beauty of their lives will continue to live in our hearts and will serve as signposts in our lives.

Translator's Footnotes

1. See page 101.

[Page 148]

Anecdotes

by Dr. Matityahu Pomeranz

Brief stories about various personalities

One of the Orthodox Jews who earned his livelihood by the sale of "banned" merchandise whose sale was permitted solely through the agencies of government, sat one Sabbath afternoon with his neighbor as they occupied themselves with Torah. A gentile entered and asked to purchase a small bag of tobacco for smoking. The Jew was not lazy. He went up to the attic, brought down a bag of tobacco, gave it to the gentile, and received his recompense. The neighbor was astonished at this deed and asked: "Is it possible, is it permitted to sell something on the Sabbath?" The Jew answered with a question, "And on a weekday, is it permitted to sell?..."

Judge M. would come to the courthouse quite late and begin hearing the cases, even though the case was set for an early hour. Once, the judge turned to one of the Jews who was involved in the case with a warning, "Is it possible, sir, when you come to the court, to concern yourself with your appearance and to shave." The Jew answered, "Indeed, I shaved, Your Honor, but during the time that we were waiting for the case to begin, my beard grew anew..." The judge laughed heartily at the wise answer, and would often mention it.

That judge had a sense of humor himself. When he came across a Jewish name that ended with "s" he would say, "Indeed they are Greeks, Hesheles, Breines, Chachkes, Socrates, Temistocles". When he once came across a Jew from Monastyrishche whose name was Azdrabel, he called out, "Here once again we have a Babylonian..."

One citizen once turned to my brother, who was a well known lawyer, and requested that he prepare an eviction notice for one of his tenants. My brother explained to him that it is not possible to win the case, since there is a law to protect the tenants. The Jew turned to another lawyer who was willing to prepare the notice. Of course, he lost the case. After some time, the Jew ran into my brother and said to him: "I, thank G-d, have more brains than the lawyers, and I found my own means against my tenant. I tied a calf under his window, which mooed at night and did not let him sleep, until he left the premises and fled for his life."

A middle aged fish merchant was invited to court. The judge wrote down his personal details, and asked among everything else: "Are you married?" The Jew answered, "No Your Honor, I am still a youth..." From that time, that Jew received the nickname of Youth.

One of the residents of the city who became wealthy during the time of the First World War did not have a great intellect, and he based his prestige primarily on his wealth. Once, he came to the train station to ship out a shipment of merchandise, the exchange of which was supposed to be paid right there. When he came to the train station, he put his hand into the pocket to take out his money, and to his great dismay, he found that he had forgotten his wallet in his home. His first reaction is, "Where is my intellect..."

One Jew named D. who was a carpenter by trade abandoned his trade and became a merchant. One of his weaknesses was his love of the "prayer leader's podium" – that is he loved to serve as a prayer leader. Once the shochet Yaakov Friedman stood next to him and pointed out, "Our D. is a great expert about the board." (That is he is an expert about the wooden prayer leader's podium). In Yiddish, the word "breitel" means "board", and serves as a euphemism for the prayer leader's podium in the synagogue.

Leibish Meier, a resident of the village of Lissa, informed the police that some wooden oak planks that he had purchased with his money from an estate had been stolen. After searches, investigations and inquiries, the planks were found hidden in the home of a villager named Tz. However, the gentile insisted that the planks belong to him. In order to prove the correctness of his claim, Meier demonstrated that all of the planks were marked with the letter M., the initial of his name. The gentile retorted: "I wrote this letter, and the letter M. stands for "moya" ("mine" in Ukrainian).

One of the residents of the city loved to spice his conversation with sentences in the German language. Not infrequently, he would stumble in his language, and use an expression that was not appropriate. When his mother died, he wished to explain this in the vernacular, and he said: "Meine mutter itzt mir niderge-komen", the correct translation of which is "My mother is about to give birth".

The residents of Podhajce were called "Podhajcer Katshkemachers" (Podhajce Duck Makers) by the residents of neighboring cities. The root of this nickname related to a Jew of our city who succeeded in convincing one villager that the calf that he brought to sell in the city is nothing more than a duck. However, our city was not the only one whose residents had a nickname. Regarding this it is said: “The distress of the many is half a comfort”.

[Page 149]

The House on the Small Hill

by Etty Gross

In memory of Leib Kressel and Aba Rubinsztok who concerned themselves with finding a hiding place for the entire family, and they themselves fell victim.

One of the villages near Podhajce is called “Stary Miasto” in Polish. This was sort of a suburb of the city. Exactly on the boundary between the city and the village, on a small hill, stood a house in which two families lived. There was a large yard around the house, in which wheat was grown, and there was a cowshed. The families that lived there created the stamp of a new life, as if it was an intermixture between the village and city life. Thus was it before the outbreak of the war.

In earlier days, only one family lived there. This is the Kressel family: a father, mother, two daughters and three sons. The children grew up and left the home. Two daughters immigrated to the United States, one son immigrated to France, and only two children remained at home, the daughter Adela and the son Leib. With the passage of time, the father died, and the mother remained with two children. Adela married Abba Rubinsztok who came from one of the villages near Podhajce, and Leib married my sister Pepa Gross.

During that time, I got to know that family. I was then a young girl, a member of Hashomer Hatzair, and everything connected with the life of the land and village life enchanted me greatly. I loved to watch how they milked the cows, filtered the milk, and churned the butter. The fields were close to the house, and the aroma of the wheat wafted up from the farm.

I loved to visit them very much. The mother, Mrs. Kressel, was a short, rotund woman. She was smart, intelligent and full of energy. Since the hospital was very close to their home, she had an interesting occupation: as a member of Bikur Cholim, she would visit the hospital. Every ill Jew, especially if they were from the area, would benefit from her caring attention. She would bring food to the ill (for there was no kosher food there) as well as sweets. She made sure that permission would be granted for visitors to enter. She concerned herself with the forsaken ones, and in general, all of the ill Jews in the hospital were under her care. The Kressel-Rubinsztok family had fields, and occupied themselves in the grain trade. The two men had decidedly opposite personalities.

Abba Rubinsztok was a tall, broad-shouldered man, with a tanned face. He worked the land with all the bones of his body. He would make the rounds through the yard with diligence and meticulousness. He would fix something here, straighten something there, and pluck every weed. He was a good homeowner in the full sense of the term. All the tasks related to the working of the land were under his supervision. Leib Kressel was his exact opposite: short, jovial, not excited about working the land but rather about business. He felt himself as a fish in the water when he was in the grain warehouse. Purchasing, selling, weighing, going to town – this is what he loved.

In the interim, children were born into both families. Thus they lived together in one house – with one complimenting the work of the other, in honor and peace, until the outbreak of the war.

Mrs. Kressel died at the beginning of the Nazi occupation. The family moved into the ghetto when it was set up, and lived in the ghetto like most of the Jews. In the ghetto, they recommended that Abba Rubinsztok join the militia, but he refused, which testified to his uprightness and propriety. Since the Kressel and Rubinsztok families had lived for all the years in the village and had connections with the farmers of the area, they began to think about a hiding place. Leib Kressel searched for and found a hiding place for my parents (the Gross family), me, his family, and the Rubinsztok family.

In the meantime, and aktion took place. They searched for men to go to the work camp, and came to search for Abba Rubinsztok. However, he succeeded in hiding. Leib Kressel was recovering from a severe bout of typhus, and was sure that they would not take him on account of his illness, but he was mistaken. They took him out of bed and told him that he would be freed if Rubinsztok presents himself. Obviously Rubinsztok would not present himself, for then they would both be held. The Rubinsztok family, Pepa Kressel and her son succeeded in leaving the ghetto exactly at the last moment, and arriving at their hiding place in Muzylow.

Leib Kressel remained at the work camp in Zagreblya near Tarnopol for four months, and then succeeded in escaping from there. He walked for eight days until he reached Muzylow, since he walked only at night and hid during the days. How great was their joy when he reached them whole and healthy and joined up with them. However, their happiness did not last long.

The farmers that agreed to hide them were Ukrainians. They belonged to the "Bondira Organization". Apparently, they did not take two things into account in their reckoning: one is that the matter would last for so long, and second is that the danger would be threatening them from both sides, from the Germans and also from the members of Bondira. In any case, they changed their mind, and one night they forced the two men to go out to find another hiding place.

At that time Max Melcer, a court official, roved around the area of Holendri. He managed to arm himself with a gun, and instilled fear upon all of the farmers of Holendri by forcing them to provide him with food and clothing. The farmers put out an ambush for him, and to the ill fortune of Kressel and Rubinsztok, they arrived in Holendri that night and were caught. They wanted to enter the hiding place of my parents. However, the farmer did not permit them,

and they were forced to remain in the field. Therefore, they were captured. The farmers who captured them were their neighbors, who had known Leib Kressel from his childhood. However, nothing helped. They beat them with death blows so that they would reveal the hiding places of their wives. Then they called the Germans, and both of them were murdered.

After the murder of the two men, the Ukrainian farmers had no choice but to continue to keep the wives and two children until the Soviets arrived. When the Soviets arrived in Podhajce in the spring of 1944, they only remained a few days and were then forced to retreat. Then the two women left the bunker and fled to Skalat. This was spring, and the snow had melted. There was mud along the routes, and they were almost barefoot. They had only rags tied around their feet. Thus they arrived in Skalat. They remained there for a few months until Podhajce was liberated, and they then to Podhajce.

[Page 150]

Then the two sisters-in-law set out on different paths. Adela Rubinsztok and her son immigrated to America. Today she is the grandmother of three grandchildren. Pepa Kressel made aliya to Israel and established a family. Today she is the grandmother of two grandchildren.

I am certain that both of them recall that house on the small hill from the good days that went by.

Life of the Jews in the Village of Zlotnik

by Dvora Shapira (Friedman)

My town was small and poor, but it had a rich name: Zlotnik – the city of gold. It is adorned with forests and fields that spread out to the horizon. A river also flows through its precincts, the Stripa River.

During days as they were, the days of peace, this river knew many romantic secrets. When the days of the Holocaust arrived, it waters were reddened with the blood of the Jews. However, the river flows along its path as always, and tries with all its might to cover the blood and appear again as clean and pure before the sun – a stream like all other streams.

Like all cities and towns in mournful Poland, our town was destroyed in the great destruction, and everything related to it arouses pain, anguish and grief. Despite all this, at times the heart recalls other types of memories, from the peaceful days before the Second World War. A joyful tremble passed over the heart as these good days are recalled.

I recall how a group of amateur players organized themselves in Zlotnik and performed the play "Ahava Kovkozit". Some of the organizers of that play are today in Israel, such as Rivka Flaszner, Tovia Feder and Chana Poker. I wanted to see the play very badly, but I did not have money for a ticket. To my fortune, I had an aunt named Bat-Sheva (Sheiva) who was close to the "Bohemian" people, and did not miss any performance. With her, I entered the hall and saw the play – without paying any admission.

I remember how the Hebrew teacher Mrs. Horowitz came to our town and began teaching the Hebrew language. I also registered for the Hebrew school, but since there was no class appropriate for my age, they included me in a class of older students. I already had a proper knowledge of the Hebrew language, and the older students were embarrassed that I exceeded them with my knowledge. Therefore, I was once again transferred to a different class of students who were younger than I. The classes under the direction of Mrs. Horowitz lasted only for a brief period, since the teacher made aliya to the Land of Israel, and she could not delay her aliya on our account.

Now, I will write a few words about our family in Zlotnik.

My parents had seven children. They were not particularly wealthy, and they saw no future for their children in the town. My sister Rivka, today living in Israel, went to Hachshara, but she remained in the town as she did not have sufficient money to obtain a certificate. My brother Moshe is also in Israel. The three of us were the only ones to survive from the family. The rest, our parents and the children who did not succeed in escaping, perished in the Holocaust.

Thus, our town is no more. The Stripa River washed everything away, and its waters are once again clear and fresh. However, in the hearts, wounds that will never be healed remain. Today we live in our Land, far from the anti-Semitic atmosphere that enveloped us in the Diaspora. We paid a dear price for our freedom. We have only one prayer in our hearts, that all that was accomplished through the toil of generations should continue on forever, as repayment for the suffering of the nation throughout many generations.

I hope that our children will not be witness for such tribulations as afflicted our generation. I tell my children about everything that my eyes witnessed, and ask that they also tell their children. For we are duty bound to fulfill the Biblical verse: Remember what Amalek did unto you.

[Page 151]

Memories of the City

From Podhajce to Jerusalem by M. Sh. Geshoury

(About the Personality of Professor Avraham Weiss of blessed memory.)

(An abridged summary of the article in the Hebrew section of the book {Hebrew article is on Page 99})

[Page 152]

The Bursztyner Rebbe in Podhajce

by Rabbi Z. Eichenstein of blessed memory

(Note at the bottom of the page: Given over through his son, Rabbi Yitzchak Izak Eichenstein.)

When my father, the rabbi and Tzadik Rabbi Yechezkel Izikel Eichenstein of holy blessed memory settled in Podhajce in the year 5668 (1909), he was a young man of 33 years of age. He settled in Podhajce with the approval of the rabbi and gaon Rabbi Shalom HaKohen Lilienfeld of blessed memory, for there was in the city a significant number of Bursztyner Hassidim of the rebbe Rabbi Nachumche of holy blessed memory, my father's father-in-law.

He quickly attracted a large number of various Hassidim. Many ordinary Jewish householders also became his followers, for his innocence convinced everyone that he was truly a tzadik. I wish to note a few well-known and prominent people who became his Hassidim: Reb Shlomo Orgel, who himself was a tzadik, and was never absent from his table on Sabbaths or festivals, summer and winter, despite the fact that he was already elderly; Reb Hershel Korenblum – a great scholar who used to conduct the Shacharit service in the rebbe's Kloiz; Reb Yehotzedekl Fried – a scholar and Hassid; Reb Feivish Peshis – a scholarly Jew; and hundreds of other Hassidim from various rebbes who became his Hassidim and dedicated friends.

With help from those Hassidim and from dedicated friends and supporters from among the householders, the large house with the Beis Midrash was built. The rebbe was a great tzadik, a wonder worker, and a great distributor of charity.

This is how it went until the First World War. The war brought a great change to the Jewish life in general, and to religious life in particular. A large proportion of the important householders who left on account of the war did not to Podhajce. The older generation passed away. The city took on a completely different face – new householders, new customs and a new intelligentsia. Zionist parties arose on the right and the left, and there were also no lack of “Reds”. Parties were also created within Orthodox Judaism. Thus was Jewish life organized after the rebuilding of the ruins of the First World War.

The Orthodox Jewish party, of which the writer of these lines was one of the founders, also created various institutions. Some existed for a long time, others stopped their activity after a brief time, primarily on account of financial difficulties. The city Talmud Torah was led for a long time by me. A Beis Yaakov for girls was also founded, and it was greatly successful.

The changes in Jewish life in the city did not have a great effect on the Rebbe's house. Sabbaths and festivals were celebrated as always with great joy, and were sources of spiritual pleasure for all who came to the Rebbe's table. On festivals, Hassidim from other cities and towns would come as well.

In the final years before the Second World War, the situation in the city became more difficult. However, the Jews of the city used all their means to ensure that the Rebbe's house could be sustained with honor. This continued until the great misfortune in the era of Nazi rule. The rebbe died in the ghetto on 13 Adar I 5702 (1942), and his entire family was murdered during the last aktion on 3 Sivan 5702. I alone was saved with the help of G-d, for I settled in New York in 1936.

Here in America there are four Podhajcer organizations.

1) “Chevra Masaat-Binyamin Anshei Podhajce”, which built its own synagogue where I am the leader.
2) “Chevra Rodef Shalom Anshei Podhajce”
3) The United Podhajcer Organization
4) Podhajce Young Men

All of the Podhajcer Jews of New York take part in the aforementioned organizations. However, in the last few years, the number of members has declined greatly, for the older generation is passing away, and their children rarely belong to the Podhajcer organizations.

[Page 153]

Dr. Michael Weichert

(May 5, 1890 – March 12, 1967)

Dr. Michael Weichert
of blessed memory

He was born in Podhajce, Staro Miasta, Eastern Galicia. After three years, he moved with his parents to Stanislawow, where he studied in a modern cheder, Polish public school, and later in a gymnasium. In 1908, he took part in the Chernowiczer Yiddish Language Conference. He studied theater and art history, literature and jurisprudence in the universities of Lemberg and Vienna (in the latter, he earned a doctor of jurisprudence). In 1916-1917, he was a guest student with Max Reinhardt in theater in Berlin. Simultaneously, he studied theater science from Professor Max Herman in the University of Berlin. Starting in 1918, he studied Yiddish theater in occupied Warsaw, where he also worked as an Austrian assistant in the Newspaper Science Institute at the German Press Committee. After the first World War, he was a teacher of German, Polish and diction in the "Ascula" Gymnasium of Warsaw until 1933. He was a jurisprudence counselor at the United Committee for Matters of Jewish Labor (of the Joint, ORT and Handworker Central). Throughout all this time, he was connected to Yiddish theater, in which he quickly became known as one of the innovators and successful artistic directors.

In 1920, Dr. Weichert directed Gerhard Haufman's "Furman Henshel" (translated by H. D. Nomberg) in the Vilna Troupe; in 1928, he directed his own stage adaptation of Sholem Asch's "Kiddush Hashem"; in 1929, Shakespeare's "Shylock", Aharon Ceitlin's "Yidden Stadt" and M. Lipschitz's "A Story about Hershele Ostropoler"; in 1930, G.

Bichner's "Danton's Death"; in 1931, Asch's "Reverend Silver" and Ch. Gotesfeld's "Livelihood"; in 1935 Friedriech Wolf's "the Yellow Patch".

Dr. Weichert was the founder of the Jewish Dramatic School (1922) and Jewish Theater Studio (1929), whose graduates created (1933) the experimental "Young Theater" (later the "Young Stage", "New Theater"), to which the most significant personalities of Jewish theater belonged. "Young Theater" performed, under Dr. Weichert's direction, among other performances: "Boston" (Sacco and Vanzetti); Goldfaden's play "Troupe Tanenzap"; Shalom Aleichem's "Napoleon's Treasury", Mendele's "Third Travels of Benjamin"; Leib Malches' "Mississippi"; Yaakov Preger's "Simcha Plachte" and "Meilech Freilech".

Dr. Weichert was also the chairman of the Jewish artists' organization in Poland and vice president of the Warsaw chapter of the Jewish Pen club.

At the time of the outbreak of the Second World War, Dr. Weichert was the founder and chairman of the Jewish Social Self-Help (J. S. A.) that helped Jews in the ghettos and camps, intervened for the benefit of arrested Jews, etc. In December 1942, the German authorities shut down the J. S. A., but a little later, he, with the agreement of the German authorities, once again opened up the organization with the name of "Jewish Support Organization" (JUS). Dr. Weichert was one of the leaders of the new organization.

With respect to Weichert's activity in that organization under German rule, the illegal Jewish Coordination Committee leveled accusations against him. After the war, in 1945, he was brought to trial in a Polish government court in Krakow. Weichert was acquitted of those accusations.

He began his literary activities when he was still a student. His debut was with critical articles in the Lemberger Tagblatt. Later he began to work with Polish and German theatrical periodicals. He took part in Der Juda (edited by Martin Buber) with his work "About the History of the development of Jewish Theater" (Number 8 - 1917, 1-4, - 1918). He published a large number of theatrical critical works in Moment, Lebens Fragen (Life Questions), Folkszeitung, Choliastra, Bicher-Welt, Literary Pages, Ringen, Theater, Jewish Theater – Warsaw. Along with alter Kaczizna he edited "Ringen" (Notes on literature, arts, and criticism), 1921-1922 (10 notes); Yiddish Theater (the organ of the Jewish Artists Organization in Poland), Warsaw 1925-1926, 4 issues; Theater – 6 issues; Yiddish Theater, quarterly book, 1-4, Warsaw, 1927-1928. Published in book form: Theater and Drama, book 1, Warsaw 1922, 184 pages, book 1 and 2, Vilna 1926, 186 pages.

[Page 154]

Dr. Weichert lived in Israel since 1958. He teaches diction in courses at the Histadrut and also in courses for beginners in dramatic circles at the Tel Aviv city administration. He is a contributor to Last News, People in Zion, Davar, and Echoes of Education, Tel Aviv.

Dr. Michael Weichert of blessed memory passed away on the 30th of Adar I 5627, March 12, 1967.

Dr. Weichert was active in the Podhajce organization in Israel, and as a member of the committee for the publication of the Yizkor Book until his death in 1967. There is an article of his memories of Podhajce in the Hebrew section of the Yizkor Book.

A memorial ceremony for M. Weichert at the conclusion of the year following his death

Z. Reizen Lexicon, book 1; Z. Silberzweig, Lexicon of Yiddish theater, book 1; A. Gurstein, Zeitschrift, Minsk, book 2-3, 1928; Y. Mestel, Archives of the History of Yiddish Theater and Drama, Vilna-New York, 1930, pages 505-506; First Yiddish Language Conference , Vilna 1931, index; G. Bader, A Country and its Scholars, New York, 1934; Dr. R Feldszwa, Yiddish Sociological Lexicon, Warsaw, 1939; General Encyclopedia of Jews, B, Paris, 1940; N Meisel, Yiddish Culture, Number 8-9, New York, 1944; There Once Was a Life, B. Ires, 1951, pages 337, 345-347, 358; B. Mark, Stories of Ruins, Lodz, 1947; El. Granach, Thus Goes a Man, New York, 1948; Y. Turkow, Thus Did it Go, Buenos Aires, 1948, Warsaw 1952, index; Dr. Y. Shatzki, YIVO pages, 1954; M. Borovitch, Aryan Papers, Buenos Aires, 1955, index; Sh. L. Schneiderman, Daily Journal, B. Y., March 4, 1956; M. Ravitch, My Lexicon, book 1, Montreal, 1941; pages 220-223, and book 3, Montreal, 1958, page 475.

[Page 155]

Synagogues, Cheders and Teachers

by Yehuda Grussgott

(A free translation of the article in the Hebrew section of the book. {Hebrew article is on page 107})

[Page 156]

Memories of the Hebrew School

by Yehudit Heller

(A free translation of the article in the Hebrew section of the book. {Hebrew article is on page 110})

Students of the Hebrew School with the teacher Rozen (1924)

[Page 158]

The General Zionist Youth Movement

by Baruch Schatten

Translated by Jerrold Landau

(Equivalent with the Hebrew article on page 114 (although the first paragraph on page 114 is not included in the Yiddish).)

A group of Hanoar Hatzioni on Hachshara
Sitting at the bottom: Anshel Roll of blessed memory, Yehuda Perl (in the United States), Tzvi Roth of blessed memory, Yosef Shechter (in Israel).
Standing in the center: Aryeh Dik of blessed memory and Yosef Hessel

[Page 159]

Hanoar Hatzioni at the time of bidding farewell to the member Freda Statmauer-Perl prior to her aliya
Standing from right to left: Shimon Kramer, Meiberger, Gruber.
Sitting from right to left: Fishel Jopiter, Mrs. Kramer, Freda Statmauer, Schatten, Bernard Poliszuk

A convention of Chalutz Mizrachi in Lvov with the participation of members from Podhajce

Members of Achva

[Page 160]

The top leadership of the Achva organization
Standing from right to left: Freda Dunkel, Isser Roler.
Sitting from right to left: Aryeh Kurtz, Munia Schatten, Moshe Erde

[Page 161]

The Activities of Hashomer Hatzair

by Avraham Brandwein

(An abridged summary of the article in the Hebrew section of the book {Hebrew article is on Page 119})

A chapter of Hashomer Hatzair, 1925

The Kinneret group of Hashomer Hatzair, 1938

A Hashomer Hatzair Chapter, 1938

[Page 163]

The Kadima Student Corporation

(An abridged summary of the article in the Hebrew section of the book. {Hebrew article is on page 124})

A group of academics
From left to right: Dr. Ber, the teacher Kestenblat, the veterinarian Dr. Matis Kohn

---

[Page 164]

Meir Mass – the Hero of the Town

by Y. Grussgott

(An abridged summary of the article in the Hebrew section of the book. {Hebrew article is on page 126})

The Market Square
Mordechai Messing and Abba Milch are standing in the center

[Page 165]

Memories of Years Past

by Dr. M. Pomeranz
by Y. Grussgott

I have beloved memories from my childhood years in Podhajce, especially from the long walks with my parents in the areas outside of the city, to the hill, to Siolko, to Zahajce or to the train station. During those walks, my revered father took the opportunity to discuss with me lectures from the synagogue, as well as issues of general education.,

Today, when I think about Podhajce, the thoughts are filled with sorrow. When I recall the souls of my kin who were murdered there, the city as I saw it for the final time before the outbreak of the Second World War stands before my eyes. This was a city with Jews, exotic orthodox ones as well as non-observant, rich and poor people – a city in which Jews lived and flourished for hundreds of years.

Aside from the city, the Podhajce area includes three towns, Zlotniki, Wiœniowczyk, and Zawalow, and approximately 70 villages. The Jews were a small minority among the Poles and Ukrainians in the region. However, the city itself was mainly Jewish. Thanks to their astuteness, the Jews took the first place in all economic endeavors.

For example, there were only 3 gentiles from among the 20 lawyers. I believe that all of our natives still remember the eldest lawyer in the city Dr. Finkel, as well as the lawyers Nutik, Pel, Gross, Salpeter, Ratner, Rotenberg, Kestenblatt, Falver, Pomeranz, Bin, Greenberg, Marbach, Abend, Rauch, Horowitz and Fein, along with their wives. The younger generation of lawyers included Lilienfeld, the Gand brothers and Sher. The lawyer Leon Pomeranz should also be noted. He died a few years before the war. He was well-known among the Jews and Poles. He was vice mayor for a few years after the First World War. A large number of lawyers left Podhajce and settled in other cities, including Binyamin Pomeranz, Yaakov Wolf, Rudolf Rusmak, and the lawyers Margolis, Messer, Milch and Goldschlag.

There were a total of two gentile doctors. The Jewish doctors included the eldest, Dr. Landau, as well as Drs. Kornowicz, Reichman, Dik, Falver, Neuman, Silberman, Heller, and three women: Roth, Aszenfeld, and Bider (in Zlotniki). From among the younger doctors, Drs. Milch, Weinles and Heller should be mentioned.

The pharmacies were completely in Jewish hands, and only Jews worked in them: Eker, Goldschlag, Nussbaum, Weintraub, Bezen, Margolis and Balin (in Zlotniki). The younger practitioners of this profession included three young women: Ornstein, Falver and Salpeter.

There was no shortage of Jews in the courthouse and other regional offices. The Jewish magistrate Dr. Aszenfeld always found the need to highlight his Judaism. A few officials remained in the courthouse from the Austrian era, including Gang, Lilla, Postel, Melcer, and Zomerstein, who died before the war. Rusmak worked in the tax office. Falver, Mrs. Alter and the mailman Zin worked in the post office. Isidor Rozmarin and later his son Tadeusz Rozmarin worked in the city administration.

There were two engineers in the city who worked in surveying: Hirschberg and Lilla, who died before the war.

The director of the insurance office was Tovia Ratner until almost the last years. He employed Jewish officers and doctors.

Despite the fact that was no gymnasium in Podhajce, a large number of Podhajce youth graduated with a Ph.D.: Welger, Trajaner, Poliszuk, Friedberg and Kestenblatt. The youngest of this group were three women: Falver, Zeidler, Salpeter and Heller.

[Page 166]

A gala evening of the local intelligentsia
Most of the participants were Jews

Jews directed very little energy to agriculture, but in proportion to their numbers, this was no small percentage. From among the largest landowners, we must include: Julius Rotenberg from Belokrinitsa, Alfred Somerstein from Burkanow, Gelber (Gelewski) from Shumlyany, Dr. Slomnicki from Bozhikowa, Adler from Szweykow, Roth from Malowud, Silberman and Zimmer from Zatuzhyn, Dolberg from Tustowawy, Blaustein and Shmirer from Kotuzowa, Mehr and Ales from Wolica, Zusman Kahn from Poplawa, Engineer Kogan from Zastowcza, Dr. Landau from Tarasowka, Leon and Eli Kohn from Buda and Michael Kohn from Sianokoski.

In truth, several of the aforementioned landowners strayed from the path of Judaism and became apostates. However, at the time of the murder of Jews, this did not help them, and they were murdered along with the rest: such as, for example, Somerstein,

Gelewski and Dr. Slomincki. Aside from the landowners, there was also a large number of land lessees. Many Jewish managers and "economists" worked also for Jewish landowners.

Many Jews were also employed in the agricultural industry, such as owners and lessees of mills and mines from Jewish and gentile landowners. I only remember a few of these: the Lilienfelds, Avraham Milch and Shimon Wassermil.

Podhajce also had a large mill, a sawmill and an electric generator. The mill and the sawmill were owned by the brothers Oscar and Yaakov Haber. The electric generator was established and run by Engineer Roth in partnership with the Habers. The Habers also owned the concession for chopping the large and ancient forest in Solewa. They cut the wood in their sawmill and then exported it.

Connected to agriculture was also the exploitation of the three ponds in the Podhajce region. One of them belonged to the Habers. The other two belonged to the landowners in Nowosiulka and Zahajce. Jews worked for them.

The grain business was completely in Jewish hands. Grain exporters included Zusman Kohn, Michael Kohn, Shmuel and Mendel Fiszer and Rachmiel Hessel. Henryk Rozmarin was known as a middleman in the grain business. Yaakov and Yosef Werfel and Fishel Milch (died before the war) were involved with land partitioning, and the farmers had complete trust in them.

Some Jews also did business with building materials, particularly with wood, and had large storehouses: Moshe-Baruch Bezen, Dr. Gross, Leon Kohn and Kune Hochman, Hirsch Leib Horowitz and Don Horowitz, and primarily the Habers. Involved in the production of bricks were Abba Fisz and Yisrael Silber, as well as Berish Welger who was also involved in bee keeping.

There were a few wholesale businesses in Podhajce, which served the entire retail business in the city and region. Chaim Lehrer, Hersch Kimmel and Avraham Milch owned wholesale food businesses. Moshe Zimet, Marcus Ohering and Dik owned wholesale iron businesses. Berel Weiss, Yehoshua Walfisz, Zelig Milch, the Ettingers, Boral and others owned wholesale leather businesses. Weintraub, Mauer, and Eisenberg were in the textile branch. Marcus Lehrer was in the haberdashery business. Sonia Schechter was involved with wine. Rabbi Lilienfeld, Hazelkorn and Tovia Ratner were involved with beer.

[Page 167]

In brief, all business was entirely in Jewish hands. However, in the latter years, particularly in 1938 and 1939, the tendency increased for the Polish and Ukrainian nationalists to take over businesses from Jewish hands. In Podhajce, a special committee was set up for this purpose under the chairmanship of the manager of the court Ritarowski. They set up Polish institutions and conducted a strong propaganda campaign toward the Poles that they should have as little as possible to do with Jews. The Ukrainians did the same thing. This continued until the outbreak of the Second World War.

The Jews also played a very fine role in the handworker trades. Despite the fact that there was no shortage of Christian craftsmen, the Christians themselves gladly hired Jewish craftsmen.

Yehuda Marbach excelled in the mechanical trade. All landowners, Jews and Poles, would hire him to construct and repair their mines, for they esteemed his abilities and honesty. The artistic workshop of Shlomo Silver, his father-in-law, Zimmerman, and Degen was involved in carpentry. Well known tailors included Kressel and Berg; shoemakers – Sekler and Lebensfeld; Kressel was known among the furriers; the entire Glazer family was involved in glassmaking; with paints and chemicals – Bergman and Bodzanower; sheet metal – Dik, Fistener, Biller and others. There were also Jewish tradesmen who worked with wood and stones for building, smiths (like Poliszuk) and various other trades.

The hotels of Gross and Schechter were known in the city. Aside from these, there were, of course, a large number of restaurants and taverns (Yosef Werfel, Shaul Friedman, Moshe Ornstein, Zeinwil Weisman and David Ajlen, Mrs. Fiszer, Haken, and others). Aside from these, there were several Christian restaurants. There were also a few Jewish bakeries: Moshe Gross, Chaim Yehoshua Beker, Statmauer, Buchwald, Wolf, among others.

There were two printing shops in the city, both of which belonged to Jews – Weinles and Moszel. The owner of the bookstore was Eli Kressel.

The saddle making profession was also solely in Jewish hands (Citron, Lew and others). Several Jewish families, such as the Goralnik family, were involved in the transport business. Shmuel Szmiczler conducted an automobile and autobus enterprise. Two workshops (Zeidler and Rohatyner) were involved in watch making, as well as with selling various electrical appliances and furniture. Sellers of firewood included Meir Falver with his son-in-law Rutin, Abba Fisz with his brothers-in-law, and several other Jews. Of course, there were several Jewish hairdressers – for example, Szmicler, Scher and Pik.

In one word – both business and the most important trade enterprises were in Jewish hands at the time that the Christian population were mainly occupied with agriculture and gardening. Only in the latter years were a few Christian cutting enterprises and grain purchasing cooperatives formed.

For generations, the owners of the houses in the city were Jews. An anti-Semitic adage used to circulate: we would prefer it if Jews purchase houses, where they will dress well and eat well; the houses will, in the end, fall into our hands... Thus did they think, and they were prepared for the time when Hitlerism came to the world, and Jewish lives and possessions became a free-for-all in all of the lands in which the nazi murderers overtook during the Second World War.

[Page 168]

Religious and Communal Life

Podhajce Jews strongly upheld tradition. Accordingly, there was a large numbers of synagogues and shtibels in the city. Today, I cannot remember them all. However, I well remember the Great Synagogue and the Beis Midrash (the city Beis Midrash), where such Jews as Binyamin Kitner, Rabbi Lilienfeld, my father Yitzchak Pomeranz of blessed memory, Moshe Liblich, Michael Kohn, Zusman Kohn and his son, Yoel Hazelkorn, Yaakov Fueurman, Hersch Leib Horowitz, the Ettingers, Abba Kremer and many more people worshipped. I have only fond memories of the Beis Midrash, for there I used to worship with my father of blessed memory from my earliest childhood. After his passing, I worshipped there until the outbreak of the Second World War. Aside from these, I recall the Husyatiner Kloiz, the Czortkower Kloiz, the Bursztyner Kloiz, the Bekerishe Kloiz, which was very beautiful and esthetically designed, as well as two other large synagogues, one near the Wide Street and the other near the Brzeszaner Street. Aside from these, there was an entire set of smaller synagogues.

While discussing the city Beis Midrash, I wish to mention here a story that took place. After the passing of my beloved parents, I searched for a way to perpetuate their memory. Since the Holy Ark in the Beis Midrash was old, simple, and worm eaten, I decided to make a new Holy Ark. I commissioned an artistic, oak Holy Ark from Shlomo Silber. However, I kept this secret, lest someone preempt me. I would inform the gabbaim (synagogue trustees) when the ark was ready. However, one of the gabbaim, who it seems was interested in obtaining this merit himself, resisted and stated that the old Holy Ark cannot be removed under any circumstances, as it would be a desecration of its sanctity. I retorted that the old Holy Ark can be placed in Pulisz, but this did not help.

A short while later the Zlotniker Rebbe, Mund came to see me in my office about some matter. In passing, I told him about the troubles that I had experienced in that they were not permitting me to put up the Holy Ark. He told me that there is a small synagogue in Zlotniki which would certainly take the old Holy Ark from the Beis Midrash. Not long thereafter, the Jews of Zlotniki came and took the Holy Ark with great honor and singing. Thus, the place for the New Holy Ark that I donated was freed up.

Near the entrance of the Podhajce cemetery there is a row of old gravestones marking the place where well-known rabbis and activists from hundreds of years ago were buried. I recall that following the First World War, the cemetery was badly damaged, especially the bricks that surrounded it. At that time, a committee was formed in which my father took part. With the financial help of an America native of our city, the cemetery was repaired.

The celebration of the festivals in our city is a chapter unto itself. During the month of Elul, we began to arise for Selichot. In the morning, the entire city heard the shofar blowing. We also visited the graves of our parents during the month of Elul.

This was all a preparation for Rosh Hashanah, when all of the Jews gathered in the synagogues and worshipped until late in the afternoon – praying for a good year. Prior to Rosh Hashanah, people sent each other “Shana Tova letters”. As we left the synagogue, we wished one and other “Leshana Tova Tikateivu Vetechateimu”. On the first day of Rosh Hashanah toward evening, almost the entire city went to Taslich at the Koropiec River.

The awesome mood of Yom Kippur commenced already on the eve of Yom Kippur, and perhaps even a day earlier, when people conducted the Kapparot ceremony. On the eve of Yom Kippur, people went to the Mincha service early, so that they could have time afterward to eat the final meal. In “Pulisz” they set up an entire row of clay plates in which the worshippers placed their charity money. In the latter years, these included the national funds. The tall, wax Yom Kippur candles already stood on the ground. They were lit in the evening, and burned throughout Yom Kippur. I recall as well that a group of worshippers would conduct the flogging ceremony after Mincha. I looked upon this custom with curiosity.

Of course, not one Jew remained at home during Kol Nidre. As well, a large number of intelligent

Christians would come to observe that solemn prayer. The image of my father of blessed memory still remains before my eyes, as he would always stand beside the cantor and hold the Torah Scroll during Kol Nidre. I must mention here the cantor Getzel Perl, who would lead the services in the synagogue every year. Many of his tunes are etched in my memory to this day.

The Jewish character of the city could best be noted on Yom Kippur. All of the streets were empty at the time the Jews were in the synagogue, and the city was as if it was dead. After the meal following Yom Kippur, many of the householders began to build the sukka, and banged in the first pair of nails.

[Page 169]

Everyone fulfilled the commandment of eating in the sukka. The children were particularly joyful, for they decorated the sukka in various ways. Almost ever Jewish home had either a sukka or a tarp.

A joyous and cheerful mood pervaded in the city on Simchat Torah. The children came with flags. During the Hakafot (Torah processions), they sang, clapped, and danced with the Torahs. Everyone received an aliya (Torah honor) during the reading of the Torah in the day. Special festive foods were served during the meal. In many houses and synagogues, they would have a "drink" in the late afternoon with beer and beans.

The holiday of Chanuka was also a lovely and long festival, especially for the children. We received Chanuka Gelt, played dreidel, and ate good things. Older children would play card games with special cards that had Jewish letters.

Then came Purim, and it was joyous in the town. In the evening after the Fast of Esther, the Megilla was read, and the children swung their graggers and stomped with their feet at each mention of the name of the evil Haman or his children. The next day, we sent Mishloach Manot (Purim food portions) to one another, and the city was filled with people in disguise and ordinary poor people, who went around to all of the houses in order to receive Purim money. There were also groups of Purim players who performed various plays, primarily the Sale of Joseph. The people in disguise and the Purim players were well received everywhere with a drink and treats, over and above the Purim money. Furthermore, various institutions and organizations utilized the day to collect for their causes. In the evening, we sat down for the feast, which was accompanied by visits from the disguised people and Purim players. A particularly joyous feast was conducted every year in the court of the Bursztyner Rebbe. His Hassidim and followers used to partake therein.

After Purim, we already began to prepare for Passover. The duck fat for Passover was already prepared from Chanuka, but the serious preparations began from Purim. People began by whitewashing or painting the house, cleaning the furniture, cleaning the silver spoons and brass pots. Then they began to purchase the matzos. Some people wished to be present as their matzos were baked. People had to purchase new clothes for themselves and the children. In brief – there was no shortage of work.

On the Sabbath before Passover, Shabbat Hagadol, there was a longstanding custom to "send the rats back to Egypt". The town jokers gathered together and walked in pairs, making a loud noise with old metal pots and lids. For them, this was the beginning. Prior to the "sacrifices" this was the "torture". At least one person in the city related to this with humor. He treated the scoundrels nicely and wished them that they should next year...

In the morning of the Eve of Passover, people burned the chometz (leavened bread) and began to prepare for the Seder. People sat down for the Seder after coming home from the synagogue following Maariv. The youngest child asked the four questions, and then the Haggadah was recited and the tasty Passover foods were eaten. A Seder was once again conducted on the second night of Passover, and then the festival lasted for an entire week. Even on Chol Hamoed, when the stores were open, a festive spirit pervaded in the city.

Shavuot was a short but beloved festival. The homes and the synagogues were decorated with greenery. In the synagogue, Akdamus was recited and the Book of Ruth was read. Tasty dairy foods were eaten after from the synagogue.

I also recall joyous Jewish weddings that were held in the hall of Gross' or Schechter's hotels. The local musicians, Dauber, Kimmel and Leizerl played. At times the Gutenflan brothers from Brzeziny or the musician Faust from Rohatyn were brought in.

[Page 170]

A farewell party for a Polish judge, with the participation of the Jewish intelligentsia

Jewish Personalities and Organizations

From among the most important personalities of the previous generation, one must first and foremost mention Rabbi Shalom Lilienfeld of blessed memory. He left behind two sons, David and Leibish, who were also well educated. They were treated with great respect. The judge Avraham Eisen was also active in the clergy. He was the head of the rabbinical court along with his son-in-law Judge Wolfe Haber. Aside from them, there were four shochtim (ritual slaughterers) and a scribe in the city.

The first Zionist organization in the city was founded just prior to the First World War. Zionist meetings were held in Hersh Freundlich's parlor. I remember that my brother Binyamin and my sister Roza used to go there for lectures. As a child, I studied in the Hebrew school of Rabbi Mordechai Brecher. Every year on the 20th of Tammuz, we would all go to the Great Synagogue for the memorial service of the late leader Dr. Herzl.

After the First World War, when the Jewish servicemen from Western Austria, the Hashomer youth organization was founded. I was also a member of Hashomer, and I wish to mention here several members whom I remember from that time: Munia Ornstein (today Mordechai Oren), Chaim and Yehoshua Marbach, Meir and Munia Zloczower, Izia Liblich, the Kestenblatts, the Friedbergs (Later Mrs. Marbach), Izia and Wilo Friedberg, Ber, Trajaner, Messer, the Poliszuk's, the Margolies's, Bunia Milch, Weinles, the Wiesenthal's, the Salpeter shoemakers, Mates Falver and his sister, Leib Dik, and many others who I no longer recall today. Some of them came to Israel and played in important role in various organizations, such as Mordechai Oren, Meir Zloczower, Dr. Chaim Marbach and Dr. Izia Liblich.

Eastern Galicia was under Ukrainian rule in the years 1918-1919. This did not last long. At that time, Ukrainian bandits began to attack Jewish stores and stalls, and even Jews on the street. At that time, a Jewish self-defense organization was established spontaneously, consisting of former soldiers of the Austrian army, under the leadership of David Lilla. When the Ukrainian state ceased to

exist, the Jewish self defense organization also disbanded.

The members of Hashomer were for the most part involved with Hashomer Hatzair, which had an extreme left leaning. Aside from them, in the city there were General Zionists, Revisionists, and various youth organizations such as Hanoar Hatzioni, Beitar and others. The head of the General Zionists was Moshe Liblich, who excelled as an orator. All of the Zionist organizations were involved in the Keren Kayemet (Jewish National Fund) committee and Keren Hayesod. They were seriously involved in collecting money for the national funds.

[Page 171]

The Zionist organizations had a well-organized cooperative bank, which was established with its own capital, without the help of the government of the city. They greatly help their members, who were primarily small businessmen and tradesmen. The Zionist organizations also had a well-stocked library called Hatikva, which also served many gentiles.

The Zionist movement also maintained the Hebrew schools, where one could study Hebrew language and literature, and Jewish history. The teachers that I recall include Mordechai Brecher, Rozenzweig, Rozen and Kurtz.

Some of the founders of the library
From right to left: Dr. Baruch Milch, Shlomo Walden, Yehuda Grussgott

There were also halls in the city where one could find and read all types of newspapers in Hebrew, Yiddish, Polish, and German. From time to time, debates, discussions and celebrations were held in these halls.

For a certain time, amateur performances were also performed in the city. They were organized and produced by Meir Goralnik. Miriam Kitner (the daughter of Binyamin Kitner) also took part in the artistic performances. She was a pianist, and very active in the field of choreography. She stood out with her high intelligence and her mastery of several languages. She also played a large role in preparing performances for children and youth for cultural and volunteering occasions.

The orthodox circles in the city were also well organized. For many years, they conducted a religious organization under the chairmanship of Tovia Ratner. They maintained a Talmud Torah and a Yeshiva. Aside from these, there were cheders where Jewish children were educated in the spirit of Jewish tradition. They were also active in the economic realm, and they had a cooperative bank, which gave loans for small businessmen and tradesmen. The bank was in a positive situation. One of its directors was David Cimet.

There was a volunteer society in the city that took upon itself the task of improving the situation of orphans and of the poor people in general. This society was founded by Mrs. Dr. Landau, who was involved in benevolent activities with her full heart. If she found a poor child without shoes on the street, she would bring him to a shoe store and purchase a pair of shoes for him. In 1929, she left the leadership of that society, and her place was taken by Mrs. Dr. Pomeranz. Mrs. Dr. Morgen headed that society from 1931 until the outbreak of the Second World War. There was no orphanage in our city, and in certain cases, orphans were sent to the well-known school of Korkis and Mrs. Klaften in Lemberg, with the Podhajcer society paying the bill.

The income of the society came from membership dues, and primarily from various campaigns and fundraisers, such as for Chanuka and Purim. Once a year, the society sponsored a

grand ball, in which the Polish intelligentsia of the city and region participated as well as the Jewish intelligentsia. First and foremost, the mayor and all high Polish officials also participated.

[Page 172]

Aside from that society, there was also, as in every city, a Bikur Cholim (visiting the sick) committee and other volunteer societies, which from time to times conducted charitable campaigns for their activities. One of the most important was the activity for Hachnasat Kalla (providing for brides). My father of blessed memory always used to stress to me the importance of enabling two Jewish children to found a family. A few days before his death, lying in bed, he found out that Yaakov Fueurman was collecting money for Hachnasat Kalla. He summoned him and gave him 25 dollars for that purpose.

I wish to conclude by stating that, despite the fact that the Jewish community in the city was not united, and there was no shortage of friction among them, they had a deep feeling of community. Ignoring the restrictions (such as "numrus clausus" which was effectively a "numrus nullus"), they achieved a great deal in all areas of societal life in the city.

A celebration for the benefit of the Society for the Aid of Orphans

Podhajce Anecdotes

by Dr. Matityahu Pomeranz

Told by Dr. M. Pomeranz

Translated by Jerrold Landau

(Equivalent with the article in the Hebrew section of the book, with the exception of 2 anecdotes that appear only in Hebrew. {Hebrew article is on Page 148})

[Page 173]

On the banks of the Koropiec

Jewish Life in the Town of Zlotnik

(Equivalent with the article in the Hebrew section of the book. {Hebrew article is on page 150})

[Page 175]

The City in its Destruction

In Eternal Remembrance

No! It is forbidden for us to forget them – the millions of our brethren who perished in sanctification of the Divine name.

From the time that Israel became a nation, we were persecuted to our necks, enslaved and exiled. A holocaust of this nature, however, with such terrible destruction, we never knew. A third of our nation was destroyed, we lost the best and dear ones of our nation. Torah giants perished, their light was extinguished from the flame of Judaism – and we hastily forget. Is not this forgetting also part of the terrible Holocaust? Is it not also a tragedy among the tragedies?

In the annals of Jewish history, there are many chapters drenched in the blood of men, women, and children. Israel knows tribulation and suffering from time immemorial. Many are the days of mourning and tribulation in the calendar of the Hebrew nation. Our treasury of song and hymns is filled with dirges, laments and bitter weeping. For just as we know how to die the death of martyrs and mighty ones, we also know how to memorialize and perpetuate those of our people who have been slaughtered. We all recall the destruction of the nation and the land long ago, but we tend to forget the destruction of the nation in our own day.

No! It is forbidden for us to forget! The memorial day for the martyrs of our city and its environs must stand at the center of our life. It must become a day of uniting with the martyrs of our city, and with the millions who perished in the European Diaspora, until each and every one of us knows and feels what was lost to us in this frightful destruction, until each Jewish child knows what the bloodthirsty wild men perpetrated upon us, and how great is the breech in the loss of the mighty people, cedars of Lebanon, who were the glory of Israel.

The great traditional command beseeches us: Do not forget! And on the memorial day we will unite with our martyrs and together call out with a loud voice along with the entire House of Israel:

"Yitgadal VeYitkadash Shmei Rabba!"
Tzvi Goralnik

[Page 176]

An Eternal Light

In memory of the pure and holy martyrs who were murdered, burned and strangled
In the fields of Podhajce, Zlotniki and environs during the days of murder and slaughter.

Call out! Even today, with the passage of years
We so wish to know
Who and who, where and when, and how, how?
You so wished to place your ears to the pages of the book,
To see if is heard
The final sigh of a father,
The cry of a mother who was being strangled for eternity...

For there is a tear on every page of the book,
Each letter is a wailing lament;
Each line is a festering wound,
Each chapter is a valley of sacrifice.
Read, and know
How before the bright, shining light of the sun
The pure souls were dragged to the pits of the masses of the community.

They afflicted the blood of fathers and sons,
The blood of merciful mothers and their children,
The blood of brothers and sisters,
The blood of grooms and brides,
The blood of men and their wives,
The blood of teachers and their students
And they were all murdered as one in the sanctification of Your Unique Name.

Earth, do not cover their blood, so that there will not be a place for their cries.
You have no grave, a stone monument was not erected for you,
Letters were not engraved upon it, gold upon black.
To you, my dear ones, I have erected a monument in my heart.
I have etched its letters with tears and blood.
A monument of grief shines with its bright light,
Fathers to children will inherit it as an eternal memory

Mordechai Feder of blessed memory

The memorial tablet in the Holocaust Cellar, Mount Zion, Jerusalem

The Memorial tablet states:

In Eternal Memory
To the martyrs of our city, the community of
Podhajce
And its environs, may G-d avenge their deaths (Galicia)
Who perished during the years of the Holocaust
Memorial day is 3rd of Sivan, 5703
May their souls be bound in the bonds of eternal life
Perpetuated by the survivors of Podhajce
In Israel and America

[Page 177]

Lament, lament, my Soul Weeps

A dirge in the form of Eli Tzion[1]
My G-d, my G-d, my soul weeps
And cry out, daughter of Israel,
Raise a cry and a lament
For a fire has consumed in Israel.
On the slaughter of the nation, which was prepared,
Tribulations of bereavement, a flood of blood,
Elderly and children without mercy,
A pure sacrifice upon the altar.
For the babes, weaned from breast,
Split upon the rocks
And for their blood that flowed
In public, before the eyes of their parents.
For the destroyed communities,
And for the destruction of the sanctuaries of G-d
Gone up in fiery flames
The cities of the glory of Israel.
Woe about the generations that were cut off,
The blood of fathers with the blood of children,
In the vale of Auschwitz they were cut off and perished
In the smoke of the chimneys.
Woe about the prisoners, dressed in sackcloth
Wasting away in their myriads,
In Treblinka and Majdanek
With no refuge for their bones.
Woe about the train cars, cramped with people,
Spread with sulfur and pitch,
Those parched with thirst, as their souls departed,
Shouted for water, but nobody gave.
Woe about the daughters who swooned
Women to whose souls the hand struck out
In their cotton robes they perished together
Without any concern for the desecration of their honor.
Woe about those frozen on the snowy fields,
Young children in the bosom of their mothers
And on the martyrs who shout out
Buried alive in pits.
Woe about the scrolls that were desecrated
By the Nazis who blasphemed G-d,
Shredded, torn and sullied
In the dung heaps, with nobody to rescue them.
Woe about the youth, the flower of the nation
Girded for battle, ready to rise up,
Against the murderous evildoers,
They shot at them with flashes of anger.

Woe about the martyrdom to G-d and the nation
And the revenge of the blood of the martyrs
With strength they gave up their souls
The fought and fell the deaths of the brave.
See, oh G-d, arise oh shriveled one,
My heart falls, my enemies rise.
Hear my prayer, hasten with a refuge
Save my soul from the men of blood.

A dirge by Y. L. Bialer, a Holocaust survivor

First published by the chief rabbinate and the committee of Polish communities in the year 5608 (1948)

Translator's Footnote

1. Eli Tzion is one of the primary dirges of Tisha BeAv.

[Page 178]

A Path Full of Obstacles and Suffering

by Henia Shourz

Translated by Jerrold Landau

At the Outbreak of the First World War

My father Aharon Fuchs and my mother Tzipi were considered to be a well-to-do couple in Podhajce. They had a meat and sausage business, and money in the bank for distribution of loans. Aside from this, my father fulfilled the role of meat provider for the Austrian army. When the Russian army entered our city in 1914, we were forced to leave our city and wander westward. We reached the city of Stryj and could not continue further, for the Russian army had filled all the connection routes. We remained in Stryj with our workers, three gentile males and three females. Our family consisted of ten children, five girls and five boys. My parents were forced to remain in their place of residence, for my father had to fulfill his role as an army provider until the last minute. Even Dr. Charupsky had to remain with the gendarmes in the place until the last moment. Finally the gendarmes fled from the city. My parents should have gone with them, but they were not informed about this, and they remained in their place along with Dr. Charupsky and the communal supervisor. A Russian guard entered the city in the morning. They went through the roads of the city, and our Ukrainian neighbors served as their guides. The first question that the members of the guard asked was: "Where do the wealthy Jews and the bourgeois live?" They showed them us, Binyamin Kitner and Yoel Rotenberg. At first they entered my parents' home. When my father answered the door, they stated their demand, "Yevrei Dovai Dyengi" ("Jew, give money"). Mother was in the back room, and she had the keys. My father's response was that he was going to get the keys. The soldiers thought that he was trying to flee, and one of them beat my father strongly over the heart with his rifle butt. He cried out in pain, stumbled, and slunk to the ground. My mother heard the shouts and brought the keys. The soldiers shot the lock of the safe a few times and wanted to open it themselves. However, the safe was too strong, and it was impossible to open it without the keys. They were only able to open the safe after my mother gave them the keys. They took all that was inside and demanded more. In the meantime my mother summoned the neighbors and Dr. Charupsky, but it was not possible to save my father. He asked that the family members gather so that he could take leave of them. My mother sent a wagon to fetch us, and we home. Father was wrapped in his tallis and wept profusely. We also wailed with the bitterness of our souls. He blessed us, passed away, and left us in grief. This was the first day of the Festival of Sukkot. My father was 42 when he died. My 36 year old mother remained a widow with 10 children.

The yoke of sustenance for the family rested on the shoulders of my mother. My sisters were Chaya, Leah, Rachel, and Libbe and Henia[1]. My brothers were Yisrael, Gedalyahu, Shraga, Leib, and Moshe Yosef. My uncle Fishi Fuchs, my father's brother, took in my two older brothers, educated them, raised them along with his children, and educated them in business. My mother continued to run the business. She fired all the workers, leaving only the lame worker whom was known throughout the city. Berel Breines also remained working with us. Since my mother was now a widow, all of the debtors who were late in their payments began to to her the loans that they had received from the bank. Thus did the business reestablish itself. Mother continued with the business and married off her children. Mother would travel each year to the Poretz (landowner) in Mozilow, who permitted no Jew to enter the threshold of his home and courtyard except for her, whom he called Mrs. "Fuchsowa". She conducted large-scale business for him. This situation continued until the Second World War.

I met my late husband in the Zionist movement. He was elected as the chairman and I was the vice-chairman. From this acquaintance, we became increasingly friendly until we got married. My husband, who was an expert in flourmills, set up a mill in the city. Thanks to this mill, we and 40 other people from Podhajce were saved from talons of death during the Holocaust.

During the Second World War

The Judenrat that was established by the German Nazis busied itself at first with the collection of small sums of money that was imposed upon it from time to time. Finally, they were no longer satisfied with money, and they demanded that my husband join the Judenrat and participate in the confiscation of furniture, silver, gold, clothes and other personal objects. My husband and his brother-in-law Leib Fink refused to participate in these odious activities, and they expressed their negative opinion and disgust with such matters. From that time, persecutions and oppression were directed against him at every footstep. Several other informers who wished to ingratiate themselves with the Gestapo joined the Judenrat. They thought that they would be able to save their skin and their family in this manner. They began to dig around our flourmill with the pretext of finding our hiding place in a bunker. However, this was to no avail. Their anger was kindled, and they demanded that my husband or my son who had not yet reached the age of 12 be sent to a death camp. However, their efforts did not succeed. Our bunker was concealed and hidden in such a way that nobody could

expose us. Two open water buckets, appropriate for my husband's profession, stood on top of the bunker. Approximately ten young girls spread out the earth that was excavated from the dig during the hours of the day in various places where nobody would pass. The excavation activity took place day and night, and lasted for 14 days. The Jewish police snatched my husband only once when he left the bunker. They immediately brought him to the basement of the Judenrat office, where a car was waiting to transport them to the camp. My husband sent a note to me, hidden in a pot of food, leaving behind a bit of the food that I had brought to him in order to hide the note. He wrote that I should flee to Blicharski, his friend from the milling profession. He was a Volksdeutsche who worked in the mill of Zahajce. He would always assist my husband when something was wrong in the mill. Now he had risen to a high level in the Gestapo, and in his time he promised my husband that he would not be among the first Jews to be sent to the camps. I jumped over the barbed wire and ran to Blicharski, as my husband instructed. Five guards ran after me with sticks in their hands and could not catch me, until I fell and broke my leg. The guards no longer saw me, and I crawled with all my energy until I reached Blicharski. He was lying sick in bed. He told me to sit down, but I lay on the floor and asked that he fulfil his promise to save my husband. At that time, a Gestapo commander sat with us, and I did not know he was. He saw how I was kissing Blicharski's feet. Blicharski immediately turned to the Gestapo commander and said that my husband had always assisted him and stood at his right hand as he saved him from uncomfortable situations, and he promised that my husband would not be among the first who would be sent to the camps. Blicharski promised the Gestapo director that he took it upon himself to send my husband in the final transport. He influenced the Gestapo commander to the extent that he hastened himself to the Judenrat to remove my husband.

[Page 179]

I should point out here that Blicharski, the Volksdeutche did a great deal for the Jews. He even sent food to the hidden rabbis. He always issued a notice about searches that were to take place. In this manner, he endangered his life and that of his family. He would also strengthen the hiding places of the bunkers. He would distribute full sacks of flour to the Jews in the ghetto. He was forced to accept the job of serving as a translator between the Polish guards and the Gestapo since he was a Volksdeutsche. Similarly, I must also point out that during the time of the third aktion that was to completely liquidate the few Jews who remained alive, Blicharski went around the street that was named after Baron Hirsch. His job was to ensure with great vigilance that our "dear" Ukrainian neighbors would not pillage the property of those who perished. The Gestapo directors related to him with complete trust, and gave him the responsibility for the Jewish property. The Gestapo forced him to accept this task. He wept and pleaded to be freed from this task, but without success. At that time, there were still a few Jews remaining who were hidden in bunkers, and the Gestapo conducted an aktion to expose the bunkers. They were accompanied by Ukrainians and perhaps also by Jewish slanderers. The Ukrainians excelled in this lowly work. They also reached our bunker, knocked and searched. From inside the bunker, we heard the voices of one of our Israelite brethren stating that there is definitely a bunker in this location, since he had heard conversation there with his own ears two days ago. The entire gang stood next to the wall, and if they had lifted it, they would have exposed all of the 40 people who had found refuge in the bunker and killed us. Once again I must mention Blicharski, who went around the streets that night and realized that they were about to expose our bunker, for they were tarrying longer than usual. He also approached our hiding place and listened to the words of the Jewish informer that a bunker should be exposed here. In response to this, Blicharski told the Gestapo men, "Don't listen to him, he himself is interested in fleeing, and he is making efforts to confuse your thoughts in order to ease his escape. I guarantee to you that here there is no bunker, and here there is no person. Thus did he save us at the last minute. We must thank him for our lives, as the adage states, "The gentile prolongs the exile..." He then went to another place which belonged to Keila Moshe and Goralnik. There as well, he answered negatively by stating that there is nobody alive there. He continued on stating that already during the second transport, he saw the local residents being transported from their homes on wagons, and it would be too bad if one wastes time on naught. There as well, he saved approximately 60 souls from destruction. Another bunker was located next to the residence of Avraham Meizes. My late mother was hidden there along with approximately 30 other souls. Blicharski expressed his opinion there as well and told the Gestapo in German, "Don't believe the word of the deceitful Ukrainians. There is nobody there, and these deceivers only want to search for places with the sole purpose of coming later to pillage the property of the Jews who perished."

I should mention here that at the beginning of the Nazi rule in our city, they had not yet come to cruelty. They satisfied themselves with forced labor, including snatching of people from the streets for labor, but without murder. They also captured me and forced me to drag heavy rocks as they stood with whips in their hand to beat anyone who was lax in their work. They immediately decided to dismantle our mill. This was a new, modern mill with the finest technological setup. Two shifts worked in the mill. At first they dismantled the most important parts and sent them to Germany. Aside from this, they confiscated all of the grits and spelt, as well as other shelled products and cereals. They loaded up everything and sent it to Germany. They gave my husband a job next to the train station. Meir Goralnik and his brother Avrahamche worked at his side. They were ordered to supervise the grain as it was being loaded upon

the transport trucks. The Ukrainians also worked there. The three Jews received transit passes that allowed them to go from the train station and back. The Ukrainians were not pleased with the fact that Jews were going around supervising the work. They turned to the Germans with the request to remove the excess Jews from there. One of the Ukrainians knew my husband. He whispered in his ear, "Don't come here tomorrow, for tomorrow they will be coming to take the Jews." My husband fled and hid in the mill, in a place where no worker knew or saw. He sent me a note from there through a Christian acquaintance, telling me to also hide with the children. Thus did we enter the bunker, and my husband joined us.

[Page 180]

When they took out the Tzadik of Berezhany with his students from the city, they brought him to Kozowa. The Rebbe sent a note to Blicharski, who made great efforts with the Gestapo to save the Rebbe. He traveled to the Gestapo in Kozowa and proclaimed to them that the Rebbe had saved his children when they were ill, and that he is a man of portents and great deeds, the greatest Rebbe in the entire country. Blicharski influenced the Gestapo to issue an edict that the Rebbe can to his home. The Rebbe came to Blicharski to thank him for his actions in saving Jews. Along with this he told the Rebbe that he would not to his home without the students, and what will happen to the students will also happen to him. Blicharski spent the entire day with the Rebbe and attempted to convince him to let him take him home, but he did not succeed in changing his decision. Blicharski alone to the city, and the Rebbe perished with his students. I should add here that Blicharski's children would bring food to the Jews in the ghetto, and did not wear crosses on their necks, as did the other Christians. Instead of crosses, they wore amulets that they had received from the Rebbe.

As I had mentioned above, my late mother Tzipi Fuchs hid in a bunker with 30 other people, including all of her daughters-in-law and grandchildren, after my brother had been transported to the death camp. My mother left the bunker and asked for advice regarding what to do now. In the interim, panic ensued in the city once again. Old men were snatched and murdered in the cemetery. My late mother came to me in my bunker. It was very difficult for an old woman such as her to crawl through the network of trenches. However, she succeeded in passing through and arriving in the bunker. She remained there for two days. The Jewish police made great efforts to capture my mother and extort money from her. Quiet after this. They succeeded in snatching old men, and again my mother to her bunker, that had been expanded and fortified further. They prepared as much food and drink as possible. After there was some calm, Mr. Buzi sent me some milk. He was one of the "important ones" in the Judenrat, and he risked his life in bringing food packages to those who had been sent to the death camps. He told my mother that he was prepared to rescue two of her children (my brothers) from the camps, and my mother paid 1,500 dollars in gold for this. They took the money but did not free my brothers. My mother still remained in the bunker with her daughters-in-law and grandchildren after Podhajce had been declared Judenrein. In the interim, three of her grandchildren died before the eyes of their mother and my mother.

Three months passed from the time that we entered the bunker. The suffering and tribulation was severe. Not one man could be found, only widows with young children. My mother could not look at the pain of the children, so every night at 1:00 a.m., she went outside to fetch water. She did this at a time when no living person could be seen on the streets. This continued until the Ukrainians informed the Gestapo that some woman, apparently a Jewish woman, comes every night. The Gestapo ambushed her one night and captured her. She was tortured with great atrocities at the guard station. The human vocabulary does not contain the words to describe this in words. At first, they demanded that she give over her gold, and then she would be allowed to live. The Gestapo men went to her home, dug in the floor, and found a suitcase with gold. They demanded more. My mother showed them two more suitcases with gold, and felt that they would all be set free on account of this. Finally, they commanded them to leave the bunker one by one, all of her daughters-in-law with their children by their side. They were all brought to the cemetery with my mother at the head. There, everyone was forced to dig a grave for themselves, and then they were all murdered. Thousands of Ukrainians stood around, enjoying themselves immensely. Paulina Dosgutch and the hunchback Pankalsi told us about this. I should point out that the Gestapo took along the bodies of the three grandchildren who had died in the bunker and were still lying there

I wish to introduce one other "personality". He is none more or no less than the Podhajce dogcatcher. He was a Volksdeutsche, and became "close to the government" when the Germans entered the city. I will relate one of the actions of this man. We had a large dog which we would hitch to a small wagon to bring water for our needs and for our animals. This dog was intelligent and faithful. Once the dog was in the yard, and the dogcatcher cast him the rope through the fence, strangled him, and dragged him over the fence. The dog's yelps reached me ears. I ran outside and saw the dog dead. I ran to him thinking that I could still save him, but it was for naught. I approached the dogcatcher and asked him why he had done this, and he laughed at my question. I approached him and slapped him over the face a few times. This took place while the Polish government was still in place. After the conquest of the city by the Germans, he came to me to kill me and to take revenge on me for the slaps that I gave him. My pleas and weeping were to no avail. By chance I was at my father-in-law's at the time, and he urged him to forgive me. He told my father-in-law that he would forgive me only because of him, for my father-in-law had loaned him several gold coins and also treated him to a glass of liquor. He was only able to forego what had happened on account of my father-in-law.

[Page 181]

Similarly, I must mention one other Ukrainian who endangered himself for my family, and on account of whom, my husband our children and I were saved from death. During the era of Polish rule, a settlement for poor Poles who received land from the government was set up in our area. They were called by the nickname "Lemks". They were brought there from the area of Krakow. Among these settlers was one Ukrainian named Dimitry Launchuk. Still during the era of the Bolsheviks, I once traveled to purchase clover and fodder around Novoselka–Pavlovo. I purchased a wagonload of these products, and this Ukrainian brought the products to our house in his wagon. He was poor, tattered, downtrodden and barefoot, in a pitiful state. My husband invited him into the house and treated him to a cup of liquor. He took down some old clothes from the attic for him and his wife. He fell at my husband's feet with feelings of thanks, and wanted to bring a present from his farm. We refused to take any, and we always gave him old clothes. We also paid very generously whenever he brought us straw. Once he came to us with weeping: "Dear sirs, news reached me that the Germans are about to come, and that they are murdering Jews. I wish to save you from their hands, for there are no people in the world as good as you." We had not yet known about the level of cruelty of the Nazis, and we thought that they would suffice themselves with taking the men to forced labor. We decided to hide my husband and son with the Ukrainian, while my daughter and I would remain at home. When the Germans entered, a ghetto was immediately established for the Jews. Freedom of movement was already difficult for the Jews. The Ukrainian came to the ghetto with a sleigh and straw for the animals, although the animals had already been taken from us, and written receipts were given to us in . The Ukrainian brought us furs to protect against the cold. My husband took with him work tools, hammers, saws, and hoes for digging – items that the Ukrainian did not have. He also took various household objects for him. The Ukrainian lay my husband down in the sleigh and covered him with straw so that nobody would see him and capture him. When they arrived at the farm, they began to dig the bunker in the barn which housed the horse, cow, goat, and pig. The entrance to the bunker was constructed under the evestrough. My husband and the Ukrainian finished setting up the bunker after three days of work. It was 2 meters by 1.5 meters, for there was no more space. My husband to the ghetto, and we were somewhat calmer for a brief period.

This calm did not last long. Every day, they would snatch people for work and send some to camps. Then the difficult days began. On account of the great hunger, we were permitted to leave the ghetto for one hour each day (12:00 – 1:00) to purchase food or barter objects for food. Woe unto the person who would be late in coming and going, for they would beat him with murderous blows. The market was next to the Great Synagogue, and the farmers of Verbova would sell a bit of food. Most of them did not want payment in money, but rather in objects. I had to give a few pillowcases for ten eggs, or give a cloak for a glass of milk, and a cloth for some potatoes. The person who succeeded in bartering his property for a bit of food was fortunate. There was a shortage of wood for fuel and straw, and the cold was fierce. The hunger also increased. The situation worsened each day. Objects for barter ran out, and we began to dream about a morsel of bread. People began to beg the farmers to bring the potato peels. We washed them with water and grated them with meat grinders. On account of this situation people became bloated with hunger. A typhus epidemic broke out in full force because of the hunger, and it was impossible to get medicine and medical equipment. Dr. Torten excelled in administering aid to the sick, and Dr. Dik was also very dedicated to this task. However, their possibilities were limited. I became ill with abdominal typhus and had a fever of 42 degrees. They took me down to the bunker, because the Gestapo chief Herman Mueller was commanded to kill those who were seriously ill. We did not even have a bit of food to keep us alive. My daughter Genia jumped over the ghetto fence to search for a bit of food to save me from death. She was caught a few times, and the "shkotzim" threw stones at her. She remained lying in the snow and almost froze from the cold. She would beg the Christian woman to have mercy on her mother who was lying gravely ill, and give her a bit of food. Thus did she save me. She was then 8 years old. Our son Aharon ran to the depot and always brought a board or twigs to be able to cook something. Once a miracle took place: he took down a board from an inner wall of one of the buildings. It began to fall, and a full bag of grits rolled down from it. It became clear that rats had prepared full meals for themselves there. The grits fell upon Aharon and almost covered him. He dug himself out of there with difficulty, and to us with a happy face. These grits sustained us in the time of difficulty and want, and saved us from dying of hunger.

It is worthwhile to note here that the porters who used to work for us liked my late husband very much. When they were bloated with hunger, they would turn to us and ask us to save them from dying of starvation. In my attic I had a sack of spices that was called "Lipowi Czweit". I would boil an urn of tea and treat them, and they were saved with this tea. Among them were Shmerel the porter, his brother Shmuel the porter, and other porters whose names I no longer remember. When my son found the grits that were hidden by the rats, we saw this as a miracle from Heaven. I cooked the grits in clean water, and everyone came to us to take a bit of grit water, with wishes for eternal life for the kindness that we did to them.

In the meantime, the state of my health improved somewhat. After my bout of typhus, I received a seamstress certificate after paying the sum of 50 dollars,

and I was permitted to be outside the ghetto for the entire day, without limited hours. The Gestapo chief signed the certificate and gave it to me, putting the fee in his pocket. Despite this, I had to be careful, and wear the Star of David mark on my sleeve. I wore a large shawl like a Christian woman, with a black kerchief on my head. I looked like a gentile villager. Thus did I obtain a bit of food every day. I would openly carry a measuring ruler and scissors, so that everyone passing by could see them. Every time I left the ghetto, I would take with me a pair of socks and some other household object to exchange for a bit of food. I must point out that most of my wanderings were in villages far from Podhajce. My father-in-law, husband and the children waited for me at home impatiently and with pained hearts. I home as if I had come from "the other world". Once I came from my way during the day, laden with food provisions. The Gestapo chief came to meet me as he was riding on his bicycle, and ordered me to halt. I did not lose my composure, and I did not enter the ghetto for I would not have anywhere to escape there. Rather, I mixed myself among the gentiles, ran in a zigzag manner and entered a burnt house, for it was impossible for him to go through the narrow alleyways on his bicycles. I stood in the ruins of the house until late at night, as the Gestapo chief was searching for me through all the streets and alleyways. I looked through the holes until he disappeared, and I entered the ghetto late at night. When I entered my house, the entire family broke into hysterical weeping. Nobody believed that they would still see me healthy and whole. It was not long before I went out of the ghetto again in the same disguise that I mentioned, for the hunger afflicted us and the desire for life urged me on. Despite the danger, I went out once again to bring food for my family in exchange for various objects that I gave to the Christians. However what type of exchange could be given for our finest and best possessions that we had, when in their eyes it was seen as a great mercy that I remained alive since they could take all that I had brought and turn me over to theGestapo.

[Page 182]

As mentioned, I had to also look after my elderly father-in-law, who was a rare type of Jew who was a scholar, a maskil, and a great fearer of Heaven. I also had to concern myself with Sani Shechter and his wife Rivka who were with us in our house. I was considered as a daughter to them, and my husband and children also held them in esteem.

I was blessed with exceptional strength of heart and fearless brazenness. On more than one occasion I looked death in the face and nevertheless I was not moved and I continued with the struggle for life and existence. The desire for life waxed greater and gave me no rest.

Another wondrous miraculous event took place with us. One day, my husband stood at the gates of the ghetto. A Ukrainian named Potra who worked in the mill with my husband during the communist rule of the city as a supplier for the "Cooperative Soyuz" passed by. When the Germans entered, he continued working there for the Germans. He had the keys to the food storehouses, and he had been promoted to the rank of chief bookkeeper. He passed by the ghetto and saw my husband standing in front of the gate. He approached my husband and said: "My dear friend, what is happening with you? I hope that good days will again come when we will both work together, and an end will come to the great tragedy." As he was talking, he placed a few boxes of cigarettes into my husband's hand. These cigarettes fell into my husband's hand life a gift from heaven. My husband asked him to provide a bit of food for us. He answered my husband: "I have great trust in you and believe that you will not betray me. I am giving you the keys to one grain storehouse. Various grain storehouses were set up by the courts, and each storehouse has a different kind of grain. The key that I gave you is for the storehouse on such and such a street, and you can take as much as you want."

I took hold of the certificate that I had that enabled me to go outside of the ghetto without time restrictions and also the strength of my heart, and I ran several times a day with two coffee mugs under my shawl. Aside from this, I sewed a corset with pockets under my dress. I ran and endangered myself six times a day. One week passed by with my daily walks, and the Ukrainians saw me as I passed through the dirty alleyways. They noticed that I was passing by too often. Among them was one enthusiastic follower of the Nazis called Tomashevski. He gathered together all of the citizens and incited them to turn me over to the Gestapo. They did not want to capture me, and only agreed that the

Gestapo would capture me. Among the Ukrainians, there was a crusading woman who was very religious. She earned her livelihood by predicting the future through cards. She also went to church often. She recognized me well. Once when I passed by her house, she stood by the window and called me (after she crossed herself as a sign that she was telling me the truth and thinking of the truth). She literally cried to me that I should have mercy upon myself and not come anymore. She was not interested to know what I was doing there, and why I was passing through the side alleys several times a day. "However, I must tell you the entire truth, that all the neighbors around are murmuring about you that there is a Zhidovka (Jewess) wandering about her too often, and they decided to inform the Gestapo so that they would capture you." I to my house in the ghetto with a heavy heart, for the small light that gave hope in our hearts to stay alive was extinguished – indeed it was locked. At night during my sleep, my late father came to me in a dream and warned me: "Enough running". I arose from my sleep in great fear. The next day I did not go, and I felt myself in a very bad state. I did not tell anyone about these matters. I later found out that on that very day that I stayed home, the neighbors in the alleys informed the Gestapo, and they closed off the path in order to capture me. They did not succeed, for I did not leave home that day. Two days later, I could not overcome the "evil inclination", and I once again went as before. Next to the storehouse, one Ukrainian stood and asked me, "Why are you coming here, Zhidovka?" I pretended not to hear, entered the washroom, and stood there for about half an hour, until the Ukrainian left. I opened up the storehouse, filled my pockets, and started to leave. Then something unexpected happened. Two young skotzim aged 12-13 ran after me and called: "Here comes Zhidovka. Gang, come to us." Several other shkotzim joined them, and this entire procession ran after me calling: "Catch the Zhidovka, and we will immediately receive sugar and oil." This was the reward that the Gestapo gave for snatching a Jew and giving him over to their hands. I started to run quickly through the gardens and orchards, hiding from the shkotzim. I finally came to a Christian woman called Pankolski who knew me well. When I went to her, she understood that I had come to hide, and she hid me. The shkotzim came to her as well to search for me and get what they wanted. However the Christian woman claimed that she did not see any person. They stood their ground, for they themselves saw the Zhidovka enter her house. They searched for me and did not find me. The shkotzim left the house and the Christian woman kept me until late at night. Then she went out first to see if it was safe to go out. After she was convinced that the path was clear she told me that I could now go. Furthermore she put many plums in a bag, and she put salted fish in my shawl. She took off the Magen David sign from my sleeve and dressed me in a white kerchief. Only then did she let me go. I went out though a narrow alleyway beside which stood next to the cross, and I to the ghetto. I threw the bag with food into the ghetto, and then went through the gate. I told my husband what had happened to me. My husband then took the key from me and ended the entire episode of bringing food from the storehouse. A few days later I went to Rinow Jablonowka, where a trustworthy Polish man lived. He lived in a nice villa which we rented every year, and spent a few weeks there with the children. My husband would visit us each week. I went through the fields, and I hid every time that I heard the sound of a wagon traveling or people walking. Finally, after great toil and fear of death, I reached the Pole.

[Page 183]

The Pole was astonished to see me so pale, and he literally wept from grief. He crossed himself many times and got down on his knees: "What is happening here and what will the end be?" He swore that he had brought various food provisions several times to the Judenrat to send to me via the gate of the ghetto, and they refused to fulfil his request. His wife crossed herself, wept, and said that such a situation is impossible, and the human intellect cannot make peace with such a situation. Is it the desire of Heaven that the Jewish nation be wiped out, without any possibility of working against this? I sat there for two hours. Suddenly, powerful sounds of movement and confusion were heard, and through the confusion – Germans and Ukrainians. The Pole hastened outside to find out the cause of the uproar. It became clear that the Ukrainians had reported that there were Jews hiding in a pit in the forest. The hidden Jews heard the uproar and hid behind the leaves and branches so that they would not be noticed. Only 8 young people who were not able to escape were snatched as they were running. The murderers thought that this was all. The Gestapo tortured the captured people util death. The Pole did not allow me to leave all day, and I remained until the next day.

The next day he packed me some food, took me on a wagon, and hid me in the straw and haystacks. He took his mother and wife with him so as not to arouse suspicion – as if they were traveling to the fair. He drove his wagon until the ghetto fence not far from the gate. Then he threw the food and other provisions over the fence into the ghetto. He then set up a ladder for me made from the small ladders of the wagon. Thus was I saved once again. When I arrived home they all wept, for nobody thought that I was still alive. All of them swore that this would be the last time that they let me leave the ghetto. They decided that if we were to die, it would be best if we all died together.

I should add that the following people were also with us in the house: Mendel Abend and his daughter Rachel, Sani Shechter and his wife Rivka, my brother-in-law David Shourz and his wife Yachtzi (Janina) with their two children Sara and Shalom, my sister Liba Fink with her husband Leib and two children Yisrael and Aharon, Bergman with his wife, two sons and a daughter, the widow Milsztok with her son and daughter, my father-in-law Reb Moshe Shourz, my husband Yitzchak Shourz, I, my son Aharon and daughter Genia, Gittel Fink of Zawolow who today is my sister-in-law and lives in America, Broncha the daughter of Slova Fink, a sister of Shlomo Gluck whose name I do not remember, Pepi Altein who is the daughter of my eldest sister Chaya and her husband Hirsch, Rivka and Pepi Heller the two daughters of Leib and Roza Heller, Tovia Breines and his wife and sister, as well as his sister and sister-in-law (Kroner) whose child was strangled at our house. The boy wept for an hour when the Gestapo men were above. They searched, and someone strangled the child, without us knowing who. Also Weisman and her sister Doncha Rozman, Mrs. Margolis the wife of Peisi Margolis (the chief "trafficker"), the sister of Yisrael Silber with her two children, Abba Fish the son of Sima Fish, and her two grandchildren Aharon and Pepi the children of her eldest son Moti Fish, Mordechai Shapira and his sister, Slop and his entire family.

[Page 184]

The Nazi Murderers Perpetuate their Victims

The murderers concerned themselves with publicizing their atrocities by issuing pamphlets denying their activities of torturing the Jewish "rebels". Two of the photos speak for themselves. The German caption under the photo on the right states: "A Jewess armed as the leader of one of the gangs of murderers."

Judisches Flintenwelb als Arfuhrerin gemeiner Mordbanditen

[Page 185]

I must tell what happened to Mendel Abend and his daughter Rachele. After the Gestapo demanded the fulfillment of the quota that was set for taking out people to be killed, the Judenrat had permission to decide for itself the types of people who would be sent to be killed. First they took the handicapped, the lame and the elderly. Among the elderly was Mendel Abend, who lived with us and hid with us in the bunker so they could not find him. They searched for him for several weeks and could not find him. Finally they took his daughter Rachele as a hostage. There were other elderly people who hid with me, but they could not find hostages in their place. They demanded that the daughter of Mendel Abend reveal the hiding place of her father, or she would be liquidated in place of her father. The Judenrat issued a final warning to her next to the grave that was dug in the Podhajce cemetery. The Judenrat rounded up the people who were designated to be killed. Later the Gestapo men came, ordered them to strip and to place themselves in the graves. While this was happening, a member of the Judenrat entered our house and said that Rachele the daughter of Mendel is about to be killed if her father does not present himself. This became known to the girl's father. He wrapped himself in his tallis and tefillin, recited the confession (Vidui), and went to present himself to the Judenrein. When the girl saw her father, she started to weep bitterly, hugged him and did not let him approach the grave pit. However the Judenrat guard forcibly removed her from her father, and he was murdered before the eyes of his daughter. She requested that they also kill her, but the members of the guard took her from there to take her to her home, to the living grave.

All of the readers of this description should know that scenes such as this were our lot each day, and whoever did not see this with his eyes could live eternally. Our eyes were suffused with tears, and the source of our tears became dried out. Every one of us lived with the hope that the Dweller on High would let us die a natural death. After the event that I described, we thought that the murderers had reached their quota and that the situation would perhaps improve. However three days later we learned that the snatching of people had resumed. We quickly hid in the bunker, except for one person who remained above to close the bunker. We were all already below, except for my father-in-law and Sani Shechter who remained above. I went into a crevice filled with harichka seeds. In the meantime, the Gestapo men and the Ukrainians came to search the mill and the house. The Ukrainians suspected very strongly that there were Jews hidden there. As proof to this they found warm excrement that still exuded vapors. This was a definitive sign that Jews were hidden there a short time ago. They began to murderously torture my father-in-law and Sani Shechter so that they would reveal the hiding place. They responded that there was nobody there aside from them. They removed both of them from the house. Why did both of them remain above in the house? The reason was that Sani Shechter suffered from asthma and he coughed violently. He was afraid that they all might be exposed because of him. My father-in-law decided that he should not remain alone, so he remained as well. Both of them were loaded on a train to be taken to the crematoria of Auschwitz. The train cars were crowded as if they were transporting animals.

The train passed through Rudnik at a great speed. During this trip, Sani Shechter jumped from the train and hastened to run into the forest. My father-in-law jumped from the train a short time thereafter, and he continued on to the Rebbe of Premishlan. He remained there for one day. An aktion took place there the next day, and the Rebbe with his Hassidim, including my father-in-law, were taken out from there. We heard this news from the women Kestenblatt and Reiter who also jumped from the Premishlan train and home. Many people jumped from the trains. My father-in-law refused to jump again, or he did not want to part from the Rebbe. Sani Shechter to his home and lay in his bed very ill. He died a week later. His wife Rivka did what was possible for him, but there was no doctor in the city who could save him. Everyone was jealous that he was able to die in his bed. Before his death he said with a smile on his face, I laugh at the entire world for my children were saved." He then recited Shema and gave up his soul. We all stood beside his bed, and brought him to a Jewish grave dressed in shrouds as is the Jewish custom.

After this news spread that the city of Podhajce is about to become Judenrein shortly. That is to say, that no Jews would be allowed to be in the city. The idea of suicide began to spread. We began to think how and from where we could obtain poison. Chaim Lehrer had obtained a large quantity of poison, and whoever was able to do so paid a hundred dollars for one dose. Apparently, 40 people purchased poison, and when the Gestapo guards came to take them from their homes, they poisoned themselves. These people lost their will to live and to struggle against the bitter and terrible fate, so they ended their lives. There was another group of people who were sick of fighting the angel of death every day, and they decided to end their lives. They gathered glowing coals and put them in the furnace. The smoke went up from there and they were asphyxiated. Approximately 20 people died this "easy" death, and everyone was jealous of these dead people.

I will now write a bit about Yisrael Silber who was the living spirit behind the idea of organizing resistance activity, of preparing defense cells in the forests with food supplies and kitchens with the help of the Subnotniks (Christians who observed the Sabbath on Saturday) who were great believers. They would provide the provisions and weapons in for payment. The money would be gathered from

people who registered with Yisrael and paid their dues to him. People also gave money to purchase weapons to resist the conquerors. There were already more than 100 men and women in the forest. There were no children, for it was difficult to bring them into the forest. In the forest they were waiting for the arrival of approximately 50 more people, who were late in coming one day. Yisrael Silber trained the men how to use the various weapons. The women also learned how to shoot. I should point out that in the forests there were various bunkers of Jews from the region of Zawalow, Roznkiche and several other cities. Each group made its own arrangements, and each communal head from those cities obtained weapons and food provisions. The Subotniks were the providers.

[Page 186]

Now I will discuss the story of Yisrael Silber in the forest. The 50 latter people were late in coming by one day, and it was already impossible to go out. Various plans were hatched, but we did not succeed in taking the people out, aside from Silber's wife and children, and Leib Ritkis with his entire family, who still succeeded in getting to the forest. The rest of the people who remained with me in the bunker began to look for various ways to save themselves after the final ordinance was issued declaring the city Judenrein. A day before this, the police of the Judenrat took out men and women without children. The mothers put their children to sleep and gave them sleeping pills, as they fled dressed as men. They carried hoes and spades, saying that they were going to cover over the pits of the martyrs who were murdered. The 50 people who were supposed to go t0 Yisrael Silber in the forest tried to escape through any means, such as jumping out of the windows that faced the outside of the ghetto. However the guard surrounding the ghetto was very strong. The Nazis placed the vilest men around the ghettos, of which nobody could imagine a worse element than them. They were called by a variety of names: Kubans from Asian Russia, sadists, murderers and criminals of the worst kind. Their greatest pleasure was cutting out the tongue from a mouth and hanging it on the fence, cutting over the stomach, cutting off the male organ, and pulling out the eyes and the brains from the head. There are no words in the human language to describe their atrocities. Only a person with a heart of stone could write down the satanic descriptions of these acts. It was specifically these types of people, who rule the netherworld, who were brought to liquidate the ghetto of our city.

I myself ran to and fro all night, for we all had to present ourselves at 11:00 a.m. They attempted to mislead us by telling us that they were taking us to Tarnopol. Only about 600 Jews remained in the city. They told us that we could take with us belongings of up to five kilograms, valuables and food for four hours. However, we already knew their ruses, and nobody believed them. I ran to and fro searching for any crack or break in a window or fence through which I could flee with my family. I stood in a narrow lane in the alley where the house of Avraham Meizes was located. Zalman Katz approached and firmly pushed me from my place, shouting at me: "Are you perhaps thinking of jumping?" I answered him: "I also want to live, I am a mother of children, and I must save myself." He answered me curtly, "You will not succeed at this." I answered him, "I desire to live more than you." I uttered these words with the hope that I would remain alive. Indeed, thus it was. I always remember these fateful words. Indeed, it was impossible to jump from that place, so we searched for a breach in different places. Many people attempted to jump from the ghetto but the Kubans caught them, and it is easy to imagine what they did with them, everything that was fitting to do to poor Jews who desired life...

I made great efforts to search for an exit from the ghetto. I attempted to find the desired place in another place, near the synagogue. I entered the home of the Lamper family near the "Kreniche". He was a grain merchant. The windows of their house faced Sziroka Street. We found many desperate people there sitting on the floor as if reciting the dirges on Tisha BeAv, to the light of small candles. These were people who lost their will to leave, and bowed their heads to the bitter fate that was awaiting them. This image left a deep impression upon us. We were already considered to be brave people who continued with the struggle for life before giving up. We stood next to the windows, looking to and fro and around us. We first attempted to lower our boy Aharon through the window. My husband and I held him with out hands. Suddenly we heard a whistle from the murderers, as a sign that a victim was arriving. We quickly raised Aharon back to us and closed the window. No more than five minutes passed before they starting throwing stones at the windows. This possibility of saving ourselves was also thereby closed off, and we came to the conclusion that we might be murdered before we succeed in saving our lives. We left there and saw people running and wandering around, each one wary of the other. We saw that they were running to the Russian monastery, and we also ran in that direction. We attempted to transfer our son Aharon through the fence. We agreed among ourselves that he should search around to see if it was possible to continue on and flee in that manner. If the answer was positive, he was to knock three times with a stone, which would serve as a sign that we should also come. If the response was negative he should knock only once. After this he entered the Russian monastery. About a half an hour passed without hearing any sign from him. Only after a half an hour did he give one knock as a negative response. We suddenly heard the source of noise around the Russian monastery. Several people were snatched from there, and the Kubans all began to run in that same direction, like a cat after a mouse. In that panic, our son succeeded in stealing away and to us in the ghetto. We immediately went to Binyamin Shochet and asked him what he thinks we should do. His answer was that they too had a place but they were too late, and they were also full of despair. From there we went to Rivka Teiner, who told us that she decided not to go anywhere. She wanted to to the bunker, for she could not stand up to the hard struggle for she has lost all of her energy. From there I went to my nieces Sheva and Golda Fuchs (the children of Mordechai and Gittel Fuchs), and found them dead. They poisoned themselves with burning coals. The windows and doors were sealed with rags. From there I went to my sister Chaya Altein, and when I entered her house I saw a frightful scene. I literally wallowed through blood. The house was full of corpses. Emil Zelemeier and his wife Dvora (the daughter of Moshe and Breina Altein) lay dead in one bed. I also found my sister Chaya Altein with her daughter Salka and son Moshe. Salka Altein attempted to flee through the fence. However the murderers caught her as she was fleeing, and she remained hanging from the fence. There were approximately 30 more corpses in the yard. The entire yard looked like a slaughterhouse. From there I home with my husband, and we found people who went out to bury the dead – that is to say they were sent for that purpose by the Judenrat. We to our house in despair, despairing of any futile effort to save our lives.

[Page 187]

As I mentioned above, Tuvia Breines, his wife Anna and sister Salka, today living in Lvov, lived with us, as well as Risia and her husband. I saw that they were preparing themselves and packing their belongings. I asked them to explain the situation, and what they were intending to do. They said that they were going to attempt to go out to bury the dead with spades, and perhaps they would find in this manner the opportunity to flee to the places that they had prepared for themselves. I asked my husband to also go to the Judenrat to see if he could also save himself and our son. My daughter and I would at least remain with the hope and faith that some of us would remain alive. My husband divided the money that we still had into four portions. Each of us hung our portion around our necks, and we all agreed that any of who remain alive would go to the "Kaplicza" on the hill.

Thus did we part from each other. My husband and son took spades and hoes in their hands, and set out for the Judenrat. They were forced to pay an advance of 50 dollars each, and in for this they received passes to leave the ghetto and bury the dead in the holy cemetery. After they paid, they set out on their way, and I remained in the kitchen. Suddenly I felt myself overcome with sadness and emptiness. My innards trembled, my teeth clattered in my mouth and I began to shout, "Geniale, hurry and get your father back, for I cannot continue on." He was everything to me, and I felt like nothing without him. Everything that he said to me was holy in my eyes, and with him I had some value, more or less. I began to scream to myself, "What did I do, why did I send him, what am I without him?" My daughter Genia was perplexed from my state. She hastened to the gate of the ghetto and began to shout "Father". My husband, who was holding the spade over his shoulder, and Aharon heard Genia's screaming. My husband ran back to the gate of the Ghetto along with Aharon, and Genia shouted to them, "Father, home, mother is screaming bitterly. Something happened to her." My father and son , opened the gate of the ghetto, and to their home. As soon as I saw them I was again overcome by an attack of sadness. I hurried to him, hugged and kissed him, and did not let him go. Later, when my state improved somewhat, I asked him to forgive me for calling him back with our son. He answered that he never thought that he would save himself without me. It was I who forced him to do this, and his sole desire was to save the boy alone, without paying attention to us adults. We sat together and could not look at each other. Our eyes were lowered to the ground. I asked my husband to listen to me this time, just as he listened to me throughout all the years. He extended his hand and said that he would do whatever I asked of him. My husband and I, our son and daughter hugged each other with great love, so that the four of us were one unit. I told my husband that when I was a young girl, I was once in the Christian cemetery and saw a family grave in which the grandfather and grandmother were resting, with room for the rest of the family. I liked this idea, and I said that whatever should happen to us should be together. It is best that we enter the bunker, where we would either remain alive together or die together. If we were to die, we would leave a note on the wall: "Here lies the Shourz family", and we would write our names.

As we were hugging each other and attached to each other, my mother of blessed memory arrived and found us in this state. She asked us what we had decided to do. I answered that we had decided that we would stay in our bunker, and what would be would be, whether for life or for death. I told my mother that after we had decided that my husband an our son would go to bury the dead in the cemetery, and they paid the required sum and went with their spades to the place, I changed my mind and asked them to at the last minute, and here they are before you. My mother said that I had done well, and she parted from us as we all wept bitterly.

In the meantime, the possibilities for salvation increased somewhat. My sister Liba and brother-in-law Leib Fink came to me, as well as my husband's brother David Shourz and sister-in-law Wonka with her children, and asked us what we intended to do. My husband answered that he decided to do anything that his wife said, and told them what we intended to do. I must inform you here that there was practically no hope or chance of the situation improving, but it seemed to me as if someone was whispering in my ear what to do and how to do it. This was a kind of push from my soul and a command of the hour to act in accordance with hidden forces. My husband explained to everyone present that Henia said that the claim that we were to be transferred to the Jewish ghetto in Tarnopol was nothing but a Nazi lie and ploy. My husband asked his brother and all present to prepare for themselves provisions for food and smoking. He did not suffice himself with those who were with him, but he ran to two of his closest friends in order to bring them to us. These were Ala and Anchia Weisman, and Rivla and Wilosh Lerer. However he was too late. It became clear that just as we had desired the previous night to escape by jumping outside through the windows or the fence, approximately 200 other men and women did so, and the Kubans murdered them all through all sorts of terrible tortures, and many of them committed suicide with their families. Those who told us in the ghetto what had transpired. They noted publicly that I, the wise Henia was the most intelligent, and my advice was the most correct. However, none of those present were initiators of any actions of salvation. I was an initiator, and I started taking anything that was possible into the bunker. The neighbors closest to us who remained alive asked me what we intend to do, and I told them that we are not going anywhere, but rather remaining in our place. They all went down with us to the cellar until it was full. We only had to beware of the Judenrat and its assistants.

[Page 188]

In the meantime, an unexpected event happened. The adage states, "The walls have ears" and thanks to this the following people came to us: Sima Weisman and her sister Danchia; Aba, Fishel Aharon my neighbors; the Margoles family with their children who were the owners of the first tobacco store in Podhajce, she was also the sister of Yisrael Silber and she also had a place prepared in the forest with her brother; Izak Fink; Gittel and Breincha Fink; and Rivka and Pepi Heller. I myself did not know how word spread to these people that we had decided to remain, aside from those who lived with us whom we told. We brought in all those who turned to us, on the condition that there would be no more chance of "", for anyone who would want to leave later would be liable to bring a disaster upon all of us. All of us who entered the bunker decided to die in the bunker and not to submit under any circumstances to the cruel murderers. All were forced to sign and to obligate themselves not to leave, even if someone would die with us or would be dying. I already mentioned the names of those who were with us in the bunker, aside from the names that I have just mentioned. There were a total of more than 50 men and women.

Translator's Footnote

1. Henia is the author herself.

A Path Full of Obstacles and Suffering (cont.)

The Situation in the Bunker

All of those present brought in what they had. Since this was unexpected, we were forced to enter through a sewage pipe. Each one entering had to crawl on his back a distance of about ten meters through the yard, until they dropped down into the place under my house. After all of them went down, my husband and son remained outside in order to hermetically seal the bunker. They sealed it with a stone set aside for this, which looked like a monument covered with a structure of tin and wood, sealed from the bottom with screws with button-like notches. Later, all of this was covered with water to a height of 4.5 meters. Thus was the bunker large and unique, and no person would be able to find it. At first, this was made for the needs of our flourmill, and the water was used for the production of grits called "harichka". First, the harichka would be boiled in a vat whose height and width was five meters, and when the vat was active, one had to bring in water in an automatic fashion from the pool of water. There were two such pools in the mill. The entrance to our bunker was under one of those pools. After all the aforementioned people entered the bunker, the bottom entrance was sealed and the pool filled with water after being sealed hermetically with a stone that prevented the water from entering the bunker. At first, the cellar was under my house. However, during the era of the Germans, when we saw that this was no laughing matter, my husband, some other residents of our house and the children enlarged the bunker. They brought out the clods of earth in baskets and scattered them in a way that this would not be noticed.

The Judenrat offered a prize of 500 dollars to any guard who would expose the bunker of Yitzchak Shourz, and the members of the guard dug around for 14 days to no avail. They followed after the children, but the children were very careful and did not fall into the trap.

What took place in the bunker? It is obvious that it was extremely uncomfortable for the group of 50-60 people who were in the cellar, in the dark without air. Everything had to be done in the cellar, including attending to one's needs. Among them there were boys and girls, old people, and religious people. A barrel that was sunken into the ground was used for a toilet. At first people were embarrassed and attended to their needs in privately. However after 14 days of sitting there without washing the face and hands, each of us felt ourselves to be a solid chunk of rotting flesh. The stench from the barrel was horrific, and the feelings of shame ceased from us. We all waited for some sort of miracle to come. There was no other hope for us.

Indeed on the designated day, at 7:00 a.m., we were already all underground in the bunker. At 11:00 we heard the terrible shouting from above. According to the order of the Gestapo, each of us was to bring a sack of 5 kilos that consisted of our most valuable and necessary items. The Gestapo set up loudspeakers and issued a command to the monasteries and churches to ring their bells at full force, so as to make a great noise that would drown out the weeping and screaming of those who were sentenced to death. The Gestapo men snatched the sacks from the Jews and threw them onto a transport truck. The people were forcibly loaded onto a second vehicle. Later, we heard the sound of the shooting of thousands of bullets in Zahajce. All of those in the bunker said that I, Henia, had foreseen this from the outset, and my words were justified by this most tragic event...

Then came the hour of the Judenrat guard. After the members of the Gestapo murdered all of the Jews of the ghetto in Zahajce, they order all of the guards to line up in the ghetto. There were approximately 30 people. The head of the Gestapo delivered a brief speech to them: "I thank you, honorable sirs, for your faithful service and assistance." He removed his revolver from its case and shot every second person in the row. He commanded the rest, who were still alive, to ascend the vehicle. An order was given to the members of the Judenrat, Leib Shapiro, Muni Fink, Dover, Trauner with their families and relatives (I have forgotten the names of the rest of the people), as well as the rest of the guards and members of the Judenrat to transfer them to Tarnopol. The head of the Gestapo promised them that he would not shoot them. Here, he showed himself as a "refined" man with polite manners. He kept his promise, and sent them to Tarnopol, to the jurisdiction of the Gestapo of that city. The Gestapo of Tarnopol brought in the heads of the Judenrat and the Jewish guards to a room. He locked them in and sealed it well, and then set the house on fire with all those who were inside. This was the payment for their faithful service of providing silver, gold, money, precious stones, and anything that the murderous Nazis desired – packages filled with all good things that were sent to their families in Germany. This was their payment as well for providing people for the aktions against the Jews in Podhajce and in other places...

[Page 189]

We, those imprisoned in the bunker, had enough food for only three days. We began to suffer from hunger on the fourth day, and people began to lose their tempers. We began to divide up the available food by weight and measure. A piece of sugar was considered as medicine for the sick. Finally, we were left without anything. Among us was an elder youth from a very important family, whose name I do not wish to mention. He had prepared for himself several loaves of bread that he held between his legs, or he might have been sitting on his sack. He sat with his head lowered and his hands over his head. Since it was dark, he would sit and eat without anyone seeing him in his disgrace. The children would search the floor to see if perhaps a tiny morsel or crumb of bread could be found. In so doing, they ran into the sack of this youth. Then, they began to watch him vigilantly, and when he went to attend to his needs, the children took out the bread from the sack and distributed a piece to everyone. They filled the sack with stones and earth. The youth took his time in attending to his needs, and in the meantime, we ate up all the bread. When he finished his "job" he to sit in his place and began to scratch through his sack in order take out some bread. His disappointment was great when he found stones in the sack. He began to shout out loud about what had occurred. However we quieted him with the threat that if he would not stop his shouting we would strangle him, and he ought to be ashamed of his narcissism, thinking only about himself at a time when all those gathered divided up their last morsel of bread, and the young children are sitting overcome with hunger and famine.

This was only the fourth day in the bunker, and the hunger and tragic suffering had only began. People turned into wild animals. Disputes and arguments broke out, and everyone began to complain about each other. For example, you are speaking too much, you cough too much, a bad odor is coming from you, you took the best spot, you should switch with me. Sima Weisman and her sister Danchia Rozman sat quietly on the ground bound to one another, as if they were stuck together. From time to time we approached them to see if they were still alive, for they were the quietest of all. I cannot mention the names of several men, women and children who went crazy. We especially suffered from the tragic women who turned the bunker into a literal hell. We had not imagined all this. Only now did we find out that it is worse to die from hunger than to die by sword.

Then a new will to live was rekindled among us. I already mentioned above that all of those who went down with us to the bunker were prepared to die there – that is, they descended into a communal grave. However, it was very difficult to live together with people who had lost their self-control, including those who had the patience of steel. The hunger gave them the urge to desire both food and life.

On the evening of the fifth day in the bunker, my late husband wanted to see what the situation as outside, since a deathly silence pervaded above. Even before this we had heard knocking, the movement of furniture and the noise of cars, upon which people were loading the booty that they had pillaged from the Jewish homes. After this silence pervaded, similar to the silence of the cemetery. My husband opened the bunker and we chose several astute youths, including our son Aharon, to go out and see what the situation was. The first task of these youths was to see if there was any guard in the ghetto, and if the Kubans are still in the city. The youths crept into the gardens of the houses, moved from one roof to the other. They and said that the ghetto is still closed, and the gate is hermetically locked. The ghetto is still as it was before, and they heard people chatting in the alleys. This was at 2:00 a.m. The youths were withered from hunger, and they decided to search for something to eat to sustain their souls. They divided the houses among themselves, and everyone went to search in a different home. They searched and found dry morsels of bread, and in one house my son found some ingredients for the making of ice cream. They also found some corn meal, chicken feed, several bags of sugar, and a number of moldy biscuits. When the murderers and pillagers removed the furniture from the homes, they left behind several morsels of rotting bread under the closets. The youths also said that the ghetto guards are still stationed around it, that the entire guard is still intact, and that there is no possibility of leaving there. The youths began to distribute the ice cream ingredients among those in the bunker. Everyone received only a small portion. They also distributed the biscuits that they had collected. We sat in the bunker in this manner for about two days. The famine did not cease. However, there remained a bit to eat – a bit of cornmeal and potato peels that the youths had gathered from here and there. We then opened the bunker, and two women took out a vat for laundry. We brought in food and lit the oven. This was at 2:00 a.m. and the youths guarded the gardens to ensure that nobody would come. However, at night it was more difficult than during the day, for at night it was possible to see embers coming from the chimney, and when the washers saw the smoke from afar they thought that a fire had broken out and they began to run in the direction of the chimney. The youths gave a sign to put out the fire. Indeed, they immediately took a bucket of water and poured it into the vat. They removed the boiling vat from its place and again sealed the bunker hermetically. The murderers reached the place, wandered around, searched and smelled, and left empty handed. Below in the bunker the residents fell on the vat. Everyone wanted to get a bit of food to sustain himself. After this we swore not to conduct this activity again, for it would be better for us to die of hunger. My sister Liba could no longer look upon the agony of her two children and the look on their faces. Here husband was also in a state of despair and oppression after seeing the terrible situation of his children, and he wished to commit suicide. However, they guarded him at all times. My husband also wished to commit suicide, for he had no more energy to continue in our dire state. Rivka Heller, her sister and others whose name I no longer remember also rose up. They demanded that we let them leave the bunker, for they can no longer tolerate the hunger. They raised a tumult and began to shout: Let's leave here. However we knew well that if we allow anyone of us to leave, we would all pay with our lives, for they would capture them, torture them severely until they could no longer withstand the trial from the beatings and sufferings, and they would reveal the hiding place. Our aim was to die in the bunker and not to fall in the hands of the murderers of Hitler, may his name be blotted out. This was the request of each of us. Now, with the shouting of those who were rising up, there was danger that the cries would be heard outside. As a result we informed the screamers that we would gag their mouths if they do not stop and become quiet. The situation reached a point of severe danger and panic. Those present tore off their clothes, tore out the hair from their heads, and bit each other's flesh. Finally my sister Liba turned to my husband with the request: My dear brother-in-law, have mercy upon me. You relate to me with complete trust. I swear to you by the life of my children that you can let me go out, and I promise you with a full heart that even if they cut my body into pieces, I will not reveal your secret. Your heart can be calm and trusting with my oath. And if you do not let me go, I will have no choice other than to commit suicide with the poison that I preserved for myself. My husband decided to let her go. However, her husband and children remained in the bunker. We all bid her farewell, for we were certain that we would not see her again. She left, and the bunker was again sealed. Those who remained in the bunker complained: why do you let her leave and prevent the rest of us from doing so? My husband retorted that he had complete trust in my sister, and he does not have similar trust in the others that wish to leave. Even before she left, my sister told us that we do not have to be afraid at all, for nothing will come from her mouth that will reveal our hiding place. On the other hand, she promised to do whatever she could to hasten aid to us, and if she could not do anything to our benefit, she would not to us. My sister left and went to the attic of the house, and from there, she looked through the cracks and saw a man armed with weapons, wandering about below whistling merrily. My sister also whistled. The gentile began to cross himself, thinking that the dead are whistling at him. My sister recognized him. This was a Volksdeutsche named Barshtash, who would purchase from us the leftovers of the mill for the pigs and fowl. My sister shouted to him: "Don't be afraid. I am still alive. I am Mrs. Finkova, the sister of Mrs. Shourz. Come to me." He held up his weapon ready to shoot, and my sister left the attic and entered the house. Barshtash entered the house and said, "I also recognize you." She told him that aside from here, there are about 50 men and women hidden in a bunker. "However I cannot tell reveal the location to you, even if you will cut my body into pieces. Even if you decide to turn me in, you will only be able to turn me in, for I do not care what happens to me." Tears streamed from the eyes of the gentile, and he said after a brief pause: "So what do you want me to do for you?" "First of all", said my sister, "Please bring me two loaves of bread with some sugar and water, with several candles and matches. Leave them all in one corner at 1:00 a.m. and whistle. After that, I want you to take us all out of here and transport us to the other bank of the river, and in for this, you will receive a bag filled with gold, watches, dollars, and diamond rings. After we are on the other side of the river, we will show you the location of the bunker, and you will find there textiles and other objects, and everything that you find there will belong to you." The gentile thought for a moment and said: "I want that you will swear to me that if they capture you, you will not reveal my name, for I am the father of six young children, and I must sustain them." He again stopped and added: "To you it won't matter any more, for you would be finished. However I stand by my demand not to mention my name in the event that they capture you." My sister promised her that she would keep her oath.

The gentile informed her that at 2:00 a.m. he would come to take us, and that we should be ready for this. With great effort and hard work, we crowded through and ascended. Everyone in the bunker was stuck together like one unit. When we sensed the air above, some began to lose consciousness and faint. A foul odor emanated from the people who sat together in the bunker and attended to their needs in their clothes. We had a difficult task in raising up two people, a man and a woman, who had gone crazy. We had to drag them up and hold their mouths closed at moments when fate was likely to be decisive between life and death, so that they would not shout or weep. Barshtash advised us to divide into two groups, for it would be difficult to transport such a large group at once. He had to do the job twice. One group organized themselves in a line with me in the yard. We then heard questions from members of the second group as to what would they do without money if the first group would cross over, and they would be left alone without means. My husband promised them that he would go with the first group, and my son and I would go with the second group. After the plan succeeded and the first group crossed over in peace, he would give a sign that all was okay.

[Page 191]

After the first group crossed over, Barshtash transported the second group. He marched in front, and we followed behind him at a distance of 30 meters. Suddenly we saw a group of drunken gentiles running and shouting at us. We began to run back. We to our yard and began to to the bunker. After that Barshtash came to us and explained to us who these gentiles were that we had met. They were Ukrainian murderers who were appointed as ghetto guards. He purchased about 20 liters of liquor, gathered them all at one end of the city, and told them to remain there and not to leave their place until he to them, for he must arrange an urgent matter. He then busied himself with transporting the people from the bunker. However, the drunks did not have the patience to wait until he , and they went out with sticks in their hands, acting wild as was their manner. Barshtash ran to them and chased them back to their place. He then to us to transport us. I chastised him, for I thought that he incited the Ukrainians. Finally I gave him the sack full of gold, silver and watches, and he repeated his urging not to expose his name in the event that one of us would be captured. I found my husband and my daughter, who was severely injured as she crossed the river. Her foot stumbled and she fell, and my husband wanted to lift her up. The Gestapo men far off saw something black move, and thought that it was a dog. They shot the girl and injured her leg. The girl remained lying down motionless. Another Gestapo man wanted to shoot her a second time. However the other said to him: "Lay off. She already has died." After they left, my husband left one of the ruins in which he had found refuge and lifted up the girl in her hands. Blood was flowing from her, and he tore off a piece of cloth from his coat to make her a bandage. The rest of the people made haste to flee into the forests, each to a different direction, and not one was caught. The entire thing was completed in peacefully.

My husband had told those who left the bunker that if circumstances cause everyone to run alone in a different direction, everyone should know and recall that they meeting point will be at the "Kaplicza" behind the bridge. This was it. I did not find my husband, for Barshtash transported us over the river in an area behind the ghetto. I began to search for him and forgot the words of my husband that in an event such as this, we should meet in the aforementioned place. With despair, I thought to run into the forest in the direction that my sister and brother-in-law had mentioned. Suddenly, my son remembered the words of his father, who told us what to do if we all lose track of each other. My son called to me: "Come and let us go over the bridge to the Kaplicza, where there is no doubt that Father will be waiting for us." I listened to my son, and remembered the words of my father-in-law who said that sometimes one must listen as well to a child, for prophecy is found in the mouths of children. I went with my son, with words of reproof prepared in my heart. We reached the area behind the Szachtowka, which was a stream of water that was deeper than a person's head, which was difficult to cross. Out of great confusion and fear, I uttered sharp words to my son: "Look where you led me, now we must throw ourselves in the water for there is no other way". As we lay on the ground we saw a German guard pacing back and forth over the bridge, and we were concerned lest they might see us, for the night was clear. It was already 3:00 a.m. As we lay on the ground in this manner, an idea went through my mind: "Why did I not run together with them all to the forest?" Now we are lying down as in prison, without being able to move forward or backward. As we lay on the ground I said to my son: "My son, our end has come. We will cast ourselves into the river if the Germans or Ukrainians approach us." I lay down and wept with tears: "Was it for this that I struggled for two years in the closed ghetto, to come to a situation where we must drown ourselves in the river so that we will not fall into the hands of the murderers?" I approached the banks of the river, and as I lay down with my head up, a long cry of "Genia" broke out from my mouth. The echo of my voice was heard as the song of a bird. I wanted to mention the name of my daughter once before my death. At the sound of this call, my son hurried to me and began to kiss and caress me. He wept greatly and did not let me jump into the river. Suddenly I heard a lengthy call of "Mama". I recognized the voice of my Genia and within a moment, the thought of jumping into the water was abandoned. I saw that my son was correct, they were not far from us.

It is interesting to point out that my son demanded of me, "Let's go to Father". My daughter also asked of Father, "Why did you go without Mother", and she never ceased to demand that he come to Mother, and gave him no rest. When they heard the echo of my long cry of "Genia", the girl was calmed slightly. My husband asked her at all times to remain lying in her place, and he would swim across the river and attempt to find us. When she heard my voice, the girl agreed to her father's advice, to not approach us. I and my son did not know about this. We lay down and looked over the straw, and on the other side we saw something like a small boat. As we watched the boat, we saw that it was approaching us, and we were trembled in fear that the Germans heard me calling Genia, and that now they were coming to see from where the sound came. I hugged my son and we whispered Shema Yisrael. Then we saw my husband descending from the boat, jumping into the water and swimming to us. We hugged and kissed, and my husband told me to hurry up, for Genia cannot lie there alone unless he to her immediately. I had no words in my mouth. My husband was an expert swimmer. He took me on his shoulders, swam with me to the boat that was about 50 meters away, and lay me on its bottom. He then to swim with our son. The strong will and desire to live was again rekindled in us after the three of us were together in the boat. Suddenly we heard the sound of the German guard: "Halt!". Immediately we heard the sound of shots. At first we thought that the call and shots were directed to us, and that perhaps they captured our daughter. She thought that they were shooting at us, and she began to wail and weep, not wanted to remain alone, and she began to run to us. Later it became clear that the guards were not directing their attention to us. We quickly entered the boat and met up with Genia. It is difficult to describe in words the joy of our meeting, as if we from death to life. We sat together and began to think about what to do further. We were suffering from cold and dampness, and we did not think about eating or sleeping. Then my husband said, "Children, we must continue with our flight and not think about food or sleep." My husband had already been several times to the Ukrainian who had prepared the bunker for us, and he began to take us to him. However it became clear that the he had not found the correct route that we needed to go on in the direction of Poplowa. Again my husband said "Children, I cannot continue on. My strength has left." The sky became very cloudy, and this helped us. For had the sky not been covered with clouds, the gentiles would have been taking out their animals to pasture, and they would certainly have found us.

[Page 192]

A heavy rain with hail fell all morning. It covered us, and we had to lie down facing upwards. We saw that the rain was indeed a miracle from Heaven, for without it, who knows if the gentiles would not have found us, turned us over to the murderers and received several kilos of sugar and kerosene in exchange for us. The rain stopped at noon, and we continued to lie down until the evening. The sky brightened somewhat, and this had a positive influence upon my husband's spirit. His energy . He began to think again about the correct way for us to go, and we continued along the journey with our last strength. My husband and son went first, and my daughter and I followed them at a distance of some tens of meters in order not to arouse the suspicion of those who might meet us. We dragged ourselves along until we were about two kilometers from the village. My daughter and I remained for I could not continue on. I remained lying down in a small ditch. My husband and son went to the Ukrainian and asked him to go with a wagon to get my daughter and I. This is what we had agreed between us, and thus it was. My son went with the gentile in the direction that my husband had described, in order to search for me. They searched for a long time and did not find me. The Ukrainian full of anger and shouted: "Where did you send me? I could not find the place." My husband was confused, thinking that he had gone to the place without finding us.

In the interim, as we were lying in the fruit orchard, the gentile woman who owned the orchard went out of her house to the garden, and my heart was pounding with fear. The gentile woman saw us and began to cross herself. She immediately recognized that I was a Jewish woman, and asked me: "From where did you come? In the name of G-d, where do you want to go?" I answered her that we were going to Buchach. He continued asking: "Today you are going to Buchach? Don't you know that the Germans are retreating and fleeing because of the heavy bombardment? Where do you want to go now in such a situation?" I went to get something to eat. However I thought that that my husband would come in the meantime with the gentile to get me, and would not find me. She then asked us if we have something to sell, and from where we were. I told her that we have nothing to sell, and we only have a few worn out sheets to cover ourselves from the cold, and that we had come from the forests. She told us that her daughter is not far from there, and she would bring us something to eat.

She distanced herself from us, and my daughter and I began to tremble with fear. We were certain that she went to call her husband, and that he would come to kill us, since she had seen us with two sacks, and she would have wondered what were in those sacks. We thought we would flee after the gentile woman left us. However, I remember that we had agreed with my husband to wait for him in that place. In the meantime the gentile woman and brought us a small basket of food and milk. However our lips were trembling to such an extent that we could not open our mouths. The gentile woman sat next to us and told us that shortly her husband would come and show us the route to Buchach. I answered her that we were both very tired, and wished to rest a bit from the travail of traveling on the roads. My daughter was trembling greatly from fear. "Please do not tell anyone about us. Not even your husband or neighbors. You yourself told us that it is not peaceful on the roads due to the retreat of the Germans. We will rest here, and only leave at the evening." The gentile woman left us and told us that she would in the evening to show us the route.

[Page 193]

In the meantime, we tired ourselves of waiting for the arrival of my husband with the gentile. I did not know that there was a misunderstanding and they had stumbled on the way. When the gentile without us, my husband said that he would drive the wagon himself to search for us. He would sit in the wagon with the gentile and indeed found us. He told us why he had been so late in arriving. The gentile drove us on his wagon and covered us in straw. He took us thus to his house. To our ill luck, at the same time the neighbor of the gentile arrived and began to enter into a two-hour conversation with him, and he could not take us out of our hiding place.

We almost choked from lack of air and weariness, but we continued to lie under the straw without moving. This was Sunday. The wife of the neighbor was also there. She sat in the yard and chatted until they had enough of sitting and went on their way. Then the gentile came to us and took us to the barn. Later he came to us and told us to trust him, and to fulfil all of his requests. "First, you must strip of all your clothes and remain only in your undergarments. All the rest of your belongings, shoes, and even gold, you must leave above." We were forced to strip and go down half-naked to the pit. The pit had room only for one adult and one child. Even as I lay alone, I was able to touch both sides of the pit with my shoulders. The girl lay in my arms, and Aharon lay in my husband's arms. We all lay down stuck to each other, like bricks in the wall.

"Life" in the Pit

For half of the first year, the gentile related to us in a more or less humane manner, and served us sufficient food. The gentile explained to us that he had heard that many Jews were captured and murdered in the forests in which they were hiding. Even Jews who had found refuge in the bunkers were murdered by those who hid them. On account of the rumors, searches were conducted at the homes of other gentiles. However our gentile was simply "crazy". He was young and did not know very much. He ran to and fro with the bug of "what should I do" eating at his brain. There were no longer any Jews hidden with the farmers of the village, and the relations of the gentile to us worsened day by day. He wanted to kill us from hunger. He would shout to us in despair: "To me you are like Noah in the ark. Where should I hide you? There are no more Jews around." He banged his head with his hands, saying: "What do you want from my life? Why did you choose me to save you? I also have a wife and children." He stopped bringing us food, and only when he prepared food for the pigs – potatoes with their peels mixed with bran – did the farmer throw us some half cooked potatoes, without giving us water to drink. The farmer wanted us to die of hunger in the pit, and then he would cover the pit upon us as if we had never been with him. We felt that the day was nearing when he would kill us. I already pointed out that the gentile was not very intelligent. He simply had no ideas of what to do. My husband called the gentile, whose name was Dimitry, and said to him: "Don't think that we are the last Jews who remain alive. Know that there will be always Jews alive, and there are still a large number of them. You should know that all my relatives are in large partisan camps in the forests. At night they or their representatives come to me, and ask if we are missing anything. Up to this point I did not want to tell you all this, for I did not want to frighten you." However apparently my husband's words had no effect upon him, and perhaps he realized that all this was simply empty talk. After this discussion he clapped his hands together and said, "To hell. What did you want from my life? Whatever way things happened, you were among those sentenced to death. Why did you cleave specifically to me? I do not want to be killed because of you." He continued to torture us with lack of food. He did not even give us a measure of water, let alone a slice of bread. He only threw us a piece of bread during the days of Christian holidays. Apparently, he waited daily for our deaths. My husband said that as long as our breath is still within us we must save ourselves. My husband still had a few dollars sewn in his collar that the gentile did not know about, thinking that he had taken everything us when he lowered us into the pit.

My husband asked the gentile to bring us a newspaper or some sections of newspapers in order to read about what was happening outside. He also wanted to use the newspapers to calculate when Yom Kippur would be. However, the gentile refused to fill his request. My husband calculated the times in the pit and finally figured out the day that was Yom Kippur. He told the gentile: "Yom Kippur will be on such and such a day. This is our holiest day. We do not eat on this day. Therefore I ask of you, Dimitry my friend, to help us with something that will not cost you money. The food that you usually bring at noon you should bring toward the evening, and tomorrow do not give us anything to eat, for it is our fast day. Only in the evening, at the end of Yom Kippur, should you give us food. The gentile did not answer this request at all. He did not bring us the food at noon but rather toward evening, and the next day, on Yom Kippur, he did not bring us anything. We thought that after it got dark, he would bring us food to restore our souls after the fast. The girl was also waiting for food, for even she, a young girl, observed the fast. However night came and the gentile went to bed without bringing us food. My husband endangered himself, went up from the pit, entered the gentile's house, woke him up and asked him: "Why did you not bring us something to eat? We did not eat all day because of the fast." The gentile answered angrily: "You wanted to fast on your festival, you can continue to fast even all night." The gentile refused to get up and prepare food. Then my husband took a few potatoes in a metal pot and brought them to the hole. He also took straw for fuel. Dimitry pretended not to see and continued to sleep. The cooking of the potatoes took until 2:00 a.m. In the meantime, my son ascended from the pit and brought a few potatoes. We ate the raw potatoes until the rest were cooked. In the morning, Dimitry acted as if nothing had happened and brought us food as usual.

[Page 194]

The gentile employed our son Aharon for the removal of manure from the barn every week. As he worked, Aharon dug a hole in the wall of the pit. Each time he widened the hole with a knife and covered the mouth of the hole with manure. The hole grew with time to the point that a person could pass through it. One harsh, snowy winter night, my husband and son set out on their way wearing only pajamas. Each of us only had a sheet. We went barefoot, for the gentile took everything from us. Instead of shoes, they tied sheets around their feet. Each of them had a stick that they carried under their shoulder as a gun – or so it looked from afar. The snow was a meter deep. They parted from us with mutual wishes that we would see each other soon.

They went to the village of Poplowa, knowing that there were Subotniks (a Christian sect that observes the Sabbath) in that village. They approached the window when they saw the first light in one house in the village. The gentile saw them and thought that they were partisans. He hid and did not want to open up for them. They continued to go on until they came to the third house, where the door was opened for them and the gentile recognized them. This was a Subotnik who was an acquaintance of my husband. The gentile crossed himself and asked him where he was located. My husband answered him: "I cannot tell you anything right now. First give us food." The gentile brought a bucket of milk from the barn. He placed the entire bucket of milk on the table before the guests. They drank the milk as a medicine that saved the life, and also tore up a loaf of bread into pieces and swallowed it. My husband did not tell the gentile where they were located, even though he was a Subotnik. He told him that they were in a pit in the forest. The gentile asked him: "What food should I make for you?" My husband gave him five dollars and asked for bread in . The gentile did not want to take the money. After a brief thought, he got up and brought two large loaves of bread and other food for the way. My husband gave him more money to prepare loaves of bread for his next visit. However the gentile wanted to make it easier for him by not making it necessary for him to visit to take the food. They agreed upon a place where he would leave the food on a specific day, and from there he would be able to take the package. My husband asked him to prepare bread, tobacco, matches, some olive oil and some potash, for he suffered greatly from heartburn. My husband and son took the packet and prepared to to where we were.

My daughter and I lay down next to the hole and looked outside. Perhaps we would see them as they . We heard the barking of dogs, and we were sure that they were captured along the way. We could not calm ourselves, and the desire to leave the pit grew in us, so that their fate would be our fate. If they were captured, we would also be captured, for even here, our lives were hanging from afar. These hesitations lasted for about two hours. Finally my husband and son in peace, and entered the pit through the hole. My son resealed the hole so that it would not be recognizable, and brought us the precious food. We divided up the bread, which was literally consumed as it was still in our palms. I secretly hid a morsel of bread under my back, and my daughter did so as well. In the corner of the pit there was a pot into which the gentile sometimes tossed in some food from what he was feeding the pigs. My daughter hid her portion in this pot. We then went to sleep. Early in the morning, at dawn, the gentile came to take the pot, for he would cook the pig food in it. This was a narrow iron pot into which he would place 18 small potatoes with some bran to prepare for the pig. He would not peel them and would not clean off the clods of earth that were stuck to them. My husband did not know about the "gold treasury" that was resting in the dirty pot, hidden by our daughter, and he passed the pot out to the gentile. When we woke up, our daughter began to search for the morsel of bread that she had hidden, and then we were concerned that the gentile might find out our secret. However, my husband calmed down immediately, recalling that he had once told the gentile about the partisans that would come to visit us at night. Now there would be proof that indeed, partisans visited us that night and left us some bread...

We began to deliberate how to save ourselves from the gentile. However suddenly the gentile came with an angry face and shouted: "Shourz, come out!" My husband immediately went out, and I followed him. My husband was the first one out. As soon as I managed to get out, I heard a scream as if someone was strangling a person at his throat. My husband shouted out "Ah- ah – ah". I wanted to get out but could not, because the gentile stood with both feet over the hole. He wore spiked rubber shoes on his feet. The gentile continued to choke my husband, and I could not get out of the pit. I bit the gentile's leg very hard until it started to bleed. Out of great pain, the gentile let my husband go and kicked me strongly with his nailed boot, so that blood flowed from my face and over my whole body. Despite the pain of the kick, I ran to the gentile and shouted to him with all my strength: "Murderer, thief. You are worse than Hitler. He immediately pillages and murders his victims, but you stole everything that we have, and now you are torturing us without giving us a morsel of bread or a drop of water, and now you have come to strangle my husband. Let us go to the Germans. I have no more strength to suffer this. Look at what you have done to us." From the great anguish and anger I lost control of myself and became hysterical. The children tried to calm me down through various means, with caresses and kisses. The gentile became very afraid from the situation, fell down before our feet and pleaded with us to be quiet and not to arouse any noise (For I shouted that the partisans would come and take revenge for us). I lost four teeth from the kick of the gentile, and later I lost the rest of my teeth that were left in my mouth. It is difficult to describe the situation of losing all of one's teeth at once. I felt like a small child.

The gentile appeased me, begged me to remain quiet, and told us that everything would improve. We went to the pit. From them, the gentile improved our portions of food and drink, added potatoes with a drop of salt, and also gave cigarettes to my husband to smoke without matches. Rather he lit it from the cigarette that was in the gentile's mouth. Then my husband transferred the fire from one cigarette to another, thereby smoking the five cigarettes one after the other. The gentile stood and laughed at the site of this chain smoking. Once the gentile told me that throughout the village it is said that partisans surround the village, and the footsteps are leading to him. "But you have not been outside?" My husband answered him: "How did you suddenly get such an idea in your heart? You took away my shoes, and how can I go outside with such snow as this."

[Page 195]

Several weeks passed, and Dimitry did not give my husband cigarettes to smoke. The situation again became more difficult. The gentile continued to restrict our portions of food until we came to the situation of "not living and not dying". This desperate situation once again roused us to action.

My husband and son once again tied their bare feet with sheets and went through the hole that was always covered with dung. They went once again to the nearby village where the Subotnik who they visited a few weeks ago lived. This time it was easier for my husband to go at night, for he already knew the way. When he reached the village he knocked on the window of the acquaintance. He crossed himself and asked: "Where were you all this time, my friend?" My husband answered that he could not come because of the danger, and he left five dollars for food on his first visit. The Subotnik started to pack two packs of necessary provisions, one for my husband and one for my son. They without problem, and we were very happy. They also brought a section of a Ukrainian newspaper. We again sealed the hole with dung after we wiped over all of our steps from around the barn. From the piece of newspaper that my husband brought, it was possible to surmise that there was "happy" news from the front. The battles were taking place on the entire length of the front, and the situation of the Germans was not bright. Almost everyone had been killed in the forests, and there were still bunkers that had not been exposed. The Subotnik asked my husband to go around less outside. "If you have already maintained yourself to this point, you must be careful that they do not kill you, for this entire 'game' will end soon." "I promise you", added the Subotnik, "that you will survive, as long as you do not wander around outside." Indeed, now we were calmer. My husband again had something to smoke, and we were not lacking in food. We continued to sit in the pit in the barn in this manner for another few months, with suffering and oppression. The lice ate us, and the gentile did not allow us to wash. We also did not change our clothing, even though he had all of our clothes. He tortured us in various ways, but he was also very afraid, for he believed that we had a connection with the partisans. Dimitry even knew of all of our brothers-in-law who were in the partisan camps, and this instilled fear in him.

One day, Dimitry asked, "Please, tell me the truth. Did the partisans visit you again? For throughout the village, they are saying that the partisans are surrounding the village again. Were they not with you again?" My husband answered negatively. "They were not with us in the latter period, since we told them that your relationship to us improved, and you give us better food." Dimitry asked my husband to tell the partisans not to come again, and he promised to keep us alive. From then, Dimitry began to relate better to us, sometimes giving us bread with some spread. We saw real signs of his improved relationship to us. Once again Dimitry turned to my husband and told him that throughout the village, people are pointing to him and speaking about him, for the footsteps of the partisans lead only to him. Dimitry explained that because of this, he has decided to arrange a party for the entire village. His intention was to bring the partisans even into his barn and to show them the cow that gave birth, the pig and the horse, that is to say his entire wealth. The intentions of the gentile were otherwise, since there were suspicions that the footsteps of the partisans lead only to him (these were the footsteps of my husband and son). He wanted to prove in this manner that he was fitting and proper.

Dimitry arranged the party, and all the Banderovchik Ukrainians enjoyed themselves nicely, became tipsy, and said that the Jewish partisans killed an entire village near Buchach, telling the victims: "We are taking revenge upon you for you turned in the Jews to the Germans. Let this serve as a warning to all of you." Of course, Dimitry's sense of worth rose when he heard such stories.

The situation became more unstable. Once my husband said to Dimitry: "Tonight the partisans came. I told them that we have no need for food, for we have sufficient. You give us enough. I asked them not to wander around any more and not to investigate further, since you, Dimitry, are to us like an angel from Heaven, doing everything for us." Dimitry heard the words of my husband and became proud. However the next day, after this conversation, Dimitry suddenly issued a command for us to get out of the pit. "What happened Dimitry, what more do you want from us?" He answered: "I want to clean the pit, for there is the danger of disease. I want to change the straw in the pit, since you have slept on this old straw for ¾ of a year. He ordered us to strip, and he would give us new clothes. We should go to the attic until he cleaned the pit. He began to examine the rags that we took off. My husband, son and daughter stripped completely, but I waited to be last. I looked through the entrance at how he was searching, and became very anxious, for I had hidden a small gold watch with a few dollars in the collar. I collected all of this and hid it deep in the ground at the threshold of the barn. Marisa, Dimitry's wife, conducted a thorough search of me. Finally she brought us all a vessel full of water, told us to wash and go into the attic. We remained there for 2-3 days. The attic was very cold, and we literally froze from the cold. When we to the pit, we were happy. In the meantime, Dimitry had aired out the pit and changed the straw. His intention was to check that the partisans had not left weapons with us. He dug and searched everywhere and did not find anything. My husband showed him that he had matches and a few cigarettes, left with him by the partisans. He took the matches from us. He suspected that we might have knives or guns. He was very afraid that we might be armed. After this, Dimitry's relationship with us again improved. He added some spread to the pig food, and he salted the food. At night, Dimitry would call my son to him to prepare and cut about ten bundles of straw. He would give him a piece of bread in . The value of the bread was worth millions to us, more than fine gold.

[Page 196]

The first time that Dimitry called my son up, I went up at night, and he showed me the piece of bread that he got from Dimitry. He took one bite of it, and while he was still holding it in his hands, the cow grabbed it from his hands. The boy screamed terribly. I approached the cow and opened its closed mouth, and the boy stuck his hands into its mouth and removed the bread from its throat. He divided the bread among all of us, but sweat was dripping from his face. How did he have the energy to turn the wheel of the cutter? Nevertheless, he performed this job with joy in the merit of the piece of bread that he received.

My husband suffered from heartburn and felt bad. At night he went to the barn and nursed from the goat's udder. The boy nursed from the cow's udder. Once Dimitry came to us in anger and asked: “Why have the goat and the cow stopped giving milk. Perhaps you have started to nurse from the cow and the goat?” My husband answered: “You do not have to be suspicious of us. Certainly you have been skimping on their food. Give them better food, and they will continue to give milk.” Among other things, he told us that his sister-in-law from the area of Krakow was coming to visit him. He added, “I told wrote to her to come to visit us. I have to go to work in the field, and I do not have anywhere to leave my three-year-old daughter. I also am afraid to leave you alone, lest you desire to leave the pit.”

About a week later, Dimitry's sister-in-law arrived, a girl of about 14. Dimitry sat with her and told him about us, that he is holding 4 Zhids, and woe unto him if anyone would find out. The girl listed to everything he said. After Dimitry and his wife went to the field, the girl wanted to get to know us. She brought us the small amount of food, and when we asked her to bring us some water, she did so. She also began to turn the cutter along with my son. We told our son to become friendly with her and tell her that she was pretty. After he won her confidence, the boy asked her to bake some pita cakes for us. The girl did so, and every day after her sister and brother-in-law went out to the field, she would bake a pita and bring it to us. The girl literally saved our lives. When my husband asked her to bring him a light so he could smoke, she would bring it to him. A great deal of good came from this friendship of ours with his young sister-in-law. The girl let me sew various things for her, and later also for her sister and her young child. As I was sewing, the girl sat in the barn to ensure that nobody would come to us. Her brother-in-law did not know about this, but later he found out. The mistress of the house wanted to pay with food for this, but she was afraid of her husband. There was a rumor in the village that wherever there was Jewish women, they would sew for the women of the village. Our mistress also wanted to benefit from this merit that a Jewess would sew for her. Indeed, I was not a professional seamstress, and I never was employed in sewing, but I knew enough to satisfy these villagers. Thus we again thought that the sun would again shine, and life would become more encouraging.

Suddenly Dimitry appeared with a new statement: "They are saying in the villages that there will be an evacuation of all the villages, including our village. Therefore, what should I do with you?" He advised us to go to his field and to dig a pit for ourselves there. His field was a large distance from here. Apparently, his intention was to take us out to the field and to murder us there. Since we did not want to act on his advice, he altered his request that at least two of us go out to the field and two of us remain. We decided not to separate, whatever would be. Here Dimitry was unable to kill us, for he was afraid of the revenge of the partisans who knew of our location, whereas in the field nobody would see and nobody would know what happened. We asked Dimitry to leave us in peace. We were already coming to the end of the war. We had heard from the partisans that the war was already reaching its final stages, and we had no intention to improve our situation. Dimitry claimed that his plan was for our benefit. We declined his favor and his concern for us, and decided to remain here as before, and to satisfy ourselves with several potatoes and a bit of water – not more. When he saw that his plan did not work out, Dimitry became very angry to the point where he did not sleep.

The next morning, Dimitry came to us and called my husband to come out to him. We became very scared. Dimitry said the following to my husband: "Shourz, you know that I do not sleep at night because of you. You are a thief and murderer. Why do you not listen to me? Why did this happen to me? I wished to save you at the risk of my life, and now my family and I are in danger only because of you. What will happen if the Germans order us to leave the village, and they send me out of the village with my family, and the Germans come in our place. What will you do then?" My husband answered: "Don't worry about us Dimitry. We will remain in the pit. And if the Germans come and find us, we will not say anything bad about you. I have given you my oath about this. If you are not here, you are not responsible for us. We will say that we decided to settle in here because the placed was empty." Dimitry answered: "But I will take everything with me and will not leave you any potatoes". My husband answered him: "Dimitry, it is not your job to worry about us. There are still some people here who will bring us food. I mean the partisans." When Dimitry heard the words of my husband, he spat strongly on the ground and knocked on the door of the barn. My husband again turned to him and told him directly: "Dimitry, do not worry about helping us and do not worry about us. I have relatives among the partisans, and they will provide for our needs."

[Page 197]

Dimitry took advantage of the new situation that he created. He expressed his initiative by decreasing the already meager allotment of food and water that he served us. To our good fortune, the heart of Dimitry's niece was with us. She would bring us food discretely, and even gave her of her own food. We promised the girl to repay her and give her a plot of land that we would register in her name. The girl's origins were from a poor family, and on account of this, she denied food from her own mouth and gave it to us, along with sniffing tobacco and paper for smoking. This had a good influence on my husband's life. I had mentioned before that when my husband and son visited the house of the Subotnik in the nearby village, they also brought a section of a newspaper aside from food. Its content gave us some encouragement. The newspaper contained news about the partisans who were active in the region of Buchach. The headline of the newspaper had news about the situation of the front, where the situation of the Nazis was not good – as far as one could determine from reading between the lines. This situation strengthened our hope for the destruction of the Nazis, and the recognition that any exit from the pit would only lead to death and destruction for all of us.

We did not see Dimitry for two weeks. After two weeks, he again appeared before us with a new byline. He had to travel to a wedding with his entire family, and nobody would be left here. He warned us not to leave the pit or make a sound. He would prepare us food for one day, that is a pot with pig food that we would keep in the pit with us. He would leave a bucket of water next to the pig, and those who would come in would think it was for the pig. Aside from this – a shepherd lad would come to take out the cow and goat to pasture, and we had to be careful not to make any sound, not even a cough, which the shepherd lad might hear. For a moment we thought that this was another ruse from Dimitry, but at dawn he traveled from the house with his entire family and locked the barn. The shepherd came only after two hours and took the cow and goat with him. He walked to and fro around the barn and whistled as he walked. We remained in fear. Finally, the shepherd took the cow and goat and closed the barn. My husband could not control himself, and he went up to the barn. We felt that he was spending too much time up there, and I also went up to the barn. To my astonishment, I saw that my husband had hanged himself with the capes that he wore on his pants.

I ran to him and began to struggle with him and to remove the capes from the tree. The children heard the sound of my shouting and they also started to shout and cry. With great effort, we saved my husband from hanging. He claimed that he had already suffered more than enough, that he has no more energy to continue to suffer, and that he was angry that we disturbed his effort to commit suicide and put an end to his life.

The thing that affected his mood the most was the plague of lice. There was not even one centimeter of our flesh free of lice. This is what gave my husband the idea of suicide, even though he was apparently as strong as a lion and he used to encourage us. After all that befell us, our situation in the pit was an ideal situation. Despite this, the effort of picking out the lice day and night influenced my husband badly. My husband had a mark all the days of his life from the suicide attempt.

We were unable to withstand the test of leaving the pot of potatoes that Dimitry left us for the next day. That day, we ate the next day's portion. Dimitry told us that he is traveling for only one day. Another day passed and Dimitry had not , and in the meantime, we were suffering from pangs of hunger. My husband nursed from the goat, which relieved his heartburn a bit. We remained without food also on the second day of Dimitry's absence. We went to the barn and attempted to gather some food with bran from the pigpen. We lapped up the crumbs. My husband said that there was no other choice than to go into the house to find something to eat. We wanted to open the door of the barn, but it was impossible. We were left with only one option, to open up the hole through which my husband and son would go to search for food from the Subotniks. We had covered the opening in dung, and it remained in place. My son began to move away the dung until the hole was exposed. My son went out. My husband could not push through the hole, for his energy had left. My son went above and wandered around the yard. We told him to try to break into the house, but this was beyond his capabilities. We advised him to take out the window from its frame. The lad tried with all his energy, but could not. Finally he found a pickaxe and began to dig under the window until it came out. The boy took out the window, put it aside, and entered the inside of the house. It was dark outside, only the moon was shining. He found the supplies of milk that the shepherd had taken from the udders of the animals for the past two days. He brought in what he found through the hole, and he literally revived us with this. He entered the house once again through the open window and began to search for something to eat. He found the apron of the wife, and placed in it whatever he found: several slices of dry bread and a bit of cornmeal. He wrapped all this in the apron and dragged it into the pit through the hole. He also brought a bucket with clean water, so that we could quench our thirst. Then my son wanted to replace the window in its frame, but he was not able to. He asked his father what to do, and his father told him to place the window on its side. He also told him to remove the small window of the barn so that there would be a bit more air. My son asked why he should also take out the window of the barn. My husband answered: "We will tell Dimitry that the partisans, headed by my brother-in-law, opened the window. They called me, and I approached the window of the barn. My brother-in-law asked me if I had enough food, and we told him that you told us that you are going away for one day only, and now the second day and night have passed, we have nothing to eat, and we are literally dying of hunger. During their last visit, we told the partisans that you are giving us food, and therefore they did not bring any food with them. Now, when they heard that we were starving for bread, they took out the door of your house and the window from the barn, took everything they found in your house, and gave it to us through the window. They told us that they would a few days later to find out what had happened to us." Thanks to this situation, my husband continued to nurse from the goat, and my son also learned how to nurse form the cow. After we satiated ourselves with the milk, the cow and the goat did not give any more milk.

[Page 198]

Dimitry only after three days, and by his reckoning, we should have all been corpses. As Dimitry approached his house, the shepherd lad ran to him and informed him that there had been thieves in the house, who removed the windows of the house and the barn. Dimitry first called my husband and asked him what had happened there. My husband told him that the partisans, headed by my brother-in-law, had come. After they found out that we had not received food in two days, they searched through the house, and threw us out the food from the window. They then said that they would to see what was happening with you. They also said that they were about to go to Buchach to attack the slanderers who turned the Jews in to the Gestapo. Not one of them or their families would be left alive. Then they would come here to see what had happened to us. They issued a warning to you through us, for there are thousands of them in various groups. They told us that our salvation is closer than we think, and all those who helped us will receive their reward. Whomever does bad to us will be repaid. Dimitry paid attention closely to these words and sighed loudly: "Now my time and your time has come".

From then it was if Dimitry had been possessed by a demon. He did not sleep at night, and he would stand by the window and look outside. In addition, he began to get drunk by drinking strong liquor. This troubled us, for he was liable to tell everything to his acquaintances while he was drunk. Once, as he was bringing us a portion of food, my husband told him: "Indeed you are right that you might indeed bring a disaster upon you and us, for you are not responsible for your actions. You are always drunk." He no longer retorted. Rather on occasion, he hosted revelries, invited his friends and acquaintances, and they drank to the point of drunkenness, and danced. He did this out of fear of the partisans. He lit up the entire yard, so that he would not have to be alone, and also with the reasoning that the partisans keep away from light that would impede their actions. They would prefer to be enveloped in darkness. As he was enjoying himself with friends, they began to discuss what is going on in the world of politics. Dimitry started, stating what the partisans had done near Buchach – that they had set several villages on fire because they had turned Jews in. Dimitry improved our food portions slightly. He gave the excuse that we cannot find ourselves in a good situation – which is to our benefit. It was only because of this that he had cut down the size of our food portions and stopped giving cigarettes. However, now a new chapter of events begins.

About two weeks after this, the Subotnik who assisted us in times of trouble and tribulation and provided us our food came. The Subotnik demanded a specific type of wheat for planting, and offered Dimitry to enter into a barter arrangement for this. They sat down on the grass, as was customary among the village farmers who love to sit and discuss politics and other matters. The Subotnik told Dimitry of the great good deed that was lost to him, and on account of this he is not able to sleep at night. It always seemed to him that a Jew and his son were with him and had requested food. He continued on that he regrets that he did not advise the Jew to stay with him so that he could hide him from the Germans. Through this, he would merit the Garden of Eden, and without this he would descend to Hell (Gehenom). The words of the Subotnik served as words of reproof to Dimitry that his conduct toward us had been merciless and full of despair. On the one hand, he was afraid of the partisans, and he was constantly restless and desperate. On the other hand, he saw no way to get rid of us. The Subotnik, as he was about to leave to his village, did not hesitate to point out: "How great would my fortune be if I would hide with me such a Jew as the man who once owned the mill. What would I be lacking then? When the Russians we will be lost in any case, for we assisted the Germans knowingly and unknowingly. The Russians are liable to cut our bodies to pieces and send us to the wasteland of Siberia, for we are considered enemies by the Soviets. Whoever hides a Jew has bought his world. I myself know, Dimitry my friend, that many Jews were hidden with the farmers in the villages, and many of them are with the partisans in the forest. Do not think, Dimitry, that the Germans will not ask for an accounting from each of us. There are already those people who will tell them everything." The Subotnik ended with goodnight wishes, and left.

We were able to overhear the entire conversation. Dimitry said to his wife Marisa: "Did you hear? It is very possible that the Subotnik is correct, and that we followed the correct path. Indeed, it is difficult to correct it now. However, we must keep them until the end, and this will be to our benefit.

[Page 199]

For I have no other choice, for the partisans know that I keep them with me, and I will have to give an accounting. Even if they were to die, they would force me to show them their bodies. It is clear that it is determined from Heaven that they will remain alive. We tried all means to do bad to them and afflict them, but Heaven protected them so that they survived. See Marisa, all the things that we did not do for them, and they stood up to the test and went through everything with strength and boundless patience. God in Heaven Himself stood at their side and gave them the strength to endure everything and remain alive."

A new phase began with Dimitry. He was very afraid of the revenge that would be exacted from him when the Russians . This discussion between the Subotnik and Dimitry caused a debate between my husband and I with respect to Dimitry. My husband said that if G-d would help us and we would leave the yoke of servitude, hunger and oppression in freedom, the first thing he would do would be to take revenge on Dimitry for all of the torments that he caused us. However, my opinion was otherwise. I saw Dimitry as the rod that was chosen by Divine providence to afflict us, and to remain alive despite everything. We had seen unspeakable acts of cruelty perpetrated against Jews by other murderers. Indeed his behavior was very far from the path of righteous and upright people. Despite this, he did give us of his bread and food in a meager fashion. As I lay in the dark bunker, I vowed that if G-d helps us and the four of us remain alive, I would forgive Dimitry with complete forgiveness, since I saw eye to eye that such was decreed upon us from Heaven. This was a difficult Divine decree from all perspectives, and we were expected to stand up to the test. It was good that we knew how to withstand the test and merit salvation and liberation from the yoke of servitude, from the yoke of the Nazis who wished to rule over the entire world, and from the yoke of other tribulations which we were chosen to endure. We must only rejoice and utter a blessing that we remained alive.

Dimitry's heart changed a bit for the better, and his relations to use improved a little. He would come to us in the pit, tell us various items of news and speak to us a bit. By nature, he was not very talkative. Two months later, he came to us again with a somewhat cheerful face. He said: "I see that it is decreed from Heaven that you are to remain alive. The Russian armies are approaching us. What will it be? I don't think you will be permitted to forget about the good life that you had here with me. Do you know what it would be like to live under the Bolshevik police? You would never eat any more roast chicken, as you used to eat before the war." My husband answered him: "Who needs roast chicken? We would be satisfied with a dry morsel of bread and a bit of tea." To this, Dimitry answered: "If you are satisfied with such a small amount, your fate will not be bad. If you do not have any aspirations for a comfortable life as in other lands, your lot in life will be good with them."

A Path Full of Obstacles and Suffering (cont.)

The Liberation

Several weeks again passed, and Dimitry came to us with a cheerful face: "Shourz! Your salvation has arrived, so it seems to me." He brought with him a section that he had cut out of the newspaper. As was his custom, he asked that we all remain quiet and not make any noise, for at the last moment, something might change, for the tension of everyone was very high, especially among the gentiles who behaved cruelly toward the Jews. These were mainly Banderov gangs, who were faithful assistants to the German Nazis. All of them, from young to old, assisted them. A few days later he came to us and said: "Behold, you are free. However, you must not hurry to leave here until I tell you that you are permitted to go. However, my husband did not want to stay a moment more, and he said that the time has finally come for us to leave here. Dimitry stood his ground: "Don't go. You need to wait a little while until the influx of the Russian army completes. If you do not want to listen to me, you will only be sorry about all your struggle." My husband said to Dimitry: "Nothing will help you." He called loudly to Dimitry: "I want our clothes, mine, my wife's and my children's, and we will leave. There is no more time for convincing, the time has come to go." Dimitry went, and about two hours passed. Then my husband began to knock on the gate of the barn. Only then did he bring us down our clothes. However, when we examined the clothes, it became obvious that these clothes were not ours. These were worn out rags of gypsies, that nobody would wear. At that moment we had the thought that they were preparing to kill us, and these rags would be sufficient to bury us. He did not even our shoes to us. It was then the harsh days of winter, with a lot of snow up to the height of a person. For food, he gave us one egg with a pita, covered in a rag. Due to our great anger we had not yet eaten supper, and we wanted to leave already. We parted from him, and we each extended our hand to him with a promise that we would never tell anyone where our hiding place was. He showed us the way that we should go. Later, it became clear that Dimitry had prepared gangs of murderers with the intention of killing us and removing us from the world. Seeing the clothes that Dimitry had prepared for us, we felt instinctively that death awaited us if we went in the direction that he showed us. He had even warned us to go according to his directions. Our heart told us not to go in the direction that he showed us. In order to confuse him, we went that way until his house was no longer in view. Then my husband called out: "Children! We are turning off the road and going in a different direction, to the right." We walked all night in the deep snow, without knowing where we were found. We continued on until we arrived at the house of a certain gentile, when dawn already had arrived. This light showed us the direction in which to continue our journey. We continued until we arrived at the window of a house in the village. We knocked on the door. of the house, and a Subotnik opened up. He was a good man of faith, and he recognized my husband. We were half naked and frozen from the cold. The gentile crossed himself and served us warm milk. He gave each of us a piece of sugar. He literally earned his share in the hereafter.

[Page 200]

After we drank the milk, the Subotnik asked us: "How did you get here, and what did you do that you remained alive? Had you come by a different way, the straight route, they would have killed you. Bands of Banderovchiks are roaming around, and every night they murder even Ukrainians and Poles." We were convinced that we had done the right thing by not following the route that Dimitry had showed us, for we would have certainly not remained alive. It is possible that Dimitry himself participated in that gang. The Subotnik went out to his yard to feed the animals and the fowl. He advised us to rest a bit after such a difficult journey in the snow. We slept for about two hours. At 8:00 a.m., he came to us. His wife had cooked potatoes with sour milk, and set the table for us, with other good food. This family of farmers fulfilled the commandment of tending to guests from the depths of their hearts. After the meal, the entire family sat down and asked us questions about what had happened to us. They expressed interest about what had happened to us during the difficult times. After we had told the family of all of the tribulations that we endured in Dimitry's pit, the entire family said together that a great miracle had happened to us, for as far as they knew, almost no Jews from Podhajce remained – neither those who hid among gentiles nor those who hid in the forests. In their opinion, we left our hiding place early. My husband asked the Subotnik to give him some tobacco leaves to smoke, a box of matches, and perhaps some sheets of paper. The gentile harnessed his horse, took us to the road where the Russian transport was passing, and let us down on the road. We parted from the Subotnik with warm words, and expressed our hope that we would yet be able to repay him for all of his kindness and good relations to us. The Subotnik went on his way, and we remained standing on the road.

Soviet army wagons passed by one after another. We raised our hands to the wagon drivers as a sign that we want to travel with them. Many passed by without paying attention to us. Finally, an old Russian passed by with his horse and wagon, and asked us what we wanted. We answered him that we wanted him to take us with him to where he was going. "Okay", he said, "Give me something to smoke." My husband gave him what he had received from the Subotnik. We sat and rode until the Zahajce farm. It was already dark, and the Gestapo was still in power in Podhajce. We descended from the wagon. The Russian battalion went to their field camp to eat. We also went to the kitchen of the farm, for we had some acquaintances there. As we entered the kitchen, we met the two brothers Yitzchak and Motia Frankel, Michael Lehrer and Fanchia Rozmarin. There were a few other acquaintances whose names I do not remember. We were very glad to see that indeed, some Jews of our city remained. We got something to eat and arranged a place for ourselves to sleep between the wagons. We tried to remain within the bounds of the transport for greater safety, and we also attempted to forge the connection with the four who remained alive. We drifted into a deep sleep as if after a great exertion. In the meantime, the Soviets retreated, and there was a tumult in the camp. We did not hear anything of this. We woke up at 3:00 p.m., and did not know what had happened suddenly, that we did not see a living soul. We were particularly angry at the four Jews and the Frankel brothers who did not wake us up, and left us sleeping, while they themselves fled, while it was very possible that we might have fallen into the hands of the Germans.

The Russians had received an order to retreat hastily at night. When we woke up, we began to search for a way to go. We approached the main road and found a tumult and shouting. The Russians were running like crazy people, whipping their horses with whips and shouting at them. The Germans were bombing without stop, and the shrapnel from the bombs was falling like hail. We stood on the way waving our hands, and the Russians paid no attention to us at all. We saw that our end was near, and it was no use waiting for any assistance. Only the Dweller of Heaven could show us a miracle. We saw that the convoy was almost ended and that nobody wanted to take us aboard. We lay on the road, and only our daughter remained waving her hands. One soldier stopped and asked what was going on here. We said that we were Jews, and that since no soldier wants to take us aboard their wagon, we were prepared to be killed and not fall into the hands of the Germans. Our daughter asked the solider to take us aboard his wagon, since we had already been standing there for a few hours, and the Germans were about to come.

The soldier had mercy upon us, took off his coat and threw it upon the girl who was frozen from the cold. He asked once again if we were Jews. Our daughter requested that the soldier also take aboard her mother, father and brother Aharon. Having no choice, the soldier, took us all aboard, shouting that we must flee quickly since the Germans were behind us. He urged the horses on very strongly. The soldier asked: "Where should I let you down? We are the last ones. I am traveling to Burkanov, where my commander is located. He is a Jew. I will give you over to his custody. He is a captain, and the entire command is located there." The soldier brought us there and apologized to his command that he violated the law and transported guests on his army wagon. He could not do anything else, for they were lying on the road, and he had no other option other than to run them over. However, the fate of the girl particularly moved him, since he had one like her at home. The captain told the soldier: "You have done well, and behaved in a humane fashion." He patted him on his shoulder and gave him a prize: a full pack of tobacco leaves that could not be obtained for any price. The soldier continued on his way, and the captain put us up with a gentile, telling him: "First of all, prepare hot water so that they can wash up well. He gave us army linens, coats, and pants for my husband and son. He ordered that the old rags be burnt, and commanded the gentile woman to prepare for us food, and not to give us anything fatty, which might injure us. Later the captain called to us and asked: "Is it true that you are Jews? It is hard to believe that any Jews remain. How and where did you hide?" We lay down to sleep on a straw mattress on the ground, and fell into a deep sleep. A short while later he awakened us and said: "We are located here on the border between the two regions. We cannot waste any time. You know about the Communist police in Russia. I am also a Communist, and I promised my father before his death that I will recite Kaddish for him, and I was not able to fulfill my promise until this point. Therefore, I took it upon myself to save as many Jews as possible. And behold, fate took you into my hands, and it seems as if from Heaven they helped me to fulfill my promise to my father. Your salvation is in lieu of reciting Kaddish. Now my dear ones, I do not have much money. I have ten rubles which I am giving to you. He took a hand made woolen shawl from around his neck and gave it to us. We felt that this was no ordinary shawl. He told us that we had received this shawl as a symbol. He told us that he had a very wealthy sister who had a large farm and a mill. "You will go to her, and she will make up what I am missing. You will feel at home with her. You are permitted and are able to remain with her as long as you wish until the end of the war. Perhaps in this merit I will also survive, come home in peace, and rejoice greatly with you."

[Page 201]

We took leave of him and kissed him literally as a fellow townsfolk. He gave us a transport truck with blankets, and food for three days. He told the driver: "I place upon you the responsibility for these four people, who are very dear to me." Aside from this he gave my husband a certain password, and if the driver does not bring the password in it will be a sign that he himself murdered us, and he will shoot him on the spot. The captain could do no more than this, and we felt that he was not a human being, but rather an angel in human form. He did not allow any of the soldiers who were present and wished to help to load us aboard the car. Rather, he himself did so, for we did not have the strength to jump up. He told the soldiers that we are his relatives. He made a place to sleep to each of us, and he gave us each several warm blankets. He did not embarrass us, even though we looked like filthy wild animals. He himself served us, and everyone stood about filled with astonishment.

We traveled all night. The driver took us to a train station, from which we could reach the Zhmerinka station. We sent the agreed upon password through the driver to the captain in a closed envelope, and asked the driver to protect it so that it would not be lost, for it is not a simple letter. This was an important letter to his commander. The driver set out on his way, and we remained for an entire day in the central station. There were thousands of other people aimlessly lying around us. They lay in a tenfold worse state than we did. Then the train arrived, and we entered it with great danger. These were ordinary transport trains that brought war provisions to the front. We traveled for an entire day and night. According to our plans, we intended to travel to the interior of

Russia, to the address that was noted on the woolen shawl. This was the clearest sign. Aside from this, the captain wrote to his sister to take good care of us. This was his only demand, and he asked that she do this for his sake. These are the few Jews who remained alive from the war of destruction of Hitler. After the end of the war they will to their home, and perhaps he would also survive in their merit.

We arrived at the Zhmerinka train station, and as we looked out of the windows, we saw that many soldiers were carrying loaves of white bread and complete sausages. My husband said: "If this is the situation, we will descend here and not continue on the journey. I do not wish to travel to the depths of Russia. If it is possible to obtain white bread and sausage here, it is a clear sign that we could live here. Aside from this, I want to be close to our country and city, and not go far off into the depths of Russia". We knew the Russians. On the other hand, I knew that if we were to begin to do business to earn our livelihood, the Russians were liable to send us to Siberia or other wasteland as a punishment. Therefore, what good would it be to flee from our city if all of these tribulations would come upon us? I began to influence my husband to change his mind to continue with the journey, by pointing out the excellent recommendation that we had in our hands from the Jewish captain, who acted to us like an angel from heaven. Furthermore, we would distance ourselves further from the front line, where the Germans do not stop to bomb and attack. However my husband stood his stand: "My children, you will not convince me. My heart says to stay as close as possible to our homeland and not to distance ourselves with a journey to the depths of Russia. Indeed, we did descend from the train in Zhmerinka.

We descended from the train and wandered around the station of Zhmerinka hungry, without a coin in our pockets. I saw a large heap of dung and garbage, and began to search for empty containers of preserves in which I could heat up some water. A soldier stood on guard not far from this garbage heap. The soldier stopped me from going: "What are you doing here? Do you not know that it is forbidden to approach here?" I answered him: "I did not know. We just arrived, and I want to warm up a bit of water, for we are hungry. I have come with young children. I am a Jewess." The soldier said: "First, I want to be convinced that you are a Jewess. Bring

your husband here, and if your words are true, I will give you something to eat. I have everything. I ran to bring my husband, and the soldier interrogated him to find out if he was a Jew." He took out a sack and filled half of it with salt, a commodity that was very difficult to obtain. Aside from this, he placed various food provisions in the sack, aside from bread. He promised to bring bread later. The soldier told him that he has many Jewish friends, and he spent half of the years of his life among Jews. He would eat at their table, and they were among his best friends. We parted from the soldier, but from our great weakness, we could not lift up the sack with food. We to the station and found a place to sit down. My husband found two bricks and an old German steel helmet. We lit some straw and warmed up the water in the helmet. We found a bit of millet in the sack. I put some of it into the helmet with some salt. We turned to the side so nobody would see us eating a bit of warm soup. We restored our spirit with this. This food was more precious to us than all the treasures of the world.

Now for some words on Zhmerinka. It is located in the Vinitza region of Podolia. This used to be an uninhabited area, upon which a central train station was located. On account of the station, some families settled in the place, including some Jews. In 1897, the population was 13,944 people, including 2,396 Jews. The place was opened up to unrestricted settlement of Jews in 1903. In 1909, there were already schools for Jewish boys and girls, as well as mixed schools. There were pogroms against the Jews after the manifesto of the Czar of October 17, 1905, as there were in dozens of other Jewish communities of Russia. There were no victims. Large army garrisons passed through this station during both the First and Second World Wars, bringing it great benefit as a central station.

[Page 202]

The soldier appeared at the train station once again at 7:00 p.m. He brought a large loaf of bread under his arms as well as a bottle of liquor. He brought two small cups and drank with us "Na Zdarovia" (Lechaim – to Life). The solider took interest in what had happened to us, and he literally wept from grief as he heard of the tribulations that we endured. As he took leave of us he gave us several rubles and told us to go to the interior of Russia, for the front was again approaching from the east, and the Germans were liable to .

We did not act on his advice, and decided to set ourselves up in Zhmerinka. However, this was no simple matter at all. There was a respectable number of Jews in the city, however nobody took interest in our fate, and nobody agreed to rent us a dwelling, not even a cellar or a barn. We ran into an abandoned cellar whose door faced the street as we wandered through the streets of the city. I advised my husband to enter into this cellar and set it up as a dwelling for our family. Having no option, my husband agreed to my advice.

After the issue of a dwelling was settled, I went out the marketplace and began to occupy myself in business. First I sold the salt that I had received from the soldier. The profit was not bad. Then I purchased eggs from the farmers of the area, cooked them and offered them to the soldiers for sale. With time we began to do business with the merchandise that we purchased from the soldiers, and we sold them for a reasonable profit. Thus, we managed to save several thousand rubles. We rented a four-room dwelling, furnished it, and began to live as members of the community once again.

However, one bright day the war again caught up with us. A large volley of German bombs attacked the city and turned it into mounds of ruins. My daughter and I were in the market at the time, and we succeeded in entering the shelter in sufficient time. My husband and son were in the house and were saved miraculously. The dwelling was destroyed, but they hid under the table and were not injured by the crumbling ruins. The house went up in flames, and the merchandise that we collected with great toil was burnt. The streets were full of victims, and those that survived fled to the nearby town of Murafa. We took the pillows and blankets that remained and joined the refugees. We were again left penniless. We did not even have enough money to rent a wagon. After wandering on the roads, we arrived in the town of Murafa with our last energy. Miraculously, we ran into a Jew who helped us rent a dwelling in the home of a widow. The dwelling had three rooms and was furnished. To our good fortune, rent was not demanded up front.

The next day, my husband went out to the market and we again engaged in commerce from whatever came to our hand. We were again successful, and within a short period of time, we succeeded in amassing some money. Even in those days, after many years of war, it was possible to obtain any good thing with money. I prepared "food fit for kings" for the Sabbath and we invited the Jews of the town to eat with us. The meal was conducted in hassidic fashion, and the "tables" that we conducted gave us renown as wealthy people. My husband was honored in the synagogue with aliyot to the Torah, and he pledged proper sums. We also distributed generous gifts to the poor. During the early period, we were forced on occasion to flee to the fields and forests during the night on account of the German bombardment. However, once the German retreat had taken place, the region quieted, and it was possible to live in peace.

After the retreat of the Germans and the movement of the front westward, the Soviet government began to concern itself with the issue of the refugees, which had turned into a "national plague". Unrestricted travel certificates were promised to anyone who wished to to their "homeland". Despite this, we were forced to give bribes, for even in Soviet Russia the power of bribery was great in hastening the arrangement of affairs. After a few weeks of negotiations, we were able to hire a wagon, to load our meager property onto it, and set out westward in the direction of Podhajce. The wagon driver brought us to the former border city over the Podwo³oczyska and then home. We wandered around there for a few days and met with several of our townsfolk, including Chaim Stamler the son-in-law of Wolf Glazer. We were very happy to see them, even though their situation was not at all bright. Most of them were emaciated from hunger and afflicted with disease.

From Podwo³oczyska we wandered to the city of Buchach. There were many partisans there, and each one had his own story about his actions in the battle against the Germans. Buchach was the center of the partisans in eastern Galicia, and they instilled their fear upon the Ukrainians who collaborated with the Germans in the murder of Jews. No small number of Ukrainians paid for their misdeeds with their property and their lives.

We wandered around Buchach for several days, and then went to Trembowla, carrying our property on our shoulders. Trembowla served as a meeting point for refugees, partisans, and survivors form the region. In a destroyed building which had once served as a hotel, relatives, friends and acquaintances who had become separated during the war reunited with each other. We also met a few of our townsfolk, and we told each other what had transpired with us. We remained in Trembowla for two weeks, until a larger group of refugees from our region gathered together, and we were able to together, for we had heard rumors and news about bands of Banderovchiks roving on the roads and threatening the lives and property of the Jewish survivors.

[Page 203]

As a result of the gathering together of a relatively large sized group of refugees in Trembowla, a difficult situation arose with providing food. In addition, rumors spread that the Soviet ruble was liable to lose its value, and the sellers refused to accept it as payment for their merchandise. The situation reached the point where, as I once passed by one yard in which I saw heaps of potatoes and beans without protection, I snuck into the yard and "pilfered" some of each type in order to sustain my family.

In "Liberated" Podhajce

Finally, we joined a group of several of our townsfolk who met in Trembowla and set out for Podhajce. We reached "home" after several days of wandering. First we turned to the mill, our former source of livelihood, and found it destroyed to its foundations. From there we went to my mother's house. We found it standing, but there was nothing in it aside from the empty walls. I remember all of the good and happy days that I had spent in that home, and a cry of despair broke forth from my mouth. At the sound of my scream, the Christians who lived around gathered together. Some of them participated in my sorrow, such as Paulina Daskocz, the old Szikurski and Pinkolski – all of them our former neighbors and customers. They came from the entire area and brought good things with them. They looked at us as if we had from the other world. Later, we approached Moshe Gross. They did not permit him to enter his home and his bakery, and only after great efforts and convincing did they do him a favor and to him one small room. With regard to the bakery – the Christian who seized it did not agree under any circumstances to it to its owners.

Only 13-14 families remained of all the Jews of the city. Fear accompanied us with every footstep, and we were not so brazen as to be seen outside more than necessary. Nobody went out to the street alone. We all went together, for we felt more secure in that manner. We all lived in one lane: the Rozman family with Goralnik; Leah Ritkis with Dr. Pomerantz; we the Shourz family with Moshe Pikola and his sister Nesia Reich; Roller with Dr. Kressel; the Sztamler family with Getzel Reiles; The Sztarmkan family with Tovia Breines; Chaik Piklora with Risia. Tovia Breines' brother was about to be shot in the head by the Russians since he acted disrespectfully toward the image of Stalin. He was saved from death only because of a malfunction of the revolver. Absolving him from this great "sin" cost him a great deal of money.

Avrahamchi Roller succeeded in hiding in his own house. The Christian woman who served him hid him in his house. He later married her and they had a daughter. Sarah, the granddaughter of Reizi Fisz, was hidden by a Christian. She later married him. Yisrael Tzines' daughter from the partisans. Among those who were Yerucham and Mordechai Szulman, Henia Freidman, Breincha the granddaughter of Szulwolf, Pesia Tabak the daughter of Moshe Gross, Lustig the shoemaker with his daughter, Rivka Silber, Shaul Silber, Gittel Fink of Zawalow who is today my sister-in-law, and several other people whose names I have forgotten.

The first thing that my husband did upon our to destroyed Podhajce was to erect monuments over the two mass graves in Stara Miasto and Zahajce in memory of the martyrs who were murdered and buried there during the liquidation actions. My husband obtained two suitable stones, and he and my son Aharon engraved the letters. All of the survivors in Podhajce at that time participated in the unveiling of the monuments.

The dwelling in the house of Moshe Pikola was poor for several reasons. Therefore we moved to the house of Mordechai Lehrer, opposite the office of the N.K.V.D., where we felt more secure. There were also several other families who followed us and settled in the home of David Zimet.

Among the people who survived and to Podhajce were the wife of Binyamin Szaar with her son and daughter, and Yisrael Muruchnik and his brother. Yisrael Muruchnik was an avowed Communist. He with his brother from Russia. He attained greatness there and was appointed as the chief overseer of the entire economic life of Podhajce, and especially over the mill of Yehoshua and Yaakov Haber. He greeted us with great joy when we arrived in Podhajce, for he remembered that we always related well to our workers and attempted to improve their lot. He set up his residence in the home in which we resided, next to our dwelling, and we spent evenings in conversation until late at night.

One day, Yisrael approached my husband with the offer of joining him in running the mill. He promised to make him his right hand man, since he did not know much about matters of milling, and my husband, as was known, was a great expert in this matter. My husband refused to accept this offer, since he knew that it was best to keep one's distance from the leadership of the new authorities. However his refusal did not work, for Yisrael hinted to him that this offer was an order of the "government" which must not be refused.

[Page 204]

The next day my husband woke up, recited the Shacharit service, and unwillingly went to accept the important position that had been imposed upon him. It was not easy to approach the great Muruchnik, who used to be a porter and now had reached the rank of commissar. Two policemen stood at the entrance and wrote down the names of all who requested entry to the commissar. Permission was only granted after receiving his approval. My husband also entered in this manner, but after he entered he told him: "I wish to inform you that my desire to leave this 'Garden of Eden' and to settle in our old homeland of the Land of Israel is very strong, and you must promise to assist me in this." Yisrael promised to free him when the time came. Later he invited all of the workers of the milling trade, the men of the N.K.V.D and the secretary Rivka Shechter to him, and in a speech before them all he advised them to accept Yitzchak Shourz as the expert in the running of the milling business. A vote was taken. All of them voted for the recommendation and ended with the proclamation of: "Long live Stalin!"

My husband remained to work in the mill, and he was given a special office. Yisrael Frisz was also accepted for work in the mill. The commissar advised my husband to set up an enterprise for the production of groats, as we had done in our mill. My husband agreed to do this after they provided him with the necessary materials and workers.

The news that Yitzchak Shourz had survived and was working in the mill spread around the residents of the neighboring villages. Many came to visit him, including the Subotnik who stood with us at our time of trouble. Through this Subotnik, my husband sent a gift of flour also to Dimitry who had hid us in the pit in his house, and asked him to inform him that he should not be afraid of us, for we only remember the good that he did for us, and we have already forgotten his bad deeds. However, it became clear that Dimitry, when he had heard about our to Podhajce, began to fear us and fled to the forests, and he only to his home sometimes at night, until he was arrested by the N.K.V.D. His wife Marisa came to us one day, fell to our feet, and begged us to have mercy upon her children and attempt to free her husband. Indeed, he was not deserving of mercy, for he was a member of the Banderovchiks. However, according to his wife, he was forced to join them so they would not suspect him of hiding Jews. "In any case", she said, "He was not one of the active members of these gangs."

My husband was not inclined to intercede for him, but I remembered by vow that if we would survive, we would forgive him all of his iniquities. My husband indeed went to the N.K.V.D. office and testified that we were saved from the Nazis through his actions. He was immediately freed. My husband also signed in his merit at the police that he be given some petty position in order to distance him from the Banderovchiks. I am convinced that thanks to the information that he gave to the police, many of the members of these gangs in our area were identified, for he knew all of their hiding places. From that time he would come to visit our house daily for about a month, and I would serve him food.

The survivors after the Holocaust next to the memorial tablet in Zahajce

The inscription on the monument (in German, with Hebrew letters):
"This memorial was erected on the mass grave where our beloved families, consisting of 800 people, were shot by the Hitlerist murderers on June 7, 1943, and were buried together. In eternal memory, erected in Podhajce on May 5, 1945

We can learn about the relationship of the Soviets to the survivors from the following incident. One gentile named Marinka Rogoszka, who worked for Leib Fink for about thirty years, promised to hide my sister and her family during the time of the Nazis. In she received a large fortune of cash and objects. However, after she received the property, she chased out my sister, her husband and their two children. She did this as well to Rivka Shechter. Relying on the testimony of her neighbors, I went to her house to retrieve from her at least the objects that I recognized as belonging to my sister. The woman turned to the N.K.V.D. and complained that I had passed judgment myself and removed various objects from her house. I was summoned to the investigator and explained the entire matter to him. However the investigator did not accept the explanation, and issued a verdict that I must everything that I had taken. I answered in anger that I would turn to higher authorities to overturn the perverse verdict. To this the investigator retorted in Russian: "It is too bad that Hitler left a few Jews alive." All of the gentiles who were present at this case smiled upon hearing this witticism.

[Page 205]

This investigator was later removed from his post after complaints against him by two Jewish sisters from another city who ended up in Podhajce after the Holocaust. They were very intelligent and knew how to act under such circumstances. They issued the complaint from Zlotniki rather than Podhajce in order to evade the censor who was sharper in Podhajce. Both of them suffered greatly from the Soviet detectives, for they complained about all the iniquity that was perpetrated against the Jews. One of them was even imprisoned and tortured severely by the N.K.V.D. Thanks to our intervention, the two sisters were freed from the guardians of Soviet justice, and left the "Vale of Weeping". Both of them survived. One of them lives in Vienna, and the other lives in the United States.

There were also more severe incidents. There was a Jewish pharmacist in the city named Chaim Weintraub. It once happened that pills disappeared from the pharmacies and the men of the N.K.V.D. sent Weintraub to bring pills from Berezhany. At first he refused to go, for he knew that mortal danger awaited the Jews from the Banderovchiks. However his refusal was not accepted, and he was accused of failing to listen to the police. With pressure from the authorities, he was forced to go on the journey. Indeed, gangs awaited him on the journey, dragged him into the forest, and murdered him with harsh tortures. The wagon driver to Podhajce with his wagon and horses.

Events such as this convinced us that we would not have any peace under Soviet rule, and that we must move out of the place at the earliest opportunity. Even in the mill where my husband worked, not everything was as it should be. He indeed brought the mill to a high level and the business was run appropriately. However as time progressed, anonymous complaints were presented that the Jewish managers were treating the mill as their own. On occasion the N.K.V.D. members came to investigate these matters that were completely contrived. My husband decided that the time had come to actualize our decision, to leave the city, and to go into the free world, and from there to the Land of Israel. He approached Muruchnik with this matter, but he explained to him that the times had changed in the interim, and he was no longer the "plenipotentiary". For such a matter as leaving a responsible position, one must turn directly to Stalin's office. My husband formulated an appropriate request, stating that during his tenure, he succeeded in running the mill appropriately and trained appropriate staff members to run it. Now, he does not see himself as fitting to continue in his position, and he wishes to be freed from it. Recommendations and permits from Muruchnik and the N.K.V.D. were added to this request. A few weeks later, an order came to the secret police to investigate this matter and see if all of the facts were correct. At first Muruchnik was summoned to the secret police, and he had to certify that he indeed signed the request and all the facts were correct. Then my husband was summoned, who also verified all the facts and explained that it was difficult for him to continue to live in a place where all his family and friends perished. The secret police issued an authorization that Yitzchak Shourz was a dedicated employee, he had received an award for his diligence and commitment, and all of his reasons were correct and logical. A few weeks again passed, and finally my husband received the notice that he is free from his position and work.

After that came the period of preparing passports, which was also quite complex. During that time, my youngest brother Moshe Yosef from Russia, and he decided to join us as well. The rest of the survivors of Podhajce reached the same conclusion, and decided to form a single group to leave this city forever.

There were several single young people among the survivors, and it was natural that they would want to get married. Several couples got married: My brother Moshe Yosef with Gittel Fink of Zawalow, Chana Rozman with Roller, and several other couples whose names I have forgotten.

Here is the place to tell the story of how Gittel Fink was saved. She was the only one who survived from among the partisan group of Yisrael Silber. Gittel Fink was a relative of ours, and on the day of the final action, she found refuge in the bunker under our mill. Our paths parted when we all left the mill. She went out to the forest with a group of people of Zawalow, and there she joined up with my sister Liba, her husband Leib Fink and their children. They sat together in one of the bunkers in which there were about twenty people. There were several other bunkers in the forest, and Yisrael Silber was the commander of them all. Among other things, he concerned himself with the provision of food and water to the residents of the bunkers. Hershele Breines, a youth from our city, would help him by going to the well to bring water for everyone.

[Page 206]

The Ukrainian murderers knew that there were Jews in the area, but they did not succeed in exposing the bunkers in which they were hidden. Once, when the youth went to the well, the Ukrainians ambushed him, approached him and began to entice him with soft words. They laid their weapons down onto the ground, and asked him to do the same. Then they told him that they themselves were partisans, whose chief command was located in Halicz. They were connected with the Russian partisans, and they wished to connect with the Jewish partisans a well. The youth was tricked into believing them. He showed them the location of the bunkers and with the good "news" that he found "brothers in arms". The Ukrainians first demanded that the men with weapons come to them, and place their weapons at the side. This seemed very suspicion, but they saw that there was no other choice other than to comply. In the meantime, Yisrael Silber and immediately understood what had taken place. The Ukrainians commanded his friends to summon him, and when he did not answer their summons, he forced his sister to call him to assuage his fear. He answered the call of his sister. Then the Ukrainians removed his weapons, led them all to a place 100 meters from the bunker, and murdered them all.

After this, the Ukrainians to the bunker and called the women to come to them, but they did not listen to them. Then three murderers descended to the bunker and shot the women and children, while the rest went to search for the other bunkers in the area. The murderers did their work completely, and when they ran out of bullets, they murdered the rest with axes.

Gittel Fink was not injured by the bullets, but she fell among the dead and did not show any signs of life. After the murderers left, she extricated from among the bodies of the dying children, some of whom were still writing with their final death throes, but she did not leave the bunker during daylight. From afar she heard the shots of the murderers in the other bunkers, and the cries of the victims. After some time, the murderers to the bunker, removed the bodies, and brought them to a burial pit that they had dug. First, they stripped the clothes from the corpses to see if there was any money or valuables that remained. Then, with two people at a time, one at the head and one at the feet, they took the corpses and tossed them up onto the wagon.

Once again, Gittel had to pretend she was dead. She was tossed onto the wagon among the first bodies, and the rest of the bodies were piled onto her. When they arrived at the pit, the murderers dumped the contents of the wagon into the pit, so that Gittel was in the top part of the pit. They began to cover the pit with earth. To her good fortune, they covered her with only a thin layer. She felt that she was about to suffocate, but suddenly the heavens opened, flooding rains came down, and swept the earth away from on top of her. She realized that she had survived this time as well.

After the murderers left and it was again quiet, Gittel rose from the grave and set out towards the fields. There, among the sheaths, she lay down and thought about what to do. Would miracles continue to happen and she might remain alive, or would it be best to turn herself in to the Gestapo? After the rain, the sun again came out, and everything dried out. Suddenly she heard the footsteps of a person approaching her. A youth approached her, the son of the owner of the field, and found her lying among the sheaths stark naked. The youth was from Zawalow. He recognized her and said: “Aren't you Genia! Why are you lying here?” She told him everything that had taken place in the past few hours. The youth comforted her and told her that she would tell this to his mother who was working in the fields, and she would certainly come to her aid. He also left her a bit of food that he had brought along and went on his way.

Gittel was not completely sure that the youth would not turn her in again to the Banderovchiks, and therefore she got up and went away from this place to a place where the sheaths were taller. However, she erred with this. The parents of the youth were Subotniks, and when the mother heard that the daughter of Yossel Fink was lying in her field, she did not rest until she found her a new place. She dressed her in farmer's clothes, placed a hoe upon her shoulder, and led her to her home. She prepared a place to sleep in a secret place, and healed her wounds with home made medication that was common among the villagers. Later, when she had recovered a bit, the gentile got in touch with other Subotniks who took care of the needs of several dozen Jews from Zawalow. Finally she transferred Gittel in a wagon covered with straw, to the bunker where Jews from her city were located. In general, it is impossible to overstate the deeds of the Subotniks in our area, and it is difficult to believe that during those dark times, there were people who literally risked their lives to save the lives of Jews, who felt themselves close to the “nation of the Bible” and who tried to do anything they could to relive their suffering.

The “Maker of Matches”[1] gave it into my hands to be the matchmaker for this Gittel, and to present her to my brother Moshe Yosel, the only one of my brothers or family to survive. The wedding was not at all like the weddings that we were used to in the communities of Galicia, attended by a large group of relatives and friends. This time the wedding was modest, without any clergy. My husband fulfilled the role of rabbi and cantor, and conducted the marriage ceremony for the young couple. The couple joined us in our journey westward. The immediate destination was Germany, but our desire was to make aliya to the Land of Israel.

[Page 207]

On the Route to Israel

After endless wanderings and tribulations, we arrived at the railway station in Kozowa, but we found it abandoned and forlorn. Nobody knew when the train was to come, and how one should proceed. It was very cold outside. However we were experienced and knew how to ease our suffering through various makeshift means. We waited that way for several days and nights, until the train suddenly arrived during the night. We crowded into the transport wagons that were meant for transporting cattle. We traveled that way for several days until the train stopped at a Bytom near Breslau (which is called Wroclaw by the Poles). We descended from the train there and obtained a nice four room dwelling in the center of the city above the central post office. We began to rest from the long tribulations of the journey.

Suddenly the men among us picked up the bug for enjoyment of life. When we reached an inhabited city after long years of suffering and tribulations, they desired to see a film in a theater. All four men, my husband Yitzchak, my brother Moshe Yossel, my son Aharon and Yidel Shechter left the house to go to the theater. This was toward evening. A short time later, as darkness fell, we heard the sound of confusion next to the entrance to our dwelling. Approximately eight armed hooligans went up the stairs and began to knock on the door of our dwelling. They presented themselves as men of the secret police, and demanded that we immediately open the door. I answered them that I could not open, for it was dark outside and the men are not at home. My claim did not help. They broke open the door and entered the dwelling. I ran outside and shouted: Help! Help! The last of the hooligans attempted to stop me, but I punched him in the face with my two fists until he fell to the ground. However, he immediately recovered and shot at me with his gun. A bullet grazed my face next to my right eye and went over my head. In the meantime, the hooligans wreaked havoc upstairs and demanded that my sister-in-law turn over all the money in our hands, and if not, they would kill her. In the meantime, the sounds of the men who were called from the street near the house reached their ears, and they began to retreat without taking anything. To this day I do not know who these hooligans are. It would seem that they were members of the illegal national underground, who were called "Armia Krajowa". These people excelled in deeds of murder and theft no less than the Nazis. They particularly were interested in "saving" their homeland of Poland from the remnants of the Jews who had from the bunkers and labor camps. The government of Poland did not lift a finger to stop their atrocities.

When the men from the movie theater and heard about what had happened when they were gone, we all decide that it would be best to continue our journey westward to the city of Breslau, the capital of Silesia. This time, we loaded our belongings onto a transport truck. In Breslau, we met several people of Podhajce, such as Hirsch Kimmel and his family, Sima Weisman and her sisters, the two Litman brothers, Roller, Dr. Trif of Tarnopol, and many others whose names I have forgotten.

We remained in Breslau for a few months. After deliberations, we decided not to remain in that city, even though there were many Jewish refugees and all the institutions needed by Jews, such as synagogues, aid organizations, a cemetery, etc. We saw the direction of the winds of the new Polish government, and we suspected that no good would come from living under its wings. In the meantime, a new factor arose that assisted us with our decision to leave Wroclaw.

After the destruction of Europe during the Second World War, the United Nations set up the UNRRA (United Nations Relief and Rehabilitation Administration) whose task was to aid those afflicted by the war and to support them in any way possible. This organization was established in Washington in 1943, even before the end of the war. After four years, in 1947, a special organization called IRO (International Refugee Organization) was set up to take care of the refugees and displaced persons. Among other things, this organization offered help to a quarter of a million Jewish refugees and aided those were interested in making aliya to Israel.

Representatives of the UNRRA were active in Breslau as well, and we turned to them for assistance. Through this organization, we were sent to the displaced person's camp in Saltzschlief near the German city of Fulda. We received a furnished room with a balcony in one of the courtyards of a former nobleman. All of our needs, including clothing, shoes and medical care were given to us in a generous fashion by the UNRRA. This was one of the finest places of comfort. The good, worry-free life that we had there was meant to encourage those who had suffered, and to instill in them the hope for a better future, that would come, even if it would take time.

We spent two years in this place in the situation of children who are supported at the table of their parents. During this period, our ties to the Land of Israel increased. The news of the founding of a Jewish State began to penetrate throughout the world, even though it was not yet clear when this would happen, and how it would work out. My husband who was known as someone whose heart was set to Zion, was chosen as one of the activists, and he was given the job of gathering together young people who were prepared to make aliya to the Land, so that they could work at jobs that would prepare them for this. In the Land, there were battles between the Jews and Arabs, and the first necessity for the youths was to be able to bear arms and to assist in the difficult battle. As a first step in this direction, a list was made of youth who desired to make aliya to the Land of Israel. A short time later, the first group of volunteers was sent. The preparation of the second group met difficulties, for an insufficient number of people had registered. It is possible that the news of the difficult battles frightened the youth, and they decided to wait until the wrath would pass. Those in charge of matters of aliya used moral means of pressure: they composed a blacklist of youth who were candidates for aliya but who had refused to register. This method was quite effective, for many of the youth began to view this remission as a form of treason to the government of Israel that was to be set up.

[Page 208]

At that time, our son Aharon was in Munich where he studied engineering. We then received a letter from my brother-in-law Yaakov Shourz, who had already lived in the Land of Israel for several years, advising us to transfer Aharon to a professional school, since engineering in the high school lasts for many years. We traveled to Munich and transferred him to the ORT school to study a profession. After some time, the Zionist idea took root among the students of the school. Several presentations about Zionism and the Land of Israel were arranged, in which they encouraged the students to volunteer for aliya. About 1,300 students of the ORT schools and gymnasiums registered for aliya at that time. One day, our son came home and informed us that he too had registered, and he had come to bid farewell to us before his aliya. I attempted to convince him to push off his aliya. Among other reasons, I claimed that he was still too young in that he was not quite 18 years old. However, he claimed that if did not make aliya now at a time when the Land needs him, he would be embarrassed to make aliya when everything was already prepared for him. Without any choice, I subjugated my will to his will, and I gave him my blessings for his aliya. My husband had agreed to this from the outset, for as an organizer of aliya to the Land of Israel, he was not able to be seen as having his own son shirk from fulfilling his duty.

According to the news that reached us after Aharon's aliya, the young volunteers were sent directly to the battlefront against the enemy in the region of Jerusalem, and no small number of them fell in battle. Aharon was among those who remained alive. He was injured in his leg, but the wound was light. He wrote to us often, without mentioning to us at all that he was located in the region of battles. In order to calm us, he sent his letters from Tel Aviv, even though he was never there at all. His letters were full of love for the homeland and full of pride that he and his friends were preparing the Land for a Hebrew state, which would be able to absorb into its bosom all Jews that wished to leave the life of the Diaspora.

About one year after Aharon's aliya, we decided to answer his call and to make aliya to the Land of Israel. At first I traveled with my daughter, for my husband was forced to remain for some time longer in order to arrange various matters. The Tamer ship, an old warship, was waiting for us the port of Marseilles, France. It took aboard about 600 people who were making aliya. The boat also carried a special cargo of great weight, and therefore it moved with difficulty and the trip lasted for 31 days. None of us knew what the cargo was. Only later did we find out that the ship was primarily intended for the transfer of the cargo, which was of great importance to the Haganah. The people making aliya served only as a decoy for the British police. The long journey caused great suffering for the people making aliya. There were storms, cold, food shortages, technical obstacles, and even a revolt among the ship staff. However, we accepted everything with love, as the pangs of the Messiah before the redemption.

My brother-in-law Yaakov Shourz and his family greeted us at the port of Haifa. Aharon was serving in the army at the time, and he did not receive a furlough to greet us. One week after our arrival, my brother-in-law transferred us to his house, after we forewent any assistance from the Sochnut (Jewish agency) and signed this explicitly. My husband arrived about one year later, on a comfortable flight in an airplane. We lived in an old, half-ruined Arab building on Hassan Bek Street for about 10 years. We married off our daughter Genia. She set up her home in Holon and she has two sons, Moshe (after my father-in-law of blessed memory) and Yaakov Dov. Aharon completed his army service and began to work as a galvanizator, a profession that he learnt in the ORT school in Munich. We assisted him in getting himself set up. He also established a family and had a son and a daughter. The son is called David after the name of my husband's brother. The daughter, who was born after the death of my husband, was called Yitzchaka after his name. After all the tribulations, we finally came to a peaceful life in the Land, and with the marriage of our children, we enjoyed the contentment of family life. Our hearts were filled with praise and thanks to the Dweller on High for all the good that he did to us in us to the Land of our heritage.

My husband lived in the Land for 15 years, and continued to live a life of purity and uprightness. He worked a great deal for the benefit of the Yeshivas, and donated a Holy Ark to the synagogue in Bnei Brak. He took interest in any matter that was for communal benefit. To our great sorrow, he was taken from us when he was only 62 years old. The news of his sudden death, when he was still with his full strength and energy, fell one bright day upon the circle of his friends and acquaintances like a thunderclap. His loss was felt primarily within the circle of his family, especially by me. From the time of his death, he did not leave my memory even for one minute, and I continue to work in his spirit to the best of my ability.

I will conclude the story of our travails and success with the note that, with all my descriptions, I have not related even one tenth of what took place with us, and what we had seen and heard during the days of the frightful rule of the Nazi enemy – with all their atrocities the likes of which did not exist since the day that G-d created the heavens and the earth.

Translator's Footnote

1. A reference to G-d.

[Page 209]

The Destruction of our City

by Nachum Pushteig

I am the man who witnessed tribulation by the staff of His wrath.
It was I whom He led to walk into darkness and not light.
To me He turned His hand against me over and over again all the day.

(From the Book of Lamentations)

I was born in 1902 in Zlotniki. I married a wife named Klara in Podhajce, and our son Munio was born there. I lived in Podhajce and earned my livelihood from my galanteria (fancy goods) store. The entire Nazi Holocaust engulfed me from 1941 until the end of the war. It is not easy to survey this terrible era with a few words; and is it even at all possible to describe in human terms the depths of suffering and despair that I endured for the entire time? This is a matter for a writer who has yet to be born, for he must stand in the company of the author of the Book of Lamentations and describe the destruction of a Jewish community with a population of 6,000 souls that was destroyed along with all the Jewish communities in sorrowful Poland.

At the outbreak of the war between Russia and Germany in June 1941, the Nazi German armies entered Podhajce. At first they did no harm to the Jews. Only with the arrival of the Gestapo did they begin to pillage and steal anything that they wanted without recompense.

The first thing that they did was to organize the Judenrat (Jewish council) whose members were appointed by the recommendation of the mayor. At first, the members of this council did not know what their task was, and what was expected of them. The members of the Judenrat were Leibish Lilienfeld, Shapira, and Dr. Margolies. Later, the Judenrat appointed the Ordenungs-Dienst (Service for the Maintenance of Order). Their first task was to collect punitive fines – money, furniture, and bedding – everything for the gendarmes and the Gestapo. The task of the Judenrat was to collect the money from the Jewish population.

Later they began to enlist Jews for labor. At first they enlisted them for work in the city, and later they established a camp in the region. The Jewish council was obligated to draft people for work. By chance, I had acquaintances in the post office who arranged the distribution of the mail of the Judenrat – only for the Jews – and through their recommendation, I began to work as a postman.

Thus did the situation continue for almost an entire year, without aktions and without any other activities. The first year went by only with forced labor, collection of fines, the removal of furniture from the Jewish homes, etc. However, the waiting was tedious, and there was great tension throughout the entire time. We knew that difficult times were awaiting us, without knowing when and how the matter would unfold. Indeed, that which we anticipated took place.

The first aktion in Podhajce was on Yom Kippur of 1942. Then, they drafted the intelligentsia for labor. They invited the young men and finest girls for "labor". They were all sent to the Belzec death camp. Approximately 1,000 people perished during this first aktion. I saved myself and my entire family by hiding.

After the first aktion, a few people who endangered themselves and jumped from the train wagons . They told us the "secret" about to where they were being sent. Indeed, we knew the secret even prior to this, in accordance with the popular adage, "A secret for all the people of the group". The people who had Polish acquaintances, who said that they were being sent directly to the crematoria.

The first aktion served as a paradigm for the following aktions. In the following aktions, a panic ensued in the city when people were snatched for labor. People hid and did whatever possible to evade the fate that awaited them. However, many fell into the trap, including my brother-in-law.

My hiding place was in the house. There was a cellar in the entrance near the sill. We lifted the trapdoor, entered, and closed it behind us. The snatchers passed over us and did not detect us. We heard them milling about and searching here and there. Finally they reached the conclusion that all of the people had already been taken from there. They began to erect the ghetto after the first aktion.

During the second aktion, I remained in the hiding place until 3:00 p.m. The snatchers did not find us. The second aktion was conducted on the 2nd day of Cheshvan. (I recall the date very well, for that is the date of the yahrzeit of my father Shmuel Pushteig of blessed memory.) My father lived in Zlotniki, a town near Podhajce, whose residents were forced to leave their homes and move to Podhajce. My father was 81 years old at the time, and since he already knew why they were all been taken, he did not want to go to the roll call. Uberstormfuehrer Mueller of the Gestapo dragged him against his will. Father did not want to go and said to him: "Why are you dragging me? For what purpose do you have a gun?" Then the German shot him on the spot and murdered him. My sister and her two daughters were also taken during that aktion.

It was told to me that when they took the family members of one member of the Ordenungs-Dienst, the Gestapo man said to him: "If you give me

such and such a quota, I will free them". This man knew my hiding place, opened it, and took us all out during the second aktion. When I arrived, the transport was prepared to depart, and we were the last ones. I was informed that when my father saw that I was not in the gathering place, he said, “It is good that Nachum and his family are not here”. When I arrived, he was already no longer alive.

[Page 210]

The member of the Ordenungs-Dienst who revealed our hiding place was a Jew by the name of Lutner, who remained to the end. He made a great deal of money. After the final aktion, he went out to hide with his family. The gentile with whom he went to hide murdered him and took his money.

My brother David and my sister Rivka with her two daughters were also taken during the second aktion. My brother fled immediately and was not sent with the transport. I went with my entire family to the train. Next to the train there were already people who began to think about how to jump from it. They took along tools for that purpose. I wanted to place myself near people who had initiative, but suddenly I was dragged from behind. A Gestapo man approached me with a big stick, dealt me a blow on the head, and blood began to drip from all sides. I still had a sum of money. I gave it to my wife and told her that if she could flee, she should flee.

The Nazis acted with deceit. They said that the men would be taken in a separate train wagon to work. They loaded 120 of us men onto one wagon, and the women and children onto other wagons. I do not know how I found the energy to board the wagon. I grabbed my hat with my two hands and the blood clotted. I boarded the wagon, and it was stifling and foul smelling. Aside from this, we had not eaten or drunk all day. My fortune was that as soon as I entered, the train began to move. I looked for a place near the wall so that I could lean. Suddenly, I heard “Shma Yisrael”, and they began to open the small window of the train; I heard how one person jumped; the second person jumped... I was the fifth one to jump. I jumped from the train as the train was moving fast. I felt that the station was close, and I jumped with all my energy.

I fell on my hands. To my fortune, I did not fall under the cars. I was tossed, and the blood began once again to fall. I do not know how long I lay there. Suddenly I woke up and I saw that I was alone there, and the train was gone. I began to walk back beside the tracks, and there I met other people who had jumped. There were people who had acquaintances in the area. There were “feld shtiber” (field rooms) in the fields. We went to someone's house, and remained there all night and all day. We to the ghetto in the evening. I to the house, and the only one I found there was my brother. When we met, I wept the entire time and asked, “Where is all the family? Where is my wife? Where is my son?” He was a five-year-old child, and was so delicate that it was difficult to cross the street with him... When they took my brother-in-law, my wife told the child that she was going to bring him something. However the child said to her, “Mother, come home, I am afraid here, we will go out when the Russians will arrive.”

I then went to live in the ghetto with my brother. Nothing was left for us in the house. After they removed the people from the house, the Volksdeutschen (local Germans) came and took everything, without leaving a thing.

Before Passover, rumor had it that there would be another aktion. My relative Yisrael Silber began to organize people to go out into the forest. He was a firewood merchant, and knew his way around the forest. At first, he took his family to his acquaintance in the forest. I went there with my brother, and we spent ten days with that man, a Ukrainian named Zacharechki. Later, it became clear that nothing happened, and we . In the interim, my brother David and Yisrael Silber began to arrange provisions of necessities and weapons.

We remained in the ghetto until before the festival of Shavuot. My brother, Silber, and his family already went out to the forest, and were supposed to come on Sunday to take us to the forest. The third aktion took place that Sunday – the liquidation aktion – and I was still in the ghetto. On the Sabbath there were rumors that there was going to be an aktion. We fled in the middle of the day – through some passageway from the ghetto – into the fields. We remained for the entire day among the stalks, which were still green. Later, it became clear that there had not been an aktion, and we to the ghetto at 10:00 p.m.

I began to get undressed to go to bed – when they came and told us that the ghetto was already closed and the Kovanchiks (in Russia there was a colony of Germans) had arrived to assist with the carrying out of the aktions. It was said that the entire ghetto was surrounded by the Kovanchiks. I jumped and went to the place where the family of the Ordenungs-Dienst Lutner was located. He prepared a hiding place for them, and I entered with them. We were approximately 50 people. There was also a cellar, but the O.D. had closed it and placed things upon it so that it would not be recognizable. It was terribly stifling there. There was a passageway from the cellar to another hiding place, so that if someone opened up at night and asked, "Are you still alive?", they would think that we had suffocated there and they would say, "You can come out if you are still alive".

We went out and everything was empty... This was not an aktion for Belzec. They had taken people to dig pits in Zahajce near Podhajce. They put planks over the pits. People were supposed to strip and walk onto the planks. They shot with machine guns and the people fell into the pit – alive or dead.

It was night. The conscience of O.D. Lutner bothered him that he had taken out my family. He knew that my brother was in the forest and he said, "Don't worry, I will arrange for you to go"...

People remained in the ghetto after the aktion, and the Germans said that whoever remained would be taken to work. There were also people who had prepared poison for themselves. The head of the Judenrat, Lilienfeld, prepared poison for himself as well. He and his wife poisoned themselves during the liquidation aktion.

[Page 211]

People ran about not knowing what to do with themselves. Among them were people who had prepared to go out to the forest but had not had the chance. They knew where to go, and took me with them. The O.D. man took money and a gold watch from us, and gave it to one of the Kovachniks so that he would not be present at the time of the passage. At 10:00 p.m. approximately ten of us set out for the forest.

We wandered around in the forest all night and all day, until my brother and Silber came during the second night and took us to the rest of the people who had fled to the forest. We were more than 100 people there.

We had a small amount of arms, but this was not a forest that was able to sustain partisans. In addition, there were also families with children, etc. They prepared a pit in which to hide temporarily. This was already the 3rd of Sivan, three days before Shavuot. I recall that there were people who took tallises with them and still recited Akdamut (a Shavuot prayer). People put up some sort of tents made of trees and leaves, but this did not help at all, and the rain fell upon us...

At first, we were all together in the forest, and later we organized into groups. We remained in contact with the Ukrainians, from whom we purchased food.

I was so despondent after I had lost my family. I arrived in the rain, and sat down to rest. I fell into a deep sleep and dreamt the following dream. I went to worship in the Beis Midrash of my city. There was a Torah scholar there by the name of Yaakov Rellis who went around all day in the Beis Midrash wearing his tallis and tefillin until 11:00 or noon. Youths studied there, and when they had questions, they approached him. He knew how to answer their questions. He came to me in a dream as he was in the synagogue, with his tallis and white beard, and said to me, "Blessed is G-d day by day" – thus did I have the strength to persevere. To this day, when I pray, I recall the elderly Yaakov Rellis of blessed memory.

Afterward they formed groups, and I remained in a group with my brother and Silber and his family. Thus things went until the 20th of Tammuz. These Ukrainians were Benderovches. They knew about our places and wanted to take our money. They attacked us at night on the 20th of Tammuz. I was not in this group, but Silber was there. First they searched him since he was a man of initiative, and they wished to get rid of him. This was a group of 39 people. They came at night and told everyone to take their things and stand in a line, for they wished to take them to the partisans. With this pretext, they then murdered them with axes. Silber was among them, but his family was not in this group. His wife, brother-in-law and three children were in our group.

My brother, I, and Silber's family were in Zacharechki's group. He told us that he would make a special hiding place at his home for us. However, when we heard what had happened to Silber and the rest of the group, fear overtook him and he told us to leave him for he was afraid. He did not tell us anything about what had happened. At night, my brother, Silber's family, and I went out to search for the people. There was still a third group that remained. Thus did we go at night. My brother already knew a little about the paths. Suddenly he heard someone approaching us. He feared that we had fallen into the hands of a band of bandits, but it became obvious that this was the third group. They thought the same about us, and one of them had a grenade in his hand to throw at us. However, my brother suddenly went out and shouted "Shma Yisrael". When they heard "Shma Yisrael", they knew that we were Jews, and we united. Then the question arose, what to do now. We said that one group would to Zacharechki, and the second would remain in the forest and make some arrangements to be able to remain. The lot fell upon the Silber family and I to go to Zacharechki. They wanted my brother to go with them, but since I had to go, my brother went together with me. One group remained in the forest, and I, my brother, Silber's children, and Mrs. Feldberg with her husband and two children all went to Zacharechki.

Zacharechki agreed to take us in. He knew that we still had money – dollars – gold – and he was a businessman. He told us that he also had a son-in-law in the forest, and he promised that he would bring us to him, that he would make a hiding place for us, and we could remain there. We went to him and remained in that situation until the 20th of Av.

Apparently, someone had informed on us, and on the 20th of Av, a Ukrainian militia with Volksdeutschen attacked us. Some of us had to remain alive nevertheless... I, Silber's three children, and the mother and two children – went into some hole and hid. My brother, Mrs. Feldberg, Silber's wife and brother in-law all remained, and the Ukrainians took them. My brother attempted to flee, but they shot and killed him. I heard the groans from my hiding place, without knowing from whom they were coming. Later, they told me what happened. They shot Silber's wife on the spot as well. His brother-in-law and Feldberg were taken to the area of Zawalow. They dug a pit for themselves, and then they were shot.

Later, Zacharechki was also afraid to keep us. We went out and scattered. There was a valley with a small grove. We entered, and I remained there all day. The children disguised themselves, and I heard them talking. I remained the entire day in the sun without a drop of water. At night I went to the son-in-law of Zacharechki, who told me that they had shot my brother. When I heard this, I said that I had no more reason to live. My brother was strong, he had taken me out to the forest, and now I remained alone, and I did not know what happened to Silber's children. Later it became clear that they survived, and they came to us. Zacharechki's son-in-law was afraid to keep us, and he brought us back to Zacharechki.

[Page 212]

Once again we were all together with Zacharachki. Silber's children included a son of 8, a son of 12, and a daughter who was perhaps 14. There was also Mrs. Feldberg with her 2 children. We remained with him for one day, and then he said that he would bring us to a place in the forest where nobody ever comes. There they made for us some sort of tents between the trees. I made a tent for myself, one for the woman and two children, and one for Silber's three children. We made a sort of roof above the tents. We placed leaves upon it so that the rain would not penetrate, and it would be warm inside. My tent was like a doghouse.

At first we still had some money. The woman still had gold dollars, and Zacharechki brought us a little food each day.

It is interesting to state that I knew that I had a small Siddur (prayer book) among our belongings. I asked that they bring me this Siddur. Day to us was like night, since we could not go out. I was fortunate that I had this Siddur. I prayed every day, and recited the entire book of Psalms every day.

Later, he organized us into groups. He said that I should come each day with a different group of children to obtain something hot to eat. We suffered so much then. It was not easy for us to get there, for we only walked when it was pitch dark. I was again fortunate. Silber's 12-year-old child had a good sense of direction, and he knew the way, so I went with him each time.

If one is predetermined to remain alive, every step leads to life – even though we were already on the way to death. We once went in complete darkness. We had to hold on to each other so we would not get lost. Suddenly the child said, "Nachum, I saw someone light up like a lamp". I told him that we need to go off from the path and walk through the fields. We walked through the fields and reached Zacharechki. He told us, "You have good fortune; this was a Ukrainian from the militia." If the child had not seen the light, we would have fallen directly into their hands.

However, in the interim, life became quite loathsome to us. We had not changed our shirts. We had no water in which to wash. I had dropped to 38 kilo. I had grown a beard like a Nazirite. Once there was a bit of sunlight. I then went among the trees and got undressed. I sat that way, and suddenly I heard the noise of some "shkotzim", but nothing mattered to me anymore and I was apathetic. I got up and . At night I went to Zacharechki and told him what I had heard. He and his wife laughed. It became clear that these were children who had gone out to gather wood to heat the house in the winter. They saw me, got afraid and fled. They came home and said that they had seen a demon. Indeed, I looked like a demon.

Zacharechki still had some hiding places. He took us to rest a bit at his home. This was on Rosh Hashanah, and he wanted to give us some festive food. At night he held us in his home, but he sent us out at night. We hid under haystacks. I recall that I had my Siddur, and I spent the entire day of Rosh Hashanah lying under the haystacks and praying.

Once, when we were all together, a group of Ukrainian and Polish partisans attacked us and snatched us. They spoke Polish. First they took Zacharechki and beat him terribly. Then they came to us and said, "All of you lie on the floor, one on top of the other, and then we will throw a grenade on you". They indeed had a grenade in their hands. However, it became clear that they were just playing a trick on us. They went out, closed the door, and left without doing anything do us. However, they did beat Zacharachki.

We went out again to the hiding place at night, and remained there until the snow began to fall. When the snow fell, it was difficult for us to walk, since our feet sank. We also felt that Zacharechki's attitude to us was no longer as it was before, and he was already tired of us. I then said in my heart, "Would it be that a miracle would take place for us, we would find a different place, and Zacharechki would not know to where we disappeared". Indeed, the Master of the World helped us.

We thought that the second group was already in America. We were seven souls and they were sixteen people. They were connected to the "Subbotniks"[1] who were in our area. These were not truly Subbotniks, but like Baptists (they had many groups). They did not believe in the Pope like the Catholics, but only in Jesus. When they wanted to worship, they went together to a house of prayer. They did not worship from a prayer book, but rather each one on his own. They regarded the spreading of their faith as their mission. These sixteen Jews were from Zawalow, and were their acquaintances. They established contact with them. The guardian of the forest was also their acquaintance, and he gave them a good place to dig a pit. They entered it and hid, and he gave them food. Thus they had come into this group of Subbotniks. I knew about this already.

When I realized that our situation was hopeless, I told the children who were with us: "Now we have no choice, for we cannot remain here any longer". For example, at night I took a bottle of water from Zacharechki that was supposed to last the entire day. If one child wanted to drink a bit more, the other would shout: "Enough!" He also gave us bread, which we divided up by lottery so that one would not suspect that the other got a larger piece. And in the winter, the water in the bottle froze...

In the group of 16 Jews there were men and women, and only one child. They did not want to take us because of the children. Nevertheless, I went with the woman and children, and we entered some small house in the forest with the risk that if there was a good gentile there, it would be good, but if there was a bad gentile there, we would suffer. He stood at the time next to the well with the cow, and he suddenly heard my footsteps coming. He said, "Yes, I already know who is coming."

[Page 213]

He brought us in and received us pleasantly. His whole house was the size of our kitchen. There was a pricha[2] there, which also served as a kitchen. The light came from a wick stuck into a bottle of oil. However, when we entered there, we felt as if we were entering a palace... The smoke covered me, and I smelled the aroma of the food that was cooking, for he was preparing dinner.

This was a small house in the middle of the forest. Afterward we were told that before the gentile joined this sect, he was one of the dangerous men. He did not have an oven for baking bread, so he baked on the stovetop. He prepared fresh bread, and mushrooms with potatoes, and gave us all of his food. I can still feel the taste of that food he gave us in my mouths today. Simchat Torah fare is no sweeter to my palate than that food.

I no longer remember the name of that man. I still had two dollars. I took them out and wanted to pay him, but he refused and said, "No thank you. You must thank the Master of the World, and I will give thanks to the Master of the World for giving me the opportunity to do this good deed. He gave us some bread for the way, and then we entered. Zacharechki no longer knew about us.

This gentile showed us the way to the guardian of the forest. We went to him. There, there was a trench that was still from the First World War. We entered it, and made ourselves a roof. We remained there for approximately two weeks. After that, we had no other options. I spoke to the guardian of the forest and told him, "If you do not want to take us into this group, I am not responsible if they catch us and I reveal something." I asked him to take only the children, and it is not important what happens to me. I told him that this group entered the forest thanks to the father of these children, for my brother and Silber were the organizers of those who went to the forest, and now we have no other options. If they would not take us in, we had no more to do. None of this helped. However, it is interesting to note that until they took us in, they had made three hiding places that had been revealed... until they took us in. Thus was the story:

They said that there was a hiding place prepared for us, but it was difficult to be all together. They would be in one hiding place, and we would be in a second one. However, this was a trick – this was the hiding place that had been revealed. However, I had no choice and we went there. They told us that they would provide us with food.

We entered the hiding place. A few days passed and they did not come. There were potatoes inside, but there was no water. There was only snow, and we did not know how to make water from the snow, for first one had to melt the snow, and then filter it. We did not know this. We cooked them in this manner, and we were unable to eat them. We fasted for approximately 14 days. I then said to the oldest child, go see where we are. We walked and walked until we reached a path, and we more or less knew where we were.

I wanted to go out the next day, but I had no strength. I went out and fainted. The woman had a black and dirty piece of sugar. She placed it into my mouth and I came to.

Suddenly one day, on a Sunday, two Ukrainians with axes came. We were all afraid of such strong gentiles... However, they said, "Do not be afraid!" It became clear that they had been drafted for work in Germany and they had escaped – at least that is what they told us. They entered out hiding place and asked us, "How do you manage? From what do you live? And if someone attacks you, how do you defend yourselves?" We answered, "Who, the children will defend?" However, I could not speak for I was so weak. They once again said, "Do not be afraid", and they left. I thought that they had already left us. Suddenly – after I had gone back in – they told me: "Go out! The women and the children saw that they were occupied with me, and they fled." I still had an Omega watch. They took my watch, my coat and a few dollars – and left.

I went out the path and the children . I then said that we should flee, and we fled. What strength did the Holy One Blessed Be He give me, for after a fast of 14 days, I ran approximately 5 kilometers. The woman and the young children fled leftward, and I and the oldest child fled straight, not knowing to where. We wanted to reach the guardian of the forest. I thought that I had already freed myself from the two Ukrainians. Suddenly they ran after us, and saw that the child still had boots. First they said, "Why did you flee? Come, the Germans are waiting there..." The child started to cry and I said to him, "What do you want from me?" They took the boots. Suddenly we felt that a wagon was approaching. They beat me and said, "Go to hell".

We did not know the way, and did not know where we were. We ran and ran until we reached the house of the guardian of the forest, without knowing the way, this was providence... The children and the woman saw some house in the field and entered the barn. They entered a stall that also belonged to a Subbotnik. Had they entered another place, they would have fallen into the hands of a Ukrainian who murdered Jews. We entered to the guardian of the forest and waited until night.

They guardian of the forest had a daughter who was as righteous as a rebbetzin. She saw the child and me, the child without boots, etc., and began to weep. She immediately took a dish of cold water and put his feet into the water, and gave him and old sweater. She made us food and said, "Do not leave here now until the group will take you".

In the meantime, they put us in the barn. It was cold there, and we thought hat we would freeze. On the second night, the Pole brought the woman and children, and we were together again. This was in the winter, December 1943.

Later, the guardian of the forest went to the group and told them, "Now there is no choice, you must take them". They came at night to take us. The 12 year old girl who was with us already had no strength to walk, so they carried her with their hands.

[Page 214]

We came there and entered into what looked like a palace. We were 23 people in the hiding place. When we entered there, they no longer recognized us, me certainly not... But there was already sufficient food there.

The guardian of the forest provided us food, but not only him. At all times, a group of the people of this religious sect came and brought us bread and other food. We cooked it there. We remained there until the liberation. This lasted for three months, until March 1944. Members of this sect, as well as the daughter of the guardian of the forest came at all times. We sang together, we prayed together – we were already one group.

Russian partisans came to the hiding place in March 1944. They came to tell us that the Russians had already arrived. We then went out of the hiding place and started to walk. We had no more energy to walk along the route – this was in the month of March – but we reached some village where their army was stationed, and where there was also a kitchen. When they saw us they realized that we were Jews. They took us in and gave us food. From there we to Podhajce.

The few survivors who remained alive gathered in Podhajce. We were 23, and there were others who from among the gentiles. We all went to one room. I went to my neighbor, and he asked, “Who is this Jew?” I looked in the mirror, and I also did not recognize myself.

We remained in Podhajce for a few days, and we heard that the Russians were retreating. It was snowing, and it was difficult to make connections, but we fled along with them. We fled to Skalat and passed Buchach as well. A few hundred people, perhaps a thousand, had remained in Buchach. They did not flee, and they once again fell into the hands of the Germans. We passed through Buchach and reached Skalat.

I was embarrassed to go among people when I arrived in Skalat. I had no button on my clothes anymore. I had some coat that I had received from Zacharechki after they took mine, and I turned it inside out. In Skalat there were storehouses with goods that the Germans had pillaged from the Jews. I went there and looked for something that I could change into, but I did not find anything. Shortly thereafter, I heard that they had liberated Tarnopol. I went to Tarnopol, and there I also went into the storehouse of the Germans. I found some shirts and soap. I also took a backpack. It was hard for me to remain in Tarnopol. I fled from Tarnopol to Mikulinitsy.

In Mikulinitsy I found a family that had survived. I went in to them and said, “Now something must be done...” Among the Russians, there was a Jew who was responsible for the bathhouse. This was an airforce battalion. I went to the bathhouse and cleaned myself thoroughly. I threw out everything that I had, I changed my clothes, and went to the barber to get a haircut.

There was a gentile from Kiev who knew how to speak Yiddish. He asked me, “What do you do, Jew? You need to earn a living; we buy and sell liquor...” I worked there for 3 months, and was already a different person. I had a bit of money. A Jewish doctor who was with the Russians helped me, and gave me some medicine. They gave me some money, and helped me with clothing.

About three months later, after Podhajce was liberated, I there. When we arrived in Podhajce, there were already about 50 people, and we lived in two houses. We had to make arrangements, and I was in charge of food distribution. This was strictly a formality, in order to receive a work permit. However, the official from Chortkov did not want to provide me with such. He said to me, “You cannot be a director here; you must open up your own store.” I told him that I was not able to, but he was stubborn and said that I would open up my store and give him a bribe. I did not open up, and he threatened to send me to Dombas. Suddenly someone from the N.K.V.D. came to take me and send me to Dombas. I said to myself, "I was saved to the Germans, and now he will send me to Dombas?"" I said to the man standing guard that I wanted to go home to get something, and I fled. I had money. I paid some gentile some money for the journey, and I reached Tarnopol. I joined the "escape" group in Krakow. We stole across the borders to Czechoslovakia and Austria. From Austria we went to Italy and from Italy to Cyprus.

I made aliya from Cyprus in the first movement. I have already been working in the post office for 16 years. I got married and have a son. I live in Kiryat Shalom, in Tel Aviv.

My Dear Town

How much did I love you, my dear town!
We lived in you for years, my parents and I;
An extended family, involved in community,
With the tradition of generations, with a Jewish essence.

And you yourself – an enchanting, delightful corner;
From you – the "valley" covered with trees,
All covered with grass and flowers,
Giving their aroma – to restore souls.

At the foot of the mountains – a stream flows,
The moon washes its face in its waters,
It sends storehouses of gold exchange,
The river hides them all in its depths.

However all of this was, and is hidden forever,
There is no forgetting and no forgiveness
For everything that was perpetrated by the impure murderers
To my people of Israel and my dear town.

Klara Reich – Elbaum

[Page 215]

The Story of One Family

by Ada Weiss (nee Gross)

Our family lived in peace and tranquility until the outbreak of the Second World War. My parents were well-to-do who attained an honorable social position due to their hard work. My father managed the bakery he owned with great success. A pleasant atmosphere pervaded in the home, primarily thanks to my father, who was an optimist by nature. He conducted himself throughout his entire life in accordance with the adage of our sages: "Who is wealthy – he who is happy with his lot". My eldest sister was already married. There were three other children at home. As I mentioned, we lived a life of tranquility and comfort until the outbreak of the war.

It is hard to know why our family began to feel the effects of the war immediately after the capture of the government by the Soviet powers. For some reason, my father was entered into the list of Capitalists, and the Soviet authorities confiscated all our property and expelled us from our home. The decree of confiscation did not affect all of the bakeries, even though most of them employed hired workers, as did we. It seems that we were expelled since my father was more successful in his business than others. It is possible that there was also some private accounting of one of the local Communists. In any case it was clear to me that the way this situation was dealt with was completely unjust.

Without having any option, we left our home and went to live in an attic in the home of the Walden family. We moved from a comfortable home to a small, cramped dwelling. Our source of livelihood was lost – we lost everything at one time. We also lived with constant fear that we might be exiled to Siberia. After some time we moved to a more comfortable dwelling in the home of the Friedman family. Thus almost two years passed in fear and distress until the entry of the Germans to the city.

My youngest sister was seriously injured in the only bombardment of Podhajce at the time of the Soviet retreat. She died from her wounds after some time. With the arrival of the Germans, we to our home and lived like all the Jews under the yoke of the Nazi occupation. The first year passed in relative quiet. We sold our clothes in order to sustain ourselves in some manner. We went out to backbreaking labor, and we comforted ourselves that the wave of tribulations would pass without affecting us.

Then came the first aktion. This took place on Yom Kippur. My parents went to worship, but it was my turn to go out to work. Suddenly, the German S.S. men arrived in automobiles and the aktion began. Before the Germans surrounded us, I succeeded in removing the band with the Magen David from my shoulder, and I set out as quickly as possible for home. I was fortunate, for despite the fact that many of the Christian residents of our city recognized me, they let me go. I arrived home, and in the interim my parents and brother also arrived home. We all hid in our house. My parents hid in the cellar next to the bakery, and my brother and I in the attic. The bakery workers knew that we were in the house, but they behaved well toward us. They closed the entrance to the bakery and told the Germans that only the employees were in the bakery, and that nobody else was there. Throughout the entire day, we heard from our hiding place the screams and weeping of the Jews who were captured by the Germans. Thus passed the aktion, and we were saved by chance and by a miracle.

After the aktion, my father insisted that our family not remain together, for if we separated, there were greater possibilities to be saved. My brother-in-law Leib Kressel had good connections with the farmers of the region, for he was a wheat merchant and lived among the farmers in Stara Miasto. He arranged a hiding place for my parents with the Babiarchok family in the village of Holendri. Our family found a place with a Ukrainian family in the village of Mozilov. My brother set out with Klar (Kral?) to work in Germany as a Pole, and I also found a place to work as a Pole.

We began to liquidate the household and prepare for our departure – to our respective hiding places or workplaces. My brother and I succeeded in obtaining forged birth certificates and identity cards as Poles.

My brother set out with Kral(Klar?), but he after a few days. He felt that it was better to live in the ghetto and be in danger only during the times of the aktions, than to live as a Pole which would imply constant danger. That very day we debated the accuracy of that claim.

My brother on a Friday morning, and the second aktion took place on Friday night. When I found out that the aktion had begun, my mother hid with our neighbor in the bunker of the Shulman family. However my father, brother and I went up to the attic, for we had our hiding place there. This time, apparently the employees of the bakery hinted to the Germans that we were hiding in the house. The Germans came with Tovia Breines. They broke down the wooden partitions and took us out of the hiding place. During the incident, my brother jumped from the roof. He broke his leg and one of the Germans shot him. The next day, when my mother left her hiding place, she immediately stumbled over his body. My father and I were taken from the attic, and we began to flee. The German raised his gun, but to our fortune, he had no bullets. When he captured us, he beat us soundly and dragged us to the concentration area in the Stara Targovicza.

From there we succeeded to escape once again (to that end, I bribed a Ukrainian guard with a diamond ring) and we hid in a cellar in one of the nearby buildings, under a pile of coal. However, at nightfall before all the people had been cleared from the area of concentration, a German entered the cellar and removed those who had hidden there.

Until the end of my days, I will not forget the gloomy march to the train station. The Jews walked in the middle of the road, men, women and children, all of them tired and broken (after having remained for almost the entire day in the concentration area). The Christian residents of Podhajce stood on both sides of the road and stared at us. At the train station, the loading of the people – men and women separately – began. My father wanted me to enter the men's car as well. He believed that he would succeed in saving himself, and that he would also save me. I refused to enter the men's car, lest they discover me and beat me or kill me. We separated, and I entered the car filled with women and children. These were cars for the transport of cattle, with two small windows on the top. It is hard to describe what took place in this car. We all stood cramped together, for there was no room to sit. The air was dense and foul smelling. The children wept and wailed.

[Page 216]

The train began to move after some time. We slowly became accustomed to the dark, and then I realized that the windows were closed with wooden boards and wire. The planks were tied from the outside on one window, and from the inside on the other. We tried to remove the boards from the inside, and with their help, we broke the boards on the outside, and tore the wire. Thus was the route for jumping from the car opened.

Mrs. Heller, a teacher in the high school, was among the women, and she suggested that I be the first to jump from the car. I hesitated to jump, for I was very afraid. I suspected that I might jump as the train was crossing the bridge in Bozhikov-Litvinov, where jumping would be a certain death. The train continued to hurry along its way. It arrived in Potutori and stopped there. Fear overtook me when the train stopped. I was very hungry, and felt a general weakness, for no food passed through my lips all day. Suddenly, I decided to jump from the train. I knew that if I would continue to travel in the train, I would arrive at the Belzec death camp and go up in smoke, and if I would jump, I would have a chance of surviving. While the train was still stopped I went to the window and jumped out. Tzipka Noss, the daughter of the shochet, followed me. We rolled to the side of the train track and started to run. The Germans shot at us, but in the interim, the train began to move and they did not touch us. We intended to run in the direction of Podhajce and to the city, but as we later discovered, we ran in the opposite direction. In the darkness of the night, we entered the house of the guardian of the forest. We told him that we were Poles, and we had traveled to Lvov with merchandise, but the Germans took all of the merchandise from us since it was forbidden to do business in agricultural products, so we fled in order to save ourselves from arrest. I do not know if the guard believed our story – he was "convinced" only when Tzipka removed her wristwatch and gave it to him. In for the watch he allowed us to remain with him until the morning. He woke us up early in the morning and sent us along our way. This was also a Sunday. We went on foot. We passed many villages in which the residents looked at us suspiciously, but they did not turn us in.

We to Podhajce in the evening. There I found out that my father had also jumped from the train and was saved. My mother had succeeded in burying my dead brother in the interim. The next day I went to my "workplace" which was also my hiding place. A short time later, my father and sister also left the ghetto.

My parents remained in the home of the Babiarchok family in the village of Holendri for 14 months. This was a proper family. They received all of the movable property of my parents, and they were promised that they would receive my father's fields after the war. The head of the household was a good and wise man, but his wife was a bad woman as well as a miser. She treated my parents like dogs. Their hiding place was in the attic above the barn. In the summer it was very hot and in the winter it was very cold. The food was bad and scanty. The potatoes that were served were for the most part hard and cold, and even water was given in an insufficient measure. My father had always liked to drink a lot, and when they came to the barn to give the animals to drink, he asked that they also give him water. However, they would first give the animals to drink, and if there was any water left in the bucket, they would give some to my father.

The relationship between them continued to deteriorate, primarily because this situation lasted longer than they had thought from the outset. Furthermore, the Germans became stricter with their punishments for hiding Jews. This situation continued until March 1944, when the Soviet army arrived in Tarnopol and remained for a day in Podhajce as well. When the Soviet army arrived, my parents decided to leave their hiding place the next morning, but in the meantime the Soviet army retreated, and they were forced to remain in their hiding place for an additional three months, until the final liberation in the summer of 1944.

The relationship between my parents and the family that hid them is very good to this day. My parents continue to send money and valuable packages to them – for after all, they endangered their lives in order to save the lives of my parents.

*

My married sister, her son, her sister-in-law and her husband Abba Rubinsztok and their son found a hiding place with a Ukrainian family in the village of Mozhilov. My brother-in-law Leib Kressel also joined them when he escaped from the work camp in Tarnopol.

This Ukrainian family belonged to the Bendera (Benderovches) organization. They regretted that they had granted refuge to Jews, and they began to pressure the two families and demand that they leave their hiding place. On account of the pressure, the two men, my brother-in-law Leib Kressel and his brother-in-law Abba Rubinsztok left the village of Mozhilov in order to find a different hiding place.

[Page 217]

They were caught by their neighbors in Holendri and murdered. This took place close to the house in which my parents were hidden, and my mother mentioned that she heard the shots and felt that someone from the family was killed.

After the murder of the two men, the Ukrainians let the women and children remain in their hiding place. They remained in the bunker under very difficult conditions, suffering from hunger and thirst. My sister became very ill as a result of remaining in the bunker, and to this day, her legs hurt her as a result of this illness.

In March 1944, when the Soviet army arrived in Podhajce for one day, the two women and their children succeeded in escaping to Skalat. They all fled barefoot, with their feet covered in fags. Only after the liberation of Podhajce in June 1944 did they to their city.

*

The work place that my brother-in-law Leib Kressel found for me was with the Czewa family. Mr. Czewa was of German origin, from the village of Bekersdorf. At the outbreak of the war, he worked as the secretary of the city hall in Staro Miasto, from where he knew my brother-in-law. During the period of the German occupation, Czewa was appointed as director and supervisor of several farms in the region of Berezany. He was an educated and cultured man, and he related to me well during the entire time that I was in his house.

His wife was also a good woman who deported herself with simplicity. To this day, it is hard for me to understand what moved them to employ me in their house and thereby endanger their lives. It is possible that they wished to prepare an alibi for themselves in the event of the change of regime. After his appointment as the director of five farms, the family moved to the region of his new work. This family had four children, and I moved along with them as a house maid and nanny to the children.

We lived on a large farm in the village of Hinowicza near Berezany. I indeed worked hard, but in I had good conditions: a clean bed, plentiful food, and freedom of movement. These were conditions that of which a Jewess could not dream of during the era of Nazi rule. At first, they were suspicions about my origins, but I told everyone that the Soviets had exiled my parents to Siberia and I remained alone. I was very afraid lest my origins be revealed, even though externally I did not look Jewish and my Polish accent was flawless. Nevertheless, I imagined every night that the Germans were liable to find me out and murder me.

Once, a strange and dangerous event took place to me During the time of the second aktion, when they placed us in the train cars, a sum of money was given to one of the Germans who promised to not lock the door of the car in for this. Needless to say, the German did not fulfil his promise. A long time after we arrived in Hinowicza, Mrs. Czewa sent me to serve tea to the German officer who had come to visit the farm. I entered the office with the tea, and to my surprise I saw before me the German who had been bribed in the Podhajce train station. I was frightened and my knees knocked, but I immediately overcame my fear. I thought in my heart: there were so many people there, and it is impossible that the German would remember me and recognize me.

We arrived in Hinowicza at the end of 1942, and remained there for an entire year. At that time, the Benderovches began to attack the farms, set them on fire, and kill the German supervisors. There, I was restricted in my movements, and I attempted to refrain from going out on the street, since the place was close to Podhajce, and someone was liable to recognize me. As the front approached to Berezany and the Germans retreated, Mr. Czewa, his wife, and two of his children fled to Lvov. Mrs. Czewa's sister and the two other children remained with me in Berezany in order to guard the family property. We all remained there until the Soviet army arrived in the summer of 1944.

Immediately after the liberation, Mrs. Czewa's sister traveled to Podhajce in order to find out if any of my family had survived. She immediately with the happy news that my parents had survived and are in Podhajce, and my sister and her son are in Skalat.

Of course I immediately hurried home on foot. The appearance of the city frightened me. Wherever one turned there was destruction and ruins. The stores in the market square were in ruins, and nobody was on the streets. Thus did I arrive on the street where our house stood. From afar I saw a barefoot woman wearing a winter robe (it was the middle of the summer), with a red tie serving as a belt. I thought to myself, “Who is this strange creature!” As I approached her, I realized that it was my mother. She was bloated, and she had a frightful appearance with this “splendid” garb. “Mother, mother!”, I shouted at her, and I did not believe that my mother looked like that.

My father sat on the steps of the house. He was also barefoot, of course, and wearing tattered pants. The joy of this reunion cannot be described. I remained at home for only one day, for I had obligations to the Czewa family. I remained with their children for two more months, until I succeeded in selling some of the property, and transferred what was not sold to Lvov. In the autumn of 1944, after I brought the Czewa children and the rest of their property to Lvov, I home. We remained in Podhajce until the end of the war, and immediately thereafter, in May 1945, we arrived in the Silesia region of Poland.

We lived in the city of Walbrzych in Silesia. There my widowed sister got married, and I also found my match. My parents made aliya to the Land in 1949, and my sister in 1950. My family and I made aliya only in 1956. My husband worked as a chief engineer in a large factory, and the Polish government was not anxious to authorize the departure of people with academic skills.

[Page 218]

From Podhajce to Soviet Russia

by Yosef Kressel

(A section of testimony from Yad Vashem)

... In September 1939, the Soviet armies entered Podhajce. The life of our family did not undergo any serious changes with regard to this. My father continued to manage his tailoring workshop, and I continued to attend the public school. Of course, with the arrival of the Soviet army, organized activities of the Zionist youth, to which I belonged, ceased.

Podhajce was a typical Jewish town in Eastern Galicia until the outbreak of the Second World War. The population of the town included 7,000 Jews, 2,000 Ukrainians and 1,000 Poles. The vast majority of the Jewish population was poor. The youth had no good prospects for the future, despite the fact that the desire of the youth was for education and knowledge even with the difficult conditions, and they streamed in their masses to technical schools and even to universities. At the conclusion of their studies, they joined the ranks of the unemployed holders of academic degrees. The only factories in the city were a factory for wood and a flourmill. The Jews worked in commerce and services. There were several Ukrainian villages and one Polish village surrounding the town.

The Ukrainian population was extreme nationalists. Prior to the war, the Ukrainians in the region of Podhajce and its environs commenced serious activity toward the aim of self-determination. As a result of this, several “pacifications” were conducted by the Polish authorities: that is, activities to promote peace and order by means of punishments and judgements – after which the Ukrainians would live in quiet.

After these regions were annexed to the Soviet Union, the Ukrainians raised their heads. The Hitlerist agents were particularly active in their regions, and the Russians revealed that Hitler's men had a particularly great influence in these regions.

Immediately after September, 1939, the Ukrainian nationalists began widespread terrorist activity, and the representatives of the Soviet government fell victim to their attacks. As a result of the counter-activity from the government, there were many expulsions of participants in these activities and Germans to remote regions of the Soviet Union.

With this situation, the war of Nazi Germany against the Soviet Union broke out on June 22, 1941. The Germans bombarded Podhajce on the first day of the war. My father was injured on his head by a piece of shrapnel from a bomb.

Even though Podhajce was located near the border, the invading Germans refrained from conquering all of the areas immediately. They conquered our city only after two weeks. In the meantime, the Russians succeeded in evacuating their families. They told the local population not to leave, so that Podhajce would not fall to the enemy. Indeed, one morning, we realized the true situation as we saw that the Soviet authorities had retreated completely from the city. In this situation, it was impossible to postpone the escape. The route to Monasterzyska was almost completely open, but there was nobody with whom to travel.

Father, Mother and two of their children succeeded in finding a place in a wagon. In the meantime, my brother and I went to search for and purchase bread. However, when we , we no longer found the wagon. I was separated from my brother during the confusion that ensued in the city. He had set out eastward, whereas I had prepared to set out with an organized group of approximately 20 youths. We succeeded in finding our way and crossing the old border with Russia. We reached the city of Zhitomir on foot. The group broke up in this city during the bombardment, and I remained alone.

I immediately presented myself to the Voynkomet and requested to be enlisted as a volunteer to the army. I was not yet 17 years old, and aside from this, I was short. The army did not want to accept me, but they turned me over to a work brigade that was sent to Melitopol. We worked there in digging ditches to protect the approach to Kachovka. Throughout the time of my work, I attempted to convince them to send me to the battlefront, but without success. Instead of this, they placed me among the guards of the armaments trains. I was slightly wounded along the way. Then, they transferred me to Stalingrad for an investigation. There, they issued a decision without the option of appeal that I was too short and too young for the army. I was fired from my assistance work in the army in November, 1941.

(The chapters that follow in this testimony include details on: a) the journey to the Polish general Anders and the kolkhoz; b) the strike of the Jews in the kolkhoz; c) meeting my brother; d) "The organization of the Jewish brigade"; e) protecting the important strategic position; f) being wounded for the second time and the hospital; g) organizational work and being turned over for judgement.)

Translator's Footnotes

1. Subbotniks refers to Sabbatarians, and would be akin to Seventh Day Adventists – although that is not how they are known in Polish.
2. I do not know to what this is referring.

[Page 219]

The Campaign of Annihilation and Destruction in Podhajce

by Shoshana Haber

I was an alumna of the Hashomer Hatzair chapter in our city. I studied sewing, and I was 16 years old when the Nazi persecution of the Jews began. As a seamstress, I received a special permit from the Germans as a "useful Jew", like other Jewish tradesmen who worked for the Germans. The workplace was located outside the ghetto and called the "work camp". People were transferred there in the company of a German guard.

At first, the work camp was located in the large house of the Bursztyner Rebbe. However, after some time, a "selection" was conducted, for it became clear that among the workers with "certificates of importance" there were also people without specific trades. The camp shrunk and was transferred to Dr. Heller's house on Pilsudski Street (formerly "The Street of the Vehicle"). Later, further aktions and selections took place. Once again the camp was shrunk and was transferred to the home of the Weinless family in the center of the city, which was well fenced in. The camp remained there until its liquidation, after the time when the Nazis had declared the city as Judenrein. We went to work with a Magen David badge on our sleeves. Girls were forced to cut their hair. I had long, beautiful plaits of hair, and I did not cut them off, but rather covered them with a kerchief. This enabled me to leave the ghetto on numerous occasions without the Magen David badge in order to obtain food during the times of great hunger in the ghetto, or a bit of milk for the children during the plagues of typhus and illnesses that plagued the ghetto.

At times I fled from the ghetto with my long hair, when news arrived from neighboring towns about an impending aktion. I hid with Christians whom I knew from before the war. My father worked for many years as an expert and supervisor in the forests of the region, and he often had helped those people with whom I found refuge. I often gave over to these "good" people the rest of my money or other possessions that I still had from home in for the hiding place, or I had to sew something for them or weave a sheet. After I finished my work they hastened to send me out, without concern for the danger that lurked around.

I remember that once during the large aktion that took place slightly before the "cleansing of the city from Jews", the Gestapo men entered the work camp in the Weinless house and shot them all next to their work machines. I lay on the floor as a corpse. Since I had a wound from before, the murderers thought that I had already received a bullet, and apparently did not want to waste another bullet on a Jewess. Thus I was saved by a veritable miracle.

My father was murdered already at the beginning of the occupation in 1941, before the ghetto was established. The Germans searched the Jewish houses to take people to work camps outside of Podhajce, and my father, who was already quite old (older than sixty) and sickly, lay in a bed, and was not able to rise from it. The Germans shot him in bed and killed him. Numerous similar deeds of murder were perpetrated that day. A fenced in ghetto was established a short time later, on two side streets that join the main street, all of whose houses belonged to Jews.

For all the days of my life, I will never forget the frightful scene at the time of the transfer of the residents from their houses to the cramped ghetto. Everyone, including the elderly, women and children, took all kinds of belongings in their hands, on their backs and on their heads. The Germans and their Ukrainian assistants stood at the side and laughed. A number of those being transferred received death blows because they lagged behind in the transfer of their property. The local Christian population and farmers from nearby villages gathered to purchase goods or to pilfer without payment. The worst part was at the end of the transfer, at nightfall, when the Germans realized that there were too many Jews, and the place was not large enough for them on the two streets that were designated for the ghetto. (This was due to the fact there were Jews from outside of Podhajce in the city, who came there from the neighboring towns and villages. Even before the command of the Germans, Jews had already gathered in the city to find refuge from the Ukrainians, who began to murder the Jews already at the beginning of the war). Then they began to shoot at anyone they wanted to as they were entering the ghetto. Several hundred Jews were murdered that day.

My mother was murdered in the large aktion in 1942. Then, the Germans snatched several hundred Jews, brought them to the train station and loaded them on train cars that were practically hermetically sealed, without provision of water and with no place to attend to one's bodily needs, crowded like fish in a pot, without air, and sent them to the furnaces of Belzec. During the journey, some people succeeded in cutting some sort of opening and jumping from the trains, to to the ghetto in Podhajce. The Germans removed my mother along with approximately fifty other people from the bunker that was set up in the Kitner house in the center of the city. That day, several dozen other people were murdered on the spot – the ill, children, or people who attempted to flee. Not all of those who were loaded upon the train reached Belzec. Many suffocated along the way.

Those who were murdered during the aktions lay scattered in the houses or the streets. Only on the second day following the murder were the victims gathered up in their clothes upon wagons and buried together.

I had another brother who was 21 years old. He was taken to the Russian army in 1941, and when they fled eastward, they took him along with other youths of his age. He disappeared in Russia. I approached the Red Cross organization and directly to Moscow many times, however to this day I no nothing about him.

[Page 220]

The first aktion that took place on Yom Kippur (most of the aktions took place on Sabbaths or festivals) left an unforgettable impression upon me. Many Jews were murdered then. The slaughter was perpetrated by the Germans along with their Ukrainian assistants. Most of the Jews had gathered in the Great Synagogue to worship, and they did not succeed in fleeing. I fled along with my mother to the fields outside the city, and thus was I saved during three aktions, almost miraculously. We almost always suspected an impending aktion, whether through rumors that arrived from the surroundings or other definitive signs. However, we did not always believe it. Those who believed it hastened to flee into the fields and forests, or they entered bunkers that had been previously prepared.

I will never forget the final aktion that took place in 1943, the result of which rendered Podhajce Judenrein. The men were murdered on the spot next to three large pits that were dug outside the city in Holendri. Several hundred men were buried in each one. I hid under the roof in an old, abandoned house, and I was again saved by a miracle. Very few Jews remained alive after this aktion: well connected ones or ones that had been gathered from their hiding places. The Germans took them to cover the communal graves with earth. I was among them. This was a difficult and frightful task. As the large graves were being covered, the earth raised itself again and again. An outstretched limb would be raised, a clod of earth was exposed with a stream of blood that began to seethe literally like boiling water – for most of the victims were naked, men, women and children together, and many of them had barely been shot. At times, a stream of blood began to flow from the pit. Surrounding the place of murder were torn money bills that had been ripped to pieces at the last minute so that they would not fall whole into the hands of the murderers.

Two or three days later, the Germans gathered up the survivors, several dozen Jews who remained alive, and transported them under false pretext to a work camp near Tarnopol under heavy guard of Gestapo men and Ukrainians. Along the way, a distance of several kilometers outside the city in the direction of Tarnopol, next to a small village called Zahajce, they shot them all. I was not among this remnant, for I fled with a Jewish friend from Stanislawow to a field, and from there we went to a small village called Rigailicha, where my friend had an acquaintance named Kranciglowa. We remained there until the liberation of the region by the Russian army. I should point out that this farmer and his friends in this village were not Christian Catholics, but rather members of a small sect whose members believed in the New and Old Testaments together. They were called

Subbotniks or Badacze Pisma Swietego (Researchers of the Holy Book). The host farmer advised us often to join their faith. They helped many other Jews as well.

I was freed from the cruel and frightful tribulations in the years 1944-1945, when I found out that very few Jews had survived. I fled from the inimical surroundings, and I made great efforts to burn my bridges behind me, as I fled from the land of darkness and the shadow of death, whose Polish and Ukrainian populations behaved like wild wolves. I went to begin a new life in the State of Israel. I found a fellow native of my city who wished to marry me. I have two successful daughters and my own home. However, my health is frail. The terrible sights that I witnessed do not leave my memory. Everything is etched in my mind as a memorial book, and I often see terrifying visions of murder and death during my sleep. I must use tranquilizers to calm me. I often ask myself from where I drew this great and powerful energy through which I was saved from a cruel death many times? I answered to those who approached me from Yad Vashem, not with great desire, for the task of bringing to the fore these terrifying events that I had endured is very difficult for me. I knew this would cause me again numerous sleepless nights. Only the idea of perpetuating the memory of all of the suffering that was caused to us by the 20th century Amalekites, and to inscribe these memories in the memorial book to our town of Podhajce enchanted me. I thereby fulfil the words of the scriptures, “Remember what Amalek did unto you”.

How I Was Saved

by Shoshana Drori (nee Rotstein)

It was July 1942. Only my brother Pinchas and I remained alive from our entire family. My father of blessed memory was sent to a concentration camp in Kamenetz Podolsk and never from there. My mother of blessed memory and my two sisters Susia and Matti (Matilda) were sent to the Belzec death camp. My brother and I lived in the ghetto with Yisrael Waltoch, who had mercy upon us and took us into his home.

The state of those who survived was desperate. We knew that we stood on the threshold of destruction, and all of us had only one thought, how to save our lives.

Since my friend Buzio Nass worked at that time in the work office of the Germans, I told him my plan: to arrive in Germany in the disguise of a Christian. During that time, the Germans enlisted young Christians and sent them to Germany to work in factories for the war effort. They would enlist volunteers for this, and if there were no volunteers, they would capture young people on the street, in the churches, or in the movie theaters and send them to work even against their will.

Since I did not look Jewish, I asked my friend Buzio Nass to attempt to “capture” me as well and send me to Germany. Buzio discussed this with his supervisor, a Volksdeutsche by origin, who promised to help actualize this plan in for a specific sum of money that would come at the appropriate time.

[Page 221]

Several months passed, and there was no progress in the actualization of this plan. One bright day, my friend Buzio Nass was killed. One of the German directors of the work office shot him for “sport” and killed him. After his death, I saw no chance of actualizing this plan, and I almost despaired of it.

One day, this Volksdeutsche who promised Buzio at that time to assist in my escape happened to pass through the ghetto by chance. I jumped outside and presented myself before him as the girl about whom Buzio had spoken. Out of feelings of friendship for Buzio and anguish about what would happen to me, he agreed to assist me. There, we set the date and time of the actualization of this plan.

Now I had an urgent problem – to find an appropriate friend who would go out with me on the journey, for I did not want to go on such a long and dangerous journey alone. At the time, I thought that I would take Bluma Stein along with me. She was my neighbor and good friend, and also a friend of Buzio Nass. However, in the interim, Bluma Stein had died of typhus, and her entire family of six had also died in various manners. I looked around me, and my eyes fell upon a friend by the name of Rivka Bin, who was appropriate according to my judgement, since she also did not look Jewish.

The designated day arrived, and late in the evening of that day in the winter of 1942, I and my friend Rivka went out secretly from the ghetto. We had only a small bundle in our hands that contained a piece of bread, soap, and a comb. I will never forget the anguish that I caused to my brother when I left him alone in the ghetto forlorn and abandoned, given over to hunger and hard work. "Can you really leave him?", I asked myself. My grandmother Perel "the baker", her daughter Rivcha and her husband Moshe and their three year old child lived nearby. They did not believe at all that I would leave the ghetto, and I myself only barely believed this...

We passed through the gate of the ghetto with the assistance of Melech Kessler, who literally endangered his life on our behalf. As soon as we had left the ghetto, we were captured on the street by a Ukrainian guard who wished to turn us in to the German police. However, his human conscience was aroused, and he gave in to our pleas. He uttered a curse from his mouth and freed us. We went to Davidzinski to sleep that night. According to the plan, the following day he would join us to a work group that was to set out by train to Lvov, and from there to Germany.

The next evening, we walked to the train station accompanied by Davidzinski's twelve-year old son. The journey was difficult. We trudged through deep snow. We were hungry, frozen from the cold, and our hearts were full of fear. To our good fortune, the officials did not stop us at the train station, even though many of them recognized us. To this day, I do not know how this transpired, that they allowed us to travel without disturbing us. The hunger afflicted us greatly. We befriended a Polish girl on the journey who had pity on us and assisted us a little.

The holdover in the central transit camp in Lvov was particularly difficult. Every day, girls who were exposed as Jews were discovered and taken out to be murdered by the Gestapo. The girls from our region suspected us as well. Firstly, we were not dressed like them. We wore coats without fur, and the fur covering was missing from the collar. This fact was enough to arouse suspicion about us, for it was known that the Jews were commanded to give over every piece of fur that they owned to the Germans. In addition, we were full of fear, tension and anxiety, which was undoubtedly recognizable in our eyes and the appearance of our faces.

After remaining for two weeks in the transit camp, we finally left the city of Lvov, which was once an important Jewish center, both from an economic and cultural perspective. Our family had a particular connection with Lvov. My grandfather Yeshayahu had died in Lvov in 1936 after a difficult illness and was buried there. When things were normal, my mother would visit Lvov annually on the yahrzeit.

The trip from Lvov to Germany was long and exhausting. We traveled in closed wagons in the company of girls who were mainly from the lowest social class (the educated and well-off girls found ways to avoid being sent for forced labor). Most of them were properly equipped for a long journey, and we had to invent an appropriate story to explain our situation.

We arrived in Germany on December 22, 1942, two days before Christmas. We were put up in the city of Essen in the Ruhr valley, which was an important manufacturing region. We were employed in an aeronautics factory. Our situation was very difficult there as well. The work was hard, the food was scanty, and we had problems in getting accustomed to the customs of the Christians so as not to arouse suspicion about ourselves. There were also other problems, such as the issue of correspondence with relatives. We constructed a detailed biography about ourselves that answered all questions, but we had to be very careful not to confuse it with contradictions. Even there we heard on occasion stories about Jewesses who were exposed and sent to Auschwitz. These stories filled us with fear and trepidation. Close to our camp there was a camp of Polish prisoners of war, who were occupied in building a bridge over the Ruhr River. The issue of relations with the prisoners was also not easy.

Thus did we live and work until the beginning of 1945. With the approach of the Allied Army, there were ever stronger bombardments. It is easy to understand that we were very happy at the scenes of ruin and destruction that were caused by the bombardments. However, on the other hand, our source of existence was in great danger. The Germans did not permit us to enter the shelters, and we were forced to remain outside, open to the danger of attack. There was also the suspicion that the Germans would liquidate us before their surrender to the Allied Army.

To our good fortune, these suspicions did not come true. In April, 1945, we were liberated by the Allied Army, which conquered all of Germany. I cannot describe the feelings of joy that filled our hearts after so many years of suffering and danger. After a few months, we joined a camp of Jewish refugees, and in 1947, we made aliya as Maapilim (illegal immigrants).

[Page 222]

*

This, in great brevity, is the story of our survival. In this story, of course I skipped over many details that have no place in this memorial book.

Thoughts of a Native of the Land

I was born in the Land eighteen years ago. I only know about the town of Podhajce from the stories of my father, Avraham Yosef Kressel. Nevertheless, the life of the Jews of that city has always interested me. I have often sat and listened with great interest to the stories of my father about life in the city before its destruction, and about the destruction that he saw when he there in 1945, after his liberation from his service in the Soviet Army.

The city was located on a relatively small area, but the scenery of the surrounding area was variegated and wondrously beautiful. The vast majority of the Jewish residents were working people, shopkeepers and craftsmen who earned their livelihoods with difficulty. No small number of them lived in literal poverty, and their prime worry was how to save a few coins to purchase challa and fish for the Sabbath. Nevertheless, most of them were satisfied with their lot, and knew how to enjoy the Sabbath rest and to joyously celebrate the Jewish festivals - each of which had its own character and theme that was forged throughout many generations.

One of the residents of Podhajce who was satisfied with his lot was my father. The entire family lived in a small house that stood at the edge of the city. The parents, children, and even married children with their children lived together. Despite the material poverty, light and warmth pervaded in the house, that shone from the souls of the people who lived therein.

The Second World War, which broke out in 1939, put an end to the tranquil life of Podhajce Jewry. The city was conquered by the Russians, who imposed new regulations which to a large degree shook up the life of the Jews in the city. They drafted many people to the Soviet Army. My father, who was married and the father of a child, was forced to enlist in the army.

This was the summer of 1941. A short time after he was drafted to the Russian Army, Soviet Russia was attacked by the Germans, and the entire region was conquered by the German army. When my father to Podhajce after four years, the city was completely ruined and destroyed. Of its thousands of Jewish residents, only a small handful of several dozen people remained. They were emaciated from hunger, lacking everything, and had almost lost their human form after the trials and tribulations that they had endured. My father was also in a pitiful state, to the point where nobody recognized him when he to Podhajce.

Thus did he stand in the street, alone and forlorn. Then an acquaintance came to greet him, wearing nice clothes and shiny boot, but he also did not recognize him, and continued on his way without stopping.

"Leibish", my father called to the passer-by.

The tall man stopped, looked at my father, but still did not recognize him.

"Who are you?", he asked in Yiddish.

"I am Avraham Yosef", answered my father.

Only then did a smile of joy appear on the man's face. He hastened to bring my father to the nearby house where several Jewish families who had survived the destruction lived. These also could not recognize my father, until Leibish explained to them who the guest was. Only then did their faces brighten, as they expressed their joy that he had survived and remained alive.

My father remained in his destroyed native city for three months. After three months, he cast his final glance at the city in which all of his relatives, friends, and family members had been cruelly murdered. He left it forever, with the hope of arriving in the Land of Israel and beginning a new life in the Land of his fathers.

I certainly know that there are thousands of people in Israel who endured the era of suffering and tribulation during the Second World War, and myriads of boys and girls in the Land were not fortunate to see their parents' parents – grandfather and grandmother – but were only able to hear about their lives in the Diaspora and about their bitter end at the hands of the murderers. I feel that all of these must, as I do, take great interest in the life that was cut off by the cruel hand, and forge the connection between themselves and the natives of this city, so that it can continue to exist for many more years.

Herzliya, January 18, 1967

Rachel the daughter of Avraham Kressel

[Page 223]

Podhajce after its Destruction

by Dr. Baruch Milch

{This article is equivalent with the English article, on page 11 of the English section.}

Dr. Baruch Milch
in the Tluste Ghetto

[Page 224]

JUDE

Eigenhändige Unterschrift
власноручний підпис
własnoręczny podpis

Nr. 1241

Name: Dr. Milch
Прізвище
Nazwisko

Vorname: Boruch
Імя
Imię

geboren am: 20.6.1907
уроджений (а) дня
urodzony (a) dnia

in: Podhajce
в
w

Wohnung: Ort Tłuste
Мешкання: місцевість
Mieszkanie: miejscowość

Strasse:
Вулиця
Ulica

Berufsstellung: Arzt
Становище в званню Лікар
Stanowisko w zawodzie Lekarz

ist Mitglied der GESUNDHEITSKAMMER
є членом Палати Здоровя
jest członkiem Izby Zdrowia

Krakau, den 1.4. 1942

der Leiter
i. V.

(Dr Kroll)

German identity card of the physician Dr. Milch in Tluste, 1942

Legitymacja nr. 47

Ob. Dr. Zielinski

Jan

ur. 20.6.1907 r. Podhajce

zam. Opola, Pl. Czerwonej Armii 5

zatrudniony (a) jest w Panstwowym Urzędzie Repatriacyjnym, Powiatowy Oddział w Opolu

w charakterze Lekarz

Kierownik Refer. Zdrowia

Ważna do 31 grudnia 1945 r.

O 17 listopada 1945

Kierownik Oddziału

własnoreczny podpis

Jprawnia do przejazdów państwowy
irodkami komunikacyjnymi według u
aryfowych dla urzędników państwowy

Polish identity card of Dr. Milch with the false name Jan Zielinski, from 1945

[Page 226]

Podhajce Holocaust survivors next to the communal grave in Stara Miasto

[Page 229]

The Gathering of Podhajce Survivors in Bad-Reichenhall

On May 22, 1947, a gathering of the Jewish survivors of Podhajce took place in Bad-Reichenhall (Bavaria, Germany), with the participation of 79 survivors from Podhajce and the region, who had come from all of the refugee camps in Western Germany.

Mr. Yehuda Weissman, who organized the committee of Podhajce survivors in Bad-Reichenhall and initiated the gathering, opened the meeting and recommended that the following be appointed to the chairmanship: Messrs. Izak Fink, Oskar Eisenberg, Yeshayahu Freidman, Yitzchak Weitreich, Yitzchak Shourz, Nathan Brecher, Moshe Zawalower, Nathan Marmisz, and Marcus Shulman. Similarly, he recommended that Mr. Izak Fink be the honorary president of the gathering, Mrs. Oscan Eisenberg as the chairman, and Mr. Yeshayahu Friedman as the secretary.

His recommendations were accepted with a small amendment: Mr. Yehuda Weissman would join the leadership.

The chairman Mr. Oscar Eisenberg read out the order of the day:

a) The arranging of a memorial ceremony to the martyrs of Podhajce and region, and the display of memorabilia from the era of the Holocaust in the ghetto of Podhajce.
b) Elections to the general committee of Podhajce Natives.
c) A discussion of the behavior of several natives of the city who participated in activities with the Nazi murderers.
d) Debates.
e) Acceptance of resolutions.

Mr. Oscar Eisenberg opened by stating:

“Brothers and sisters! We, Jews of Podhajce, Zlotniki, Wiœniowczyk, Zawalow, Gorzhanka and Tustowawa, have gathered here today to survey and understand who from our city and region has remained alive after the barbaric murderous deeds of the Nazis and their assistants. Similarly, we must establish a memorial day for the martyrs of our city, and recite Kaddish in their memory.”

All of the assembled rose to their feet in memory of the martyrs. Cantor Roner recited “El Moleh Rachamim”, and the elder of the community Mr. Izak Fink recited Kaddish in their memory.

Mr. Yitzchak Shourz received the right to speak, and said:

“Dear brothers! It fell in my lot to be in Podhajce throughout the entire era of the Holocaust, to see the blood of our brethren spilled as water outside the city. I myself suffered no small amount, and it was a great merit for me that I survived and stand among you today.” As he surveyed the events, Mr. Shourz reminisced that the majority of the Ukrainian population participated in the murder of the Jews of Podhajce with their full heart and soul. He concluded with the call, “Jews! Do not forget this! We must pursue these war criminals and take revenge about them!" (By bringing them to judgement before the authorized institutions.)

Mr. Yehuda Weissman took the right to speak and said:

"Dear brothers and sisters! Four years ago at this time, our city passed through its final death throes. The last Jews, who survived the aktions and slaughters, walked broken and crushed along their final path. With false promises and deceit, as was their way at all times, the Nazis gathered the last Jews, pretending to transfer them to the ghetto of Tarnopol. However, the "transfer" concluded very quickly, not far from the city in Zahajce. Thus were all of our dear ones gathered up within the brief period of two years, approximately 5,000 residents of Podhajce and environs."

Mr. Weissman showed the gathering the form of a monument upon which was written: "Remember what Amalek did unto you! Let the nation of Israel remember the 6,000,000 martyrs who were murdered and burned in sanctification of the Divine name and the nation. Avenge the spilled blood of your brethren!" He continued on saying, "Dear brothers and sisters! At the top of the slope, we are standing today before the communal monument for 6,000,000 of our brethren. We recall the tribulations and hellish suffering that were the lot of our unfortunate brethren. We cannot forget the war criminals who murdered our dear ones in cold blood."

Aharon Shourz (from Zlotniki) stressed in his words that the place for the survivors is in the Land of Israel. "We must not continue to be a nation scattered in all corners of the earth! We must remain together and build our home, our Land! I express the wish that next year, we will be able to arrange our memorial in our Land, in the Land of Israel."

In his words, Mr. Moshe Zawalower discussed the terrible tragedy of the Holocaust that has no equal in the annals of world history. He recalled the fact that Jewish blood was not only spilled in ghettoes, but also on all the fronts. Thereby, they gave their part in the attainment of victory over the fascist murderers.

The chairman moved over to the second section of the program: the selection of a general committee for the survivors of Podhajce. After a brief debate, seven members were chosen for the committee: Yeshayahu Friedman, Yehuda Weissman, Oskar Eisenberg, Yitzchak Shourz, Yaakov Gross, Motia Shulman, and Moshe Zawalower.

The chairman opened up the discussion of the third section of the program: the behavior of the members of the Jewish militia during the Holocaust era.

The members Yitzchak Shourz, Getzel Blecher, Yerucham Shulman, Leib Frankel, Sala Sperber, Yitzchak Frankel, Yosef Pistreich, and Zigo Lateiner pointed out that a few of the members of the Jewish militia (who survived) were saved by performing their task in a malicious manner, and they caused great troubles to Jews. During one of the aktions, Riva Har also exposed a bunker where approximately 50 Jews were hidden. However, one can assume that she did this out of fear lest she be taken to be killed if she tried to mislead the Germans.

[Page 230]

We moved over to the acceptance of resolutions, and the following resolutions were accepted.

a) The 3rd of Sivan will be the memorial day for the martyrs of Podhajce and the

region.
b) The members Yitzchak Shourz, Getzel Blecher, Leib Frankel, Yerucham Shulman, and Yosel Pistreich were requested to compose a description of life in Podhajce during the time of the war, and of the murder aktions that were perpetrated in the Podhajce ghetto during the German occupation. This composition will be sent to the committee for assistance of the Podhajce Natives in the United States, and the Podhajce natives of Israel.

c) Those gathered expressed their heartfelt thanks to the members Yehuda Weissman, Yeshayahu Friedman, Shimon Fink and Yaakov Gross, who were the forces behind the memorial gathering.

d) The committee that was chosen at this meeting was asked to turn to the assistance committee of Podhajce natives in the United States with the request of material help for the needy among the refugees of Podhajce.

e) Those gathered decided that some of the members of the "Ordenungs-Dienst" who survived carried out their tasks with maliciousness during the period of Nazi occupation.

f) The committee must pursue with great persistence several Ukrainian war criminals who are walking around free in Germany, and ensure that they are brought to judgement before the appropriate authorities.

g) Yeshayahu Friedman was asked to produce the minutes of the gathering and send copies of it to the assistance committee in the United States, the Podhajce natives in the Land of Israel, and all members of the committee who were chosen at that gathering.

The aforementioned minutes were signed by Izak Fink, honorary chairman; Oskar Eisenberg, chairman; and Yeshayahu Friedman, secretary.

The gathering of the Holocaust survivors of Podhajce Jewry in Bad Reichhall

[Page 231]

The Annihilation[1]

A Letter from Hell

by Yehoshua Weiss

Footnote at the bottom of the page:

> This letter was written by Yehoshua the son of Berl Weiss shortly after the first aktion. He signed it with the pseudonym Bin-Nun[2] and sent it to his brother Professor Avraham Weiss in New York. After the war, Professor Weiss gave it to the Yad Vashem Archives in Jerusalem.

First Intermediate day of Sukkot, September 28, 1942

From the great misfortune on Yom Kippur until now, I have not been able to collect my thoughts. I should realize in what type of a situation we find ourselves. I cannot now comprehend the tragedy of the recent events, but I can only see now the 1,100-1,200 victims of Yom Kippur, which includes my own two victims, namely our parents, Father and Mother. G-d's wrath has not yet completely quieted, and dark clouds float farther. As recollections flash by, I will express my bitter heart and my feelings on paper. Maybe I can describe this in words for my readers.

The clouds of a pogrom had been fluttering over our skies for several weeks already, with everybody worried about not being able to find a place to hide where they might be able to be saved. I myself was also worried about this. At that time, Father was overtaken with toil and fear of death. Mother intended to remain in the house, for she had enough of suffocating in the hiding place every time. I also realized that we would be separated, for one cannot know if it would be good and if there would be enough time for me to come. I had indeed surmised the situation correctly, for things indeed happened that way. A few days later, on Yom Kippur, they took us away. Two days later, every area was closed off. Father also did not want to go to the hiding place anymore. His state of health had declined and he had become completely bedridden to the point where he could no longer leave his bed. The eve of Yom Kippur arrived. It was completely calm. I was with him one time. That last time, I told him that he must not fast even for a brief time[3]. On the Monday of Yom Kippur, at 7:00 a.m., they came. I was still in bed. We remained in hiding that night for a long time, and we went to sleep when the day began. It was said that the city was surrounded and the pogrom was raging. I only had a few seconds to go into the hiding place, and I could no longer think about my parents. If I were to have resisted, I would have certainly fallen and lost the chance to get to the hiding place, I reckoned. My discussions with my parents had been proven correct by the statements of the co-residents. The co-residents further said that they went to him in bed – and suddenly wild shouts were heard from the (one word is not legible) murderers. I jumped up and took a look from the window, and they already saw how they were taking out the victims. During the same glance, they entered to my parents, who were already worshipping, for it was indeed a holy day. My mother and the other residents quickly entered the hiding place. Mother then went up to the roof. Suddenly, to her great misfortune, she decided to inside. Immediately thereafter the murderers went inside and shot Father while he was in bed, enwrapped in his tallis. His soul departed with "echad"[4]. Mother also prepared to become a victim. The other residents remained in the hiding place for two days and two nights, and were saved. I was also in the hiding place for two days, under the fear of death. Only on the second day in the afternoon I unexpectedly encountered the many unfortunate victims, among whom was also my mother.

At the same time I was informed that the Judenrat, whom this time did not let people know, had gathered together the martyrs and was preparing to bury them in a mass grave. My holy father was among them.

[Page 232]

After our fright, I ran to the cemetery and searched for the holy martyr. I removed him with my own hands from among the corpses which had already begun to decompose. I helped the uncircumcised one to dig the grave. Then I went into the grave, and with my own hands I laid the martyr to his eternal rest, and covered it over. The uncircumcised one did not move a finger. He would not show me anything, so I bid farewell to the martyr for the last time. Kaddish was not recited for there were only two Judenrat members present. There were only 9 people at mincha, so I included my almost 9 year old son and recited the first Kaddish. I did not know how much longer this could last, so I finished up with my holy father[5]. Things were much worse with my mother.

When my holy father gave up his holy soul, my mother was immediately led to the gathering place, where she languished with everyone outside for the entire day. Their dark fate was known. They were led on foot to the train station like sheep. The elderly, children, and ill people were sent by bus to Belzec. They had a premonition that this was to be their death journey to martyrdom. As one says, they had something up their sleeves. As I was told, the victims were ill treated, beaten badly, and treated like material. Approximately 1% succeeded in escaping, some of whom did not make it. You can imagine my feelings when I found out that somebody saw our mother, when she had the merit of having a place and location to end her life[6]. There were more difficult situations, where parents lost all of their grown up children, and were completely bereft of their children, but they continued to live on...

My voice also became hoarse. But one sickness does not heal the other one. The survivors were put to work for as long as the terrible situation and oppression will last. We were locked up, there was terrible hunger, there was a lack of means of living (one word is illegible) and so on. The youth collected the few things that were left over from the Jews. The threat of death overwhelmed every section of the imagination. This added to our insecure life. As well, I must say a few words about the Judenrat. The Judenrat was an institution that had a bloodthirsty spirit for Jewish blood. It went way beyond the bounds. It was responsible for many victims, not only on Yom Kippur, but indeed throughout the entire time. It has Jewish tears and indescribable agony on its conscience. For anyone that survived, the Judenrat is a cause of "weeping for generations", a terrible word that cannot be described in any human language. When one says "a member of the Judenrat", one understands this to mean Jewish robbers and Jewish tormentors. When one would hear about a Jewish institution or a Jewish home with Jewish leadership – one should flee to the wilderness of the "Sahara", where one would not encounter a single living soul. People understand this to be the worst thing in the world, living with wild beasts from the wilderness. I could portray this in much darker terms, but unfortunately, I do not have the power of words to express it.

I have not only described this particular Judenrat, as far as I hear. Good things do not come to my ears, for word travels from ear to ear. The Judenrat does indeed move around in this region.

With this very short portrayal, I have described only "a drop from the sea of tears". After this all ends, then all the accusations will come out in detail. I am not a professional writer, and do not possess literary talents. Second, human life is too short to describe on paper all the events in general, and the Judenrat in particular. Perhaps G-d will help me and I will be able to give it over orally. Amen.

Bin-Nun

Translator's Footnotes

1. This article is written in very atypical Yiddish, and many words and phrases were hard to identify. Furthermore, it was obviously written under a great deal of stress. Parts of my translation may not be accurate, but I hope that I was able to portray the ideas appropriately.
2. Bin-Nun is a reference to Joshua (Yehoshua) the son of Nun, of the Bible.
3. On Yom Kippur, a critically ill person is not supposed to fast.
4. Echad is the last word of the first line of Shema – so this reference means that he died as he recited the Shema.
5. I believe that this means that he found it impossible to continue to recite Kaddish.
6. A difficult phrase, but I believe this means that she ended her life among her own people and surrounded by people she knew.

[Page 233]

Four Years of War and Destruction

by Genia Shourz

The Germans came to us in 1941. I was 9 years old when I began to experience the terrible times. During the first days after their arrival, the Germans did not behave so badly. The Ukrainians organized a Ukrainian police force and began their mistreatment of the Jews. They dragged children in chains to the harshest labor. They beat, murdered and mocked. However, this did not last long, and the Germans took control after a week.

It is impossible to write how we suffered. I remember one day when I went with my brother, and they took him away from me. I did not know where they took him. I shouted after him that he should run flee. He listened to me and escaped. They shot after him. He hid in a barn. They asked me in which direction he ran, and I pointed them in a different direction. They saw that I tricked them and one of them beat me over the face with a whip to the point where I started to bleed. I remember how the blood sprayed from my face onto the wall. However, this still was not the worst. After two weeks of hard labor and great fear, the Germans decided that this was too difficult for them, so they approached the Jews with a project – that they should set up a Jewish police force that will carry out all of their orders. Shortly thereafter, a Jewish police force was founded that carried out every order that was issued by the Gestapo. In the Gestapo promised them that they would remain alive and nothing would happen to them. This was even worse – to be captured for hard labor in the camps by our own brethren.

This lasted for an entire year. Then an order came that the Jews from the entire city must gather in one street that would be designated as a ghetto.

It was very crowded there, with ten people living in one room. A typhus epidemic broke out, from which many people died. The Germans would come to search the ghetto, and they would shoot in bed anyone who was ill. I was very afraid, for there were many sick people among us, including my mother and father. I saw that my mother was languishing from hunger, so I jumped out of the ghetto in order to purchase some food. I purchased a loaf of bread, but on the way back my former schoolmates saw me and beat me until I bled. I did not let the bread go from my hands, for I knew that I could save my mother with it. I arrived home bloodied and caused my mother's heart to palpitate.

I forgot to write that when the ghetto was created, our house was included in the ghetto. We owned a mill, and my father made a plan to build a bunker in the mill. After two weeks of hard labor from all of the 50 people who lived with us, the bunker was ready. The bunker constantly saved the men from the conscriptions to the camps. Our bunker was not only the best in the city, but also the best in the entire region of the city. Once more that one night, the Germans dug through the entire house. They were anxious to find the bunker but they did not succeed. Our Jewish police also did not succeed in finding it, even though they made every attempt, to the point of life and death, to find it. They said that they would not send the men to the camps if someone would show them where the bunker was located. However, we did not tell, for we knew that what they said was a lie. Thus did it go until Yom Kippur. People worshipped at our house. I went out onto the street and waited for my friend who was supposed to come to me. I already saw her from afar, but she quickly began to flee to her home. I looked around and saw that she had fallen down as she had been shot. At the same time, I heard cries of mothers who were searching for their children. I ran home and told everyone to go hide in the bunker. They immediately stopped the services and entered the bunker. We heard shouts and automobiles traveling around for the entire night and throughout the day. We went out onto the street in the morning and saw that blood was flowing throughout the ghetto. 600 Jews had been transported to Belzec. This was the first pogrom in the city.

[Page 234]

From that day and onward, we stood on guard day and night. One night, I was standing with a girl on the attic. Suddenly, we saw that the entire ghetto was lit up with reflectors. We realized that this was a pogrom. We quickly woke up everybody from bed, and everyone fled in their shirts. My grandfather, who could no longer look at this, told me: "I do not want to go into the bunker. I do not wish to live anymore." I begged him to come, but then the Germans began to knock on the door, and I fled while he remained. One child suffocated on my knees, for he was crying and someone placed a rag in his mouth. The aktion ended after 24 hours, and then I first realized that the child was dead. I became crazy from fright, for I also wept about this.

During the second aktion, 2,000 Jews were shot in one pit behind the city. The third aktion came after some time. We once again remained all together. When we came out after the third aktion, everything was completely different than after the previous actions. The ghetto was surrounded by Kubans – who were Russian captives who helped the Germans murder the Jews. An order was quickly issued that within 24 hours, a Jew must not be found in the ghetto. Where should we go? They said that if we do not go somewhere within 24 hours, any Jew who would be found in the ghetto would be shot. We realized that they wanted to shoot us all. 600 Jews remained in the ghetto, and all fled like wild men, for everyone had seen death before his eyes. We counted the hours, how long remained for us until death. We tried to bribe the guards, but it was not possible. We saw that they were preparing knives with which to slaughter us. We saw that there was nothing else to do other than await death. This was the most terrible moment in life, to await death. People went crazy. My friends ran about wildly in the streets. Blood flowed. People poisoned themselves, and whoever did not have any poison felt unfortunate. Very few people remained. Everyone poisoned themselves, killed themselves or stabbed themselves. We had no poison with which to poison ourselves. We bid farewell to each other and wept because our lives were about to end. I recall that the will to live of the children who bid farewell to me was very strong. We went out the nearby window and could not believe that we must go to death in a short time.

I remember the conversation among the children. One said, "It is so nice outside, but not for us." A second one said that his joy would be to eat to satiation once in his life, and then die. One said, "Who knows if we will meet again in the next world." We said that as soon as they would shoot us, we hope to immediately meet again in the next world. Thus did we converse until morning.

Germans entered the ghetto in the morning and issued an order that all the Jews in the ghetto must present themselves in the place at 11:00, and then they would go through the ghetto to see if there are any other Jews. We were somewhat happy with the hope that they might set us free. We could not go to the place because my mother had broken her foot. She told us, "Children, let us go into our bunker, and stay there until we die, for we will not survive in a different ghetto." We agreed with this course of action, and the entire house decided to remain in the bunker. We had two hours. We began to bake crackers in the kitchen. We had water in the bunker, for there was a spring there.

We entered it quickly. We took as much food as possible, and we spread the best things on the floor of the bunker.

[Page 235]

An hour later we heard a great deal of shooting. The Germans shot the Jews who presented themselves at the designated place according to their command.

Thus did we sit in the bunker for two weeks. We choked because there was a shortage of air. However, it got worse later when the food and water was used up. The situation was indescribable. Everyone was almost like dead. People tore at the walls and beat one another, until two young people, including my brother, left the bunker. They quickly with the news that nobody was wandering around the ghetto, but it was still surrounded by guards. First and foremost, they brought various scraps of food that they had collected from the ghetto. We remained in the bunker in that manner for a few more days. When this food also ran out, we all went out to search for something to eat. We found some flour and other dry products, which we decided to cook. As we were cooking, Germans came and knocked loudly at the door. Within one second we to the bunker. They searched thoroughly and did not find the entrance to the bunker.

On one occasion, my brother went out of the bunker and met a local German (a volksdeutsche). The German wondered how we were able to hold out for such a long time and told him that since they were able to hold out for such a long time, he would not turn them in. He further said that we should wait until he , and then he would lead out from the bunker out of the ghetto. We waited for two days until he came around midnight and told us to divide ourselves into two groups and come to the fence of the ghetto. There, upon receiving his signal, we would begin to jump out. We gave him a great deal of money, gold and jewels even though he did not request it. The first group exited out successfully. Then it was our turn. I recall that I was the first to leave the house, and a group of people followed me. In the interim, Germans came and I became separated from the group. I began to flee, and they pursued me. I did not even look for my parents. I ran and felt that they were catching up to me. However, I soon heard them running in the other direction. I turned around and saw that they were running after the group and not after me. I fell down on the street and relieved myself. I had received a strong knock on the head from a German. I thought that I had been captured, but he thought that I was dead and left me. I stood up and ran farther from the ghetto. I stopped in a destroyed Jewish house to catch my breath a bit, and there I met my father who succeeded in escaping from the group. I was very happy that I was not alone. We both began to flee in the direction that our eyes led us.

We sat down in a small grove, and there I first noticed that we were without my mother and brother, so I did not want to go further. I wept at why I had fled from them. I felt the childlike attachment for my mother. As we were sitting and weeping, we heard some shooting. I began to cry out, "Mother, they are shooting you." I was full of terror and cried out for Mother the entire time!

I recall that terrible moment that I endured. Then I heard a voice calling my name from afar, "Genia!" I was so happy, like a person who had lost her mother and she suddenly came back from the grave. I could not lift myself up out of weakness, so my father left me and ran in the direction of the voice. Thus were we once again united. I could not believe that I still had a mother and a young brother, for in truth I could not conceive of this. This must only be a miracle, or a dream...

They told us how they were saved. Germans chased after them and almost captured them. However the German who led us out and led the Germans further away from the ghetto. Mother did not know where we were. All of the people went into the forest where there were already groups of Jews who were organized with weapons against the Germans. I hoped that this would end our experiences. We went into a field and sat down until night fell. It was raining hard, and we had to remain motionless, hiding in the hay.

When night fell, we decided to go to a gentile acquaintance. The gentile was actually a stranger, he only saw us in the ghetto through the fence, and we liked him... He told us that if we ever find ourselves in a hopeless situation, we should come to him; not all of us, but only two of us. However after such an experience we decided not to separate. Either we would all live or we would all die.

[Page 236]

We began to go. Our clothes were wet from the rain. Thus did we drag ourselves on for 10 kilometers until we came to him. He took us into the attic and gave us food and drink. The gentile was 24 years old. We were afraid of him, but we had no other choice. We gave him gold, money and other objects, asking him to hide us until the liberation. He dug a bunker for us in the barn. It was so small that we sat in it one on top of the other. The only consolation was that we were all together. He gave us food for the first few days, but later he told us that two can remain and two must leave... We all got dressed and wanted to leave together. He took a look at us and did not let us leave. He almost stopped giving us food, and we began to endure difficult times.

Our suffering was indescribable. Once a day, we received a small pot of food, without bread and without water. We had no change of clothes, so we became filthy. We remained there for five months. We did not see any light for the entire time. I remember that I found a small mirror, and when I looked in it, I wept and cried out that this was not a human visage at all. We could not hold out anymore. I became ill and could not stand up on my feet. The weather became freezing, and my father and brother went out without the gentile knowing, and they brought food from other gentiles. Once I left a bit of bread in a pot, and Mother gave the pot with the piece of bread to the gentile. The gentile saw the bread, and realized from where we were obtaining bread. The gentile became angry and began to choke my father. We took control, and my mother began to run to him and fight with him. He left us alone, and we shouted at him that he should leave us alone, for he is worse than Hitler. He wanted to kill us with hunger.

From that time, he related to us a bit better. However I was already sick, and we looked like skeletons. We said that if one of us were to die, the rest of us will take revenge on the gentile after the liberation and not let him live. However, after ten difficult days of hunger, thirst, cold and illness, the long awaited day arrived. On March 28, 1944, the gentile came with the news that the Russians had marched into our city. We did not even rejoice, for we looked like corpses from the other world. They dragged me by hand 10 kilometers to our city, for I could no longer stand on my feet.

When we arrived in the city, we found several Jews. From our bunker, only one girl remained, a cousin of ours. The rest were murdered by the Germans, the Ukrainians and the Poles. She alone survived from among the 600 people who were murdered by the Ukrainians. She dug herself out of the pit and remained alive. One can write a book about how she survived. One can become grey listening to the stories of what she experienced.

However, the Russians retreated on March 15, 1944, and we followed them.

In 1945, we to our city of Podhajce. The only thing that we could do was to erect a monument over the pits where our dear, 10,000 unfortunate Jews were buried. Now I live in a camp. I am now finishing the sixth grade in the school where we study Hebrew. Our common objective is to set out for our own country, the Land of Israel.

(From the Yad Vashem Archives).

[Page 237]

Baptists Save Jewish Refugees

by Sima Weisman

I was born in Podhajce in 1913 to religious parents. The city had 6,000 Jews. In October, 1939, on Yom Kippur, the Russians entered our city. We lived calmly and peacefully until July 6, 1941.

The Germans entered our city on that day. From the first day of their arrival, a series of difficulties and tribulations began for us. On the first day, the Ukrainians ruled over us. They immediately began to steal Jewish property and goods which they found in the homes. Their second task was to capture males between the ages of 16 and 50, and send them to the camps of Borki Wielki, Globaczow and Kamionka, where they were forced to work at very hard labor, such as digging clay in deep quarries, forest work and building highways. There were cases where the men were buried in the clay quarries.

One week later, on July 13th, the Ukrainians summoned a convocation of farmers from 72 villages around Podhajce, and began their known anti-Semitic agitation and incitement to the point where they prepared for an actual pogrom against the Jews in Podhajce. A terrible bloodbath was averted thanks only to the great efforts of the Podhajce priest Aidikewicz, who worked against this with all his strength.

In the camps where the men worked at very hard labor, the rations were 100 grams of bread with a watery soup in which a few moldy potatoes were swimming around. Obviously with such work and with such rations, people quickly became sick, but they were afraid of lying in bed for whoever did not show up for work was quickly shot. At this time, women and children between the ages of 13 and 16 were employed in the city at various jobs: gardening, field work, cleaning for the Germans, etc.

One month later, on August 6, 1941, when the Germans took control of the government, the German gendarmes ordered that white armbands with blue Magen Davids 10 centimeters high must be worn on the left arm. At the same time, the Germans set up a Judenrat with 24 Podhajce Jews, consisting of fine householders and members of the intelligentsia. Leibush Lilienfeld was the chairman.

The Judenrat served as the intermediaries between the German authorities and the Jewish victims. On August 10, 1941, the Germans imposed on the city a contribution of a half a million zloty in addition to other products including one cubic meter of soap (this had to be "layered" soap), two cubic meters of sugar, coffee, manufactured goods and even eau de Cologne. The Judenrat and the Ordnunsdienst worked faithfully for the benefit of the German authorities. They helped to search for Jewish means and made sure that the contribution would be paid in full. These Jewish officials always demanded the contribution with an extra amount, for they often behaved immorally and filled their own pocket with money. On September 25, 1941, an order came from the German authorities via the Judenrat that all men's furs, pelts, women's furs, valuables, etc. must be turned in. When a Jewish woman named Vishe Roth hid her fur with the Pole Dinawski, the Pole reported her and she was shot. Thus did things go for almost the entire latter half of the year, with the Judenrat religiously carrying out all orders of the authorities, whether to provide people or to turn over materials, and products. There were two well known murderers from Tarnopol among the Gestapo men, who were the commanders of the upcoming actions. They oppressed and turned the screws on the contributors with taxes until the last breath. The name of one of them was Herman Mueller.

On Rosh Hashanah 1942, the Judenrat requisitioned 50,000 zloty as a second contribution. As they later explained, the 50,000 zloty was intended to pay for the bullets for the first aktion. On the afternoon of the eve of Yom Kippur, the liaison man and militia commandant Avrumche Milch came to us and assured us that no harm would come to us. After this assurance, the Jews gathered together to worship. In the morning of Yom Kippur, when all of the Jews were dressed in there tallises and kittels, praying to G-d in heaven, the first terrible aktion began. It took place as follows: They removed all Jews from the Beis Midrashes and private dwellings and took them to the designated place in the market. Everyone had to sit on the ground. They sat in that manner from 8:00 a.m. until 4:00 p.m. Then they were taken by transport truck to the train station, and loaded on the wagons. The doors were locked behind them, and they were taken to Belzec. Children suffocated along the way due to the great crowding and poor air quality.

[Page 238]

In Belzec, the 1,200 people were tossed into the electric rooms[1], and soap was made from their fat. I and my family, which consisted of five sisters, two brothers, our mother, and a brother-in-law, were saved from the first aktion, since we were well hidden in a bunker. One of my sisters, Chana Rosman, was already loaded upon the transport truck and being taken to the train station, jumped off the truck. She was slightly injured, but she to Podhajce in the morning.

On the morning after Yom Kippur, the ghetto in our city was created. The ghetto was created in the following manner: They designated a side street, surrounded it with tall wooden fences, and placed barbed wire on top. The remaining Jews were enclosed there, 20 people to a small room. The residents of the ghetto were let out twice a week for two hours at a time so that they could purchase things. Whoever would be found on the street after the two hours, or in other days when it was not permitted, would be shot. The camp was guarded by the Jewish militia. We lived from our stored reserves or from the things that we sold in order to purchase necessities. Whoever had no reserves or things to barter went around the ghetto begging for donations. Various epidemics, such as typhus, scabies and various fevers, broke out on account of the hunger, cold, and filth. Those who were ill could not lie in bed, for anyone who lay in bed was shot.

The Germans gathered Jews from all the towns and villages around Podhajce and stuffed them into the ghetto. Thus, there were up to 4,000 Jews there. After approximately six weeks, that is on November 1, 1942, the second aktion began. After the first aktion, almost all of the Jews went into hiding in well designed bunkers, for they anticipated further actions. Thanks to the devoted, diligent assistance of our Jewish militia who went around with axes and crowbars, all of the bunkers and hiding places of the unfortunate Jews were exposed, and they were given over to the hands of the German murderers. This time they were led by foot to the station, where they were loaded on wagons and taken to Belzec. There, they were murdered in the same manner, in electric rooms. This time there were 1,400 people, including my mother and my sister Taube.

The winter of 1942-1943 began, a difficult, cruel winter of hunger and cold. Through the means of the Judenrat, all elderly men and women were gathered and sent to the camps of Borki-Komionka and Globaczow, where they were killed. The remaining young women and men remained in the Podhajce ghetto, where the Germans used them for a variety of jobs.

This continued until Shavuot, 1943. Then they gathered together all of the Jews, men, women and children, and took them to the Podhajce cemetery to shoot them. Thus did they finish off the Jews from our city of Podhajce.

On the day of the last aktion, when all the Jews were gathered together by the Judenrat according to the command, we – three sisters and 33 other men, women and children – were hidden by an acquaintance of mine, who was a volksdeutsche, a student named Barshtash. We sat in a bunker in the ghetto for 14 days. Barshtash brought us food and drink throughout the 14 days, in exchange for money. After 14 days, that selfsame Barshtash led us out from the bunker into a forest behind the city, we found 40 other people. We remained there for three weeks. The farmers from the villages gave us food in exchange for good money. After three weeks, a Podhajce Jew named Yisrael Silber came and led us out from this forest into a second forest 12 kilometers further, for Silber said that the camp here was not secure. Indeed, the next morning, the selfsame farmers who had provided us with food surrounded the forest and murdered everybody. Yisrael Silber as well, who had gone there to provide a few people with some food to save them from starvation, was murdered there along with 34 people. We, three sisters, were together with 12 others, together making 15 Jews. Silber left behind three children.

[Page 239]

One of our group, Grau from Podhajce, knew a about a group of "believers" of Ukrainian extraction who were called "Baptists". He went to them to discuss our situation, and from where we could obtain food supplies so that we could survive until the liberation. The Baptists were located in a village not far from Podhajce. Then one of the Baptists, Sev Biletzki, came himself to us in the forest, took with him a Bible, and read to us about their creed. He read to us that the Jews are a sinful people who were rejected by God. Therefore, they came to such a fate. "And if you to believe in God", he told us, "You will be saved from death". He sung to us holy songs and Psalms, preached morality, spoke to us words from his heart, and indeed related us in a good natured and honest fashion. Willingly or unwillingly, we began to believe in them. Then, when this Baptist saw that we were his people, he led us further into his forest, for he told us that it was dangerous for us here. He found us an appropriate location there, brought us all sorts of implements, helped us to build underground bunkers, got us set up, brought us pots so that we would have in what to cook and conduct our household, brought us straw in a wagon so that we would be able to sleep – and most importantly, he brought sacks with food every day.

Aside from this, they would sit with us for the entire night, sing songs, read the Bible, and preach religiosity and belief. They told us that we, brothers and sisters, would only be saved in that merit. Later, when they saw that we were already their believers, all the Baptists would come to visit us. They called us sisters and brothers, and talked only about belief, about God, and about good deeds of man. They brought food not only to keep us alive, but also lots of butter, cheese, herring, meat, eggs, white pastry, etc. They also brought four more lost people from the forests, who were almost at the point of death. They also found the three young orphans of the aforementioned Yisrael Silber and brought them to us. We were already 22 people.

We three sisters supported almost all of the 22 people. Then something took place that made us lose hope. They began to track us. The Baptists noticed this and took us to their home, where we were hidden in a hiding place for six months.

In one word: we cannot describe it enough. The pen cannot write so much to describe what these people did for us. No father, no mother, no sisters or brothers would have been able to do what they have done.

Thus did things continue until the liberation came in March 1944.

Bad Reichenhall, November 12, 1946

[Page 240]

In the Borki Wielki Work Camp

by Shlomo Teicher

Translated by Jerrold Landau

(From the Yad Vashem archives)

It was the beginning of November, 1941. In accordance with an order from the S.S. command in our city of Podhajce, the Judenrat had to provide 500 Jews for a special work assignment over and above the contingent that had to be provided daily for work. Only 150 men were gathered by the designated time. The only people who came were those who had families and were afraid of persecution that might come from their closeness to the German military authorities. I was also among those who gathered together.

Shortly after our arrival in that place, we were surrounded by the armed S.S. and Ukrainians. The highest in command of the S.S. group ordered us to line up five in a row and march. We went for two kilometers and arrived at the train station. There we were forced into wagons. A short time later, our train started to move. We traveled from our station to Tarnopol. The train stopped in Tarnopol and we were forced off the wagons. This was at night. The night was dark, and we heard an order to mount the tall, open wagons which were located close to our train. It was impossible to climb onto the wagons, especially for the elderly Jews who were with us. When the S.S. men noticed that we slipped back when we tried to climb, they began to beat our heads with the butts of their guns. Three Jews who did not climb quickly enough were beaten for so long that they died. Shortly thereafter, our train started to move.

We arrived in Borki Wielki after another day and a half. The work camp was located close to the railway station, near a stream. At first when the authority was taken over by the Germans, the camp was used for Russian prisoners of war. Then it became a work camp.

After entering the camp, we went through an inspection by the S.S. guard. Each of us received beatings over the head by a gun. Many fell down bloodied, and they were immediately taken away.

After we entered the camp, we were met by the representative of the camp veterans, a Jew from Lemberg. Without any questions, he took everyone and beat them over the head with a thick stick, accompanied by various curses. Then he told us to gather together in one place. He then began to deliver a speech to us in Polish: "Sons of bitches, do not think that you are here in your homes... You did not come here for rest. Here you must work and be obedient, and we have sufficient means here to make you into people. And if any of you attempts to escape, another ten will be shot." After the lecture, some S.S. men came and ordered us to line up five in a row and march into the barracks. When we arrived in the interior of the barracks, the air was stifling with a terrible stink. As we looked for places in the dark, we only found places on the rear cots; the rest were already occupied by Jews from Lemberg, Buczacz, Mienica, Ozerna, Skalat and Wodszemolow.

There were already 1,000 Jews in the camp. We were awakened before dawn to go for coffee. After drinking the meager, bitter coffee, we went to role call. It was autumn. The seasonal strong rains had already lasted for weeks. We were forced into a field which was in a ploughed up state after harvest time. There we were held for two hours every day, performing various exercises until the point of torture, until the S.S. leader came and counted us with the light of a flashlight. Then we were divided up into workgroups, and we marched to work under the vigilant guard of the S.S. and Jewish police.

[Page 241]

Our work was to build a railway line. Day broke by the time we had reached the work place. That is when we first realized the terrible appearance of the Jews who had arrived earlier. During the short period of time that they were in the camp, they became terribly emaciated. Their hair grew wild, their clothes had become disheveled, and they looked like people who had given up on life. The area in which we worked was full of clay. If one unfortunately put a foot in the clay, it would be impossible to remove it. When we carried the planks or the rail links, we had to rush through it. We would indeed leave our shoes or boots sticking in the clay, moving only in bare feet. If we wanted to retrieve our shoes later, we would be beaten by the Jewish police or the S.S. to the point of unconsciousness, for they said that we were holding up the work that had to be conducted at a quick pace. We were also forced to carry 12 meter rail links with a small number of people. It was impossible even to lift them with such a number of people. Whoever displayed any weakness was beaten to the point of bleeding, or was even shot. People who could not run quickly back to the camp after a 12 hour workday would also be shot. Every day there were about ten victims who died of shooting, beatings, hunger or hard labor. Most of the arrivals were Jews from Lemberg. The Jews from smaller towns of the regions would somehow have food sent to them from their relatives, but the Jews of Lemberg would have to live off the 200 grams of bread and the bit of watery soup that we received in the camp. Indeed, almost every month, transports of Jews would arrive to replace those who died.

Once when there was an ambulance with a large number of sick people, they were shot before our eyes as we were standing at role call and being sent out to the field. This served as a warning for us that we must not become ill...

If a person fled from the camp, the remaining people would be held responsible. The first time that someone fled from the camp, the remaining people would be placed ten in a row during roll call, and every tenth person was shot. This was the penalty for escaping and as a warning if we were going to prepare to escape. In a second case of escape, when the person who escaped was caught, he was hanged publicly in the yard. With the passage of time, the S.S. guard was replaced by Ukrainian and Polish police. From that time, the camp was no longer crowded. Jews were shot on a daily basis when they needed a target for target practice. When one of the workers would ask the police during work hours for permission to go to rest, the police would shout at him, "Run faster", and immediately shoot him in the head.

As we were from work, they would shoot at the group, and we had to take the shot people with us.

At the beginning of July 1943, we heard strong sounds of dismantling at night. The next day, we found out that the partisans who were in the area had conducted a large aktion. They tore down all the railway bridges and freed the Jews that they found from the Kamionker forced labor camp. The partisan aktion caused a panic among our camp leaders, and they began to talk about the work ending, and that we would be transported to Tarnopol.

On July 10 at night, the work ended. A Polish policeman came to my group and said that we would not be going there to work tomorrow, and it is possible that we would not have to work at all. It was further possible, he said, that we would have to give over to him the valuables that we were hiding. We regarded this as a sly trick, thinking that his intention was to deceive us out of our valuables, despite the fact that we did not have any. That very night, as we were sitting in the barracks, we heard the loud noise of trucks. Immediately thereafter, armed S.S. men came to us in the barracks and began to force us outside. As we in the yard, we received an order that we must sit down half kneeling, five in a row. After receiving the order, the first group of Jews was forced back into the barracks. Two S.S. men accompanied them. Shortly thereafter, we heard a series of shots, accompanied by human cries. The two S.S. men , took another group of five, and the same thing repeated itself. A group of men tried to escape, however they were immediately shot by the S.S. men and Ukrainians who had surrounded us. They even shot the Jews who made the slightest movement.

[Page 242]

I was sitting among the last groups, opposite the window of the barracks. The window on our side was open. As one of the S.S. men was driving us out he could not stand the bad smell in the barracks, so he broke the window. Seeing that my turn to be killed was coming up, I thought about how to save myself. The first thing that I did was to remove the wooden shoes from my feet. I then removed my work clothes, and immediately jumped out of the window into the barracks through the open window with great speed in a swimming position. I heard shots over my head. One bullet even grazed my back. Then I fell on top of a mound of shot Jews. The S.S. took me for dead, because one who was standing at the side of the window shouted out, “He is kaput”. I was afraid of lying near the window, so I snuck into the rooms that were further on, which were already filled with shot Jews. I heard the wheezing of the dying people. I snuck into the corner of the room of the work supervisor. In that room, I noticed an open door to the attic. With extraordinary strength I quickly climbed up and lay down in a corner of the attic. I waited for the end with a fluttering heart.

After all the Jews were shot, the commanding voice of the camp director Wojciech was heard, stating that he was going to burn straw. The straw was to be spread out next to the barracks and ignited. The S.S. guards responded that they have no straw. They only had straw sacks. The camp director agreed to spread out the straw sacks, and they immediately began to drag the sacks. The barracks in which I was hiding stood near the fence. The straw was spread to on the side of the yard. After bringing the straw sacks, the camp director ordered that the barracks be spread with the kerosene that was located on the trucks, and the straw was set on fire.

A few minutes later, the thick smoke began to choke me. I jumped outside through a small door in the attic and lay on the ground for several minutes. When the smoke got thicker, I began to shuffle in the direction of the fence. I shuffled to the lavatory and went inside. As I came in, I heard that a man was crawling quickly back through the lavatory pit in the closet on the other side. I realized that he was also a Jew who saved himself. I waited for several minutes, and then crawled to the other side through the pit in the closet. When I was already outside, I began to run with wild speed after seeing that they were throwing rockets in all directions around the camp. I threw myself prone on the ground and slithered on my stomach until I came to the corn stocks. I lay there until the second evening, and when it got dark outside, I set out on my way.

Through the 18 months of the existence of the work camp, more than 4,000 Jews died there.

[Page 243]

Podhajce Under German Occupation

by Leah Feldberg

Shortly after the outbreak of the Second World War in September 1939, a large stream of Jewish refugees who were fleeing from western Poland arrived in our city. Our community made strenuous efforts to help the homeless families whose fate brought them to Podhajce. Many of the local families gave over a room for the refugees. Efforts were made to find employment for them, and thus were they helped to endure the difficult days of the war.

A short time later, the entire area of Eastern Galicia was taken over by the Red Army. Shortly thereafter, the Sovietization of the entire life began. Business was nationalized, Jews lost their sources of livelihood and had to change their entire way of life. This caused a great unrest among the Jewish population.

On one occasion, the Soviet offices announced a sensational piece of news: the refugees who wish to home can register, and they would be granted the opportunity to travel home. However, it turned out that this was a trick from the regime. One night, those refugees who registered were taken from their houses, transported to the train station and sent to Siberia and other far off places in Russia.

On a hot summer day in June, 1941, we suddenly heard the powerful detonations of bombs in the nearby region. It quickly became clear to us that the Germans had declared war on the Soviet Union, and they were bombarding the flight locations in the region. The panic among the Jewish population was indescribable. Anyone who was able fled eastward to Russia. Unfortunately, only a few were able to flee, and a few days later the city was occupied by the German army.

The hell for the Jewish population began immediately after the arrival of the Germans. The first to demonstrate their animalistic instincts were the Ukrainians and Volksdeutschen. They began by extorting money from the Jews and beating them mercilessly without any reason – solely to express their sadistic tendencies. Later, when the S.S. men began to busy themselves with their bloody work, the Ukrainians and Volksdeutschen helped them faithfully and diligently.

The first night with the Germans was completely peaceful, but everyone was very tense, knowing that no good was awaiting them from this. The military civic authorities came the next day and the commandant summoned the Jewish representatives and ordered them to set up a Judenrat. At the same time, an order was issued that all Jews must wear an arm band with a Magen David.

After the establishment of the Judenrat, S.S. men came from Tarnopol and imposed a large contribution which the Judenrat had to collect from the Jews in the city. Everyone gave what he could, thinking that thereby they would redeem themselves from their hands. A short time later, S.S. men came again and ordered that they must provide 80 workers; otherwise they would kill 500 Jews. The Judenrat had no choice but to carry this out. My husband Yehuda Tzvi Feldberg of blessed memory and my brother-in-law Chaim Baruch Ridkes of blessed memory were among the unfortunate workers. They were all taken to the Borki Wielki forced labor camp, where they were worked to death and then murdered.

Thus did things go for over a year. Every time the S.S. men came with new orders which one had to fulfill in order to save one's life. The first large scale aktion took place on Yom Kippur, 1942. The streets were abruptly surrounded by armed Germans, Ukrainians and Volksdeutschen. They tore into the homes and the synagogues, and ordered everyone to come with them. Whoever attempted to stand up to them was shot on the spot. The aktion lasted for the entire day. From among my neighbors on Schlossegasse they took away at that time the Horowitz, Fiszer, and Kohen families, the two Fuchs brothers with their families, their sister and her family, and many others whose names I do not remember. An S.S. General named Mueller led that aktion. Upon his order, they forced the unfortunate people onto trucks and drove them to the train station, from where they were taken to the Belzec extermination camp. I was hiding with my children in the attic, for I did not want to leave young children in a better hiding place, lest they cry and thereby betray the hiding place. A great miracle happened to us then, for they ran by my house like wild beasts many times, but they did not open the door and did not go searching. Throughout that day, I heard from my hiding place the weeping of the unfortunate people who were dragged out of their hiding places.

[Page 244]

A great fear pervaded in the city after the aktion. Everyone was making a fuss. Many families were affected by the aktion. There were husbands without wives, wives without husbands, and children without parents. However, the Germans did not let us be. They came with new demands every day. Once time, they demanded that everyone who has gold or silver turn it in. The second time, they ordered everyone to give over their entire set of food serving utensils. The penalty of not carrying out the order was death. My husband was in Borki Wielki at that time, and I gave over our entire set of food serving utensils in order to not risk my life and the lives of my beloved children.

After the large aktion, the survivors were forced into the ghetto which was created in a small section of the city. The crowding was very great. Several families had to crowd into one room. The hunger got worse, and a typhus epidemic broke out that did not skip over even one family. Every day, there were victims from malnutrition and the lack of medical care. From time to time, there were also victims of the German murderers.

Everyone began to realize that the only place to hide from the Germans was in a well fortified bunker or somewhere outside the ghetto. Such a bunker was prepared in almost every house, but this was no simple matter. There was a big problem with the elderly who would often cough in the bunker, and with young children who would cry in the bunker, and might thereby turn in all of the people. Indeed, people gave cough medicine to the elderly, and the children were injected with medicine that causes drowsiness. There were also cases where young children suffocated during the aktion, for their mouths were covered so that they would not cry.

A short time before the last aktion, I went out to the forest with the help of Yisrael Silber and Breines. They built a large bunker in the forest, primarily to save young people who would survive the misfortune and then go to the Land of Israel. They took me because I promised to help them with money.

This did not last long, for the Ukrainians discovered that there were Jews in the forest, and they began to search for them. Every night we had to wander from one grove to another, until we found a large forest. There we were divided into three groups in order to make it easier to escape in the event that we were discovered.

The Benderovches somehow found about the second group, of which I was not a part. They disguised themselves as Russian partisans and thereby approached the bunker of the second group with the pretext of uniting with them. Silber and Breines were not in the bunker at that time, for they had come to us. They shortly and began to shoot at the Benderovches when they saw them. This barely helped, for there were a larger number of Benderovches. They brought everyone out, two at a time, to a pit and shot them. Silber was also murdered at that time. This was told to us by a Jew who was hiding in the forest not far from the place where the misfortune took place. Only one girl was miraculously saved out of all the people. She is now a sister-in-law of Mrs. Shourz and lives in America.

When we heard about this, we ran to Ukrainian acquaintances that night. We fell into the hands of a bandit who gave us over to his brother-in-law. He apparently said he would make a hiding place for us, but before the bunker was ready, he went to the police to turn us in. Jews who were hiding in his attic saw him from the police at 6:00 a.m. Shortly thereafter, German and Ukrainian policemen attacked us. When we heard the police we fled, but two of us, one of them a pharmacist and a brother of Pushteig, fell into their hands. The police took them out to be killed.

[Page 245]

After they took them away, the murderer who had apparently hidden us came and ordered us to leave the bunker. As we were leaving, we encountered the policemen who began to shoot at us. Silber's wife and her brother unfortunately fell, and the children – my two children and Silber's three children – succeeded in escaping. The bullets did not hit me, but I fell onto the ground like a corpse. Later, two Ukrainians passé by, and I heard one say to the other, "The woman is dead, we must bury her..."

After they approached me, I crawled father away from that place and waited until it got dark. In the evening, I went out to search for a bit of water and something to eat. I encountered an old Ukrainian woman who took me in to her barn and brought me food and drink. She held me for three days until I calmed down somewhat.

I left the woman, and did not know where to go and where to search for my children. I did indeed decide to go to the gentile to whom we went in the first place, to see if he perhaps knows something about the children.

When I came to him, I did indeed find all five children with him. We remained with him for a long time, but we suffered very greatly. On one occasion a Jew came and told us that there is a bunker nearby which he left behind, where there are potatoes and a kitchen to cook. We could go there if we wished. I did not think for very long, and we went with the Jews so that he could show us the bunker.

This was at night. In the morning, a Ukrainian came. He seemed like a good man, and said that he would go to fetch us something to eat. I believed him, and I told the children to go into the forest to bring some wood so that we could cook something. In the interim, I saw the Ukrainian with an axe in his hand. I immediately shouted to the children to escape, and began to escape myself. The gentile caught us and captured Silber's older son. He removed the boots from his feet and wanted to drag him to the police. However some people came by in the meantime, and he let him be. The child escaped from him.

We fled into the forest and waited there until it was dark. Then we began to think about where to go. We ran into a Pole who treated us well. He told us, "It is good that you did not run into my neighbor. Just yesterday he turned a Jewish family in to the police."

Thus did we have a different adventure every day, and life was dangerous. We could write an entire book about the miracles that the Master of the World performed for us. For example, once we were quite frozen, and we dared to approach a gentile to ask him to give us something warm to eat. He left us in the barn. As we were sitting there, suddenly a number of people came with flashlights in their hands. We did not have any time to escape. The people entered the stable and shone the light in our faces, but they did not say anything, as if they did not see us.

Thus did we live with miracles and great suffering – so much so that we often thought about turning ourselves in to the police. We had some contact with a few Jews who were hiding in that region – altogether 23 Jews from various cities and towns.

Finally we survived until the day of the liberation, and we to Podhajce. There we found a small group of surviving Jews who, like us, miraculously survived the total destruction. Like all of the cities and towns in Poland, Podhajce gave up its part to the altar of the murdered Jewish people.

[Page 246]

Family Reflections from Zlotnik

by Chaya David (Rauch)

I, Chaya David (nee Rauch) lived for many yeas in the town of Zlotnik. Hundreds of Jews lived there and the Jewish settlement there existed for centuries. In the town there was a large synagogue, a kloiz, a Jewish community, and every Jewish family there was well and properly established.

The First World War broke out in 1914, and the calm life and property were ruined. The wild war took no account of sentiments. The Jews suffered greatly from the Russian invasion. After the war, we began to rebuild everything anew. Our energy and zest for life in the wake of the bloody war. People worked diligently and industriously. It was not long before the image of the past had changed, and a new life was built up. My father was among those who rebuilt our destroyed home and set it up anew. However, unfortunately, Father did not last long. He died young, and left behind four children – three daughters and a son – along with our mother. The house which we had built up served as our fabric store aside from our residence. We continued to conduct our household and our business, and thus did several years pass.

In the meantime, my older sister got married. My sister's husband was a liquor distiller by trade, and was commissioned by the regime in the manufacturing of liquor. Sorrow once again afflicted our house. Our dear beloved mother died. Our only brother obtained independent work and left our house, so only I and my younger sister were not taken care of. At that time, I decided to go to the land of Israel. After leaving the town, my younger sister went to live with my older married sister.

I recall those fortunate days when we were all together in the home, in the bosom of our family. Everything changed in the month of May. In truth, we were left alone after the death of our beloved parents, but there were close relatives such as Dr. Nachman Rauch, Yaakov Grynberg, and other more distant relatives. Prior to my departure for Israel, our family decided that my younger sister should also go to Israel. To our great regret, that fine and good hope did not come to be. Merely one month after I arrived in Israel, the criminal Nazi hordes entered Poland and destroyed everything. They robbed our dearly beloved ones from us. Everything was destroyed and burnt. All of our close relatives and friends were murdered with a cruel and unusual death.

I came to Israel with the illegal immigration, having only what I was wearing on my body plus another two pounds. This constituted my entire possessions. This was around the month of July, 1939. From that time on, I bore with me the fantastic idea that perhaps, just perhaps, someone of my dear family might have been saved from the hands of the murderers. However, unfortunately, the Nazi murderers devoured even the one year old son of my brother. I am the only survivor of my entire family. Only the yahrzeit, which falls out three days before Shavuot, will always remain etched in my memory and also in the Yizkor book that will be published by the natives of our area in Israel as a memorial.

G-d should punish the murderers and murderous nation for the innocent and precious blood that was spilled for no reason.

This Yizkor book must serve as a monument that the murder of six million Jews by the Nazis is not a legend. It is possible that in a future generation, some people will ask about what type of people these were, who could not defend themselves. Indeed, these were people with understanding, but they had nothing in their hands with which to defend themselves from the murderers.

My memories of my family members are still fresh, and I am certain that I will never be able to forget them.

Translator's Footnote

1. Evidently, this is referring to gas chambers.

[Page 247]

The Memorial in Bad-Reichenhall

On May 22, 1947, a gathering took place in Bad-Reichenhall (Bavaria, Germany) from 10:00 a.m. until 4:00 p.m.

This was a memorial for the martyrs who were murdered in the Podhajce Ghetto during the Hitlerist German occupation (1941-1944).

At the same time, a meeting took place with the participation of those people who came to the memorial. The following protocols were issued.

1. 79 members were registered who took part in the gathering (the list is given at the end of the protocols).

2. Yehuda Weissman, the member and founder of the provisional Podhajce committee in Bad-Reichenhall, the initiator of the memorial, opened the meeting and proposed the following persons to the presidium: 1. Izak Fink, 2. Oskar Eisenberg; 3. Yeshaya Friedman, 4. Yitzchak Weitreich, 5. Yitzchak Shourz, 6. Nathan Brecher, 7. Moshe Zawalower, 8. Nathan Kermish, 9. Marcus Shulman.

At the same time, the member Yehuda Weissman proposed that Mr. Izak Fink should be the honorary president of the gathering, and that Mr. Oskar Eisenberg should lead the gathering, and that member Yeshaya Friedman should be the secretary.

The decision motion was taken by the gathering, and they demanded that the member Yehuda Weissman also take a place on the presidium.

Mr. Oskar Eisenberg read the proceedings of the day:

1. Yizkor, Kaddish. Reflections on the experiences in the ghetto.
2. Elections to the Landsmanschaft committee.
3. The behavior of the Jewish militia in Podhajce.
4. Discussions.
5. Resolutions.

The proceedings were accepted by the gathering without change.

Oskar Eisenberg said the following:

"Brothers and sisters! We, Jews of Podhajce, Zlotniki, Wiœniowczyk, Zawalow, Gorzhanka and Tustowawa, have gathered here today in Bavaria in Germany, in Bad-Reichenhall, where fate has by chance brought us together, to survey and understand who from our city and region has remained alive after the barbaric murderous deeds of the Nazis. We have undertaken to determine the exact time when our beloved fathers, mothers, brothers, sisters and children were murdered by the German murderers, and thereby, throughout our entire lifetimes, we will know when to say Kaddish."

At the time when the appropriate honors were offered to the fallen martyrs, Cantor Ronner recited the appropriate prayers accompanied by "El Maleh Rachamim"[1]

The eldest member of our committee, Mr. Izak Fink, recited Kaddish for the murdered Jews of the city of Podhajce.

Mr. Yitzchak Shourz received the right to speak, and said:

"Dear Podhajcer brothers! It fell in my lot to remain in Podhajce when the Germans entered our city. It was my lot to see Jewish blood flowing through the streets of Podhajce. I was hunted and harassed. I did not know where to hide in order to save my life. Despite this, I am among the living, and I survived the attacks of the murderers."

As he briefly surveyed various images of the Podhajce Ghetto, of the life and deaths of the Podhajce residents, Yitzchak Shourz mentioned that those present must always bear in mind that the majority of the Ukrainian population helped the Hitlerist German barbarians in Podhajce to murder Jewry. Therefore, he shouted out: "Jews! Do not forget. Seek out the war criminals and take revenge on them." (By bringing them to justice before the authorized institutions.)

[Page 248]

The member Yehuda Weissman received the right to speak and said:

"Dear brothers and sisters! Four years ago at this time, our city passed through its final death throes. Four years ago at this time, the last Jews, who survived all the slaughters, walked broken and crushed along their final path. With false promises and deceit, as was their way at all times, the Nazis gathered our weary brothers and sisters, pretending to transfer them to the ghetto of Tarnopol. However, the final journey of our brothers and sisters soon ended. Behind the city, in Zahajce, our beloved ones gave up their lives. Tortured, shot, plundered by the Nazi Germans and Ukrainian and Polish Volksdeutschen – thus departed 5,000 Jews, our dearest and most beloved."

"We, the small group, are gathered today from all over Germany in order to recall and remember our close ones who were so cruelly murdered."

Mr. Weissman showed the gathering the monument upon which was inscribed: "Remember what Amalek did unto you! Let the nation of Israel remember its 6,000,000 martyrs who were murdered and burned in sanctification of the Divine name and the nation. Avenge the spilled blood of your brethren!" He continued on saying, "This is our Kaddish, our Shloshim[2], and our ancestral grave! We stand today with bent heads in front of the communal monument. Recall well what our beloved endured; never forget the war criminals who murdered our beloved people."

Aharon Schwartz (of Zlotniki) received the right to speak, and said:

"My heart weeps inside of me as a look around at the small group of Jews from Podhajce, Zlotniki and Zawalow who remain after they lost their dearest and most beloved people. I have no place of rest. I am in the midst of a journey. Two weeks ago, I was at the Warsaw memorial ceremony. One week ago, I was at the Lemberg memorial ceremony. And today I am at the Podhajce memorial ceremony. The Jew weeps and weeps! I believe, dear brothers and sisters, that our place is in the land of Israel! We must not be scattered and dispersed in all corners of the world! We must be together, and create our home, our Land! Today I recite Kaddish here, and I express my heartfelt wish that next year we will recite Kaddish in the Land of Israel."

In his discussion, Mr. Moshe Zawalower (of Zlotniki) pointed out that there is no equal to the tragedy of the Jews during the German occupation in the annals of world history. However, the world must know that Jewish blood was not only spilled in the ghettos and the crematoria. Jews also gave of their blood on all the fronts, where our brothers and children fought heroically for freedom and against injustice, and helped with the defeat of the German fascists murderers.

The chairman, Mr. Oskar Eisenberg, moved over to the second section of the program (elections to the landsmanschaft committee).

It was proposed that a committee of seven members be chosen, with its headquarters in Bad Reichenhall. The following natives of our city were proposed as candidates: 1. Oskar Eisenberg, 2. Izak Fink, 3. Yeshaya Friedman, 4. Yehuda Weissman, 5. Nathan Brecher, 5. Munio Schwartz, 7. Moshe Zawalower, 8. Marcus Yatshes, 9. Yitzchak Shourz, 10. Motia Schulman, 11. Hersh Rellis, 12. Yitzchak Weitreich, 13. Yaakov Gross.

After a brief discussion, the following townsfolk were selected for the committee: 1. Yeshaya Friedman, 2. Yehuda Weissman, 3. Oskar Eisenberg, 4. Yitzchak Shourz, 5. Yaakov Gross, 6. Motia Shulman, 7. Moshe Zawalower.

The chairman moved on to the third agenda item.

The member Yaakov Gross received the right to speak about that point.

"You, friends, were in the war during the time of the German occupation. However, we know that certain residents of Podhajce collaborated with the Germans and did evil to Jews. I request that those present who know about any of them speak up."

The members Yitzchak Shourz, Getzel Blecher, Yerucham Shulman, Leib Frenkel, Sala Sperber, Yitzchak Frenkel, Yossel Pistreich and Zigo Lateiner noted that some of the Jews of Podhajce who survived were members of the militias during the German occupation of Podhajce and inflicted a great deal of harm upon Jews. There was even a case where a Jewish woman revealed where 50 Jews were hiding during one of the aktions.

[Page 249]

Then the proceedings ended, and there were discussions about the resolutions. The following were the resolutions.

a) The 3rd of Sivan will be the memorial day for the martyrs of Podhajce and the region of Zlotniki, Zawalow, Wiœniowczyk, Zawalow, Gorzhanka and Tustowawa.

b) The members Yitzchak Shourz, Getzel Blecher, Leib Frankel, Yerucham Shulman, and Yosel Pistreich were requested to compose a description of life in Podhajce during the time of the war, and of the murder aktions that were perpetrated in the Podhajce ghetto during the German occupation. This composition will be sent to the committee for assistance of the Podhajce Natives in the United States and Israel.

c) Those gathered expressed their heartfelt thanks to the members Yehuda Weissman, Yeshayahu Friedman, Shimke Fink and Yaakov Gross, who were the initiators and organizers of the memorial gathering.

d) The committee that was chosen at this meeting was asked to turn to the assistance committee of Podhajce natives in the United States with the request of material help for the needy among the refugees of Podhajce. The relief committee should send the assistance individually to those in need, and should communicate this to the Podhajce committee in Bad Reichenhall. The newly selected committee should inform the Podhajce relief organization in America about who from our members are in the greatest need of assistance.

e) Those gathered determined that the aforementioned Podhajcers (who are alive) were members of the militia during the German occupation and thereby helped the Germans. A Jewish woman revealed to the Germans where 50 Jews were hidden. However, we wish to believe that she did this out of fear that she should not lose her life.

f) The committee must take the necessary steps in short order to turn in to the appropriate authorities the Ukrainian war criminals who are walking around free in Germany.

g) The gathering asked Yeshayahu Friedman to produce the minutes of the gathering and send copies of it to the assistance committee in the United States and in the land of Israel, and to all members of the committee who were chosen at that gathering.

Honorary president – Izak Fink
Chairman – Oskar Eisenberg
Secretary – Yeshaya Friedman

Members of the committee: Yehuda Weissman, Yitzchak Shourz, Yaakov Gross, Motia Shulman, Moshe Zawalower

The List of the Podhajce Survivors who were present at the Memorial in Bad Reichenhall

Eisenberg Oskar
Blumenfeld Shimon
Blumenfeld Mina
Blecher Getzel
Bloch Edzia
Berg Marcus
Brif Moshe
Brecher Nathan
Ginszberg Moshe
Gross Yaakov
Gruber Mietek
Horowitz Hersch
Hutes-Hirsch Misia
Wassermil Binyamin
Weissman Yehuda
Weissman-Rozman Sima
Weitreich Yitzchak
Zawalower Moshe
Zawalower Feivish
Tenenbaum Yehuda
Yotshes Marcus
Yotshes Dova
Lateiner Zigmund
Lifschitz Fani
Lifschitz Munia
Lipman Zalman
Mandler Sala
Mandler Yisrael
Milch Dr. Bunio
Milshtak Mordechai
Meltzer Moshe-Yossel
Segal Leib
Etlinger-Kover Chaya
[Page 250]
Fogel Zigmund
Fogel Mendel
Polak Yeshaya
Pasternak David-Shlomo
Ptashnik-Meltzer Uka
Fink Izak
Fink Genia
Fink Shimon
Pistreich Yossel
Pistreich Leon
Feldberg Leah
Peltz Meir
Friedman Yeshaya
Frenkel Yitzchak
Frenkel Leib
Zimmerman Yaakov
Zimmerman Krantzia
Korn-Weinstein Chaya
Kupfer Hersch
Kupferman Zigmund
Klein Yitzchak
Kermish Nathan
Kermish Gusta
Rozman Choma
Rozman Donia
Roth Moshe
Roller Isser
Reibel Adam
Reibel Yosef
Reibel Perl
Reibel Mina
Rinder (Mossberg) Aharon
Rellis Hersch
Shulman Marcus
Shulman Yerucham
Shourz Yitzchak
Shourz Henia
Shourz Aharon
Schwartz Aharon
Schwartz Immanuel
Shtamler Aharon
Shtamler Fishel
Shtarkman Marcus
Sher Yaakov
Sperber Hela
Sperber Sali

The gathering of the Holocaust survivors of Podhajce Jewry in Bad Reichhall

Translator's Footnotes

1. The traditional prayer for the souls of the dead.
2. Shloshim is the traditional 30 day mourning period for close relatives.

[Pages 251-264]

{Translator's note: This section of names of those who perished is translated in the Necrology section , and is sorted alphabetically in English. The opening paragraph on page 251 is translated there. The concluding paragraph on page 264 is the traditional Kel Maleh prayer, adapted for Podhajce. It is translated as follows:

[Page 264]

El Maleh Rachamim

G-d full of mercy, who dwells on high, find proper rest under the wings of the Divine presence, in the heights, holy and pure as the splendor of the shining heavens, for the souls of the natives of our city, the martyrs of Podhajce and its region, men, women, boys and girls, who were murdered, burned, slaughtered, and strangled by the enemy in the European Diaspora. All of them are pure and holy, among them were sages and pious people, cedars of Lebanon and mighty in Torah. May their repose be in the Garden of Eden. May the Master of Mercy bind their souls in the bonds of eternal life, G-d is their memory, and may their sacrifice be remembered for us, and may their merit stand for us and all of Israel. May the land not hide their blood, and may there be a place for their outcry. In their merit, may the dispersed of Israel to their homeland, and may the righteousness of the martyrs be constantly before Your eyes. May peace come, and may they rest in peace, and let us say Amen.

[Page 265]

Old Monuments in the Podhajce Cemetery

The Monument of the rabbi and Gaon, the author of "Masaat Binyamin" of holy blessed memory, from the year 5380 (1620)

The monument reads as follows: Binyamin Year 5380

This monument and marker is from the great Gaon who is buried here, as well as all of the monuments from here were fixed and erected by the local Chevra Kadisha in the year 5591 (1831).

The monument of his wife Malka the daughter of Reb Shmuel

The monument reads as follows:

Sunday, The eve of the new moon of Tammuz 5384
{Much of the rest of the monument, except for the name, is not fully legible.}

Below, from right to left: the monument of the grandson of the author of the "Masaat Binyamin" Reb Yeshaya the son of the rabbi and Gaon Rabbi Avraham, who died in the year 5398 (1638);
The Monument of the martyr Rabbi Moshe the son of Rabbi Nachman from the year 5431 (1671);
The monument of the martyr Reb Natan the son of Reb Yechezkel from the year 5443 (1683)

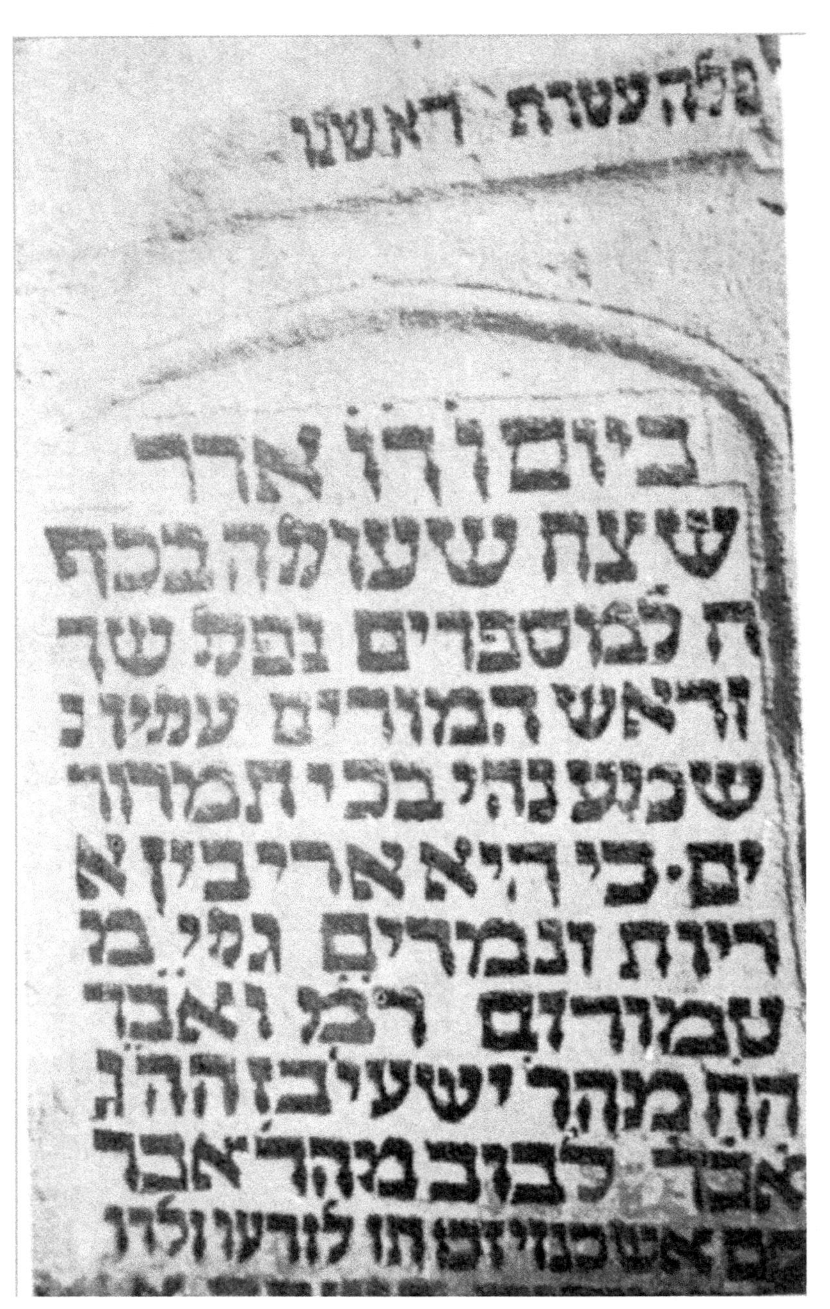

The monument reads as follows (some phrases are omitted).

The crown of our head has fallen
On Friday, 7 Adar 5493, the head of the teachers fell. Bitter weeping and lamentation is heard. For he was a lion among lions, the rabbi and head of the rabbinical court Rabbi Yeshayahu the son of the Gaon the head of the rabbinical court of Lvov, Rabbi Avraham Ashkenazi, may his merit protect us

The monument reads as follows:

Here is buried
A pious and faithful man
Like Darda and Heiman[1]
This is the holy man Rabbi
Nachman who was killed in his house, and his
Soul left him in holiness
And purity, like Rabbi Akiva and his friends
With him. May his soul be bound in the bonds of eternal life

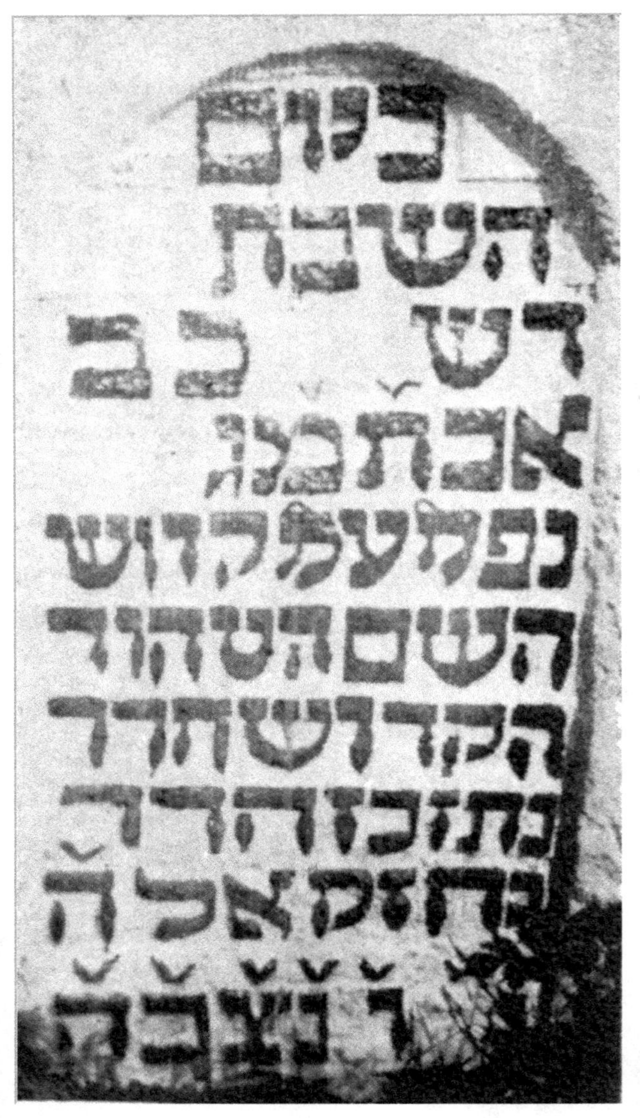

The monument reads as follows (some phrases are omitted)

On the day of the Sabbath
{date cannot be made out}
He fell in Sanctification of the Divine
And Pure Name
The martyr, Natan the son of Reb Yechezkel
May his soul be bound in the bonds of eternal life.

Translator's Footnote

1. Names of two pious Biblical personalities known from the books of Chronicles and Psalms. Rabbi Akiva, mentioned a few lines below, was a Talmudic sage who met his death by martyrdom.

[Page 266]

About my City Podhajce, About My Parents and Brother Who Perished in the Holocaust

by Menachem Ettinger

May G-d remember the soul of my revered father Reb Aharon Shmuel Ettinger and the soul of my revered mother Chaya Ettinger, and their young son Abba Ettinger, who were murdered at the hands of the Nazis, and the souls of my brothers Gedalya and Yitzchak who went to their eternal world.

I was ten years old when I first left my native city of Podhajce. I fled to Hungary along with my mother, my eldest brother and my grandfather, on account of the tribulations of the First World War, and especially on because of the fear of encountering the Russian Cossacks. The fact that our journey, along with the journey of the rest of the refugees, was arranged by the Austrian government, or as we used to say – by the Kaiser Franz Josef himself – is etched in my mind. At that time, my father was serving in the Austrian Army, and had been sent to Czechoslovakia.

We home after about four years. The town was almost completely destroyed. The good name of Franz Josef was again mentioned as the one who gave the money to restore the ruins. Slowly, life to its normal course, but I had become a different person. I no longer had the calm of a child living under the wings of his parents. The feeling of lack of security grew in me day by day. I would often say to my father of blessed memory: "I cannot remain here, for here there is nobody we can trust. The Poles are on one side, the Ukrainians on the other side – (These were the residents of Podhajce in addition to the Jews), is it possible to believe that we can trust them?" I did not realize at that time how correct my words were, not only with respect to the situation that pervaded after the First World War, but primarily with respect to the great Holocaust.

I remained with my parents for only another two years, and I tried to assist them to the best of my efforts. However, I finally decided to actualize my desire and to leave the place. I set out toward Vienna, the capital city of Austria.

My father of blessed memory accompanied me to Lvov. As we sat on the train car, he said sadly, "Who knows if I will see you again?"... My dear father was indeed correct! However, I did not think at all about that at the time – that I would never visit my native city again nor see my beloved family again, Mother, Father and my brothers.

They stand before me as if alive: Father with a refined countenance and melancholy nobility etched on his face. Sadness peered from his good eyes even when he would smile. Indeed, from where would the happiness come? He lived with the constant pressure of the livelihood of the family, especially when we to the town after the war. In order to sustain his family of seven – five sons and a wife – he had to toil very hard. The livelihood of the family came from a store which stood in the market, in one line with similar stores owned by Jews. The store sold shoes and hides, merchandise for the farmers of the region who would come to this center for purchases, especially on the market day, which was Thursday. Every storeowner attempted to attract the purchasers, to speak to the gentile in the language that he would understand, to make promises and lower the prices – for the most important thing was to sell and to receive cash. Father spent most of the hours of the day in the store, and often also the evenings. The Sabbaths and festivals were dedicated to Torah, for my father was a scholar, who could understand the small letters. I can see him sitting next to the table in the large room, with a Gemara opened before him. He would study the page quietly, without raising his voice. My late father had a very sweet voice. Father was the regular Torah reader and prayer leader in our synagogue, the Temple. Father would often stir up the hearts of the worshippers with his prayers, for he understood the content of the prayers and would worship with deep religious emotion. He would often move the hearts of his listeners to the point of tears.

Mother of blessed memory was a typical Jewish mother, "A Yiddishe Mama". She would help father in the store with all her strength, as is written, "a helpmate for him"[1]. In the home she was a merciful mother who spread her wings over her five sons in order to warm them and protect them. Poor mother did not succeed in saving them from their bitter fate! My mother spent all the days of the week with my father in the store. However, after the market day on Thursday she would spend all of her time, day and night, preparing for the Sabbath. She would bake challas for the Sabbath every week, and prepare special delicacies that we loved – puddings, dumplings, stuffed fish, and of course cholent. Nothing was lacking on the Sabbath. The food was like that of a king, as if she wanted to pacify us on account of the ordinary food of the week. She also cleaned the house on Fridays. Everything was shiny and polished in the house. How did she have the strength for all of this? We never heard any complaint from her mouth, not against us and certainly not against father. The relations between them were of honor and love, and they served as an example for us.

I recall my eldest brother Gedalya very well. He had a difficult fate. He became seriously ill in his childhood, and he suffered for many years. Whenever he had the strength, he tried to help our parents, but at the end of his life he could not even do this. Only one mercy came to him – he died a natural death during the first year of the Second World War, and the hand of the cruel enemy did not touch him.

I did not know my two young brothers in Podhajce; for they were born after I left the town. However, the bitter fate did not pass over them, even though I succeeded in bringing them to the Land while there was still time. My brother Fishel remains seriously handicapped after being injured during his service in the brigade. My youngest brother Yitzchak perished in a fatal accident while he was fulfilling his duty as a captain in the Israel Defense Forces.

I did not know my youngest brother Abba at all. He was the youngest child in the family, and was brought with my parents to the death camp of Sobibor. He perished along with them at the age of 21.

How and when did this take place? It seems to me that there is no accurate testimony about this to this day. I only know what is known to the rest of the people who lost their dear ones in Podhajce. On the eve of Yom Kippur of 1942, the Gestapo surrounded the Jews of the city who had gathered for the Kol Nidre prayer, and took them out cruelly from the house of prayer, to take them on their final journey...

The prayer hall from which the worshippers were taken was in the home of my parents in the ghetto. Father of blessed memory, the regular cantor of the Temple synagogue, stood on his duty, fulfilling his final task.

Thus do I remain as almost the only survivor of a large family that was cruelly killed. I remain, to remember everything – and I will not forget anything.

May G-d avenge their deaths.

The Ettinger family in 1928
From right to left: Reb Aharon Shmuel Ettinger of blessed memory, his wife Chaya Ettinger of blessed memory, and the sons Abba of blessed memory and Fishel, may he live. Standing, the eldest son Gedalya of blessed memory, and Yitzchak of blessed memory

[Page 268]

Berta Enis of blessed memory (nee Kleinrok). Wife of Dr. Enis. Murdered during one of the aktions

Moshe Erde of blessed memory. An important Zionist activist. Perished along with his wife Klara (nee Velger), and their son David

Blumenstein family
Most of them perished in the Holocaust

Translator's Footnote

1. From Genesis, the description of Eve's relationship to Adam.

[Page 269]

In Memory of the Brandwein Family, may G-d avenge their blood

Efraim Brandwein of blessed memory and his wife Sara (Sali) of blessed memory

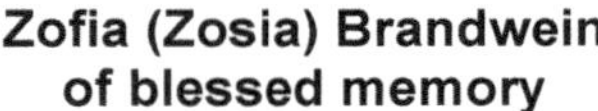

Zofia (Zosia) Brandwein of blessed memory

Sonia Brandwein of blessed memory

My father Efraim Brandwein of blessed memory was a respected communal activist, who got along well with people in our city of Podhajce. He was an active Zionist, and participated in the Zionist institutions of the city. On occasion, he served as a mediator during various disputes, when the two sides preferred to accept his decision rather than presenting their case to arbitration or the rabbinical court.

He was an intelligent man, who knew how to find common language with members of the younger generation as well as those older than he. He earned his livelihood as an accounting director at a beer factory. On occasion, he also worked with his own hands in that company. Mother also did her share in supporting the family at the appropriate level by managing a small grocery store. The sisters also attempted to increase the family income by giving lessons and doing any other job that came their way.

The atmosphere in the home was warm and pleasant. This was especially felt during the Sabbath and festival evening meals, which were filled with joy and exalted spirits. Every event in Jewish life in the Land of Israel or the Diaspora had an appropriate echo in the family discussions around the table. The link was thereby forged, and the feeling of a common lot with all the members of our nation, wherever they were found, intensified.

Their fate was the fate of all the natives of their city. Woe over those who were lost and who will never be forgotten.

May their memories be blessed.

Munio Brandwein

[Page 270]

In Memory of a Prominent Family – the Walden Family

Yaakov Walden
of blessed memory as a soldier in the Polish army

Yaakov Walden
of blessed memory

His young daughter Julia
Both of them perished
in the Holocaust

The Zionist activist
Moshe Lieblich
of blessed memory

May the memory of my dear, pure, martyred family, men, women, and children, be brought to the fore. They were murdered, killed, and slaughtered in sanctification of the Divine name by the impure Hitlerist Nazis and their accomplices, may their names be blotted out, and especially by the murderous Bendera gang, may its name be blotted out.

I will remember my father Avraham the son of Shlomo-Zalman of blessed memory, and my righteous mother Chava the daughter of Mordechai and Freda of blessed memory (nee Heiden), who died a natural death in their homes and on their beds, and were brought to eternal rest in the Podhajce cemetery, next to the graves of their parents and family members.

I will remember my brother Tzvi Walden of blessed memory, who perished in one of the death camps, and his family members who were slaughtered in one of the large-scale massacres in Podhajce.

I will remember my brother Yaakov (Koba) of blessed memory who was murdered by the Bendera gangs, may their names be blotted out, and his family members who were murdered in the large-scale aktion.

I will remember my sister Shoshana of blessed memory, who died of hunger in the ghetto during the era of atrocities.

Thus did all of the members of my family perish and die. They were all people of toil and work, who lived modest lives, and whose prime desire was to help their fellow. They were murdered through no fault of their own, only because they were members of the downtrodden and persecuted Jewish people. Only I myself survived of all this wide branched family – as the final scion of a branch that was cut off from the tree of life.

I bow my head in their memory, and I will not forget them until my soul ends.

May their memories be blessed, and may their souls be bound in the bonds of eternal life.

Shlomo the son of Avraham and Chava Walden.

[Page 271]

The Household of Mordechai and Feiga Lehrer

Mordechai and Feiga Lehrer of blessed memory in the year 1922

We were a large, jolly family. Father was a wheat merchant. He also ran a grocery store, in which Mother assisted. Mother was an exemplary housewife. In addition to all of her business, she found time for social action, for offering assistance and support to the needy.

Our house was the center of this wide branched family. Mother was a native of the town of Gnilobody, and was very connected to the members of her family who were spread out in all the villages and towns of the region.

All family members knew that in our house, they would find proper counsel and advice that was appropriate as a solution to their problems. Every family event, whether happy or sad, was brought first and foremost to the adjudication table of our family. Therefore, our home was always bustling with a large number of visitors – uncles, aunts, cousins, and other relatives. Our family had the name of a beloved and united family.

The first breech in the unity of our family took place in May 1926, when I moved to live in Krakow after my wedding. Later, my sister Aliza (Freida) left the home and made aliya to the Land. During my first visit to our home after my marriage, my mother uttered a broken hearted sigh over the two empty seats at the table, and asked sadly: "How were you able to leave the home?"

Father died suddenly in 1932, and my family and I made aliya to the Land in 1934. However, the house was not emptied, and it bustled with life as always. My two eldest sisters got married and lived in our family home. The two families gave birth to children, and Mother had satisfaction from her grandchildren.

When I came to bid farewell to my family before I made aliya in 1934, I did not imagine that I would be taking leave of them forever, and would never see them again. Our last greeting arrived to us in the form of a postcard from my brother-in-law Yehoshua Landman. He wrote that their situation was good. They were all alive, but that the situation of Mordechai Lehrer was better than any of them... From this I understood how bitter and terrible was their fate, if they were jealous of our dead father...

May their memories be blessed, and may their souls be bound in the bonds of eternal life.

Yafa Shulwolf, nee Lehrer

In Memory of Dr. Arnold Landau of blessed memory

Dr. Arnold Landau was the son of Immanuel Landau, the publisher of the first Hebrew newspaper in Tarnopol. His mother was Berta of the Rozmarin family, a progressive family who owned the lease of the Nowosiulki estate in the region of Podhajce.

Dr. Landau was born in 1868. He concluded his course of studies in medicine at a school in Krakow in 1891. That year, he settled in Podhajce, where he worked as a doctor for 50 years. He was an expert diagnostician and a faithful physician for the residents of the city, four generation of whom enjoyed his dedication medical service.

The honor, medical ethic, fulfilling of his promises and complete fulfillment of his duties – these were the main trait of his life. Through his strong connection with Judaism, he was very familiar with the Jewish mentality. Every tragic event that took place with the ill people whom he tended caused him personal suffering. During the era of the First World War, when he was a military physician in the hospital for communicable diseases, he greatly assisted the Jews, with personal sacrifice. Those people coronated him with a title of love and honor – our father.

In his daily personal life, he went along his usual path: upright, faithful to those who depended on him, pursuing peace, and distancing himself from any feeling

[Page 272]

of jealousy or hatred. He was modest, and never looked for greatness or personal benefit. He was a devoted and dedicated father to his three children, and dedicated most of his free time to them. His wife was from the Bernstein family, the daughter of a well known banker and estate owner from Warsaw, who was a scion of the family of the Gaon of Vilna.

He died in Lvov in 1941 as a result of a heart attack, at the time that the German troops were taking their first steps in the outskirts of the city. He left behind a son named Edmund, who was the manager of the large machine factory in Przemysl, a daughter named Halina who was married to the engineer Zigler, a daughter named Janina who is married to the pharmacist Hesheles, and three grandchildren. Of three generations, only the writer of these lines, Janina Hesheles, survived. I live today in Jerusalem along with my husband the pharmacist Hesheles.

Janina Hersheles

Memories from Father's House

I remember the pleasant spring days in our town, which were days of great interest and joy. The people of the town would be working at their respective jobs and tasks – and the entire town bustled with life. A textile shop appears before my eyes on one of the streets, and behind the counter, the eyes of my parents of blessed memory are smiling at me.

A splendid beard adorned the face of my father Reb Avraham. Many charitable deeds were concealed within him. He was busy with his livelihood from morning until night without rest, and even at times without a meal – however he never forgot the times of prayer – a time when nothing else was more important. Then, he would leave his business and commune with his Creator for several minutes. Synagogue affairs were as important to him as his own affairs. He concerned himself primarily with the cleanliness, heating and light of the synagogue, and anything that was for the comfort of the worshippers.

With longing and yearning I recall the Sabbath eves and Sabbath days in our city and our home. It was as if the entire world desisted from its normal course and went out to greet the Sabbath Queen. The house took on a new look, and it was as if its residents were born anew in order to greet this day. Everything was cleaned and polished in the house, and everyone wore festive clothes. Mother of blessed memory even wore a "sheitel"[1] in order to greet this day that is honored above all days. The Sabbath candles that were lit twinkled and spread their light in all corners of the house, and added a unique sparkle in the eyes of its residents.

Father from the synagogue, and to our joy, he always brought a guest for the Sabbath meal. The table, covered with a white tablecloth, was spread with tasty Sabbath delicacies that were prepared tastefully by Mother of blessed memory. Men wearing "streimels"[2] were hurrying to and from the synagogue, with the joy of the Sabbath and the "extra soul"[3] beamed from their eyes.

Thus did life go for generation after generation – a life of Torah and Divine service, of days of festivity and days of mourning – until the "Days of Awe" came, the days of the Second World War and the Nazi conquest, that destroyed and eradicated this entire life off the face of the earth within a few days.

Many tragedies occur to a person during the time of his life, and he succeeds in overcoming them. However a tragedy such as this, the spilling of clean blood in such great proportions – cannot be forgotten or silenced for the life of the entire generation.

All the members of my family fell prey to the cruelty of the Nazis and their accomplices, and only I alone remained alive – a lone scion of an entire family. With a grieving heart, I hereby recall my dear ones, whose pure blood cannot be weighed in gold:

My father Avraham of blessed memory and my mother Itta of the Kornbaum family.

My brother Berl of blessed memory and my sister Sala of blessed memory.

May their souls be bound in the bonds of life, Amen and Amen!

Uri Milshtock

Translator's Footnotes

1. A wig worn by Orthodox Jewish women in observance of the traditions of modesty. During the week, she probably wore a more simple kerchief (tichel)
2. Hassidic fur hats
3. Jewish tradition states that a person attains an "extra soul" on the Sabbath

[Page 273]

A group on vacation in a summer farm in Truskawiec
Second from left – Mrs. Roza Milch of blessed memory (the mother of Dr. Baruch Milch)
The fourth from the left is Mrs. Slova Milch of blessed memory

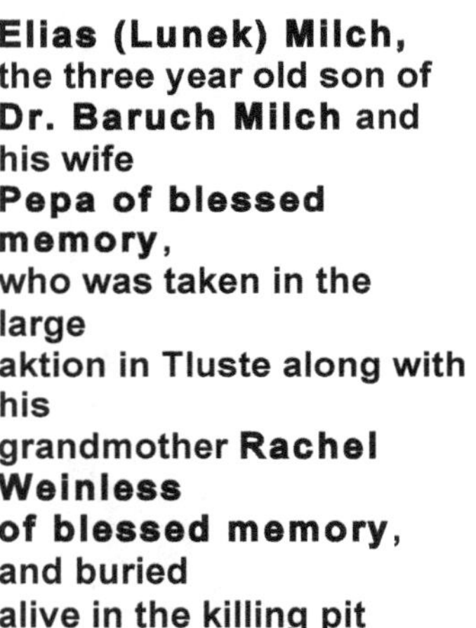

Elias (Lunek) Milch,
the three year old son of
Dr. Baruch Milch and
his wife
**Pepa of blessed
memory**,
who was taken in the
large
aktion in Tluste along with
his
grandmother **Rachel
Weinless
of blessed memory**,
and buried
alive in the killing pit

Pepa Milch of blessed memory
(the wife of **Dr. Milch**, second from right),
and her sister-in-law **Ava Weinless** of
blessed memory (second from left),
accompanied by two friends who
survived and remained alive

Six grandchildren of Zelig Milch of blessed memory (the father of **Dr. Baruch Milch**). All of them perished in Podhajce during the Holocaust era

[Page 274]

Libchia Milch at four years old

Libchia and Malchia Milch – two daughters of Yosio Milch (the brother of Dr. Milch) and his wife Mintzia, murdered in the large aktion in Podhajce

The family gravestone in memory of the family of Dr. Milch who perished in the Holocaust

Fishel Milch of blessed memory and his wife Chava of the Zeida family (the parents of Klara Stop)

The gravestone reads as follows:

In eternal memory for my family
My father Mr. Zelig the son of Yehoshua
Milch of blessed memory and my mother Mrs.
Shoshana the daughter of Shmuel of blessed memory
My brother and sister who were murdered
In sanctification of the Divine name
By the German murderers
During the annihilation of the ghetto
Of Podhajce on the 3rd of Sivan 5703 (1943)
May G-d avenge their death
May her soul be bound in the bonds of eternal life

[Page 275]

Nathan Milch of blessed memory and his friend Avraham Mosberg of blessed memory, who perished in the Holocaust (seated)

Natan Milch of blessed memory (the brother of Dr. Milch). He served in the Soviet army and fell near Stalingrad

The Moshel family of blessed memory
All perished

Members of the Zahler family (most of them perished in the Holocaust)

[Page 276]

Standing from right to left: **Dunia Shotten of blessed memory, Liba Fuchs of blessed memory**, and **Pepi Goralnick of blessed memory**, who perished in the Holocaust. The fourth is **Freda Perl-Shtatmauer** who is living in Israel. Sitting on the right **Golda Shotten** and on the left **Henia Fuchs (Shourz)**

Liba Fink of the Fuchs family (the sister of **Mrs. Henia Shourz**) who perished in the Holocaust

Gedalia Fuchs of blessed memory, (the brother of **Mrs. Henia Shourz**), who perished in the Holocaust

Yitzchak Shourz of blessed memory
(first on the right) with a group of friends in a vacation spot. Most of them perished in the Holocaust

[Page 277]

Chana Kressel
of blessed memory
(Elu Kressel's mother)

From left to right:
Leib Feldberg, his brother
Yehuda Hirsch and their sister
Yeti of blessed memory

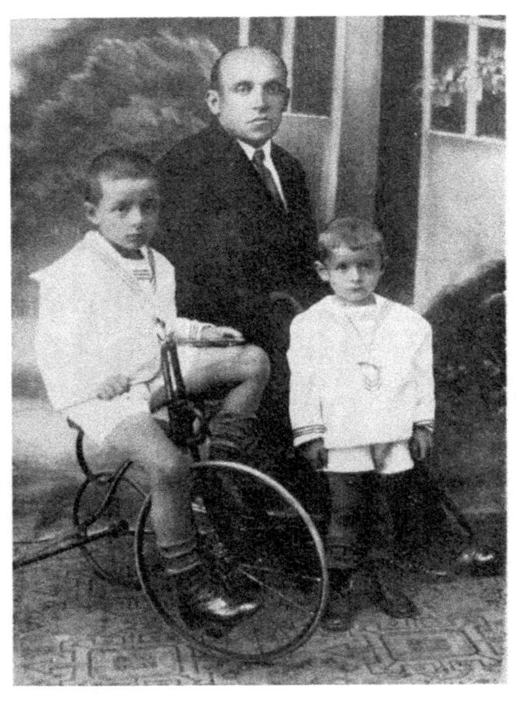

Elu Kressel of blessed memory
and his two sons Adolf and Leon.
The three of them perished in the Holocaust

Bronia Reich of blessed memory and her son Hersch Reich of blessed memory

[Page 278]

The Roth family
Sitting – Simcha Roth of blessed memory and his wife.
Standing – their son Yankel Roth and his wife Chaya of the Goralnick family. In the center is a photo of the young son Hirsch Roth

Standing from the left: Moshe Kaufman of blessed memory, Pepi Rozman may she live, Gittel Zuban of blessed memory. Tzvi the son of Pinchas Rosenberg of blessed memory. Seated: Moshe-Yossel Rideks of blessed memory and his wife Yeti of the Feldberg family of blessed memory

[Page 279]

In Memory of the Shotten Family

Our family home in which I was born and raised stood on Baron Hirsch Street. The synagogue stood at one end of that street, at the corner of Pansak Street, and the Greek Catholic church stood at the other end, at the corner Brzezanska Street. The street was raised, but there was no paved roadway or sidewalk. On rainy days and when the snow was melting, we sank into the mud every time we left our house. During the winter, in the season of ice and snow, the slope served as a sledding area for the children of the city.

There were eleven people in our family, including Grandmother Malka of blessed memory. The atmosphere in the home was tradition, and saturated with popularity. My parents related to the Zionist movement with understanding, and they also did not spare any effort to impart Jewish and general education to us. This helped each of us to find our way in life.

Our home was open to everyone on weekdays, Sabbaths and festivals. My mother of blessed memory would offer assistance to the needy in a discrete fashion. Her personality exemplified the "Jewish mother" (Yiddishe Mama) in the full sense of the term.

The dear members of my family perished in a tragic manner in the ghetto, like all the people of our city. When I made aliya to the Land in 1939 and bade farewell to my family members, my dear ones said to me: "Who knows if we will see each other again alive..." To my great sorrow, the suspicions were actualized and became the bitter truth. From that time, I bore their last words in my heart, and their memory will not leave me forever.

Baruch (Bunia) Shotten

The Shotten family in 1939
Sitting – in the center **Avraham Shotten** and his wife **Rivka**.
At the left the eldest daughter **Mina** and on the right, her husband **Gedalya**.
Standing from left to right: the eldest son **Moshe Yossel** and his wife **Chaichia**, the daughter **Dunchia**, the son **Baruch (Bunia)**, the daughter **Golda**, the son **Bernard (Berchia)** and his wife, and the youngest daughter **Leah (Leika)**

[Page 280]

In Memory of Our Son Yigal of Blessed Memory

Uncaptioned
Yigal

From the distance of many years, the bright image of our only son Yigal of blessed memory looks upon us.

I remember him from his earliest life, when he was still in his diapers. He was a ruddy, healthy child with beautiful eyes, upon which the azure skies of the homeland peered and imparted their color. From the time he first saw the light of the world, he spread his nest with great love, warmth, and boundless dedication.

The child grew and became a lad – head and shoulders above his friends. The three links in our small family became a wonderful chain, in which our son Yigal became the chief link. With the passage of time, true friendship and deep mutual understanding was forged within our small family, forming the unique character of relationships among us.

The lad grew up and became a tall, bright youth, dreaming, visualizing and content with his lot. He had a good heart, feeling the burdens of his fellows and behaving pleasantly to every person. What was most wonderful about him was the wonderful blend of youthful dreams and healthy logic, with a developed sense of justice and correctness. There was always an enthusiastic smile on his face. A sensitive heart hid behind the smile, prepared at all times to help anyone in need of assistance.

Thanks to his clear mind and sharp intellect Yigal succeeded in becoming an excellent student without a great deal of effort. He read a great deal, and was also a good sportsman. Yigal was a member of the scouting organization, and was sent by them to be a counselor for children who were having difficulty with education. Yigal invested a great deal of effort and energy until he succeeded in imparting scouting values to these children, and to make a life of work combined with a life of the spirit dear to them. All of this was done with seriousness and persistence, as was his way with any task that he undertook.

Our son Yigal was blessed with talents. He was talented in handiwork. He wove cloths and created many useful tools for the household. He had unusual artistic talent, to the point where he succeeded in completing his studies in a school of art and sculpting. Nothing was too difficult for him, and it seemed that he had sufficient time for anything that he chose to do.

[Page 281]

His artistic talents were accompanied by deep commitment and dedication to the difficult daily work. We once asked him if he was preparing for a career as an artist, since he devoted so much time and energy to this. His answer was: “For me, this is only a hobby. I see my future in medical research, and it is to that that I wish to dedicate my life.” Indeed, he read a great deal of medical books, and he devoted most of his free compositions in school to those topics.

Suddenly – there was a convention of the scouting movement which was accompanied by a tour throughout the land. He from the convention tired, sick and feverish. He went to the hospital, but the source of the disease was unclear. The disease progressed quickly in an unexpected manner – until the bitter end.

The last days of our son Yigal are etched in our mind. We will not forget them until our last day. We stood by his bed as evening was falling, before the bitter and despised day. Our son was discussing the convention with us, and he suddenly said, “The birds are chirping outside – and I am going to die...” “What are you talking about Yigal? You will recover, and you will live.” “Yes, yes, the penicillin will save me...”, he added and smiled at us.

The next morning, when you saw us standing at both sides of the bed, you extended your hands as a sign of farewell, looked at us, and two tears rolled down your eyes. We understood – this was the end...

Our son Yigal was ill for a number of days, and at 6:00 p.m. on the 19th of Tishrei 5607 (1948), he his soul to his creator. He was only 17 years old. Our son died in the prime of his life, and we were left bereft and bereaved, having drunk the cup of agony in its fullness. **May his memory be blessed.**

Bluma and Menachem Ettinger

Uncaptioned
The gravestone of Yigal Ettinger

[Page 282]

In Memory of Yitzchak Ettinger of Blessed Memory

Uncaptioned
Yitzchak Ettinger

Yitzchak the son of Aharon Shmuel and Chaya Ettinger was born on 22 Adar, 5681 (April 1, 1921) in the city of Podhajce, Poland. He made aliya in 1935, joined the Haganah, and was a member of the guards of "Kofer Hayeshuv". He served in the coast guard starting from 1939.

During the War of Independence, he fulfilled a senior role in the military command in Acre (Akko). Later, he was appointed in charge of security information and smuggling in the entire Galilee region.

Yitzchak spent the best of his years in the service of the nation: in the Haganah, in Aliya B and in the information corps, where he served as a captain during his final years He was a dedicated and very active captain, who fulfilled his roles with excellence. On more than one occasion, he risked his life during his service on the borders.

Yitzchak fell in fulfillment of his duties on 13 Sivan 5719 (June 18, 1959). He was brought to eternal rest in the military cemetery in Nahariya. He left behind a wife and three children.

May there be honor to his memory, and may his soul be bound in the bonds of the nation, for which his entire life was dedicated to its protection.

The Family

The Admor of Bursztyn in Podhajce

by Rabbi Z. Eichenstein of blessed memory

My father, the righteous rabbi Rabbi Yitzchak Eizikl Eichenstein of holy blessed memory, settled in Podhajce in the year 5669 (1909) at the age of 33. He came to settle in that city with the approval of the rabbi of the city, the rabbi and Gaon Rabbi Shalom Lilienfeld of blessed memory, for there were many Jews in the city who were Hassidim of his father-in-law Rabbi Nachumche of holy blessed memory of Bursztyn.

When he came to Podhajce, many Hassidim of all streams drew close to him. As well, many householders who were not members of any Hassidic sect supported him and followed him, since they were impressed with his demeanor and were convinced that he was indeed a righteous, pure and upright man.

With the assistance of his supporters and Hassidim, a large house was set up, in which the rabbi lived with his family. There, there was also a Beis Midrash for Torah and prayer. The Rebbe was a great Tzadik, worker of wonders, and unparalleled charitable person.

Thus was life conducted until the outbreak of the First World War. The war brought in its wake many changes in the lives of the Jews in general, and in religious life in particular. Many of the householders of the city who left their city on account of the tribulations of the war, did not after the war. The elders of the generation passed on, and the face of the city changed in a very great fashion. There were new householders, new customs, and also a new intelligentsia. Various Zionist factions blossomed and rose up – people of the right and people of the left – as well as factions whose color was Red. Various factions were also formed within Orthodox Judaism. Thus was the face of Jewish life that took root in the city after the recovery from the destruction of the First World War.

However, these changes did not have much influence on the way of life in the Rebbe's court. The house was filled with light and joy on the Sabbaths and festivals. The large congregation who came to the Rebbe's "table" drew a full measure of spiritual bliss. Hassidim from cities and towns close to Podhajce would recline around his table on festivals.

The situation in the city became increasingly severe during the final years before the Second World War; however the people of the city assisted the Rebbe in maintaining his household in an honorable fashion. Thus did things continue until the days of the major Holocaust during the era of Nazi rule. The Rebbe died on 13 Adar I 5702 (1942), and his entire family was murdered during the final aktion on 3 Sivan 5702. I alone was saved through the help of G-d, since I had been in New York from 1936.

[Page 283]

Rabbi Yitzchak Izak Eichenstein of holy blessed memory,
the Admor of Bursztyn (the Bursztyner Rebbe).
He died in the Podhajce Ghetto on
13 Adar I, 5702 (1942)

Rabbi Zeida Eichenstein of blessed memory,
the son of **Rabbi Yitzchak Izak of holy blessed memory.**
(See his article in Yiddish on page 152)

The son-in-law of the Rebbe, the husband of his daughter **Babele**, with a group of young men who were close to him. The first on the left is **Eli Kohn**. Next to him is the son of the rabbinical judge **Eisen**

From the right: **Yitzchak (Yitzchakl)** the Gabbai of the Admor of Bursztyn. In the center: the son-in-law of the Rebbe and two of his grandchildren, **Naftali** and **Avraham** in the year 1938

From left to right: The rabbinical judge **Rabbi Avraham Eisen** and his brother-in-law **Rabbi Yaakov-Yitzchak Weisselblum**. The first on the right is **Reb Leibish Perl**

In the center, the wife of **Reb Zeida Eichenstein** with family members and friends of the family. (1938)

My Grandfather Yaakov Shechter and my Father Moshe Gross

by Etia Gross

My grandfather Yaakov Shechter was a goodhearted man. He tried his luck in the United States at a young age, but he to Podhajce and continued his work. He stopped working during his old age, and supported himself from the money sent to him by his sons from the United States.

He was noted for his deep faith and desire to help other people. He would lend money without interest to those in need. However, his crowning trait was his hosting of poor guests.

Who does not recall these poor people, those who rely on donations, who would go from door to door? Among them were people who lost their livelihoods, fathers who were collecting a dowry for daughters who had come of age, as well as regular loafers whom, without delving into the reasons that brought them to that state, were for the most part destitute, bitter of spirit, and hungry for bread. The chief concern that they had when they entered the city was to find for themselves a place to sleep, for there were few people in the city who would run to invite them into their homes for the night, and they did not have money for a hotel (even at a low price). Thus began the blessed work of my grandfather.

My grandfather had only a room and a kitchen. Nevertheless, two or three people always spent the night with him. It was no simple task to set up two or three beds each night and to make them in the morning. Aside from this, there was the concern that the guests not be hungry for bread.

These donation collectors (called in Yiddish "Di Oreme Leit" – the poor folk), would go from door to door throughout the entire day. They would gather together individual coins, and were not willing to spend on food the money that they had collected with so much effort. They would arrive in our home at night tired and hungry. My grandmother and mother would always cook a warm soup for these needy people, and prepare coffee and a roll for them in the morning. The lives of these people were not simple – every person had his own troubles. Just as they differed in their troubles, they differed in their customs. Among them were quiet people who recognized the goodness of their hosts and offered their thanks. There were also those who received everything that came to them without expressing gratitude. However, my grandfather was not waiting for thanks, for he performed his deeds with great love for these needy people, and out of a soulful duty to assist his fellowman.

Many people passed through my grandfather's home, and among them were people of interest. Among them was one man who knew how to tell splendid stories. On account of this, he read before us "The Man of Stories" (in Yiddish; Der Mayse Yid). Another of them was skilled at imitating the sounds of various animals. There were also people of bitter spirit who did not open their mouths. We children loved to hear their stories. After dinner, we would run to Grandfather's home, sit on the bed, and listen attentively to the stories of the adventures that they experienced.

After my grandfather's death, my father continued on with this activity. Grandfather's entire residence served only for the hosting of poor guests. Mother from the store in the evening tired, but she would always serve dinner to these needy people. My mother worked very hard. We had a large bakery with many workers. Despite this, she found the time and energy to concern himself with these people. In addition to a place to sleep, they would also receive a plate of warm soup at night, and a cup of coffee and a roll in the morning.

My father continued on further in this manner, and distributed challas to the poor of the city every Friday. He would even bring a guest for the meal every Friday. I recall that one of the wealthy men of the city said that he would not take any guest for the Sabbath who had eaten at the home of Moshe Gross, for they were finicky and used to good food. I remember the following incident: Once, some Jew came to us for the Sabbath meal. My mother used to place on challa next to each guest. The meal began, and fish was served as the first course. The guest did not know that he would be served several other courses, so he ate a great deal of challa and fish. As was the custom in those days, after the fish course, chicken soup with noodles, meat, stuffed cabbage and dessert were served. However, this poor guest could not enjoy this bounty. After some time, this guest once again came to us for the Sabbath eve meal. When my mother placed the challa before him, he smiled and said, "I fell into this trap only once. Now I know that you eat to the fill, and there is no need to eat a great deal of challa."

However, those good days passed, and the terrible Nazi era came. My parents, my sister and I were saved only through a miracle. My father made aliya to the Land in 1949. His first years in the Land were difficult, for he was not young, and he did not have any money. He worked hard and became rooted, and when he had amassed a sum of money, he immediately placed it at the disposition of the community. He founded a modest charitable fund, and he continued to assist his fellow by giving interest free loans to people in need.

[Page 285]

Moshe Gross may he live (living in Israel), and his wife **Rivka of blessed memory**

Leb Kressel of blessed memory and his wife Pepa of the Gross family

Aba Rubinstock of blessed memory and his wife Adela of the Gross family

Michael Goldberg of blessed memory
Born in Podhajce on June 28, 1897.
Died in Tel Aviv on 4 Shvat 5673 (January 7, 1973)

[Page 286]

The Grave of Rabbi Yosef Aryeh[1] and Chana Brecher

The Inscription on the grave of Rabbi Yosef Aryeh Brecher

The inscription on the grave of Rabbi Chaim Mordechai Brecher of blessed memory, who was the first Hebrew teacher in Podhajce

Here is buried
An upright and pure man, an example of an active person
A man of feeling, and preciousness of the spirit
Dedicated to studying of Torah
Observant – correct and assured.
He supported the poor with his fortune
He died with the name of the shining light
Rabbi Yosef Aryeh the son of Reb Dov HaKohen
Brecher of blessed memory
Died 25 Sivan 5706
About the age of 89
May his soul be bound in the bonds of everlasting life

After our terrible destruction in Europe
A memorial is engraved here
Also in memory of our pure and upright mother
Chana the daughter of Reb Chaim Mordechai
Fueurstein may she rest in peace
Who died in Podhajce on 16 Adar I, 5673
May her soul be bound in the bonds of eternal life

Here is buried
Rabbi Chaim Mordechai
The son of Rabbi Yosef Aryeh HaKohen
of blessed memory
Of the Brecher family
Who died on 14 Cheshvan 5726
At the age of 86.
He was of noble spirit and a precious man
Expert and sharp in all areas of Torah
The author of the Yehoash glosses on the Bible,
Torah Shleima Mishe Torah, Chizkuni
The Heichal HaKodesh Concordance, and others.
All the letters of the Torah were etched upon his heart
A genius in the research into Torah and tradition
His mouth did not desist from learning day and night
May his soul be bound in the bonds of eternal life.

Translator's Footnote

1. The caption reads: "Rabbi Aryeh-Yosef Brecher, but from the grave photo and the transcription of the inscription, it is evident that this was an error, and Rabbi Yosef Aryeh Brecher was intended

[Page 287]

In Memory of Dr. Simcha Margolies of blessed memory

Hirsch Margolies and his wife of blessed memory

Fania Margolies
of blessed memory
(wife of
Dr. Simcha Margolies)
Perished in Drohobycz

Dr. Simcha Margolies
of blessed memory
Died in Israel in 1968

The two sons of Dr. Simcha Margolies
On the right is Ulrich and on the left is Hendik
Both of them perished in the Holocaust

Dr. Shlomo Margolies was born in Podhajce, Galicia in 1888, where he received his early Jewish and general education. Like many of his era, at the beginning of the 20th century, he went to complete his education in the universities of the city of Vienna, where he completed a law degree before the outbreak of the First World War

In Vienna – the city where Binyamin Zeev Herzl took his first steps as the Zionist leader – the young Simcha joined the Zionist movement, to which he remained faithful until the day of his death.

At the beginning of the 1920s, Simcha Margolies came to the regional center of Drohobycz, where he opened a law office. He quickly became involved in the cultural and social life of the vibrant Jewry of that city. He took an honorable place in the Jewish society, and with the passage of time, he became their representative on the city council.

Along with his friends Dr. L. Tennenbaum and Dr. P. Adlersberg, Dr. Margolies served as the force of nationalist Jewry on the city council of Drohobycz. From that time on, he knew how to express concern for the small man and the worker. He set up a loan fund for their purposes in Drohobycz.

Dr. Margolies spend the terrible years of the Second World War in Drohobycz. He endured all the tribulations of the war in flesh, and he lost his wife and two sons.

At the end of the war, he ended up in Silesia, which was to Poland, where he began a short but most important era of his life. The activists of the "Habricha" could tell many stories about how Dr. Margolies was involved in rescuing the survivors.

The final, and certainly most pleasant, era of his life began in 1950 when he made aliya to the Land of Israel with his only surviving son and his daughter-in-law. His age (above 60) did not stop Dr. Margolies from sitting at the student's desk and studying the language of the Land and its laws. After a short time, he passed his tests, and obtained a permit to open a law office.

Even here, in Israel, he did not forego his greatest love – to occupy himself faithfully with the needs of the community. He found many people here from Drohobycz and the surrounding area. Along with them, he established the organization of Drohobycz natives, founded a benefit fund for the needy, published a memorial book for the destroyed community, and served as the address for new immigrants who were natives of Drohobycz and the area, several hundred of whom came to Israel during that era. The memorial evenings that were conducted under his direction, with the participation of hundreds of natives of his city, were very significant.

Dr. Simcha Margolies his soul to his Creator at an old age on April 1, 1961. His memory will not depart from the midst of the many who knew and appreciated him.

[Page 288]

In Memory of my Father Yitzchak Pomerantz of blessed memory

Elyakim-Getzel Perl of blessed memory, the son of **Zeinwil Perl**, a shochet and cantor in Podhajce

Zeinwil Perl of blessed memory (the son of **Reb Gershon Perl)**

Reb Gershon Perl of blessed memory

My father of blessed memory was born into a rabbinical family in the city of Brzezany in the year 1859. He married Esther Kohn of the city of Podhajce in 1883, and settled in that city. He was involved in business, and was the owner of lands in Poczmiestrowka near Siulki. He sold these lands a few years prior to the First World War, after dividing them into small lots.

Yitzchak Pomerantz of blessed memory was the possessor of a broad Torah and secular erudition. He was familiar with world literature and was comfortable in all areas of science. He was also fully fluent in the German and Polish languages. He would interpret the Talmud according to his fundamental style, and his commentaries were often cited by rabbis of renown.

The mastery of general erudition did not come easy to him. He never attended the public school, and he was forced to acquire this knowledge discretely, in the attic or far from his house, so that this matter would be concealed from his pious father.

On account of his great expertise in Talmud and its commentaries, he maintained correspondence with famous rabbis. Among others, he maintained correspondence with Rabbi Shapira of Lublin and other famous personalities until the outbreak of the second World War.

As a modest man with a pleasant disposition, he always tended toward compromise. He displayed love and affection toward all people, and any feelings of dislike or hatred were foreign to his spirit. He supported Zionism with a full heart, and participated in all deeds of charity and benevolence.

He would flee from honor in his public life. He frequently pushed aside the recommendation of the townsfolk who urged him to serve as the head or vice-head of the community. Despite this, he willingly accepted the honors that were given to him in the local synagogue, such as the rights to be the Chatan Breishit[1] on Simchat Torah every year, and other honors of this nature.

His feelings for justice and righteousness, and the faith that the residents of the city placed in him can be shown by the fact that they would often turn to him with the request to serve as a mediator in various disputes, some of which were quite important. He always did this without any benefit to himself. The gabbaim (trustees) of the synagogue also often turned to him with requests for advice in matters related to their duties. Similarly, he was sensitive to the suffering of poor and lonely people, and he stood to their right at any occasion. Within the circle of his family, he displayed great understanding with regard to the education of his children, and he concerned himself with imparting appropriate education to all of them.

My father of blessed memory died in 1933. He had three sons and one daughter. One, Dr. Eliezer Pomerantz, was a lawyer in Podhajce, and died in 1930. The second, Dr. Binyamin Pomerantz, was a lawyer in Kolbuszowa, and perished along with his wife Anna at the hands of the Nazi murderers. The daughter Shoshana (Roza) died in Jerusalem in 1970, whereas her husband, Magister Chaim Kahana, who was a director in the treasury department in Lvov, was murdered by Hitler's troops. The third son is the writer of these lines, Dr. Matityahu Pomerantz, who lives with his wife Shoshana and two children in Jerusalem, the capital of Israel.

Dr. Matityahu Pomerantz.

[Page 289]

Yitzchak Shourz
of blessed memory
who died in Tel Aviv
on 27 Sivan, 5623 (1963)

Reb Moshe Shourz
of blessed memory
who died in Podhajce prior
to the Second World War

Mrs. Henia Shourz next to the gravestone of her late husband, **Yitzchak** the son of **Moshe Yechezkel Shourz**

The Torah dedication ceremony in the Ramah Synagogue on Ben Yehuda Street in Tel Aviv in memory of Yitzchak Shourz of blessed memory, with the participation of the family members

Translator's Footnote

1. The honor of being the first to be called up for an aliya in the new annual Torah reading cycle

[Page 290]

Activities of the Memorial Book Committee

An anthology of minutes that were sent to members of the organization in Israel and the Diaspora.
The Organization of Natives of Podhajce and the Region in Israel
Tel Aviv, Elul, 5625 (September 1965)

First round of correspondence

Regarding: The publication of a book in memory of the martyrs of Podhajce in the region (Zawalow, Wiœniowczyk, Gorzhanka, Zlotniki)

In the recent meeting of the natives of our city in Tel Aviv, a special committee was established for the publication of a book in memory of the martyrs of Podhajce and the region.

So that we can stand up to this task that we have taken upon ourselves, we request assistance from all members in the following areas:

1. Please check the list of natives of our town that is included herein, point out any error, and add the names and addresses of natives of the city that are known to you but do not appear in our list.
2. Please send us lists of natives of our city who are found in the Diaspora, including correct addresses.
3. Please inform us if you know of any people who are prepared to participate in the editing of the material for the memorial book, or who can contribute in any fashion to the success of the task. First and foremost, let us know if you are willing for such.
4. If you have written matter regarding Podhajce (photographs, documents, etc.), we request that you send them to us. We will photograph the originals and them to you immediately.
5. Please send us any practical ideas or advice that can contribute to the success of this task.
6. All members are requested to prepare a list of their family members who perished, including details (dates and circumstances).
7. Please let us know the number of books that you wish to order.

We request that you the responses along with the requested material to one of the following addresses:
Dr. B. Milch, Ahad Haam Street 14, Haifa
Yehuda Weisman, Chovevei Zion Street, Tel Aviv
With blessings for the New Year
In the name of the Committee for the Publication of the Memorial Book
Y. Weisman Dr. Milch

Every native of our city and its region is requested to transfer the amount of 20 Israeli Lira to the accounts of those responsible for the publication of the book. Please send to the following address:
Menachem Ettinger. Buki Ben Yagli Street 11, Tel Aviv
{The text below is a reproduction of a photocopied page.}
The Organization of Natives of Podhajce and its region in Israel
To whom it may concern
We hereby inform you that we are about to actualize
THE PERPETRATION OF THE MEMORY OF THE MARTYRS OF PODHAJCE AND ITS REGION
By planting trees in a special grove that will be given to us by the Jewish National Fund for this purpose, within the general area of the Martyr's Forest.
We are hereby including several forms, which we ask you to fill out and to us with the fees (1 Israeli Lira for each tree – with no restrictions on the number of trees per person), to the following address:
M. Merker, King George Street 56, Tel Aviv.
You are hereby requested to sign up and to donate in memory of friends and acquaintances who have no family members in the Land.
We will send receipts promptly.
Donate and urge others to do so!
With friendly regards
The Organizing Committee
Israel 5714 (1954)
{End of photocopy}

The Committee for the publication of the Memorial Book of the community of Podhajce and its region in Israel.
Tel Aviv, December 1965.

Round Two

Dear esteemed friend:

Unfortunately, many of the natives of our town have not to this date responded to our first call, that we sent out to everybody two months ago. Nobody has sent any material or photographs. Nobody has sent any money, or has answered the questions about their murdered friends and acquaintances.

Therefore, we turn to you with request number two, and beg you to answer our questions which we have sent to you in our first call as soon as possible

[Page 291]

and also to send as much as possible for the needs to the address of Mr. Menahcem Ettinger, Buki Ben Yagli 11, Tel Aviv.

In general, we request that all of our friends become more active in the matter of the Yizkor Book, the importance of which we all recognize.

We take this opportunity to present to you a brief accounting of our activities to date.

a. We have been in touch with Dr. Kermish of Jerusalem, who serves as the secretary of Yad Vashem. (He had relatives in Podhajce). And he has taken it upon himself to edit the material of the Yizkor Book, and help us in general with the publication of the book.
b. We have increased and improved the list of our natives, and their addresses.
c. We have succeeded in obtaining several photographs, narratives and facts about Jewish life in Podhajce.
d. We have gotten in contact with people who come from Podhajce, as well as with Podhajce natives in America.
e. We have obtained exact details from Yad Vashem about the events in Podhjace during the Holocaust.
f. We have collected some money, primarily from the members of the book committee and also from several natives whom we canvassed in person.

With the passage of time, we have held several meetings with the members of the book committee in Tel Aviv and in Jerusalem. At the last meeting, we selected a broader book committee, composed of the following people: Dr. Weichert, Dr. Pomerantz, Dr. Marbach, Dr. Weinless, Dr. Heller, Dr. Weiss, Dr. Baruch Milch, Mr. Weisman, Mrs. Klara Stoop, Shragel Hessel, Nathan Brecher, Mordechai Merker, Yehuda Grussgot, Yehoshua Stamler, Menachem Ettinger, Bunio Shotten, Bunio Brandwein, Aharon Shourz, Shlomo Walden, Yitzchak Walden-Breines, Tzvi Goralnik, Mrs. Henia Shourz (Fuchs), Mordechai Fedder, and others.

We once again request you to send us photographs and material in Hebrew, Yiddish or other languages, which we will translate and edit.

We request that each of our members contribute to this endeavor according to your means. The money should be sent to the address of Mr. Menachem Ettinger. (We note that some of our members have contributed 100 Israeli Lira.)

We wish to stress that the expenses to create the Yizkor Book are very large, and to this time, we have not received any financial assistance from America.

With friendly regards
In the name of the committee
Dr. B. Milch M. Ettinger
The Committee for the Publication of the Yizkor Book
By the organization of Natives of Podhajce and its Region
December 28, 1966

Round Three

Dear Member!

We are pleased to inform you that in the last year, every effort has been made by the committee to expedite the publication of the Memorial Book of the Community of Podhajce and Region. We hereby present to you a brief accounting of the recent activities.

a. We have strengthened the connections with the Yad Vashem institute, and especially with Dr. Kermish, one of the heads of Yad Vashem in the Land (who is also a native of our region, and has taken great interest in our activities).
The following are participating with us in this activity: Dr. Weichert, Professor Weiss from the United States, the writer G. Kressel, Dr. Pomerantz, and Dr. Margolies.
At one of the meetings in Jerusalem at the home of Professor Wish, the following people participated: Dr. Kermish, Dr. Milch, Dr. Pomerantz, Mr. Menachem Ettinger, and Mrs. Walden. At that meeting, many important decisions were made regarding the publication of the book.

b. An additional meeting took place at the home of Mr. Ettinger, in which the following people participated: Professor Weiss, Dr. Kermish, Dr. Milch and other members of the committee. A final decision was made to commit a significant sum of money, which would be given to Dr Kermish in order to take the first steps in the publication of the book. Similarly, all of the material that has been collected to date by Dr. Milch was given by him to Dr. Kermish for classification and editing.
We must point out the warm feelings that have been expressed by Professor Weiss regarding the activities and dedication of Dr. Milch to the holy task of the publication of the book. Professor Weiss has promised to also work personally and to solicit support in the United States for the idea of the publication of the book.

c. Natives of Podhajce and the region! We are only at the beginning of the journey, and its success depends solely on you. In the accompanying list, we present you the detailed financial accounting of the sums that have been collected to this date. This sum is only a portion of the funds that are necessary to realize the goal. Therefore, we turn to you with the call: Please join us in this holy task that is close to your hearts, in order to perpetuate the memory of your parents, friends, and all the martyrs of our city who perished during the era of the Holocaust

[Page 292]

Similarly, you must make efforts to help us gather the material for the book, and to write in any language about various topics connected with the past of our city. The material will be edited by experts, who will translate it and render it fit for publication. The topics about which you should write include: Zionism in our city, youth movements, rabbis, people and personalities, synagogues, etc.

We have enclosed a personal questionnaire which you are asked to fill out and to the address of Dr. Milch, Ahad Haam Street 14, Haifa.

Please send donations in cash and pledges to Mr. Menachem Ettinger, Tel Aviv, Buki Ben Yagli Street 11.

With Great Honor,
In the name of the committee.
Dr. Milch M. Ettinger
The Organization of Natives of Podhajce and the Region in Israel
Sivan 4727 – June 1967

Round Four

(Includes an invitation to the memorial ceremony.)

With great satisfaction we hereby inform you that the preparation efforts for the publication of the Yizkor Book for our destroyed community is progressing.

Much material has been received from the Land and the Diaspora, including pictures and photographs. We can determine that the book will include four sections:

a. A Historical section about Podhajce from the beginning of its existence and about its Jewish community.

b. Surveys and descriptions about institutions, personalities, schools, movements, communal personalities and well-known families (including photographs).

c. A section on the Holocaust era, according to stories and testimonies from survivors of our city.

d. A memorial section, which will include the names of our dear ones and all the members of our city who were murdered by the Nazi criminals and their accomplices.

At the end of this section, everyone will be able to publish a photograph of their relatives who perished along with words of memorial (for a special fee).

We turn to all members who have not yet to us their questionnaires which were sent to you with the urgent request to them to us promptly and to include any material that you have in your hands. You must hurry to send the material, for we will be unable to receive further material after we give it over to the printer. Similarly, we ask our members to give us their generous donations, so that we can pay the significant expenses that are tied in with the publication of the book.
With honor and friendly greetings:
The Organization committee

Mordechai Feder of blessed memory

A native of Zlotnik. A member of the organization committee in Israel. He made aliya in 1933. He volunteered for the brigade, served in the Israel Defense Forces at the rank of a captain during the War of Independence and the Sinai Campaign. He participated in the efforts for the publication of the Yizkor Book and composed an elegy for the victims of the Holocaust in Podhajce and its environs (see page 176). He died in Tel Aviv in 1969

The Organization of Natives of Podhajce and Region in Israel
Tel Aviv, November 11, 1968

Round Five

To all natives of Podhajce and its region, much peace.

Since the time of the annual memorial for the martyrs of our city is approaching, and we once again cannot fulfill our promise of publishing the Yizkor Book on time, we have decided to turn to you once again and request your help so that we can bring the matter to a conclusion.

To this date, we have gathered approximately 90% of the material and greatly edited it. However, in order to bring it to its conclusion, we are short a sum of close to 10,000 Israeli Lira. Therefore we turn to you with a request to donate significant sums to this need, for it would be unfortunate for us if all the material that was gathered, and the work that was invested to this date would go down the drain.

Anyone interested in having photographs of their family members published in the book must pay us a special fee for us (the price of every plate is 20 Israeli Lira). Everyone who has additional material is requested to send it to us at the address of Dr. B. Milch, Ahad Haam 14, Haifa. Similarly, we request that all those members who have not yet to use the questionnaire with names of their relatives who perished to it to us promptly.

Member! Even if you already donated, please repeat your donation and send it to us promptly, so that we can conclude our work.

With friendly and faithful greetings

The Committee

[Page 293]

The Yizkor Book Committee in Israel

Tel Aviv

July 26, 1969

Beloved natives and friends

Of the Podhajce Relief in America!

We thank you very much for the heartfelt greeting and report that you sent us through the esteemed member Isser Roller, and especially for the generous sum of 900 dollars that he brought as a contribution from the American committee in order to publish the Yizkor Book. Isser Roller added his own check of 100 dollars to the aforementioned sum – despite the fact that he had already given 100 dollars in his own time. Therefore, we must thank him heartily.

The support of the American Relief demonstrates that you appreciate the importance of our work and the holy duty to perpetuate our destroyed town. We are certain that the following people played a great role in this: the member Mitzio Frisch, the vice president and secretary Paul Klein, our diligent assistance Isser Roller and his wife Chanale, Rabbi Wolf Feuerstein, and probably others of whom we do not know. We extend to all of them our heartfelt thank you for their assistance.

The member Isser Roller is able to relay to you how far we have come in our work. We are still missing many names from the list of those who perished, as well as a bit of material for the book. We are also still short some money for our further activities. In the past while, everything has become more expensive, and furthermore, we wish to publish a part of the book in English, which will increase the expenses. We hope that the American Relief will be able to assist us further, for there are still many of our natives who have not contributed anything, or have contributed insufficient amounts for this purpose. The member Isser Roller has told us that he would help collect the needed sums, and he will certainly do this.

We are sending you a list of all who have contributed to the book to date, from which you can see that our townsfolk in Israel have also given fine sums. However we are still 20,000 Pounds short of the sum that is needed to publish the book. We send you our best wishes, and await your prompt reply.

In the name of the book committee

Dr. B. Milch A. Ettinger

A List of our Members and Townsfolk who have Contributed to the Publication of the Yizkor Book

With the conclusion of the publication of the memorial book, we see it as our duty to thank all of our townsfolk in the Land and in the Diaspora who have helped financially to the publication of the memorial book.

The general income to the date of December 31, 1972 is the sum of 18,980 Israeli Pounds. Of these, 3,780 Israel Pounds (900 dollars) were donated by the Landsmanschaft of natives of Podhajce and the region in the United States. The remaining amount, totaling 15,200 Israeli Pounds, was received from various members in Israel, the United States, and France.

The following is the list of our members and natives of our town who have participated financially in the publication of the book.

The Podhajce Landsmanchaft in America

Avraham Pels
Henia Shourz
Isser Roller (United States)
Rabbi Wolf Fueurstein Brecher
Dr. Baruch Milch (United States)
Menachem Ettinger (United States)
Reuven Margolis (United States)
Halpern brothers (United States)
Berger (United States)
Lucia and Bernard Milch (United States)
Sali Klang (United States)
Leon Reibel (United States)

[Page 294]

Dr. Max Sherr (United States)
Eliezer and Freda Perl
Aryeh Kopler
Yisrael Roth
Gruber (United States)
Sporer (United States)
Yehuda Weissman
Chaim Kessler
Berta and Izak Weitz (United States)
Leon Fistreich
Adela Frankel (United States)
Schulman brothers (United States)
Fanny and Michael Lehrer (United States)
Klara Reich
Leah Feldberg-Rafael
Klara Stoop
Yehudit Weinleger
Yaffa Shulwolf
Aharon Stamler
Chaya Ettinger-Kanner (United States)
Avraham Geller (United States)
Heshels –Halitzka
Yitzchak Liblich
Meir Morbach
Moshe Fogel (United States)
Dr. Matityahu Pomerantz
Shourz family
Yosef Fistreich (United States)
Sara Drori-Rotstein
Helen Epstein (United States)
Simon Blumenfeld (United States)
Zelda Grau (United States)
Moses Meltzer (United States)
Uri Milshtok
Reiss (United States)
Ella Stein-Lilienfeld
Baruch Shotten
Eliahu Ehrlich
Sam Fried (United States)
Arthur Fried-Patrick
Oscar (United States)
Shimon Kubs (United States)
Moshe Roth (United States)

Dvora Blumberg
Phillip Glazer (Germany)
Herzl Greenberg (France)
Yitzchak Wetreich (United States)

Professor Avraham Weiss of blessed memory
Shalom Lilienfeld
Feibish Mossberg
Dr. Simcha Margolies of blessed memory
Shlomo Mendler
Yishayahu Polk
Mendel Zeiler
Mina Fisch-Streifeld
Akiva Schwartz
Chaim Steinberg
Malka Roth-Goralnik
Sarah Blumenstein-Polishuk
Shmuel Horowitz
Etka Glazer
Shlomo Walden
Avraham Tunis
Yaakov Zimmerman
Aharon Schwartz
Yehuda Shechter
Shraga Hassel
Shaul Silber
Yitzchak Frankel (United States)
Leib Frankel (United States)
Nachum Pushteig
Shimon Farb
Rachel Abend
Golda Erde
Munio Brandwein
Sarah Banner-Lang
Elka Bronstein
Malka Globos
Etia Weiss
Tzvi Weizman
Rivka Yankelevitch
Hella Lubel-Messing
Sarah Marbach
Yitzchak Mintzes ?
Tzila Sobel
Slova Zinkover
Moshe Friedman
Freda Fisch
David-Shlomo Pasternak
Menachem Mendel fleshner-Shnier
Malka Kaufman-Hessel
Avraham Kressel
Aliza Rottenberg
Yehoshua Stamler of blessed memory
Meir Shechter
Nathan Brecher
Felix Bin
Yosef Hessel
Mordechai Feder of blessed memory
Genia Kugler
Anna Reiss
Leah Stamenberg
Yosef Shechter
Hella Steg-Citron
Hela Foder-Kiniover
Yitzchak Bin
Mordechai Breines
Grussgot
Tzvi Goralnik
Elka Gishes
Avraham Glazer
Chaya David-Rauch
Getzel Hessel
Malka Hessel
Manhard Hessel
Shoshana Chetzroni
Ada Levin
Yosef Must
Miriam Nadler-Tuchman
Henka Friedman-Klug
Chana Peleg
Meir Pelz
Dora Tzeiler-Pantzel
Yaakov Kessler
Yitzzhak Rotenberg-Mayberger
Yehuda Roll
Hella Shmok
Sender Stern
Chana Teib-Frisch

[Page 295]

List of Our City's Natives Who Died in Israel

Yitzchak Ettinger
Yigal Ettinger
Eker (the pharmacist)
Liobi Buchwald
Esther Goldberg
Michael Goldberg
Tzvia Goldberg
Tovia Breines
Efraim Brandwein
Rivka Gross
Dr. Meichel Weichert
Professor Avraham Weiss
Dr. Yisrael Weiss
Meir Zelchower-Zerubavel
Yosef Tunis
Melech Teicher
Menachem Jopiter
Freida Lehrer
Munio Lilienfeld
Dr. Aryeh Morbach, physician
Sarah Morbach
Dr. Simcha Margolies
Mordechai Fedder
Meir Fink
Shimon Fink
Mendel Fleshner
Shimon Farb
Yossel Frisch
Yaakov Zimmerman
Yosef Ruf
Yitzchak Shourz
Meir Schwartz, the Rabbi from Zawalow
Izik Stamler
Meir Shechter

Errata

{Translator's note, the obvious typos would have already been rectified in my translation. Errors in names would not have been. For completeness, I included the entire errata as it appears in the book.}

25	Column 1, row 22: Hakatar written in error. Should be Hakatan
48	Row 34. Instead of Binyamin Kutner, it should be Binyamin Kitner
49	Column 1, Row 9. The author should be Rabbi Wolf Fueurstein Brecher
52	Column 1, row 9. Instead of the Responsa of the Maharsha, it should be the Responsa of the Maharsham (Rabbi Shalom Mordechai)
98	Members of the Beitar in Podhajce. Add: In the center, the commander of the troupe Nathan Milch of blessed memory (the brother of Dr. Baruch Milch)
104	Instead of the home of Dr. Pik, the home of Weintraub (the shochet), it should say: The home of Dr. Dik, the home of Weintraub, the home of Cimet
104	The houses of Dr. Pik, Weintraub (the shochet), should say: the homes of Dr. Dik, Weintraub and Cimet
107	Column 2, row 14. To the death camp of Blutz. Should say Belzec.
120	Column 1, row 27. Instead of Dov Kutner of blessed memory, it should be Binyamin Kitner of blessed memory
125	The caption under the photo at the end of the page should say: A group of academic youth in the home of the Weinless family, not Moshe Weinless.
127	Column 2, row 19: instead of the suburb of Halicz, it should say Holhocha
141	A group of Gordonia members. The following should be added: seated, from right to left, Yisrael Glazer, Nathan Brecher, Uri Milshtok, and Izik Gotstein. Standing from right to left: Hirsch Schwartz, Yoel Lustigman, Dik, Brecher, and Izik Ettinger
147	The names of two of the standing people were omitted: the first from the right is Mrs. Pepa Milch (nee Weinless), and the first from the left is the court official Mr. Shleicher.
157	The caption under the photograph; students of the Hebrew school with the teacher Goldstein (instead of the teacher Rosen)
159	It should say: standing from right to left: Shimon Kremer, Mayberger, Gruber, Berish Burl.
160	It should say: standing from right to left: Freda Dunkel, Isser Roller, Mrs. Feldberg
183	Column 2, row 25. Instead of Mendel Abend and his daughter Rachel, it should say, with his daughter Dvora
185	Column 1, row 3. Instead of Mendel Abend and his daughter Rachela, it should say, and his daughter Dvora. Also in the continuation.
216	Column 2, row 42 (second from the bottom): My brother Leib Kressel should be my brother-in-law Leib Kressel
228	Column 2, row 12: instead of Dombas it should say Dunbas

Necrology

Translated by Shlomo Sneh
Edited by Francine Shapiro

Yizkor Am Yisroel – Prayer for Israel

The Jewish people will remember
Their sons and daughters, the saints of
Podhajce community and the area: men, women
And children who were killed, slaughtered
And burnt by the German onslaught
During the war and Holocaust during the years 5700-5704
May their souls be bound up in the everlasting life of their people

Surname	Given Names
	Avremele der Kruma, (the lame man)
	Beile de Mishugene (Baila the crazy woman)
	Chaim, "Paklor" and his mother, (from Halich)
	Sara "the princess" and her family
	Sheindel the water carrier and her family
	Shimele the porter and his family
	Sosia (a woman baker)
ADLER	and his family from the village Alhutsye
ADLER	Bronya (née Beeder)
ADLER	Shimon (Dr. Adler)
ADLER	Yetta (née Polishuk), widow, and her two daughters
AKEN	and his family (owner of a restaurant)
ALFENBEIN	his wife and his children
ALTEIN	Hirsh, his wife, Chaya, their son Moshe, and their daughters Sara (Salka), Henya, and Pepi.
ALTER	(the porter)
AVERBACH	Batsheva
AVERBACH	Ephraim
AVERBACH	Rifka
AVERBACH	Shlomo
AVERBACH	Shoshana
AVERBUCH	(from Zlotnick) and all the family
AVRAHAM	Hugo, (son-in-law of Dr. Notick), his wife and son
BALTUCH	Esther and her family
BALTUCH	Israel and his family
BALTUCH	Melech and his family

BALTUCH	Shalom (egg merchant)
BALTUCH	Shalom, his wife Chana and their children
BALTUCH	Shmuel (flour merchant)
BALTUCH	Yakov (flour merchant)
BARUCH	Zaide and his family
BAUM	and his family (from Rudnickie)
BECHER	Yehuda Hirsh (the scribe) and his family
BER	and his family
BERCHER	Berl
BERCHER	Chana
BERCHER	Mendel
BERCHER	Raizia
BERCHER	Tova
BERCHER	Yente
BERCHER	Yosef
BERG	Gershon, and his family
BERG	Getzel and his family
BERG	Israel
BERG	Leib
BERG	Yosef
BERGER	Baruch, his wife and his two daughters
BERGMAN	and his family
BERL	Yosef, his wife Manya and three children
BERTZIA	Hinda-Rochls and his children
BEZEN	Arye, and his wife Esther, and their children
BEZEN	Berl and his wife
BEZEN	Chana (daughter of Yerucham), her husband, two children
BEZEN	Lipa (the son of Yerucham), wife and one boy
BEZEN	Moshe Baruch and his family
BEZEN	Moshe, his wife Tzilla and three children
BEZEN	Yerucham and his wife
BILLER	Bashe (Batia) and her children Rachela and Yossele
BILLER	Mordechai, his wife Chaya (née Shulman) with two children
BILLER	Moshe, his wife Brantzia, and their children
BILLER	Rachel
BIN	David
BIN	Freide
BIN	Leah (née Haaken)

BIN	Liba (the daughter of Nissan), her husband and children
BIN	Moshe
BIN	Nissan, his wife and their children
BIN	Rachel (the daughter of Nissan), her husband and children
BIN	Rifche (Rifka)
BIN	Rifka
BIN	Shimon
BIN	Shmuel
BIN	Wolf, and his family
BIN	Yosef
BIN	Zalmon
BITTERMAN	Chaya, and her daughter Seeta
BLANK	and his family
BLANK	Yashe and his family
BLECHER	Hava
BLECHER	Leibish and his family
BLECHER	Meir and his family
BLUMENFELD	and his family (from Zbalov)
BLUMENSHTEIN	and his family
BRANDWEIN	Berl, and his wife Bryna
BRANDWEIN	Efraim, his wife Sara, and their daughters Zusia and Sonia
BRANDWEIN	Leib, his wife Chana, and their daughters Tonya, Sonia, and Rifka
BRANDWEIN	Yakov, his wife Sima, their son Yoshua, and their daughter Rosa, their daughter Hansia and her husband
BRANDWEIN-FEIGENBAUM	Zisl, Munyo, and Yoel
BREEYAN	Yehoshua, his wife Etya, their son Moshe, and their daughter Tzila
BREINS	(the mute)
BREINS	Alte and his family
BREINS	Berish, his wife Etya, and their children
BREINS	Getzel
BREINS	Haitzia
BREINS	Hirsh and his wife, and their daughter Clara and their son Benny
BREINS	Israel
BREINS	Leib and his wife Toibe
BREINS	Manya, (the daughter of Alte), and her family
BREINS	Sara (the wife of Shlomo), and their daughter Aliza

BREINS	Shlomo Leib
BREINS	Uri (the shohet-the ritual slaughterer), the son of Alte
BREINS	Zalman Ronyes
BRIEF	Israel, and his family
BUCHBINDER	Lazar, and his family
BUCHSBAUM	(veterinarian) and his family
BUCHWALD	(grain merchant), and his family
BUCHWALD	Chaya (the baker)
BUCHWALD	Moshe, his wife Charna (née Stadmuer), and two children
BUDZARNOVER	Avram David
BURL	Motya, his wife Clara, and their sons Isaac and Berish
BUTIELI AND SHENDELE	water carriers-pumped water and sold it
DAUBER	all the family
DEGEN	Meir and Rachel
DIAMONT	Dora, her husband and their child
DIK	David (merchant)
DIK	David (tinsmith)
DIK	Leah
DIK	Leib
DIK	Malka
DIK	Rifka
DIK	Zalman, (the physician Dr. Dik) and his wife
DIK	Zvi
DIRENFELD	Luncia and her family
DIRENFELD	Patachia (lawyer) and his family
DIRENFELD	Shlomo and his family
DIRENFELD	Yehoshua (lawyer) and his family
DREXLER	Yente and her family
DREXLER-POLISHOK	all the family
DUNKEL	Alta and his wife Dvora
EICHENSHTERN	Rabbi Itzhak Isaac, the Rabbi from Burshtein, and his family
EILEN	David
EILEN	Mina Eva and Mendel, his wife Perel-Sara and daughter Dvora
EISEN	Rabbi Avram (the head of the Rabbinical Court), his wife, his daughter, his son-in-law, and their children.
EISENBERG	(seller of eggs) and his family

ELICH	Henya
EMARANT	Avraham and his wife
ENGEL	Zvi (Dr.)and his family
ERDE	Moshe, his wife Clara (née Valger), and their son David
ERLICH	Baruch, and his wife
ERLICH	Bertzie, and his sons Itchie Mayer and Gershon
ERLICH	Bryna Dvora
ERLICH	Ephraim, his wife Laytzee and their children Doba, Shlomo, and Meir
ERLICH	Fishel
ERLICH	Haim
ERLICH	Hirsh
ERLICH	Ita
ERLICH	Leib
ERLICH	Regina
ERLICH	Zvi
ERTLINGER	(from Zlotnick) all the family
ESCHENFELD	Ignatz (the judge), his wife, (the physician), their son and daughter
ETTINGER	Aron Shmuel, (son of Yitzhak), his wife Chaya, (née Goldberg), and their sons Gedalia and Abba
ETTINGER	Daniel,(son of Yitzhak), his daughter Meltzia Geeps, and her husband, Moshe Geeps.
ETTINGER	Mendel, (son of Daniel),his wife Faiga (née Direnfeld), and their son, Hirsh
ETTINGER	Mordechai (son of Yitzhak), and his wife Mina (née Brandwein).
ETTINGER	Toibe, the widow of the late Itzhak Ettinger.
EVAND	David (Dr. Evand), and his wife
EVAND	Mendel, his wife Perel-Sara, and their daughter Dvora
EVAND	Toibe, her husband, and their daughter
EVAND	Zvi (Hersh), lawyer
FEDER	Avraham and family.
FEDER	(merchant), his wife, (née Dick), and their two daughters
FEDER	Chaim, his wife Esther, (née Schimmel),with six children.
FEDER	Dov, his wife Rifka (née Stern), and their daughter Nechama, the parents and the sister of the late Mordechai Feder
FEELING	David, his wife (née Milch) and his family
FEIFELD	Zengvel, and his wife, Fani
FEIGENBAM	Hanzia

FEIGENBAUM	Munio
FEIGENBAUM	Yoel
FELBER	Chaya-Ita, her son Mattes, and her daughters Feiga and Chana
FELBER	Itzhak, his wife Rosa (née Fink) with two children
FELBER	Mendel (the son of Chaya-Ita-Dr. Felber) with his wife and their son
FELDBERG	Mela
FELDBERG	Rachel, and her daughter Chana
FELDBERG	Shlomo, and his family
FELDBERG	Todres, with wife, daughter and son
FELDBERG	Yehuda-Zvi
FELSCHNER	Aharon (the son of Yechiel Anschel), his wife Blima (née Freibrun), and son Mordechai (Matziush)
FELSCHNER	Yechiel-Anschel
FIDRER	Esio and his family (his mother and his two married sisters with their husbands and children)
FINK	Rosa, her daughter Brancia, and sons Yerucham and Isaac
FINK	Haim Munio (son of Yati) and his wife, Frieda
FINK	Leib, his wife Liba (née Fuks) and their sons, Israel and Aharon
FINK	Vaveh, and his wife, née Weintraub, and their daughter
FINK	Yati
FINK	Yossel, his wife Rachel and their son Zalmon
FINKEL	Adolph, lawyer (Dr. Finkel), his wife Sophia
FINKELSTEIN	Melzia (née Milch) and her family
FIREBERG	Bernard, (brother-in-law of Ratner) and his wife.
FIREMAN	(son of Ester Fireman), his wife and their children
FIREMAN	Yakov and his wife and their son Avigdor
FIRESTEIN	Ahron-Hirsh
FIRESTEIN	Mosh and his family
FIRESTEIN	Yakov, (Der Russiche Shohet) and his family
FIRESTEIN	Yoshua and his family
FISH	Feivel and his family
FISH	Haim-Yitzhak and his family
FISH	Meier-Aba
FISH	Motya, his wife Chana, their son Aharon and their daughter Leytaie
FISH	Yeshaya, his son David and his daughters Zlata, Sara (Serel) and Shoshana
FISH	Yisroel

FISHER	(the owner of a restaurant) and his family
FISHER	Chana-Bina
FISHER	Haim, the son of Shmuel and his family (Lawyer in Lvov)
FISHER	Mendel, the son of Shmuel
FISHER	Minna
FISHER	Shmuel and his family
FISHER	Sima
FISHLER	Fishl and his family
FISTREICH	all the family
FISTREICH	Mutzio, and his family
FLESHNER	Motka, and his son Zalmon (from Zlotnik)
FLESHNER	Yitzhika (from Zlotnik)
FLIK	Salka (née Milch) and her family
FOGEL	the whole family
FRANKEL	(ex-merchant) and his family
FRANKEL	Beila
FRANKEL	Pavel and his family
FRANKEL	Shimon, the son of Yitzhak- Arie
FRAYD	Lazar (teacher) and his wife
FRAYD	Leon
FRAYD	Munio (lawyer)
FREIBRUN	Yakov-Yahuda, his wife Ita (Bupzia) (née Gold)
FREIDBERG	(from the center) all the family
FRIEDBERG	Motya, his wife Minna, their sons Shlomo and Chaim and their daughter Rifka
FRIEDMAN	Chaim , his wife Peia (daughter of Moshe), their son Avrham, their daughters Malka, Sara, and Shoshana.
FRIEDMAN	Kalman, his wife Haya and their children
FRIEDMAN	Lazar (Lazer Klazmer) and his wife, their daughter Matel Walden and their daughter Leitzie Valash
FRIEDMAN	Naftali,
FRIEDMAN	Shaul, his wife Rifka (née Fisher), and thei daughters Genya and Clara
FRIEDMAN	Yeshayahu, his wife Zill and their children
FRIEDMAN	Zippora
FRISH	(from the village of Vieshbov) all the family
FRISH	(the owner of a restaurant, and his family)
FRISH	Fanni (the daughter of Arie)
FRISH	Hirsh, and his family
FRISH	Leib and his family

FRISH	Leib the son of Zvi
FUKS	(owner of a restaurant) and his family
FUKS	Aharon and his wife, Zippi, (née Meltzer)
FUKS	Feivish (son of Aharon), his wife Genya, and their sons Menyus, Tilzia, and Fishl.
FUKS	Gedalia, son of Aharon , his wife Minzia, son Aharon, and their daughters Melzia, Etia, and Tzilla.
FUKS	Isroel, son of Aharon, his wife Busia (née Kraus), their sons Moshe and Leib, and their daughter Melzia, and another child who died in a bunker, and was taken in an Aktion with his parents
FUKS	Lea (Lortzi), and her family
FUKS	Leib (the son of Aharon) his wife Salka (née Moshl) , their daughters Fanya and Rosia, and their son Hershele.
FUKS	Leib, his wife Rachel, and all their family
FUKS	Mordechai, his wife Gittel, their son Beryl (Bezie), and their daughters Sheva and Golda.
FUKS	Pesie, his wife and their son Izio.
FUSHTEIG	(from Zlotnik), all the family
GANG	(government official) and his family
GANG	Adzio (lawyer) and his family
GANG	Shlomo
GELBER	Efraim Elisha, his wife Lea (née Fuks), and their sons Visia, Mundek, and Puldek, their daughter Rosia Nagler and her husband (Dr.Nagler)
GELBER	Leib, his wife Sara, and their sons Falik and Yitzhak
GELLER	Issachar and his family
GELLER	Shmuel
GELLER	Sumer
GLANZ	Sheindel and her son, Dov
GLAZER	Haim Ber and his family
GLAZER	Haim Wolf and his family
GLAZER	Isaac and his family
GLAZER	Shlomo and his family
GLAZER	Shmuel, and his family
GLAZER	Yehuda and his family
GOLDBERG	Zaide
GOLDENBERG	Binyamin, his wife Rechl (Rahel) and their sons Dolki, Paysi, and Izio
GOLDENBERG	Gershon, his wife Sara, and their sons Binyamin and Yisroel
GOLDFELD	Isaac and his wife, Hensia (nee) Rotshayn)

GOLDSHTEIN	Yehuda and his family
GORALNICK	Avraham, and his family
GORALNICK	Bejji
GORALNICK	Hirsh and his family
GORALNICK	Mayer and his wife Mintzia (née Katz)
GORALNICK	Shmuel and his family
GORALNICK	Shmuel and his wife Sofia
GORGEL	Levi and his family
GORGEL	Mendel and his family
GORGEL	Yetta
GOTTESMAN	Hirsh
GOTTESMAN	Laya
GOTTESMAN	Moshe (Motyo)
GOTTESMAN	Oziash
GRAD	Israel, and his wife
GREENBERG	and his family
GREENBERG	Avraham (Dr. Greenberg) and his wife Sabina
GREENBERG	Henya
GREENBERG	Mali
GREENBERG	Nachman (Dr. Greenberg)
GREENBERG	Yakov and his family (from Zlotnick)
GREENBERG	Yehuda
GREENBERG	Yidl and his family
GREENSHPAN	Sara, her sons Shlomo and David, and her daughter Ita, her daughter Esther Huber and her daughter Chana Weinberg
GREESGOTT	Moshe
GREESGOTT	Shprinza
GREESGOTT	Yoshua Zvi
GROSS	Berl and his family
GROSS	Leon (Dr. Gross), his wife Sala, and their son Yulyush
GROSS	Max and his wife
GROSS	Oziash and Rosa (The sons of Moshe Gross)
GROSS	Zvi (lawyer), his wife and his son
GROSSKOPF	Lipa, his wife and two children
GROSSKOPF	Sender and his family
GRUBER	and his family
GRUBER	Yakov, his wife Henya, and their children Minna, Hava, and Ephraim
GUTMAN	Chaya, and her husband and four daughters

GUTMAN	Fayge and her family
GUTMAN	Hinda and her son Yolek (Rol)
GUTMAN	Hirsh, his wife Chana, and their son, Mottel
GUTMAN	Marcus
GUTMAN	Moshe
GUTMAN	Moshe and his son
GUTMAN	Mottye
GUTMAN	Rifka
GUTMAN	Yente and her family
GUTSHTEIN	Israel Hirsh, (the son of Rahel) his wife and one child
GUTSHTEIN	Perl (the baker), her daughters Rifche and Susia, and her son, Mayer
GUTSHTEIN	Rahel, her son Aharon and all the family
HAITZIE	a milkman (but she was a woman), her husband (cart driver), and their daughters Hodia, Matl
HAKEN	Gerson and his wife
HAKEN	his wife Chana (née Shtemler) and two children
HAKENLEIB	and his family
HAKENWOLF	and his family
HAKENZEIDE	his wife Faiga (née Kronish) and their child
HALPERIN	(iron merchant) and his family
HALPERN	Nachum, his wife and two children
HAR	Asher and his two children
HARBER	(the judge in the rabbinical court) and his family
HARBER	Minio, his wife, (née Miller) aand their daughter Annitchka
HARBER	Yakov and his family
HARBER	Yishaiahu (the owner of the Tartak? Meaning?)
HAZELKORN	(beer merchant) and his family
HECHT	Chana
HECHT	Munyo
HECHT	Pinchas (Pinyo)
HEIDEN	David and his wife, their son Shaul, and their daughters Leidzie and Salka
HELLER	(née Horowitz), the widow of Zvi Heller and her son
HELLER	Herman (Dr. Heller), his wife Rosia and their son Yolek
HELLER	Leib, his wife Reji, and their daughters Rifche, Freedl, and Pepi
HELTZELL	Moshe and his family
HELTZELL	Yakov, his wife Adela (née Streisand) and their children

HENDMAN	Mundek (the teacher), his wife and their sons; his mother and his sister
HERBER	(iron merchant) and his family
HERSHEL	Baruch Shatans, (the rabbi) and his family
HESSEL	David, the son of Avraham and his wife Rifka (from Iviromka)
HESSEL	Moshe (the son of David), his wife Chana, and their children, Yakov and Minna
HESSEL	Yerachmiel (the son of Avraham) and his wife Chana
HESSEL	Zvi (the son of David), his wife Leah and their children Avraham and Doni
HIRSH	"Klosnik" and family
HIRSHBERG	Shmuel (engineer) and his wife, their daughter Clara Fein and her husband
HIRSHHORN	Hirsh, his wife Duncia, and their family
HOLDER	Hirsh, his wife Toibe (the daughter of Wolf Kohn), her daughter Miriam, and two more children.
HOLLANDER	(from Zlotnick), all the family
HOLLANDER	Israel
HOOTES	(from Zlotnick), all the family
HOROWITZ	David, and his family
HOROWITZ	Hirsh Leib and his wife Etl
HOROWITZ	Leib (Leon) and his family
HOROWITZ	Levi
HOROWITZ	Malka
HOROWITZ	Shamai and his family
HOROWITZ	Yakov (lawyer, Dr. Horowitz) and his family
HOROWITZ	Yitzhak, his wife Beila, and their daughter Rifka
HOROWITZ	Yona, his wife Salka, his daughter, his father and mother, and his sister
ITZIEDRANG	(the carpenter)
KAHANE	Chaim (magister), Karl Kahane
KAHANE	Lilian and her family (from the village Malaboda)
KAMERLING	the whole family
KARSEL	Alo, wife of Dr. Haya Karsel (née Tortin) (a woman doctor), and their sons Adolph and Leon
KARSEL	Chana
KARSEL	Leib (son of Feivish) and his family
KARSEL	Malka, and her son Leib
KARSEL	Mendel
KARSEL	Miriam

KARSEL	Rachel
KARSEL	Ronya
KARSEL	Yitzhak
KATZ	Liba
KATZ	Mintzia
KATZ	Motya and his family from the village of Malaboda
KATZ	Shlomo Yakov, his son David and his daughter Zvia
KATZ	Zalman
KELER	Dolek, and his wife Manya
KELER	Shaul, his wife (née Berl), and their two sons
KELER	Shimon, and his wife Zlata
KENDEL	the whole family
KENIGSBERG	Meir, his wife Rachel, and their daughters Rayzl and Bluma
KESLER	the whole family
KESTENBLET	mother of Zeev and Zvi
KESTENBLET	Zeev (teacher)
KESTENBLET	Zvi (Dr. Kestenblet the lawyer)
KIMEL	Itzi, ("Itzele Bader"Also a violinist, and his wife Yocheved
KIMEL	Izio
KIMEL	Marcus (son of Itzi) and his wife Hava (née Gruber)
KIMEL	Miriam
KIMEL	Mondek
KIMEL	Rachela
KIMEL	Roma
KIMEL	Yehuda, his wife Dvora, and two children
KIMEL-LOVISH	Ita (daughter of Itzi), and her daughter Salka
KIRSHENBAUM	Meir
KIRSHENBAUM	Yakov
KIRSHNER	Klara
KIRSHNER	Rayzia
KIRSHNER	Rifka
KIRSHNER	Yunta
KITNER	Miriam (Manya, daughter of Benjamin Kitner)-piano teacher
KLANG	the whole family
KLEIN	Hirsh and his family
KLEINROK	Berta (wife of Dr. Anis)
KLEINROK	Rachel

KLEINROK	Sara, Betty, and Marcus
KLEINROK	Yehudit, her husband and their children
KOBS	Yitzhak, his wife Sara-Gittel, their daughters Keindel, Elka, Dvora, and Frieda, and their son Matityahu (Matyas-university graduate)
KODISH	Hirsh, his wife Yenta, and their children
KOHAN	Elo, (Zusio's son), his wife, and thieir son and daughter
KOHAN	Fayga (university graduate)
KOHAN	Leon, (Zusio's son), his wife, and their son and daughter
KOHAN	Matityahu (Matyas), veterinarian
KOHAN	Michael (merchant)
KOHAN	Michael, (Mechel, son of Zelig), his wife and two children
KOHAN	Michael, son of Wolf
KOHAN	Yitzhak, (Zusio's son), his wife Visia with three children
KOHAN	Zusman (Zusio), and his wife Sara
KOPFER	(Kirshner) and his wife, their son Bunia, and other children
KOPFER	Lazar-Hirsh and his family
KOPLER	Arie-Leib and his family
KOPLER-BABAD	Berel and his family
KOPLER-BABAD	Mendel and his family
KOPLER-BABAD	Michael and his family
KOPLER-BABAD	Moshe and his family
KOPLER-BABAD	Shlomo and his family
KOPLER-BABAD	Yisroel (son of Avraham), and his wife Adele (née Weinshtok)
KOPLER-HERZOG	Fayga (daughter of Yisroel), her husband Zusia and their daughter Adele
KORN	Nisan, (son of Sara Korn), his wife, and their daughters Rachel and Liba
KORN	Sara (née Lehrer), and their daughter Yonta
KORNWEITZ	Yoshua, (doctor for the area Dr. Kornweitz), and his family
KORTZ	(the Hebrew teacher) and his family
KREIZLER	Arie
KREIZLER	Menachem
KREIZLER	Miriam
KREIZLER	Sara
KREMER	(daughter of Moshe Shaten) his daughter and granddaughter
KREMER	Aba, his wife Fayga and their families
KREMER	Shimon, his wife Hava, (née Klein) and their son

KREMISH	Yitzhak, his wife Haya, and their children
KROCHMAL	Asher, his wife Mindel and their sons
KROCHMAL	Shimon, his wife Gittel and their daughter
KROMISH	(from Zlotnik), and other families
KRONISH	Hirsh, his wife Batya (Basia)
LAMPER	Danya, and family
LAMPERT	and his family
LANDAU	(the physician Dr. Landau), and his wife; their married daughter and her family
LANDAU	Hirsh, his wife Rahel, and their daughters Malka and Etl
LANDMAN	Yoshua, his wife, Berta, (née Lehrer), and their sons, Issachar (Rauzi), Ozer and Natan
LANG	Abraham
LANG	Aharon
LANG	Chana
LANG	Cilla
LANG	Henya
LANG	Shlomo
LATEINER	Munya, and his wife, Ribtzia (née Relis)
LATEINER	the whole family
LEHRER	Fayge (widow)
LEHRER	Haim and his wife, Rontzia (née Milch)
LEHRER	Machtzia
LEHRER	Reuven, his wife Fayge (née Fisher), with son and daughter
LEHRER	Sheindel
LEHRER	Shmuel, and his wife Batya
LEHRER	Yankl
LEHRER	Zisia, and his wife, with two children
LEICHTER	(from Zlotnik), all the family
LEIMBERG	Haim, his wife Hanzia (née Lippe) and their son, Avraham (Avrumzi from the village of Chepanov
LEINVAND	Feiga, and her two children
LEINVAND	Yitzhak
LEV	Eli
LEV	Haim Ber (the son of Moshe Leib), and his daughters Ita and Chana-Freide
LEV	Hirsh, and his family
LEV	Hirsh, his daughter, Elka, and son, Haim Ber
LEV	Meier, and his wife, Rifka (née Blasberg)

LEV	Moshe
LEV	Moshe Leib
LEV	Shmerl, and his wife, Hinda (née Goldberg)
LEV	Zelig, and his wife, Chana
LIEBLICH	Moshe, his two sons, his two daughters, and his son-in-law, Josef Lipschitz
LIFSCHITZ	Abush Shalom (lawyer in Berzezany) and his wife (née Milch)
LILA	David (engineer), his wife, and their son, Mitzio (lawyer)
LILIENFELD	David (the last rabbi in Podhajce) with his wife and two sons
LILIENFELD	Leibish (the rabbi from Zlotnick)
LINGEL	and his family, from Zablov
LIPPE	Manya, née Brins, the wife of Leopold, and her two sons, Shmuel and Moshe
LIPPE	Moshe, and his family, from Kalno (Kuzova)
LIPPE	Moshe, and his wife and their son Noach; their daughter Dvora with her husband and two children, (from the village of Cherpanov)
MARGALIT	Ero (the lawyer, Dr. Margulies), his wife (née Zeidler), and their son
MARGALIT	Fanya (the wife of the late Doctor Simcha Margalit), and her sons Ulrich and Henryk
MARKER	the whole family
MAS	Chana, and her son,Meir Mas; her daughter Sheindl with her husband and their children
MAUER	the whole famly
MEIBERG	his wife, his daughter, and his son-in-law
MEIR	the cart-driver, his wife Inda-Rahel, their daughters Hodya and Chana, and their son Shlomo
MELTZER	Isroel, his wife Manya and two children
MELTZER	Moshe, his wife Perel, and their daughters Ronzia and Leah; their daughter Shloma (Shlomit) and her husband, Henik; their daughter Rahel Wunderlich with her husband and their sons Junk and Luzia
MELTZER	Motya
MELTZER	Shimon, his wife Dvora and their sons David and Beinish; their married daughter Chaya and her family
MENDLER	and his family
MENHARD	and his family
MENSH	Mundek (electrician) and his family

MERBACH	Yehuda and his family
MILCH	Aba, his wife and four children
MILCH	Avramzi, and his wife Etl (née Lehrer)
MILCH	Bronzia (the daughter of Moshe), with her husband and two children from Teapopolka
MILCH	David (from Talzia) with his wife and two children
MILCH	David (the son of Moshe from Teopopolka)
MILCH	Fishl, and his wife Hava; their daughter Salka Falik and her family; their daughter Marzia Finkelstein
MILCH	Leon, (veterinarian), and his wife Lorka (née Weinglass)
MILCH	Moshe (from Teopopolka) and his family (the brother of Zelig Milch)
MILCH	Oro (the son of Aba), and his wife and two children
MILCH	Pepzia (née Weinless), the wife of Doctor Baruch Milch, and her son, Lunek (Eliash)
MILCH	Ptachia, and his wife and two children
MILCH	Yosef, the son of Zelig), his wife Minzia, (née Hecht), and their daughters, Marzia and Lipzia
MILCH	Yoshua (from Talzia) and his family
MILCH	Yosio, the son of Yoshua, and his wife, with their daughter, their son-in-law, and their grandson
MILCH	Zelig (the father of Doctor Baruch Milch), his wife Rosa (née Lippe), and their son, Natan, (fell in battle near Stalingrad)
MILSHTOK	Avraham, his wife Ita (née Kornbaum), their daughter Sara (Sala) and their son Berel
MILSHTOK	Dvora (the daughter of Mechl Vidiker)
MILSHTOK	Hirsh
MIR	Yisroel (from Rudnik)
MORDECHAI	the water-carrier and his wife Zelda
MORDECHAI-OREN	the piakernik and his family
MORGEN	Mundek (clerk), and his sisters
MORGEN	(the lawyer), and his whole family
MOSBER	Yoshua, his wife Hanzia, their son Moshe, and their daughters Sara and Ita
MOSHE	Haim and his mother Rifziale
MOSHEL	Matyek
MOSHEL	Adela
MOSHEL	Adolf, and his wife Inza
MOSHEL	Bernard
MOSHEL	Fanya
MOSHEL	Herman

MOSHEL	Pnina
MOSHEL	Rosa
MOSHEL	Shlomo and his family
MOSHEL	Yosef
MOSHEL	Zalmon-Hirsh, his wife Kayla, their daughters Luba, Feiga, and Esther, and their son David
MOSHEL	Zelig
MOSHEL	(Most), Meir, his wife Henya, their daughter Sara, and their sons Mordechai, Ahron, and Eliahu
MUND	the rabbi from Zlotnik, and his family
NACHTIGAL	Shabtai and his family
NADLERDOV	and his family
NAS	Binyamin (the ritual slaughterer) and his wife
NAS	Yakov and his wife, their daughter Golda and their son Buzyo
NOTIK	Henryk (the lawyer Dr. Notik), his wife Clara and their son David
NOYMAN	Wilhelm (the physician Dr. Noyman) and his family
NUSBAUM	(the pharmacist) and his family
OBERLANDER	(the carpenter) and his family
OHRING	Marcus, his wife Bronya (née Milch, the sister of Dr.Baruch Milch), their daughter Golda, and son Puldek.
ORAM	Tzilla, and her family (from Zlotnick)
ORNSHTEIN	Moshe, his wife Heiche, their daughter Sara, and their sons Yehoshua and David.
OYZERKIS	Avrah
PASTERNAK	Ettl
PASTERNAK	Pepi
PASTERNAK	Yatka
PEL	his wife and their son
PEREL	Leibish and his wife, Alta, their son Yair and his family
PETRANKA	Shlomo, and his family
PIK	(the barber), and his family
POLISHUK	Aharon and his family
POLISHUK	Henya (daughter of Pesach, married) and her daughter Regina
POLISHUK	Hirsh, and his family
POLISHUK	Leib (the smith) and his wife the midwife
POLISHUK	Pesach, his wife Dvora, their son Zeev, and daughters, Miriam and Yitka
POLISHUK	Shmaryahu and his wife

POLISHUK	Yakov and his family
POLISHUK	Yehoshua and his wife, (née Klein)
POLLACK	(lawyer), his wife, a teacher in school, and their son
POLLACK	(the caretaker of the synagogue), and his family
POLLACK	Dvora
POLLACK	Ita
POLLACK	Sara
POLLACK	Shalaom
POMERANTZ	Binyamin, lawyer, (Dr.Pomerantz, and his wife, Chana (Anna)
POMERANTZ	Maximilian (lawyer)
POPOVITCH	and his family
PRINTZ	Chana (from the village of Bukov)
PRINTZ	Chanah-Freia and her daughter
PRINTZ	Hirsh
PRINTZ	Lea (from the village of Bukov)
PRINTZ	Volf (from the village of Bukov)
PTCHENYAK	Rifka
PTCHENYAK	Yakov
PTCHENYAK	Yidl
RAFAEL	(the porter) and his family
RAT	Bronya and her family
RAT	Isidor, his wife Manya, and his daughter Bella (from Melo-Boda)
RAT	Kuba and her family
RAT	Lunya and her family
RAT	Mulo and her family
RATNER	Tuvia and his wife
RATNER	(lawyer) and his family
RAUCH	Nachman (Dr. Rauch the lawyer), his wife Franziska (née Folk) and their son
RAVENSHTOK	Aba
RAVENSHTOK	(from Zlotnik) , and other families
RAVICH	(from Zlotnik), and the family ...
REIBEL	the whole family
REICH	Avraham
REICH	Avraham, son of Yakov, his wife Feiga, and children Haya and Rosa
REICH	Baruch (the son of Michel), his wife Henya, and their daughters Malka and Rosa

REICH	Bryna (Bronya)
REICH	Hirsch (the son of Michel) and his wife, Gittel; their son Haim and his wife Clara
REICH	Michel and his wife Haya (from Novosiolka)
REICH	Moses (from Zlotnik)
REICH	Moshe,(son of Michel) his wife, Chana, and their children Yakov, Yeheskel, and Shulamit
REICH	Nachman and his family (from Zlotnik)
REICH	Shabtai (from Zlotnik)
REICH	Yakov (the son of Michel), his wife Bronya, and thir children Hirsh and Malka
REICH	Yeheskel (the son of Michel), his wife Bayla, and their children Tonya, Lena, Clara and Yitka
REICH	Zecharia, his son Tuvia and his daughter Helena and Cilla (from Zlotnik)
REICH-ZIMET	Sarah, daughter of Michel, her husband Fishel-Zimet, and their children Yoel, Avraham, Vita and Rosa
REIZBERG	A.
REIZBERG	Ahron-Leib, his wife Mirtzia and their sons Yosef and Yehoshua
REIZBERG	Chana
REIZBERG	Malka
REIZBERG	Max
RELIS	Avram and his daughters
RELIS	Bertzia (the son of Avraham) his wife Zelda, their sons Itzie and Ze'ev, and daughters Kayla, Bina, and Leibzie
RELIS	Brontzie and her family
RELIS	Lipa and his sister Toibe (Tontzia)
RELIS	Miriam
RELIS	Yakov
RELIS	Zelda and her family
RIDEKS	Avraham-Moshe and his wife Frumzi (née Feldberg)
RIDEKS	Chana
RIDEKS	Haim-Baruch
RIDEKS	Layzi
RIDEKS	Moshe, his wife Esther (née Shparer), and their daughters Feiga, Rifka, and Manya
RIDEKS	Moshe-Yosef, his wife Iti (née Feldberg)
RIDEKS	Sender
RIDEKS	Yisroel
RITER	Leib and his family

RITER	Vava (Wolf) and his family
ROL	Anshel (from Halich)
ROL	Hinda
ROL	Lazar (from Halich) and his son Yitzhak
ROL	Shlomo
ROL	Yehuda
ROLLER	Eliahu (son of Sara, his wife Leah (née Weinleger), and their daughters Penina Pepsia), Yehudith (Dzunia) and Tzila (
ROLLER	Sara, her sons Meir and Avraham, and her daughters Dvora, Feiga, and Duba
ROSEMAN	Hirsh his wife and their children
ROSEMAN	Shmuel, his wife Leah (from the village of Muzilov)
ROSEN	(from Zlotnik), the whole family
ROSEN	Shimshon (the Hebrew teacher), his wife Leah, and two boys
ROSENSHTOK	(veterinarian) and his family
ROSENSHTROICH	Moshe his wife Dvora, and their son Avraham
ROSMARIN	Zvi-Hirsh, his wife Gusta (née Zeller)
ROTENBERG	(Lawyer) and his wife, their daughter, her husband, and son Stephan
ROTENBERG	Todrus and his family
ROTENBERG	Yoel, his wife and their son Dziunk
ROTENBERG	Yutka
ROTSHTEIN	Aba, his wife Roza (née Gutshtein), their son Pinchas, and their daughters Susia and Matilda
ROTSHTEIN	Meir (brother of Aba Rotshtein)
ROTSHTEIN	Moshe
RUBEL	Shmuel, his wife Zisia and their son Nisan (from Zlotnik)
RUT	Herman, his wife Hinda, and their children Visia and Sara
RUT	Sincha and his family
RUT	Yehuda (son of Lipa), and their sons David, Shimon, Mordechai, and Yitzhak Lipa, and their daughters Esther, Frida, and Pepi
RUT	Yitzhak- Natan and his wife (née Goralnik)
RUT	Zvi
SALPETER	(the lawyer)
SALPETER	Dolek
SALPETER	Hirsh, his wife Freide (née Zilber), their daughter Taube, and their son Israel
SALPETER	Moshe and his family

SALUP	and his wife and his five children
SATANOVER	(from Zlotnik) and the family
SCHECTER	Natanel son of Yosef Gershon-Sani Schecter
SCHECTER	Rifka daughter of Israel Fink
SCHECTER	Yakov
SCHER	Aharon
SCHER	Binyamin (a dentist)
SCHER	Hersch
SCHER	Klara
SCHER	Reuven
SCHER	Rosa
SCHER	Vili (a dentst)
SCHER	Volf and his wife and their daughter Salka
SCHER	Yakov
SCHINDLER	Baruch and his family
SCHNEIDLER	Hinda, her sons Anschel and Shmul, and her daughters Rachel and Rifka
SCHOR	Freidel
SCHOR	Moshe
SCHOR	Penina
SCHOR	Rifka
SCHOR	Shimson, his wife Hudl (née Kopler), and their daughters
SCHULMAN	Avram, son of Yeheskel
SCHULMAN	Bina and her family (the sister of Abba Rotshein)
SCHULMAN	Feivish and his wife Bryna, their sons Binyamin and Yoel, and their daughters Rifka and Leah
SCHULMAN	Haim (the son of Yehuda), his sons Shlomo and Israel and his daughters Hava, Ettie, and Tzipora
SCHULMAN	Hava and her children
SCHULMAN	Malya
SCHULMAN	Pini, his wife Manya, their daughter Sara and their son Fishl
SCHULMAN	Razia
SCHULMAN	Schraga-Feivish, (son of Yehuda) and his children
SCHULMAN	Yeheskel, son of Yidl
SCHULMAN	Yerucham
SCHULMAN	Yidl, and his wife Charna
SCHULMAN	Yoel and his wife Yente
SCHULMAN	Zvia, and all the family
SCHULTZ	Moshe and his wife Mintzia

SCHULVOLF	Devora and her family
SCHULVOLF	Leib
SCHULVOLF	Moshe, his wife Rayzie (née Velish), their son Yakov and their daughter Sara (Salka)
SCHULVOLF	Sara and her family
SCHULVOLF	Shlomo and his daughter Doba (Yotis) and all her family
SCHULVOLF	Shulamit
SCHUTZ	Brontzia and her daughters Hava Gittel and Yanka
SCHUTZ	David, his wife Yanina (Yachtzia), their daughter Lucia and their son Shalom (Shuni)
SCHUTZ	Shalom, his wife Rifka, and their daughters Gittel and Hava
SCHWARTZ	Ahron and his family
SCHWARTZ	Avigdor, his wife Minna and two children
SCHWARTZ	Berrel
SCHWARTZ	Ettl and and her family
SCHWARTZ	Feibish
SCHWARTZ	from Zlotnik, some families
SCHWARTZ	Hirsh, the son of Aharon and his family
SCHWARTZ	Shimon, his wife Mizia, his daughter Zosia, and another six children
SCHWARTZ	the Dayan, and his family (the son of the Rabbi from Zablov)
SEKLER	all the family
SFARD	(from Zlotnik), all the family
SHAPIRA	Chaya and her daughter Dvora
SHAPIRA	Leib (egg seller)
SHAPIRA	Leib, his wife Perla (née Lehrer), their son Yosef, and their daughters, Hadasa, Cilla and Rachel
SHMITZLER	the whole family
SHOTTEN	Avraham, his wife Rifka and her mother Malka: their sons Moshe-Yossel, and Bertzia (Bernard), and their daughters Mintzia, Golda, Dontzia, and Lea
SHOTTEN	Beryl-Hirsch and his family
SHOTTEN	Moshe
SHPARAR	Bertzia, his wife Bynzia (née Weiss), thir daughters Faygie and Rifka, and their sons Nisan, Avraham and Aron
SHPERBER	and his family
SHPIGEL	Avrham-Yankel, his wife Fayga, their sons Moshe and Manzi and their daughter Leibtzi
SHPIGEL	(the owner of a bakery) and his family

SHTAMLER	Bronya (wife of Aron Shtamler), and her son Munya
SHTATMAUER	Yitzhak, his wife Etti (née Pines) and their son Hayim
SHTEIN	Itzhak and his family
SHTEINBERG	all the family
SHTEMLER	Herman , his wife and one child
SHTEMLER	Klara and her son Munya
SHTERN	Avraham
SHTERN	Berta
SHTERN	Bryna
SHTERN	Hava, Yenta and Mizia, daughters of Rabbi Avraham Shtern (from the family of Mordecai Feder of Zlotnick)
SHTERN	Hutzia
SHTERN	Odzi
SHTERN	Pesil
SHTERN	Rachel
SHTERN	Shlomo(Solomon)
SHTERN	Yakov
SHTERN	Yitzhak
STEINFINK	Israel and his family; their daughter Frieda, her husband Hirsh Leinberg and their son
STREISAND	Moshe and his family
STREISAND	Yeheskel, his wife and their son Yitzhak
TANNENBAUM	Batia (née Roll)
TANNENBAUM	Rachel (Berel's daughter)
TAUBENKIBL	Anshel and his family
TAUBENKIBL	Fanny
TAUBENKIBL	Izak
TAUBENKIBL	Tzirl
TAUBENKIBL	Yona and his wife Yente
TAUNBENKIBL	Fishl and his family
TAUNBENKIBL	Moshe
TEICHER	Elimelech
TEICHER	Leib
TEICHER	Rintzia
TEICHER	Rozia
TEICHER	Shmuel
TORTAN	Michael
TORTAN	Miriam
TORTAN	Natan

TORTAN	Nechama
TRAUNER	(Izio (the son of Rahel)
TRAUNER	Rachel (nee) Milch
TRAUNER	Yeshua (Rachel's son, the teacher Dr. Trauner)
TUNIS	all the family
TUNIS	Anshel and his family
TUNIS	Berlish
TUNIS	Dvora
TUNIS	Rachel
TZAHLER	Avraham-Yakov
VALDEN	Abrahamche, his wife Hava (née Heiden), and their daughter Rosa (Shoshana)
VALDEN	Shlomo (the bakeshop owner and his family)
VALDEN	Yakov (Kuba), Abramche's son and his family
VALDEN	Zvi (Hirsh), Abramche's son and his family
VARMAN	and his family (from Zlotnik)
VEIBERG	Chana (née Greenshpan)
VEICHART	Zvi (Hirsh), his wife, Zissel, their sons Tuvia and Haim, and their daughters Razel(Rahel) and Esther
VELGER	and his family (from the village of Ohrinov)
VELGER	Haim (the physician Dr. Velger from Ohrinov)
VELGER	Haim (the teacher Dr. Velger)
VELGER	Shlomo, his family and his parents
VELVL	"Glak" and his sister Sarah
VERFEL	Yosef, his wife Ettl, and their son Yakov; their daughter Nuncia Lipa and her husband Yosef; their daughter Esther Dlugatch, her husband Yosef, and their son
VETREICH	and his family (painter)
VIDERKEHR	and family, grocer
VIDERKEHR	Asher
VIDERKEHR	Michael (Mechl)
VIDERKEHR	Shandel
VIDERKEHR	Sonia
VIRIKS	Toibe
VIRIKS	Yente
VOLISH	Hirsh, his wife Sara, and their daughters Laytzie and Rayzel
WACHSHTEIN	Miriam-Laya
WALFISH	Yehoshua, his wife Dvora (Bupzie), née Milich, their sons Leon (Lucia) and Fuldek and their daughters Maltzia and Hantzia

WASSERMIL	Shimon, and his family
WASSERMIL	Yosef and his family
WEIDMAN	Feiga and her family
WEINGLAS	(goldsmith, silversmith)
WEINLESS	Rahel and her daughter Clara
WEINSHTOCK	Kalman and his family
WEINTRAUB	David and his family
WEINTRAUB	Feige
WEINTRAUB	Feivish and his famiy
WEINTRAUB	Golda
WEINTRAUB	Haim, his daughter-in-law and all their family
WEINTRAUB	Heimke (the pharmacist)
WEINTRAUB	Hircsh Moshe and his family
WEINTRAUB	Israel and his family
WEINTRAUB	Melech, and his family
WEINTRAUB	Moshe Noach and his family
WEINTRAUB	Rifke (née Mauer)
WEINTRAUB	Shaul and his fa,mily
WEINTRAUB	Yakov and his family
WEINTRAUB	Yente
WEINTRAUB	Yidl and his family
WEISS	Berel and his wife, Sarah (née Geller)
WEISS	Leibl and his wife
WEISS	Meier and his family
WEISS	Moshe and his family
WEISS	Nechemia and his family
WEISS	Nuni (Meier's son) and his family
WEISS	Yoshua, his wife (née Shulwolf), with two children
WEISSMAN	Bernard, his wife Janet, and their children Clara, Wolf, Pepi, Gedalyahu, and Pesach
WEISSMAN	Frieda (née Biller)
WEISSMAN	Yakov and his wife
WEISSMILCH	David and his family
WEISSMILCH	Eliyakum (Yakov's son)
WEISSMILCH	Ita (Yakov's daughter)
WEISSMILCH	Moshe
WEISSMILCH	Rachel (née Gelber)
WEISSMILCH	Yakov and his family
WEITZ	Dvora and her daughter

WEITZ	Israel
WIESENTHAL	and family
WITELES	Yakov
WITS	and his family
WITS	Berel
WITS	Meir and his brother
WITS	Yakov, wife, Gusta (née Fink) with two children
WOLF	(Dr, the lawyer)
WOLF	Abraham, his wife Toni and their son
WUNDERLICH	and his family (dance teacher)
WUNDERLICH	and his family (merchant)
YEFTIS	and his family (clerk)
YEFTIS	and his family (merchants)
YOSEVE	(water carrier) and his family
YUPITER	all the family (soap factory owner)
YUPITER	Fishl
YUPITER	Leib
ZABLOVER	Beila, her daughter Michla, and his son, Hershl
ZABLOVER	Eidl
ZABLOVER	Natan (from Zlotnik), his wife Golda, and his son Shalom
ZABLOVER	Shulki
ZAHLER	Adela
ZAHLER	Avraham-Yakov
ZAHLER	Bernard
ZAHLER	Hava
ZAHLER	Melzia
ZEIDA	all the family
ZEILER	(owner of the grocery), and his family
ZEILER	Meir and his wife Roza (née Fisher)
ZELERMAYAR	Emil, his wife Dvora and their children
ZEMMELMEL	Wolf-Isaac, his wife Heina, their daughters Etti and Gittel, and their sons, Motya, Simcha, and Berel
ZEPTEL	Herman, his wife Toiba (née Goldenberg) and their children
ZILBER	Chaya –Sarah (wife of Shaul Zilber) and her son, Moshe
ZILBER	Henya-Dvora
ZILBER	Israel, his wife Bryna and his mother
ZILBER	Shlomo (the carpenter)
ZILBER	Shlomo, his sons David and Haim, and his daugher Eydel

ZIMERMAN	Chana (née Zilber) and her children Yerucham and Zvia
ZIMERMAN	Yakov and his family
ZIMERMAN	Yoshua and his family
ZIMT	Hinda
ZIN	(post office clerk) and his family
ZIN	Yosef and his family
ZITRON	Haya, (daughter of Lipa), sister of Hirsh Zitron).
ZITRON	Hirsh, his wife Rifka (née Weinshtok), their sons Avraham and Lipa, their daughters Sara (Salka), Gittel and Esther
ZITRON	Lipa and his family
ZITRON	Shimon and his family
ZITRON	Zvi and his family
ZONNENSHEIN	Yehoshua and his wife, their daughter Feiga, and their son Hershl
ZUSSMAN	Litman, his wife Reva (née Rellis), their son Israel, and their daughter Bazia
ZVIKER	Gershon, his wife Sara (née Kopler), and their son Shmuel (Milo), and daughters Hodel and Beila Alter

Table of Contents of the Original Yizkor book

Notes from Translator:
[Y] denotes a Yiddish section.
[Y – number] denotes Yiddish, which corresponds to an equivalent section in Hebrew.
[Y – number S] denotes that the Yiddish article is a summary of the equivalent section in Hebrew.

Introduction to the Book

Chapters from the Past

From the Past [Y]

Chapters of Memories

Memories of the City [Y]

The City in its Destruction

The Annihilation [Y]

English Section

Necrology

Translator's Footnotes

1. This entry is not in the table of contents of the book.
2. There is a typographical error in the table of contents. This page is listed as page 48 by mistake. Note, this section is a summary of the corresponding Hebrew article on page 49, rather than a full translation.
3. There is no note in the text about this section being a summary of the corresponding Hebrew section on page 47 – but it appears to be. It misses numerous dates, and does not appear to be a translation.
4. In this case, the Hebrew is a brief summary of the much longer Yiddish article.
5. The Yiddish appears to be missing the first two paragraphs that are in the Hebrew.
6. Two anecdotes are missing in the Yiddish.
7. Appears to be largely a translation of the Hebrew on page 229, but there are some differences.

Podhajce Yizkor Names

Last Name	First Name	Page of Original Yiddish Yizkor Book
		Find page in text by "[page number]"
Abend	Rachel	295 errata (p.183)
Abend	Rachel	295 errata (p.185)
Abend	Mendel and Rachel	183
Abend	Mendel and Rachele	185
Abend	Rachel	294
Abend	.	165
Adler	Dr. Herman	86
Adler	Dr. Herman	English 5
Adler	Rabbi Herman	57
Adler	.	166
Adlersberg	Dr. P.	287
Aidikewicz	(Priest)	237
Ajlen	David	167
Alerhand	Maskilim Yehuda Leibush	44
Alerhand	Reb Yehuda Leibush	61
Alerhand	Yehuda Leib	77
Ales	.	166
Altein	Chaya, Salka, and Moshe	187
Altein	Moshe and Breina	187
Altein	Pepi	183
Alter	Mrs.	165
Amnon	Rabbi	129
Aranska	Franciska Benedictus	70
Aszenfeld	.	165
Avner	Dr.	111
Babiarchok	.	215
Bachinski	Dr.	75
Balaban	Professor Meir	99
Balin	.	165
Bananenzis	Roza	70
Banner-Lang	Sarah	294
Barshtash	.	239
Beker	Chaim Yehoshua	167

INDEX

G

L

M

N

www.ingramcontent.com/pod-product-compliance
Lightning Source LLC
Chambersburg PA
CBHW082007150426
42814CB00005BA/254

* 9 7 8 1 9 3 9 5 6 1 0 5 3 *